World Wide Web Connections

The companion website continues to offer additional inform
including links to sites with teaching ideas and to sites of pro
tions that are important to early childhood educators. A mar
icon identifies the places in the text where visiting the websi
specific information or links would be especially useful.

Children with Special Needs

A section entitled Children with Special Needs relates the given chapter content to
teaching children with a variety of disabilities and exceptionalities, ranging from
language delays to physical limitations.

Celebrating Diversity

Celebrating Diversity sections encourage teachers of young children to think about
the benefits of diversity in their classrooms and to ensure that they are sensitive to
diversity in their schools and communities.

Theory into Practice

At the end of each chapter, a section called Theory into Practice provides a variety
of activities intended to help readers apply the information in the text to the real
world of teaching and decision making.

A Teacher Speaks

To further strengthen the
connection to real practice,
each chapter ends with A
Teacher Speaks, which presents the observations and
suggestions of practicing
teachers.

A Teacher Speaks

Pamela Pottle   Happy Valley Elementary School
Bellingham, Washington

Engaging First Graders in Science

According to Webster's *Beginning Dictionary*, *science* is
"Knowledge about things in
nature and the universe. Science is based on facts
rned fr   ents and

placed their first-impression drawings with realistic
drawings reflecting their observations of wetlands.
In order to build opportunities for conversations about the wetlands, I posed this question to
my stude   habitat die   you find

FIFTH EDITION

Introduction to Early Childhood Education

Preschool through Primary Grades

Jo Ann Brewer

University of Massachusetts Lowell

PEARSON

Boston ■ New York ■ San Francisco
Mexico City ■ Montreal ■ Toronto ■ London ■ Madrid ■ Munich ■ Paris
Hong Kong ■ Singapore ■ Tokyo ■ Cape Town ■ Sydney

Series Editor: Traci Mueller
Editorial Assistant: Krista E. Price
Marketing Manager: Elizabeth Fogarty
Editorial-Production Administrator: Annette Joseph
Editorial-Production Service: Omegatype Typography, Inc.
Photo Researcher: Katharine S. Cook
Manufacturing Buyer: Andrew Turso
Composition Buyer: Linda Cox
Cover Administrator: Linda Knowles
Cover Designer: Suzanne Harbison
Electronic Composition: Omegatype Typography, Inc.

For related titles and support materials, visit our online catalog at www.ablongman.com.

Copyright © 2004, 2001, 1998, 1995, 1992 Pearson Education, Inc.

All rights reserved. No part of the material protected by this copyright notice may be reproduced or utilized in any form or by any means, electronic or mechanical, including photocopying, recording, or by any information storage and retrieval system, without written permission from the copyright owner.

To obtain permission(s) to use material from this work, please submit a written request to Allyn and Bacon, Permissions Department, 75 Arlington Street, Boston, MA 02116 or fax your request to 617-848-7320.

Between the time Website information is gathered and published, some sites may have closed. Also, the transcription of URLs can result in typographical errors. The publisher would appreciate notification where these errors occur so that they may be corrected in subsequent editions.

Many of the designations used by manufacturers and sellers to distinguish their products are claimed as trademarks. Where those designations appear in this book, and Allyn and Bacon was aware of a trademark claim, the designations have been printed in initial or all caps.

Library of Congress Cataloging-in-Publication Data

Brewer, Jo Ann.
    Introduction to early childhood education : preschool through primary
grades / Jo Ann Brewer.—5th ed.
      p.   cm.
    Includes bibliographical references (p.) and index.
    ISBN 0-205-39861-8
    1. Early childhood education—United States.   2. Early childhood
education—History.   3. Child development—United States.   I. Title:
Early childhood education.   II. Title.

LB1139.25.B74   2004
372.21—dc21

                                           2003049609

Printed in the United States of America

10 9 8 7 6 5 4 3 2 1   RRD-IN   08 07 06 05 04 03

PHOTO CREDITS: p. 34: Paul Conklin/PhotoEdit; p. 100: Jonathan Nourok/PhotoEdit; p. 148: Corbis/Stock Market; p. 359: Will Hart/PhotoEdit; p. 422:BILL LOSH/Getty Images, Inc.—Taxi; p. 455: Charles Thatcher/ Getty Images Inc.—Stone Allstock; p. 462: Mary Ellen Lepionka; pp. xxii, 12, 21, 59, 69, 108, 178, 202, 238, 244, 264, 300, 328, 331, 347, 364, 397, 434, 476, 491: Will Hart; pp. 3, 48, 72, 81, 128, 136, 140, 165, 170, 223, 234, 251, 287, 380, 406, 412, 441, 467, 496: Will Faller; pp. 95, 112, 113, 155, 210, 285, 344, 446: Brian Smith; pp. 179, 183, 482: Robert Harbison; pp. 198, 401: Laura Dwight/Laura Dwight Photography; pp. 280, 305, 329: T. Lindfors/Lindfors Photography.

To my family
With love and gratitude for each of you

BRIEF CONTENTS

CONTENTS

CHAPTER *5*

Play: Learning at Its Best   136

CHAPTER *6*

Guiding Behavior through Encouraging Self-Control   170

CHAPTER *7*

Observing and Assessing Young Children   198

CHAPTER *8*

Working with Parents and Paraprofessionals   234

PART TWO   **CONTENT AREA CURRICULUM**

CHAPTER *9*

Celebrating the Magic of Language   264

CHAPTER *10*

Developing Literacy   300

CHAPTER *11*

Manipulation and Discovery through Mathematics   344

CHAPTER *12*

Manipulation and Discovery through Science   380

CHAPTER *15*

PREFACE

Being an early childhood teacher has never been easy, and as I have said in the preface of the previous editions, it continues to be a challenging and complex task. More teachers teach more children who are poor, who speak languages other than English, who have social and emotional needs that reflect the stress on modern families, and who are trying to cope with the social changes of life today. It is the skill, knowledge, and dedication of our teachers that give us hope for the future of this country.

Teachers of young children have always needed a solid foundation of knowledge on which to base their educational decisions. They have to know about children and their development, about learning and how it takes place, and about the content of the academic disciplines and how to make that content accessible to young learners. In addition, early childhood teachers must work sensitively with families and communities that are diverse in many different ways. All of these needs are critical to the success of young children as learners and members of a democratic society.

If the challenges are enormous, so are the rewards of helping children as they learn about themselves and their communities and as they develop a concept of themselves as successful learners.

Plan for the Text

This book defines *early childhood* as the period from birth through age eight and focuses on the school experiences of children in this age range. The early childhood years are more important than any other eight-year period in the life of a human being in terms of the learning that occurs, the attitudes about learning and school that develop, and the social skills that are acquired that will enable the individual to succeed in today's world. The problems of the future will be solved by today's children only if they value learning, know how to cooperate with others, and appreciate a democratic way of life. Teachers can help young children develop these attitudes and skills.

The primary goal of this text is to provide a comprehensive knowledge base for teachers of young children so they can make decisions that are founded on more than educational traditions or their own experiences as students. This text is also designed to encourage early childhood teachers to consider the child, the family, and the community when planning experiences for each individual. Finally, this text will help readers prepare for the Praxis Exam, which some states require teachers to pass before they can become certified. The content of each chapter reflects the newest standards and research coupled with practical suggestions and activities.

The first eight chapters are grouped together as foundation chapters, offering basic information that guides good teaching practice. Chapter 1 gives a brief overview of child development. This material is presented first in the text because knowing about how children's growth and development are related to providing appropriate experiences for them is basic to teaching young children. Chapter 2 provides a historical context for the schools of today and describes what are currently the most common approaches to early childhood education, including the Reggio Emilia schools of Italy. Chapter 3 offers guidelines for making good decisions when planning learning environments for children, and Chapter 4 provides suggestions for planning appropriate learning activities and experiences. Chapter 5 focuses on play and the critical role it has in how young children learn. Chapter 6 explores the topic of discipline, with the emphasis on guiding children's behavior and teaching them self-control. Chapter 7 on assessment offers sections on observing young children, including techniques for recording observations (including electronic recording) and using them to inform instruction. Observation, assessment, and reporting are discussed as complementary processes. Chapter 8 offers strategies for promoting parent involvement and for working well with paraprofessionals and volunteers in the classroom.

Chapters 9 through 15 are the content chapters, offering information about the various disciplines and content areas that make up the curriculum in early childhood programs. Even though the disciplines are presented in separate chapters, the emphasis is always on an integrated, meaningful curriculum. To that end, most content chapters contain a section on integrating the curriculum around a theme.

The theme illustrated in this edition is Who Are We? This theme was selected because it is so adaptable to different groups of children and stresses the importance of connecting with the families and communities of the children. Such a theme provides children with the opportunity to explore their own identities as well as the identities of their families and communities. Multiple opportunities for reading, writing, social studies, math, and science can be connected to the theme. There are suggestions in each of the chapters about the theme, but the expectation is that teachers will think of many more connections that will be useful to the children they teach.

Chapter 9 highlights the development of language and the strategies for incorporating language development into all elements of a program. Because literacy is a critical component in today's early childhood program, Chapter 10 offers brief overviews of the various programs designed for teaching literacy that are common in modern schools and a discussion of phonics and phonemic awareness as well as a basic look at how children develop as readers and writers. In both the mathematics and science chapters, the emphasis is on hands-on activities that are intellectually challenging and interesting to children. The arts, social studies, and health and wellness are also important components in the curriculum, and these chapters suggest not just activities, but also a way of thinking about activities in these areas that will contribute to children's development and offer them appropriate content knowledge.

Many activities appropriate for children of various ages are recommended throughout the text. These activities have been tried by real teachers in real classrooms. They are presented not as isolated units or events (something to do on Monday) but as applications of theory. When teachers understand theory, they can design their own learning activities and evaluate other activities presented in the many publications aimed at teachers of young children.

Included at the end of the book are three useful sections. The glossary lists key terms (which are bolded in text) along with their definitions. The references section lists the professional works and children's literature cited and discussed in the text. And a comprehensive index provides ready access to specific topics covered in the text.

Features of This New Edition

The features of this fifth edition reflect the many challenges faced by teachers of young children in today's world:

■ In this edition, as well as in previous editions, the goal has been to help readers view *developmentally appropriate practice (DAP)* as the process of choosing learning experiences that are individually appropriate for each child, that recognize the strengths of each learner, and that involve children actively in their own learning. In each chapter, readers are presented with a "Developmentally Appropriate Practice" box that asks them to respond to questions or statements designed to help build a strong understanding of DAP and what it means when implemented in classroom settings. These boxes and other comments about DAP, which appear throughout the text in relevant discussions, are identified with an icon representing the National Association for the Education of Young Children (NAEYC). Readers should look for this icon alongside references to DAP and other connections to the NAEYC.

NAEYC

■ Another focus of this text has been to demonstrate the importance of integrating subjects within the early childhood curriculum. Toward that end, the theme of Who Are We? is developed in each content-area chapter (Chapters 9 through 15) in a feature called "Integrating the Curriculum." This feature demonstrates that any well-chosen topic can incorporate all the content areas and that young children learn best when the experiences and activities planned for them are not divided into discrete subject-matter areas.

■ A new feature in this edition is the inclusion of "An Expert Speaks" pieces written by experts in their respective fields. These "An Expert Speaks" features are designed to foster discussion and thought about the field of early childhood education. Except for length, we have not edited these pieces, as we want the authors to freely express their opinions.

■ Short "Parents" boxes, found throughout each chapter, provide suggestions for teachers on communicating with parents of children in their classrooms. Although this has always been the responsibility of teachers, it can no longer be discharged simply by sending home report cards every six weeks. These boxes offer innovative ways to help parents understand what is happening at school and why.

■ A section entitled "Children with Special Needs" relates the given chapter content to teaching children with a variety of disabilities and exceptionalities, ranging from language delays to physical limitations.

■ "Celebrating Diversity" encourages teachers of young children to think about the benefits of diversity in their classrooms and to ensure that they are sensitive to the diversity in their schools and communities.

■ A chapter-ending "Summary" gives an overview of the chapter content using concise bulleted points.

■ Following each "Summary," a section called "Theory into Practice" provides a variety of activities intended to help readers apply the information in the text to the real world of teaching and decision making.

■ To further strengthen the connection to real practice, each chapter ends with "A Teacher Speaks," which presents the observations and suggestions of a practicing teacher.

Supplements to the Text

Continuing in this edition is a **companion website** (www.ablongman.com/brewer5e) that contains additional information and resources, including links to sites with teaching ideas and to sites of professional organizations that are important to early childhood educators. A marginal icon identifies the places in the text where visiting the website to find specific information or links would be especially useful.

An **instructor's manual** (prepared by Sharon Milburn of California State University at Fullerton) is also available to adopters of this text. This resource will be of use to teachers in education programs who want to make their classes as meaningful as possible for the students they teach.

The Allyn and Bacon Interactive Video for Child Development and Early Education illustrates real-life applications of the textbook topics and provides a springboard from which to start classroom discussions, facilitated by on-screen critical thinking questions. An accompanying video guide is also available, to make classroom use of the video even more effective.

Every teacher makes important decisions every day. This book is designed to help teachers of young children make wise decisions that will benefit the children they teach and, therefore, all of us.

Acknowledgments

No book can be completed without the work of many people, and this one is no exception. Many teachers have helped me with ideas and offered me opportunities to be in their classrooms. I wish that I could list all their names, but I cannot. One of these people is Dr. Ann Benjamin, who has been willing to help me with my many requests for assistance. I also want to thank all my students, who push me to think of new ways to explain concepts and see applications of theory in the classroom. I am also grateful for the contributions of the various people who wrote the "An Expert Speaks" pieces and the classroom teachers who contributed new "A Teacher Speaks" pieces for this edition. There is no reward for doing this work other than my appreciation and the knowledge that they are helping other teachers.

The editorial staff at Allyn and Bacon also has provided support and encouragement at every stage of producing this book. I wish especially to thank Traci Mueller for her work in guiding and supporting the publication of this fifth edition.

Without the help of reviewers, it would be difficult to choose direction and focus for a new edition; therefore, I am very appreciative of the work of the reviewers who helped with this edition: Gerard Buteau, Plymouth State College; Kathryn Jenkins, University of Houston; Ann M. Bingham-Newman, California State University–Los Angeles; Linda Peacock, Southwest Missouri State University; and Delores Stegelin, Clemson University.

I would like to thank once again those individuals who reviewed previous editions. For the first edition, the reviewers included Donna M. Banas, Moraine Valley Community College, Illinois; Julie K. Biddle, University of Dayton; Sheila M. Cole, Garden City Community College; Carol R. Foster, Georgia State University; Mary-Margaret Harrington, Peabody College of Vanderbilt University; Joan Isenberg, George Mason University; Kathy Lake, Alverno College; Donna L. Legro, University of Houston; Betty Mason, Ohio University; Nancy Russell, Texas A & I University; Sandra L. Starkey, West Virginia Graduate College; Beverly Tucker, Valdosta State College; Betty Watson, Harding University; Deborah Webster, Mount Mary College; and Nancy Winter, Greenfield Community College. And for the second edition, the reviewers included Tabitha Carwile Daniel, Western Kentucky University; Carol S. Huntsinger, College of Lake County; Marilyn McWhorter, Marshall University; and Marilyn Moore, Illinois State University. For the fourth edition, the reviewers included Deborah Glasgow, Towson University; Lorelie Olson, Seattle Pacific University; Patricia Otis, Kirkwood Community College; and Beth Row, Southeastern College.

Finally, I appreciate the love and support of my husband and colleague, Bill Harp. Bill keeps the household running and is always generous with his advice and praise.

CHAPTER 1

Young Children Growing, Thinking, and Learning

After reading this chapter, you will be able to do the following:

- Define the term *developmentally appropriate practice (DAP)*.
- Describe the three major theories of child growth and development.
- Describe the physical, social, emotional, and intellectual development of children.
- Describe appropriate activities for encouraging development in all four areas.
- Explain the relationship between child development and diversity.

*W*hen you enrolled in the program to become a teacher of young children, you knew that you had much to learn about planning activities for children, keeping records of children's progress, and handling all the other responsibilities of a teacher. You were pleased when your first observation was to be focused on children's growth and development because that seemed to you to be basic information that every teacher would need to know.

You selected a second-grade classroom in a school where the population was diverse and the school was in a low socioeconomic area of the city. After your observation, when you looked over your notes you found many indicators of development in all areas. The children in this classroom exhibited their physical development through skillful ball throwing and catching, jumping rope, hanging by their knees from bars, and other physical skills. They also had the fine motor skills to make writing, drawing, and painting easy for them to manage. You noted evidence of social growth as children settled a disagreement about who was responsible for cleaning up the art center by talking about their points of view and listening to the other person's perception of the problem. You noted that indications of frustration or anger were rare in this classroom. You also found that these children could attend to a task for an extended period of time. You watched in amazement as they worked on their research projects for an hour.

When you talked with the teacher, she explained that for children ages seven and eight she plans many activities that give the children a choice about what they will do to achieve a goal, she invites children to share their ideas and discoveries with one another, she plans regular sessions in which classroom problems are solved, and she is sensitive to the cultural expectations of the parents. She knows that second graders still need to move around and talk to one another.

Developmentally Appropriate Practice

This chapter is meant to be a review of the principles of child development, not a comprehensive treatment of the topic. A basic knowledge of child development is critical to appropriate planning, teaching, and evaluating in programs for young children. Just as we would never plan a meal or vacation without knowing something about the ages and tastes of the participants, we cannot plan curricula without knowing what children of a given age will likely be able to do and be interested in doing.

The National Association for the Education of Young Children (NAEYC) defines *early childhood* as the period from birth to age eight (Bredekamp 1987). Some child-care programs serve infants and toddlers as well as preschoolers (three- and four-year-olds) or primary children (five-, six-, seven-, and eight-year-olds). Most of this chapter will discuss normal growth and development. Keep in mind that to determine the average age when a child is able to perform a task or behave in a certain way, some children must perform that task earlier than the average and some later than the average.

You will meet many children in your teaching career who have special needs, ranging from severe mental or physical challenges to slight delays in the development of language. You also will meet children who are gifted and talented in a variety of ways, who have attention deficits, and who are wise beyond their years in relating to people. Children come in all sizes, colors, and places on the developmental continuum. Our job as teachers is to recognize each child's abilities and growth and plan for the next steps as she grows physically, intellectually, socially, and emotionally.

The term **developmentally appropriate practice (DAP)** will be used throughout this book to mean practice that is age and individually appropriate for each child in a program. Planning a developmentally appropriate curriculum means that teachers have to know each child—where he is developmentally and what his individual talents and interests are. DAP also requires that teachers think about children's basic needs for play and rest, that they focus on children's development in all areas, that they plan an inclusive program that honors the cultural differences each child brings to school, and that they work to support parents and families (Bredekamp 1987, 1996).

Programs for young children can vary widely and still be considered DAP programs. However, some practices are not appropriate for young children. These practices include timed tests, a focus on academic skill development through worksheets or workbooks, or a schedule that ignores a young child's need to move physically and expects her to sit for extended periods of time.

The chapters that follow will provide more detail about developmentally appropriate practice and ask you to reflect on what makes one choice developmentally appropriate and another inappropriate. Please remember that although some basic guidelines help define DAP, in classrooms across the United States, DAP looks quite different. DAP requires that teachers and chil-

A variety of developmentally appropriate toys should be provided in the preschool classroom.

dren work continuously to determine the best practice for a group of children at a given time. DAP is dynamic, not static. It cannot be the same for all children or all groups of children.

The purpose of this chapter is to review briefly some theoretical lenses through which child development is seen and to outline typical patterns of development. This knowledge is most useful when it can be consciously applied to selecting and organizing curriculum experiences. Often, teachers choose activities or organize those activities in ways that can be traced to the different theories of child growth and development, but they are unaware of these connections. As a teacher, you need to recognize why you choose one activity over another or one organizational scheme over another.

Theories of Development

Children's growth and development can be described from several theoretical points of view. Each of these points of view has its supporters among practitioners in early childhood education, and each offers explanations of human growth and development. These theoretical positions include behaviorism, maturationism, and constructivism. Throughout your career, as you read and think about children and about planning programs that will be beneficial to them, reflect on the points of view expressed by authors of articles and reports and notice how their suggestions differ depending on what they believe about children's development.

Parents AND Development

■ Each month, find an article on some aspect of child development related to the age of children you teach. Make the article available to parents by summarizing it in the class newsletter or letting those who are interested check it out.

Behaviorist Theory

Behaviorist theory suggests that behavior can be shaped by the response that follows any particular action. John B. Watson (1878–1958), Edward Thorndike (1874–1949), and B. F. Skinner (1904–1990) are well-known behaviorists. Skinner is the best known of the modern behaviorists. He wrote extensively about learning as controlled by a system of rewards and punishments. His name is synonymous with the terms **stimulus-response theory** and **operant conditioning** (W. F. Hill 1977). The basic elements of stimulus-response theory include reinforcements, punishments, operant conditioning, and extinguishing behavior.

In *classical conditioning,* a learner is presented with a stimulus and a reward and learns to expect the reward whenever the stimulus is presented. This type of conditioning is exemplified by the classic Pavlovian experiment of ringing a bell and immediately presenting a dog with food until the dog salivates at the sound of the bell. *Operant conditioning* differs from classical conditioning in that the behavior precedes the reinforcement. For example, a pigeon may learn to push a lever to get a food pellet. Presenting a reward after a response provides positive reinforcement of the behavior. Negative reinforcement can also be used to elicit behavior. If the floor of the pigeon's cage were electrified and pushing the lever stopped the shock, the pigeon would learn to press the lever to avoid an unpleasant stimulus; that is negative reinforcement. Behavior can also be punished rather than reinforced. A pigeon might be punished by an electric shock for failing to push a lever on a set schedule.

In the classroom, reinforcements are often used to shape behaviors. Reinforcements in the classroom can be positive or negative. A *positive reinforcement* is something the learner views as desirable. If a child completes a task or exhibits a behavior that is desirable, the teacher may positively reinforce that behavior by verbal praise, a token such as a sticker, or some other treat. *Negative reinforcement* involves allowing a child to avoid or escape from an undesirable consequence or situation if certain behaviors are exhibited. For example, the teacher might give a child the option of leaving the "time-out" chair more quickly if she does not talk at all for five minutes. Finally, *punishment* in the classroom need not necessarily be corporal (physical) punishment but can be time outs, exclusion from the group, withdrawal of privileges, and so on.

In a classroom, operant conditioning might be used to shape children's performance on an academic task. For example, suppose a class of second graders has been assigned the task of completing twenty arithmetic problems. Those children who complete the task promptly and correctly get a token, which can be redeemed for objects in the class store on Friday. With those children who do not complete the task either promptly or correctly, the teacher may take one of several approaches. If he knows that three of the children have never completed twenty problems, he may choose to reward their performance if they complete more than they have completed before. He may choose to provide neither positive nor negative reinforcement to children who complete the same number of problems they have completed in the past.

If he believes that some children deliberately did not attempt the task for some reason, he might punish them by reducing their recess time.

Operant conditioning can be used to shape behavior by providing reinforcements when the learner's behavior moves closer to the target behavior. Shaping behavior involves the following components (Pellegrini 1987):

1. *targeting the desired behavior*
2. *fixing a behavioral baseline*
3. *selecting reinforcers*
4. *analyzing the task and sequencing the segments*
5. *systematically applying the reinforcers* (p. 113)

In the classroom example just discussed, by rewarding a child who completes more problems than in previous assignments the teacher is rewarding closer approximations to the target behavior of completing twenty problems. Teachers often use such techniques to help children gain control of their classroom behaviors. If a child is hitting other children, for example, the teacher will first collect baseline data through observations to determine how often the child is hitting and then provide rewards as the hitting behavior decreases.

Behaviors can be extinguished by failing to provide reinforcements for them. If a child is behaving in ways the teacher deems inappropriate, then the teacher can ignore the less desirable behaviors while consistently rewarding more desirable behaviors.

The goal of employing behavioristic techniques is for the desired behavior to become rewarding to the child so that the teacher or parent need not continue to provide extrinsic rewards. Most teachers, even those who believe strongly in other theories of development, employ some behavioristic strategies as they ignore some behaviors and praise others. Most teachers have had experience with children who prefer negative attention—that is, punishment—to no attention; the usual strategy for dealing with such children is to make every effort to ignore their misbehavior and to reward their appropriate behavior.

Behaviorist theory does not say much about physical development because most authorities agree that physical development is genetically determined and thus does not affect a child's behavior, at least in an optimal environment that includes good nutrition, lack of disease, and safety. Behaviorists are more concerned with how children develop socially, emotionally, and intellectually.

Maturationist Theory

The roots of the **maturationist** point of view are found in the work of Jean-Jacques Rousseau (1712–1778), who believed that children should be allowed to "unfold." A child is like a seed that contains all the elements to produce a wonderful apple if given the proper amounts of nutrients from the soil and water along with sunshine and an ideal climate. The modern maturationist point of view is most often associated with the work of the Gesell Institute (Ilg and Ames 1955). The Gesellian literature describes growth and development in terms of children's maturity. Experience plays a much less important role in development in the maturationist point of view than it does in the behaviorist point of view. Maturationists believe that each child's physical, social, emotional, and intellectual development follows an individual schedule that is basically predetermined. They believe that a child will develop to his potential when placed in an optimal environment and that his development will be slowed or retarded if the environment is not optimal.

Maturationists believe that a child's developmental level is the most important determiner of social and intellectual success, especially in school settings. They suggest that the child will have difficulty in school if he is "overplaced," that is, placed in settings where the requirements do not match his developmental level. Maturationists emphasize the child's own schedule of maturation rather than rewards and punishments, experiences, or interactions with the environment. Experience, in the maturationist point of view, is always filtered by the child's maturation level.

Even though this theoretical position has been criticized, many schools continue to screen children for entry into programs on the basis of developmental tests developed by the Gesell Institute (Meisels 1987).

Constructivist Theory

The **constructivist**, or developmentalist, point of view is founded on the work of Jean Piaget (1896–1980) and Lev Vygotsky (1896–1934). Modern constructivists—such as Jerome Bruner, George Forman, and others—continue to refine the theories of Piaget and to clarify concepts about children's development.

Jean Piaget

Piaget believed that children create knowledge through interactions with the environment. Children are not passive receivers of knowledge; rather, they actively work at organizing their experience into more and more complex mental structures. Piaget and Inhelder's (1969) descriptions of children's thinking include the concepts of assimilation, accommodation, and equilibrium.

Assimilation is fitting information into existing schemas or categories. If a child has developed a schema for "dog" and is presented with a new example of a dog, such as a St. Bernard, the new example can be assimilated, or included, in the existing schema. If presented with a cat, the child may create a new schema for "furry pets that are not dogs." Creating a new category is the process of *accommodation*. Through a series of repeated assimilations and accommodations, the child eventually creates a mental structure that will account for all animals.

Equilibrium is the balance achieved whenever information or experience is fitted into a schema or a new schema is created for it. This balance is very short lived, as the child constantly encounters new experiences and information. *Disequilibrium* describes the mental state in which there is an imbalance between assimilation and accommodation. Disequilibrium is motivating in that it drives the learner to achieve equilibrium. *Equilibration* is the process of moving from disequilibrium to equilibrium. Equilibration allows the learner to employ assimilation and accommodation as tools for achieving equilibrium (Piaget 1985). In the "dog" example, if the child is presented with a basenji, a dog that rarely barks, disequilibrium may result as the child is confronted with a dog that does not exhibit one of the usual dog behaviors. The child must then assimilate this dog into her schema of dogs. Some theorists agree that equilibration is one process that contributes to cognitive growth but question the idea that one process can account for all cognitive development.

Piagetians categorize knowledge as physical, social, or logico-mathematical. Forman and Kuschner (1983) postulate a fourth kind of knowledge: knowing what one knows. The term used in the literature to describe this category of knowledge is **metaknowledge.** If a child knows about the number system, for instance, then his knowing that he knows the system is another type of knowledge that is not social, physical, or logico-mathematical.

Wadsworth (1989) describes the definition of *learning* in Piagetian terms as follows:

> *Two usages or meanings of the word learning are differentiated by Piagetians. The first usage can be called learning in the broad sense, and it is synonymous with development. It is appropriate to talk about the development of, or the learning of, physical knowledge, logical-mathematical knowledge, and social knowledge. The second usage of learning is narrower. It refers to the acquisition of specific information from the environment, learning that is assimilated into an existing schema. Most content learning is the second kind. Both forms of learning imply comprehension.*
>
> *Rote memory, or memorization, is not considered learning because it does not involve assimilation and comprehension. Some theories, such as behaviorism, consider rote memory as a form of learning and do not differentiate between it and the two kinds of learning defined here. For Piagetians, learning always involves construction and comprehension.* (p. 156)

Wadsworth goes on to explain that even though rote memory is not considered by Piagetians to be a kind of learning, it is valuable. Rote memory is certainly useful for knowing one's address or telephone number, for example, but comprehension is not necessarily a component of memorization. A child who comprehends place value is intellectually different from one who has simply memorized the algorithm for solving addition problems that require regrouping.

Lev Vygotsky

Lev Vygotsky was a contemporary of Jean Piaget, and the two men agreed on many points about human growth and development. Whereas Vygotsky died as a young man, Piaget lived into his early eighties and thus produced a greater volume of work. Moreover, Vygotsky's work remained relatively unknown for many years, as U.S. scholars rarely read the work of Soviet scholars during the cold war era. In more recent years, Vygotsky's work has been translated and studied, such that it is now influential in our understanding of children.

Vygotsky (1978) described learning as the construction of knowledge within a social context. He believed that development could not be separated from its social context and that learning could lead development. Vygotsky viewed the learner as an active participant in constructing his own learning within the context of interactions with caregivers, a family or community, and a society. For example, a child in a society that depends on technology will learn to think differently than a child in a society that depends on agriculture.

Vygotsky also believed that language plays a central role in cognitive development, as learning language influences the way a person thinks about the world. For example, a child who learns the scientific language of classification will think differently about classification tasks than one who has not learned such language. Vygotsky agreed with Piaget that learning is dependent on the child's development, but he believed that learning new strategies (when presented at the appropriate level for the child) could lead to increased development. Bodrova and Leong (1996) describe a three-year-old child who is learning to classify objects but cannot keep the categories straight. When the teacher helps her by providing two boxes, one labeled "big" and one labeled "little," the child is able to keep the categories straight. Learning to classify in terms of *big* and *little* will aid the child's development of categorical thinking. As summarized by Bodrova and Leong (1996):

> *The highest level of development is associated with the ability to perform and self-regulate complex cognitive operations. Children cannot reach the level through maturation or the accumulation of experiences with objects alone. The emergence of this higher level of cognitive development depends on the appropriation of tools through formal and informal instruction.* (p. 19)

For early childhood educators, one of the most significant elements of Vygotsky's theory is the **zone of proximal development (ZPD).** The ZPD is the gap between what the child can do independently and what he cannot do even with the assistance of someone (such as an adult or peer) who is more skilled than he is. For example, if a child can independently solve addition problems involving regrouping, then he does not need instruction in solving these types of problems but could learn to solve subtraction problems that require regrouping. However, he probably would not be able to solve problems that involve long division, even with assistance. The skill range in which the child *can* work successfully with some assistance is the ZPD. Clearly, it is a waste of time to teach children what they already know as well as what they cannot do, even with assistance.

Piaget and Vygotsky agreed that learning involved "major, qualitative transformations in thinking" (Berk and Winsler 1995, p. 111). And even though Piaget and Vygotsky did not agree on other points, both of their theories are valuable to early childhood educators. Namely, both can help us understand that teachers must recognize the development of individual children, provide activities and experiences that will enhance children's thinking, and remember that all learning takes place in a social context.

Howard Gardner

The theories of Howard Gardner (1943–) in explaining the growth of human intelligence are very important to the work of early childhood teachers. Gardner has identified nine intelligences that meet the strict criteria for being labeled as such. Gardner (1997a) describes these multiple intelligences as follows:

1. *Linguistic intelligence* is the individual's capacity to use language—her native language and perhaps other languages—to express herself and to understand other people. A poet really specializes in linguistic intelligence, but any kind of writer, orator, speaker, lawyer, or person for whom language is important to her trade demonstrates high levels of linguistic intelligence.

2. *Logical-mathematical intelligence* is highly developed in someone who understands the underlying principles of some kind of causal system—the way a scientist or a logician does—or who can manipulate numbers, quantities, and operations—the way a mathematician does.

3. *Spatial intelligence* refers to a person's ability to represent the spatial world internally in her mind—the way a sailor or airplane pilot navigates the large spatial world or the way a chess player or sculptor represents a more circumscribed spatial world. Spatial intelligence can be used in the arts or in the sciences. If someone is spatially intelligent and oriented toward the arts, she will more likely become a painter, sculptor, or architect than, say, a musician or writer. Similarly, certain sciences, such as anatomy and topology, require spatial intelligence skills.

4. *Bodily-kinesthetic intelligence* is the capacity to use the whole body or parts of it—hands, fingers, arms—to solve a problem, make something, or put on some kind of production. The most evident examples of people with well-developed bodily-kinesthetic intelligence are those in athletics or the performing arts, particularly dance and drama.

5. *Musical intelligence* is the capacity to think in musical terms—to be able to hear patterns, recognize them, remember them, and perhaps manipulate them. People who have a strong musical intelligence do not just remember music easily—they cannot get it out of their minds, it is so omnipresent. Some critics argue that musical ability is a talent, not an intelligence. However, the genius of individuals such as Mozart and Beethoven would seem to demonstrate the existence of musical intelligence.

6. *Interpersonal intelligence* is understanding other people. It is an ability everyone needs, but it is vital to success for anyone who is a teacher, clinician, salesperson, or politician. Anybody who deals with other people has to be skilled in the interpersonal sphere.

7. *Intrapersonal intelligence* refers to a person's understanding himself—knowing who he is, what he can do, what he wants to do, how he reacts

to things, which things to avoid, and which things to embrace. People are drawn to individuals who have a good understanding of themselves because they tend to be confident and successful. They know what they can and cannot do, and they know where to go if they need help.

8. *Naturalist intelligence* is the human ability to discriminate among living things (such as plants, animals) and to be sensitive to other features of the natural world (such as clouds, rock formations). This ability was clearly of value in humans' evolutionary past as hunters, gatherers, and farmers; it continues to be central in such roles as botanist and chef. Much of consumer society also seems to exploit naturalist intelligence in discriminating among goods such as cars, sneakers, kinds of makeup, and the like. The kind of pattern recognition valued in certain of the sciences may also draw on naturalist intelligence.

9. *Existentialist intelligence* is the most recent type of intelligence proposed by Gardner. He describes this intelligence as the "proclivity to ask fundamental questions about life: Who are we? Where do we come from? Why do we die?" (1999). Questions such as these underlie much of religion, art, science, and philosophy. Children are often intrigued by these questions, as well.

In a classroom for young children in which the teacher believes that the theory of multiple intelligences is a meaningful guide to making curriculum decisions, the program would include various ways of learning material, but lessons would not be repeated to address every type of intelligence. At least once during each week, however, information would be presented through all the intelligences so that each child could learn through her strongest skills some of the time. For example, if the children were investigating simple machines, they would take apart old appliances looking for the simple machine parts, work in small groups to invent their own appliances using simple machines, write descriptions of their appliances, and present their appliances to the class and try to persuade others to buy them. On another day, the children would learn about the life cycle of the frog through watching a video, put together a puzzle depicting the life cycle, listen to a recording of the sounds of various kinds of frogs, and examine the back legs of a frog on a computer simulation that compares the frog's leg muscles to those of a human being, measuring the distance each can jump from a standing start, and so on.

The significance of multiple-intelligence theory for early childhood teachers is that it gives them the opportunity to look for learning strengths in all children and to justify providing a wide variety of learning experiences so that each child will have the chance to learn through areas of strength. Gardner explains that all learners need all the intelligences and opportunities to grow intellectually in all areas. However, initial learning or entry-point learning is most easily achieved through employing individuals' personal areas of strength. In sum, by understanding and applying multiple-intelligence theory, teachers affirm that every child has abilities that can be recognized and honored.

Theoretical Influences

The different theories of development provide points of view through which to interpret observations of children as they grow and develop (see Table 1.1). Depending on our theoretical orientation, we would look at examples of children's development differently. If a child were observed throwing a ball at a target, a behaviorist might point out the reinforcements that make the child seek closer approximations to the most effective throwing techniques. The maturationist observing the same child might focus on the child's physical maturity, as indicated by her ability to grasp and release the ball appropriately. The constructivist would view repeated attempts to hit the target as evidence that the child was actively seeking information about velocity and angle of release in order to hit the target (although the child would not be expected to be able to verbalize these concepts).

A child develops as a whole. Development in one area certainly influences development in other areas. For example, when a child becomes mobile, he opens up many more possibilities for exploration and learning about the environment. Children who feel that they are learning successfully or who feel confident about their physical abilities develop more positive self-esteem. Children who learn to control their impulsive behaviors may be able to sustain interactions with people and materials longer than children who do not, which affects their intellectual development. A child's social, physical, emotional, and intellectual development are always interrelated.

Table 1.1 General Overview of Different Theoretical Orientations

	Behaviorist	**Maturationist**	**Constructivist**
Physical Development	No special attention	Indicator of readiness for social and intellectual tasks	Internally motivated; influences other areas of development
Intellectual Development	Learning is achieved through reinforcements and rewards; is incremental	Learning is unfolding of child's potential if in optimal environment	Learning is a continuous process of assimilation and accommodation; results in changes in thinking rather than incremental growth of facts
Social Development	Shaped by reinforcements	Dependent on optimal environment	Learned through process of testing hypotheses; same as learning in other areas
Emotional Development	Shaped by reinforcements	Dependent on optimal environment	Learned through internal process; developmental
Motivational Development	External; rewards and punishments	Internal; child follows own program	Internal; child is active in own development

Children's Development

This section provides brief overviews of patterns in children's physical, social, emotional, and intellectual development. Table 1.2 (pages 14–15) summarizes and gives examples of these patterns.

Physical Development

Patterns of Development

Physical development is orderly, not random. Infant development is marked by the change from undifferentiated mass activity to controlled activity. It is easy to observe undifferentiated mass activity in an infant. If she is excited, her whole body moves and her arms and legs flail. Gradually, the baby becomes more capable of differentiated movements, such as deliberately reaching for and grasping a rattle. Movements that become controlled and deliberate also become organized into patterns, such as pulling oneself to a standing position, releasing the hands, and moving the legs and feet to walk. The patterns then become available to the child as possible responses to different situations. If the child wants a toy that is across the room, at first the only option for getting there is scooting and rocking. As development progresses, crawling and finally walking and running become patterns of physical movement

Physical growth is an important part of a child's overall development.

available to the child. The physical development of children in the infant stage proceeds rapidly. The child learns to control head position, to grasp objects, and perhaps to stand and walk in the first year. As children grow, the development of their motor skills is not quite as rapid as it is in infancy, but it continues throughout childhood.

Observations of physical development reveal that growth is *cephalocaudal* (it proceeds from head to tail) and *proximodistal* (it proceeds from the center of the body outward) and that gross motor movements are developed before fine motor movements. Control of head and arm muscles is achieved before control of leg muscles. Similarly, children are able to control the muscles of their arms before they can control the fine muscles in their hands that are needed for tasks such as writing and cutting with scissors.

The rate of children's physical development is variable and related to environmental features such as nutrition and the freedom to practice movements. Some behaviors, such as walking, tend to emerge at about the same time in children, even if they have been confined as infants; others, such as throwing, seem to depend more on practice opportunities. Most children are encouraged to practice their developing skills through interactions in daily life. The parent may encourage the child to progress from letting go of support, to standing alone, to walking a step or two, and finally to walking several steps across the room. Children give their caretakers clues about what to encourage at any given time by attempting the behaviors. Thus, for example, most caretakers would not attempt to encourage walking in children who are not yet showing they are ready to walk by pulling themselves to a standing position.

By the time they are three, most children can walk backward and on tiptoe and can run. They can throw a ball and catch it with their arms extended. They can also ride a tricycle and hold a crayon or pencil with their fingers rather than their fists. Four-year-olds continue to refine their skills; they can bounce a ball, hop on one foot, climb ladders, alternate feet while walking downstairs, and jump from a standing position. Some five-year-olds can skip, and some learn to jump rope. By the time children are six, most can throw fairly accurately, and many learn to ride a two-wheel bike.

Children seven and eight continue to refine the skills they have acquired and learn new skills. They are physically active, running, skipping, hopping, and climbing—rarely just walking. Their fine motor abilities increase so that they can draw, write, and learn to play musical instruments. Practice in motor skills is important in this period, especially for newly acquired skills such as swimming. Age and practice have more effect on the development of motor skills in this period than does gender. Girls can run as fast and throw as far and as accurately as boys during this period.

Implications for the Curriculum

It is important during the preschool and early elementary school years for children to have many opportunities for engaging in physical activities. Three-year-olds are in a constant state of motion, and it is important that

Table 1.2   Overview of Patterns in Children's Development

	Birth to Three Years Old	Three to Four Years Old	Five to Six Years Old	Seven to Eight Years Old
Physical Development	Physical skills develop rapidly Sits and crawls Walks and begins to run Fine motor skills develop; can stack and pick up small objects Manages spoon or fork for feeding Grasps and releases objects	Physical skills increase Rides a tricycle Walks up and down stairs, alternating feet Runs Jumps with both feet Walks on balance beam Climbs on playground equipment Undresses and dresses self Catches ball with arms extended Walks backward and on tiptoe Holds crayon with fingers	Skips on alternate feet Rides two-wheel bike Skates Throws fairly accurately Catches ball with hands Turns somersaults Participates in games requiring physical skills Small muscle development increases; eye–hand coordination develops Fine muscle control increases; can use hammer, pencil, scissors, etc. Copies geometric figures Cuts on lines Prints some letters Pastes and glues Begins to lose teeth Handedness is well established	Physical skills become important in self-concept Energy levels are high Rate of growth slows Fine muscle control is good; can form letters well Permanent teeth appear Body proportions, facial structure change More mature throwing and catching pattern Increases accuracy in throwing and kicking
Social Development	Responds to others Enjoys company of other children Can maintain involvement with another for a very short period Is unable to share without coaxing Shows very little ability to postpone gratification Imitates actions of others Begins to engage in parallel play	Becomes more aware of self Develops more altruistic feelings Becomes aware of racial/ethnic and sexual differences Is able to take direction, follow some rules Has strong feelings toward home and family Shows a growing sense of self-reliance Parallel play is common; cooperative play begins Imaginary playmates are fairly common	Expresses rigid ideas about sex roles Has best friends but for short periods of time Quarrels often but anger is short lived Is able to share and take turns Is eager to participate in school experiences Considers teacher very important Wants to be first Becomes possessive	Is more competitive with peers Depends on parents for expansion of interests, activities Is influenced by peer opinions Plays with opposite sex less often Needs teacher approval Is able to share Wants to please Is more independent at work and play Forms more enduring friendships Peer groups begin to form

	Birth to Three Years Old	**Three to Four Years Old**	**Five to Six Years Old**	**Seven to Eight Years Old**
Emotional Development	Cannot tolerate frustration Cries easily Is often unable to control impulses Begins to express affection Needs routines and security Begins to perceive emotions of others Expresses self, sometimes emphatically	Can tolerate some frustration Develops some self-control Appreciates surprises and novel events Begins to show sense of humor Needs overt expressions of affection Fears the dark, being abandoned, strange situations	Expresses and labels feelings Controls aggression better Expresses less concern when separated from parents Expresses sense of humor in jokes, nonsense words Learns right from wrong Develops a conscience	Expresses reactions to others Is sensitive to ridicule and criticism Expresses more worries: war, loss of parents Shows more persistence Expresses more empathy; is able to see others' viewpoints
Cognitive Development	Sensorimotor investigation of environment is predominant Development of concepts is rapid Develops a sense of object permanence Develops language May use some number and color words but may not understand them	Follows instructions of two commands Makes impulsive judgments and frequent mistakes Develops vocabulary rapidly Uses numbers without understanding Has difficulty differentiating fantasy and reality Begins to classify, especially by function Begins to use some functional abstract words "Why" questions are constant Thinking is very egocentric	Shows a growing attention span Is able to seriate objects Is able to group objects Is more deliberate, less impulsive in judgments Differentiates between fantasy and reality Uses language aggressively, in categorization Is aware that words and pictures represent real objects Becomes interested in numbers and letters Knows names of colors Does not spontaneously use rehearsal in memory tasks Follows three unrelated commands Some children begin to conserve number, length	Differences in reading and language abilities widen Transition to concrete operational thinking begins Talking and discussion are important Is able to plan Can sustain interest over long periods of time Begins to understand cause and effect Develops a growing understanding of time, money Uses slang and profanity Understands and uses more abstract terms Expresses more awareness of community, world

Sources: Association for Supervision and Curriculum Development 1975; Berk 2000; Tudor 1981.

teachers and parents provide opportunities for safe physical activity and not expect motor control that is beyond what the child can achieve. Fours and fives still need much more movement in their programs than sitting, although they can sit still for short periods for such activities as story time.

Teachers and parents need to think carefully when planning activities for young children. For example, writing on a line requires excellent fine motor control, and most fives and sixes cannot perform this task without considerable difficulty. Children who engage in organized sports such as tee-ball and soccer when they are very young may face the same sort of difficulties. Some parents and coaches expect coordination beyond what five- to eight-year-olds are capable of. If children do participate in organized activities, parents and coaches need to be aware of the abilities that the activities require and to match their expectations to children's capabilities.

All young children need vigorous physical activity every day, and no child should be deprived of the opportunities for such activities because he must complete other tasks or because he is being punished. There is a growing concern that children in the United States are less physically fit than previous generations of children (Berk 1996). This trend seems to reflect the time that children spend in passive activities, such as watching television and sitting quietly at desks, and the lack of vigorous exercise in their daily lives.

The following suggestions may help teachers plan activities that encourage the physical development of children:

- Provide outside play every day that it is possible. Equipment should encourage climbing, running, jumping, and so on.
- Make sure children have access to an inside play area that contains a tumbling mat, Velcro balls and targets, and other materials to encourage movement.
- For very young children, indoor equipment for physical development can include rocking boats, steps, and low slides and tunnels. As children mature, appropriate equipment includes more complex climbing apparatus, balance beams, and so on.
- Provide balls that are age appropriate. For very young children, balls should be large and made of soft materials such as foam and yarn. As children learn to catch and throw more easily, they can use balls made of soft rubber. Durable rubber balls should be provided for children of about five and six who are learning to kick a ball.
- Beginning around five years of age, children can use jump ropes and hula hoops for experimenting with movement and control.
- Many classroom activities help children gain fine muscle control: painting, cutting with scissors, manipulating clay, stringing beads, sewing cards, using pegs and pegboards, and so on. Teachers must encourage these activities as the children's development indicates.

Social Development

Patterns of Development

As noted in the section on physical development, the child's first physical actions are not differentiated—she moves all over, all at once when excited. The infant's social and emotional development is also undifferentiated, in the sense that responses to stimuli such as being cold or hungry evoke crying behaviors that are not specific to the stimuli. In a matter of weeks, the child's crying becomes differentiated so that the primary caregiver can distinguish between the cries that indicate that the child is hungry, bored, or in pain. By six weeks or two months, the infant is able to respond to an adult by smiling and begins to imitate behavior such as sticking out her tongue or closing her eyes. By eight months or so, the child has developed a strong attachment to the primary caregiver and is anxious about separation from him or her. Toddlers begin to develop attachments to their families. Two-year-old children are trying to establish their own identities, and "Me do it" is one of their most frequent statements.

By the time they are three, children have established relationships with their families and with others outside their families. They have also developed some strategies for achieving what they want and some ideas about sex-role identification.

Development of Personality   One element of social development is development of personality. Erik Erikson (1902–1994), a psychoanalytic theorist, concentrated on studying the development of the ego—a sense of self (Ambron 1978). His description of stages in ego development are especially useful to teachers. Erikson viewed the child's developing identity as a reflection of relationships with parents and family within the broader context of society.

Teachers who think about children's behavior in Erikson's terms will plan programs that provide many opportunities for children to build trust and to make choices and feel successful in the choices they make. Building friendships is important in early childhood. Cooper and McEvoy (1996) state that forming friendships offers children the chance to learn skills in negotiation and compromise that are necessary for mature social interactions as adults. In addition, having good peer relationships as a child is an excellent predictor of achieving adequate social adjustment as an adult.

Helping children recognize their own needs and the feelings and emotions of others are important steps in building trust. The child must feel that his ideas are good ideas and that others respect them. If too much of the time spent in school or child care is directed by the teacher, children will begin to feel that their ideas are unacceptable. Older children need to be able to participate in activities in which their achievements are obvious and celebrated. For example, four- and five-year-olds need to know that if they suggest activities, the teacher will listen and help them carry out their ideas, if possible. If the

■ Basic Trust versus Basic Mistrust (first year of life)

Experiences and sensations that give the infant a sense of familiarity and inner certainty provide him with a sense of self. He feels that the world is benevolent or at least reliable, and he likewise trusts himself and his own capacities. He has established basic trust. If the individual develops basic mistrust instead, he may tend to behave irrationally or to withdraw into schizoid or depressive states in later life.

■ Autonomy versus Shame and Doubt (second year of life)

During the second year of life, the infant develops muscular control; she moves about and begins toilet training. She needs firmness now, as a protection against the potential anarchy of her own impulses. The sense of self-control (autonomy) learned at this stage leads to a lasting sense of goodwill and personal pride. A failure to achieve well-guided autonomy can lead later in life to compulsive neurosis (a pervasive sense of shame before the world) and compulsive doubt of the self and others.

■ Initiative versus Guilt (the preschool years)

During the preschool years, the child has a boundless supply of energy, which permits him to learn all kinds of activities and ideas quickly and avidly. He concentrates on successes rather than failures and does things for the simple pleasure of the activity. Autonomy becomes more focused and effective. The child becomes "more himself." The danger in this period is that the child's exuberant and aggressive explorations and conquests may lead him into frustration. His new physical and mental strengths encourage ambitions that may turn out to be beyond his abilities—inevitably, he sometimes fails or is defeated. Unless he can come to terms with these disappointments, he may be overwhelmed by resignation, guilt, and anxiety.

activity cannot be incorporated into the classroom, the teacher will still treat the idea with respect and perhaps help the child modify the idea or accomplish some part of the activity.

Development of Self-Esteem   Another element of the social development of the young child is the development of self-esteem. The concept of self is developed gradually; the young child develops a concept of himself as a separate individual over a period of years. Through interactions first with the parents and family and then with peers and others outside the family, children gradually develop a concept of who they are and what they are like. In a classic study of children's self-esteem, Coopersmith (1967) found that children, especially boys, with high self-esteem had parents who were accepting, affectionate, and genuinely concerned about their child. The parents also enforced rules carefully and consistently and insisted on high standards of behavior but used noncoercive methods of discipline. They also demonstrated more democratic interactions with their children.

Teachers of young children often plan experiences in which improving self-esteem is the primary goal. However, such plans for activities often ignore the pervasive nature of the development of self-concept. Katz (1986) discusses the futility of planning an activity based on "me" (a booklet about my favorite food, my pet, my favorite dress, my best skill, and so on) as a means of improving self-esteem. Such an activity might contribute to the child's self-

Perhaps the best way to help the child at this age is to encourage him to play constructively, to do some chores around the house, or to help care for younger children. In this way, the conflict between initiative and guilt may be resolved by the establishment of a constructive moral sense; it can set the individual on the road to goals that are not only possible for him but also deeply satisfying. If the conflict remains unresolved, in adult life the individual may be inhibited or impotent (socially as well as sexually), or he may overreact by compulsive showing off.

■ Industry versus Inferiority (middle childhood)

Building on the previously developed trust, autonomy, and initiative, the child can achieve a sense of industry. In school, she learns the basic tools of literacy and cooperation that will enable her to become a productive member of society, and a sense of achievement becomes important to her. She learns the satisfaction of persisting at a task until it is completed and of using her skills to perform according to her own and others' expectations. In a culture like that in the United States, in which achievement is often measured in terms of doing better than someone else, she also learns to compete and to measure her productivity in relation to that of others.

The dangers of this period are twofold. On the one hand, the child may learn to value achievement in work above all else; she may alienate her peers by excessively competitive behavior. On the other hand, she may feel unable to perform the tasks required of her and develop a sense of inferiority that prevents her from trying. Experiences of failure may lead to the child's feeling that she is inadequate, that she cannot be successful as a worker. In extreme cases, this sense of inferiority can affect the child's attitude toward work for life.

Source: Adapted from Erikson 1963.

esteem if it is conducted in the context of a classroom environment in which children have choices and opportunities to participate in a variety of activities in which they can feel successful and in control. But if the classroom environment is generally structured so that children feel unable to be successful, then even a series of self-esteem lessons will not be effective.

Kostelnik et al. (1993) state that "fifteen-minute activities or the adult's gushing remarks will not infuse children with a sense of well-being or inoculate them against negative self-perceptions. Because esteem-influencing experiences pervade all aspects of children's lives and are ever-present, authentic esteem enhancing efforts must be pervasive too" (p. 78). Therefore, a teacher who wishes to build self-esteem in children will consider how children are treated all through the day. The kinds of experiences regularly provided for them are much more important in the process of building self-esteem than isolated lessons or activities designed to focus on positive feelings about oneself.

The Role of Play   Play experiences are very important in the social and emotional development of young children. Children can "play" various roles and behaviors and get feedback about the appropriateness of the behaviors in play. They can play "bully" or "baby" and find out what kinds of responses their behavior elicits in nonthreatening situations. They can also play various adult roles. Young children often play the roles of family members, and with experience, they begin to play roles of those outside the family. They might play "grocery clerk," "filling station attendant," "dentist," or "garbage worker" and explore the behavior patterns that they believe are appropriate for those individuals.

Because play is so important in the lives of children, an entire chapter will be devoted to the topic of play (see Chapter 5).

Social Skills and Social Relationships   Research continues to emphasize the importance of fostering children's social development in the early childhood years. In summarizing the effects of peer relationships in childhood, Hartup (1992) states that these relationships contribute greatly to our successful adaptation as adults:

> *Indeed, the single best childhood predictor of adult adaptation is not IQ, not school grades, and not classroom behavior but rather the adequacy with which the child gets along with other children. Children who are generally disliked, who are aggressive and disruptive, who are unable to sustain close relationships with other children, and who cannot establish a place for themselves in the peer culture are seriously at risk.* (p. 1)

Rogers and Ross (1986) describe *social skill* as the "ability to assess what is happening in a social situation; skill to perceive and correctly interpret the actions and needs of the children in the group at play; ability to imagine possible courses of action and select the most appropriate one" (pp. 14–15). Children who are popular and most successful socially demonstrate these abilities, but children who lack social skills may need direct instruction through modeling, role-playing, or the use of puppets to help them develop these abilities. Roopnarine and Honig (1985), in a review of research on the unpopular child, add that teachers can help children become more popular by helping their families focus on more positive discipline techniques and making sure that positive social development is a major program goal. Katz and McClellan (1997) believe that the child's capacity for developing close, caring friendships, not just her popularity, is the best indication of a child's social competence.

Teachers and parents are concerned with the development in young children of *prosocial behaviors:* helping, cooperating, and empathizing. Kostelnik et al. (1993) report that prosocial behaviors increase rapidly during the preschool years. In the classroom setting, teachers can help children develop these behaviors through modeling the desired behaviors, setting up situations that require cooperation, and suggesting specific ways that children can be cooperative or helpful. Some play equipment should be selected that can be used by more than one child, such as telephones, jump ropes, and board games. Teachers can model caring and empathy for each child and discuss with the children how some actions make others feel. Teachers can also demonstrate how to be cooperative by helping build a block construction or helping dig in the garden.

Katz and McClellan (1997) suggest that building prosocial behavior has several components. One is to alert children to other people's feelings and interests. Teachers can help children think about others who share their interests or

Getting along with others and relating interpersonally demonstrate prosocial behavior.

help children think about how others might feel. Another component of building prosocial behavior is to encourage children to accept alternative interpretations of others' behavior. For example, if one child accidentally knocks over another child's block structure, the teacher may need to help both children recognize the difference between accidental and purposeful behavior. Teachers may also need to help children develop verbal skills by providing them with models for what to say to facilitate interactions. For instance, the sensitive teacher can encourage taking turns through teaching the child who wants a turn how to ask and through appealing to the resisting child's sense of generosity and reason. If the child continues to resist, the teacher may have to intervene. The resisting child needs to be offered some other interesting choices of activities so that the resistance does not become a significant behavioral style.

Aggression   Another aspect of social development that receives attention is aggression. Teachers and parents are concerned with children's aggressive behavior. The results of studies indicate that aggressive behavior in the classroom can be reduced by providing enough space and materials so that children do not have to compete with one another. These studies also suggest eliminating toys that lend themselves to aggressive themes and not allowing children to benefit from aggressive behavior by either controlling the victim or getting the teacher's attention. It is also important to model cooperative behavior and discuss and demonstrate solutions to problems other than aggression (Potts, Huston, and Wright 1986; Yarrow 1983).

Aggression can be manifested as either a reactive or a proactive action. A *reactive* action is usually accompanied by anger, as when a child defends himself or his belongings through aggressive actions. A *proactive* action is not always accompanied by anger but involves the child's use of aggressive behavior to get something he wants, such as a toy from another child. Bullying is usually proactive aggression.

Helping children manage their anger will help eliminate much aggressive behavior. Marion (1997) suggests teachers take these measures to help children manage their anger:

1. *Create a safe emotional climate.*
2. *Model responsible anger management.*
3. *Help children develop self-regulatory skills.*
4. *Encourage children to label feelings of anger.*
5. *Encourage children to talk about anger-arousing interactions.*
6. *Use appropriate books and stories about anger to help children understand and manage anger.*
7. *Communicate with parents.* (pp. 65–66)

Stopping the behavior of a bully can be especially complex. It may involve helping the child make the connection between her behavior and her rejection by the other children. The teacher may need to directly intervene and then indicate her dislike for the bullying child's behavior. Asking the child how it would feel to be bullied requires a cognitive analysis that the child may be unable to perform, so direct action is usually more successful (Katz and McClellan 1997). Farver (1996) has found that aggressive children tend to play with other aggressive children and suggests that regrouping the children for projects or outings might change the aggressive patterns. Hektner, August, and Realmuto (2000) found that aggressive children who choose other aggressive children for playmates often do so because they have been rejected by other, more nonaggressive children. Teaching children how to become friends with nonaggressive playmates can reduce the amount of aggressive behavior.

Violence in schools is an area of growing concern. There is evidence that aggression and violent behavior begins early in children's lives; therefore, many schools have adopted violence prevention programs. Anderson (2001) suggests that schools can help prevent violence by providing experiences that

- help build and foster relationships that support learning
- promote social and emotional competence
- provide frequent and positive interactions between adults and children
- strengthen children's skills to interact meaningfully with others
- demonstrate good and positive role models
- foster problem solving with respectful words and actions. (p. 60)

One of the assumptions in early childhood care is that aggressive behavior will increase if there are not enough toys or attractive activities for the number of children in the group. Blair and Kwang-Sun (2000) found that the incidence of aggression could be lowered after children were trained in social skills even when the number of toys was not adequate. Reducing aggressive behavior in situations in which aggressive behavior is frequently demonstrated lends strong support for teaching social skills.

Bullies and their victims can both benefit from what Shure (2000) calls "problem-solving dialogue." In lieu of punishment for bullying, she suggests helping bullies learn more positive interaction patterns and helping victims learn to be more assertive. Shure believes that children from ages four to seven can learn to solve interaction problems and that by about age eight, children gain new skills in understanding the point of view of others. She suggests that teachers get children actively involved in questioning their behavior and finding solutions rather than simply telling them what to do (as in "Tell him with words what you want"). Leff et al. (2001) examined violence prevention programs for young children and found that teaching positive social skills was an effective means of reducing violence.

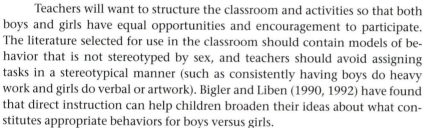

Parents AND *Development*

■ If parents are interested, ask a speaker to focus on the relationships among child development, discipline, and routines or some other area of development.

Sex-Role Identification Sex-role identification is yet another important element of social development. Before they are three, children begin to identify themselves as boys or girls, and at around three years of age they can identify others as boys or girls. They continue to develop their concepts of sexual identity and their attitudes about appropriate roles for males and females. In fact, preschoolers may be quite rigid about what is appropriate play or an appropriate task for males or females.

Teachers will want to structure the classroom and activities so that both boys and girls have equal opportunities and encouragement to participate. The literature selected for use in the classroom should contain models of behavior that is not stereotyped by sex, and teachers should avoid assigning tasks in a stereotypical manner (such as consistently having boys do heavy work and girls do verbal or artwork). Bigler and Liben (1990, 1992) have found that direct instruction can help children broaden their ideas about what constitutes appropriate behaviors for boys versus girls.

Implications for the Curriculum

Teachers do not usually plan activities in which the sole purpose is social development; instead, they think about social development as one facet of children's participation in a variety of classroom experiences. Teachers who want to help children develop socially will be aware of children's social abilities and take advantage of the classroom routine to further their development. Activities should encourage children to cooperate, to develop their self-esteem, and to gain skill in interacting with other children. The following are only a few suggestions of ways to promote growth in social abilities:

■ Provide dress-up corners where children can take on a variety of roles. Simple costumes such as aprons and hats can help children explore new roles. Threes and fours need more family-oriented props; older children need more props for roles found in the larger community. Sixes, sevens, and eights may respond to props that help them reenact stories from literature.

■ Involve primary children in solving social problems in the classroom through role-play and discussions of how to find alternative solutions, how to disagree without being aggressive, and how to make changes in rules they believe are inappropriate or unfair.

- For threes, popular play materials should be plentiful so that fewer arguments arise and children do not have to wait long for a turn. As children mature, teachers may help them work out approaches to taking turns and sharing toys and equipment, such as using waiting lists or a timer.

- Use puppets to model appropriate techniques for entering a play group. For example, the teacher could use a puppet to demonstrate how a child might ask a group playing with blocks if she could play, too.

- Encourage children to make as many decisions as possible. In free play, allow children to choose activities and experiences. In more directed times of the day, such as music or story time, encourage children to choose songs or stories.

- Model empathy and caring behaviors, and encourage children to display these behaviors.

- Role-play solutions to problems in social interactions. For example, children might role-play how to make an introduction when a guest comes to the classroom or how to ask another child to share materials.

Emotional Development

Patterns of Development

Emotional development, like physical and social development, follows fairly predictable stages of growth (Berk 2000). The infant responds to any emotion with undifferentiated crying. As the baby grows, this crying becomes differentiated to reflect various emotions. By the time the baby is a few months old, he may scream in anger but produce none of the tears that accompany crying caused by physical pain. Infants have almost no capacity to wait for someone to attend to their needs; their reactions to feelings are immediate. Some researchers (Thomas and Chess 1977) have found that children have distinct temperaments early in life and that temperament tends to be stable over time. Other researchers (DeVries and Sameroff 1984) believe that temperament is responsive to environmental influences. If a baby is difficult and irritable, for example, the parents may not handle the baby as much as they might have handled a more responsive or easy-going baby—and this, in turn, will further affect the baby's temperament.

Toddlers are compulsive in their behaviors. They have little control of their impulses and are easily frustrated. By the time children reach three years of age, they have developed some tolerance for frustration. They can wait for short periods of time. If their mother explains that dinner will be ready very soon, they can manage to wait for it. They are also developing some self-control; they do not respond to every impulse. Three-year-olds have been observed talking themselves out of doing something they would have done without thinking a year earlier.

Threes and fours like surprises and novel events. They need the security of knowing that there is structure to their day—that they are going to play, have a snack, and so on—but they respond well to some surprises in the day. When someone dressed as Mother Goose stops by the classroom to share some nursery rhymes, they can handle the change. Three- and four-year-olds are also beginning to develop a sense of humor. They often laugh when they hear a word that sounds funny to them or when they see something incongruous. They are not embarrassed when they laugh at inappropriate moments because they cannot analyze their own behavior in order to determine that it was inappropriate.

By the time children are in kindergarten and first grade, they are able to express and label a wide variety of emotions. They can describe their own sad, angry, or happy feelings and can describe situations that produce given emotions in others. These children become more capable of controlling their aggressive feelings and, with some guidance, can learn to work out their frustrations with other children using words rather than hitting. Five- and six-year-olds also begin to develop a conscience and a sense of right and wrong.

Fives and sixes express their sense of humor in jokes or nonsense words. They often tell jokes without punch lines and still laugh at their own stories. They repeat jokes they have heard, often without understanding them. "Knock-knock" jokes are favorites, and children frequently make up their own versions. They also have great fun creating nonsense words or making rhymes with other words. These tend to be especially funny if they are a little naughty.

Children in the primary years, seven- and eight-year-olds, continue to gain even more control of their emotional responses. They are much less impulsive than younger children. They have strong responses to other individuals and usually like or dislike them immediately. Children in this age group are quite sensitive to criticism or ridicule. They demonstrate embarrassment at their own behavior. They tend to have more worries than younger children as they become more aware of world conditions and attend more to news stories they see on television or hear being discussed by adults. They worry about war, about things happening to their parents (death or divorce), and about accidents.

Seven- and eight-year-olds demonstrate persistence in trying to achieve their goals. This often drives their parents mad, as the child asks to do something again and again after it has been denied. Children this age develop much more empathy for other people and feel bad when someone else is hurting, either physically or emotionally. They offer comfort to family or friends without being prompted to do so.

Implications for the Curriculum

Emotional growth can be encouraged through typical classroom experiences if the teacher is aware of the child's level of development and what can be done to encourage development. The following are examples of classroom activities that can help children:

- Have children dramatize situations in which anger or frustration are handled appropriately.
- Use puppets to model appropriate responses to emotions. For example, with younger children the teacher might use puppets to model the use

of language rather than hitting to express anger. With older children, the teacher might model different responses to frustrations, such as not winning a race or a game.

- Help children learn to acknowledge and label their feelings as they participate in classroom activities.
- Choose literature in which the characters respond to emotions appropriately, and discuss how they felt and how they acted.
- Provide empathy for children's fears and concerns. They are real to the child and should not be belittled.
- Allow children to share their humor; appreciate the growth in their sense of humor.
- Primary children may be helped to express their feelings through writing. Select examples from literature that illustrate how children have written about their frustrations or stresses and learned to cope more effectively with them through the writing process.

Intellectual Development

Patterns of Development

Berk (2000) defines *cognition* as "the inner processes and products of the mind that lead to 'knowing.' It includes all mental activity—remembering, symbolizing, categorizing, problem-solving, creating, fantasizing, and even dreaming" (p. 221). **Cognitive development**, then, refers to the development of the child's thinking and reasoning abilities.

The cognitive development of young children is described by different theorists in different terms. The behaviorist point of view is that children grow intellectually through accumulating more and more information. Most measures of intelligence are based on this idea of accumulating knowledge. Another point of view is that of the constructivists, or developmentalists, who describe knowledge as being constructed from children's interactions with the environment. According to this viewpoint, intellectual development is influenced by both maturation and experience (Piaget and Inhelder 1969). Cognitive development is indicated by a growing ability to plan, to employ strategies for remembering, and to seek solutions to problems.

Piaget and Inhelder (1969) described the cognitive development of children as progressing in several stages, including the *sensorimotor stage,* the *preoperational stage,* and the *concrete operational stage* (see box on pages 28–29). The stages evolve with the child's growing maturity and experience. Although approximate ages have been attached to these stages, the rate at which individuals pass through them is variable; the sequence of stages, however, is invariant. In other words, a child must pass through each stage, but different children may pass through the stages at different ages. The transition time between stages is lengthy. Children do not move suddenly from one stage of thinking to another—changes may take months or years, as the child constructs and integrates knowledge. A child may be performing some tasks in ways that indicate preoperational thinking while performing other tasks in very stable operational ways.

Vygotsky (1978) believed that children's intellectual development is influenced more by social context than by individual experiences. His theory places a great deal of emphasis on effective social interaction. One characteristic of such effective interactions is what Vygotsky called *intersubjectivity,* which describes a process in which two people are engaged in a task and begin it with different understandings but come to a shared understanding. With infants this process is illustrated when the caregiver follows the infant's gaze and talks about or hands the object of the gaze to the child. The nature of these encounters changes over time, especially with the development of language.

Another hallmark of effective interactions is *scaffolding:* the support given the learner in the social context, which changes with the growing ability of the child or with the situation. For example, an adult helping a child learn to cut may hold the scissors with his hand over the child's hand and help the child move them, pointing out what happens when they are moved in a certain way. As the child becomes more skilled, the adult offers less help and more challenging cutting tasks.

Vygotsky also emphasized the role of make-believe play in children's cognitive development. Children involved in pretend play learn to act in accordance with their internal ideas, not just their external environment. Children must also follow the rules of the social situation they are playing—for example, riding on a train, going to church, and so on.

In addition to the theoretical explanations of cognitive growth, an increasing amount of knowledge is available from biology as scientists study the human brain. Using sophisticated imaging techniques and other investigative strategies, scientists can determine how the electrical activity in the brain differs from one experience to another. This is the beginning of a revolution in the field of education. When we have answers about how the brain works, teaching will radically change.

At this time, however, our knowledge of the brain is limited. Some proponents of so-called brain-based learning are making claims that cannot be proven. For example, Bruer (1999) argues against the generally accepted belief that the two hemispheres of the brain have different functions, such as the processing of music and math. He believes that scientific evidence proves that different areas of the brain do different kinds of processing, but it is much more refined than the proponents of left- and right-brain teaching would have us believe, and that both hemispheres are involved in almost every processing task. He also finds no scientific support for the idea that learning takes place more quickly and easily when children are young. According to Bruer, there is no evidence that a five-year-old brain learns more quickly than a fifteen-year-old brain.

What we *do* know about the brain is that it is "wired" to process information in different ways. Some of this wiring happens prenatally when cells differentiate into the different areas of the brain. Human brains are prewired for some

■ Sensorimotor Period (birth to two years)

The sensorimotor period is characterized by interactions with the environment based on the child's reception of sensory input and muscular reactions. The period begins with reflexive actions, which are gradually controlled by the child, and ends with the child's having developed a concept of separateness from others and the beginnings of symbolic thinking. The task of this period is to develop the concept of *object permanence*, the idea that objects exist even when they cannot be seen or heard.

■ Preoperational Period (two to seven years)

The beginning of the preoperational period is characterized by emergence of the ability to represent objects and knowledge through imitation, symbolic play, drawing, mental images, and spoken language. One outstanding characteristic of preoperational thinking is lack of conservation. *Conservation* is defined as the knowledge that the number, mass, area, length, weight, and volume of objects are not changed by physically rearranging the objects.

Children whose thinking is preoperational are egocentric in that they cannot easily take the points of view of others. A preoperational child believes that everyone thinks as she does and that everyone thinks the same things she does. *Egocentrism* is not exclusive to the thinking of preoperational children but is most prominent then. Egocentrism is a factor in the child's reasoning at this stage because children do not question their own thinking and therefore do not change schemata readily.

Another characteristic of preoperational thinking is *centration*. The preoperational child tends to pay attention to one element of a problem at a time and cannot coordinate information from multiple sources. Centration is related to classification, seriation, and other such tasks. The following anecdote describes an example of centration:

> A child was visiting with a family friend, and they were going out in a boat. The friend's boat was beside an identical boat at the dock. One boat was tied up about three feet farther in the slip than the other one. The child walked up and down the pier several times, observing the two boats. After a few minutes, he remarked, "Your boat is longer on this end, and that boat is longer on the other end."

A fourth characteristic of preoperational thinking is the difficulty a child has in trying to reverse capabilities, such as oral language (Brandt 1999). And some of this wiring happens because of experience or need. For example, people can learn to interpret the messages from the nerves in the eyes differently, as when they learn to wear one contact lens to correct for distance vision. In doing so, the pattern from one eye is always fuzzy, either at a distance or close up. After a few weeks, the brain learns to ignore the fuzzy message and interprets only the clear message.

It is also safe to say that providing an enriched environment encourages many more connections between the neurons of the brain, creating more possibilities for solving problems (Jensen 1998; Sylwester 1995). It cannot be said for certain, however, just what an *enriched environment* is and what cultural biases limit the descriptions of enriched environments currently being published.

Even though we have much to learn about the brain and its functioning, we can observe children's development and offer them opportunities for many kinds of experiences under emotionally comfortable circumstances. If we do this and continue to read and learn about the biology of the brain, we can make schools better and learning more accessible to all children.

thinking. *Reversibility* is defined as the ability to follow a line of reasoning back to the beginning point. In the problem of conserving number, a child is presented with two rows of eight plastic chips and observes that they are equal. When the space between the chips is lengthened, the preoperational child believes that the number has been changed because the row is longer. When the child is able to reverse the reasoning process, he will be able to determine that moving the chips does not affect the number. A child may be able to reverse an operation physically before being able to reverse operations mentally.

Preoperational children have difficulty in reasoning logically about transformations. The child tends to concentrate on the elements of change and not on the transformations of objects or materials from one state to another. Piaget found that children had difficulty thinking about successive changes in states and about the relationship of one event to another. Piaget made this observation when walking with a child through the woods and drawing the child's attention to the snails that could be seen at various points along the path. The child could not determine if the snails were all the same snail or different snails. Children can observe the beginning point and the ending point of transformations, but they often have difficulty follow-ing all the points in between. If a child is asked to draw what happens to a pencil as it falls off a table, she can draw the pencil on the table and on the floor but not all the steps between the table and the floor.

■ Concrete Operational Period (seven to eleven or twelve years)

Children begin making the transition from preoperational thinking to operational thinking at various times. In most kindergarten classrooms, a few children will be beginning to think operationally. In the primary grades, more children will be operational thinkers, even though many may still be preoperational on some tasks. Piaget and Inhelder (1969) describe the operational thinker as one who employs "identity or reversibility by inversion or reciprocity" (p. 99) in solving problems.

Concrete operational thinkers are able to solve problems of conservation and reversibility. They can *decenter*, or coordinate information from more than one source, in solving problems. They are not as egocentric in their thinking. Because they are aware that others may come to conclusions that differ from theirs, they are much more likely to examine their own conclusions.

Sources: Piaget and Inhelder 1969; Wadsworth 1989.

Implications for the Curriculum

Planning for the intellectual growth of children is dependent on the knowledge of children's cognitive development. A child who is preoperational, for instance, would not be expected to solve problems in the same way that an older child would solve them. Also, children need chances to learn in ways that are active and that provide opportunities to learn in ways that suit their individual techniques for organizing and remembering information.

One challenge for teachers is to avoid what Lilian Katz (1986) describes as "learned stupidity," which occurs when children are given tasks that they cannot do and, through failure at those tasks, learn to believe that they are stupid. No young child has the life experience to evaluate an inappropriate task and determine that it was the task that was at fault, not the learner.

Young children learn best through manipulating objects and being reflective about those manipulations, not through passive experiences in which they listen to someone tell them how something works. Young children need the stimulation of their peers in solving problems, and they need to be able

Developmentally Appropriate Practice

Knowing the child or the learner is absolutely necessary for planning a developmentally appropriate program. Several questions about DAP are directly related to children's development:

- Are the activities planned usually of interest to children of the age for which the activities are intended?
- Can most children complete the activities successfully?
- Will some children be allowed to choose more challenging activities?
- Will some children be allowed to choose activities that require less skill without being censured?
- Will expectations for performance reflect knowledge of child development?

to use what they already know in learning new information. Throughout this book, you will find suggestions for encouraging the intellectual growth of children; the following activities are merely a small sample of the endless possibilities:

- Provide old machines (toasters, TVs, radios, and so on) that children can dismantle and explore. (Be sure to remove the electrical connections and any springs that could be unsafe.)

- Set up problems to be presented to the class in ways that encourage divergent thinking and multiple right answers. For example, ask children how many different ways they can sort the blocks rather than ask them to sort the blocks by color.

- Give children the opportunity to choose as many of their own activities as possible. Children can learn to classify by playing with blocks, leaves, keys, items from the supermarket, and articles of clothing. When children are given a choice, they are more likely to learn.

- Provide materials that are open ended so that the challenge and complexity can be increased as the children grow. For example, given beads, children at different ages can string them, use them to create patterns, or use them to create models and designs.

- Encourage children to follow their interests. Jacque Wuertenburg (1993) calls it "leading through life." If a child is interested in spiders or snakes or computers, use that interest to help build skills and concepts.

- Assist children in understanding the application of what they are learning in school to real life. Learning without a purpose is difficult.

Celebrating Diversity

The work of Vygotsky supports the notion that children from different cultures learn different things at different ages. Teachers need to recognize that children learn to use language in ways that are appropriate for their own culture and to perform tasks that are significant in their culture. For example, some Asian children can manipulate chopsticks successfully long before their European counterparts have the fine motor control to do so.

In celebrating the diversity of the children in their classrooms, teachers must also think about the expectations that children's families have for them and for their behavior and learning in the school setting. Although it is not acceptable for teachers to engage in practices they feel are inappropriate for children, teachers must always respect the parents and their culture. For example, corporal punishment of children is advocated in some cultures. Suppose some parents suggest that if their son does not attend to task or misbehaves in school, you, the teacher, should hit him. Of course, you should not hit the child, but you should respect the parents' desire for their child to be successful in school. In addition, you should make sure that you keep the parents informed about their child's progress and behavior as well as what you are doing to help him.

The time you spend learning what parents expect of their children in terms of social and emotional development will benefit you in planning activities and experiences. For example, if a child's family encourages cooperation rather than competition, then they need to know that you are also interested in using cooperative behavior to solve problems and that you will not try to change their child.

> ## *Parents* AND *Development*
>
> ■ Communicate with parents about their children's accomplishments in all four areas of development: physical, social, emotional, and cognitive. For each child, keep a column in a notebook or a file of observations labeled with the four areas so that you can tell at a glance if you are not observing growth in one area as much as in others. Share this information with parents, and ask them to provide information across all areas as well—particularly cultural expectations.

Chapter Summary

■ Development can be described in different terms, depending on one's philosophical point of view. The major philosophical orientations are represented by the behaviorists, the maturationists, and the constructivists.

■ Development is an orderly process of moving from undifferentiated movements and reactions to finely differentiated and controlled movements and specific responses.

■ Physical development is most rapid in infancy but continues quite rapidly through the preschool years. Children in the primary grades continue to develop their physical abilities, but the rate is not as rapid as it is with younger children.

■ Ideally, as their social development progresses, children become capable of successful interactions with others, develop prosocial behaviors such as helping and cooperating, learn to control aggression, and develop a positive concept of themselves.

■ Emotional development is observed as children evolve from expressing undifferentiated responses to emotions to being able to express their emotions in socially acceptable ways and to control their impulses. Children grow more capable of understanding how others feel and develop a sense of right and wrong.

- Cognitive development describes the changes that take place in children's thinking and reasoning. Very young children learn best from handling objects, preschoolers need to manipulate objects and reflect on the outcomes of their manipulations, and elementary school children still need to use concrete materials in their reasoning processes.

Young children do not employ adult logic in making sense of their environment, nor can they reason in abstract terms.

- The different stages of child development have implications for planning a curriculum for young children. Teachers need to think about children's physical abilities and the cognitive requirements of different tasks when they select learning experiences. They also need to plan activities that will help children develop social skills.

Theory INTO *Practice*

For about thirty minutes each, observe a group of three-year-olds and a group of eight-year-olds at play. Make a list of what you see as the most obvious changes in children between the ages of three and eight. Consider all areas of the children's development.

Observe in a preschool or a primary grade, and list those activities you believe encourage physical, social, emotional, and intellectual development. (That is, make four lists.) Discuss the activities with your group. Do members agree about whether each activity should be listed? Do any activities appear on all four lists? Discuss differences among members' lists.

In your group, read two articles that describe some element of cognitive development. List the points on which the authors agree and disagree. Is their philosophical bias evident in their writing? If so, how? Do all authors who write about children's development have a bias in terms of their philosophical viewpoint? Why or why not?

Darla Wood-Walters

Elk Meadow Elementary
Bend, Oregon

Using Developmental Knowledge in Planning

My classroom brings together children who are assigned to a specific grade level. However, whether I am teaching kindergarten or first grade for a given school year, my focus is always on the developmental needs of the individual children in my classroom, not their grade-level placement.

It is my challenge to identify and celebrate what a child can do well, build a foundation of confidence and pride, and from there guide and support him as he takes the next step. Although I can present lessons and activities that are well prepared, organized, and appropriate for my grade-level curriculum, if they are not within reach of my students' present understandings, they are nothing more than a lesson taught, not a lesson learned.

The concept of developmental appropriateness has received much attention in past years, with general definitions being assigned to each of the primary grades. However, I teach the child, not the grade level. It is as developmentally inappropriate to fail to challenge students as it is to frustrate other students. My goal is always to match instruction to the developmental needs of my students, providing a task that is just beyond what they think they can do and giving them the support they need not only to be able to do it, but also to do it well.

For example, I want young writers to know that writing is talking on paper. Rather than spoon-feeding them with fill-in-the-blanks and specific structures to make them all sound like writers, I want to recognize each child's first steps to becoming a writer as they share their thinking and talking voice through an illustration, letterlike marks, random letters, phonetic spelling, conventional spelling, or edited writing and revising. As I conference with a young writer, I applaud what she does well and focus her attention on what she can do to make her next writing even better. For one child, this might be to put spaces between words, for another it might be how to use a word card to edit for spelling, and for yet another it might be how to extend the story to make it more interesting.

Just as the instructional focus reflects the writing development of the student, the book size and format also reflect the writer's needs. Emergent writers need large, blank paper, providing space for the untamed pencil and crayon. Developing and fluent writers use smaller formatted, lined paper as the illustration becomes less important and the print carries more of the message. A variety of writing materials would be used in kindergarten and first grade, providing each child with the support he or she needs for success.

There is no set time in the year when I begin instruction on handwriting. Until a student has a good grasp of directionality, spatial awareness, and motor control, learning to make letters correctly is unnecessarily difficult. I focus a student's attention on handwriting when these concepts and skills are in place, when a child is confident in putting pencil to paper, and when he has had enough writing experiences to understand that good writing is much more than how the print looks. I teach handwriting on an individual basis, embedding it in meaningful print, beginning with a child's name, pulling letters out of their daily writing, and then attending to capitals/lowercase as needed to support understandings of punctuation. This focus on handwriting might begin with one student the first month of kindergarten; it might begin with another midyear of first grade. Always instruction is based on the development of the child.

CHAPTER 2

Designing Schools
for Young Children

After reading this chapter, you will be able to do the following:

- Briefly describe the history of early childhood education.
- Describe the contemporary models in early childhood education: Montessori, behaviorist, and constructivist.
- Relate the research on various program models.

*W*hen you entered the kindergarten classroom in which you observed this week, a child asked, "Do you want to see my book?" You admired the child's book and were then invited to observe other children's accomplishments: a replica of the fire station they had visited several days ago; a painting of a bird's nest; a melody played on bells; and a plant along with a growth chart, starting from the day the seed was planted. Everybody in this busy classroom seemed to be doing something interesting, but you did not see anyone doing the lessons you had expected to see.

When you shared your observations with members of your class, you found that the school settings your peers had observed varied a great deal. Some had observed lessons in which small groups of students were learning the alphabet and the sounds represented by the letters. Others had observed in classrooms in which children worked independently with materials they selected from neatly arranged shelves.

When you finished sharing observations with your peers, you did discover some elements that the programs had in common. For example, all the programs were promoting learning in children. Even so, the content of the learning and how the instruction was delivered varied greatly. You have many questions now: Who makes the decisions about how programs are organized? Who determines the focus of the instruction? Who determines what role the teacher in the program will play? What is the best kind of program for young children?

Early Schools for Young Children

As an early childhood educator, you will be asked to make many decisions in your career. Many of those decisions will be about the programs and activities that you will provide for the children you teach. The decisions you make will reflect your own view of how children learn best and the most effective ways to teach them. You will want to know that early childhood education has a long history and that for many years philosophers and teachers have been thinking about these same questions.

Early childhood programs today can trace their development back to early philosophers. For example, Martin Luther (1483–1546) believed that all boys should be educated (a radical thought in his day) and insisted that music and physical education should be integral parts of the curriculum (Frost and Kissinger 1976). A century later John Comenius (1592–1670) suggested that all children should attend school, and he recommended an integrated, hands-on curriculum. He believed that children should learn to speak by speaking, to write by writing, and to reason by reasoning (Comenius 1642; reprinted 1969). Later educators such as Dewey, Montessori, and Piaget have echoed Comenius's call for active learning.

Two other philosophers, Jean-Jacques Rousseau (1712–1778) and Johann Pestalozzi (1746–1827), also made important contributions to early childhood education. Rousseau thought that educational decisions should be made on the basis of the child's nature. He also developed a stage theory of child development based on his belief that children from birth to age five learn best from physical activity and that children from five to twelve learn best by direct experience and exploration of the environment (Rousseau 1780; reprinted 1950). When educators advocate hands-on learning, they are agreeing with Rousseau. Pestalozzi wanted to rid the schools of cruel punishment and rote learning. He believed in having children participate in real, meaningful activities and in grouping children of various ages so that the older ones could help the younger ones (Pestalozzi 1885, 1894).

Friedrich Froebel

Friedrich Froebel (1782–1852) is credited with founding *kindergartens:* "children's gardens." He studied with Pestalozzi but believed that Pestalozzi did not go far enough in matching teaching to the nature of the child. Froebel began his school for young children in Blankenburg, Germany, in 1837. He believed that everything in the universe functions in relationship to God and that each person has a specific purpose to fulfill in this life. He wrote, "Education should lead and guide man to clearness concerning himself and in himself, to peace with nature, and to unity with God" (Froebel 1826, ch. 5). The importance of the individual and the respect that must be accorded to each person is central to Froebelian thinking.

Froebel believed that play is the foundation for children's learning and envisioned the kindergarten as the child's bridge between home and school. He believed that appropriate play helps children think about the interactions between "life and self-activity, thought and action, representation and cognition, and ability and understanding" (Ransbury 1982, p. 104). Froebel believed that materials in forms found in nature—spheres, cubes, cylinders, squares, triangles, circles, and lines—help children explore the properties of matter and understand the relationships in the universe. He called these materials "gifts." He also designed sequences of activities that he called "occupations"; they included folding paper, drawing, and weaving. Froebel distinguished between what he called "thoughtless copying" and "deliberate imitation." He believed that when children perform the occupations, they restructure their own ideas and do not merely copy actions without thinking about them.

In Froebel's school, children often learned verses to accompany the occupations. Froebel encouraged these "Mother rhymes," which were what we would call *fingerplays* today. Children said the rhymes while they performed actions with their hands or bodies. Froebel believed that to teach young children, it was necessary to arouse and maintain interest and attention, use the child's curiosity, and plan for motivation to learn.

Although Froebel's structured approach to kindergarten instruction has been discarded, modern teachers of young children do employ fingerplays and play materials designed to encourage learning. Modern teachers also recognize the value of play as a mode of learning and the importance of recognizing the individual child. All these ideas can be traced to Froebel and his kindergarten.

Patty Smith Hill

Patty Smith Hill (1868–1946) was trained as a Froebelian but soon challenged the rigid Froebelian curriculum. Her most important contributions to the profession of early childhood education include her dedication to the scientific study of children; her belief in play as a way of learning; her insistence on creative approaches to art and music; and her commitment to the goal of an individualized curriculum. Hill's belief in the value of play was articulated in a speech she gave at her college graduation ceremonies, when she commented that Adam and Eve deserved sympathy because they never had an opportunity to play as children. Others have continued to develop her ideas about the meaning of play in children's lives. She designed "hollow blocks"—big blocks that children can use to build structures large enough to play inside—that were later manufactured commercially. She also invented other play materials that encouraged children to construct a variety of items (Garrison 1926).

In addition to promoting free play as a valuable learning experience, Hill believed in free expression in art and music. She and her sister introduced children to bells, triangles, and other instruments to "call the children's attention to the beauty of sounds" (qtd. in Fowlkes 1984, p. 48). One of the songs created by the Hills is the song most frequently sung in English, "Happy Birthday to You." (The rights to this song sold for about 12 million dollars in 1988.) Hill also rejected the formal art lessons that were standard in her time. In these lessons, children were instructed to draw horizontal lines followed by diagonal lines and were told that when all the lines were drawn correctly, they could be combined into a house. Hill believed that children should express themselves in their artwork and that formal lessons in which all the products were the same were not appropriate.

The curriculum that grows out of observation of the children and their needs, along with the interactions between the teacher and the children, is described by leaders in early childhood education today as *emergent* or *appropriate*. Patty Smith Hill would approve of current efforts to fit the curriculum to the child.

Another of Hill's contributions to early childhood education was her emphasis on the importance of the child's home and the learning that took place there. In 1926 she wrote an article (Hill 1926; republished 1987) in which she described the function of the kindergarten teacher as ministering to the natures and needs of children by looking forward to their needs as they develop through the sixth year and looking backward to the home to study the experiences and types of learning that have taken place there. She also wrote an article entitled "The Home and the School as Centers of Child Life" (1928), in which she defined the differences between home learning and school learning and advised teachers to pay attention to home learning and use information about it in their own teaching.

NAEYC

Hill founded the National Association for Nursery Education (NANE) in 1926. This organization is now the National Association for the Education of Young Children (NAEYC).

John Dewey

John Dewey (1859–1952) is most often connected with the **progressive education movement.** He was the most influential educational philosopher in the United States in the early 1900s, and his influence is still being felt—and debated—in U.S. schools. Dewey established a laboratory school at the University of Chicago at about the turn of the century and tried to implement his educational theories in the school. The progressive movement gained momentum until the time of the Great Depression and then lost credibility with the public, but many of the ideas of the movement are now considered traditional, especially those in early childhood education.

Education for children in Dewey's time was very teacher centered, in that the teacher had absolute control of the activities in the classroom and selected those in which each child would participate. Most schools relied on a subject-matter orientation in selecting curriculum experiences and on rote learning as the teaching method. For example, facts in biology would be learned from a text and teacher lectures. Students would then be expected to repeat the information either orally or in writing. Dewey and the other leaders of the progressive movement believed that curriculum experiences should be based on children's interests and should involve children in active experiences. In learning about biology, children might explore a limited area of their schoolyard, collect specimens of the plant and animal life, learn to classify these specimens, compare their collections with the collections of others, learn about how their specimens fit into larger ecological systems, and so on. In the process of investigating their own area of the schoolyard, they would read, write, solve mathematical problems, and learn to work successfully with others.

Dewey's ideas have often been misinterpreted to mean that children should do only what they are interested in and that any kind of experience is valuable for learning. In fact, Dewey believed that activity itself was not enough for learning. He believed that children needed to be engaged in real and meaningful activities that would lend themselves to a wide variety of learning possibilities and that would be vehicles for learning to think and reflect. Dewey was concerned that in the democratic United States, the schools failed to reach large segments of the population and that the teaching methods stifled individual growth and development (Dewey 1900, 1902).

Early childhood education has benefited from Dewey's work in developing an active curriculum for young children that is integrated, rather than divided into subject-matter segments. Dewey's influence is also evident in curricula that reflect the interests of the children. Such curricula cannot be set ahead of time but must be built on knowledge of children and their interests. Teachers are responsible for achieving the goals of the school, but the specific topics to be studied to meet those goals cannot be determined in advance. Children are also encouraged to learn to work in groups and to learn about the interdependence of people in a community and a nation.

Lucy Sprague Mitchell

Lucy Sprague Mitchell (1878–1967) founded the Bureau of Educational Experiments in 1916. The bureau eventually grew into the Bank Street College of Education, a leading institution in the study of children and play and the development of curriculum materials.

Mitchell was a student of John Dewey, who greatly influenced her work. When the progressive movement began, typical school conditions involved harsh punishments, a curriculum that was established without regard for the individual child, teaching methods that relied on rote memory, and a subject-matter orientation to learning. Those involved in the progressive movement emphasized the needs of the individual child, believed that children learned best when they were interested in the materials, felt that learning was best achieved through active involvement with materials, and were concerned with the development of the whole child—physically, socially, intellectually, and emotionally. "Whole child" was one of Mitchell's phrases.

Mitchell's philosophy of education proposed that the education of young children should be based on these principles:

- *stimulating each child to unfold as fully as possible, but at her or his own pace;*
- *welcoming individual children's conversation and other forms of self-expression (art, music and movement, story creating, etc.);*
- *promoting learning through play (always child-initiated and child-directed) and through meaningful self-initiated or teacher-initiated planned experiences and projects (e.g., attending to how young children learn);*
- *individualizing; and*
- *avoiding teacher-given external rewards, because the reward of learning through meaningful activity is in seeing a challenge and solving the problem oneself.* (Greenburg 1987, p. 73)

Although Mitchell did not create any of these principles, she served as a leader in promoting them. For instance, she opened a laboratory school to implement and experiment with the teaching principles in which she believed. She also organized a laboratory to study how and why children function as they do and a teacher's college to educate teachers about these principles. She organized a workshop for writers of children's literature—a field not recognized as important in that time—and published bulletins to inform people about what she and others in the progressive movement were accomplishing. Like Dewey, Mitchell believed that the education of the young is important in a democratic society, and she placed great importance on helping children learn cooperation and group skills.

Mitchell was also a leader in educational research. When she began her work, psychology was a new field of study and psychologists were just beginning to try to explain human behavior. Mitchell's goals were to bring together researchers from a broad range of disciplines to study normal children in a setting in which they were offered a curriculum made up of experiences as well as information. She wanted to support educational experiments and make information about these experiments available to the public.

Lucy Sprague Mitchell was an influential leader in early childhood education because of her contributions in developing and implementing a hands-on curriculum and because of her dedication to the scientific study of education (Antler 1987).

Other Influences on Early Childhood Education

New ways of thinking about children have evolved from the research of leading educators such as G. Stanley Hall, J. McVicker Hunt, Benjamin Bloom, and Jerome Bruner. The results of their research and child study have certainly had an impact on thinking in the field of early childhood education.

G. Stanley Hall was an advocate of the scientific study of children and adolescents in the late 1800s. He urged psychologists to study education and teaching, which were not especially interesting topics to most psychologists of that time. He also wanted to create a professional base of knowledge for education. Although Hall's studies focused on the nature of the child, he never tested his conclusions in real school settings. His work would not meet current standards for scientific studies.

Hall was very critical of the Froebelian approach to kindergarten and wanted more emphasis on free play and attention to physical health than was common in the traditional kindergarten. His real concern for the study of children contributed to the development of the field of educational psychology. He and his many students pushed educators to learn more about children and the psychology on which teaching decisions are based (Ross 1972).

Historically, educators had believed in the fixed nature of intelligence. It had been believed for years that the intelligence of each child was fixed at birth and could not be altered. Building on earlier studies, J. McVicker Hunt demonstrated in the late 1950s that at least what we *measure* as intelligence is not fixed but, rather, responsive to experience. This finding gave added impetus to the early childhood education movement, especially to intervention programs such as Head Start (which is discussed in more detail later in this chapter). Such programs were designed to provide experiences for children who might otherwise miss out on what is available to middle-class children. For example, children in intervention programs who had never seen a farm would be stimulated through field trips to a farm and follow-up language experiences revolving around the trip. The idea that a child's measured intelligence quotient (IQ) could be raised by participation in given experiences provided early childhood educators with support for the importance of their programs (Hunt 1961).

The research of Benjamin Bloom also had an impact on early childhood education programs. One of Bloom's major studies, *Stability and Change in Human Characteristics* (1964), looked at intelligence over a period of time and concluded that much of what can be measured as IQ at age seventeen is developed in the child's early years. His findings, like Hunt's, gave early childhood educators more reasons to be concerned with the quality of educational experiences for young children and more support for the importance of experience in children's early years. Bloom developed a taxonomy of objectives by which experiences and questions can be ordered in a hierarchy from recall to application. Also important is his concept of *mastery learning*. Bloom believes that children can master the tasks presented to them at school, but some children will need more time and more activities or guidance in order to do so. He proposed that curricula be organized so that each learner can move at his own pace in mastering the objectives.

It is difficult to summarize the work of Jerome Bruner because he has been involved in so many kinds of educational research over the years. He has studied the development of language, play, thinking, and curriculum. Bruner wrote that "any subject can be taught effectively in some intellectually honest form to any child in any stage of development" (Bruner 1960, p. 32). This statement has often been misinterpreted, leading some people to believe that he meant that children of any age can learn any subject—that all teachers need to give them is more practice or more drill and they can master anything. Bruner believes the key to good teaching is to understand the child's development and how she views the world and then to translate the subject to some form that fits the child's current views. A teacher who understands development would not believe that two-year-olds should be taught multiplication but would help young children begin to recognize that some objects in their environment, such as their shoes, come in sets. This concept of sets is the basis for learning multiplication.

The Child-Care Movement

The earliest **child care** was established in the settlement houses of big U.S. cities at the turn of the twentieth century "to provide a shelter for the children of mothers dependent on their own exertions for their daily bread; [but] also to rear useful citizens among the class represented by the children we reach" (Steinfels 1973, p. 29). Even though most mothers who worked outside the home did so for economic survival, the belief persisted that mothers should take care of their own children, so the availability of child care declined as the century progressed.

Other efforts at providing child care have been in response to national emergencies. During the Great Depression, the Works Progress Administration created nursery schools to provide teaching positions for unemployed teachers, and during World War II the Lanham Act established nursery schools so that mothers could participate in the war effort. At the end of each of these periods, the federal funding ended, and so did the programs (Grubb 1989).

During the 1970s, there were repeated efforts to pass legislation to support child care. Progress on child-care legislation stalled during the 1980s, but some positive steps were made in the 1990s, such as providing more federal funding for programs that benefit children.

Kindergarten

Kindergarten—defined as "a specialized school adapted to the nature and needs of young children from the fourth to the sixth year" (Hill 1992)—began with the Froebel kindergarten in Germany in 1837. The first kindergarten in the United States was opened in 1855 by Margaretha Schurz, and the first English-speaking kindergarten was opened by Elizabeth Peabody in 1860. The first publicly supported kindergarten was opened by Susan Blow in St. Louis in 1873 (Frost and Kissinger 1976).

Publicly supported kindergarten is now available in almost all the states, and many states provide funding for public school programs for four-year-olds, especially those deemed at risk of failing in public school for any reason (Grubb 1989). In a few states, attendance in kindergarten is compulsory; that is, state law requires that parents send their children to school at five years of age. In most states, even though school districts are required to *offer* kindergarten, attendance is not mandated by law.

Changes in Early Childhood Education

Head Start

The charity schools of the early 1800s (nursery schools supported by philanthropists to save children from poor families from disadvantaged environments) and the settlement house programs of the early 1900s shared the goal of trying to change the lives of young poor children. Modern-day programs continue this effort.

One component of the War on Poverty in the early 1960s was **Head Start,** a compensatory program that was a major feature of the plan to break the cycle of poverty in the United States. Head Start provides educational, social, medical, dental, nutritional, and mental health services to low-income preschool children. In 2000, Head Start celebrated its thirty-fifth anniversary, but the program continues to be able to serve only a portion of the eligible children. Since the beginning of the Head Start program, over 17 million children and their families have been served. Currently, over 800,000 children are enrolled in Head Start programs, and appropriations have been increased over previous years. Many different programs have been developed and evaluated as part of Head Start, and much research in early childhood education has been undertaken in Head Start programs. Thus, Head Start has been beneficial not only to the millions of children who have attended programs but also to the profession of early childhood education.

Because some of the positive effects of Head Start did not last once the children were in elementary school, Project Follow Through was developed. Follow Through attempts to maintain the gains made in Head Start by continuing family education and health care and by emphasizing success. Follow Through programs have never been as widely available as Head Start programs, however.

Programs for Children with Special Needs

The education of children with special needs has undergone radical changes in the last few decades. Early in the twentieth century, children with disabilities were often excluded from school experiences. Later, they were identified but segregated into special classes in schools. Often, all children with disabilities from a given school district were housed in a special school so that they had no contact with typically developing children.

In 1975, Public Law (PL) 94-142, the Education for All Handicapped Children Act, was passed in the United States. This law is often called the "mainstreaming law," but it does not mention the word **mainstreaming**. What the law does say is that every child is entitled to an education in the **least restrictive environment (LRE).** Separate schools or classes are appropriate only when the "nature or severity of the handicap is such that education in regular classes with the use of supplementary aids and services cannot be achieved satisfactorily" (PL 94-142 20 U.S.C. 1412, 5, B).

Public Law 99-457, enacted in 1986, reauthorized PL 94-142 and extended its provisions to younger children. The intent of the original law had been to provide services to children with disabling conditions from birth to school age, but the law had been written so that states were not required to provide services to children younger than school age. PL 99-457 extended the services to children from ages three to five and added incentives for states that served children from birth to age two, as well. Services can be provided by public or private agencies, but providers must demonstrate quality and integration. Key elements in PL 99-457 are its emphasis on the role of parents and its recognition of the importance of the family in the child's development.

Recognizing that labeling young children can be a harmful practice, PL 99-457 does not require or emphasize categorical labels. Safford (1989) states the following reasons for avoiding labeling:

> *Young children's needs are difficult, if not impossible, to categorize with traditional labels.*
>
> *Especially during the early years, these needs change rapidly.*
>
> *Categorical labels have no utility for young children, since categorical programs may not be appropriate.*
>
> *Early labeling of children may limit and restrict them, since others may respond to these labels in limiting and restricting ways.*
>
> *Labels tend to follow the child, even after they are no longer applicable or appropriate. A label is a hard thing to lose!*
>
> *Least restrictive services for young children, required by P.L. 99-457, are intended to foster the interaction of handicapped and nonhandicapped children. Labels tend to impede that interaction. (p. 10)*

Federal law also requires that a minimum of 10 percent of the children enrolled in Head Start programs be children with disabilities and that services be provided to meet their special needs (Head Start, Economic Opportunity and Community Partnership Act of 1974, PL 93-644, 1974). To meet enrollment quotas, children who are disabled but not otherwise eligible for Head Start may be admitted (Safford 1989).

PL 94-142 was updated in 1990 and is now known as the Individuals with Disabilities Education Act (IDEA). IDEA expanded the categories of children eligible to receive special education services to include those with autism and traumatic brain injury. The new law continues to mandate parental involvement in educational decisions, education in the least restrictive environment, and individualized education programs (Hardman et al. 1993).

Early Intervention Programs

Most states have programs for children deemed at risk for any number of factors. Many of these children are identified because their mothers are poor, received little or no prenatal care, or are substance abusers. Other children who qualify for intervention are those with disabilities or other special needs. Many states have programs that seek to identify eligible children at birth and to provide home-based services to these children from birth to age three. At age three, most states provide center- or school-based programs for children with special needs.

The support for early intervention programs is based on the idea that preventing a problem from occurring is more efficient than trying to correct a problem that already exists. In other words, if children who are at risk can be identified and provided with needed services early in their lives, many problems can be prevented. Early intervention specialists usually focus on helping the family provide an environment that promotes healthy growth—both physically and intellectually. For example, caretakers are aided in planning children's diets and visits to physicians for immunizations as well as taught how to talk to children to promote language development.

Available services, procedures for identifying children, and funding vary widely across the states. Some states attempt to provide services for a broad range of conditions, whereas others provide services only for children with identified disabilities.

Contemporary Models

Today, many models describe goals, materials, teacher roles, and appropriate instructional practices for early childhood education. Roopnarine and Johnson (2000) describe thirteen models, including home-based models. It is not a simple task to group the programs commonly found in early childhood into model designations. Goffin and Wilson (2001) discuss models in four basic categories. All of these authors believe that knowledge of the models can lead to a more professional approach to developing curriculum and activities for young children.

Models can serve as guidelines for planning and organizing experiences, but they are rarely, if ever, implemented totally. Uncritical acceptance of any model certainly does not encourage the professional growth and development of teachers and curriculum planners. As teachers use models and theories, they construct their own understanding of the teaching–learning processes and should be able to incorporate their experiences into any model to make it a more cohesive or complete explanation of how children develop and learn.

Most knowledge of models in early childhood education grew out of work done in the late 1960s and early 1970s in Head Start programs. Financial support for developing and testing models has been much more difficult to obtain since that period; therefore, fewer models have been developed. Of the thirteen models described by Roopnarine and Johnson (2000), the center-based models fall roughly into three categories: *Montessori models, behaviorist models,* and *constructivist models.* In this chapter, we will describe each of these three basic approaches to early childhood education. Although some of the models have been extended to address both younger and older children, for the sake of comparison each program in this chapter will be described as it applies to four- and five-year-olds; notes about applying programs to younger or older children will be included.

Each section will include a description of the theoretical foundation of the model and the beliefs about teaching and learning on which the model is based, the goals of the model, a typical day in a school based on the model, and a brief evaluation of the model.

The Montessori Model

Maria Montessori left her mark on the world in many ways. She was the first woman in Italy to become a doctor of medicine and the first woman to earn a doctorate in anthropology. She established the method of education that bears her name and continues to be used today in schools all over the world. Even schools that do not claim any particular kinship to Montessori education use materials and methods of teaching that were influenced by Montessori and her inventions (Kramer 1976).

Montessori became interested in education as she worked with children who were labeled "feebleminded." She soon discovered that her methods of teaching could be applied to children who did not have mental retardation. She opened her first school in a poor district in Rome in 1907 and in a very short time drew worldwide attention to Montessori education.

Interest in Montessori education in the United States was very strong in the early 1900s. Montessori came to lecture at Carnegie Hall as the guest of Thomas Edison, and shortly afterward the Montessori Society was formed, with Alexander Graham Bell as its first president. Montessori schools, at both the preschool and elementary levels, are now common in most U.S. communities. Although most Montessori schools are private, some public school systems offer Montessori programs as alternative schools.

How Children Learn: Montessori

Some key elements of Montessori philosophy include the ideas of the absorbent mind, the prepared environment, autoeducation, sensitive periods, and the principle of freedom for the child. Each of these elements is a factor in explanations of how children grow and develop.

The concept of the **absorbent mind** is important in Montessori philosophy. The prevailing idea in Montessori's time was that children do not do anything mentally during infancy. Montessori, however, believed that infants unconsciously absorb all that is around them and that gradually this process becomes conscious. As the child becomes conscious, he begins to organize experiences and make generalizations. For example, after several experiences with cups of various kinds, the child comes to understand "cup" as a category that includes not only all existing cups but also all possible cups. Montessori philosophy also holds that the child's construction of a sense of self is accomplished if he is free to develop the pattern inherent in him (Standing 1962).

In a Montessori program, the teacher is responsible for the **prepared environment:** that is, for selecting and arranging the materials that make learning possible. Materials for learning must be carefully chosen and displayed to catch the child's interest. The tables and chairs must be child sized and lightweight so that a child can arrange them in the way that is most comfortable for her. The environment must be orderly so that the child develops a sense of order and control. It must also be attractive so that the child develops a respect for beauty. Most Montessori classrooms are decorated with plants and objects from nature as well as colorful displays and tasteful pieces of art.

The teacher is responsible for sequencing the child's experiences so that he learns concepts logically. The materials for instruction are arranged so that the child can select from among them the ones in which he is interested, but it is the teacher's role to bring out and demonstrate new materials at the optimal time in the development of each child. Once the teacher has demonstrated the procedures for using materials, the child can choose to work with them. It is within this carefully planned framework that **autoeducation**—the organizing of information into logical patterns—takes place. Children learn to clarify their perceptions and organize their experiences through certain activities. The teacher's role is not to present information through direct instruction but to demonstrate the materials and guide the child's selection of materials and activities.

A basic premise of the Montessori philosophy is that the child copies reality rather than constructs it. From watching and then doing activities, the child organizes the world and her own thinking. One of the primary roles of a Montessori teacher is to demonstrate how materials are to be used and tasks are to be completed. These demonstrations are very specific in that there is an exact procedure for using each set of materials; children are not allowed free expression with the materials until they have mastered the exact procedures (Montessori 1914).

Most Montessori materials are self-correcting in that they are designed to give the child feedback on the correctness of his actions. An example of self-correcting material is the Pink Tower, which is a set of cubes of graduated sizes. The child begins building the Tower by placing the largest cube on the bottom; each additional cube is placed on the Tower in order by decreasing size, such that the smallest cube is placed on the top. In demonstrating how to use the Tower, the teacher first shows how it is constructed; then he takes it apart and allows the child to construct it. The teacher does not supply information or cues to the child while he is attempting this construction. If the Tower is constructed correctly, each cube will be used and every cube placed on the Tower will be smaller than the preceding cube. If the child makes an error in construction, one or more cubes will be left over or will not fit properly. The purpose of the Pink Tower is to help the child develop abilities in seriation. Once the child has mastered the Tower, other materials are introduced in a careful sequence to aid him in transferring the ability to seriate from one situation to another and to further his thinking and reasoning abilities.

Montessori materials and exercises are basically divided into four categories that promote the development of daily-living skills and sensorial, academic, and cultural and artistic abilities:

1. *Daily-living exercises* involve the physical care of oneself and the environment and include tasks such as washing a table and polishing shoes. The purpose of these tasks is not simply to develop a skill but also to aid the "inner construction of discipline, organization, independence, and self-esteem through concentration on a precise and completed cycle of activity" (Lillard 1972, p. 71).

2. *Sensorial materials* are designed to encourage refinement of the senses for the purpose of aiding the child in developing intelligence. Montessori

Daily-living exercises, such as tying shoes, are an important part of the Montessori classroom.

believed that intelligence is developed as the child organizes and categorizes perceptions into a mental order. An example of sensorial materials is a collection of seven different fabric samples: velvet, silk, wool, fine linen, coarse linen, fine cotton, and coarse cotton. The teacher is to take care that these samples are pure. The child is encouraged to play with the samples, to learn the names of the fabrics, and then to identify a given sample by touch.

3. *Academic materials* include the movable alphabet, sandpaper letters, and plane geometric insets. After the child has learned to recognize the individual letters of the alphabet and to compose some words with help from the teacher, she is presented with the movable alphabet. There are several duplicates of each letter, and the child is encouraged to compose words with them. The child is freed from the difficulty of forming letters by hand and so can progress more quickly in composing and recognizing words.

4. *Artistic or cultural materials* and exercises are designed to help children learn to love and appreciate music and to learn to control movements of their hands and feet in preparation for dance. Rhythm and then harmony and melody are introduced. Children are taught how to use musical instruments and to recognize musical sounds through the sensorial exercises. Although drawing is never taught directly, children are taught about line and color before painting is introduced.

Freedom to choose activities and when to change activities is very important in Montessori education. The teacher may guide the child by demonstrating new materials she thinks might interest or challenge the child, but the child must choose which materials to use. The choice of materials is the child's, but how the materials are used is clearly defined. If the child chooses to use materials in unacceptable ways, the teacher may remove the materials and ask the child to make another choice. Freedom of choice is related to the concept of *autoeducation;* the child must educate himself. Standing (1957) summarizes this concept in the following statements:

1. *The child must learn by his own activity.*
2. *He must be granted a mental freedom to take what he needs.*
3. *He must not be questioned in his choice—since the "teacher should answer the mental needs of the child, not dictate them." (p. 364)*

Another important concept in Montessori education is that of **sensitive periods**, which are periods when a child is capable of and interested in learning specific things. This concept is much like that of *readiness*. For example, if a child is in a sensitive period in which she is fascinated with details, the teacher might supply materials that have many small parts to put together. Montessori teachers are trained to observe these sensitive periods and provide experiences appropriate for each period.

Montessori believed that young children want to be obedient and that they desire order in their environments. If a child becomes agitated or experiences "brainstorms" of activity, then he is to be removed silently and gently from the environment and encouraged to rest quietly until he has calmed down. Teachers in a Montessori school maintain discipline by expecting children to respect one another's work and workspaces and by removing children who lose control of their impulses.

Goals of Montessori Education

The most important goal of Montessori education is to develop the individual. The facts a child learns are not as important as her mental or intellectual development. Therefore, the goals of Montessori programs emphasize development of general intellectual skills and general, rather than particular, subject-matter concepts. As stated by the American Montessori Society (1984), the goals of Montessori programs include development of the following:

- Concentration
- Observation
- Awareness of order and sequence
- Coordination
- Perceptual awareness and practical skills
- Mathematical concepts
- Language skills
- Writing and reading skills
- Familiarity with the creative arts
- Understanding of the world of nature
- Experience with and understanding of the social sciences
- Experience with critical-thinking skills through problem-solving techniques

9:00 – 9:20	Arrival, group time
9:20 – 10:20	Choice time
10:20 – 10:45	Outdoor play
10:45 – 10:55	Group time, preparation for snack
10:55 – 11:10	Snack
11:10 – 11:30	Story time, one group in rhythms

In Susan's group, there are twenty-eight children, a head teacher, and two assistant teachers. The children in this group are between three and five years old. As Susan enters the light and airy classroom, she goes immediately to the area with open cupboards containing hooks and hangs up her coat while her mother signs her in for the day. Susan waves good-bye to her mother and joins the children who are gathered on the "blue line," a line of blue tape that forms a square in the middle of the largest room in the building. Susan is greeted by her teacher and says hello to her friend, who is already sitting on the line.

When all the children are gathered, the teacher sits at a small table containing a plastic mat, blue and brown clay, a rolling pin, and two identical trays about five by eight inches in size. The teacher tells the children they are going to learn about the words *island* and *lake*. She tells them that an island is land surrounded by water and that a lake is water surrounded by land. She then asks about the colors of water and land, and the children respond "blue" and "brown." She makes a model of a lake by rolling out some of the blue clay and some of the brown clay and placing the brown clay around the blue clay on one of the trays. She repeats the process to make an island on the other tray. Then various children are called on to come up and point to the representations of the island and the lake. At the conclusion of the lesson, the teacher tells the children that this material will be available in the art room so that they can construct their own lakes and islands today.

The head teacher then tells the children that they may choose to work today in the solarium, the art room, or the large room. One of the teachers will be in each of these areas. The head teacher asks the children to go one at a time to choose their favorite things to work on and to get started working. All the children go immediately to an area and choose an activity.

One boy chooses a carpet square, places it on the floor, and selects from the shelves a tray containing a corkboard, a small hammer, and small wooden shapes, each with a hole drilled through it. Using the pegs on the tray, the child begins to attach each shape to the corkboard.

Susan takes a circular felt mat from a stack and places it on a nearby table. She then selects a basket containing a wooden board divided into six squares, with a picture of an animal on each square. She finds small squares with matching pictures and places one on each square. When she has completed this task, she places the pieces back in the basket, places the basket on the shelf, places the mat back on the stack, and chooses a carpet square, which she puts on the

Montessori programs are concerned with children's development physically, socially, emotionally, and intellectually. The importance of physical development is reflected in an emphasis on outdoor play and participation in rhythmic activities. Social development is emphasized in discussions of appropriate behavior on the playground and in the focus on respecting the individual's work and space in the classroom. Intellectual development is achieved through activities designed to help children organize, classify, seriate, and heighten their perceptual awareness.

In the classroom described in the panel on pages 50–51, some children are developing perceptual abilities by matching pictures or completing puz-

floor. She selects a puzzle from the shelf and begins to work on the carpet.

Meanwhile, some children have chosen to work in the solarium, where many science-oriented activities are available. Some children are working with the teacher using a scale to weigh various objects and find out whether they are heavier, lighter, or the same weight as other objects. Other children are filling containers with water from a tub; some are sorting objects based on the materials they are made of. In the art room, some children don painting smocks and paint at easels; one works with the clay to make islands and lakes; and other children choose paper and clay for drawing and molding experiences.

A few children in the large room are working with the teacher on recognizing letters. The teacher places white letters (upper- and lowercase) on a black background and tells the children the name of each letter and its sound. Then they look at a small set of pictures of objects whose names begin with that sound and name each one, emphasizing the sound. Another teacher moves around the room, working with individual children, for example, asking them the names of colors after they have matched color strips. Each child works with an activity as long as she chooses.

The children work with their activities for about an hour and are then instructed to put their materials away and get their coats for outdoor play. They play outside for about twenty minutes on the swings, a climber/slide, and balance beams and also with some large outdoor toys. Susan walks the balance beam several times. One of the teachers holds her hand the first time, and then she walks with the teacher walking beside her but not touching her. Then Susan joins a group playing on the climber/slide and plays there until it is time to go inside.

As the children return to the room, they are instructed to wash their hands for a snack and to sit on the blue line again. As the children are washing up, one of the assistant teachers beats the rhythm of a child's name on a drum, and then all the children clap the rhythm. Each child called on is asked what name to beat—some supply only their first names, some their full names. When all the children are on the line, the head teacher discusses a problem that occurred outdoors: Someone threw a rock. She asks the children to explain why they cannot throw rocks and concludes by having them think of things they *can* throw outdoors. The children are dismissed to have their snack by getting up one by one as the teacher describes their clothing.

After the snack each day, one group stays in the large room for movement exercises. Susan goes with a small group to one of the small rooms for story reading. The small groups are selected on the basis of maturity and experience in listening to stories. The teachers read the stories and ask questions about them. They then read stories selected by the children, if there is more time.

By this time, parents are beginning to arrive. Susan's father signs her out, helps her collect her coat, and takes her home.

zles. Others are learning the difference between lakes and islands by constructing models with clay. The outcomes expected from each of the experiences differ. Not all children share the same experiences, but all are guided to learn some concepts and to develop some abilities. Subject-matter concepts, such as the vocabulary to describe islands and lakes or the names of the letters of the alphabet, are conveyed through group or individual instruction. Content areas such as science and social studies are included in the program in the form of materials or equipment such as scales and maps. Math concepts are also developed through materials such as the Tower and beads. Literacy is promoted through materials such as alphabet letters of different textures and the movable alphabet. Some activities, such as listening for syllables in names, are also designed to promote the development of literacy. Stories are read daily to encourage children's interest in books.

When children younger than three are accepted in Montessori programs, they usually attend two or three mornings each week, and the programs are modified by having smaller groups and fewer choices for the children. The Montessori approach also includes elementary programs (and a limited number of secondary programs). Programs for children in the primary grades are fundamentally the same as preschool programs in that children are presented with materials and allowed to work with those they select. In the primary grades, there is much more emphasis on literacy, as children create words from the movable alphabet. They begin writing by copying words and then move on to writing sentences and stories. Instruction in reading often emphasizes a phonetic approach. Many Montessori materials are available for helping children develop concepts in mathematics, social studies, and science.

Two publications offer additional information about Montessori education: *Montessori Life,* a journal published by the American Montessori Society, and *Public School Montessorian,* published by Jola Publications (2933 North 2nd Street, Minneapolis, MN 55411). Montessori Internationale also publishes a small journal once a year.

The Behaviorist Model

The behaviorist model of schools for young children is based on the learning theories of Edward Thorndike and B. F. Skinner (described in Chapter 1). Basically, these theories explain behavior in terms of a stimulus and a response and operant conditioning. Three other key components in the behaviorist model—also known as **direct instruction**—are reinforcement schedules, shaping of behavior, and extinction of behavior:

- A *reinforcement schedule* is established after a specific response has been achieved; at that point, the learner is rewarded on a schedule rather than for every response. The learner might be rewarded for every two responses, then every four responses, and so on; eventually, the learner will not need a reward to continue the response.

- *Shaping of behavior* is changing behavior by controlling the rewards and punishments. If a child is disruptive to the group, the teacher might decide to change the child's behavior by ignoring all disruptive behavior and rewarding more appropriate behavior. Even calling the child's name when she is disruptive can be rewarding to a child seeking attention.

- Behaviors can be *extinguished* just as they can be encouraged. For instance, if a child throws a temper tantrum in order to get something that has been denied, the teacher can ignore that behavior until it is no longer exhibited. If a behavior does not result in the child's getting what he wants, he will try another behavior.

How Children Learn: Behaviorist

In the behaviorist view, a child acquires knowledge as the result of repeated interactions with the environment. The consequences of the interactions—reward or punishment—determine whether the interaction will be repeated. The most effective teaching presents a carefully selected stimulus and then controls the rewards or punishments connected with the child's response to the stimulus. The behaviorist view is that a child accumulates knowledge through repeated exposures to stimuli and that the learning process is directed by the adult who controls the sequence of stimuli and the reward system (Roopnarine and Johnson 2000).

In the direct instruction model, the focus is on achievement of academic goals, especially in reading, arithmetic, and language. The lessons presented to children are designed to be conducted in small groups and are carefully sequenced. Each lesson includes an activity designed to motivate students and attract their attention. Following this part of the lesson, new information is presented and responses are elicited from students. If their responses are correct, the students are rewarded. If their responses are incorrect, the students repeat the lesson until the correct responses have been elicited and then rewarded.

The children's behavior is also controlled by a system of rewards and punishments. For example, when a child comes into the room in the morning and hangs up his coat without being reminded, the teacher might reward the child by giving him a token. Tokens can be redeemed later for extra play time or special activities or used to purchase items from a class store. Children who fail to follow the rules may receive no tokens or have tokens taken away.

Teachers who follow the direct instruction model are expected to understand and be able to use reinforcement schedules, shaping of behavior, and extinction of behavior in achieving academic and behavioral goals. Bereiter and Engelmann describe the hallmarks of their method as follows:

1. *Fast pace. During a twenty-minute period as many as 500 responses may be required of each child. Usually five or more different kinds of tasks are presented during a single period.*
2. *Reduced task-irrelevant behavior. The teacher controls the session relying only incidentally on spontaneous exchanges to dictate the direction of instruction. Efforts of both teacher and children are focused on the tasks being studied.*
3. *Strong emphasis on verbal responses. These are often produced in unison, so that each child's total output can be maximized.*
4. *Carefully planned small-step instructional units with continual feedback. The teacher is not receptive to irrelevant exchanges but is very sensitive to possible areas of difficulty, possible ambiguities that arise from her presentation. She quickly corrects mistakes. She tries to anticipate and avert them.*
5. *Heavy work demands. Children are required to pay attention and to work hard. They are rewarded for thinking; half-hearted or careless performance is not tolerated.* (qtd. in Spodek 1973, pp. 177–178)

With the direct instruction model, the classroom is simplified and the number of activities is limited. Bereiter and Engelmann (1966) offer this rationale for setting these limitations:

> An object-rich environment stimulates a culturally deprived child to attend to a glitter of superabundant stimuli. He darts from one object to another, treating each only in terms of sensory gratification. When the toy no longer "feels good," another one is selected. By minimizing the inducement of noise in the environment, the preschool can be far more effective in directing the child not to the vehicle of the concept but to the concept itself. Sterilizing the environment is a firm requirement of the work-oriented preschool. Toys should be limited to form boards, jigsaw puzzles (which are usually favorites with the children), books, drawing and tracing materials, Cuisenaire rods (to be handled during free time under the direction of the teacher), and a miniature house, barn and set of farm animals. Paper, crayons, and chalk (but no paint) should be available for expressive play. Motor toys, such as tricycles and wagons, and climbing equipment are not necessary for the program. (p. 72)

More recently, Neisworth and Buggey (1993) have summarized the basic procedures of the teacher in a behaviorist program:

- *Reward constructive behavior; ignore undesirable behavior. The best rewards are those that are natural or intrinsic to an activity. Add-on, contrived rewards (e.g., tokens, extra praise) should only be used when necessary, much as crutches should be used.*
- *Teach skills in simulated settings or in the actual circumstances in which the skills are expected.*
- *Practice what you teach. Children will imitate teacher behavior.*
- *Behavioral teaching is by definition individualized. Plan developmentally appropriate sequences for each child.*
- *Choose rewards that are appropriate and motivating to the child. Children's preferences differ; not all children enjoy the same activities, rewards, or circumstances.*
- *Learning occurs when the child is interacting with the environment; maximize interaction.*
- *Plan for generalization; use shaping and stimulus-control. Evaluate acquired skills across settings, time, and persons.*
- *Make sure that children have opportunities to practice (and experience reinforcement for) learned skills periodically to maintain them. Optimally, what children learn at one time is used as part of more sophisticated behavior learned later. (p. 130)*

Goals of Behaviorist Models

The most important goals of behaviorist models are to achieve academic competencies in language, reading, and arithmetic. Children are also expected to learn to answer questions from the teacher articulately and in complete sentences and to perform on cue. The developers of direct instruction models believe that children who are academically capable will have improved self-concepts. Motor development is not among the primary goals of direct instruction models.

In the description on pages 56–57 of a typical day in a behaviorist preschool, the children are engaged in activities designed to teach content knowledge or facts and to help them develop the skills necessary for success in school settings, such as answering questions posed and responding to cues provided by the teacher. Other activities are included to accomplish specific academic goals, to complement the teacher's instruction, or to reward performance.

Parents AND School Design

■ Provide parents and other visitors to your school with references for articles or books that support your program philosophy and perhaps explain the differences between your program and others.

The behaviorist models focus primarily on *intellectual development,* which is defined as the learning of content and facts, not as the development of generalized intellectual abilities. Physical development is not a primary goal of this type of instruction, nor are social and emotional development. Behaviorists believe that children will achieve more positive self-esteem if they feel that they are successful learners. Children are assumed to develop emotionally as they learn to control their impulsive behaviors and respond appropriately in school settings.

Subject-matter content in language, mathematics, and reading is broken down into small, discrete steps, which children must master in sequence before going on. These subject-matter areas are emphasized because they are considered basic to the children's success. The curriculum is tightly sequenced but not integrated. Children learn each subject without regard for what is being learned in other subjects. Science and social studies are rarely included in the curriculum, and the arts are included in a limited fashion as part of the choice activities.

When implemented with older children, the fundamental behaviorist model remains intact. Basically, the changes for older children are found in the content of the lessons presented in subject-matter areas.

Many elements of the behaviorist models are evident in current elementary programs. Specification of limited objectives, emphasis on the sequence of materials or activities, and mastery of small steps as a method of achieving larger goals are all behavioristic in origin. In many elementary schools that do not claim to be behavioristic, tokens or stickers are used as reinforcers, and grades are often viewed as rewards or punishments.

The Constructivist Model

Constructivist models are based on the learning theories of Jean Piaget (1896–1980) and Lev Vygotsky (1896–1934). Examples of constructivist programs include the School for Constructive Play, developed by George Forman; the High/Scope program, developed by David Weikart; the Bank Street College of Education, developed by Lucy Sprague Mitchell; the Reggio Emilia programs in Italy, and Project Construct in Missouri and elsewhere. There are points of

9:00 – 9:15	Arrival, group time
9:15 – 10:00	Rotating instructional groups
10:00 – 10:25	Outdoor play
10:25 – 10:45	Snack
10:45 – 11:10	Instructional groups
11:10 – 11:25	Choice of activities
11:25 – 11:30	Dismissal

The school Alan attends has separate classes for fours and fives. The classroom in which five-year-old Alan works each day is a large room with three smaller rooms that open off it. For Alan's group of thirty children, there is a teacher and two assistant teachers.

The teacher greets Alan at the door with a smile and tells him how glad she is that he is at school. As Alan hangs up his coat, the teacher slips him a red token, and with a grin he puts it into his pocket. Alan joins the other children sitting in a circle on the floor. In a few minutes, when all the children are present, the teacher joins the group and calls the roll. Alan responds to his name with "I am present." Then the teacher reviews the days of the week and the months of the year. Alan raises his hand to say the days of the week. He repeats the names successfully and receives another token. He also gets a smile and praise from

the teacher. After a child is selected to pin the correct numeral on the calendar and move pointers on the weather chart to indicate today's weather, Alan is instructed to go to the language room with his group. Alan's group membership is based on his ability level. There are high, middle, and low groups.

One of the assistant teachers conducts Alan's language lesson for twenty minutes. Alan and the other members of his group sit on small risers to be as close as possible to the teacher and to facilitate their choral responses. The first part of the lesson is a warm-up in which the teacher tells the children that when she taps her pencil three times, they should clap their hands. Some children do not clap on cue, and the exercise is repeated. The children are reminded that paying close attention and responding quickly are very important.

Today's lesson is on the use of pronouns: *I, he, she, we.* The teacher opens a paper bag and removes a comb. She says, "I comb my hair." The children are instructed to pretend combing their hair and to repeat, "I comb my hair." Each child who responds correctly is rewarded with a token. The teacher then goes through sentences using the pronouns *he, she,* and *we* with descriptions of other self-care actions, such as brushing the teeth, washing the face, and so on. When the lesson is completed, Alan and his group leave their

agreement among constructivist programs as well as some differences. Among the points of agreement are the following:

1. *All contend that a basic objective to be drawn from Piaget's work is to foster structural change in children's reasoning in the direction of operational thought.*
2. *All emphasize the fundamental importance of the child's action for learning and development.*
3. *All borrow ideas from the child-development tradition in early education for materials, equipment, and activities that permit children to be active (for example, painting and other art activities, blockbuilding, pretend play, singing, and sand and water play).*
4. *None of the . . . Piagetian programs is just "Piagetian." Each recognizes certain limitations in using Piaget's theory alone as a basis for educational practice.* (DeVries and Kohlberg 1987b, p. 51)

Programs differ in their definitions of action, the extent of emphasis on logic in language, the extent of reliance on child development traditions, and how cooperation and interest are fostered. Some developmentalists define *ac-*

room and walk with the teacher to the next room for their arithmetic lesson.

In this lesson, Alan's group is learning to recognize and complete simple addition equations. As the teacher holds up flashcards showing equations such as 3 + 1, the group responds, "Three plus one equals four." Today, the teacher repeats combinations whose sums do not exceed six. When the children have reviewed these sums, they are given a worksheet, listing the same equations, and asked to complete it. Alan mumbles something to Brad, who is sitting beside him at the table. The teacher quickly reminds him that this is work time and that talking to friends is not appropriate now. She tells Alan that a token will be taken away if he talks again. Alan writes the answers to the problems and is rewarded when he does them correctly.

For the next twenty-minute period, Alan and his classmates play outside. The playground has swings, climber/slides, tire swings, and climbers. Alan chooses to swing and takes turns with Brad.

When the children return to the classroom, they are instructed to wash their hands before the snack. The snack today consists of apples cut into fourths and crackers scored into fourths. The teachers introduce and reinforce the use of the fractional terms as the children eat their snacks.

After the snack, Alan's group goes into a small room for the reading lesson. Again, the teacher gets the children's attention with a warm-up exercise, and when all have responded correctly, he begins the lesson. Today's lesson is on the sounds represented by the letters *b, m, l,* and *d*. The teacher presents a letter on a card and says, "This letter is *b* and its sound is 'buh.'" The children repeat the name and the sound several times. They already know the long vowel sounds, and today's letters are combined with each of the vowels in succession and pronounced.

When the reading lesson is finished, Alan and his group return to the large room, where all the children are gathered. They now have the opportunity to spend their tokens on some special activities. Alan chooses to spend three of his tokens for drawing with paper and markers. When he completes his drawing, he spends three more tokens to play with the jigsaw puzzles. Then he and the assistant teacher build some sets with the Cuisenaire rods. The teacher blinks the lights to indicate that it is time to put away all the materials and get ready to go home.

In a few minutes, the room is clean and orderly, and the children have put on their coats and are out the door.

tion as physical action; some broaden the definition to include mental action. Some programs place more emphasis on children's being able to articulate their understanding; others emphasize performance. Some programs allow more time for free play and free expression than others. Some programs rely on free-play activities to help children develop cooperative behaviors; others specifically plan for interventions in behavior cycles.

How Children Learn: Constructivist

Recall from Chapter 1 that Piaget and Vygotsky described *learning* as a process that is under the control of the learner, or intrinsically motivated. According to Piaget, not all knowledge is acquired in the same way. Some kinds of knowledge, such as the concept of *hot,* can be learned only by experience with objects. We don't learn *hot* until we are burned. Thus, the properties of objects—texture, shape, function, and so on—are learned through experiencing them. Language and social customs, however, cannot be learned from experience but only from other people. Logico-mathematical knowledge—which includes what we know about mathematics, seriation, classification, and so on—can only be acquired by interacting mentally with physical objects.

For example, if you let a three-year-old loose in your classroom, he would explore everything about the desks. He would soon know that they have hard, smooth surfaces; that they balance on four legs; that they are heavy; and so forth. However, no amount of exploration would help the child discover the label "desk" that we apply to this piece of furniture. He would have to learn the word from someone in his social group who knows what we have agreed to call this thing.

Vygotsky (1978) recognized that children learn a great deal about their environments from manipulating objects; he called this kind of learning *spontaneous*. He also identified another kind of learning—what we typically think of as school learning (the freezing point of water, for example)—as *scientific* learning. Vygotsky believed that all learning is mediated by the social group, so if counting is important in the social group, then the child will learn to count. Recall from Chapter 1 that Vygotsky also believed that children are only capable of learning certain things, even with assistance, at given ages or skill levels; this notion is the foundation of the **zone of proximal development (ZPD).** An application of the ZPD is shown in the description of a typical day in a constructivist school (see pages 64–65), when the teacher sends two children to the library to find information about the praying mantis. The teacher must know whether these children can use materials from the library to further their own learning. If they cannot use printed materials or other library information, then this strategy will not be appropriate for them.

Constructivists believe that children want to learn and are, in fact, always learning. They also believe that children construct their own understandings and are continually refining them in terms of new experiences and knowledge. For example, at age two, most children have no concept of *time*. By age four, however, most know that a watch or clock tells time and that certain things are done at certain times of the day, such as eating breakfast in the morning and going to bed at night. By age six, the child may be able to read a watch or clock or to say the time on a digital clock. Children become increasingly aware of time and by about age ten or eleven have developed a stable concept of time, in which they know that time passes at an even rate that is not related to activities. Developing this concept of *time* as a constant takes several years and probably thousands of experiences.

Instruction in a constructivist program is provided primarily to individual children and to small groups; whole-group instruction occurs less often. Also, instruction rarely involves the teacher giving information to the students. More frequently, the teacher has arranged an experience in which to engage the learners and then asks them questions as they participate in the task. Supplying students with answers is not the goal in a constructivist program; in fact, unanswered questions are important in terms of continued interest and continued learning.

In a contructivist program, curricula are planned and learning experiences are selected to follow children's interests or expose them to new areas in

In the constructivist classroom, children are often instructed in small groups.

which their interest might be aroused. The process of finding information, analyzing data, and reaching conclusions is considered more important than learning facts. An emphasis on process does not mean that content is lacking, however. Children learn a great many facts and concepts, but they are always embedded in meaningful contexts. For example, children who are learning about trees might "adopt" a tree and visit it on a regular basis in order to record changes over time. They might learn to identify and classify leaves of various trees and participate in experiments to discover the function of leaves. The children might examine the rings in a tree stump, draw conclusions about their observations, and so on. They might locate books about trees in the library, and the teacher might read to them about trees. In other words, the curriculum experiences would focus on children's learning how to find, analyze, and evaluate information, but facts would be presented in the process.

Constructivists believe that it is important to select curriculum experiences containing content that can be acted on in various ways. The teacher must also consider the developmental stage of the learner and the complexity of the tasks required to be successful in learning the material.

Goals of Constructivist Programs

The goal of any constructivist program is to stimulate children in all areas of development. Physical development, social and emotional development, and cognitive (intellectual) development are all important. Language development and an emphasis on the process of learning are also important. Programs attempt to keep a balance so that all areas of development are addressed and none are neglected. Encouraging children to become actively involved in their own learning and developing children's desire to continue to learn are also important goals.

Piaget on Early Education Kamii and DeVries (1977) state that education must be based on the long-term objective of developing the entire personality, with particular emphasis on intellectual and moral autonomy. Their emphasis on intellectual development is based on Piaget's own statements:

> *The principal goal of education is to create [people] who are capable of doing new things, not simply of repeating what other generations have done—[people] who are creative, inventive, and discoverers. The second goal of education is to form minds which can be critical, can verify, and not accept everything they are offered. The great danger today is of slogans, collective opinions, ready-made trends of thought. We have to be able to resist individually, to criticize, to distinguish between what is proven and what is not. So we need pupils who are active, who learn early to find out by themselves, partly by their own spontaneous activity and partly through material we set up for them; who learn early to tell what is verifiable and what is simply the first idea to come to them.* (Piaget 1964, p. 5)

In the short term, constructivist programs also strive to help children achieve the following socioemotional goals:

1. *To feel secure in a noncoercive relationship with adults*
2. *To respect the feelings and rights of others and begin to coordinate different points of view (decentering and cooperating)*
3. *To be independent, alert, and curious; to use initiative in pursuing curiosities; to have confidence in his ability to figure things out for himself, and to speak his mind with conviction.* (Day and Parker 1977, p. 393)

Finally, such programs encourage children to achieve cognitive objectives:

1. *To come up with interesting ideas, problems, and questions*
2. *To put things into relationships and notice similarities and differences.* (Day and Parker 1977, p. 394)

Despite their general similarities, the goals of different constructivist programs can vary. The descriptions that follow will help clarify some of the differences in programs based on Piagetian theory.

The School for Constructive Play In George Forman's program, the goals are to help children develop cognitively through activities selected specifically to help them with the ideas of correspondences (identity and equivalence), transformations, functional relations, and changing perspectives. Forman (1993, pp. 143–144) recommends that teachers find ways to induce conflict in children's thinking. For example, in a game called Wedges and Wheels, the teacher plays with a set of wheels attached to a single axle and two wedges that form a ramp. When the child becomes interested in the game and wants to play, he is encouraged to do so. After a few experiences of rolling the wheels down the ramp, the teacher moves one of the wedges so that the wheels no longer fit on the wedges. She then watches to see how the child solves the problem of fitting the wheels on the wedges.

High/Scope   The High/Scope program, developed by David Weikart, is known for emphasizing careful and systematic observations of the child and for organizing the curriculum around key experiences. *Key experiences* have been identified in the categories of social and emotional development, movement and physical development, and cognitive development:

> *Key experiences provide a composite picture of early childhood development, are fundamental to young children's construction of knowledge, take place repeatedly over an extended period of time, and describe the concepts and relationships young children are striving to understand. They occur in active learning settings in which children have opportunities to make choices and decisions, manipulate materials, interact with peers and adults, experience special events, reflect on ideas and actions, use language in personally meaningful ways, and receive appropriate adult support.* (Hohmann and Weikart 1995, p. 299)

The categories of key experiences are creative representation, language and literacy, initiative and social relations, movement, music, classification, seriation, number, space, and time.

Most activities lend themselves to several key experiences. For example, a child might choose to paint. Such a choice would give the teacher the opportunity to observe how the child was able to understand the routine of getting paper, paint smocks, and so on and then putting away the paper when she was finished. If the child needed instruction, it could be provided. Painting would also be an activity that allowed the teacher to observe how the child represented objects and related to other children involved in the same task.

Key experiences provide teachers with a basis for planning and organizing the curriculum so that activities are not random. Through observing individual students, teachers are also able to assess how children are growing in their abilities, as categorized by key experiences (Bredekamp 1996).

The Bank Street College of Education   The Bank Street program grew out of the work of Lucy Sprague Mitchell, who had been a student of the famous educator John Dewey. Mitchell began a school for young children in which play would be taken seriously—namely, one in which children could play and researchers could study them doing so in a naturalistic setting. The Bank Street program is dedicated to fostering children's development, not simply to promoting specific learning. The following principles are the framework of the program:

1. *Development is not a simple path from less to more; and it is not an unfolding, like the unfolding of a flower. Development involves changes or shifts in the way a person organizes experience and copes with the world, generally moving from simpler to more complex, from single to multiple and integrated ways of responding. The concept of stages of development is crucial, and is also a convenient way of talking and thinking about developmental change and growth. Stages are approximate and are only loosely related to age. . . .*
2. *Individuals are never at a fixed point on a straight line of development, but operate within a range of possibilities. Earlier ways of organizing experience are not erased, but become integrated into more advanced systems. While people*

will want to function at the highest possible level, they are also able to use less mature ways appropriately. (Even after a child knows how to hop and jump, there are times when it is a good idea to crawl; even adults find moments when it is appropriate to be silly.) . . .

3. *Developmental progress involves a mix of stability and instability. A central task for the educator is to find a balance between helping a child consolidate new understandings and offering challenges that will promote growth. . . .*

4. *The motivation to engage actively with the environment—to make contact, to have an impact, and to make sense of experience—is built into human beings. The growing child gradually adds more ways of actively engaging with the world as she develops. Generally, the progression is from more physical, body-centered ways of responding to perceptual and then more conceptual, symbolic ways. . . .*

5. *The child's sense of self is built up from his experiences with other people and with objects; knowledge of the self is based on repeated awareness and testing of one's self in interaction. . . .*

6. *Growth and maturing involve conflict—conflict within the self, and conflict with others. Conflict is necessary for development. The way conflicts are resolved depends on the nature of the interaction with significant figures in the child's life and the demands of the culture.* (Mitchell and David 1992, pp. 16–17)

The Reggio Emilia Schools   In recent years, the thinking of early childhood educators has been influenced by the Reggio Emilia schools of northern Italy. These community preschools are based on the following principles:

- All children construct their own learning and are capable of learning.
- The community is an integral force in the school, providing both monetary support and involvement with programs and children.
- Collaboration, sharing, and personal relationships are valued.
- The environment—the "third teacher"—is important in stimulating interest and encouraging creativity.
- A child's personal sense of time is respected, and the pace of the day is determined by the children.
- Teachers consider themselves learners and work with other teachers and parents.
- Children have access to a wide variety of media materials that foster creativity; the emphasis is on the arts as a way of knowing.
- The curriculum is emergent, as children select projects, continue with them by choice, and return to them as they gain new insights.
- Documenting children's work is crucial to the success of the program (Cadwell 1997; Edwards, Gandini, and Forman 1993; Gandini 1993).

The Reggio Emilia schools are housed in beautiful and well-cared-for spaces that invite children to engage in activities. Each school has teachers, a *pedagogista,* and an *atelierista.* The *pedagogista* works with teachers to consider what experiences mean to children, how to help children learn more, and what additional experiences should be planned. The *atelierista* is the art director, who helps teachers and children express their interests and knowledge in many different media. For example, children studying flowers might create paintings, drawings, clay models, sculptures, and so on. Each time they create something in a new medium, they are expected to think about what they know so that each new representation will express their growing understanding. Teachers usually stay with the same group of children for several years, which allows them to get to know the children and their families very well.

One of the key elements of the Reggio Emilia schools is the documentation of children's learning:

> Careful consideration and attention are given to the presentation of the thinking of the children and the adults who work with them. Teachers' commentary on the purposes of the study and the children's learning process, transcriptions of children's verbal language (i.e., words and dialogue), photographs of their activity, and representations of their thinking in many media are composed in carefully designed panels or books to present the process of learning in the schools. (Cadwell 1997, p. 6)

This documentation, which is shared with parents and the community, creates a history of the child's learning and is used by teachers to explore possibilities for future experiences.

Another key element of the Reggio Emilia schools is the ongoing nature of the projects. Typical projects in U.S. schools tend to be rather short lived— for instance, a study of animals will go on for two weeks and be followed by a study of plants for another two weeks (or less, in some schools). In a Reggio Emilia school, the projects often last for months and the children continue to add to and revisit them again and again.

U.S. educators have wondered how the Reggio Emilia model can be implemented in U.S. schools. Some have actually attempted to transform the model and use it in their own schools (Cadwell 1997; Staley 1998). There are several obstacles to such a transformation, however. One is money. Most school budgets do not have the funds for hiring an *atelierista* and *pedagogista* to help teachers. Another obstacle is the pressure in U.S. schools to cover a wide range of content material rather than focus on one or two projects for a year. Lack of community support and parent involvement are other obstacles for implementing the model in U.S. schools. Nonetheless, some educators continue to try to implement as much as they can of the model, believing that it is a worthwhile endeavor and that the results are well worth the effort (Cadwell 1997; Gerson 2000; Staley 1998).

Overview of Constructivist Programs

Although the goals or emphases of these constructivist programs are not identical, they are all concerned with the development of children's thinking and reasoning abilities and their abilities to represent experiences in meaningful ways. Each program depends on children's active involvement with materials and teachers' guidance in helping children reflect on their experiences.

In examining the activities of a typical day (see pages 64–65) in a constructivist classroom, we find that playing with blocks offers children opportunities

9:00 – 10:00	Arrival, choice time
10:00 – 10:15	Group time
10:15 – 10:40	Outdoor play
10:40 – 10:55	Snack time
10:55 – 11:10	Group time for optional activities
11:10 – 11:30	Story time and dismissal

Michelle bounces into her classroom, carrying a milk carton with a praying mantis in it. In Michelle's class of four-, five-, and six-year-olds, there are twenty-four children, a teacher, and an assistant teacher.

The classroom she enters has only one area large enough for all twenty-four children to sit down at once. The rest of the space is filled with areas arranged for different explorations or interactions. There is a large area for blocks; an area for dramatic play that contains dolls, child-sized kitchen equipment, dress-up clothes, and costumes; an area that contains easels and many kinds of art supplies; an area that contains a water table and sand table; an area that contains puzzles and games; an area for reading books that is furnished with two rocking chairs and some floor pillows; an area with many kinds of paper and writing utensils; an area that has baskets of math manipulative materials; an area that, at the moment, is filled with a large collection of old clocks and other small appliances; and another area where there is a table, which today is covered with paper and has some blocks and cardboard milk cartons on it.

Michelle's teacher notices her entry into the classroom and smiles a greeting. She notes that Michelle has signed in on the clipboard by the door and that she has hung her coat in the cubby labeled with her name. The teacher is helping two girls find a way to remove the levers and springs from an old toaster but turns her attention to Michelle and her box when Michelle approaches. The teacher listens while Michelle tells how she and her brother caught the

praying mantis and made a container for it. She suggests that Michelle place the container on a display table near the door for other children to observe, if they choose.

Michelle does so and then decides to spend some time in the blocks area. She selects a tagboard circle with her name on it and places it on one of the pegs beside a picture of blocks on a pegboard near the door. When she gets to the blocks area, she tells her friend Amy that she would like to build an apartment building. They decide to work on it together and find that it needs a strong base to support the ten stories that they want to add to it. The teacher observes their construction and offers them a pulley, a small box, and some cord so that they can make an elevator for their building.

After about thirty minutes of animated block building, the girls put away the blocks and Michelle checks on her praying mantis. She finds three children at the table and tells them about catching the insect and making the milk carton container for it. She takes her name from the "blocks" peg and moves it to the "art" peg. She gets a friend to help her fasten her paint smock and attaches paper to an easel. She paints a picture of her praying mantis. When the teacher observes her painting, she suggests that perhaps Michelle would like to write about the insect. After Michelle has cleaned the painting area, she goes to a table where there are many kinds of paper, pencils, and markers. She finds her journal in a basket and writes about the insect and draws pictures of it. The teacher helps her date her paper and painting. The teacher and her assistant have been moving from area to area in the classroom, asking questions, providing guidance, and suggesting activities to individual children.

The teacher rings a little bell, which is the signal for the children to finish their work and clean up the areas. After that has been done, the children meet on the rug, where the teacher is leading some fingerplays and songs. When all the children have gathered, the teacher asks them to think about some of the things they learned this morning. A few children tell about the parts they found in the appliances. Others tell about how they solved some problems in their play. The teacher says that she noticed that not everyone who wanted to do so could play in one of the areas where a new set of materials was available. She asks if they can think of some ways to solve the problem. The children finally decide to take a survey to determine who has already had a turn with the new materials and to make a sign-up sheet for those who have not yet had a turn. Some children make comments about the praying mantis and ask questions about it. The teacher asks how they could find out more about these insects. Two children decide that they could go to the library and ask the librarian for help in locating information. The teacher suggests a good time later in the morning for them to go.

Next, the children review the calendar for any special celebrations that are coming up and for the symbol that indicates the day the eggs in the incubator are expected to hatch. They recall their trip to the bakery last week and their plans for sharing time the next day.

After these activities have been finished, the children go outside to play. They can choose riding toys, swings, climber/slides, climbers, and some large blocks and tunnels for play. Michelle and a small group of friends climb and swing, shouting joyfully most of the time.

After about twenty-five minutes, the teacher signals the children to return to the room. As the children enter, each is asked to choose a snack: apple juice, orange juice, apple slices, or orange slices. They wash their hands and begin to help serve the snack. When they have finished their snack, the children construct a graph of their snack choices with help from the teachers and discuss all the relationships that are illustrated on the graph.

After the graph has been finished, the children get their coats again because today they are going on a walk around the neighborhood. Each child has a clipboard and pencil and chooses something to look for. Some will observe the number and kinds of houses they pass; others will observe the number and kinds of businesses. A few children want to record the number and kinds of plants they see, and some will look for all the printed words that they can find. They know that tomorrow they will begin to transfer the information they collect to the map of their immediate neighborhood that they are building on the table.

When the class returns from the walk, the children gather on the rug again for singing and movement. Two children go off to the library to get praying mantis information; the others learn some new songs and review the lyrics to other songs that are printed on large charts. The children also use some little books in which they have illustrated a few of the songs.

The teacher then shares a story from a "big book," with large illustrations and type so that all the children can see while the teacher reads. As the teacher reads the story a second time, some children join in on the words that they recognize. The teacher tells them that they may choose to write their own stories tomorrow.

The two children return from the library with several books and some posters. The teacher places these books on the display table with the praying mantis. Several children are really interested in the insect, and the teacher promises that they will have time to observe it and read about it tomorrow.

As the children gather their coats and papers and get ready for dismissal, they review patterns and arrange themselves in line according to their coat colors. It takes some time, but they form a pattern of red, blue, green, and yellow coats; then they add the children who do not fit that particular pattern. Michelle has on a red jacket and gets in line to help complete the pattern. She has her painting in her hand and hurries to share it with her mother when the teacher dismisses the class.

to develop concepts in mathematics, such as length and equivalence. The addition of the pulley provides opportunities for developing concepts related to simple machines. Representation of experience is achieved through building the model of an apartment building. Several activities offer children opportunities to use their developing skills in literacy (signing in on arrival, recording comments about the painting, recording observations on the walk in the neighborhood) and to represent understandings. In exploring the numerical patterns in the room, the teacher attempts to aid children in the development of number concepts. Other activities require children to solve problems using reasoning (taking apart the toaster, deciding who can play in the new area).

Constructivist programs focus on development of physical, social, emotional, and intellectual competence. The curriculum is based on children's interests and is integrated so that content is not arranged by subject-matter areas. Many activities and experiences are selected to help children think about solutions to social as well as cognitive problems. The interrelationship of all areas of development is important in developing the *whole child*. The content areas of science, social studies, mathematics, the arts, and health and safety are all integrated into themes of interest to the children. Literacy is taught in the context of children's other activities, as they extend their language to reading and writing. Constructivists assume that literacy skills are best learned within a context in which they can be applied.

Because the selection of materials and experiences is based on the children's developmental level, extending the program to younger or older children requires adapting materials and experiences; nonetheless, the basic tenets of choice, intrinsic motivation in learning, and a balanced program remain constant. With younger children, the choices of activities are more limited and the guidance of the teacher is more apparent. Projects for older children are selected so that in-depth explorations of topics is possible. Teachers make a conscious effort to teach subject-matter content in meaningful contexts and to select experiences in which children can apply skills being learned.

Summaries and Comparisons

The program models described in this chapter have some common goals, but each has a different view of what is the best and most appropriate learning environment for young children (see Table 2.1). One goal common to all three models—Montessori, behaviorist, and constructivist—is for children to learn. The models differ, however, on the means used to reach this goal. Educators who follow the Montessori philosophy believe that children learn best through interactions with materials in a prepared environment; there is little child–child interaction. Behaviorists believe that children learn best in a highly structured environment in which the information presented is carefully sequenced and the rewards are controlled. Those who hold a constructivist view of learning also believe that children learn through interactions with objects and people but that children must reflect on their actions, as well.

Table 2.1 Overview of Program Models

	Physical Development	Social/Emotional Development	Cognitive Development	Other Emphases
Montessori	Emphasizes fine motor tasks	Focuses on individual, self-control	Emphasizes individual; tasks are selected by the child	Shows great respect for the child's work; teacher observes more than talks
Behaviorist	Gives little attention	Believes self-esteem is developed as child gains cognitive competence	Focuses on learning facts and responding to questions; lessons are highly sequenced	Emphasis is on learning; environment is controlled to avoid distractions
Constructivist	Focuses on both gross and fine motor development	Believes social interactions are critical; emphasizes peer learning and problem solving in relationships	Focuses on skills needed at the time and on teaching skills through projects child chooses	Believes knowledge is constructed by learner; teacher is facilitator

Other goals of the programs also vary. An additional goal of Montessori programs is to develop the child's intellect and control. Constructivist programs focus on development in all areas: physical, social, emotional, and intellectual. Behaviorists generally focus on academic knowledge and place less emphasis on physical and social development. These differing views of how children learn (and the varied program goals based on these views) translate into very different experiences for children who attend these programs.

Parents AND School Design

■ In the school's entry or main hallway, post your teacher's certification, accompanied by a short statement of your philosophy of teaching.

Research on Program Models

Attempts to compare the effectiveness of different program models have been inconclusive. It is not an easy task to control all the variables that influence such research. For example, we could argue that it is invalid to compare the academic achievement of children who attend preschools based on the different program models just described because the focuses of some of the programs

Developmentally
Appropriate
Practice

NAEYC

In Chapter 1, we introduced the concept developmentally
appropriate practice (DAP). Although DAP may look very
different in different situations, some basic criteria are critical
to such practice, including choice, activities based on children's
interests, and activities appropriate for individual children. Think about the critical
elements of DAP as you respond to the following questions:

- Are all the program models described in this chapter equally developmentally
  appropriate? Why?

- Some people argue that a kind and nurturing teacher is the most important
  element in any program. No one would suggest that teachers should be other
  than kind and nurturing, but is such behavior enough to counterbalance a lack
  of choice or a lack of individual appropriateness? Why?

- Must a program for young children give up academic goals in order to be
  developmentally appropriate? Why?

- Are the guidelines for developmentally appropriate practice a good yardstick
  for measuring programs? Why?

are much broader than academic achievement. Proponents of such broadly focused programs would argue that even if their children did not score as well on
standardized tests as children from more academic programs, they learned
other things that such tests do not measure. It is difficult to assess the academic
achievement of young children accurately. It is also difficult to control for family involvement, teacher effectiveness, children's motivation, and so forth in
studies that compare different program models.

Attempts to find differences between program models have produced
mixed results. Children who show initial gains in skill levels as the result of a
particular preschool experience may later show declines. Lilian Katz (1988)
suggests that educators attend to the long-term, cumulative effects of programs, as evidenced by children's interest in learning. Not many long-term
studies have been done, but one of the most significant research studies on
the effects of preschool experience is the Perry Preschool High/Scope research,
conducted by Schweinhart, Weikart, and Larner (1986).

The High/Scope curriculum used at the Perry Preschool was based on a
developmentalist approach. The research compared High/Scope to traditional
and direct instruction (behaviorist) preschool experiences. When children
were studied in 1988 at the age of fifteen, those who had either a High/Scope
or a traditional nursery school experience reported engaging in about half as
much delinquent behavior as children who had experience in a direct instruction program. This study also found that children from constructivist and traditional programs exhibited much more prosocial use of time (holding offices
in school, participating in sports) than those from the direct instruction
group. Another long-term study (Karnes, Shwedel, and Williams 1983) com-

Each teacher's educational philosophy shapes the activities and experiences she offers to children.

pared five preschool curriculum models and found that students who had direct instruction did poorly on several measures of school success by the end of high school. None of these differences was statistically significant, although 70 percent of the nursery school students completed high school compared to only 47 percent of the direct instruction group.

In a recent review of the research on the effects of preschool programs (including Head Start), Schweinhart (2001) states "Growing evidence that preschool programs contribute to the short- and long-term development of children living in poverty" (p. 1). He concludes that programs for four-year-olds contribute to children's readiness to enter school and remain on grade level. Oden, Schweinhart, and Weikart (2000) report that children attending Head Start programs following the High/Scope curriculum had higher grade point averages in elementary school and fewer criminal convictions than children attending a regular Head Start program.

An earlier study by Schweinhart and Weikart (1999) found less criminal behavior, more involvement in volunteer work, and less need for treatment of emotional impairment among children who had experience in the High/Scope program compared to children who attended a behaviorist model program. In addition, more members of the High/Scope group planned to graduate from college and were married and living with their spouses. The High/Scope students also reported feeling that people "gave them a hard time" less often. In criticism of these findings, Engelmann (1999) suggests that the numbers are too small to be conclusive and that there are errors and discrepancies in the data reported. He argues that the amount of time a student spent in the

Parents AND School Design

- Create a brochure or welcome letter to share with parents your philosophy about learning in a school setting.

program was not considered and that individuals' experiences in later years of school varied considerably yet were not considered when reporting the study results.

The conclusion we *can* draw from research is that much remains to be learned about the development and learning of young children. Teachers and parents must think carefully about program choices and expectations for children. And researchers must continue to attempt to solve the complex problem of evaluating different approaches to instruction for young children.

Chapter Summary

- Three models for early childhood programs were described in this chapter: Montessori, behaviorist, and constructivist.

- The key concepts in the Montessori program include the absorbent mind, the prepared environment, sensitive periods, autoeducation, and the importance of self-correcting, didactic materials. Montessori philosophy assumes that children need freedom to make choices and that they desire order and beauty in their lives.

- The behaviorist model of instruction is based on stimulus-response learning theory and operant conditioning. The instruction is primarily teacher directed and academic in focus.

- The constructivist, or developmentalist, model focuses on the child's development physically, socially, emotionally, and intellectually. Key elements include opportunities for the learner to construct knowledge and active manipulation of objects accompanied by reflection on that activity.

- The results of research that has attempted to compare the models of early childhood programs are mixed. It is extremely difficult to control all the variables that impinge on children and their school experiences in order to actually compare the programs. The long-term effects on children's interest in learning must be considered when examining research findings.

Theory into Practice

Interview a Montessori-certified teacher about the training required for this certification. Determine the focus of the training, and compare it with your own experience in learning to become a teacher of young children.

Find out what early intervention programs are available to children in your state and what qualifications are necessary for receiving these services.

Observe in at least two programs for young children that have different emphases. (You can often determine the focus of a program from its advertisement in the Yellow Pages or from brochures about the school.) Find both common elements and differences between the two programs. Discuss your observations with your group and share your comparisons.

Different program models require different skills and abilities from teachers. Choose the program model that you think best fits your own skill profile or the skill profile you hope to attain. Discuss with your group why you think this model best fits your skills.

Interview five parents to determine how each made the decision to send his or her child to a particular school. Compare your findings with those of others in your group. What do these parents' responses mean to you as a teacher?

Nancy Birkenmayer

Christa McAuliffe Elementary School
McAllen, Texas

Individual Growth in a Mixed-Age Classroom

Our K–1 classroom is deep in the heart of Texas, only seven miles from the Mexican border. Our enrollment is predominately Hispanic and Anglo children from all levels of socioeconomic backgrounds. My team teacher and I decided to try mixing my kindergarten class and her first-grade class the year before we were scheduled to mix the two grades completely in two K–1 classes. Doing so convinced us both that Vygotsky's social learning theory (1978) is indeed correct: *Children grow into the intellectual lives of those around them.* As the result of seeing the progress made by the younger children as well as the development of self-esteem in the older ones, we have now mixed our two classrooms, such that we have K–1 in both. Most of our kindergartners from the first year were promoted into our first grade, so we have been able to see the continuity of learning over a two-year period. The younger students benefit from observing what they will be able to do next year, and the first graders benefit from being the role models of that learning. Another benefit is that rapport with parents and students was well established during our first year together; thus, we can take up where we left off at the end of the previous schoolyear.

Although the mixing of ages makes for a wide range of ability, individual children do not feel stigmatized if they are not able to do what others may be doing. They know that they are not the only ones—others are learning, too. As a result, they are less likely to compare themselves to their classmates. We celebrate the progress of each child at his or her own developmental rate.

Since the children in our classes are together for two years, we have seen traditions established in which the younger ones look forward to their own "rite of passage." Each of our classrooms is more like a family than a school. We share in each other's successes and struggle with each other's problems. The children establish relationships with each other and with their teachers, which are nurtured by a two-year involvement.

Perhaps the greatest reward of teaching in a mixed-age classroom has been watching the kindergartners mature into first graders and observing the learning that takes place over a two-year period. We would not want to do it any other way.

CHAPTER 3

Creating an Environment for Learning

After reading this chapter, you will be able to do the following:

- Plan a classroom environment that reflects program goals and objectives.
- Select instructional materials that are appropriate for a given group of children.
- Make decisions about using computers in the early childhood curriculum.
- Plan an outdoor learning environment.
- Promote safety, both indoors and out.
- Adapt the learning environment for children with special needs.
- Celebrate diversity in the classroom environment.

Your assignment this week was to focus your observations on the physical environment of the classroom. To do so, you needed to sketch the arrangement of the furniture and list the materials and equipment available to the children. When you went to the first-grade classroom where you were to observe, you found about what you had expected: The children all had desks, which were arranged in a U shape around the classroom. There were shelves along one wall, where materials such as art supplies and books were stored. The teacher's desk was at the front of the classroom and to one side. There were chalkboards on two walls and bulletin boards on the other two.

When you got back to your own class and heard from your classmates, you found that the physical environments everyone had observed varied greatly. Some had tables and chairs and no desks. Some had been arranged in work areas for art, blocks, sand and water, and so on, plus a library. Some had many materials readily available to the children; others had almost none.

Now you are much more interested in the physical environment provided for children. You have questions about how teachers make decisions about furniture and room arrangements, and you also want to know how such decisions affect the children's learning and behavior.

Goals and Objectives

Some planning decisions can be made before the children arrive. Teachers can decide on the basic learning areas to be set up, the basic materials to be used, and the initial room arrangement. Other planning decisions must be made after the teacher and children become acquainted. Planning is never really finished. It is a continual cycle of making and implementing plans, observing, evaluating the effectiveness of your plans, and using that information for more planning.

The decisions you make about **room arrangement** and **instructional materials** and equipment will reflect your goals and expectations for the children. It is fairly common during an interview for a principal to ask a prospective teacher of young children to sketch a room arrangement that she would use. Much of what a principal wants to know about a candidate's curriculum priorities is reflected in how the prospective teacher chooses to arrange the room. If your program goals include encouraging children's exploration of a variety of materials and investigation of the phenomena around them, then you will not choose to set up your room with a desk for each child and the teacher's desk as the focal point of the classroom.

Environmental decisions reflect the philosophy and goals of the teacher. Thus, you will find contrasts among the instructional materials and room arrangements designed to accomplish various sets of objectives. For example, assume that one of Teacher A's beliefs is that children become more literate through participating in a broad range of activities that include read-alouds, journal writing, exploring books, playing games such as Go Fish, and reading interactive stories on the computer. Given this belief, this teacher will make sure that his classroom has a comfortable library area, that the children can access many materials without asking for them, and that they have table space for playing games. Suppose that Teacher B, on the other hand, believes that children need to have lessons on various skills. Her classroom might be arranged in a more traditional way, with a separate desk for each child, a space where a small group could sit for instruction (horseshoe tables were once common in primary classrooms), and fewer spaces open to the children.

As noted in Chapter 2, the teachers of the Reggio Emilia schools consider the environment the "third teacher," in that many explorations and ideas can be inspired by the environment itself. Of course, the opposite is true, as well. A dull, uninteresting environment can stifle children's imaginations.

The general goals of many programs include helping children to do these things:

1. Learn that they are capable learners, that they can make choices, and that their ideas are respected.

2. Learn and apply skills in a meaningful context.

3. Explore a variety of materials.

4. Become able to communicate their needs and feelings.

5. Learn to use and appreciate many sources of information—people, printed materials, visual materials.

6. Become able to express themselves creatively.

In order to meet these goals, teachers have many decisions to make. Be aware that the decisions you make about the learning environment can either foster or hinder achievement of these goals.

Structuring the Physical Environment

Often, many of the physical characteristics of the classroom in an early childhood program do not reflect the choices of the teacher—the room may be too small for the number of children, have a sink that the children cannot reach, have a bathroom down the hall, have chalkboards on every wall, or have only one electrical outlet. However, teachers can make other decisions about the physical environment, including how the furniture is arranged. Although teachers may not be able to choose the furnishings for the room at the outset of a program, they may be able to make changes over time. Teachers should also keep in mind that children need to be involved in planning the space, as well. Teachers should make preliminary plans and arrangements, but they must always address the needs of the children once they are working in the classroom.

The furniture selected must be of appropriate size for children and should be easy to rearrange to meet changing classroom needs. The most flexible furniture includes tables and chairs and shelf units on wheels. Rarely will every child need to sit at a table at once, so there need not be places at tables for everyone. Every child does need a space for her own things; this could be a cubby or a portable tub of some kind. Figure 3.1 shows one design for storage cubbies.

Figure 3.1

Storage Cubbies

Room Arrangement

The way the furniture is arranged and the way the room looks communicate to children what they are expected to do and how they are expected to behave. Furniture or the lack of furniture provides all of us with clues about what is expected of us. Think of bank lobbies that are cold and hard, telling us to get our business done and leave; a typical college classroom telling us to sit, listen, and take notes; and a comfortable family room that invites sitting or lounging and participation in a variety of activities such as watching television, playing games, snacking, reading, and relaxing.

For years studies have shown that the environment affects children's behavior and attitude. As the quality of the environment (as measured by adequate space and materials) decreased, the number of rules imposed by the adults and the amount of conflict among the children increased (Hill 1989; Midjaas 1984; Prescott, Jones, and Kritchevsky 1967; Weinstein 1979). Researchers have recommended softer spaces (Vergeront 1987), more natural light (Grangaard 1995; Schreiber 1996), and the use of ethnic colors in the environment (Caples 1996). It is clear from the research that the environment is important and that environmental influences are strong. In fact, Hubbard (1998) states that "access to a range of spaces, access to materials, access to other children and other adults; in short, the ability to access their own creative process" (p. 30) is the key to successful classroom arrangements in which children can think.

In choosing how to arrange furniture in the classroom, the first consideration—beyond the locations of doors and windows—is the locations of electrical outlets. In new schools, outlets are usually plentiful; outlets are often in short supply in older buildings, however. Areas that require electricity obviously must be located next to outlets. Usually, this means that videocassette recorders (VCRs), computers, tape recorders, aquariums, and other items that use electricity must be placed in the classroom first. Teachers should keep in mind these general guidelines for room arrangements:

1. Space must accommodate multiple uses. Few classrooms and centers have enough space for each activity to have its own area; therefore, areas must serve more than one purpose. For example, blocks can be placed in a corner that is also used for story time during another part of the day.

2. Areas in which water is used should be as close to the water supply as possible. These include art, science, and water table areas.

3. Quiet areas should be close together so that children who want to work quietly can do so. *Quiet* does not mean that children cannot talk, but activities in such areas as the library, the writing table, and a listening station are quieter by nature than activities in some other areas.

4. Noisy areas, such as the blocks and dramatic play areas, should be grouped on the other side of the room from quiet areas.

Vertical space is often overlooked in classrooms for young children. The backs of room dividers, walls, and other vertical surfaces can be used for interactive activities, such as matching activities, in which children match dresses to dolls or cookie monsters to cans; dressing activities, in which children lace, tie, zip, and button various pieces of clothing; flannelboard or magnetic story activities, in which children create and retell stories; and so on. By using vertical spaces, teachers can provide an extra activity or two in areas that would otherwise be decorative or perhaps even wasted (Readdick and Bartlett 1994/1995).

Figure 3.2 shows an example of a room arrangement for a preschool or kindergarten classroom, and Figure 3.3 shows one for a primary-grade classroom.

Figure 3.2   Room Arrangement for a Preschool Classroom

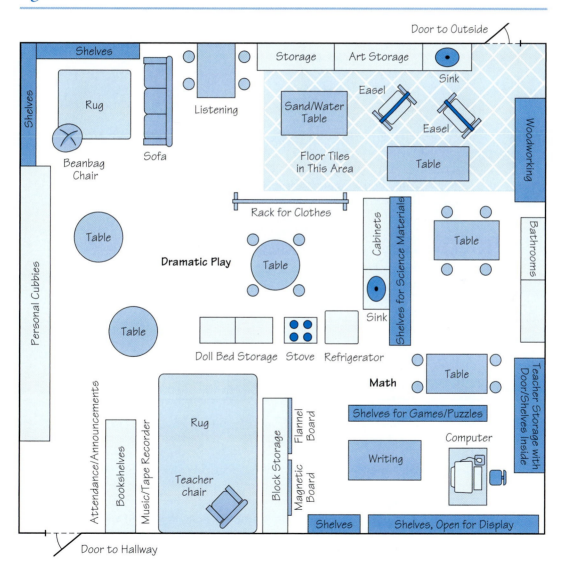

Figure 3.3   Room Arrangement for a Primary-Grade Classroom

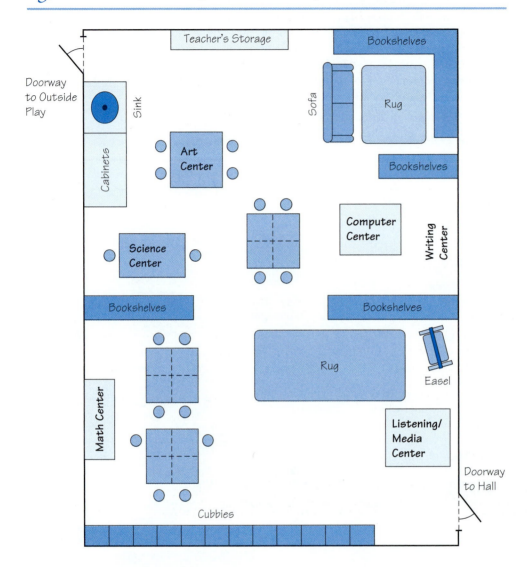

Evaluate these plans in terms of use of space, how well they would accommodate your objectives, and what traffic patterns you think would develop. Please note that these room arrangements do not have a teacher's desk. Most teachers of young children do not need a desk; they just need a shelf or table to store supplies and to keep their records together. Teacher's desks take up an extraordinary amount of floor space that can be put to better use.

Assessing the Environment

One method of assessing the learning environment is to examine activity areas in terms of their simplicity or complexity (Kritchevsky and Prescott 1969). A *simple unit* for play or activity has one obvious use and does not have subparts for children to manipulate or improvise with; examples include rocking horses, swings, and vehicles. A *complex unit* has subparts made of two essentially different play materials that children can manipulate or improvise with. A sand table with tools is a complex unit; art activity tables with paint or clay and tables with books are also classified as complex. A *super unit* has three or more play materials juxtaposed. Examples include a tunnel with movable boards and boxes, a sand table with tools and water, and a blocks area with hollow blocks, unit blocks, and block accessories. A super unit is about eight times as effective in holding children's attention as a simple unit; a complex unit is about four times as effective.

In analyzing your own room plans, count the variety of possible activities and the amount of things to do per child. Table 3.1 may help you analyze your own space. It shows Kritchevsky and Prescott's (1969, p. 13) analysis, in which the number of play spaces represents the number of children who can comfortably play in a given unit. Divide the total play spaces by the number of children to find the ratio of play spaces to children. If there are at least two play spaces for each child, children will be much more likely to find play spaces for themselves without teacher help than if the ratio were smaller. If the number of play spaces is less than the number of children, children will have difficulty finding something to do, other than grabbing something from someone else. An analysis of your room will provide information about whether there are adequate activities for the number of children and how you might rearrange the environment to make it more complex.

Table 3.1 Analysis of Play Spaces

Number of Play Units	Type of Unit	Number of Play Spaces
12 vehicles	Simple	12
1 rocking boat	Simple	1
1 tumble tub	Simple	1
1 jungle gym with boxes and boards	Complex	4
1 dirt area plus scoop trucks	Complex	4
1 equipped sand table with water	Super	8
	Total Play Spaces = 30	

Source: Kritchevsky and Prescott 1969, p. 13.

Harms (1970) suggests that in addition to assessing the environment for the complexity of play spaces, teachers should consider these questions:

- *Can quiet and noisy activities go on without children disturbing one another? Is there an appropriate place for each?*
- *Is a variety of material available on open shelves for the children to use when they are interested? Are materials on shelves well spaced for clarity?*
- *Are materials stored in individual units so that children can use them alone without being forced to share with a group?*
- *Are activity centers defined so that children know where to use the materials?*
- *Are tables or rug areas provided for convenient use of materials in each activity center?*
- *Is self-help encouraged by having materials in good condition and always stored in the same place?*
- *Are cushioning materials used to cut down extraneous noise—rug under blocks, pads under knock-out bench?*
- *Are setup and cleanup simple? Are these expected parts of the child's activity?*
- *Is the children's work displayed attractively at the child's eye level?*
- *Do the children feel in control of and responsible for the physical environment?* (pp. 305–306)*

In assessing the environment for a primary-grade classroom, the teacher must think about adequate space and materials for completion of projects such as a study of animals or birds. Ask questions such as these about a primary environment:

1. Can a child or small group get materials (paper, markers, scissors, and so on) and find a space to work comfortably?

2. Is it possible to move around the room without disturbing the work of others?

3. Is there a quiet place for a child or small group to read or think quietly?

4. Is the furniture arrangement flexible enough to allow moving from large group to small group to individual instruction without major disruptions and loss of time?

5. Are necessary items (such as a pencil sharpener) placed in the room so that a child needing to use them can do so without disturbing others?

6. Have the children been involved in solving the problems they encounter in getting their work done?

Most classrooms are not going to be ideal, and you will have to do some thoughtful planning to make the space work for you and the children. You may have to think about combining some centers, finding ways to move some centers to the middle of the room, and generally using the space you have in

*From Thelma Harms, "Evaluating Settings for Learning," *Young Children* 25 (May 1970): 304–309. Used with permission of NAEYC.

creative ways. If you keep in mind what your goals are for the children and for a space that helps them be comfortable and happy, then you will be able to solve most problems. All teachers want more space, and good planning will not achieve that, but it can help you make the best use of the space you have.

Instructional Materials

Materials for the classroom can be quite expensive. In addition to purchasing materials, most teachers ask for contributions from parents, go to garage sales, and scrounge materials from community sources. For example, some teachers get boxes and scrap paper from businesses that generate numerous computer printouts or wood scraps from local construction sites or cabinet shops.

The following guidelines will be helpful when you are selecting materials for the classroom:

1. Choose materials that can be used for more than one experience. Single-use materials like windup toys do not invite children to use them again and again, each time in a new or creative manner.

2. Select materials sturdy enough to withstand use by many active children.

3. Select materials that serve many instructional purposes, such as small blocks that can be used for constructing, for counting, for sorting by color, for arranging into patterns, and so on.

4. Select materials that can be used by children of varying ages and abilities. Sand, for example, can be used by very young children, who like to feel it and pour it from container to container. Older preschoolers can use sand

Children should have opportunities to make choices in the learning environment.

to compare quantities and to measure. Primary-age children will be more sophisticated in their sand play. Barbour, Webster, and Drosdeck (1987) report observing one group of second graders creating a desert environment after listening to their teacher read *The Desert Is Theirs* (Baylor 1970).

5. Choose safe materials; those with broken parts or rough edges should be discarded.

Learning Areas

One common technique for organizing instructional materials in classrooms is to place materials into learning centers or **learning areas.** Use of the phrase *learning centers* is sometimes criticized because it seems to imply that learning takes place only in those specific centers. The assumption underlying this discussion is that learning takes place all over and outside the classroom.

The phrase *learning area* will be used to indicate a specific location where related materials are arranged in a classroom. The basic learning areas in early childhood classrooms include areas for art, music, library/listening/writing activities, blocks, dramatic play, science/discovery activities, manipulatives/mathematics/games, woodworking, sand and water tables, and quiet activities. If space and equipment allow, an area for physical education is also important. These areas should reflect the children's ages, development, growing abilities, and changing interests; learning areas are not static.

See the panel on pages 84–85 for an overview of what materials and equipment should go in the basic learning areas. The following sections will discuss these areas in more detail.

Art Area

Teachers who want to encourage children in art experiences will think carefully about the materials and classroom environments that promote participation in art activities. If the goals of an art program are to be achieved, materials for many art experiences must be readily available to children. In choosing a place in the classroom for art, consider sources of light and access to water. An area with a sink is ideal so that children can clean up easily, but a container of warm water will serve if no sink is available. Low shelves for storage of materials, easels for painting, and tables for working with other materials are also important. Traffic patterns must be considered when deciding where the art area will be located. If the area cannot be in a corner, other pieces of furniture can be used to isolate the space so that children do not walk through it to get from one part of the classroom to another.

Setting up an art area also includes deciding on smocks and floor coverings that will help children be most comfortable as they explore art materials. Smocks can be made from plastic or from old shirts. The point is to protect the children's clothing so that they are free from the worry of getting their clothes dirty. Floor coverings should be tile, if possible, so that floors can be cleaned easily (see Figure 3.4). Floors can be covered with newspapers to aid in cleanup. Materials for cleanup—water, sponges, a small broom and dustpan—should also be readily available to the children.

In selecting materials for art experiences, teachers must think about developmental appropriateness and possibilities for multiple uses. Chalk, markers, and crayons should be easy to grasp and should not break easily. Children should be allowed to use materials in a variety of ways. For example, some teachers allow children to use crayons only as they would pencils. But the wrappers can be removed from crayons so they can be rubbed across the surface of a paper on their sides. The fewer rules that are attached to materials, the more children will be encouraged to think for themselves and be creative in using them.

Just because art materials are arranged in one place in the classroom does not mean that art experiences cannot take place in other areas. Be open to a variety of places and possibilities for art activities. In nice weather, children might be offered the chance to do art outside; for example, they might do rubbings on outside surfaces. They might also choose to draw in other places in the classroom. On the other hand, even though art activities are not limited to one area of the room, it is convenient for all the supplies to be stored together in the art area so that children always know where to find what they need. Figure 3.4 is a sketch of an art area that illustrates some of the suggestions in the preceding paragraphs.

NAEYC

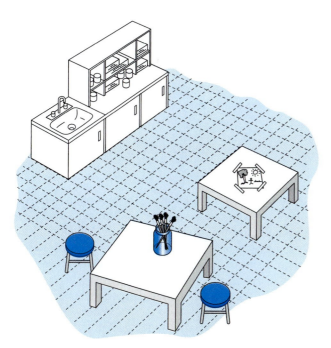

Figure 3.4

Art Area

Some materials will not be appropriate for all age groups. The teacher must select those most appropriate for his group of students.

Basic furniture in any classroom should include tables and chairs of appropriate size, shelf units, storage units, an adult-sized rocking chair, sofas, child-sized rocking chairs, floor pillows, and a full-length mirror. The following lists include additional materials that teachers in preschool and primary grades have found to be useful. Teachers will also want to provide other materials to enhance the presentations of specific topics or themes.

Dramatic Play

- Child-sized kitchen equipment (with pots and pans)
- Dishes and silverware
- Tables and chairs
- Telephones
- Child-sized ironing board and iron
- Child-sized cleaning equipment (brooms, mops, dustpan, and so on)
- Assorted dolls
- Doll clothes
- Doll bed, carriage
- Doll house, furniture
- Assorted tubs, buckets, dishpans
- Assorted dress-up clothing and costumes

Blocks

- Blocks (unit and hollow)
- Block accessories (people, cars, safety signs, and so on)
- Small blocks (sets of cubes, small colored blocks)
- Sturdy wooden vehicles (cars, trucks, boats, planes, tractors, fire engines, buses, helicopters)

Art

- Adjustable easels
- Brushes (half-inch to one-inch widths)
- Liquid tempera paint (in a variety of colors)
- Painting smocks (purchased or homemade)
- Crayons
- Colored chalk
- Clay
- Scissors
- Glue, paste
- Paper (glazed for fingerpainting, newsprint, white drawing paper, construction paper in a variety of colors, tissue paper)
- Drying rack for paintings
- Miscellaneous supplies (fabric scraps, rickrack, yarn, ribbon, glitter, buttons, natural materials)

Library/Listening/Writing

- Computer and printer
- Typewriter
- Paper (various colors, sizes, shapes) and writing instruments (pencils, markers)

Music Area

A piano is often the center of the music area. If you are lucky enough to have a piano and can play a simple tune, you can use it in many different ways to encourage children's music skills. Although a piano is still very valuable in an early childhood classroom, many teachers today use guitars and autoharps. These instruments are much easier to play and allow the teacher to face the children while playing. Still, many teachers like to have record players or tape recorders in the music area to be used in group music experiences or by individual students.

Exploration of music can be encouraged by making a limited number of musical instruments available to children. If the classroom is equipped with a

- Tape recorder, tapes, books with tapes
- Record player
- Flannelboard with stand and flannel pieces
- Books (professional and published by classroom authors)
- Magazines

Manipulatives/Games

- Hand puppets
- Puzzles
- Games (Lotto, checkers, chess, dominoes, Candy Land, Chutes and Ladders, Hi-Ho Cherry O, and so on)
- Beads and strings
- Sewing cards
- Manipulative materials (ranging from stacking rings to very complex materials)
- Tinkertoys (regular size and large size)
- LEGO blocks, bristle blocks

Science/Discovery

- Aquarium
- Terrarium
- Magnets of various kinds
- Magnifying glasses
- Prism
- Metric measuring equipment, test tubes, slides, petri dishes
- Pattern blocks
- Pegs and pegboards

- Geoboards
- Geoblocks
- Base 10 blocks
- Unifix cubes
- Scales (balance and other types)
- Rhythm instruments
- Sandbox
- Water table with top
- Workbench with equipment

Physical Education

- Balance beam
- Tumbling mat
- Rocking boat
- Steps
- Walking boards
- Jungle gym
- Fabric tunnel
- Sawhorses (sturdy metal)
- Climbing ladder, climbing rope
- Balls of various sizes
- Ropes
- Hula hoops
- Bowling set
- Outdoor equipment (wheeled toys, gardening tools, sandbox)

piano, a low shelf area near the piano is adequate for storing other selected instruments. A listening center with headphones gives children opportunities to listen to CDs and tapes without disturbing the rest of the class.

The teacher might also keep a file of songs that children know along with charts of the lyrics. When these materials are made available, children can select songs for group singing or review songs they especially like.

Usually, the space used for movement experiences is used for other purposes during other parts of the day. If possible a space can be provided for movement during the time children choose their own activities. A shelf with scarves, hula hoops, large circles made of elastic (often known as *Chinese jump ropes*), a small drum, and ankle bells will encourage explorations of movement.

Library/Listening/Writing Area

An area for language arts activities should be located in a quiet part of the classroom and should have open shelves for storing books and a table for writing activities. Children may or may not need chairs for the listening center; sometimes the unit can be placed so that children sit on the floor to use it. It is better to display books standing up, with their covers showing, than to store them stacked on a shelf. Storing books standing up takes more space than stacking them, but children are much more likely to be enticed to choose a book if they can see its front cover. Because the number of books that can be displayed at once in this manner is limited, the books on display will need to be rotated frequently and selected to support topics of study.

In addition to a table for writing, a storage area for different writing papers and writing instruments is necessary. Pencils, pens, markers, and so on should be stored in small baskets or cans to make it easy for children to choose the ones they need. Paper in different colors and sizes should be available and can easily be stored in open boxes. Dictionaries should also be kept in this area. Picture dictionaries are especially useful for young writers. Children's personal dictionaries can be kept in a basket in the writing area.

Typewriters and computers can also be housed in the library/listening/writing area. Children working with such equipment need the same supplies (word lists, dictionaries, and the like) that other writers need, so it is sensible to locate such equipment in this area. Use of typewriters and computers can generate a lot of talking and interaction, so they should be placed where students using them will disturb those in the quiet reading area as little as possible.

Blocks Area

Blocks require storage shelves and a large floor area for construction. A smooth carpet can help reduce the noise in this area and will not interfere with balancing the blocks. Larger blocks, such as hollow blocks, can be stored directly on the floor rather than on shelves. As Hirsch (1984) reminds us, the block storage area should be neither too neat nor too messy. If it's too neat, children will be intimidated and worry about cluttering the area when they use the materials; if it's too messy, children will find it difficult to locate the exact blocks they need, which is frustrating. Unit blocks should not be stored in carts or boxes. Such storage makes finding the needed block almost impossible and encourages children to toss the blocks back into the box, thereby denting them and reducing their useful life.

Parents AND *Learning Environment*

■ To help parents understand the purposes of learning areas, post a sign on the wall in each area that describes its goals. For example, in the blocks area the sign could list intellectual goals, physical goals, and social goals that can be met through playing with blocks. Such signs can be useful to parents and other classroom visitors as they observe in the classroom.

You will have to decide if you want to mark the block shelves (for example, with silhouettes of the blocks to be stored on each shelf) or if you want the children to determine the storage. Children do learn to recognize the shapes of the blocks and match them to the silhouettes, but they learn more about size relationships and classification when they are responsible for making storage decisions. Figure 3.5 illustrates a blocks area.

Dramatic Play Area

The dramatic play area is often called the *housekeeping corner* or the *doll corner*. It is an area that will reflect the development and changing interests of the children as they grow. For example, threes and fours may need child-sized kitchen equipment, dishes and pans, dolls and doll beds, and other materials for acting out the roles in a family. As children grow and develop, they are able to assume the roles of people outside the family. Although they may still enjoy the kitchen equipment, they will often use the dramatic play area to act out roles of people in such locations as a grocery store, a gas station, a beauty or barber shop, a doctor's office, a hospital, an airport, or other areas that are part of their experience.

The teacher will need to be flexible in providing the materials and assistance to support children's ideas. Primary-grade children often use this area for dramatizing characters in stories they have heard or read. They will need a variety of costumes, dress-up clothes, and props to support their play as their knowledge expands. If the dramatic play area stays the same throughout the year, then the teacher will need to take special steps to encourage children to develop and expand their interests.

Science/Discovery Area

Science activities do not take place only in the science or discovery area, of course, but the tools for investigations are kept on shelves in this area. Most

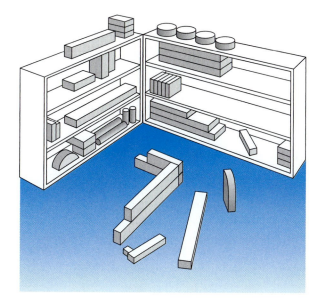

Figure 3.5

Blocks Area

teachers also like to have a table where interesting displays can be arranged and where children can explore materials—plants, soils, rocks, shells, leaves, or whatever. The area should be equipped with shelves that contain magnets, magnifying glasses, measurement containers, and other materials for investigating scientific topics. Teachers often include an invention corner in this area, where old appliances such as television sets, radios, toys, clocks, and toasters can be dismantled and reassembled, perhaps even using the parts to create new objects.

Manipulatives/Mathematics/Games Area

The math area is another area that will need to change to meet the needs and interests of children. This area should be the storage place for puzzles, beads, sewing cards, and other materials designed to help younger children develop fine motor skills. Older children will still be interested in puzzles and manipulative games and will also begin using pattern blocks, Unifix cubes, base 10 blocks, and other manipulatives used in mathematics. All ages will need construction toys and tabletop blocks. Games designed for individuals or small groups are often stored in this area. Playing cards, dice, and other game materials should also be available here; children will not only play with them but also use them for inventing games. This area needs shelves for storage and a table on which to work with the materials.

Woodworking Area

Woodworking areas require a workbench, storage areas for wood scraps, and shelves or a pegboard for holding tools. Young children who have not had much experience with woodworking are often satisfied with a sturdy log or other large piece of wood into which they can hammer nails. Children do not necessarily need to be able to make something until they have had more experience. Tools should be real tools designed on a small scale and sturdy enough to work well. Saws should really cut wood, and hammers should really drive nails.

Sand and Water Tables Area

Good-quality sand and water tables are available from supply catalogs, but they are expensive. A sand table can be constructed by adding a frame to the edge of a low table. Sometimes teachers substitute rice or cornmeal for sand in order to make cleanup easier. However, in addition to the fact that some teachers may be reluctant to use food in activities that render it inedible, neither of these materials has the same qualities that sand offers. For example, children cannot add water to these materials and mold them. Teachers should also recognize that individuals from some cultures may be offended by this use of food.

Many sand and water tables are equipped with covers so they can be used for other purposes when not being used for sand and water play. Accessories for sand and water tables depend on the developmental level of the children using them. Younger children may only pour and scoop, so precise mea-

suring equipment is not needed. Older children will need materials to make measuring, comparing, and other investigations possible. Storage for accessories is often in boxes under the tables.

Water tables are more difficult to make than sand tables. The newest models of water tables are made of clear plastic and are often round with drains in the bottom that allow for easy draining and cleaning. Teachers often substitute a tub or a child's wading pool for a water table. These substitutes are better than not having water tables, but because children lean over them rather than stand around them and could easily fall in, even more supervision is required. The water in water tables should be replaced daily, so draining and filling conditions should be considered when purchasing a table. Water play accessories should include objects for filling and pouring, tubes and connectors, and materials that sink and float. Specific materials can be added to sand and water tables to help children explore topics in the curriculum.

Physical Education Area

An area where children can use a tumbling mat and engage in other physical activities is important. Some teachers like to place equipment that encourages gross motor development around the room rather than in one area because it takes up so much space. For example, balance beams and tunnels can be placed so that children can use them to get from one area of the room to another. Physical development is enhanced with beanbags, Velcro darts, Nerf balls, tunnels, bowling pins and balls, and so on. These materials should be stored on shelves or in a closet near an area large enough for children to use them without disturbing the work of others.

Quiet Area

Every classroom needs a small area where a child can go to be alone for a time. This area needs no special equipment—perhaps just a chair or a floor pillow. Some teachers like to make the quiet area inviting with flowers (nothing elaborate, just one or two), a piece of sculpture, or a drape of fabric. A child should be able to take a game or a book to this quiet area whenever she needs to.

Specialized Learning Areas

Some learning areas are set up for specific purposes and are not designed to be part of the classroom all year. Such specialized centers might be used for activities such as following up on stories, sorting and classifying objects, and demonstrating skills.

Activities to follow up on stories include placing pictures from the story in correct sequence, listening to a tape recording of the story while following along in the book, drawing a picture of a favorite part of the story, and so on. Sorting and classifying or problem-solving centers might offer collections to be sorted and explained (shells, keys, leaves, and so on) or materials to be grouped (paper and pencils, stamps and envelopes, keys and locks). Skill

Developmentally
Appropriate
Practice

Reflect on different classroom environments you have observed in terms of what you now know about planning a learning environment:

NAEYC

- Do any elements of the classroom environment indicate developmentally appropriate practice? Why?

- Can a classroom environment be developmentally appropriate when the desks are arranged in rows, with each child facing the teacher's desk in the front of the room? Why?

- Could a more flexible furniture arrangement fail to be developmentally appropriate? Why?

- In addition to furniture arrangement, what else in the environment would indicate DAP? Why?

activities might be finding pictures of sets of objects whose names rhyme or finding the matching cylinders in a sound game. (Canisters from 35-mm film containing beans, rice, nails, stones, or other materials and having the lids taped on work well for this activity.)

Many magazines for teachers describe learning activities such as these. Teachers have to decide how they fit the program goals, if they suit the individual needs of children, and if so, where to locate the activities in the room.

Storage Areas

Each classroom needs an area in which materials not currently in use can be stored. A closet lined with shelves is ideal. If no storage facilities are built into the classroom, perhaps a storage unit can be purchased from a school supply firm. If the room contains no closet and a unit cannot be purchased, the teacher may have to improvise a storage area in one corner. Fabric can be used to cover the fronts of shelf units so that the contents are out of sight.

Beginning the Year

Teachers can begin the year by arranging materials in basic areas, knowing that they will make changes as soon as the children actually begin to work in the classroom. Teachers should try to simplify areas so that only the very basic materials and equipment are available for the first few days or weeks of the schoolyear. Materials that are easy to put away should be used until the children learn the routines of cleaning up work areas. Some materials should also be kept back initially and brought out later to add interest and novelty throughout the year; for example, large blocks and a few unit blocks can be put out in the blocks area right away, but other unit blocks and accessories can remain put away for use later.

For the first few days of school, activities in the art center should be limited to the use of crayons, paper, and clay. Unless classroom assistance is available—such as a parent volunteer or paraprofessional who can help children learn where to find paint smocks and paint, where to place their paintings until they dry, and how to clean up the art area—paint and easels should be brought out only after children have learned to handle the materials in other areas. Similarly, such areas as music, water tables, and carpentry can be set up when the teacher knows the children better and feels they do not require such close supervision.

Managing Learning Areas

More often than not, children will distribute themselves among learning areas without any problems of overcrowding. If new materials are added, the teacher may have to help children solve the problem of who has a turn first. If some areas do not attract children, the teacher's responsibility is to determine what the area needs and why it is not interesting to the children. The youngest children will need teacher guidance in choosing areas for play; older preschoolers may be able to plan their activities more independently, with the help of a few guidelines for managing the learning areas; and primary-grade children can take most of the responsibility for distributing themselves.

Many teachers have an activity time when children first arrive for the day; this allows children to choose an area and begin their activities without waiting for everyone else to arrive. Other teachers begin activity time after a group meeting, during which they have reviewed the calendar or completed other discussions with the group. To avoid having everyone trying to get to an area at once, many teachers use some scheme for deciding who chooses first and how choices are made during the play period. Some teachers group children randomly into two or three groups and rotate the group that gets to choose first. For example, the groups might be labeled red, yellow, and blue; if the red group has first choice today, the yellow group will have first choice tomorrow, and the blue group, the day after.

Teachers of very young children should try to allow them to play where they choose. When their choices cannot be honored, then the teacher should suggest another area and perhaps play there with the children for a few minutes. Some teachers of older preschoolers manage the number of children in each area by posting a number that defines how many can be in that area at a time. A child is free to join others in that area if the number of children allowed will not be exceeded. For example, if the blocks area will hold six children comfortably, a 6 is posted on one of the shelves. A child coming to the blocks area must decide if she can play with the blocks, given the number of children already in the area.

Other teachers like to use a pegboard system (see Figure 3.6). A pegboard is prepared so that the learning areas are displayed down the left side. Pictures

Figure 3.6

Pegboard

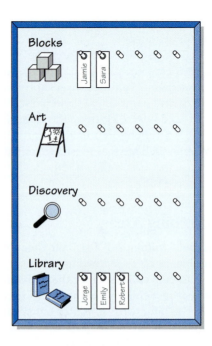

representing learning areas are added to aid the children in identifying each area. The number of pegs for each area is determined by the number of children that area can accommodate easily; pegs are placed in the row beside each picture to indicate how many children can use that area at one time. Again, if six children can use the blocks area, there will be six pegs beside the picture of blocks. Each child will have a tag with his name on it; he will place his tag on a peg when he wants to play with the blocks. If there are no empty pegs for the blocks area, he will have to make another choice. There should be more total pegs than there are children in order to give children as many choices as possible. And when an area is not available for some reason, the pegs for that area can be removed for the day.

Such a pegboard system also allows some subtle guidance in helping children make new choices. For example, if a child always chooses the art area and the teacher feels that she has developed enough confidence to work in another area, the teacher might limit the number of art pegs so that the child will have to make another choice. The teacher should make sure that choices are available that will interest the child and perhaps go there with her to play for a few minutes.

Teachers may want to involve primary-age children in more formal planning. One way to do this is to provide each child with a planning sheet on which the scheduled events for the day are listed (see Figure 3.7). After reviewing the events, each child can check what he plans to do that day.

Figure 3.7

Planning Sheet

Name: _____

- ☐ Independent Reading/Writing
- ☐ Writing Conference with Teacher
- ☐ Reading Conference with Teacher
- ☐ Buddy Reading
- ☐ Special Activity
- ☐ Math Activity
- ☐ Outdoor Play
- ☐ Work on Project with Group
- ☐ Library
- ☐ Listening Center
- ☐ Games Center
- ☐ Special Lesson

Children with Special Needs

Some areas and materials may need to be adapted for children with special needs, for instance, to make them wheelchair accessible or to add visual or auditory information to help all children work as independently as possible. Teachers should analyze the room arrangement and material storage areas in terms of the needs of all children in the class. Some spaces may need to be enlarged or more clearly defined to facilitate children's movement, some materials may need to be placed on more accessible shelves so they are within children's reach, or some materials may need to be organized so that children who have trouble hearing receive the maximum visual information.

For example, Sheldon (1996) recommends making adaptive equipment available in the dramatic play area so that children will experience what adaptive equipment actually feels like and be less wary of it. Of course, the children using these materials will require close supervision so the materials are not damaged and no children are injured. Bromer (1999) suggests that teachers find diverse props and play materials and that props be tailored to meet children's needs, such as having dress-up clothing that opens in the front, has large openings, and fastens with Velcro closures.

Clutter may be distracting for children with perceptual difficulties. Some common supplies may need to be stored in several locations throughout the room so that children who have problems moving around have easy access to them. Room arrangements, materials, and schedules must be adapted for each group and for each individual child.

Computers in Early Childhood Programs

Parents AND Computers

■ Encourage parents to observe their children as they interact with computers. Make sure that parents who are unable to buy computers for their children do not feel that having a computer at home is necessary for a child's success in school.

In today's world, computers are a part of almost every early childhood program. Having a computer, or many computers, in the classroom may mean that the children are frequent and active users of computers, that children who are good get to use computers as a reward, that children use computers to reinforce skills lessons, or that the computers are gathering dust because none of the adults feels comfortable using them. It is obvious that computers are a vital part of modern life. So the question is: How can they be used in early childhood programs to benefit children?

Teaching and Learning with Computers

NAEYC

The National Association for the Education of Young Children (NAEYC) has recognized that computers are common features in early childhood classrooms and thus issued a position statement on technology and young children. The statement assumes that computers can be misused, as can any other learning tool. The tenets are as follows:

1. *A professional judgment by the teacher is required to determine if a specific use of technology is age appropriate, individually appropriate, and culturally appropriate. . . .*
2. *Used appropriately, technology can enhance children's cognitive and social abilities. . . .*
3. *Appropriate technology is integrated into the regular learning environment and used as one of many options to support children's learning. . . .*
4. *Early childhood educators should promote equitable access to technology for all children and their families. Children with special needs should have increased access when this is helpful. . . .*
5. *The power of technology to influence children's learning and development requires that attention be paid to eliminating stereotyping of any group and to eliminating exposure to violence, especially as a problem-solving strategy. . . .*
6. *Teachers, in collaboration with parents, should advocate for more appropriate technology applications for all children. . . .*
7. *The appropriate use of technology has many implications for early childhood professional development.* (NAEYC 1996)*

*From National Association for the Education of Young Children, "NAEYC Position Statement: Technology and Young Children—Ages Three through Eight" (adopted April 1996), *Young Children* 51(6): 11–16. Reprinted with permission from the National Association for the Education of Young Children. The full text of the NAEYC statement can be found on the website of the NAEYC.

Computers are not necessary for very young children (Haugland 1999), and their use needs to be carefully planned and observed when they are used with older children. Computers should not be used as electronic workbooks and they should not be used as a reward for good behavior. Computer use should be child initiated, not teacher directed, and children should be allowed to leave the computer when they choose. Davidson and Wright (1994) believe that computer use is likely to be more appropriate for children if the following assumptions and attitudes are followed:

1. *Computer use is a social activity.*
2. *Computer use is a child-initiated and child-directed activity.*
3. *Computer software allows children to explore, experiment, and problem solve.*
4. *Computers offer new learning opportunities when unexpected things happen.*
5. *Computers are one of many materials in a developmentally appropriate classroom.* (p. 78)

Children generally prefer using computers with other children. Both language development and social skills can be improved when children explain to each other what to do to achieve certain results and negotiate turns. Kent and Rakestraw (1994) found that "computers appear to be a valuable tool for facilitating language use within the classroom. When used appropriately, they can provide a genuine, real world context for children's exploration" (p. 336).

Computers in early childhood classrooms should be one of many materials offered for children to explore and use as tools to accomplish their goals. Computers, especially those with voice synthesizers that read what has been keyed in, can help children make discoveries about written language. Computers are much more effective in classrooms where they can be integrated into the curriculum rather than in a lab where instruction is not related to classroom activities. The question of how many computers are enough must

Children often prefer—and should be encouraged—to use computers in groups.

be answered by deciding how the computers will be used in the program and what children actually do with them. Many teachers find that one computer is adequate and that they can schedule time for every student to use the computer weekly.

Computers can be used in ways that are inappropriate for young children. For example, research has shown (Clements, Nastasi, and Swaminathan 1993) that the use of drill-and-practice programs can lead to children's loss of creativity. The use of skills programs might increase ability in some areas, but the importance of obtaining such skills is not consistent with a more wholistic view of how children learn to read and write. A better use of computers in early childhood classrooms is to create stories and pictures, as opposed to practicing discrete skills. Teachers can help individual children meet their own learning goals through adapting their interactions with computers (Samaras 1996).

Selecting Software

Teachers need to carefully evaluate software before purchasing it for their classrooms. Several guides and newsletters are available for helping teachers as well as parents make good decisions about their purchases. Isenberg and Rosegrant (1995, p. 29) suggest that teachers should think carefully about software that is purchased for classroom use. They recommend that teachers keep the following features in mind as they evaluate any computer program:

Parents AND Computers

■ Share the list of software programs you have found to be appropriate for young children so that they can use them at home or at the library.

- *Technical features* include how function keys are used, how learners can manipulate the program, and whether learners' work can be saved or printed.

- *Learning features* include the voice or visual supports provided, the rate at which items are presented, and the amount and types of feedback available.

- *Content features* include what children learn—information, processes, or skills—and the level of difficulty within each area.

- *Developmentally appropriate features* include whether the program is suitable for the given children's ages, how complex the activities are, and whether children can be playful with the program.

Teachers should use these evaluation criteria not only before ordering software but also after observing children actually using the programs.

Adaptations in technology for special-needs children might include modifying the standard keyboard or providing touch-sensitive screens or voice-input capabilities. Stickers on keyboards can be used to help children learn which keys to use for particular programs. And for children who have difficulty with the keyboard, solutions include providing a template that allows only certain keys to show or a keyguard that allows use of only one key at a time. All children should be allowed to participate in open-ended activities so that special-needs children can interact with their classmates in positive play situations at computers (Sheldon 1996).

Young Children Online

In addition to deciding computer use in general, teachers today must make decisions about children's use of the World Wide Web. Haugland (2000) recommends that teachers install one of several screening devices before children are allowed to use the Web—for instance, Kid Desk: Internet Safe, Net Nanny, and Cyber Patrol. She also recommends that for safety reasons, children use pen names or the names of pets on the Web and that they never give out any information about their home addresses, parents' names, or phone numbers. The NAEYC (1998), in their *Child Health Alert* bulletins, offers the same precautions plus two additional suggestions: Children should be taught that (1) not everything on the Internet is necessarily true and (2) they should report it immediately if they get a threatening or inappropriate message.

NAEYC

Planning the Outdoor Environment

Outdoor environments, like indoor environments, require planning if they are to achieve the best results for the children (Herlein 1995). Ideally, outdoor play areas should be adjacent to indoor areas, with easy access to toilet facilities. Outdoor areas should be securely fenced and should have covered sections for play on rainy or very hot days. Outdoor areas should include sections with different surfaces: grass, concrete, areas for digging, and sand. Play areas should include different terrains when possible; hills and inclines provide interesting terrains for riding toys, rolling downhill, and so on, as well as visual interest. Paved paths and large areas are ideal for wheel toys or riding toys. In addition to the physical exertion required by riding toys, they offer children many opportunities for dramatic play.

WWW

Apparatus for swinging, climbing, sliding, and crawling should also be provided in the outdoor environment. Some apparatus should have higher bars for swinging while hanging by the hands and lower bars for hanging by the knees or elbows. Studies have shown that children develop more upper-body

> ### *Parents* AND *Playgrounds*
>
> ■ Invite parents to observe children playing on the playground. Provide a guide sheet that will help parents identify various kinds of play and activities.
>
> ■ Provide resources so that parents can read about what makes playgrounds challenging, fun, and safe for children of various ages.

WWW

An Expert Speaks

Suzanne Thouvenelle
John Hopkins University

Computers in the Early Childhood Program

The debate over computer use with young children rages on. Advocates for computers maintain that even young children can benefit educationally from their use (Becker 2000; Clements and Samara 2002; Wright and Shade 1994). Just look at how children gravitate to the computer—surely their curiosity and motivation count for something! Nonbelievers say that computers are just one more high-priced fad that promises a quick fix for educational ills and that computers for young children destroy creative thinking and social interactions (Alliance for Childhood 2000; Cuban 2000; Elkind and Whitehurst 2001; Healy 2000).

As with many educational issues, the "truth" lies somewhere between these distant positions. When school budgets shrink and technology begins to consume a greater proportion of resources in schools, we early childhood educators are forced to seriously consider the implications of acquiring and using technology in our classrooms. We need to question the impact and effectiveness of instructional technology for young learners. The research in this area offers little real help in settling the issue. For the most part, we educators tend to be optimistic about the value of educational technology, yet we often act based on incomplete information.

Children at home and in school already spend extended periods daily with computers and other technology-based devices. Still, we do not know exactly how technology affects children's cognitive, social, emotional, and physical development. There are large gaps in published literature in all these areas. Small sample size and limited research designs are characteristic of studies that involve young children. Little research has focused on the impact of computers in classrooms of young children, those between the ages of three and eight years old.

So what should we early childhood educators do about classroom computer use? I believe a balanced use of computers can be effective for young children. In the last decade, I have visited hundreds of classrooms where many teachers used technology with young children in outstanding and educationally meaningful ways. These classrooms incorporate two common elements: (1) quality software and (2) an educator who takes responsibility for mediating the computer learning experience for young children. I am confident that in time the formal research studies will document these exciting events and provide clear evidence that appropriate use of computers does make a difference for young children. Regardless of the educational medium used, effectiveness still depends on what teachers have students do with the materials. This applies to technology, too.

Only when early childhood educators accept the challenge of learning how to integrate computers into their classrooms, through thoughtful software selection and creative use with children, will we begin to develop a base of effective professional practice. Educators can advance everyone's knowledge by documenting and sharing their own successful technology practices. I encourage you to adopt effective practices and take the risks required to learn—even if it's about classroom computers and you remain skeptical.

strength when they play on playgrounds equipped with overhead ladders (Gabbard 1979). In selecting apparatus, the teacher should think about providing a balance of equipment so that children will use all the large muscles as they play. The hull of a rowboat or the body of an old car can stimulate dramatic play and offer something to climb on. Boards for walking and balance beams are also useful pieces of equipment.

Many playgrounds leave nothing for children to use in planning, arranging, or creating. Jones (1989) recommends that play areas have "loose parts" that children can move around and with which they can build and be creative. With movable equipment, children can construct their own play environment; boxes, boards, barrels, sawhorses, and short ladders work well. Tires and tubes are also useful for rolling around and stacking.

An outdoor play space should include a gardening area, a sandbox, a water play area or water table, a storage area for tools and toys, and tables or easels. (If need be, portable easels can be moved from the classroom for outside use.)

Having a gardening area does not mean that the entire area must be used for planting. At least some of the space should be reserved for impromptu digging. When children dig, they learn about the composition of soil, the differences between dry and damp soil, the insects and worms that live in the soil, and the pieces of organic matter that decompose to produce soil. A garden that includes an area for planting and caring for the plants, in addition to a digging area, can extend many classroom experiences.

An outside sandbox has advantages that an indoor sand table cannot offer. Children can climb into a sandbox, sit in the sand while playing in it, and create play areas on a much larger scale. An outdoor sandbox should have a cover to keep the sand clean, preferably one that folds back in sections to make handling easier. In many areas of the United States, a sandbox also should have some kind of roof so that the sand does not get too hot or stay wet all the time. Baker (1966) observed that the sandbox was frequently the place children started playing while they watched the more vigorous play around them. When they gained enough confidence, they joined the more active play.

Opportunities for water play outdoors can be provided with a small wading pool or a water table. Pools of water must be carefully supervised. Children can use the water outside much as they do in the classroom—pouring, measuring, and comparing. The differences are that outside, much more splashing is acceptable, and water can be carried all over the play area. Practically everything outdoors can be "painted" with water. A few large paintbrushes and some buckets are essential water play accessories outdoors.

Finally, many fine arts activities can be conducted outdoors if portable easels or tables are available for painting, creating collages, and other art projects. When the weather is pleasant outdoors, art experiences can be especially satisfying because children do not have to be as concerned about paint spills or drips. Cleanup is simple.

Outdoor play is an important means of achieving social development goals.

A shed for storing outdoor materials is a must. It can hold garden and digging tools, sandbox and water toys, riding toys, balls, and other materials used outdoors. Teachers tend to be much more relaxed about allowing children to dig in sand and mud when they know that the tools do not have to be clean enough to take back indoors when the play ends. A shed will also protect the toys and tools from exposure to the elements and prolong the life of materials.

Odoy and Foster (1997) suggest that teachers extend indoor play activities to the outdoors by using play crates, which are large, plastic boxes that hold materials used in various kinds of play. For example, a collection of shovels, watering cans, buckets, and scoops would encourage children to dig and garden. Other boxes might hold PVC pipes and elbows from which children could construct systems for carrying water or sand. Hoops, streamers, and scarves would encourage movement and imaginative play. The number and kind of crates is limited only by the teacher's imagination.

Playgrounds should be planned to help children with different physical abilities. A study by Barbour (1999) found that playgrounds designed primarily for exercise activities were not appropriate for all children. In particular, those children who are not as capable physically cannot use the equipment and have few or no other options for interacting with their peers. Children who have limited physical competence therefore fall further behind those peers who can accomplish physical feats.

Figure 3.8 (on page 101) is a diagram of a playground appropriate for children in preschool through second grade. Analyze this playground using the same criteria used earlier for analyzing room arrangements (see pages 77–78).

www.ablongman.com/brewer5e

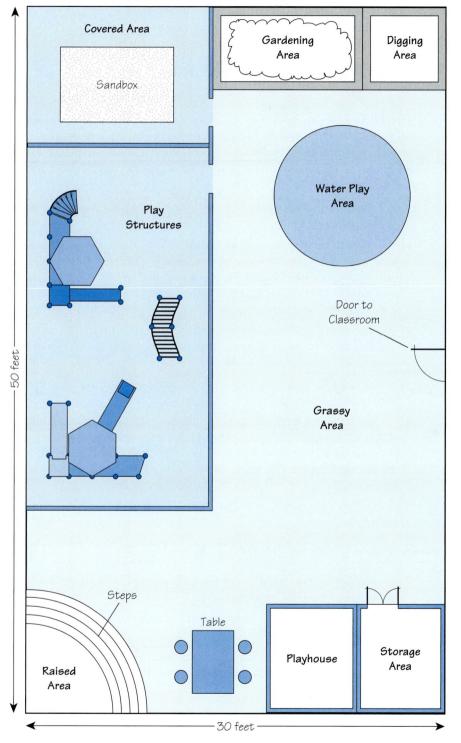

4' chain-link fence around entire area

Covered Area

Sandbox

Gardening Area

Digging Area

Play Structures

Water Play Area

50 feet

Door to Classroom

Grassy Area

Steps

Table

Raised Area

Playhouse

Storage Area

30 feet

Figure 3.8

Playground for Children in Preschool through Second Grade

How well is the space used? What developmental objectives can be met using this playground? What traffic patterns do you predict?

Planning for Safety—Inside and Out

In choosing any room arrangement or collection of instructional materials, one of the critical criteria is safety. Teachers must make every effort to provide a safe learning environment, both inside the classroom and on the playground. In addition to the safety considerations already mentioned for individual pieces of equipment, the following list will help you analyze the environment for safety:

A Safety Checklist

1. Check the environment, both inside and outside, for any hazards. Check electrical outlets and cords; make sure children cannot pull over any equipment (television sets, projectors, and so on); remove dangerous plants; cover sharp edges; make sure fences are sturdy and exit gates are childproof; and eliminate any other hazards to children's safety.

2. Practice emergency procedures on a regular basis. Children's and teachers' responses to fire drills (and in some areas, tornado and earthquake procedures) must become automatic.

3. Make sure that the classroom contains a fire extinguisher and that all staff (and children who are old enough) know how to use it.

4. All teachers and staff members should be trained in first aid and cardiopulmonary resuscitation (CPR). At minimum, one person with such training should be present at all times. Staff should be required to have special training for CPR with infants, if the program accepts children that young.

5. Post a list of the names of all children and a map of fire exit routes near each exit.

6. Keep a first aid kit adequately stocked at all times. Keep it in a specific place so that any staff member can locate it quickly.

7. Keep an up-to-date list of emergency phone numbers (parents, relatives, doctors, and hospitals) for each child.

8. Keep the number for the nearest poison control center posted near the telephone.

9. Post a list of children's allergies (including reactions to wasp or bee stings) so that it can be checked before planning any food experiences or outdoor activities.

10. Keep a list by the door of the adults authorized to pick up each child. Do not release a child to any unauthorized person.

11. Make all posted information readily available to substitute teachers.

Teachers must consider a number of factors in assessing playground safety. Frost and Wortham (1988) devised the following checklist, which you may find helpful:

- *A fence (minimum four feet high) protects children from potentially hazardous areas (e.g., streets, water).*
- *Eight to twelve inches of noncompacted sand, pea gravel, shredded wood, or equivalent material is in place under and around all climbing and moving equipment.*
- *Resilient surface is properly maintained (e.g., in place, noncompacted, free of debris).*
- *The equipment is sized to the age group served, with climbing heights limited to the reaching height of children standing erect.*
- *There are no openings that can entrap a child's head (approximately four to eight inches).*
- *Swing seats are constructed of lightweight material with no protruding elements.*
- *Moving parts are free of defects (no pinch, shearing, or crush points; bearings are not excessively worn).*
- *Equipment is free of sharp edges, protruding elements, broken parts, and toxic substances.*
- *Fixed equipment is structurally sound—no bending, warping, breaking, or sinking.*
- *Large equipment is secured in the ground, and concrete footings are recessed in the ground.*
- *All safety equipment (e.g., guard rails, padded areas, protective covers) is in good repair.*
- *The area is free of electrical hazards (e.g., unfenced air conditioners and switchboxes).*
- *The area is free of debris (e.g., sanitary hazards, broken glass, and rocks).* (p. 24)*

The National Playground Safety Institute (NPSI) notes that 40 percent of injuries are directly related to lack of supervision. Be alert and engaged with the children at all times. The Consumer Product Safety Commission does not recommend heavy swings, multiple-occupancy gliders, free-swinging ropes, exercise rings, or trapeze bars for public playgrounds.

The Americans with Disabilities Act (ADA) requires that playgrounds be accessible to children with disabilities and that schools and programs modify playgrounds to make them accessible. Sorohan (1995) suggests that the

*From Joe L. Frost and Sue C. Wortham, "The Evolution of American Playgrounds," *Young Children* 43 (July 1988): 19–28. Reprinted with permission from the National Association for the Education of Young Children.

following elements should be considered when thinking about playground adaptations:

- **Support:** Some children need back supports to play in sandboxes or with spring toys.
- **Reach:** Avoid placing elements too high or too low for children in wheelchairs to reach.
- **Diversity:** Think about materials that will enhance development of social and cognitive skills as well as gross motor skills. Materials that can be manipulated and those that require two or more children to play are both useful.
- **Cues:** Provide visual, tactile, and auditory cues to help children move around the playground safely.
- **Getting on and off:** Ramps and transfer platforms might be needed for some students. Think about equipment that will allow a child to return to his wheelchair without assistance after use.
- **Location:** Place playgrounds close to buildings for easier access.

Although many schools have attempted to make playgrounds accessible and enjoyable for all children, much is still needed to achieve the goal of fully integrated playgrounds. Malkusak, Schappet, and Lawrence (2002) remind us that one in ten children has some type of disability that usually prevents him from having a full play experience. They state,

> *Playgrounds for children of all abilities are essential to the healthy development of all children. Play is how children learn to navigate the world. All children need outdoor play environments to build their strength and socialization skills, learn to be independent, take turns and meet challenges, gain a sense of self-determination and esteem and enhance cerebral/motor development.* (p. 71)

Celebrating Diversity

Teachers can show respect for the community and the cultures of children in their classrooms by asking for information and help from various school patrons and parents. Some special materials can be selected for learning areas that will help children feel more at home. For example, the dress-up center could include several pieces of clothing that are typical of that worn by certain ethnic groups in the community. Some traditional clothing may be too rare or expensive to use for children's play, but if it can be obtained, it will be valuable for the children. Pictures can be taken around the community and used as illustrations in student-made books or as posters for the classroom.

Play materials, such as puzzles and dolls, also need to reflect the various cultures of the community. If they are not available commercially, perhaps some members of the community would be willing to help make them. Sears and Medearis (1993) describe a project in which community members helped schools develop materials, art projects, science activities, and so on that were culturally appropriate for local American Indian groups. With some effort, teachers could replicate the work of this project with their own local cultural groups.

Chapter Summary

- Program goals and objectives are reflected in room arrangements and choices of materials and equipment.

- The basic learning areas found in early childhood classrooms include art, music, library/listening/writing, blocks, dramatic play, science/discovery, manipulatives/mathematics/games, woodworking, sand and water, physical education, and quiet areas. These areas are designed to help children develop their interests; each should include storage areas for materials.

- Specialized learning centers are designed to help children master one activity or task. They are designed for temporary use in the classroom.

- Learning areas can be streamlined for the beginning of the schoolyear. Teachers must decide which areas and materials will be most important for children at the beginning of the year and which can be added later.

- Room arrangements help communicate to children what is expected of them and are related to attitudes and behaviors of the children.

- In planning room arrangements, teachers should consider multiple uses of space, the need for water, the need for quieter areas, and the need for areas where noisier activities can take place.

- Environments can be analyzed in terms of the number of play spaces per child. This type of analysis will help teachers determine the complex-

ity of the environment and what, if anything, should be done to change it.

- Teachers should try to select instructional materials that can be used for multiple experiences, can contribute to many instructional uses, are sturdy, and can be used by children of varying ages and abilities.

- Computers are increasingly likely to be included in programs for young children. Above all, teachers must think of computers as a tool for learning. Accordingly, software should be evaluated in terms of its appropriateness for the children and in terms of what is required of the learner in using it. And with a few precautions, children can go online to explore the information and activities available on the Internet.

- Outdoor play environments require careful planning to ensure that the experiences and activities conducted outdoors will be as productive and satisfying as those conducted indoors.

- The regular classroom environment should be adapted as required to allow children with special needs to have access to different areas and materials.

- In selecting materials for their classroom, teachers must consider the diversity of the families represented in the schools. Instructional materials should reflect the variety of cultures in the community and also perhaps the world at large, regardless of the school population.

Theory INTO Practice

Select a preschool or primary-grade classroom in a local school or center. Measure the dimensions of the classroom, and sketch the arrangement of furniture, equipment, and learning areas. Be sure to include the doors, windows, electrical outlets, and water sources. Analyze this classroom arrangement in terms of the complexity of its activity areas, how well it fosters independence, and its level of aesthetic appeal. If this were *your* classroom, what changes would you make? Why?

Assume that you have the basic furnishings for your classroom (including copying paper, tempera paint, and scissors) and that you have $2,000 to spend on other supplies. Check the prices in early childhood supply catalogs, and make a list of what you would buy. Compare your lists with those of the members of your group. Discuss the reasons for your choices with your group.

Observe for at least an hour in a preschool classroom that has one or more computers. How many children used the computers? How was use determined? What did the children actually do at the computers? Did equal numbers of boys and girls use them? What kinds of social interactions did you observe around the computers? From your observations, would you recommend buying a computer for a preschool program? Why?

Visit two or more playgrounds in your area, and make a sketch of each. Also note the surfaces under any equipment and what kinds of play would most likely occur in different areas of each playground. What changes would you make in the playground if you had control of it? What adaptations would you make for special-needs children? Why?

Planning the Classroom Environment

One of the ongoing struggles I have had as a classroom teacher is the design and maintenance of the ever-evolving physical environment of the classroom. I consistently ask myself how I can ensure that all students have a safe, productive place to learn and grow. If only the answer were simple and clear-cut!

Every year I seem to go through the same process of questioning the design of my classroom, in part to improve on the previous design and in part because I have not had the same room for more than one year. I first begin by reviewing the curriculum goals for the grade level along with the needs of the students. I also must take into account how both of these variables might change throughout the year. From there, I decide which learning areas will be necessary to meet those goals and needs.

With the list of essential learning areas, I can proceed through the numerous sketches of floorplans. During this phase, I take into consideration research and expert advice. For instance, I know that each learning area needs a workspace for students, a storage space for materials, and a display area for artifacts, essential information, and student work. I also need to group learning areas based on the noise level of the activities to be completed in those areas. Although experts provide a clear, logical method of designing classroom space, I struggle with conditions that may not be ideal.

When I read about classroom arrangement, the possibilities seem endless, but when I step into the classroom, the possibilities seem to dwindle. One example from my current classroom is that the furniture arrangement seems to be more fixed. The computer area must be against one whole wall because of the Internet hookups. Therefore, the writing center must be adjacent to the computer area so that it can also serve as the publishing area. If I group together quiet learning areas, then the reading area needs to be in close proximity. Although I have read many articles and books on physical environment, I must base the arrangement of a large portion of the room on the location of the computer wiring. Every teacher must work through these types of constraints. Classroom design is a compromise between the ideal and reality, but with effort, creativity, and thought, it can be successful.

Throughout my journey in classroom design, I have found that the key to creating better student-centered classrooms is overcoming functional fixedness. When I first started teaching, I looked at a desk and saw only a space for an individual student to work and to store materials. Now I see a desk in many more capacities: as part of the work surface and storage space of a learning area, as a base for student mailboxes, or as a shelf in a closet. An open space with an area rug that was once just a meeting area could now be strewn with pillows or beanbags to create a reading nook or could be an area for building with engineering sets during science.

Sometimes the only limits we have in classroom design are the ones we place on ourselves and on the materials and space we have available to us. Although it is sometimes difficult to view the classroom and its contents with a fresh eye, I have found that overcoming functional fixedness leads to new and bountiful ideas that can grow and evolve into even better ideas when I start the process all over again the next year.

CHAPTER 4

Planning and Assessing Learning Activities

After reading this chapter, you will be able to do the following:

- Define and explain the term *developmentally appropriate curriculum.*
- Define and explain the term *thematic curriculum.*
- Define and construct a learning plan.
- Plan a schedule for activities.
- Assess the quality of a program.
- Celebrate diversity in your planning.

*Y*ou observed in a kindergarten this week. You were amazed at the variety of activities the children had to choose from during most of the morning. You noticed that the teacher encouraged children to choose a project that interested them and that some children continued to work on the same activity for the entire time. One child built an elaborate block structure to represent the harbor the class had visited last week. She labeled all the parts with signs. She smiled happily when the teacher photographed her construction, asked the teacher for a blank book in which to mount the photograph, and told you that tomorrow she would write about the construction in the book. You wondered how building this block structure fit in with the teacher's goals and objectives for the class. Other children were involved in such activities as creating animals from cardboard boxes, painting at easels, observing and recording the behavior of a large frog, and following the directions in a book for making an appropriate home for a box turtle.

The teacher showed you his plan book, and you found lesson plans that did not follow the outline you learned in your first education class. How do teachers select learning activities? What does a lesson plan that includes many different activities look like? How does a teacher evaluate a program?

Curriculum Planning

In planning a **curriculum** for young children, the teacher must select objectives, select and organize content, choose the appropriate learning experiences, determine the most appropriate sequence for the learning activities, and determine how to assess both children's growth and the program itself.

Curriculum is a term that has many definitions: It can mean all experiences that happen at school; a written plan for learning; a syllabus that lists learning topics and the order in which they will be presented; or a program, such as a drug abuse prevention program, that specifies a sequence of activities. In this chapter, *curriculum* is defined as a written plan for learning experiences in which children will be involved.

In designing a curriculum, the teacher must begin by thinking about the goals of the program. What will children know or be able to do when they finish the program? Will the focus of the program be on learning specific information or on learning how to find information? Will the focus be on academic learning or broader goals of development and growth as a whole child? If we assume that the program sets broad goals for development in all areas—physical, social, emotional, and intellectual—that will be the framework for the curriculum.

Next, the teacher should analyze the options for achieving the goals. For the broad goals described, the options would include taking field trips, having classroom visitors, conducting demonstrations and experiments, and participating in activities such as classifying, problem solving, reading aloud, doing hands-on projects, and others. Over the course of a year, each of these options might be selected several times. For example, suppose the children are learning about the life cycles of plants. A seed specialist might be invited to the class to share information about seeds with the children, or the children might take a field trip to a nursery or arboretum and classify seeds and plants in a variety of ways. The children might also plant seeds and care for the seedlings, or they might chart the growth of their plants and check the parts of their plants against a diagram provided on the computer. The outcomes of the study of plants would be intellectual development in learning facts about plants and seeds; physical development in planting and recording plant growth; social development in learning how to behave on a field trip or how to interact with a visitor; and emotional development in learning how to inhibit impulsive responses or develop control in a group setting.

For each part of a study of plants, the teacher would select objectives that would help achieve the purpose of the specific study and be related to the overall program goals. Objectives should not be too broad or vague (e.g., "The children will learn to love reading") nor should they be so narrow that they limit the possibilities for children's success (e.g., "Every child will learn to count to ten"). Suppose that our objective is as follows: "Children will develop increased skill in classification and in communicating their own criteria for classification categories." Assume that various classroom materials are usually available to the children for classification, such as buttons, keys, seashells, and so on, but for this experience, children

Parents AND Planning

■ Keep parents informed about the topics studied at school. Provide suggestions for activities they might do at home to enhance the projects being done at school. For example, if the children are studying how plants change, you might suggest that parents gather seeds and other materials from plants and make a collage of them or that they take a family walk, looking for changes in plants.

also will be provided with collections of seeds that can be classified in a variety of ways. The children might also classify leaves; if they are responsive to the leaves, they might invite a botanist to explain how scientists classify leaves.

After choosing the content (knowledge of plants) and the objectives (increased skill in classification and communication), the teacher should select possible activities that will help children achieve the goals of the program. Knowledge of the content area is critical here, as the teacher must decide the sequence of activities and experiences that will be most beneficial to the children. Will going on a field trip to get an overall view of plants be more beneficial at the beginning of the plant study, when children are introduced to the subject; in the middle of the study, when they will have had some experiences with plants; or at the end, when children may need help consolidating their knowledge? Some experiences must precede others. For example, children could not be expected to communicate their criteria for classifying leaves without having had some experience in actually classifying leaves.

In short, when planning the curriculum, the teacher is responsible for selecting the objectives and the content, determining how it is organized, selecting the learning activities, and then assessing the activities. The teacher must also consider the interests of the children when selecting curriculum experiences. If the teacher who selects plants as content finds, after a day or two, that the children have absolutely no interest in plants, she should select another topic. Suppose the children had expressed interest in the caterpillars they found on the playground. Caterpillars and other insects could be just as useful as plants in helping children understand and apply classification abilities. Children should also be encouraged to choose what they would like to do from the many learning activities available and to make some choices about what they would like to learn about any given topic.

Although the sequence of planning a curriculum has been presented as a linear process, in reality it is usually more recursive: Teachers plan content and activities, adapt them for individual children, select other activities, evaluate, and plan again. All the steps are there, but the process is rarely completely linear.

Curriculum Organization

When designing curriculum, teachers have several options for choosing how to organize learning experiences. The most common approaches for young children are a facts approach and a skills approach. With a *facts approach,* experiences are arranged so that children learn a given set of factual information, such as the days of the week or the names of colors. With a *skills approach,* experiences are selected and arranged so that children learn to cut on a line, to share, or to find information in a selection of reference books.

In elementary schools, the most common organization has been the *subject-matter approach,* whereby children learn reading or math or social studies. Another approach is *thematic organization,* in which skills, facts, and subject-matter knowledge are integrated around a unifying theme, such as community.

The curriculum in elementary schools is often centered on subject matter; these children are completing an activity as part of learning social studies.

The Developmentally Appropriate Curriculum

NAEYC

In 1987 the National Association for the Education of Young Children (NAEYC) issued a statement defining *developmentally appropriate practice* in *Developmentally Appropriate Practice in Early Childhood Programs Serving Children from Birth through Age 8* (Bredekamp 1987). In order to provide examples of what developmentally appropriate practice should look like in the early childhood classroom, two more volumes were published: *Reaching Potentials: Appropriate Curriculum and Assessment for Young Children,* volume 1 (Bredekamp and Rosegrant 1992), and *Reaching Potentials: Transforming Early Childhood Curriculum and Assessment,* volume 2 (Bredekamp and Rosegrant 1995). Furthermore, the original statement on developmentally appropriate practice has been revised and issued in *Developmentally Appropriate Practice in Early Childhood Programs,* revised edition (Bredekamp and Copple 1997). All of these titles are mentioned here so that you can appreciate the long struggle to define and explain frameworks for programs in early childhood education.

Remember that the NAEYC represents a broad spectrum of professionals in the field of early childhood education; therefore, you should consider the following statements of guidelines as distillations of the thinking of all these people, not simply statements of single points of view:

Guidelines for Developmentally Appropriate Practice

A. *Developmentally appropriate curriculum provides for all areas of a child's development: physical, emotional, social, linguistic, aesthetic, and cognitive.*

B. *Curriculum includes a broad range of content across disciplines that is socially relevant, intellectually engaging, and personally meaningful to children.*

C. *Curriculum builds upon what children already know and are able to do (activating prior knowledge) to consolidate their learning and to foster their acquisition of new concepts and skills.*

D. *Effective curriculum plans frequently integrate across traditional subject-matter divisions to help children make meaningful connections and provide opportunities for rich conceptual development; focusing on one subject is also a valid strategy at times.*

E. *Curriculum promotes the development of knowledge and understanding, processes and skills, as well as the dispositions to use and apply skills and to go on learning.*

F. *Curriculum content has intellectual integrity, reflecting the key concepts and tools of inquiry of recognized disciplines in ways that are accessible and achievable for young children, ages 3 through 8. . . . Children directly participate in study of the disciplines, for instance, by conducting scientific experiments, writing, performing, solving mathematical problems, collecting and analyzing data, collecting oral history, and performing other roles of experts in the disciplines.*

G. *Curriculum provides opportunities to support children's home culture and language while also developing all children's abilities to participate in the shared culture of the program and the community.*

H. *Curriculum goals are realistic and attainable for most children in the designated age range for which they are designed.*

I. *When used, technology is physically and philosophically integrated in the classroom curriculum and teaching.* (pp. 20–21)*

An important part of planning is ensuring that the activities and objectives are developmentally appropriate.

*From Sue Bredekamp and Carol Copple (Eds.), *Developmentally Appropriate Practice in Early Childhood Programs*, rev. ed. (Washington, DC: National Association for the Education of Young Children, 1997). Reprinted with permission from the National Association for the Education of Young Children.

Although at times a content-area study might be appropriate, these guidelines support an integrated, **thematic approach** to curriculum. As explained in the next section, this approach is believed to be the most productive in helping teachers design a developmentally appropriate curriculum.

Rationale for an Integrated Curriculum

The idea of integrating curriculum is not a new one. At the turn of the century, John Dewey (1859–1952) (1902) advocated the organization of curriculum around projects that would interest and involve children. The most common approach to curriculum organization in schools in the United States, however, continues to be subject-matter organization, in which learning is segmented into math and science and language arts (Jacobs 1989).

You probably remember that in elementary school you had reading first thing in the morning, math right before lunch, and science in the afternoon. Yet when children learn outside of school, they learn in wholes. For example, a child visiting tide pools could learn about many things at once: language arts (learning vocabulary for the animals and plants of the tide pools); physical skills (staying on top of the slippery rocks); classification (noticing which animals are related); the environment (noticing pollution or litter); family stories (hearing parents tell about when they visited these tide pools as children); and so on. A child's learning experiences outside school are not divisible into subject-matter areas.

An integrated curriculum can help a child make sense of the world more easily. If a child is learning the names of the letters of the alphabet, that knowledge must be placed in a context that makes sense to him. When the child learns the names of the letters by hearing the teacher read alphabet books and by exploring the forms of the letters in writing, he knows that the names of the letters communicate information about the printed form of language. He recognizes that this information is personally useful, not something learned to please an adult but that has no other utility for him.

An integrated curriculum provides opportunities for the following:

1. In-depth exploration of a topic and learning that is more than just superficial coverage

2. More choices and therefore more motivation to learn and greater satisfaction with the results

3. More active learning

4. An opportunity for the teacher to learn along with the children and model lifelong learning

5. A more effective use of student and teacher time

Organizing learning experiences around a theme can be productive, but if thematic teaching is to be successful, the theme must be carefully selected, activities carefully planned, and evaluation of the theme and of individual children's progress carefully monitored.

Selecting a Theme

The selection of a worthwhile theme is critically important if thematic instruction is to be successful. There are several considerations in selecting a theme:

- The topic must be worthy of study. It should be an important topic that would be studied even if you were not doing thematic instruction. A theme will take several weeks to complete, and the topic should be worth the time.

- The theme should be one for which the learning standards in your state and the curriculum goals in your district can be met.

- The topic should be of interest and relevant to the learners. Children must find the learning applicable to their world outside of school. For example, children who have no experience with deserts will not be able to apply what they are learning to their lives outside of school. If children live in the desert, they will see the plants and the animals of the desert, and what they learn about the desert will be useful every day.

- There must be opportunities for the application of skills the children are learning. If the children are learning to cut with scissors, to take research notes, to put words in alphabetical order, or to write a poem, the theme study should allow them to use the skills they are learning.

- There must be adequate resources to support the topic of study with realia, people in the community who can be guest speakers or resource people, and places in the community for field trips that will add to the study.

Thematic instruction can be done poorly. If teachers choose a theme with no real content, if they apply the theme without considering the previous knowledge of the children, or if every child is required to complete the same activities, then thematic instruction will not be any better than a poorly conceived curriculum organized by subject matter. Teachers can be tempted to do "cute" themes, such as apples or teddy bears, but such topics rarely offer any real learning for children that will be useful to them in their lives. Some early childhood programs send out a list of their themes for each week before school begins each year. But thematic instruction cannot be done well if the themes are planned before the teacher even knows the children or their needs. Themes are often available on the Web or in teacher supply stores, but themes planned by someone who does not know your children and that do not involve children in the planning cannot achieve the goals of good thematic instruction.

One of the major reasons for selecting a thematic organization is to offer children the opportunity for in-depth rather than superficial study of various topics. Therefore, the theme selected must be one for which the activities are worthwhile. Thematic organization alone does not guarantee a well-planned, thoughtful curriculum. There are trivial approaches to thematic organization as well as to other types of curriculum organization. A teacher could decide to focus on mice as a theme and provide meaningful activities in which children learned about nutrition, training, building mazes, genetics, and so on. Or the teacher could choose mice as a theme and focus on it simplistically: covering the container where the children place their work with paper to represent cheese, decorating the bookmarks children use to mark their places in the reader with mice, using pictures of mice to enliven math worksheets, and having children make paper mice in art. A theme cannot be implemented solely through classroom decorations.

Implementing the Theme

Once a topic has been selected, the teacher (and the children, if they are old enough) will brainstorm areas of interest related to that particular topic. Older children will be able to see more relationships than younger ones.

After a topic and related subtopics have been chosen, the next step is to select activities that will help children learn content and apply their skills in meaningful contexts. What can be learned on a field trip? What can resource people share with the children? What play experiences can be facilitated? Are there construction possibilities? What skills can be applied in this study? What curriculum goals can be met through the study of this topic?

Let's assume that one of the teacher's curriculum goals is to help children become familiar with a variety of reading materials: narrative, poetry, expository writing, and so on. In studying corn, for instance, the children can read (or listen to the teacher read) information books about corn and perhaps stories and poems about the importance of corn to some American Indian groups. Another goal might be for children to participate in the writing process on a daily basis. They could write records of the growth of corn plants, describe in writing what happens to corn when it is popped, or create their own informational books about corn. Yet another goal might be for children to increase their ability to recall and retell significant details. Participating in activities such as popping corn could be the basis for recalling and retelling meaningful details.

Once a theme has been tentatively selected, the teacher and children can create webs of things the children know and might want to know (see Figure 4.1). Jones and Nimmo (1994) describe the value of webbing:

> It gives a staff of adults the chance to explore the possibilities of any material or idea in order to make decisions about use: Is it worth doing? Is it likely to generate developmentally appropriate activities? What are the ways we might want to enrich the activity by being prepared with other materials or questions? How long might children's interest continue?
>
> A web is a tentative plan. It doesn't tell you exactly what will happen or in what order. That depends in large part on the children's response. So, first you plan and then you start trying your ideas, paying attention to what happens, evaluating, and moving on with further activities. (p. 11)

Once curriculum goals have been reviewed, the teacher (and children) can determine activities that will be possible in this study. Not every child will participate in every activity; choices will be available to the children. The

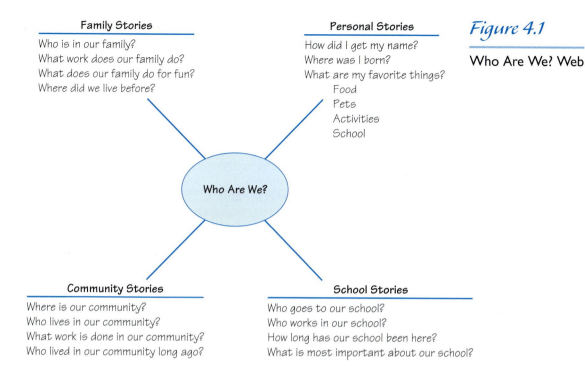

Figure 4.1

Who Are We? Web

Family Stories

Who is in our family?
What work does our family do?
What does our family do for fun?
Where did we live before?

Personal Stories

How did I get my name?
Where was I born?
What are my favorite things?
  Food
  Pets
  Activities
  School

Who Are We?

Community Stories

Where is our community?
Who lives in our community?
What work is done in our community?
Who lived in our community long ago?

School Stories

Who goes to our school?
Who works in our school?
How long has our school been here?
What is most important about our school?

teacher must think about the objectives of each activity and the relationship of the objectives to the curriculum goals. If an activity cannot contribute to the curriculum goals, it should be eliminated as a choice.

Classroom learning areas should be used to enhance particular themes. For example, in a study of plants, materials such as flowers (not poisonous), leaves, and seedpods could be placed in the art center; books and computer software about plants could be available in the library; puzzles with plant content could be available in the manipulatives area; and accessories could be added to the blocks area so that the children could create a farm. Enhancing learning areas in these ways does not mean that children will be assigned to do certain tasks in the areas; rather, materials will be available to help children complete their investigations or follow up on their interests.

Many teachers try to follow the children's lead in planning curriculum. If the children are interested in a certain topic, then the teacher will help them explore that topic and develop their interests until their questions and activities lead them to another topic. Several authors have described this **emerging curriculum** approach and their own ways of implementing it (Byrum and Pierce 1993; Edwards, Gandini, and Forman 1993; Jones and Nimmo 1994). These teachers believe that the best curriculum is that in which the children are fully engaged and their interests are fully explored. The challenge, however, is to build a curriculum that not only follows the children's interests but also meets the goals of the program.

The most famous of the emerging curriculum schools are those of Reggio Emilia, which are municipal schools in a city in northern Italy. As noted in Chapter 2, much has been written about these schools and the project approach that they use (Bredekamp 1993; Edwards et al. 1993; Gandini 1993; Kennedy 1996; Malaguzzi 1993; McCarthy 1995). These projects grow out of simple experiences, such as the children's visit to a poppy field. The children examined the flowers, drew them, painted them, sculpted them, discussed them, created murals of them, and otherwise continued to focus their activities on the poppies for a long period of time. The teachers continued to guide the children by asking questions, offering new materials, and helping the children refine and rethink their work.

The quality of the work that the Reggio Emilia children have produced is what has led to so much investigation of the processes employed in these schools. The teachers who implement this sort of emerging curriculum have support from colleagues and administrators. In Reggio Emilia, they also have support from parents, who often attend teacher planning meetings and feel comfortable making suggestions. (These parents also know how hard the teachers work!)

A child-centered curriculum that produces outstanding products while focusing on the process of learning and doing is the ideal in early childhood education. A teacher, especially a new teacher, who wants to implement a child-centered curriculum should find a colleague who also wants to implement such a program. That way, all of the questions, problems, failures, and successes can be shared with someone else struggling to achieve the same goals. A solitary teacher without support will find implementing such a program nearly impossible.

Evaluating a Theme

Teachers will want to evaluate their thematic instruction in a variety of ways. First, teachers must always be accountable for the progress of individual children. Assessment strategies for monitoring the progress of children will be discussed in detail in Chapter 7, but you will want to keep records that help you know what curriculum goals have been met and what kinds of instruction have been provided. One way to accomplish this is to keep a chart such as the one illustrated in Figure 4.2. Prepare a sheet for each child with the curriculum goals listed down the left side and columns for each topic of study on the right. As the child meets various goals, you record the progress. You need a sheet for each child because not all children will choose the same activities during the theme. (Assessment possibilities are described in Chapter 7.) In evaluating the theme, the teacher would observe the children's interest and record the contributions of the theme to overall goals.

Although a teacher may choose to repeat a theme another year, rarely can a theme be repeated in the same form. The interests and experiences of different groups of children vary considerably, and some themes that work well with one group are not at all interesting to other groups. Even if topics are

Figure 4.2

Child's Name __Jamie__

	Plants	Insects	
Reads a variety of materials: reference materials, narrative stories, poetry	10/6	11/15 11/20	
Participates in writing process: personal writing, letter writing, narratives, expository writing	10/8	11/10 12/1	
Recognizes adaptation as a factor in all plant and animal life (habitat, camouflage, food chain)	10/12 10/15 10/16	11/20 11/23 11/24	
Uses computation to solve problems			
Uses the scientific process to solve problems			

repeated, the activities chosen by the children are likely to vary so much that one year's implementation of the theme will not be the same as that of a previous year. When a teacher simply applies a theme to the children, it becomes mechanical, and the classroom routine fails to reflect children's interests and experiences. Theme studies require considerable investments of time and energy by the teacher, but the result—meaningful experiences for the children through which they gain not only knowledge and skills but also the disposition to learn—is well worth the effort.

As you read the chapters in this book about language, literature, literacy, math, science, social studies, the arts, and health and physical education, remember that although these content areas are presented in discrete chapters, the underlying assumption is that knowledge of each subject-matter area will help you integrate curriculum. You do need to understand the goals and objectives in each area in order to plan appropriately, but you should use this knowledge to plan meaningful and conceptually important themes. Throughout the content-area chapters of this book (Chapters 9 through 15), the topic "Who Are We?" will be the focus. So even though the discussion in each chapter will be about a discrete subject (math, science, music, and so on), the emphasis will be on an integrated curriculum.

However the curriculum is organized, teachers are responsible for developing the plans for learning experiences in their classrooms. The following section provides some advice on creating those plans.

Learning Plans

A **learning plan** differs from a lesson plan in that often a lesson plan outlines only one lesson. In early childhood programs, however, learning experiences are not usually confined to single lessons. As Elkind (1982) reminds us, "Clearly children learn in many different ways and what mode of learning is employed depends very much upon what is to be learned" (p. 7). Learning plans involve long-term planning, unit or theme planning, and short-term goals. Each day's activities should contribute to the unit or theme goals, and each unit or theme should contribute to the overall goals of the program.

As the teacher of the program, you may not have much control over the program goals. They are often established by the administration of the center or school—hopefully, with the collaboration of the teachers. These are the kinds of goals that centers advertise on their consumer brochures or that are printed in the curriculum guides of school districts. However, goal statements do not define how goals are to be achieved. The "how" is up to the teacher and should reflect knowledge of the children's development, the children's abilities and interests, and the teacher's own interests.

A daily learning plan may indicate the materials to be placed in the learning areas, include notes about guiding specific children's learning, and suggest plans for evaluation of activities. If one of the daily goals is learning to use the concept *line* in talking about art, the learning plan would note the pieces of art to be displayed, specify that strings and strips of paper should be made available in the art area, and call for an emphasis on line in movement experiences. Teachers would work with individual children as they participated in art or movement to emphasize the concept of line and would talk with those who were looking at the art examples about how the artists had used lines. This plan would fit into the larger theme of lines and space being explored in a variety of areas and support the overall goals of increasing children's ability to communicate effectively and to explore a variety of materials.

Several daily learning plans for preschool and primary children are presented in Figures 4.3 and 4.4. Take some time to review them, and as you do, keep this in mind: Learning plans should always be as complete as possible but should never be so rigid that **incidental learning** cannot be included in the day's schedule. For instance, if a child brings a pet rabbit to school, obviously time must be allotted to observing and discussing the rabbit. If the children are really interested in the rabbit, then the teacher might make some plans for additional experiences with rabbits in a few weeks. The point is to take advantage of what the children want to know now as you keep the over-

Figure 4.3

Program Goals: Improved communication skills, improved fine motor skills

Theme: Who Are We?

Topic: Our Family

Objectives: Children will be able to make drawings of their families and identify the members of their families.

Activity Time:

- *Art:* Provide paper and crayons. Give children the opportunity to draw a picture of their family. If they draw a picture, ask them to tell you who the people in the picture are and label each individual for the child or let him label his drawing.
- *Fine motor:* Make available puzzles with family themes. Provide dolls for the dollhouse to represent various family configurations. Make adult and child figures for the flannelboard available.
- *Blocks:* Make available as accessories in the block area wooden figures that can represent various family configurations.
- *Library:* Display books about families.
- *Dramatic play:* Make available some of the work costumes of the families in your community. You might arrange for parents to loan you some of these materials for a while.
- *Movement:* Choose a movement activity that the children's families enjoy, such as biking, walking, dancing, and so on.

Read-Aloud: *Whose Mouse Are You?* (Kraus 1970)

Small Groups: Invite each child to share her picture of her family and tell the other group members who is in her family. Ask children to define *family* and write down their responses. Read back their responses to them.

Evaluation: Observe the student's ability to represent the people in his family and to tell who the members of his family are.

all goals in mind. When Alice came to the Cheshire Cat and asked which road to take, he told her that it did not make any difference, because she did not know where she was going. Teachers of young children need to know where they are going—and they need to plan which road to take but be prepared to take another one if it appears to be better for the children.

Although learning plans are more appropriate than isolated lesson plans in terms of planning for instruction, lesson plans may sometimes be designed to teach specific elements of a broader learning plan. Some plans will provide

Developmentally Appropriate Practice

Reflect on plans for learning experiences for children. Review the framework for developmentally appropriate curriculum as you think about these questions:

- Can a teacher of young children purchase a curriculum that is developmentally appropriate? Why?

- Given what you know about developmentally appropriate practice, can a teacher plan the topics of study for the year before meeting the children? Why?

- Can a teacher incorporate the topics/goals of the school curriculum guide into a developmentally appropriate curriculum? Why?

- If a first-grade teacher wanted to study transportation with her students, would that be developmentally appropriate? If your answer is no, under what conditions would the topic be appropriate? If yes, explain why the topic is appropriate.

for whole-class activities, others for small groups, and still others for individual children. For example, from the learning plan for six- to seven-year-olds, the whole class might listen to the teacher read *Grandfather's Journey* (Say 1993). After that, small groups might work on research projects about their families, and individuals might write poems and create art projects. In every learning plan, there should be a good balance of whole-group activities, small-group activities, and individual activities. Figure 4.5 is a lesson plan for a whole-group activity.

Mandated Lessons or Goals

If the school district has **mandated goals** and corresponding materials to be used, the professional teacher must decide if the materials are appropriate for his particular group of children and, if not, how the children could achieve the mandated goals in a more appropriate manner. For example, in one school district, kindergarten teachers were told that all kindergarten children should have mastered eighteen basic sight words from the adopted basal reader by the end of kindergarten. A professional teacher would be accountable for teaching the sight-word vocabulary to all the children for whom this goal was reasonable, but given his knowledge of emerging literacy, he would choose a meaningful context for helping children learn to recognize the sight words. These basic words (*boy, girl, I, ran, look,* and so forth) are common in children's writing and in the stories and poems that a teacher would use in the classroom. The teacher would use the words as they occurred naturally and help children

Figure 4.4

Program Goals: Increased ability to use print to solve problems and meet personal needs and increased skill in collecting and evaluating data

Theme: Who Are We?

Topic: Our Families

Objectives: Children will be able to:
- Plan and implement a survey to learn about the size of families represented in the class.
- Plan and create a graph to illustrate the size of families represented in the graph.
- Research the average family size in their community and state and compare their findings to the average in the class.

Group Time: Read-Aloud—*Grandfather's Journey* (Say 1993) or select from the list in Chapter 10.

Activity Time:
- *Art*—Provide materials and models for constructing family trees.
- *Library*—Display books about families and how to research your family history.
- *Computer*—Bookmark some websites that would be appropriate for doing research on family names and/or family history.
- *Social Studies*—Locate on a map the origin of all the families represented in the classroom.
- *Math*—Find the average size of the families represented in the classroom. Find out how the school predicts the number of school-age children in the district each year. How accurate was their prediction this year?
- *Science*—Learn about the major systems of the human body: the circulatory system, pulmonary system, digestive system, skeletal system, and reproductive system.
- *Movement:*—Learn folk dances from the cultures represented in the classroom. Ask parents or other members of the community to teach these dances to the children.
- *Language Arts*—The children will be reading and writing about their families. They can create an interview form to solicit information about their own families and then present the information in a report. The information will be used for collecting data for math, developing mapping skills and knowledge, and writing their own family stories.

Note: This theme of Who Are We? will continue for the entire year as children actively explore their own characteristics, the characteristics of their families, and the characteristics of their community.

Figure 4.5

Sample Lesson Plan
for Activity on
Family Interviews

Objectives: Children will participate in creating an interview form, will interview one or two individuals in their family, and will record the answers on the form.

Materials: Whiteboard or chalkboard, an interview with an author whose works the children are familiar with (from a journal or from the Web)

Procedure:

1. Call the children to a meeting in front of the whiteboard.
2. Remind children that we need to get information about the families represented in our classroom, and describe an interview. Define an interview as asking certain questions so that we will have comparable data with which to work on later topics. Use an author interview as a model, read two or three questions, and discuss the kinds of answers one might get.
3. Ask the children for suggestions for questions that could be asked of a family member.
4. Record the suggestions on the board.
5. Evaluate the questions in terms of the information that will be obtained and select the ten most important questions.
6. Tell the children that you will provide them with a copy of the questions and space for the answers tomorrow so that they can begin their interviews.

Accommodations: Make sure that every child has a chance to contribute a suggestion for a question.

Evaluation: Observe the group for suggestions of questions to be asked.

recognize them in these contexts. Keeping good records of the children's work helps the teacher discuss the learning that is taking place and the reasons that the choice of instructional materials is important to the children's success.

The professional teacher of young children depends on assessment of program goals and the growth of individual children to make decisions about what instruction is most appropriate for them. Materials and programs must be carefully evaluated in terms of children's needs before they are used for instruction. Most goals can be reached by many routes; the teacher must choose the one that suits the children best.

Scheduling

One professional task that helps the teacher manage the activities of the class in an appropriate manner is setting up the daily class schedule. Like room arrangements, furniture, and choices of areas, the schedule can be planned before the teacher knows the children, but plans should be made with the knowledge that the schedule will change to reflect the needs of the group and of individuals.

A schedule must allow children to move around and select materials and activities as easily as possible. In planning a schedule, the teacher should begin by noting any fixed times, such as the time the class can use the outdoor play area, lunchtime, or time with specialists (music, physical education, or art). The teacher should try to arrange for a large block of the time to be a period in which children have a choice of activities and materials. Other activities that the teacher wants to include can then be added: a story time, a music time, a group time, and a snack time.

The time allotted for these activities will depend on the children's ages. Threes and fours need much shorter story and music times than older children and probably do not need group time at all. Fives and sixes can benefit from longer story and music times and from group time, as well. Teachers in primary grades experience more intrusions in their schedules (fixed recess periods, visits from various specialists, and so on), but they still have long periods during which they can schedule activities. One source of tension in planning any schedule for young children is attempting to balance large-group times and times for self-selected activities.

One purpose of a schedule is to provide routine and structure for children so that they know basically what to expect each day (Lund and Bos 1981). Another purpose is to provide balance in the day. For instance, activities in which children are relatively passive should not be scheduled back to back so that children have to sit quietly for long periods of time.

Table 4.1 shows samples of schedules for younger children and older children on half-day programs, a full-day program for kindergarten children, and a full-day schedule for primary-grade children. Note that none of these schedules includes time for cleanup or toileting. Teachers should involve children as much as possible in cleaning up the room and putting away materials before moving to other activities. Ideally, all rooms for early childhood programs should have bathrooms attached so that children can just go to the bathroom when they need to. Teachers in some older buildings (where this arrangement is often not the case) may have to arrange to take the class to the restrooms in groups. If possible, the teacher should send a few children at a time with an aide or volunteer while other children continue working.

Details of the Schedule

Activity Time

Experiences that are appropriate for children will be discussed in more detail in the content-area chapters (Chapters 9 through 15). Children usually participate in these experiences during activity times. For example, if the topic was a study of how insects change, children would work puzzles depicting insects in the manipulatives area; observe insects on display in the science area using a

Table 4.1   Schedules for Various Programs

Program	Times	Activities
Half-Day Program for Younger Children	9:00–10:00	Activity time
	10:00–10:10	Music time
	10:10–10:40	Outdoor play
	10:40–11:00	Snack time
	11:00–11:10	Quiet time
	11:10–11:20	Movement activities
	11:20–11:30	Story time
Half-Day Program for Older Preschoolers	9:00–10:00	Activity time
	10:00–10:20	Music and movement
	10:20–10:40	Group time (calendar, weather, discussions)
	10:40–11:00	Outdoor play
	11:00–11:10	Snack
	11:10–11:30	Story, poetry
Full-Day Kindergarten	9:00–9:15	Opening, singing, planning for the day
	9:15–10:15	Activity time
	10:15–10:45	Snack
	10:45–11:15	Outdoor play (gross motor play indoors in bad weather)
	11:15–11:45	Story time, literature study
	11:45–12:30	Lunch and recess
	12:30–1:30	Rest period
	1:30–1:40	Group time (discussions, planning for afternoon)
	1:40–2:15	Activity time
	2:15–2:45	Library, music, art, or physical education
	2:45–3:00	Evaluations of activities, dismissal
Primary Children	9:00–9:15	Opening, singing, planning for the day
	9:15–10:15	Reading workshop
	10:15–10:30	Recess/snack
	10:30–11:30	Writing workshop
	11:30–12:30	Lunch and recess
	12:30–1:30	Theme activities and math
	1:30–2:00	Library (alternating with art or music specialists)
	2:00–2:30	Physical education, outdoor play
	2:30–2:45	Read-aloud, creative dramatics
	2:45–3:00	Sharing events of day, discussions, plans for next day, dismissal

magnifying glass and record their observations; read (or look at pictures in) books about insects in the library; sort pictures of insects; examine sequence boards showing the life cycles of insects in the language arts area; and play with puppets and flannelboard cutouts of insects in the language arts area. Children might paint or draw insects or build insect homes in the art area. Whatever the topic, it would be incorporated into as many content areas as possible and reasonable. Activity times are scheduled so that children can participate in small-group and individual activities.

Group Time

Some traditional group time experiences are not especially meaningful to children. As noted earlier, threes and fours probably do not need group time at all. Trying to get them to learn about the calendar is not the best use of their time. Fives and sixes can review the calendar and daily weather, but these should be brief reviews, not extended drills. Other activities appropriate for group time for fives and sixes include planning and evaluating their experiences during activity time, participating in some short group experiences (such as viewing a videotape that relates to a theme topic), listening to a resource person, discussing a problem in the room, having specific instruction in fire safety rules, and so on. Whole-group instruction is not an appropriate teaching strategy for content areas; lecturing on a topic to children of this age is of little value.

Group time with primary children may be used for some of the same activities as those suggested for fives and sixes. It may also be used to help children recognize the choices they can make for their theme studies and to do more formal planning of their day. Some limited group instruction with primary children is useful. For example, the teacher may teach the whole group to recognize story structure or to recognize particular strategies that an author has used in a story the children are reading. Group discussions of books the children are reading are also important. Likewise, having children present work they have completed can be a valuable component of group time in the primary grades.

Show-and-tell, or sharing, is often a regular part of group time, especially with five- to eight-year-olds. Show-and-tell often becomes "bring-and-brag," as children bring their newest toy to show off. The teacher usually controls the audience for the speaker and directs the children while they speak or ask questions. If sharing time is to achieve the goal of promoting more effective communication, however, teachers must structure the time so that children do the talking and organizing, rather than the teacher.

One technique is to have the sharing focus on the children's work, rather than on objects brought from home. Children may also need to share something especially meaningful to them from time to time, but not every child needs to share something every day. Another technique is to organize sharing time into small groups so that children share with three or four others and do not have to sit while twenty-five children share, one at a time. It is important to evaluate sharing experiences on the basis of what the children are actually learning, rather than simply to state that sharing is an important means of children learning to communicate more effectively.

Snack Time

Very young children need a snack during the morning or afternoon. Snack time should be considered a teaching time, as children learn about new foods, learn to carry on conversations, and learn how to help prepare and serve the snack. Snacks should always be nutritious and help children learn about good nutrition.

Snack time for fives and sixes can be time consuming in a half-day program when time is so limited. By the time all the children have washed their hands, been served, eaten their snacks, and cleaned up, twenty to thirty minutes out of a two-and-a-half-hour day have been used up. Therefore, some teachers prefer to have snacks available on a table so that two or three children can serve themselves and then go back to their activities. Other teachers prefer to incorporate snack time into the activity time by making food preparation one of the activities. In this way, the activity time can be extended.

Transitions

Transitions from one activity to another are the most likely times for behavior problems or disruptions in any program. What can the teacher do when one or two children are ready to begin a new activity and the others are still cleaning up their work areas? Or what can the teacher do when the class is ready to go to the cafeteria for lunch and the principal asks her to hold her class for exactly two more minutes? The teacher can have children who have completed their cleanup help others finish. Those who have finished can then sit in the group area and listen to a tape recording of nursery rhymes, folk songs, or fingerplays; others will join as they finish. With older children, one child can begin a rhyme, the second can say the next line, and so on; the last child can begin another rhyme.

When moving children from one area to another, the teacher should try having them move in groups by color or kind of clothing (all children wearing yellow, all children wearing sandals, and so on). Playing rhythms on a drum or piano also helps in moving children from one area to another; they can march around the room and then out the door to go outside or to the lunch-

The transition times between activities need to be planned just as carefully as the activities themselves to avoid disruptions in the schedule.

room. There are many memory games that children can play in line, such as Going on the Train, in which the first player takes something beginning with the letter *a*, the second something beginning with *b*, and on through the alphabet. Children can also play guessing games, such as Twenty Questions or Who's in My Family? or they can listen to tapes of jokes or short pieces of poetry (Alger 1984).

The teacher should involve the children in solving transition problems. If it is time to go outdoors, the children might be asked to think of ways they can all get their coats without bumping into anyone or crowding. It is also helpful to have the activity that follows cleanup be something the children are anxious to do; dawdlers are not encouraged to finish their tasks when what they are going to do next is not exciting to them (Alger 1984).

Simplifying Routines

The routines of checking attendance, counting the children who will purchase milk, and so on can take up a lot of time. Some teachers choose to make these routines learning experiences for the children and as simple as possible for themselves. One way to check attendance is to have the children sign their names on a paper attached to a clipboard by the door. The teacher can see from the child's signature what he knows and is learning about writing.

Another technique is to divide a board in half, labeling one half "Present" and the other half "Absent." Nails or pegs are added below the label on each half, enough for all the children in the class. Each child is given a nametag with a hole in it, which he will hang on the board, or a name on a magnet and a magnetic board. As the children come in every day, they move their nametags from the "Absent" side to the "Present" side of the board. In preparation for the next day, the teacher reverses the "Present" and "Absent" headings.

Taking a count for milk can be accomplished by having each child who is purchasing milk place a marker with her name on it in a pocket marked "Milk." The same technique works for lunch counts.

Adapting the Schedule

For the first two weeks or so of the new schoolyear, the schedule may be adapted to help children make a more comfortable adjustment to school. Some schools have only half of the children assigned to each classroom come each day for the first week; the other half of the class comes to school the second week. This way, children have a chance to learn about school routines and get more attention from the teacher while they adjust. Some schools for younger children divide groups in half and ask each half to attend for half of each day for the first two or three weeks; other schools begin the year on a staggered schedule, so that there are five children the first two days, ten the next two days, and fifteen on the fifth day. Teachers should work with the administration and parents to make the beginning of school successful for all involved;

Parents AND Planning

■ Make sure that parents are aware of your typical daily schedule. Invite them to come to class at different times of day so they can observe individual activities as well as small- and whole-group activities.

sometimes parents are willing to help more at the beginning to ensure a good start for all children.

Teachers may also have to adapt schedules to fit the children's developing abilities. Children may not be able to sustain their play for as long as the teacher predicted at the beginning of school and may need two short play periods rather than one long one. Children may need more rest than was predicted. They also may be able to engage in activities of their choice for longer than might have been predicted. Teachers, with input from the children, may need to adapt schedules to fit the individuals' needs.

Kindergarten: Half-Day, Full-Day, and Alternate-Day Programs

This section applies specifically to kindergarten because there is so much debate about the values of different schedules for kindergarten children. The schedule for threes and fours is generally either a morning or an afternoon session of about two and a half or three hours, whereas schedules for primary grades are usually set to match the full-day elementary school schedule. Some schools have two sessions of kindergarten each day. Because of transportation problems and the need for full-day child care, some schools have adopted an alternate-day schedule, so that kindergartners attend for a full day but only on alternate days. Other schools provide full-day programs for some kindergartners, especially those deemed at risk of academic failure. What does the research say about these different schedule patterns?

The research on the various programming choices for kindergarten remains mixed. It is difficult to keep constant the skill of the teacher, the child's motivation and interest, the parental support, and the kind of measure used to judge success as well as other factors that can influence the outcomes of studies. Clark (2001), in her review of the research, states that the research from the 1990s is more positive about all-day kindergartens, but she admits that much of that research had serious problems. Several studies have shown that attending an all-day kindergarten is beneficial for academic achievement, especially for children deemed at risk of school failure (Elicker and Mathur 1997; Fusaro 1997; Hough and Bryde 1996). Nelson (2000) looked at half-day and full-day kindergarten, multiage grouping, and class size as influences on achievement. She concluded that for low-income, urban schools a full-day program with smaller classes was the best choice. Both teachers and parents seem to feel that there is more time for individual instruction and more opportunity for social development in a full-day program (Elicker and Mathur 1997).

When evaluating schedules, the best approach is to determine what is best for the children involved, to plan for excellent experiences no matter when the children are in school, and to evaluate continuously. A full-day program that involves children in inappropriate activities is not beneficial to children, even though they are there longer than children in half- or alternate-day programs. Decisions should not be made on the basis of convenience; rather, the guideline should be to provide optimal environments for children.

Other Scheduling Issues

An ongoing problem for kindergarten and primary teachers is *pull-out programs,* in which children are removed from class at certain times for special lessons or activities, such as speech therapy. Removing children from the class makes it difficult to schedule large-group activities and also complicates having all children participate in small-group or individual activities.

One solution to the problem, which is being used in an ever-increasing number of schools, is to have the special teachers come to the regular classroom to work with individual students, rather than have the students go to the teachers. In schools in which this solution has not yet been implemented, the regular classroom teachers might approach the special teachers with the idea and agree to help solve any problems that arise. If this solution is not applied and pull-out programs remain a fact of life, regular classroom teachers should try to arrange activity time for that part of the day when the most children will be in the room. Classroom teachers should also try to work with the schedules of the special teachers in order to achieve a more reasonable day for the class. Regardless, there does not seem to be an easy solution to the problem of pull-out programs.

Program Assessment

When teachers evaluate an early childhood program, they are looking for evidence that the program is appropriate for the children enrolled and that it is effective in bringing about their growth. The following questions will help teachers evaluate their programs:

1. Would you like to be a child in your classroom?
2. Is there a balance of small-group, whole-group, and individual activities?
3. Do children spend more time in self-selected activities than in teacher-directed activities?
4. Do the children's interests influence activities and learning experiences?
5. Does every child find success and challenge every day?
6. Is there a balance of emphasis on intellectual, social, emotional, and physical growth?
7. Are skills taught in a meaningful context?
8. Can children withdraw from activities without penalty?

9. Are activities and experiences selected on the basis of their relationship to the goals of the program?

10. When planning activities, is the information gathered from observations and assessments used to guide planning?

11. Do individual children show evidence of growth in all areas of development?

12. Are interactions with parents supportive of children's growth?

Answers to these questions will be derived from evaluating the schedule, the lesson plans, and the instructional materials and observations of interpersonal relationships in the classroom. A teacher who respects children's interests will not determine a list of topics to be studied before getting to know the children. (This is not to imply that a teacher cannot make tentative plans for topics he predicts will be of interest to the children.) Further, in a good program, materials will be readily available to help children learn a variety of facts and skills in a playful manner. Finally, other evidence that the program is a good one is found in the attitudes of the children. If they see themselves as a learners who seek support for their own learning, rather than waiting for the teacher to tell them everything to do, the program is effective.

If you are interested in reviewing a much more detailed evaluation of a program, consult the *Accreditation Criteria and Procedures of the National Academy of Early Childhood Programs* (NAEYC 1998b).

Parents AND *Planning*

■ Adapt the twelve questions listed on pages 131–132 so that they ask parents about their activities with their children. For example, adapt question 1 to ask: Would you like to be a child in your family? (Note that parents might not be able to answer question 10.)

WWW

NAEYC

Celebrating Diversity

To celebrate the diversity of the classroom, teachers should plan for experiences and activities that reflect the diversity of society. For example, in selecting themes, teachers should think carefully about the meanings of the activities for the children involved. For example, what will a two-week theme with a focus on St. Patrick's Day mean to a class of three- and four-year-olds who are Hispanic or Southeast Asian? On the other hand, St. Patrick's Day may be an important holiday to a child from an Irish household. Perhaps implementing a theme about this holiday could be justified if there were Irish children in the class and the theme focused on the holidays of all the ethnic groups represented in the class. In sum, the themes selected must be relevant to the lives of the children. Teachers should consider that by focusing on holidays, they may be denying children experiences with more interesting and relevant themes, such as those focusing on animals, insects, plants, and other children's interests.

Diversity can be celebrated in many of the activities and experiences that teachers plan for young children. For example, when planning cooking experiences, teachers can prepare foods that are typical of the various ethnic groups represented in the class. Members of the community can be invited to share special ethnic foods, traditional clothing, stories, and games. Community members whose work is nontraditional for their gender also can be invited to share information about their work with the class. Teachers should not advocate a curriculum that simply adds a "diversity feature." Rather, their goal should be the authentic integration of people and other resources that will help children explore topics in ways that naturally include diversity.

Experiences with literature can enhance children's knowledge and appreciation of racial and ethnic differences if they are planned carefully by teachers. Namely, teachers should select pieces of literature to add information or interest to themes, ensuring that the works of authors and illustrators of various racial/ethnic groups and both genders are included. Books, both fiction and nonfiction, and poetry that include a wide variety of characters should also be selected. In one second-grade boy's reading-response journal, he explained that he really liked a particular book because he was Hispanic and had never known about a book with Hispanic characters before. Children should be able to find characters like themselves in books that are part of the classroom experience.

Chapter Summary

■ *Curriculum* can be defined in many ways: as a program, as a written plan for learning experiences, as a syllabus listing topics and sequences of topics, or as everything that happens at school. In this chapter, *curriculum* was defined as the written plan for learning experiences.

■ The steps in planning a curriculum include determining the purpose of the curriculum, analyzing the options available, selecting the features to be included, producing the design, and evaluating the design.

■ Teachers developing a curriculum must select content and sequence activities so that children can use the information they have already learned to learn new information.

■ Assessment of a curriculum must be appropriate for the age and level of development of the children and for the activity.

■ A curriculum can be organized around facts, skills, subjects, themes, key concepts, or common human needs.

■ A thematic organization of a curriculum provides learning opportunities that are not divided into segments and that better match children's learning experiences outside the school setting.

■ In selecting a theme, the teacher must consider relevance, opportunities for application of skills, availability of resources, his own interests, and the time of year.

■ Evaluation of themes and experiences is necessary. One technique is to record on charts the curriculum goals met by a theme and the goals met by the activities in which each child actually participated.

■ A learning plan differs from a typical lesson plan in that a learning plan encompasses much more than one lesson. It may specify a variety of activities, long-term goals, theme goals, and short-term goals.

■ When teachers are faced with mandated goals, they must use their professional judgment in meeting those goals and must document children's progress very carefully.

■ A schedule is designed to offer children the security of routine and to add structure to the day. Teachers must create schedules that contribute to meeting the goals of the program.

■ Findings of research on the effects of half-day, alternate-day, or full-day kindergarten programs have not been conclusive. Much depends on the goals and objectives of the program and the actual experiences of the children while at school.

■ Teachers must evaluate the progress of individual children as well as the program itself. Important areas for evaluation include teacher–child relationships, the opportunities for children to make choices, and the balance of activities provided for the children.

■ Teachers who are planning activities and experiences should make sure that children are learning about their own culture an the cultures of others. Diversity can be addressed through experiences with literature, cooking, play, and various content areas.

Theory INTO *Practice*

Develop a list of possible themes for a specific group of children. Evaluate your themes against the criteria listed in this chapter. Develop one of these ideas into a learning plan that describes the activities you would make available to children in various centers in the classroom.

Select one of the activities from your learning plan, and create the lesson plan for it. Prepare a 5" × 8" card with directions for the activity, including enough detail that a parent or paraprofessional could supervise it. For example, if the activity involves planting seeds, what supplies are needed? Where are they? Should the table be covered with newspaper? How many children can work at the activity at one time? And so on.

Interview several teachers about their daily schedules. What daily schedule does each follow? How are their schedules similar? How are they different? What, if any, parts of the schedule would the teachers like to change? How much control do they have over scheduling?

In the theme that you developed earlier, how could you include activities that would be culturally appropriate for a group of children whom you have observed? Describe the children and what you know about their culture. In particular, what topics or issues should you be sensitive to?

Discuss the meaning of the term *emerging curriculum*. How does the teacher plan for a curriculum that the children will initiate?

Does the learning plan you developed allow for adapting instruction for children with special needs? If so, how? If not, how could it be changed to include such adaptations?

A Teacher Speaks

Beth Peter   Neill Elementary School
Burnsville, Minnesota

Planning for Success

My classroom is a multiage classroom that houses first through fourth graders who are constantly in different places on the continuum of learning development. However, meeting a wide variety of needs and matching different stages of development in the classroom is a challenge that is not unique to multiage. I've taught in single-grade classrooms where the needs of the students are also quite diverse.

I'm certain there are many "teachable moments" that happen throughout my day, but the majority of my instruction is carefully planned ahead of time. I believe that planned instruction is a vital element in taking a student to his next learning step. This planning takes a variety of forms and a variety of time frames, but it all has a common thread of building upon a student's strengths in the area in which I want new learning to occur.

I plan on a daily basis. Each day, for as many students as I am able, I examine what he has done today to enable me to plan his instruction for tomorrow. Let me use writing as an example. My students write daily. As I look through their writing for that day, I record in a notebook what I see them doing successfully in regard to the content of their writing, the surface features like their spelling and structure, and their handwriting skill. I carefully examine their writing for evidence that they are attempting to gain control over these same areas. Common strengths, attempts, and needs can be seen, from which I plan writing conference groups, editing conferences, modeled writing lessons, spelling lessons, handwriting groups, and reading material that might take them to the next learning step. I also need to have a strong understanding of the writing process, the broad stages of writing de-

velopment, the reading process, and the stages that readers go through. My students become the guides of what will be next in my instruction.

I also use observation of their reading and writing behaviors to ask myself if there is a part of the process that needs instruction. I cannot wait until the teacher's manual tells me that it is time to teach contractions, because I think teaching at the point of a student's need is where true learning occurs. You might think that it would be an impossible task timewise to meet individual learning needs, but I find that students naturally fall into groups with common needs. These groups change as fluidly as the needs of the learners change. Obviously, I do not have the time to meet with each of my students individually on a daily basis, but through small-group *and* individual instruction, I am able to see each of my students daily.

I use "running records" and the information I receive from their analysis to guide my reading instruction and to form groups for guided and shared reading experiences. The information from a running record allows me to meet the learner with a text that is at her instructional level and will allow her to build on what she is currently doing as a reader. Again, my students fall into groups that have common needs.

Even though the majority of my planning for instruction takes place on a daily basis, I still need to have a strong picture of where I want my students to go and how I am going to get them there. This planning is more global and is the umbrella for what I plan on a daily basis. I keep in mind the skills that a lifelong learner needs as I plan and write down what I expect to see happening with a student as a result of my instruction.

CHAPTER 5

Play: Learning at Its Best

After reading this chapter, you will be able to do the following:

- Define and describe the term *play*.
- Describe the roles in play.
- Explain the purposes of play.
- Explain the value of play in a school setting.
- Explain the connections between play and academic learning.
- Plan for outdoor play experiences.
- Plan for adaptations in play equipment for children with special needs.
- Plan for the play of children from diverse cultures.

This morning you visited a second-grade classroom to observe children's play. You found the children busily working on various projects. One group had written the script for a play and were making the puppets they would need to present their drama. Another small group was constructing a habitat for an insect collection using the directions they found in several reference books. They were also creating small posters that described the care the various insects would need. Another small group was working on a three-dimensional map of their community made from cereal boxes. Four children were playing a board game they had created based on the story The Lion, the Witch, and the Wardrobe *(Lewis 1951). Two pairs of children were using the computers to create final copies of the stories they had composed earlier. Several other individual children were involved in tasks such as building a dodecahedron from Popsicle sticks and putting a colorwash on paper to be used for mounting poetry selections.*

You were amazed that these children were playing in second grade. However, as you observed more closely, you realized they were learning academic as well as social skills through their play. You want to know how the teacher manages all these play activities and how play can help achieve the goals of a developmentally appropriate program.

Back in your campus class, the discussion of play in the classroom was a lively one. Many of your classmates felt children should play in school, but they were worried about justifying play when teachers are held accountable for achieving so many academic standards these days. You want to find answers to your questions about the nature of play and how it can contribute to realizing curriculum goals.

Defining Play

Teachers, parents, and administrators need continued support in their efforts to include play in the curriculum and to defend its use to those not as knowledgeable in early childhood education. Almy (1984) has published statements in several sources about the child's right to play. She writes that the distinguishing characteristics of play make it essential to the child's development. She believes that adults must provide opportunities for children to play and to learn from observations and actions as well as from being told things.

In a position paper approved by the Association for Childhood Education International (ACEI), Isenberg and Quisenberry (1988) state that "play—a dynamic, active and constructive behavior—is a necessary and integral part of childhood, infancy through adolescence." The ACEI also asserts that teachers must take the lead in articulating the need for play in children's lives, especially as a part of their school life.

Play in a school setting can be described on a continuum that runs from free play to guided play to directed play:

- *Free play* can be defined as play in which children have as many choices of materials as possible and in which they can choose how to use the materials (within bounds, of course; for example, they cannot hit others with the blocks).
- *Guided play* is defined as play in which the teacher has selected materials from which the children may choose in order to discover specific concepts. If the goal is to learn to classify objects as large or small, then the teacher will provide several sets of objects to play with that could be classified as such.
- *Directed play* is play in which the teacher instructs the children how to accomplish a specific task. Singing songs, engaging in fingerplays, and playing circle games are examples of directed play (Bergen 1988).

Describing Play

Social Play

Teachers who observe children playing will notice several different levels of involvement with other children in play episodes. In her classic study, Parten (1932) describes these levels as *solitary, onlooker, parallel, associative,* and *cooperative play.* Table 5.1 summarizes Parten's descriptions of levels of social play.

Children of different ages exhibit different levels of social play. Very young children are not cognitively capable of assuming different roles and playing cooperatively. They do not possess enough information about roles or enough social skills to work together for a single purpose. Older children do not engage in cooperative play exclusively. They may engage in any of the levels of play; they simply have a much broader repertoire of possible play behaviors.

Table 5.1 Levels of Social Play

Level	Description
Solitary Play	Play in which children play without regard for what other children around them are doing. A child may be constructing a tower with blocks and be completely oblivious to what other children in the room are doing.
Onlooker Play	Play in which the child who is playing individually is simultaneously observing those playing in the same area. The child may be talking to peers. Children who watch other children play may alter their own play behavior after watching. Children engaged in onlooker play may seem to be sitting passively while children around them are playing, but they are very alert to the action around them.
Parallel Play	Play in which several children are playing with the same materials, but each is playing independently. What one child does is not dependent on what others do. Children working puzzles are usually engaged in parallel play. They usually talk to one another, but if one leaves the table, the others continue playing.
Associative Play	Play in which several children play together but in a loosely organized fashion. Several children might decide to play "monsters," for example, and run around the playground, chasing each other. But there are no definite roles, and if one child does not run and chase, the others can continue to play.
Cooperative Play	Play in which each child accepts a designated role and is dependent on others for achieving the goals of the play. When children want to play "store," for instance, one child must accept the role of store clerk and others must be shoppers. If a child refuses to play unless she can be the storekeeper, the play episode will end.

Source: Based on Parten 1932.

Play with Objects

There are levels of play with objects as well as levels of social play. Piaget (1962) and Piaget and Inhelder (1969) have described different types of play with objects, including practice play, symbolic play, games with rules, and games of construction. **Practice play**, or functional play, is play in which children explore the possibilities of materials. Even adults engage in practice play when the materials presented are new to them. For instance, children using dominoes in practice play would stack them and stand them on end. After playing with the dominoes for some time, children might begin to use them *symbolically.* They would use a domino to represent something else. Perhaps they would make a corral of blocks and pretend that the dominoes were cattle in the corral.

These children are engaging in onlooker play; the girl on the right is watching the others play with their toys.

In a *game with rules,* children might play according to rules they have made up themselves or according to the rules that are generally agreed on for playing the game. If the children were playing with dominoes, for example, they might decide that the rules were to match all the ends but not play the doubles across; if they know the conventional rules for playing dominoes and keeping score, they might follow those rules instead. Anyone who has ever tried to play a game with rules (such as Candy Land or Concentration) with a three- or four-year-old knows that a child this age will usually play the way she wants to and that following the rules is almost impossible.

Games of construction are described by Piaget as growing out of symbolic play "but tend later to constitute genuine adaptations (mechanical constructions, etc.) or solutions to problems and intelligent creations" (Piaget and Inhelder 1969, p. 59). Levels of object play depend on the children's maturity and experience. As children mature, they become more capable of using materials symbolically and of playing a game with accepted rules.

Vygotsky on Play

In their important work on the theories of Lev Vygotsky, Bodrova, and Leong (1996) have summarized his views on play. In sum, play develops from the manipulative play of toddlers to the socially oriented play of older preschoolers and kindergartners and finally to games. Vygotsky would label as play behavior by toddlers in which they begin to use objects in imaginary situations and label the actions with words. For example, using a spoon to bang on a table is not play, but using a spoon to feed a teddy bear and asking the bear to eat is play. Most five-year-olds focus on the social roles of their play rather than on the objects. For example, they can pretend to have a pad of paper and pen for taking orders if they are playing "waiter" or "waitress." Games, as a type of play, emerge in children's play behavior around age five. Games involve explicit and detailed rules in which the imaginary situations are hidden. For example, soccer is a game in which the players agree not to use their hands, although they could use them (Bodrova and Leong 1996).

Vygotsky believes that play is extremely important in the child's development in three ways:

1. *"Play creates the child's zone of proximal development."* In a play setting, a child can control behavior such as attending to a task before she is able to control that behavior in another setting.

2. *"Play facilitates the separation of thought from actions and objects."* In play, the child can pretend that a block is a boat; this separation of object from meaning is critical to the development of abstract thinking.

3. *"Play facilitates the development of self-regulation."* In developing self-regulation, children in play are required to make their behavior match the role they have accepted. For example, a child playing "dog" can stop barking or sit still on command (quotes from Bodrova and Leong 1996, p. 126).

According to Vygotsky:

> Play creates a zone of proximal development in the child. In play, the child always behaves beyond his average age, above his daily behavior; in play it is as though he were a head taller than himself. As in the focus of a magnifying glass, play contains all developmental tendencies in a condensed form and is itself a major source of development. (1978, p. 102)

Sociodramatic Play

Sociodramatic play is of particular interest to researchers. Smilansky (1971) has studied sociodramatic play and methods for facilitating such play and observed that it has the following elements:

1. *Imitative role play.* The child undertakes a make-believe role and expresses it in imitative action and/or verbalization.
2. *Make-believe in regard to objects.* Movements or verbal declarations are substituted for real objects.
3. *Make-believe in regard to actions and situations.* Verbal descriptions are substituted for actions and situations.
4. *Persistence.* The child persists in a play episode for at least ten minutes.
5. *Interaction.* There are at least two players interacting in the framework of the play episode.
6. *Verbal communication.* There is some verbal interaction related to the play episode. (pp. 41–42)

Sociodramatic play is especially important in the development of creativity, intellectual growth, and social skills. Not all children will have had experience with sociodramatic play. Therefore, teachers may need to assume more responsibility in fostering such play with these children. Teachers can look carefully for the elements of sociodramatic play and encourage it by intervening and helping children achieve any missing elements.

Research findings support the value of sociodramatic play:

> *A vast amount of research indicates that imaginative play (symbolic play) is a significant causal force in the development of a multitude of abilities, including creativity, sequential memory, group cooperation, receptive vocabulary, conceptions of kinship relationships, impulse control, spatial perspective-taking skill, affective perspective-taking skill, and cognitive perspective-taking skill.* (Gowen 1995, p. 78)

The abilities to take on the role of another person and to shift perspective are important basic skills for academic learning. For some children, sociodramatic play occurs if time is allowed for it; for others, the teacher may have to be much more involved to get children to participate. This can be accomplished by providing time and often props to get children started in sociodramatic play. The dramatic play area and the housekeeping center are often settings that encourage sociodramatic play by providing costumes, furniture, and other props. If children have ideas about play themes, the teacher can help them carry out these ideas by providing needed props.

Teachers might consider asking parents to help them collect materials that could be used for any number of play situations. Materials for given situations might then be stored in individual boxes so that they are available when the children's interests dictate use. Such boxes might include materials for playing "repairperson," "beauty shop," "office," and so on. Myhre (1993) suggests prop boxes containing materials to recreate a bakery, a flower shop, and a beach party, as well as a jewelry and accessory box and "dentist," "police," and "firefighter" boxes.

In addition to providing time and props, the teacher might have to model appropriate play behavior for children with little or no experience in sociodramatic play. He may have to assume a role and play it for a few minutes, at least long enough to demonstrate the behavior so that children will understand and be able to perform the behavior themselves. The teacher might also suggest roles others could play or ask questions to get the children started on a play episode. The line between assisting children and dominating play is a fine one. Teachers must develop skills in listening to and responding to children, following their lead, rather than imposing their ideas about what children should be playing.

Reifel and Yeatman (1993) urge teachers to think of play in broader categories than those described by Parten and Piaget. They note, for example, that rough-and-tumble play, word play, and jokes are not covered in either theorist's description of play, although these behaviors are certainly part of children's play experiences. A play episode may begin with one type of play, move to another, and then back again, so teachers need to think about how children are relating to materials and to one another throughout play episodes, rather than make quick judgments based on short, isolated observations.

Finally, teachers should look for opportunities to encourage sociodramatic play that stems from real events in children's lives. For example, suppose one of the children has been in the hospital. When she returns to school and tells of her experience, the children will likely be anxious to play "being in the hospital." The teacher might ask some questions to help the children think about what they need to play "hospital" and then help them find appropriate props, such as clipboards to use for patient charts, stethoscopes, boxes for furniture, and so on.

Roles in Play

Role of the Child

Children in free-play situations choose to become involved in the play, are active in their involvement, can suspend reality, have no extrinsic goals for their activities, and bring their own meaning to the play (Spodek, Saracho, and Davis 1987).

Play Is Personally Motivated

In order for an activity to be called *play,* the player must choose to participate. If a child chooses an activity, it is usually play, although what is being done may appear to be work. For example, a child may load up a wheelbarrow with sand, move it across the playground to a new sandbox, and dump it. Similarly, children often "work" for hours gathering materials and building forts. The difference between play and work is that a play activity is self-chosen: The child controls how long she will participate and defines the goals of the activity. Ceglowski (1997) found that kindergartners had no trouble in identifying activities that were play versus work. Children described as *play* only those activities they selected and directed. Activities that were teacher selected or teacher directed were described as *work*. Play is always pleasurable to the participants. The feelings may be the satisfaction of having achieved internal goals or the pure joy of running freely. The player experiences pleasure in play.

Play Is Active

All play experiences require some active involvement on the part of the player. Play is *not* a passive activity, such as watching television, although play does not require active physical involvement. Children are playing when they participate in a "tea party" or investigate the hardness of rocks. Children playing are engaged in thinking, organizing, planning, and interacting with the environment. If the involvement is passive, then the activity is probably not play.

Parents AND Play

- Ask parents to keep a play diary for a few days, recording the time their children spend in active play and the materials used in the play. Arrange for a speaker to talk with parents about the need for active play in a child's life and to help them find a strategy to increase play if the child is not engaging in active play. Be sure that the parents make the distinction between active play and passive activity, such as watching TV.

Play Is Often Nonliteral

Children at play can suspend reality, usually with the magic words "Let's pretend." Time, setting, and characters involved in play can be negotiated at the moment and are not tied to reality. They need not even be possible; children might pretend to fly, to be from outer space, or to be monsters.

Play Has No Extrinsic Goals

Suppose a child is arranging and rearranging a set of letters on a magnetic board. If this task has been assigned for the purpose of helping her learn alphabetical order, it is not play. If the child is arranging the letters to suit goals that are her own, then it is play. In playing, the process, or means, not the end result, is most important. The outcome of play is not as important as the *participation* in it.

Players Supply Meaning to Play

Children sometimes explore or use materials in ways specified by others, but when they play, they provide their own interpretations of materials. A child might use base 10 blocks to build models of numbers if directed to do so by an adult. But if allowed to use the materials freely during another portion of the day, the child might use the blocks to build houses or roads.

Play Has No Extrinsic Rules

If an activity is to be considered play, the players must be able to alter the rules of the activity as needed. In a game of tag, for example, the players negotiate where the "safe" areas will be. Similarly, children playing with blocks may establish rules about spaces for building, but these rules are negotiated by the players.

Roles of the Teacher

The roles of the teacher in play within the classroom setting are very important. The teacher must be an observer, an elaborator, a model, an evaluator, and a planner of play (Bjorkland 1978).

Observer

In *observing,* the teacher should watch children's interactions with other children and with objects. He should observe the length of time that children can maintain play episodes, and he should look for any children who have trouble playing or joining play groups. These observations should then be used in planning additional play experiences, in making decisions about whether to enter play situations, and in making assessments of the play of individual children. In a review of studies concerning the effects of the physical environment on children's behavior in preschool settings, Phyfe-Perkins (1980) concludes that if a setting is to provide support for developmentally appropriate activities, the teacher must engage in systematic observation of children at play.

NAEYC

Elaborator

Another aspect of the teacher's role is that of *elaborator*. If the children are playing "going to the hairdresser," the teacher might help them collect items that could be used to represent those found at a hairdresser's shop. She might find photographs or magazine illustrations that would help the children construct a beauty salon. The teacher might even join in the play briefly and ask questions that would guide the children in thinking through their roles or their conceptions of a trip to the hairdresser. If older children were involved in a study of insects, the teacher might supply a film or videotape of insects so that the children could recreate insect movement or sounds in their play.

Modeler

Teachers who value play are often *modelers* of appropriate behaviors in play situations. For instance, a teacher may choose to sit in the blocks area for a brief time and join children in building in order to model ways in which the blocks might be used. Or he might choose to join dramatic play in order to model behaviors that are useful in entering a play group and responses that are useful for helping play continue. Sometimes, the teacher might model play behaviors that will get a play episode started or back on track if it has gone in a direction he considers negative. For example, children playing characters from a television program might begin to chase and catch one another rather aimlessly. The teacher might ask some questions about the purposes of the characters and demonstrate how they might handle interactions without running and chasing inside the room.

Evaluator

As an *evaluator* of play, the teacher has to be a careful observer and diagnostician to determine how different play incidents serve the needs of individual children and what learning is taking place as children participate in play. It is the teacher's job to recognize the academic, social, cognitive, and physical growth that takes place during play and to be able to communicate these changes to parents and administrators. Evaluation means that materials, environments, and activities must be carefully considered in light of the curriculum goals, and changes must be made if needed.

Planner

Finally, the teacher has to serve as a *planner*. Planning involves all the learning that results from observing, elaborating, and evaluating. The teacher must plan for new experiences that will encourage or extend children's interests. For example, a parent who was a shoe clerk could come to the classroom to share her occupation. She might measure the children's feet and demonstrate that part of her job is to show the customers several choices of shoes in the proper sizes and to help them try on shoes. In planning to continue the children's obvious interest, the teacher might do several things: gather a collection of many

Parents AND Play

■ Invite parents to observe a play time at school. Provide a guide sheet that will encourage parents to look for those academic skills being learned in play. For example, list classification, grouping, seriating, analyzing, and so on to help parents notice these skills. On the back of the sheet, you might describe examples of these skills in housekeeping play, block play, and other play areas. The guide sheet might also list social skills, such as sharing, turn taking, cooperating, and others.

kinds of shoes, find a rack suitable for storing them, borrow several of the instruments used for measuring feet, and so on. The teacher's careful planning will result in days of active play involvement by the children as they arrange chairs to make a shoe store, write up sales, and bag shoes to send home with the "customers." The teacher can encourage the children to talk about the different kinds of shoes and who wears them, to draw shoes, to create signs for their shoe store, and even to write stories about shoes. When the children tire of the shoes and no longer demonstrate interest in playing with them, the shoes should be removed. By that time, the teacher will have already planned other experiences that will pique the interest of the children and can be extended in play (Ford 1993).

In planning for play that contributes to development, teachers should consider the following guidelines:

1. *Make sure children have sufficient time for play.*
2. *Help children plan their play.*
3. *Monitor the progress of play.*
4. *Choose appropriate props and toys.*
5. *Provide themes that can be extended from one day to the next.*
6. *Coach individuals who need help.*
7. *Suggest or model how themes can be woven together.*
8. *Model appropriate ways to solve disputes.* (Bodrova and Leong 1996, p. 132)

Development of Play Behaviors

Infancy

The play of infants is *sensorimotor:* They explore objects and people and investigate the effects of their actions on these objects and people. At about the end of the first year, children begin to exhibit play behaviors such as pretending to eat or sleep (Rubin, Fein, and Vanderberg 1983). They are also able to begin playful interactions with others, such as playing peek-a-boo.

Preschool

Preschoolers spend most of their play time in exploratory or practice play. They are focused on the process, rather than the product, of their play. For example, they might mix the colors of paint or the colors of clay, but their interest is in what happens to the materials, not in the painting or sculpture that later results.

Preschoolers often engage in fantasy play, but it is generally focused on their own experiences. For example, they may play "Mommy" and "Baby" or other family roles. In fantasy play, they like to have materials that resemble the real things in the fantasy setting, such as a small broom for sweeping or a play telephone or grocery scanner that resembles the actual equipment.

Threes and fours also begin to involve others in their play. For instance, they may want someone to drink the tea or eat the cookie. This involvement gradually becomes sociodramatic play, which depends on others for the success of the play episode.

The play of preschoolers is vigorous; they like to chase one another and climb and jump. But they are not usually very interested in games with rules. They need a great deal of support in playing simple games such as Duck, Duck, Goose and have difficulty following rules about turns and procedures.

Early Primary Grades

Kindergartners and first graders engage in sociodramatic play that involves several children in the play episode, and they play without needing the objects they use to be so realistic. A block, for example, can be whatever they need it to be. At this age, fantasy play likely focuses less on home roles and more on roles observed in the community, such as "police officer," or on stories heard or read, such as "Three Billy Goats Gruff."

Practice play and the time spent exploring new objects decrease during the early primary grades until only about 15 percent of play can be labeled as practice (Ellis 1979). Most play of primary-grade children is constructive play, involving building or making something. They like to punch holes with the hole puncher, but they also like to glue the cutouts on a piece of paper to create a design or greeting card. Children may begin their play with the goal of constructing a boat or an airplane. Unlike threes and fours, who just move the materials around, fives and sixes like to have their play result in products.

Games with rules become more important in the play of early primary students. They may believe that the rules are made by some unknown authority and are usually very rigid in enforcing them. Children of this age cannot adapt rules to account for present conditions, such as the number of cards each person gets when playing with different numbers of players. They need adult help in learning to apply and understand rules.

Parents AND Play

- For children in primary grades, plan homework that involves family play, such as thirty minutes of playing a board game or creating a puppet with materials from around the house. For younger children, encourage parents to set aside some time each week to play with their children.

Middle Childhood

Sevens and eights still enjoy constructive play with LEGOS and other construction materials, although they usually play less with blocks than younger children. Less construction play may be observed simply because children have less access to construction materials in the classroom.

The play of older children can often increase their understanding of the subject-matter areas.

Practice play becomes more cognitive as children learn to use their literacy skills to create stories and learn information. Sociodramatic play tends to disappear and be replaced with creative drama, such as acting out stories or scenes. Children in middle childhood may act out historical scenes or create dramas to help them understand scientific facts, such as the molecular behavior of gases, solids, and liquids.

Games with rules dominate the play of sevens and eights. Board games, computer games, and athletic games, such as soccer and baseball, become important parts of the play experience. Children of this age can apply the rules of games more flexibly and can integrate their growing cognitive knowledge and social abilities more easily.

Purposes of Play

Play contributes to cognitive growth, aids social and emotional development, and is essential to physical development. Many of the abilities required to succeed in school settings are gained through play experiences. Eheart and Leavitt (1985) state that play offers young children opportunities "to master many fundamental physical, social, and intellectual skills and concepts" (p. 18). Other researchers have come to similar conclusions about both younger and primary-age children (Garvey 1977; Sylva, Bruner, and Genova 1976).

Parents AND *Play*

■ Emphasize the value of play in your reports to parents. Mention play activities that children especially enjoy in school and what they learn from such play. Select a type of play for each issue of the newsletter, and explain how this play contributes to a child's cognitive, social/emotional, and physical growth.

WWW

Intellectual Development

Both *exploratory play*—play in which the child has no objective other than exploration—and *rule-governed play*—play in which the child has objectives such as finding solutions to problems or determining cause and effect—contribute to cognitive growth. *Cognitive growth* is defined as an increase in the child's basic store of knowledge (Lunzer 1959); it occurs as a result of experiences with objects and people (Piaget 1952b). Many studies support the positive relationship between play experiences and the development of children's cognitive abilities. Cognitive abilities include identifying, classifying, sequencing, observing, discriminating, making predictions, drawing conclusions, comparing, and determining cause-and-effect relationships. These intellectual abilities underlie children's success in all academic areas.

Play helps children develop organizing and problem-solving abilities. Children playing must think about organizing materials in order to meet their play goals. For example, a child who wants to play "visiting the doctor" must decide where the doctor's office and the waiting room will be, what will be used for a stethoscope, and so on. Children must also organize tasks, deciding how to move and arrange materials so that they can play. Some of these organization tasks require very fine discriminations, such as sorting by size, shape, or color. Children playing must also think about the other players involved. Older children playing the roles of characters in books they have read must think about the roles being assumed by other players and take those into consideration when creating their own roles.

Children playing are often engaged in problem-solving behavior. They might experiment with adding water to sand to make it the proper consistency for holding its shape when molded, or they might search the room to find suitable materials for something needed in play. Children playing "riding on the bus," for example, might look for things to use for seats and perhaps something to be the steering wheel of the bus. They might also look for props to serve as tickets and baggage. They might find old purses in the dress-up area to be suitcases or a pie pan to be the steering wheel.

Because they will also need people to participate as passengers, the children playing "riding on the bus" will have to solve the problem of how to persuade enough other children to join the play. Sylva et al. (1976) found that children who played with materials were as capable of solving a problem as children for whom the solution had been demonstrated. Children who play with materials are more likely to assume that there are many possible solutions to a problem and to continue trying to solve a problem longer than children for whom a solution has been demonstrated. Older children as well as younger ones are actively engaged in problem solving when they attempt to create a structure to match the image they plan. For example, children learning about triangles might build structures supported with triangles and test their strength; children learning about hexagons might build dodecahedrons from Popsicle sticks.

Children at play certainly demonstrate creative thinking and creative problem solving. During play, children must put together information from previous experience, from the real world, and from other play participants. Frank (1968) concludes that play "is a way of learning by trial and error to cope with the actual world" (p. 436). In a review of current research on play, Bergen (2001) states that the connection between play and cognitive development is clear for children under age five but is less clear for primary-grade children. Very little research linking play and cognitive development for primary-grade children has been done. It is worrisome to see play time reduced as the push for more academics for younger children gets stronger.

Social and Emotional Development

In the Piagetian view, play pushes children out of **egocentric thought patterns** (Piaget 1962). That is, children in play situations are forced to consider the viewpoints of their playmates and therefore become less egocentric. If Susan and Juan are pretending to cook dinner, each may have definite ideas about how the task should be done. They will each have to accommodate the other's thinking in order to continue their play. Children learn to cooperate to achieve some group goals during play. They also have opportunities during play to learn to delay their own gratification for a few minutes—for instance, while someone else finishes playing with a drum.

Children often play out their fears and concerns. One study reports the reactions of a group of children after they witnessed an accident on their playground and describes how they worked out stress through their play (Brown, Curry, and Tittnich 1971). Children in different age groups (threes, fours, and fives) incorporated the accident into their play differently, but each group revealed some fear and tried to relieve it through "hospital" play or other play involving someone being injured. In another instance, children who had experienced a tornado played various forms of "hiding from the tornado" or "the tornado is coming" for a long time after the experience. Barnett (1984) found that children who were anxious showed reduced anxiety after enacting their fears in play episodes.

Although most teachers are not trained to be play therapists, they can be aware of how children explore different emotions (anger, sadness, and so on) and different social roles in their play. For example, children might "try on" the role of "bully" in a play situation; after they get feedback about how other people react to them in that role, they can alter their behavior.

Physical Development

Children achieve both fine and gross motor control through their play. They can practice all the gross motor skills of running, jumping, and hopping while playing. Children at play can be encouraged to lift, carry, and walk or hop, spin, and move in response to rhythms. They can also practice fine motor skills as they string beads, fit together puzzles, hammer nails into wood, or paint at easels.

Not only young children need active play; older children should participate in this type of play, too. They can throw, catch, kick, bat, balance on two-
wheel bikes, and skate. Today's children often spend a great deal of time in
passive behavior, such as watching television or videos. These children especially need to have the chance to climb, swing, pull, push, run, hop, jump,
and walk in order to gain control of their bodies.

Play in School Settings

Play at school usually differs from play at home in several ways. Generally,
there are larger numbers of children in play groups at school than in play
groups at home. The materials at school are often different from those at
home; only a few children would have access to unit blocks or easels for painting at home. Toys and play materials also differ in the degree to which they
must be shared. In a large group, children must learn to work cooperatively
with others. Some of the differences between play at home and play at school
are summarized in Table 5.2. Thinking of play at home and at school along

Table 5.2   Differences between Play at Home and at School

	Home	School
Peers	Mixed ages Self-selected	Age peers Selection within the group
Group size	Alone or small group	Large group
Materials and equipment	Restricted by expense, space, messiness	Larger selection Less restricted
Guidance and supervision	Guidance often focused on safety	Guides development of specific concepts Models play behaviors Questions about learning
Adult–child interactions	Purchases materials Listens to child's requests Attends to safety issues	Facilitates play Interacts with individual children Determines child's goals
Time commitments	Must fit family schedule Shorter periods	Regularly scheduled time Longer periods
Planning	Guided by family budget "Go play" is common direction	Choices of materials, equipment Evaluation of experience
Space	Typical bedroom, family room, or living room space	Larger spaces for blocks, climbing, etc.

Source: Jo Ann Brewer and Judith Kieff, "Fostering Mutual Respect for Play at Home and School," *Childhood Education* 73 (February 1996/1997): 95.

these dimensions will also help teachers explain to parents why play at school is necessary and not a duplication of children's play at home.

Play is often more restricted at school than at home. Play activities at school tend to be more guided and more closely observed. Teachers are more likely to plan specific ways of enhancing play than are most parents. For example, if the teacher observes a group of children attempting to build a space rocket, he may collect materials from around the room, such as boxes or paints, that will assist the children in achieving their goal. He may also find books in the library, pictures of spacecraft, or websites or videotapes to extend the play to other activities.

Teachers will select play experiences that match the goals of their programs. If program goals emphasize discovery, then free play is most appropriate. If objectives require children to explore concepts, then guided play is most appropriate. Finally, directed play experiences are best if the teacher wants children to demonstrate specific skills. In learning concepts about sound, a child in a free-play situation might discover that he can produce sound by striking a surface. The alert teacher would help the child verbalize his discovery and continue to explore sounds, if he still showed interest. Guided play would be appropriate for teaching children the concept that the pitch of sound varies with the length and size of the string that is vibrated. The teacher might display cigar boxes with rubber bands of various lengths and thicknesses stretched over them. Whenever a child expressed interest in these materials, he would be encouraged to discover the differences in sounds produced by the various rubber bands. In directed play, the teacher might have the children listen to sounds produced by various instruments and indicate with hand movements the changes in pitch.

Van Hoorn et al. (1993) describe play at school as instrumental or illicit. *Instrumental play* is that which the teacher plans and encourages, such as the sociodramatic scenarios of playing "hospital" and "shoe store," described earlier. *Illicit play* is not sanctioned and may even be expressly forbidden by the teacher. Examples of illicit play include children creating guns from Tinkertoys or passing secret notes behind the teacher's back. Although such play may make the teacher uncomfortable, Sutton-Smith (1988) reminds us that it also contributes to a child's developing social skills.

Should illicit play be banned from early childhood classrooms? There are no clear-cut answers to this question. Teachers who try to ban "war" play or "superhero" play realize that children find ways to engage in these activities anyway. It tends to go underground but not stop. The teacher then loses any opportunity to influence children's ideas about violence and how to manage power in a social community (Boyd 1997). The result is more tension and management problems. On the other hand, some educators believe that "war" play stimulates children to believe that violence is an acceptable means of solving problems. "Sociopoliticalists argue that war play and war toys glamorize fighting and killing, promote excessive materialism, and foster unnecessary aggression" (Isenberg and Jalongo 1993, p. 246).

Some teachers recommend redirecting "war" play or "superhero" play to focus on the positive things that soldiers or heroes can do, such as saving people who are trapped by natural disasters or building hospitals to help people who are hurt. Teachers must also help children learn to solve their everyday conflicts peacefully (Rogers and Sharapan 1991). Parents should be involved in making decisions about how to handle "war" toys and other types of violent play in the classroom so that teachers will have their understanding and support.

Play in the Primary Classroom

Most teachers are aware that play is much more acceptable in classrooms of preschoolers and kindergartners than it is in classrooms of primary-grade children. The expectation that only serious learning should take place in primary classrooms is prevalent among parents and also among some teachers. Others believe, however, that play can be serious learning for primary-grade children. Granted, the play of first and second graders does not look like that of preschoolers and kindergartners; nonetheless, many play experiences are appropriate for primary-age children.

For example, children in the primary grades enjoy exploring and building with various materials, creating new machines from old parts, inventing toys, building robots and models, and working out basic physics problems (such as dropping different materials from different heights and measuring the speeds with which they fall). Activities for primary-grade children usually must be based on the children's special interests in order to generate enthusiastic participation, which is not so much the case with preschoolers. Children in primary grades certainly continue to play, although that play may be illicit and hidden from the teacher.

Wasserman (1992) tells stories of the Wright brothers and Frank Lloyd Wright and their early play experiences, "messing about." Sadly, these ingenious and productive individuals, who contributed so much to our knowledge and our lives, often had to stay out of school in order to indulge their curiosities and play. Wasserman asserts that "messing about" is essential for developing children's creative-thinking and problem-solving skills. Teachers should encourage children to discover and explore what really fascinates them, whether that be building with blocks or exploring chemical processes.

Primary-age children are also interested in games with rules and enjoy learning to play a variety of board games. Although this type of play may not provide as many opportunities for exploring problems and creating solutions as "messing about," playing board games can help children develop social and communication skills.

Benefits of Play at School

When play is accepted as a vehicle for carrying forward the curriculum, children can learn organizational skills, develop oral language skills, and learn to

- How does play contribute to a developmentally appropriate program?
- Would it be possible to have a DAP classroom without play? Why?
- Would it be possible to have a play session that was not developmentally appropriate? Why?
- If play is important in developmentally appropriate practice, what are the most effective means of facilitating it?
- Does all play contribute to DAP? What about rough-and-tumble play? Solitary play? Explain your answers.
- What aspects of play that are developmentally appropriate for eight-year-olds would not be appropriate for four-year-olds? Why?

take risks in solving problems (Perlmutter and Burrell 1995). Play that aids children in their development can be achieved at school if teachers provide time, space, materials, and sanction for play activities. Obviously, children need time to plan and carry out play episodes if they are to develop knowledge and skills in play. No child can get organized and complete a satisfying block construction in the ten minutes allotted to play in some classrooms. Christie, Johnson, and Peckover (1988) and Christie and Wardle (1992) found that the play patterns of children in longer play periods were more mature than those of children in shorter play periods. Space and materials are also prerequisites for productive play. Materials such as sand, water, blocks, and paint take up large amounts of space. Teachers may have to arrange the classroom so that the same space is used for different activities during the day.

Sanctioning play is important, as children will pick up subtle hints from the teacher that play is important or not important. One way for the teacher to make sure the children feel that play is important is to join in. It is a real art to know when and how to join in without disrupting the play or changing it to meet adult definitions of appropriate play. Other ways a teacher might indicate that play is important are to talk about play when children evaluate their day and to share the products of play. Often, teachers share and display only the products of work activities, such as drawings or pieces of writing; as a result, children come to believe that play is unimportant in comparison. To validate the importance of play, a teacher might take photographs of block constructions or of children discovering the attributes of water and share these along with artwork and stories.

As children gain experience and maturity, play in the classroom should reflect these changes. Children of different ages and different developmental levels use materials in different ways, so teachers must be alert in providing materials that will challenge the children to develop more in their play. For example, if the housekeeping center for five-year-olds is exactly the same as that for four-year-olds, play in that area by five-year-olds may stagnate. It is the responsibility of the teacher to add materials that will stimulate new play or allow children to play out their fantasies.

Selecting Materials for Play

Teachers have many choices when selecting materials for play. *Open-ended materials*—those that allow multiple outcomes and unique uses in each encounter—are the most useful. Such materials may be fluid materials that have no inherent structure, such as sand and water, or structured materials, such as various forms of blocks. Blocks, sand, and water do not have built-in functions that limit the possible outcomes of playing with them. Therefore, they are conducive to creative thinking and problem solving in children.

Children playing with blocks can create structures that represent their own understandings of the real world or that represent their fantasy worlds. Players can reproduce known structures or design totally new ones; they can control the outcomes and determine when the structure is complete without fear that it will be criticized or rejected. Players with blocks are free to make discoveries about the relationships among the block shapes and sizes and

Open-ended play materials encourage creative thinking and problem solving in children.

about the physics of stacking blocks. These children can experience the aesthetic pleasure of the feel of blocks and the symmetry of their constructions.

Children playing with sand and water are free to explore the properties of the materials and to learn how the materials respond under different conditions. They are in charge of the outcomes and derive satisfaction from playing to meet their own goals. Sand and water allow for individual experimentation and also group interactions. Children using sand and water establish their own goals and feel satisfaction when those goals are met.

Materials that allow children to make play choices and allow multiple outcomes are necessary for the best play environments. Many materials can be considered open ended if it is possible for children to use them in different ways. For example, teachers might supply rollers, boxes, balls, and targets that will help children develop concepts in physical science (Kamii and DeVries 1978). These materials are open ended to the extent that children have choices in exploring the arrangements and outcomes that can be achieved with them. Many commercial materials, on the other hand, are limited in terms of what children are able to do with them, providing only one or two options. When dollars for purchasing materials are limited, open-ended materials are the best investment.

Play as a Teaching Strategy

Teachers have a choice when deciding how to present new information or concepts to children. Some information must be presented in a teacher-directed format. For example, safety rules, such as those about fire, cannot be explored; they must be stated firmly. But generally speaking, *telling* is the least successful strategy for presenting information to young children. Even young children can repeat words or phrases, but verbal responses only indicate that they have learned the words; such responses do not measure children's understanding at all.

Play is one of the **teaching strategies** available to teachers as they plan for children's learning. The following examples illustrate goals that could readily be achieved through play:

- To encourage children to learn about appropriate clothes for the weather, provide many different pieces of clothing in the dress-up area.
- To encourage children to learn how to create secondary colors, provide paints in primary colors.
- To encourage children to demonstrate the ability to classify, provide leaves, shells, keys, buttons, and models of farm and zoo animals.
- To encourage children to learn the characteristics of three-dimensional shapes, provide the shapes in boxes, geoblocks, and regular building blocks.
- To encourage children to learn about water erosion on landforms, provide water in containers (so that the flow can be varied) in the sandbox or gardening area.

An Expert Speaks

Jim Johnson
Pennsylvania State University

"Play" at School

Play has a privileged status in early childhood education (ECE). Indeed, some view play as the "gasoline" needed to get the "engine" of developmentally appropriate curriculum and teaching for young children "all revved up"! Before you step on the accelerator, however, please consider the following precautions.

ECE teachers need to take care to distinguish play from other behaviors that are related to play—but that are not play itself. Consider the difference between play and exploration and the difference between play and imitation. Exploring and playing often go hand in hand. Sometimes you see a child engaged in exploratory play, sometimes in playful exploration. A well-known pattern is the so-called "examine, reexamine, transform (play) cycle." First, a child explores a new object or situation in a general way, then in more specific ways, and then finally begins to act on or change the object to make something different. For example, a child approaches a new puzzle, checking the pieces and board to see how they look and feel, and then investigates particular pieces and the relations among them. Only then will the child begin to engage in the constructive play of putting the puzzle together, or maybe even turning the pieces over and pretending they are something else all together. In either case, playing (what can I do with this?) follows exploring (what is this?).

Imitating and playing are also distinguishable and serve different purposes. A child can playfully imitate another, as in a lighthearted game of copycat. At other times, the child imitates a model, not in a playful way but in earnest, as a way to learn how to do or say something new. In general, quality playing is transformative and generative of new learning or realizations and emanates from within the child acting on and assimilating experiences, whereas imitation is accommodation to external stimulation in order to learn something new or to practice or to repeat what is already known.

Children learn by playing, by exploring, and by imitating, yet the processes and purposes of playing, exploring, and imitating differ. It does not help to lump them all together. If you do, you run the risk of stretching the meaning of play and giving too much credit or blame to play.

Sometimes you hear early educators referring to simplistic slogans such as "play is the business of childhood" or "play is the child's way of learning." The teachers voicing them are perhaps unaware of the important conceptual distinctions noted above. Inadvertently, these teachers are inviting those who are opposed to play in education (and who prefer a nonplay traditional didactic approach) to dismiss the case for the use of play on the grounds that the idea seems too broad and vague to be a valid basis for ECE. Many of these play opponents are already convinced based on seeing too many low-level, unchallenging activities called "play" occur in ECE settings.

Except for pretend play and group games, behaviors at school should be called "activities." Perhaps restricting the use of the word *play* in this way is too radical, that ECE as a profession is not ready for this yet—and maybe never will be or should be. Perhaps it is sufficient to always use the adjective *educational* in front of the word *play*, assuming this expression is only used to refer to high-quality activities. As a way of putting this idea across, please remember that developmentally appropriate and enhancing practices in ECE are not based on low- or even medium-grade, but on high-grade, super-premium "educational play gasoline"!

Using play experiences as teaching strategies requires that the teacher observe how children use materials and that he ask questions to guide children's thinking and reflections. Sutton-Smith (1986) reminds us that

> *although we use play in various ways in the classroom for our own purposes, we need to remember that the children have purposes of their own, and need to deal with purposes largely by themselves (even if under distant supervision), making use of this vital and universal kind of communication [play].* (p. 13)

Teachers can make plans for play experiences, but children's needs must be honored and they must be allowed to use play for their own learning. In other words:

> *Play, then, offers the child the opportunity to make sense out of the world by using available tools. Understanding is created by doing, by doing with others, and by being completely involved in that doing. Through play, the child comes to understand the world and the adult comes to understand the child.* (Chaille and Silvern 1996, p. 277)

Vygotsky's belief that representational play includes rules for behavior is obvious even to untrained observers when they watch children who assign or accept roles and are then chastised if they fail to behave according to those roles. For example, the child playing "dog" cannot go to work nor can the "baby" watch television. As summarized by Berk:

> *From this perspective, the fantasy play of the preschool years is essential for further development of play in middle childhood—specifically, for movement toward game play, which provides additional instruction in setting goals, regulating one's behavior in pursuit of those goals, and subordinating action to rules rather than impulse—in short, for becoming a cooperative and productive member of society. Play, in Vygotsky's theory, is the preeminent educational activity of early childhood.* (1994, p. 33)

Teachers have many opportunities to plan environments and materials so that learning goals can be achieved in playful activities. Observations of children at play will help teachers choose other play materials that will help children learn concepts and clarify and extend their understandings. Selecting guided play as a teaching strategy does not imply that play is assigned; it means that careful thought is put into the selection of materials and intervention in children's play. A teacher might put out an assortment of materials that she expects will invite children to explore a new concept. If children do not learn the concept from interacting with the materials, then the teacher must choose other materials or select a different approach. Assigning a child to complete a task means that he no longer has a choice and that the teacher has chosen a strategy other than play.

Cooper and Dever (2001) found that sociodramatic play was an excellent vehicle for integrating the curriculum. They asked children to choose a theme for the dramatic play area and then used that theme to engage children in writing, oral language development, mathematics, and other content areas. Through their work, the children developed and enjoyed the selected theme.

Thus, teachers must be thoughtful when intervening in children's play and avoid trying to force their own agenda on the children. For example, the teacher can begin to play with a small group and propose a theme for the play, but the children must be allowed to reject that theme or convert it to one following their own interests. The teacher can also assume a role in sociodramatic play, such as the "neighbor coming over for lunch," but such an intervention must be done carefully. Moreover, the teacher will need to think about how to leave the play so that the children can continue on their own (Ward 1996).

Communicating the Benefits of Play

Teachers have an obligation to explain to parents and administrators the benefits of the time children spend playing during the schoolday. Teachers are and should be accountable for children's learning. Part of that responsibility is to be able to provide specific information about individual children and their play experiences. The following section applies specifically to assessment of play; a more comprehensive discussion of assessment is included in Chapter 7.

One form of data to be shared is the *anecdotal record*. With this type of record keeping, the teacher or another adult records the child's behavior and verbalizations for a brief period of time. Judgments about the child's intentions or motivations should be clearly labeled as such in the record and distinguished from descriptions of the child's overt behaviors. At the end of the day, these notes are placed in the child's file. Over a period of time, the notes should reveal some patterns that will help the teacher talk to others about the child's growth through play. For example, the teacher might have noted that Jennifer played alone with the blocks and made horizontal patterns with them. A few weeks later an observer might note that Jennifer had started to use vertical patterns along with the horizontal ones. Later, Jennifer might be seen building a vertical structure with a friend. Still later she might build a vertical and symmetrical structure. An observer might note that Jennifer had talked about her building before she began the construction and completed a structure that matched her plans. These records would clearly reveal Jennifer's growth in building more complex structures and in planning her activities.

Another technique for recording play is to record where the children are in the classroom at given time intervals. For example, every ten minutes the teacher or an adult records on a grid which children are playing with blocks, in dramatic play, in art, or in reading. Over time these records will reveal children's patterns of choice and, in combination with anecdotal records, will be useful in planning other activities. Figure 5.1 is an example of such a record.

A third technique is to keep several checklists scattered throughout the room. As an adult observes a child engaged in particular behavior, he notes it on the record. For example, the following behaviors might be listed across the top of

Figure 5.1

Sample of
Time–Activity
Record

	9:00	9:10	9:20
			Date ___4/17___
Unit blocks	Sara Carlos Hillary Jason	Sara Hillary Brian Michael	Sara Michael Brad Gretchen
Easels	Cheri Karen Phil Juanita	Dolores Cheri Juanita Jason	
Clay			
Dress-up			

the form: "Completes puzzles with 10 pieces," "Strings beads in a pattern," "Plays cooperatively with at least 2 others," and so on. The children's names are listed down the side of the form. Whenever a child is observed completing a puzzle with ten pieces, the date is recorded on the form. Such records are helpful because they offer flexibility in selecting what to look for in observations and make it quick and easy to record information. Figure 5.2 is an example of such a record.

Finally, teachers can keep samples of products from some play activities. Selected paintings, for instance, can be kept in a file for comparison with previous artwork. Obviously, it is impossible to keep samples of block constructions or sand play. Some results of these activities can be recorded in photographs, but most will have to be described in anecdotal records. As children talk about their experiences each day, the teacher can record some of the students' own evaluations. The teacher will also want to add to the child's file her own insights and interpretations of the child's play.

Before a teacher can share what children are learning in play experiences, he must be actively involved while the children are playing. If the teacher is busy doing other tasks while the children are playing, he will miss chances for observations and insights. We cannot share what we haven't seen or heard; therefore, play time is a very busy time for the teacher of young children.

	Completes puzzles with 10 pieces	Strings beads in a pattern	Plays cooperatively with at least 2 others	
Geoffrey				
Judith				
Leslie				
Michael				

Figure 5.2

Sample Record of Behavior

Play and Academic Learning

Sometimes observers of young children think that children will not learn academic skills if they spend their time playing. The truth is that play contributes to the development of academic ability. Children who are ordering objects by length or size in free-play situations, learning rhymes and chants in directed play, or exploring rhythms or constructing with LEGOS in guided play are all involved in activities that contribute to reading ability. Reading is a complex process that involves eye coordination, visual and auditory discrimination, and the cognitive ability to work with parts of wholes. Play is an important means of developing such abilities. Collier (1983) found that play assists the development of representational skills and the formation of the symbolic foundations that are necessary for reading. The following list provides only a few examples of the many kinds of academic learning that are developed during play:

Language Arts

- Develop oral language abilities (vocabulary, language in different situations such as arguing and explaining, and imaginative language)
- Develop visual discrimination skills as they sort, compare, classify
- Develop auditory discrimination skills as they listen to others, explore sounds produced by different materials, engage in musical play

- Create stories for puppets, create signs to use in their play, make books related to their play
- Take the perspective of others
- Develop the fine motor skills needed for writing through painting, drawing, cutting, shaping clay, building with LEGOS, assembling puzzles
- Write as part of the play experience as they take orders at the restaurant, fill out a patient information form at the doctor's office, make signs for their buildings, and so on

Science

- Develop the science skills of observing, making predictions, gathering data, and testing hypotheses
- Learn physics as they build with blocks and learn about stress, mass, and weight
- Learn about simple machines as they experiment with ramps, levers, and gears
- Learn earth science as they play in the sand, observe the weather
- Learn biology as they observe classroom animals and their life cycles
- Learn chemistry as they observe the mixing of materials in a solution, the effect of salt on ice, and the results of the application of heat to various compounds
- Investigate the various consistencies of paint and the results of using these on different kinds of paper with different brushes or painting techniques

Mathematics

- Learn about equal lengths, open and closed spaces, topography, and solid geometric shapes as they play with blocks
- Learn about set theory as they group, sort, and classify
- Learn to compare sets, develop one-to-one correspondence, and solve problems using mathematics (such as counting the pieces needed for each child to play a game)

Primary-age children engaged in project work can be involved in play experiences that will help them consolidate their learning and explore possibilities in given topics. Children learning about seeds can sort, group, and classify seeds; pretend to be sprouting seeds; create board games with facts about seeds; create models of seeds from clay or other materials; paint seeds; use seeds in counting and other mathematics activities; and so forth. Play should not be limited to the preschool years, as it is also an important tool for teaching children in the primary grades (Stone 1995/1996).

In planning for play experiences that enhance the curriculum, teachers must be careful to make play available, not to assign experiences that they perceive as playful. Many playful experiences can be offered that correspond with themes of instruction, such as sorting rocks to accompany a theme of rocks (Stone 1995/1996). If such an experience is provided as a choice and children choose to participate, it is play; however, if the teacher assigns the task, it is not play. As mentioned earlier, one of the criteria for determining whether an activity is play is the element of choice. If choice is not present, then by definition the activity is not play.

Children understand this. Consider how often children classify what they do at school as "play" or "work." The usual definition is that *work* is something assigned by the teacher, although older children may say it was *play* if it was fun (Perlmutter and Burrell 1995).

Outdoor Play

Outdoor play offers children many opportunities to solve intellectual problems, such as how to make the water flow down the rows in the garden, and also how to solve social and emotional problems. Children on the playground have many opportunities to problem-solve ways to move from one place to another, ways to use various materials, and ways to help other children achieve their goals (Rivkin 2001). Children playing outdoors often have more freedom than is typical of indoor play. Many teachers have observed that leadership in play activities is more readily observable outdoors than in the small-group play in a classroom. Thompson, Knudson, and Wilson (1997) found that recess provided for social growth. They held group meetings to help children learn to solve problems, to interact more successfully with their peers, and to negotiate with their classmates more successfully. Even though some schools have reduced or eliminated recess, teachers of young children should remind administrators that it is not developmentally appropriate to do so and should provide them with good reasons why children need to play outdoors.

In order to be productive, outdoor play needs the planning, observation, and evaluation accorded to indoor play. Outdoor play may offer benefits that are not available in the classroom, such as large muscle activities and less teacher control of shouting, running, jumping, rolling, and climbing. These activities can be encouraged outdoors where the children will be safe and other children will not be in danger, as they might be indoors. Theemes (1999) describes the benefits of outdoor play as "contact with nature, opportunities for social play, and freedom of movement and active physical play" (p. 4).

Many indoor activities can be brought outdoors, given the right materials. For example, children might set up easels and paint pictures outdoors, or they might use water to "paint" buildings and sidewalks, using big brushes that encourage large, sweeping strokes. Children might enjoy block building outdoors when provided with large plastic or weatherproof blocks, ramps, ladders, and other equipment. Such materials lend themselves to building structures that are large enough for children to get inside.

Although teachers of young children often discourage or forbid rough-and-tumble play because they believe it turns into negative or aggressive behavior, research reveals that such play is age related. Specifically, the incidence of rough-and-tumble play increases as children move from preschool into kindergarten and the primary years and then decreases as children reach middle childhood (Kostelnik et al. 1993). Other research shows that children who are typically rejected by their peers are more likely to misinterpret rough-and-tumble play and to participate aggressively. Popular children, on the other hand, are more likely to participate in a playful, unaggressive manner (Pellegrini and Boyd 1993). Teachers should be aware that rough-and-tumble play is developmental in children's play lives. When such play becomes aggressive, teachers should intervene and help children modify inappropriate behavior (Bergen 1994; Carlsson-Paige and Levin 1995).

Ideally, children should be able to play either indoors or out. However, lack of supervision and the fact that few schools have outdoor play areas connected to classrooms make such choices difficult.

Parents AND *Play*

■ Provide parents with information about the importance of outdoor play, and ask them to help you make sure that recess and other outdoor play times are not reduced or eliminated in your school.

Children with Special Needs

Planning play experiences for children with special needs may require some adaptations to the playground and/or to the materials used. The suggested adaptations in Figure 5.3 will be helpful as you plan for outdoor experiences for all children.

As with planning for any successful experience, you will need to think about individual children and their needs in order to plan adequately. However, making outdoor play accessible to all children will be worth the time and effort that it takes.

Celebrating Diversity

Play is a part of every culture, but there are cultural variations in how children participate in play and at what ages they are expected to play in certain ways. Some families may believe that play is not appropriate at school, and therefore their children may play in less complex ways (Kieff and Casbergue 2000). Other children may not recognize the play materials offered if they have no experience with the materials or the materials are arranged in new ways. Researchers suggest that the themes of dramatic or pretend play vary by culture. For example, Farver and Shin (1997) found that Korean American children

Play experiences must be carefully planned to meet the special needs of all children.

played more everyday activities compared to Anglo American children, who played more fantasy and suspected danger in the environment. The Korean American children also used more polite requests and fewer commands than their Anglo American playmates.

Teachers should think about culturally appropriate play materials such as dress-up clothing, musical instruments, and household items. In addition, teachers should recognize language differences that may be significant in play. Heath (1983) reported that different cultural and socioeconomic groups used language differently with their children and expected different language production from them. Of the various groups, the African American group was much more likely to expect their children to learn how to tease others verbally. Given this, some verbal teasing will probably be an important part of the play of some African American children. Teachers should accept this play and help children learn other play interactions without trying to prohibit the verbal teasing or thinking the children are being disrespectful.

Chapter Summary

■ Play in the school setting can be defined on a continuum that runs from free play to guided play to directed play. *Free play* is defined as behavior that is personally motivated, active, and pleasurable and that has no extrinsic goals or rules that cannot be negotiated by the players; free play is often nonliteral, and players bring their own meanings to the play experience. *Guided play* is play in which the teacher has selected materials from which the children may choose in order to discover specific concepts. *Directed play* is play in which the teacher instructs the children in how to accomplish specific tasks.

Figure 5.3   Adaptations for Children with Special Needs

POSSIBLE ADAPTATIONS

. . . for the child who is blind or has low vision

- Orient the child to the major playground features (e.g., the walkway, climbing equipment, water table, sandbox, garden, and fence) that can be used as points of reference. Take a tour of the playground. With adult supervision, a sighted friend can assist the child by offering her arm/elbow to guide the child who is blind.

- Describe what is happening in different areas to help the child who is blind find her friends and join in their play. When the child enters the playground, tell her which children are playing on the climbing structure, which are in the sandbox, and which are gardening or playing on riding toys.

- Use the child's name when verbally directing activities, as he will not be able to see a physical gesture such as pointing.

- Make certain the walking space is free from toys left unattended or other potential falling hazards.

- Mark the location of different outdoor areas or structures with audible cues. Different types of wind chimes or bells can help a child locate a particular area. For example, hang a wind chime from a tree branch above the sandbox. At first, physically assist the child to move into a desired area. Gradually decrease physical assistance and use verbal prompts to direct the child.

- Place toys underneath the child's hands to encourage exploration rather than pulling the child's hands forward to touch or hold the toys.

- Provide outdoor toys that use the senses of hearing, touch, smell, and movement and encourage activities that other children enjoy. Toys that address the sense of hearing are balls that beep or have noise-makers inside. Toys and materials that promote exploration through touch are those with interesting textures such as Koosh balls and bumpy balls. Smell can be incorporated into many materials by adding extracts/flavorings to paints and water. Movement can be experienced through swinging. Additional support to ensure safety and comfort may include the use of an adaptive swing.

. . . for the child who is deaf or has hearing loss

- Obtain a child's attention through touch or gestures before giving a direction.

- Make sure the child can see your face and your lips with no shadows obscuring them when giving directions. Be sure the child who is deaf and the other children are positioned so that their faces and gestures can be easily seen by one another.

- Use gestures, prompts, and visual cues to communicate information. Gestures may include pointing and sign language. Prompts may include physically assisting. Visual cues may include the use of concrete materials and modeling (e.g., demonstrating digging with a shovel in the garden).

- Learn basic signs and teach them to the other children if sign language is the child's mode of communication.

- Make sure that the child can see most areas of the playground from any given spot. Remove extraneous walls, fences, or hedges that might block her view of the other children's play and further isolate her.

- Provide outdoor toys and materials that use the other senses available to the child, including touch, smell, and movement, and encourage activities that other children enjoy.

. . . for the child who has physical challenges

- Position a child with physical challenges so that he can achieve maximum range of motion, muscle control, and visual contact with materials and other children. A child may need to lie on his side or use a bolster to access materials and interact with other children during activities such as gardening and painting.

- Furnish specifically adapted play and recreation equipment when necessary. This may include modified swings, tricycles, and tables for independent participation in activities.

- Encourage the child to use her own means of getting around—whether a wheelchair, walker, or scooter—to participate in the activities and games of the other children.

- Provide activities for the lower body and feet, such as foot painting, splashing in a wading pool, digging in the garden or sand, and kicking a ball, for a child with limited use of his hands and upper body.
- Provide activities including painting, water table, sandbox, and gardening that a child with limited use of her feet, legs, and lower body can do independently and successfully with her upper body. Always ensure correct positioning of the child's torso.
- Increase the width of balance beams and modify slippery surfaces to support better balance.
- Use softer balls (e.g., foam balls) or lightweight objects to facilitate throwing and catching when a child lacks strength and endurance.
- Use large balls (e.g., beach balls) and other large objects to make catching easier for a child who is unable to grasp smaller objects.

. . . for the child who has autism spectrum disorder

- Be aware of situations and events, such as inconsistent and unstructured environments, new situations, overstimulation, and internal changes including illness or extreme fatigue, that may trigger undesired behaviors.
- Make sure the child is aware of playground modifications prior to experiencing the change. For example, if a flat-bottomed swing is removed from the swinging tree and a tire is put in its place, tell the child ahead of time about the change. Show her a picture of the new swing and describe it before going out onto the playground. If the child is willing, accompany her to the new swing and allow her to touch it, push it, and perhaps take a turn at swinging on it.
- Limit the number of outside rules, communicate them clearly and in multiple ways, and enforce them firmly, kindly, and consistently.
- Provide extra support during new or difficult tasks and break playground activities into simple, sequential steps.
- Increase predictability and consistency in outside routines and prepare the child for what comes next through verbal and concrete prompts. For example, put a ball in a child's hand to indicate it is time to go outside while simultaneously using words to describe the next change. When it is time to transition inside, ring a bell on the playground, tell the child it is time to go inside, and put an inside toy in his hands to carry.

- Include repetition and modeling when giving directions to children who have difficulty with perception and sensory input.
- Provide structured activities that are away from distractions for children who have difficulty paying attention or controlling bodily movements.
- Organize sections of the playground that provide physical boundaries for the child. These may include a tunnel, large barrel, tent, or huge cardboard box made into a playhouse.
- Include pets in the outside play area. Some children may interact with pets before they will interact with people. Including pets in the outside play area allows children to touch the animals, feed and water them, clean their cages, and be responsible for their welfare.

. . . for the child who has cognitive delays

- Keep vocabulary at the child's level and sentence structure simple.
- Remind the child of the various types of play activities available and offer choices rather than determining places for the child to play.
- Adapt materials or vary the difficulty of an activity so that the child can succeed. For example, modify or shorten an obstacle course to encourage independent, successful completion.
- Lead the children in noncompetitive games so that the child can feel successful and enjoy her individual achievements.
- Reduce the number of concepts presented at one time.
- Use repetition and examples to explain an idea.
- Teachers, family members, and other team members should determine the most appropriate modifications for each child. . . . Not all activities require modifications. Adaptations are used only when necessary to support the child's optimal level of outside play.

Source: Linda L. Flynn and Judith Kieff, "Including Everyone in Outdoor Play," *Young Children* 57 (May 2002): 20–26. Reprinted with permission from the National Association for the Education of Young Children.

- Play contributes to the development of gross and fine motor skills, to cognitive growth, and to social and emotional development. In playing, children strengthen many problem-solving abilities, learn to express emotions in socially acceptable ways, and learn the social skills necessary for success in groups.

- Play can be described in terms of how the player interacts with other people. Play can be solitary play, onlooker play, parallel play, associative play, and cooperative play.

- Observers of children's play have noted developmental trends in play behaviors. Younger children exhibit much more exploratory play, preschoolers engage in sociodramatic play and constructive play, and elementary-age children are most likely to be involved in games with rules.

- Play in a school setting and play at home usually differ in terms of the guidance offered, materials available, and number of children involved in the play situations.

- Play contributes to academic achievement. Teachers who are concerned with academic success do not have to force children to give up play in order to gain abilities in math, science, and reading.

- Teachers have a very complex role in children's play. Teachers must observe, plan, and evaluate play experiences. They must also plan learning experiences that are best achieved through play. Finally, they must learn to communicate the benefits of children's play to parents and administrators.

- Carefully planned outdoor play experiences can provide many of the same benefits of indoor play and often allow more freedom for children than play indoors.

- Planning play experiences for children with special needs may include adapting the physical environment; special instruction in play skills may also be necessary. Children who are developmentally delayed may exhibit play behaviors that are typical of much younger children.

Theory INTO *Practice*

Observe the play of three-year-olds, five-year-olds, and seven-year-olds for an hour each, and record your observations. Label your observations using the levels of social play defined by Parten in Table 5.1. What is the most frequent level of play for each age group? How much time is spent in each kind of play for each of the three groups? If there are differences among the groups, how do you explain them?

Interview three children: one each age three, five, and eight. Ask them to tell you what they like to play. Do their answers match the developmental trends described in this chapter? If not, why do you think they differ? What implications does this knowledge have for planning classroom experiences?

Use a chart similar to the one in Figure 5.1 to record the number of children of each sex in each play area. Record your observations at ten-minute intervals for an hour. Discuss your findings with your group. Does the information suggest that changes should be made in the available play materials? Is intervention needed to address the play behavior of an individual child?

For half an hour each, observe a group of children playing indoors and then playing outdoors. What differences, if any, in play behaviors can you identify in the two settings? If you observed differences, can you explain them? Do the same children take leadership roles inside and outside? Are the children consistent in their play behaviors inside and outside (quiet and passive, rowdy and loud, and so on)?

Create a brochure for parents that explains the benefits of play for children. Discuss growth in physical, cognitive, and social/emotional areas, and offer practical examples for illustration.

Respecting Children's Play

Respecting the complexity, value, and form in children's play takes much more from adults than just making time in the daily schedule for play to take place. Respecting children's play implies that we, as teachers, do not know all of the answers and that children can be counted on for some of these answers. Respect also implies children's right to privacy.

> It is true that if we are interested in children we must look to them and listen to them as a matter of course. And as we pay attention to their play, we must never violate its complexity by presuming to "decode" or oversimplify it. (Koste 1987, p. 44)

In my pre-K classroom, children learn by playing. Watching four- and five-year-olds play allows me to expand on their interests, their knowledge, and their play. Watching children play on the playground and providing them with different balls, bats, and/or building tools enables me to facilitate learning and enables the children to build new knowledge on their existing knowledge. Watching children interact in the dramatic play center and providing new and different props allows me to extend students' language and play without "telling" them what to do. Being the audience in a library corner as children act out their favorite story using puppets, costumes, or flannelboard pieces allows children to demonstrate their knowledge in a playful manner and gives me the opportunity to talk with them about the story. Paying attention to my students, their individual interests, and their varied skills allows me to build on what they know in supportive ways, fostering a love of learning in every student.

Assessing children's play by observing, taking anecdotal records, videotaping, and taking photographs allows me to give parents accurate information about the nature of their children's play and opportunities to extend play in my classroom. I observe my students interacting with each other and often initiate games with them; then I back away and observe them continue to play these games. I take anecdotal records daily on computer labels that I can file in each child's folder. This enables me to look at each child every day and compile an ongoing record of the child's play behaviors. Using videotapes and photographs is the best way that I have found to bring the classroom home. Parents enjoy seeing their children in action, and often these forms of assessment provide insight into how much learning is accomplished through play. Assessment is key when it comes to helping parents value play as an avenue for learning in the classroom.

I feel that we must respect our children's play and trust them to learn from their play. I see it as my job as a pre-K teacher to show parents how important play is to their children, and the most effective way to do this is through sharing my observations and talking with parents about what their child is learning as he or she is playing.

CHAPTER 6

Guiding Behavior through Encouraging Self-Control

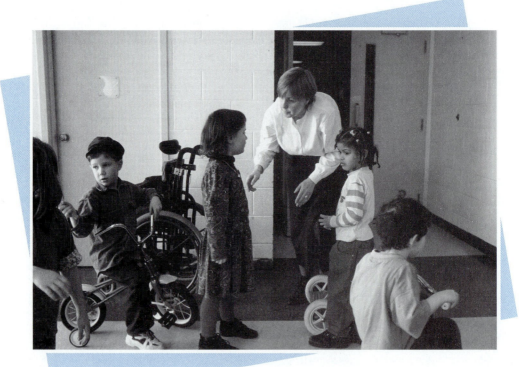

After reading this chapter, you will be able to do the following:

- Define the term *discipline*.
- Plan for discipline that enhances self-concept.
- Evaluate behavior-management systems.
- Plan strategies for both individual and group guidance.
- Plan discipline that is appropriate for children with special needs.
- Plan discipline that is appropriate for children from diverse backgrounds.

Your most recent observation assignment was to look at discipline strategies in the classroom. You were excited about this observation because all your classmates had been worrying about how they were going to control the behavior of the children in their charge more than they worried about any other element of teaching. You have also noticed how often discipline is a topic in journals for teachers and how many sessions at conferences for teachers of young children focus on the topic of discipline, so you know that even experienced teachers have concerns about classroom discipline.

You chose to visit a first-grade classroom. When you entered the classroom, you could not find the teacher for a few minutes. He was helping a small group of children with their plans to construct a display of what they had learned about penguins. In the two hours you spent in the classroom, the only interaction you would have called discipline was when the teacher reminded one youngster to remember that other people needed to hear and that he needed to use a quieter voice when speaking to his partner. You were thinking that discipline was highly overrated as a problem.

Discussion with your peers after the observation made it clear that other people had not shared your experience. Some people reported that they had observed teachers who made a checkmark beside the child's name if the child disobeyed a rule. This system had been adopted by the entire school. Another observed a chart with each child's name and a pocket, like those in library books, under the name. If the child was being good, a card with a green dot was under his or her name; if they had committed one infraction of the rules, their card had a yellow dot; and if they had more than one infraction, the dot was red. A red dot meant that the child was not allowed to participate in recess or any other class activity that was not academic work. Other students reported that they had observed a "time-out" chair where students were asked to sit if they misbehaved.

Discipline was the topic of a lively discussion with your peers, and you know that it will continue to be an important issue.

Guidance, Discipline, and Punishment

Discipline and **punishment** are not synonymous terms. Often, members of the public and even teachers use the word *discipline* when what they are referring to is *punishment* designed to enforce obedience to those in authority. Table 6.1 contrasts discipline and punishment.

The title of this chapter uses the word *guiding* because the best discipline consists of guiding children in developmentally appropriate ways to achieve self-control and eventually become self-disciplined individuals. Guidance is not punishment—it is helping children learn. Teachers must consider carefully how to guide and discipline children's behavior. Just as teachers would think about children's needs and developmental levels in planning for growth in literacy or any subject-matter area, they must think about how children can best learn to achieve self-control.

Corporal punishment is physical punishment; when the term is used in schools, it almost always refers to spanking. Ramsburg (1997) has reviewed the research on spanking and concluded that other disciplinary alternatives are more beneficial to children than corporal punishment. The Association for Childhood Education International issued a position paper supporting a ban on corporal punishment (Cryan 1987). The paper traces the historical and legal perspectives on corporal punishment and then briefly cites the research on the effects of such punishment. The effects are so negative, especially over the long term, that it is clear that corporal punishment is not an effective method of discipline and does not help children learn self-control.

Table 6.1   Discipline versus Punishment

Discipline	Punishment
Children are *disciplined* when . . .	Children are *punished* when . . .
they are shown positive alternatives rather than just told "no" . . .	their behavior is controlled through fear . . .
they see how their actions affect others . . .	their feelings are not respected . . .
good behavior is rewarded . . .	they behave to avoid a penalty or get a bribe . . .
adults establish fair, simple rules and enforce them consistently.	the adult only tells them what not to do.
Children who are disciplined . . .	Children who are punished . . .
learn to share and cooperate . . .	feel humiliated . . .
are better able to handle their own anger . . .	hide their mistakes . . .
are more self-disciplined . . .	tend to be angry and aggressive . . .
feel successful and in control of themselves.	fail to develop control of themselves.

Source: From *Helping Children Learn Self-Control* (brochure). (Washington, DC: National Association for the Education of Young Children, 1986). Reprinted with permission from the National Association for the Education of Young Children.

Punishment is not always corporal punishment, however. Children can be punished by being confined to their rooms, by having privileges restricted, or by a variety of other means. Some punishments are natural consequences of behavior. If a child breaks the crayons, then he will not have any when he wants to draw. If a child bullies her friends, no one will want to play with her. A later section of the chapter will discuss the use of natural consequences in a system of discipline (see "Dreikurs Model"). This section covers a punishment commonly meted out by early childhood teachers to control children's behavior: being confined to the "time-out" chair.

Time Out

The original theory behind *time out* was sound: Taking time out gives children an opportunity to gain control of their own behavior and to choose when they are ready to return to the group. Unfortunately, that is not the way time out is used in most classrooms. In many classrooms, the time-out chair is clearly punishment that is overused to obtain obedience. Betz (1994) states that he has "seen it misused so often that it has become unbearably trivialized" (p. 11).

Although many experts in early childhood education have criticized the use of time out as a discipline strategy (Betz 1994; Katz 1984; Miller 1984), many teachers continue to use it. Gartrell (2001, 2002) suggests that teachers replace time out with strategies focused on building an "encouraging classroom." He suggests that teachers begin by using the four guidance basics of conflict management, class meetings, guidance talk, and comprehensive guidance. Conflict management is used when there are two or more children involved and class meetings are employed when a conflict may affect the whole class. Guidance talk is used for dealing with conflicts with the adult or when additional work is needed after a conflict is solved. The steps Gartrell (2002) recommends in comprehensive guidance are the following five:

1. *Cool down*—The teacher and all the children involved take a few minutes to cool down as preparation for talking.
2. *Identify the problem*—The children agree on what the problem is and put it into words (they may need help doing this).
3. *Brainstorm solutions*—Children come up with possible solutions (they may need help here, too).
4. *Go for it*—The solution is tried.
5. *Follow-up*—The teacher continues to monitor, encourage, and guide the children involved.

The work of guidance is important in helping children learn how to handle conflicts and disappointments. Children have to be taught what to do when faced with conflicts, and punishing them, with or without a time-out chair, does not teach them what to do the next time.

Punishment may stop a behavior temporarily, but it may also interfere with teaching children appropriate behavior (Schickedanz, Schickedanz, and Forsyth 1982). Punishment may reduce children's initiative if they do not know which behaviors will be punished, and it may result in children's avoiding new situations in order to avoid punishment (Clewett 1988).

Discipline is important—how teachers respond to children's behavior is crucial in helping them grow and feel competent. No one would suggest that discipline be ignored; chaos in the classroom is not healthy for children or for teachers. Neither would anyone be naive enough to suggest that discipline is easy.

There are no clear-cut rules to follow, because every situation and every child are different. The same behavior from two different children might (and probably should) elicit different responses from the same teacher. So much depends on the child's age, development, previous experience, and present situation that no rules will ever apply to all situations. Good discipline helps children gain self-esteem, learn to be cooperative, and gradually learn the skills necessary for taking responsibility for their own behavior.

Teachers and Discipline

Every teacher has faced or will face situations in which children's behavior is inappropriate or hurtful. It would be unrealistic to expect children who are still growing and learning to behave in ways that always please the other people around them. A professional teacher knows that some behavior management will be required when working with children and thinks about how different situations can be handled most successfully.

Parents AND Guiding Behavior

■ Make sure that parents are aware of your program goals in terms of developing appropriate social skills, and highlight the guidance strategies that lead to achievement of those goals.

Teachers must consider the long-term effects on children's self-esteem rather than just the immediate results when making discipline decisions. Teachers must also think of discipline situations as teaching opportunities—opportunities to help children learn how to solve problems, how to negotiate differences, how to handle frustrations, and so on. Effective discipline requires thinking and planning, not only to prevent problems but also to prepare reactions that will be most appropriate when problems do occur.

A knowledgeable teacher also understands what is normal behavior for children of different ages and does not have unrealistic expectations. For example, very young children may scream or throw tantrums; four-year-olds may use foul language; five-year-olds may call each other cruel names; and eight-year-olds may form tight groups that gang up on outsiders. Children in one kindergarten class were often punished for lying. A sound knowledge of child development would have helped the teacher understand that many five-year-olds do not have well-developed concepts of truth and that most will deny any deed to protect themselves. Teachers have to think about what lying and other behaviors mean to the children they are teaching.

Guiding the behavior of young children is related to building self-concept, to curriculum planning and organization, and to teachers' beliefs about how children learn best. Guidance requires that teachers make decisions about individual and group behaviors. In some teaching situations, guidance may also require that teachers make decisions about discipline plans that are adopted by the school. The goal of all of this decision making is to plan carefully in order to prevent as many problems as possible.

The following scenarios illustrate the difference between a teacher who focuses on guidance and one who focuses on punishment. Assume that the children are four to five and that the teachers know Tommy and Susan well.

Scenario 1

Tommy throws a block and hits Susan on the leg.

Teacher A sends Tommy to the time-out chair and tells him he must sit there until she tells him to get up. He is instructed to think about his behavior and how the block hurt Susan.

Teacher B removes Tommy from the blocks area and discusses with him the rule against throwing blocks, emphasizing the reason for that rule. If Tommy threw the block in anger, then she helps him think of acceptable outlets for his anger. If he threw the block to see how far he could throw it, she may help him think of better materials to throw and places to throw them. The teacher helps Tommy understand that Susan was hurt by the block. She helps him make a decision about what to do now in terms of behavior.

Scenario 2

Susan yells words that are deemed unacceptable in the classroom.

Teacher A removes Susan from the classroom and puts her in a chair in the hall for fifteen minutes with instructions to think about her behavior.

Teacher B moves close to Susan and tries to determine why she used inappropriate language: Was she angry at another child? Frustrated by her inability to complete some task? Playing a role? Depending on the reason for the outburst, the teacher will ask Susan to find more acceptable words to express her anger, help her think of what to do when she is frustrated (ask for help, choose another play material, and so on), or help her think about other words that a character might use.

In sum, neither teacher ignores inappropriate behavior nor lets it continue. But Teacher A's approach is to punish without teaching, which will not help the children make better decisions in the next situations. Discipline, when interpreted as *guidance,* focuses on teaching children what to do and helping them make better choices in the future.

Guidance and Self-Concept

WWW

Self-concept is a broad term usually referring to the "perceptions, feelings, and attitudes that a person has about himself or herself" (Marshall 1989, p. 45). Self-concept includes perceptions of our physical characteristics, gender, personality traits, ethnic identity, and so on. *Self-esteem* is a much more specific concept that refers to feelings of self-worth. Most of these perceptions are shaped initially by our parents and other significant adults. As children mature, their self-esteem is shaped more and more by their evaluation of the responses of their peers.

High self-esteem is developed when children believe that significant people in their lives view them as valuable and worthwhile. Self-esteem is also increased when children feel competent, capable, and in control. High self-esteem is important; research has shown that low self-esteem is related to a number of problems, including lack of academic achievement, delinquent behavior, and poor mental health (Zigler and Finn-Stevenson 1987).

Cordell (1999) believes that self-esteem can be raised in children through help from teachers. Some hallmarks of high self-esteem are the ability to begin and maintain friendships, engage in laughter and joking, effectively join group activities, end conversations appropriately, and relate effectively to different types of people. For younger children, teachers will need to model appropriate behaviors and guide children toward these competencies. For example, helping a child learn how to enter a group can be accomplished through role-playing, puppet plays, and modeling followed by discussion. Some children can relate to different kinds of people seemingly without effort, while others need help addressing what people might expect from them. Again, teachers may need to model and discuss or role-play situations so that children can learn appropriate behaviors. Teachers must also keep in mind the developmental appropriateness of their instruction. A child may understand that other people have feelings and be able to label those feelings without being able to relate the feelings of others to the social context.

NAEYC

Discipline that encourages the development of self-esteem is marked by several principles: giving children choices, demonstrating natural and logical consequences, ensuring follow-through, and encouraging problem solving. Children can be given choices when two (or more) acceptable responses are available. For instance, a child might be guided to choose to play in another area or to play alone if he is having trouble in his current location. A child who is throwing the sand from the sand table on the floor might be asked to clean up the sand. The teacher must follow through on this request, however, or the child will not see the need to respond as asked. Most important, children need to learn how to solve their own problems. Successful problem solving leads to children's confidence in their abilities and more empathetic responses to the feelings of others (Eaton 1997).

In a classic study, Sears (1970) found that children of parents who were authoritative (as opposed to authoritarian or permissive) had more positive self-concepts. *Authoritative* parents are in charge but do not make unreasonable demands; provide reasons for expecting given behaviors rather than asserting their authority; and help children make decisions about behavior. *Authoritarian* parents demand obedience because of their authority position, and *permissive* parents fail to set and enforce limits for their children.

Parents AND *Guiding Behavior*

■ Talk with parents about the growth of their child in terms of self-control as well as academics.

■ Help parents appreciate the positive qualities of their child's behavior.

Social context is extremely important in children's development of self-concept. Caregiver responsiveness can help children learn that they are valuable and that they can influence their environment. Freedom to explore the physical environment and materials that provide children with challenges and successes are also important (Bredekamp 1987). Play can help children learn to delay gratification and deal with frustrations (Cordell 1999).

For the early childhood teacher, several implications arise from the research on self-concept. One is that children need to feel competent; teachers must select materials and experiences thoughtfully to ensure both challenges and successes. Another implication is that children need to feel in control; therefore, as much of the day as possible should be spent in self-selected activities. Finally, teachers should approach discipline from an authoritative point of view, not an authoritarian or a permissive point of view.

Guidance and Curriculum Planning

Often, when teachers are having discipline problems, they look at the children to determine what is wrong with them. At times, teachers may need to look at the *programs* instead, to see if they are meeting children's needs—not just academic needs, but also social, emotional, and physical needs.

Preschool children need an environment in which they are safe to explore, in which they have enough materials to minimize conflicts, and in which they face few demands to sit still or attend to teacher-directed instruction. Primary children also need to be able to move about the room and to have activities available that are interesting and appropriate for their level of development. Both age groups need a minimum number of rules. Nothing is harder than trying to make a group of children do something that is inappropriate for their level of development *and* be good while they are doing it. Appropriate curriculum activities, room arrangements, and routines will help prevent many discipline problems.

NAEYC

Curriculum activities need to be interesting and engaging for children. When caught in dull or boring situations, adults can play mental games, plan what they are going to do later, do something else (as when college students study for upcoming tests during boring lectures), or at least pretend not to be bored (as when employees chat politely with the boss at a dull office party). But children simply do not have the skills to look attentive while they are doing something else. When bored or frustrated, they pinch their neighbors,

Taking part in interesting and engaging activities will offset the boredom that often leads children to misbehave.

fall out of their chairs, or get out of their seats. In one second-grade classroom, two children were disrupting the teacher's lesson on the basic food groups. Their behavior resulted in being removed from the classroom. Later, the teacher admitted that these boys were gifted and already knew all the information being presented. If the curriculum had been more individualized, these two boys would have done their own experiment involving food, which would have engaged them intellectually and eliminated their disruptions and the need for punishment.

In addition to examining curriculum activities for appropriateness, teachers also need to examine materials and classroom arrangements. If, for example, only two wheel toys are available for a large group of children, there will be disputes because of the unreasonable amount of time children must wait for a turn. Similar problems will arise if there are not enough blocks for several children to be building with them at one time. Children become extremely frustrated when they start a project and then find they do not have enough materials to complete it or when storage areas are so congested and unorganized that they cannot get the materials they need.

Room arrangements are also important in preventing discipline problems. If the blocks are in an area through which children must walk to get from one part of the room to another, the teacher will spend an inordinate amount of time mediating disputes over toppled structures. In primary classrooms, the pencil sharpener often seems to be a source of contention. The pencil sharpener should be located where users will not disturb other children and disrupt the class as little as possible yet allow children to sharpen their pencils when needed. Nagging and making rules about such little things as using the pencil sharpener seems a waste of teacher energy in comparison to the time it would take to prevent the problem in the first place.

One technique to discover traffic patterns or areas of congestion is to make a map of children's movements. The teacher should make a copy of the floorplan of the classroom and draw lines to show the paths children take during given five-minute periods; observations should be repeated every thirty minutes to show patterns throughout the day. These traffic maps will help teachers make decisions about where to locate storage and program areas.

The arrangement of the classroom space should also make it possible for the teacher to scan the room frequently in order to deal with problems before they escalate. For example, if the teacher sees too many children playing in the housekeeping corner, she should redirect some of them into another activity. Perhaps this is the time to get out some new materials and encourage several children to use them. If the number of children in the housekeeping center continues to be too large, a more lasting solution may be needed. If the teacher sees the children are getting too rowdy for indoor play, she should move to the area and help the children regain self-control by offering play suggestions for quieter activities. For example, she might ask two or three children to join her in a plan for building a robot at the art center.

Large, open spaces sometimes invite children to run or to get more exuberant than the teacher would like. To avoid this, the classroom furniture can be arranged so as to break up the large spaces into several smaller spaces. Bookshelves on wheels and lightweight tables can be moved easily if a larger space is needed at another time of the day.

Once the teacher has examined the curriculum and the room arrangements in an effort to prevent problems, another step is to establish routines so

This watchful teacher is silently making sure that children take turns on the playground equipment.

*Reflect on the connections between discipline and
developmentally appropriate practice as you respond
to the following questions:*

NAEYC

- Can discipline be developmentally appropriate if it is not based on understanding the child and what is normal behavior for her given stage of development? Why?

- Should a system of discipline be instituted without considering the match between the child and the curriculum? Can discipline be appropriate if the curriculum is not? Explain your answers.

- Discipline must be considered as an opportunity for teaching. If it is not, can it be developmentally appropriate? Why?

- If you read about a conference presentation called "Developmentally Appropriate Discipline," what information would you expect to be covered?

that children feel safe and know what to expect. We would all be exhausted if we had to start from scratch to organize our time each day. We know that most of what we do is routine, and we do not have to put energy into deciding about most of our activities (eating, working, sleeping, and so on). Children also need routines in which activities are predictable but not rigidly set. Children need to know that there will be play time, snack time, outdoor play time, and other basic elements in their day. A mentally healthy person can change daily routines without undue stress. When they are secure about basic routines, children, too, can adjust to changes—the arrival of a guest speaker, a field trip, and so on. Complete lack of routine, however, leads to frustration, insecurities, and behavior problems.

Teachers might also need to examine their attitudes and feelings about autonomy and what constitutes obedient behavior from children. Kamii (1982) describes *autonomy* as the ability to make decisions for ourselves. She believes that schools generally reinforce children when they obey without thinking and therefore "unwittingly prevent them from developing autonomy" (p. 85). Having autonomy does not mean that children do not have to obey rules or respect other people and their property. It does mean that children learn to make decisions and think clearly about their behavior and their learning.

Guidance and Beliefs about Learning

Teachers who advocate a constructivist approach in explaining how children best learn content material will also advocate a constructivist view of guiding behavior. That means that teachers will think about the role of errors in children's learning to control their behavior just as they would think about errors in children's learning to speak, read, and compute. Strategies such as providing demonstration, modeling, and giving specific feedback will be as appropriate in helping children learn self-control as they are in helping them learn content. And as with content material, teachers have to make decisions about what can be learned at the children's developmental stage and what teaching strategies will be most effective in achieving the desired behavior. For example, if a two-year-old grabs a toy from another child, the most appropriate reaction might be to offer the first child another toy, and explain gently that he cannot take things from others without their permission. However, if a four-year-old takes someone else's toy, then the teacher might suggest that the two children need to solve their problem. She might help them discuss their feelings and needs and guide them to come up with alternative solutions (Dinwiddie 1994).

Suggesting alternatives to aggressive behavior—such as how to use words in a conflict—is one of several effective guidance strategies (Wittmer and Honig 1994). Demonstrating and modeling prosocial behaviors can be accomplished through using puppets to role-play what is appropriate. Teachers can also provide direct instruction in skills such as using "nice talk," saying thank-you, and so on. Schickedanz (1994) also suggests that teachers emphasize what effects children's appropriate and inappropriate behaviors have on others.

Guidance and Teaching Skills

In addition to thinking about children's developmental levels, professional teachers should respond to problem situations by analyzing what can be taught in them. Katz (1984) categorizes what can be taught as social skills, verbal skills, social knowledge, and dispositional learning.

Social skills include taking turns, negotiating, and coping. Taking turns is not limited to sharing toys but is important in all social situations. During language activities, for example, children must learn to read the signals from a speaker that tell them when they can have a turn talking—eye contact, body language such as inclining the head, and so on. Children must also learn when the speaker is not willing to give up the floor—when he says "ah, ah, ah," avoids eye contact, and so on (Wells 1981). A similar kind of reading of the situation is helpful when one child wants a toy that another child has. The teacher might suggest that the child who wants the toy observe the child who has it and look for signs that he is tiring of it and might be ready to give it up. The teacher might help by modeling language to be used in negotiation, such as "I'll pull you in the wagon later if you'll let me have the truck now." Children also need to learn coping skills because not every request that they make will be honored. The teacher might say, "Well, perhaps you can play with the truck tomorrow. For now, you might want to listen to a record or draw a picture." We have all seen adults who cannot cope with not getting what they want, when they want it. Teaching children to cope gives them a valuable life skill.

Verbal skills that can be taught in problem situations include making appropriate assertive statements and talking about disagreements. For example, a child who has just had a toy snatched from her can learn to say firmly, "I was not finished playing with that boat. Please give it back." Being able to be assertive without being aggressive is a skill that will serve the child well for the rest of her life. Carrying on conversations about disputes is often difficult for children because they lack the words to continue the discussion. Teachers may have to model the conversations by speaking for both children, as described by Katz (1984):

> Using this technique, the teacher might say to Leslie, "Robin really wants a turn," to which Leslie might grunt a refusal. The teacher might then say to Robin something like, "Leslie does not want to give up the tricycle yet." Robin might respond to this with a whining protest, in which case the teacher can paraphrase to Leslie what Robin is feeling by saying, "Robin really would like a turn now," and so on. In short, the teacher keeps up the conversation, verbalizing to each child what she infers to be the feelings of the other. (p. 31)

Social knowledge includes the ability to put incidents into perspective and an initial understanding of the concept of *justice*. If one child fails to get a turn on the swing, the teacher might say, "I know that you are disappointed, but there are other things you can do." The tone of voice should be empathetic but not tragic. Children who hit learn about justice when they are restrained from hitting and told, "I won't let you hit anyone. If anyone else hits, I will stop them from hitting, too." The child then begins to feel safer and to feel that the environment is a just one.

Dispositional learning in discipline situations includes learning to be more empathetic, to try different techniques, and to avoid negative dispositions (sulking, temper tantrums, whining, and the like). Children can be taught to be more empathetic (Honig 1985; Marantz 1988). One of the best strategies for teaching empathy is modeling accompanied by discussion. For example, if one child falls and hurts himself, the teacher can model appropriate empathy in her response. Concern for the feelings of others must be a priority in the early childhood classroom.

Children can also learn that problem-solving strategies can be applied in conflicts with others. The teacher might recommend a strategy to a child and then follow the recommendation by saying, "If that doesn't work, come back, and we'll think of something else to try." Children must learn to accept that their first efforts may not always be successful while realizing that they can try again. Sometimes, a child may have adopted a negative behavior that the teacher would like to help her change—for example, tattling or complaining. The teacher must make a decision about how best to respond to a child's complaints to help her learn that complaining is not always successful and to learn when an adult should be told about an incident. Children are usually six or seven before they can understand the difference between tattling to get someone in trouble and telling the teacher about something that it is important for an adult to know.

Guiding Groups

Children in groups must be given some rules. The fewer and more flexible these rules, the better. As soon as children are old enough, they should have a part in making group rules. Some children as young as three can be involved in rule making.

Rules must be clearly stated. Leatzow, Neuhauser, and Wilmes (1983) observe that many early childhood educators have only one rule: "You may not hurt yourself or anyone else" (p. 83). This kind of rule covers many situations and is understood by the children. Other teachers add a rule that children cannot destroy property.

Sometimes, the teacher must manage the group in addition to guiding individual children. The younger the children, the fewer the group-management techniques that should be needed. As children are able to participate in more group activities, group-management techniques will become more useful to the teacher. One rule for group management is not to call attention to an individual child. For example, a teacher might say, "You all need to sit on your bottoms so that everyone can see the pictures while I read the story," rather than "Julian and Hope must sit down so that others can see." It also helps in this particular situation to reassure some children that they will get to see a book later if they are very excited about it. The teacher might say, "You all need to sit flat on your bottoms now, but after I read the story, I'll leave the book here on the table if you want to look at the pictures more closely." With older children who are anxious to see something, the teacher might say, "When you leave this table, put your name on the list if you want to see the book again later." Just as

When managing groups, teachers should be careful not to call attention to individual children. How should these teachers address the two children who are not paying attention?

public criticism is to be avoided, so, too, is public praise inappropriate in group-management situations. For example, the teacher might say, "Almost everyone is ready for the story; in just a minute, we will begin," rather than "Sara and Randy are sitting nicely, waiting for the story."

In using group-management strategies, teachers must be careful to preserve children's self-esteem and to use techniques that help children learn acceptable behaviors—the same concerns that apply when guiding individual behavior. Gartrell (1987b) acknowledges that learning these techniques takes commitment and practice on the part of teachers. Teachers must "deal with the young child's need to feel safe and secure, through personal acceptance, sensible limits, gentle correction, and genuine encouragement" (p. 55).

The same considerations of appropriateness of activity must be applied to group-management situations as to individual guidance situations. When children are in group situations too long or when group activities are inappropriate, behavior problems will result. One teacher of five-year-olds had a group lesson on the beginning sound of "r." The teacher had twenty-three children sit in a circle to listen to a recording about the letter *r*. The teacher held an inflatable figure representing *r*. During the thirty-minute lesson, the teacher had to discipline children many times—"Stop leaning back in your chair," "Don't pull her hair," "Pay attention," and so on. Clearly, this activity was inappropriate for five-year-olds, and the time spent on it was too long. The teacher could have saved much frustration for himself and the children by choosing other teaching strategies.

Planning for Key Points in the Schedule

Experienced teachers will agree that discipline problems are more likely at certain times of day than others, including arrival times, transition times, and departure times. Planning for these key times is essential.

For *arrival time*, the teacher might ask that children wait until everyone has arrived or until a set time has been reached before activities begin. The fact is, though, that children are not good at waiting. Alternatives to waiting might be to plan an activity to occupy children who arrive early or to allow these children to begin working in learning areas.

Music and fingerplays can be used to help children make *transitions* from one activity to another without nagging and reminding by the teacher. Often, children will put away toys and materials if the teacher helps and makes up a simple song ("This is the way we put blocks on the shelf" or "This is the way we wash the paintbrushes"). Playing a record or tape of a march song will encourage the children to march around the room until they come to the area for group activities; while marching, they will have no time to become bored and get into trouble. If the children are old enough, one child can begin to lead either a song or a fingerplay, and each child can join when she is ready. Fingerplays led by the teacher can encourage children to do what is necessary without being reminded. For example, the fingerplay "Two Little Hands Go Clap, Clap, Clap" ends with the line "And one little child sits quietly down." By the end of this fingerplay, all the children will be sitting, and the teacher will not have nagged anyone to do so.

Departures also need to be planned. Teachers need to think about how to distribute notices and work at the end of the day so that children do not have to wait too long. A routine of getting coats, distributing materials to take home, and delivering some short closing message can help keep children on track during departures.

On occasion, an activity might be appropriate for most of the group but not for an individual child. If a child is having difficulty, it is usually appropriate to allow him another choice. The teacher might whisper to a child, "You can stay here if you choose, or you may work quietly with the puzzles or books if you want." Individualizing curriculum means attending to the needs of different children. The sensitive teacher is usually aware of when a child may need to leave a group and tries to arrange for that before an incident happens.

In sum, many discipline problems can be avoided by anticipating when they are likely to occur and planning to circumvent them. Crosser (1992) uses the acronym BASIC to describe such planning:

> *Before school begins*
> *Arrival and departure times*
> *Schedule transitions*
> *Interactions with equipment and materials*
> *Conflict management* (p. 23)

In other words, the teacher plans the environment, plans for special times in the day, plans to help children learn to work with classroom equipment and materials, and teaches children how to settle conflicts that arise. Figure 6.1 is a summary of planning strategies to support positive behaviors.

Guidance Decisions

When teachers are confronted with misbehavior, they must make decisions about whether to respond, how to respond, and how to evaluate the growth of the children involved.

Weighing the Situation

In some situations, the most effective response is no response at all. Children sometimes behave in ways that are not appropriate but are not harmful to anyone and are not disruptive if they are ignored. For example, suppose the teacher asks the children to come to group time and sit on the floor for a story. Maria comes to the group but stands instead of sits. The teacher comments to the group that she is almost ready to start reading and makes eye contact with Maria, who remains standing. Rather than call her name and force her to sit, the teacher should do nothing and begin reading, as if Maria

Figure 6.1

Checklist for Supporting Positive Behaviors

Strategy	Yes/No	Notes
Physical environment		
1. Design clearly designed areas		
Interest areas		
Group meeting time		
Pathways		
2. Provide adequate space for interest areas		
Set limits for number of children using area		
Discuss rules with children		
3. Monitor potential problem areas		
Blocks		
Dramatic play		
Sand/water play		
Woodworking		
Other		
4. Maintain relaxed, calm, interesting environment		
Engaging activities every day		
Images/words at eye level		
Materials on low, open shelves		
Neatly organized items		
Labeled shelves and containers		
Programmatic environment		
5. Assess structure of activities		
Open-ended activities		
Balance between unstructured/structured activities		
6. Follow age-appropriate schedule		
Alternate active and quiet times		
Group times short		
Group times spread throughout the day		
Children's cues used to assess group time limits		
Adequate choice time		
7. Establish routines		
Consistent yet flexible		
No wait times		
Posted schedule with pictures and words		
8. Plan transitions		
Use consistent signal for end of choice time		
Allow 5 or more minutes for ending activities/cleanup		
Give verbal warning to all children		
Plan and use transitions every day		

Source: Nancy Ratcliff, "Use the Environment to Prevent Discipline Problems and Support Learning." *Young Children* 56 (September 2001): 84–89. Reprinted with permission from the National Association for the Education of Young Children.

were sitting quietly. Maria may soon sit down and join the group, or she may keep standing, but as long as she is not interfering with others, little will be gained from making her sit. If Maria continually refuses to do anything that she is asked, the teacher will need to take steps privately to find out what makes Maria feel so defiant.

Effective teachers know when to ignore behavior and when to deal with it. No rules determine what to ignore and when—only professional judgment provides the answers. In weighing a given situation, the teacher should ask herself these questions: What will be gained in terms of teaching and increased self-control by responding to the behavior? What will be lost in terms of the child's self-concept or feeling of autonomy?

Making the Choice to Respond

Once a teacher has decided to respond to a child's behavior, he must decide how. In this case, there are certain rules to follow:

1. The response should be private, if at all possible. A child who is hitting another child will have to be restrained immediately, but then he can be removed and the behavior can be dealt with privately.

2. The response should be developmentally appropriate—for example, redirecting a toddler, appealing to the empathetic feelings of a five-year-old, or explaining rationally to an eight-year-old.

3. The response should be aimed at helping the child increase her self-control. The teacher should express acceptance of the child's feelings and provide guidance in finding a socially acceptable way of expressing them.

4. The response should demonstrate caring for the child but firmness in rejecting the behavior: "I'm sorry that you are frustrated because you can't have the doll now, but you cannot spit on anyone. You can spit in the sink."

5. The response should involve as much knowledge about the child and his situation as the teacher can summon in the split second that is often available for making a decision. For instance, suppose that the teacher knows that Derek's father has just moved out and that his family is under stress. When Derek behaves in a way that is not typical for him, such as throwing sand on a friend, the teacher can quietly take him aside and explain gently that he knows that Derek feels like throwing something, that he can tell him how he feels if he wants to, but that he cannot hurt other children.

Withitness is a term that has become popular in the literature on discipline; it was derived from the work of Jacob Kounin, a well-known educational researcher (Charles and Barr 1989). Withitness is knowing what is going on in the classroom at all times. If students observe that the teacher chooses to correct the wrong child's behavior, they will assume that the teacher does not know what is going on. Teachers with withitness also know to stop misbehavior before it spreads to others; timing such as this requires that teachers observe carefully.

Examples of Effective Responses

The following scenarios demonstrate effective responses to real-life problems in the classroom:

- You are reading a story to a small group. Several children start to whine that they do not like the story. One child puts her hands over her ears. Others notice and start to put hands over their ears. You could ignore the behavior and do a little editing of the story to finish it quickly. Or you could stop reading and say, "I know that some of you like other books better. Perhaps we will read a book that you like better tomorrow. But some people like this book, so I'm going to finish reading it now. You can wait quietly for the few minutes it will take."

- You find several children in the bathroom exposing themselves. You could say, "I see that you are interested in the differences between boys and girls. Would you like to have me read this book to you that explains some of the differences?"

- One child pulls all the blocks off the shelf and refuses to help put them away. You might say, "I know that it is much more fun to pull these blocks off the shelf than it is to put them away. We all have to do things that are not much fun sometimes. I'll help you begin, and you can finish." If the child still refuses to help, you could say, "I'm going to put away these blocks now. Then you and I must talk about why you are not feeling like helping today."

- A child bites another child. First, you must restrain the child so that no more biting can occur. Then you might say, "You cannot bite Sidney. You know that biting hurts very much, and the rule is that you cannot hurt anyone. I will not let you hurt anyone, and I will try not to let anyone hurt you. I know that you are angry, and I know that Sidney grabbed your toy. You must tell Sidney that you do not like it when he grabs your toy. Use words to tell him how angry you are."

Evaluating Growth

Evaluating children's growth in handling conflicts and in managing their own behavior requires that teachers keep anecdotal records of children's behavior over time and be able to document their growth in behaving in more acceptable ways. Gartrell (1995) relates the story of a child who said, "you damm sunnamabitch" to another child. When the teacher got to the children, she comforted the second child briefly and then whispered, "I'm proud of you" in the ear of the swearing child. She explained later to an observer that until last week, this child had hit or kicked others whenever he was angry; his teachers had been trying to get him to use words to express himself in these situations. When the teacher whispered in the boy's ear to congratulate him on his language use, she also supplied him with some words that would not bother people as much as the swear words.

Children's growth usually takes time and comes in little steps, but teachers need to be able to see the changes, even when they are small. Teachers must also evaluate their own growth in responding to children's behavior. Teachers must remember that both children and adults get tired and become angry. If teachers occasionally respond in ways that are less than professional, they should forgive themselves and learn from their experience.

> ## Parents AND Guiding Behavior
>
> ■ Help parents evaluate possible solutions to their children's difficult behaviors. It might be helpful to provide some guidelines that include thinking about long-term goals for behavior and possible outcomes (Heath 1994).

Behavior-Management Systems

Several behavior-management systems have been designed to help teachers control children's behavior. The following sections will describe assertive discipline, the Glasser model, the Ginott model, and the Dreikurs model.

Assertive Discipline

Designed by Lee Canter (1976), *assertive discipline* is a system in which the rules for classroom behavior are established by the teacher and posted in the classroom. The consequences for breaking any of the rules are also posted. If a child breaks the rule against speaking out in class, for example, her name is written on the chalkboard. (In subsequent publications, Canter has recommended that the names be written on a clipboard or in a book, rather than on the board [Hill 1990].) Another offense results in a checkmark being placed after the child's name. Usually, the consequence of receiving two checkmarks is being sent to the principal's office or having the teacher call the child's parents.

Because disruptions prevent teachers from teaching effectively, Canter believes that use of the assertive discipline system enables teachers to be more effective and solves the management problems in any classroom. This system is in use in many elementary schools, which means that many early childhood teachers are required to follow assertive discipline. Administrators who believe that the system helps teachers feel more comfortable about discipline are likely to promote its use.

One of the first things any teacher of young children must do is assess the validity of the assumptions of any behavior-management program. Canter based the assertive discipline system on the assumption that children want to disrupt the teacher and prevent teaching (Canter 1988; Hitz 1988). Teachers who believe that children have an inherent desire to learn and who have observed the eagerness with which young children approach learning will deem this an invalid assumption.

Another problem with assertive discipline is that it assumes that young children can operate according to rules. Experienced teachers know that young children can learn that some behaviors are acceptable at school and others are not. They also know that this learning usually takes time, guidance, and repeated experience. The assertive discipline system assumes that telling children that there is a rule and punishing them for breaking the rule will prevent unacceptable behavior. This approach may prevent the behavior at a given moment, but children will not know why the behavior is unacceptable, nor will they learn to make better judgments about how to behave in future situations.

Behavior-management systems that enforce rules established by adult authority do not help children learn to be responsible. Such systems do, however, teach children to obey authority that is exercised through "power assertion" (Hitz 1988). There are situations in which adults must assert their power and demand instant obedience—for example, in order to prevent injury or cope with an emergency, such as a fire. Adults exert such control until children are old enough to learn rational reasons for controlling their own behavior in like situations. However, controlling children by power and demanding instant obedience should not be typical means of behavior management. Gartrell (1987a) expresses concerns that assertive discipline damages children's self-concepts and turns teachers into "managing technicians" (p. 11). Perhaps a larger concern is the danger that children will not be able to determine appropriate behavior and to develop a sense of responsibility for their actions.

The assertive discipline model also fails to examine the causes of disruptive behavior. The system is applied regardless of the curriculum, the room arrangement, or the schedule. No system of discipline should ever be applied without careful assessment of all the factors and individuals involved in a teaching situation.

Jones and Jones (1990) report that some schools that began assertive discipline programs several years ago have moved away from them, for several reasons:

> Many teachers are frustrated because problem students seem to be relatively unaffected by the procedures, and students who do not need such repressive methods tend to find the method insulting or anxiety provoking. Our own concern is that too frequently the method creates a "sit down, shut up, or get out" philosophy in classrooms in which teaching methods are failing to meet students' basic personal and academic needs. Too often teachers use the Assertive Discipline procedures rather than examining their own teaching methods to consider how to prevent disruptive behavior. (p. 412)

Glasser Model

The Glasser model (Glasser 1997) is based on providing good choices for children and handling disruptions that do occur in a calm and logical manner.

Glasser believes that good choices produce good behavior and bad choices produce bad behavior. He believes that behavior represents individuals' attempts to meet their needs and that if schools are to have better discipline, they will have to become places where fewer children and teachers are frustrated in getting what they need. Some of the important needs that Glasser identifies are the needs to belong, to have power, to be free, and to have fun. Schools in which children do not feel a sense of belonging or have no power to make choices are schools in which discipline problems are common.

Glasser recommends that teachers structure learning experiences so that children have high motivation to work on behalf of the group and that stronger students help weaker students, thus fulfilling the stronger students' need for power and the weaker students' need to contribute to the group. One of the hallmarks of Glasser's model is the class meeting, in which students discuss class rules and behavior. Although Glasser's model is used more often with older students than with young children, his focus on problem solving, on the choices provided by teachers, and on teachers' persistence in helping children with problems is appropriate for young children. More recently, Glasser (2000) has written about violence prevention programs in schools. Even though this work is focused on older children, the same principles of respect and thoughtful guidance apply to young children as well.

Ginott Model

The Ginott model (Ginott 1972) is based on setting up a classroom climate that is conducive to good discipline through effective communication between teachers and children. Ginott believes that discipline is an ongoing process that is achieved over time. One of the principles of his model is that corrective messages to children should attack the problem and not the child. Ginott uses the term *congruent communication* to describe responses that are in harmony with children's feelings about situations or themselves. He also advocates inviting cooperation, not demanding it. Teachers applying Ginott's recommendations do not label children and communicate their willingness to help children solve problems.

Charles and Barr (1989) report that even teachers who are sympathetic with Ginott's views feel that more structured management is needed in many teaching situations. Nonetheless, Ginott's emphasis on the ability to communicate well with children is of value to early childhood teachers. Another component of Ginott's model that is of value to early childhood teachers is its emphasis on the self-esteem of the child and the importance of the teacher's behavior.

Dreikurs Model

The Dreikurs model (Dinkmeyer and Dreikurs 2000) is best known for its emphasis on logical consequences. Dreikurs defines *discipline* as teaching students to impose limits on themselves. He believes that all children want to belong and that their behaviors represent efforts to achieve a sense of belonging. Misbehaviors are the result of mistaken goals such as seeking attention, power, or revenge or wanting to display another child's inadequacy. Dreikurs suggests that the best method of discipline is encouraging positive behavior.

When teachers encounter behavior problems, Dreikurs recommends that they point out to students the logical consequences of their actions. In describing *logical consequences,* Charles and Barr (1989) use examples that apply to older children, but their explanation will suggest applications for younger children, as well:

> *Logical consequences must be differentiated from punishment. Punishment is action taken by the teacher to get back at misbehaving students and show them who is boss. Punishment breeds retaliation and gives students the feeling that they have the right to punish in return. Logical consequences, on the other hand, are not weapons used by the teacher. They teach students that all behavior produces a corresponding result: good behavior brings rewards and unacceptable behavior brings unpleasant consequences. If a student throws paper on the floor, that student must pick it up. If a student fails to do work as assigned, that student must make up the work on his or her own time.* (p. 83)

Gartrell (2002) believes that the terminology used can influence the mindset of the teacher toward guiding children's behavior; thus, he promotes using the term *mistaken behavior,* rather than *misbehavior. Misbehavior* makes teachers think of punishing, whereas *mistaken behavior* encourages thinking about guiding and teaching. Gartrell credits Dreikurs's thinking about behavior as the stepping stones that led to development of the concept *mistaken behavior.*

In evaluating different models for managing behavior, Charles and Barr (1989) state that "Dreikurs' views have the greatest potential for bringing about genuine attitudinal change among students, so that they ultimately behave better because they consider it the proper thing to do" (p. 85).

Assessing Behavior-Management Systems

It is the teacher's responsibility to assess any management system or discipline policy based on the following criteria:

- ■ *Respect for children*—Not every teacher will love every child, but each child deserves respect as a human being. If it is hard to respect the child because of constant problems, the teacher should seek help from co-teachers, counselors, parents, or administrators. Using a behavior-management system that does not respect the individual child will cause more harm than it attempts to address.

- ■ *Knowledge of individual children*—Discipline cannot be applied fairly if it is applied without knowledge of the individual child. For example, enforcing a rule against bad language with the child discussed earlier, who swore instead of hitting, would leave him without an acceptable way to express his frustration. As the child shows more growth, the teacher can continue to help him find more acceptable classroom words for expressing anger. Behavior-management systems often make it easy for teachers to gloss over the need to know each child.

- *Knowledge of normal growth, development, and behavior*—Children who are behaving in ways that are normal for their age may be helped to learn more acceptable responses to be used at school. But such behavior will not be irritating to the knowledgeable teacher because he will realize that it is a normal part of working with this particular age group.

- *Willingness to accept discipline as an opportunity for teaching*—Discipline is not punishment. Teachers sometimes have to work hard at helping children control their behavior in ways that teach them new strategies for interacting successfully in groups or with individuals.

- *Avoidance of judgmental words*—Calling children "good" or "bad" does not help them learn alternative ways of behaving. More appropriate descriptions of behavior guide children without judging them.

- *Limited but cooperative rule making*—Being well-behaved in a classroom where there are long lists of rules is difficult for children because too many things are against the rules. As soon as children are old enough, they can begin to help teachers decide on rules that the group will follow.

Children with Special Needs

Many children with special needs require only guidance that is typical for their age, whereas others may require more support from the teacher. For many special-needs children, arranging the environment to facilitate their access to materials and equipment will greatly reduce their frustration and thus their inappropriate behavior, as well. Once children have equal access to materials and equipment, teachers can generally use the same guidance strategies they use with the children's peers. Some children, however, may require more support, so teachers may need to use guidance strategies that are usually more appropriate for younger children. For example, consider a child with a physical disability who is in a wheelchair; she is chronologically and developmentally age four. Given this, her teacher should be able to employ the same problem-solving strategies in guidance that are applied to other children of the same age. If the child needs additional support, such as having just one or two options rather than a more open-ended approach, then the teacher can provide that support.

Guidance for children with disabilities may focus on teaching them social skills. In addition to making environmental arrangements, Lowenthal (1996) suggests several strategies: using group affection activities, such as modifying games and songs in which children touch or hug one another in affectionate ways; teaching typically developing peers to initiate play with special children by offering toys or extending invitations to play; and using teacher prompts to help children recognize elements in social situations that they might not pick up on their own. Obviously, the strategies selected must be individually appropriate for the child.

Brown, Althouse, and Anfin (1993) found that guided dramatization was an effective strategy in encouraging children with disabilities to interact in positive ways with other children. These authors guided the dramatization of a familiar story by teaching it to a child with disabilities through interactive reading, telling the story with a magnetic or flannelboard, and then asking the child to choose someone else to help tell the story. As the children dramatized the story, the teacher took photographs and used them in retelling the story again. The target child was photographed playing with the other children and asked to tell about the play. These authors found that this sequence helped the child with disabilities learn how to interact with others and that the child initiated play experiences with other children based on the story.

Celebrating Diversity

Guidance always entails values. We all select what is important to us and what is supposedly correct behavior through the lens of our own culture and family. Teachers must always keep this in mind as they make decisions about which behaviors are acceptable or appropriate and which behaviors are not. In addition, teachers must learn about the values and expectations that certain cultures have for the behavior of children and what children's families support within their cultural group. This learning is not supposed to result in teachers' feeling that they cannot make decisions about guidance. Rather, when teachers make decisions that conflict with children's cultural norms, they have an obligation to explain to the children (and their parents) why school behavior is different from home behavior. If parents understand the need for certain behaviors, they can help their children yet not feel that their own values and patterns are being ignored (Johns and Espinoza 1996).

Gender differences in expectations for behavior in educational settings are also an issue when thinking about diversity. Gordon and Browne (1996) have reported that teachers typically pay more attention to boys, give them more positive feedback, and give them more attention and praise for achievement. The same study found that aggression is tolerated more in boys, that disruptive talking is tolerated more in girls, that teachers use physical discipline more with boys, and

Parents AND Guiding Behavior

■ All guidance decisions must be made with knowledge about and sensitivity to the individual child's family and culture. Working with families in an open and caring relationship is a prerequisite to guidance that is appropriate for each child.

www.ablongman.com/brewer5e

that teachers use more negative comments or disapproving gestures with girls. All these findings should strengthen the resolve of teachers to pay equal attention to all children, to base standards of behavior on developmental and cultural information rather than on gender, and to discourage dependent helplessness and excessively conforming behavior in both boys and girls (Gordon and Browne 1996).

Chapter Summary

- Discipline is a major concern of teachers. It is perceived by the general public to be the most important problem in schools.

- The professional teacher views discipline as integral to the teaching process. Discipline must be based on knowledge of children's normal development, and the teacher must be aware of the effects of disciplinary decisions on children's self-esteem.

- The curriculum may contribute to discipline problems if activities are not appropriate for children. Children need both challenges and successes. They also need interesting, engaging activities that they select themselves.

- Room arrangements may be a source of discipline problems. Too little space to work, traffic through play areas, and spaces that are difficult to supervise may be sources of frustration to both teachers and children.

- Teachers who view discipline as a teaching opportunity can help children learn social skills, verbal skills, coping skills, and the disposition to use positive strategies in relating to others.

- Good group-management techniques require that the teacher avoid calling attention to individual children for either positive or negative behaviors.

- Often, teachers have the choice of ignoring inappropriate behavior. The decision to respond to behavior must be based on the teacher's professional assessment of the situation and what a child can learn from it.

- When teachers decide to respond to behavior, their responses should be private, developmentally appropriate, aimed at helping children achieve self-control, expressive of concern for children, and based as much as possible on knowledge of the individual children involved.

- In the last few years, many schools have adopted behavior-management systems that all teachers, even those in early childhood classrooms, must apply. In assessing any such system, teachers should examine the assumptions on which the system is based, its effects on children's self-esteem, and the cognitive requirements the system makes of young children.

- *Discipline* and *punishment* are not synonymous terms. Punishment often has long-term negative effects and does not teach children self-control.

- The goal of learning to control their own behavior must be set for special-needs children as well as typically developing children. Moving toward this long-term goal means that each child will learn problem-solving strategies that are developmentally appropriate.

- Teachers should respect children's cultural backgrounds when making decisions about behavior. In addition, teachers should help parents and caregivers understand the importance of having certain behaviors at school and the differences between what behaviors are acceptable at home versus school.

Theory INTO Practice

Interview four different early childhood teachers about their discipline problems and solutions. What are the most common problems? What are the most common solutions? Would you choose the same solutions? Why or why not?

In your small group, have each person think of a problem that he or she believes might come up in the future and write a brief description of it on a sheet of paper. Pass each paper to another member of the group, who should then write what he or she might do in response to the problem. Continue exchanging papers until everyone has written a response to each problem. Then discuss each problem and the suggested responses. Is there a consensus on some solutions but not others? What factors seem to influence the solutions?

Most teachers are calm about handling problem situations, but certain behaviors may make them uncomfortable. Think about the following list of behaviors. Does any of them make you especially uncomfortable? If so, try to determine why and what you would do when faced with this situation. *Possible behaviors:* Spitting, biting, kicking, hitting, screaming, sex play, swearing, saying "I hate you!," grabbing a toy, refusing to obey a request, teasing another child, not answering when asked a question, or deliberately breaking a toy.

If possible, observe in a school that has adopted one of the behavior management systems described in this chapter. How effective is the system for young children? Does it help teachers teach children how to control their own behavior? If you cannot observe, find more detailed information about one of the behavior-management systems and discuss it with a small group. List the positive and negative aspects of each system.

A Teacher Speaks

Rick Coxen Pringle Elementary, Salem-Keizer district, Oregon
Pam Coxen James R. Schirle Elementary, Salem-Keizer district, Oregon

Helping Children Learn to Manage Their Own Behavior

It's the beginning of a new schoolyear for us; time to reflect on the past and plan for the future. When we think about classroom management issues, we look at the outcomes and then determine what we need to do in order to achieve them. As we choose our adult friends, we know we enjoy people who are respectful, empathetic, cooperative, honest, good problem solvers, and show integrity. Assuming that others enjoy these qualities as well, we look at how to help children build these traits.

Guiding our whole philosophy is the underlying tone of the classroom. We work to maintain a positive, safe environment for children. We expect children to become risk takers and to celebrate success, as well as learn from mistakes. We celebrate positive social choices and help children learn to compliment others (and receive compliments) for good choices.

One of the most important things we do as teachers is to model what it is we expect of children. This applies not only to academic areas, but to social and emotional arenas as well. When children observe us interacting with other adults—staff members, parents, student teachers—they watch us show respect and display a cooperative nature. When we work to solve problems that arise, they see how cooperation and problem solving are applied. When we follow through on our commitments and maintain high personal standards, they understand integrity.

Beyond modeling the behaviors we want, we directly teach skills that will help children build the traits that will help them throughout life. Discussions about real classroom situations, or discussions built around photos representing social problems, begin most lessons. Role-play of difficult situations that result in problem solving, compromise, and solution play a big part in helping children apply what they have discussed. In just the same way that woodworking or sewing can be explained to you but not fully understood until you actually have to perform the task, social skills can be discussed but not really understood and made usable until the application process. Role-plays help children apply skills in nonthreatening, neutral situations before they are called on to apply the skill when the circumstance is a bit more personal and possibly filled with emotion.

In the same way that we show children, through our daily interactions, that all of their classmates are treated fairly, we also guide children to treat others fairly and equally. Since "fair" is often in the eye of the beholder, we often must have conversations about what really does constitute fairness in various situations. Compromise often plays a significant role, and helping children negotiate is part of our role.

To the extent possible, we try to let children become independent problem solvers. We must give them the skills to verbalize a problem, to see possible solutions, and to negotiate settlement along the way. When adult intervention is the only option, we intervene in order to help reach a compromise, rather than to provide the solution.

Taking the time to plan for and teach social skills benefits everyone. There are fewer classroom problems and more time for academics, and we have helped children develop the traits that will help them throughout their lives.

CHAPTER 7

Observing and Assessing Young Children

After reading this chapter, you will be able to do the following:

- Define assessment.
- Define different types of tests and explain the purposes of each.
- Explain the various strategies for observing young children.
- Explain the various strategies for assessing young children.
- Plan assessment strategies for children with special needs.
- Plan assessment strategies that are culturally sensitive.

The local newspaper has just reported the test scores of children in area schools. Reading, mathematics, and writing scores are given by school and grade, with the percentages of increase and decrease since last year printed in bold type and the national averages highlighted. The almost full-page newspaper article is accompanied by an interview with the superintendent of schools, who emphasizes that the district will focus all future staff development efforts on raising those scores before the next test.

The local TV stations have also reported the story about the test scores. One interviews an education professor from the university, who is critical of the newspaper article. As she points out, nowhere in the article is there any discussion about the match between the tests and the local curriculum, between the norming samples and the population of the community, or the appropriateness of using standardized test scores as the only measure of progress in area schools. She also cites several critics of such "high-stakes" testing, who feel it is doing more harm than good in educating children (Andersen 1998; Kohn 1999; Ohanian 2000). They argue that such testing narrows the focus so that instructional programs are based on children's memorizing sets of facts, rather than understanding processes and developing concepts of how the world works.

You are really confused about these issues. What should be the role of testing in early childhood programs? How can children's growth be measured? How should educators respond to community pressure to prove that children are learning in school? These are difficult questions, and there are no easy answers.

Definition of Assessment

Assessment and *testing* are not synonymous terms. Although testing is only one of several components of assessment, in recent years testing seems to have been misused and to have become the major determinant of the value of schools and the abilities of children.

Assessment is more than just testing, however; it is using a variety of strategies in an effort to uncover the understanding and determine the development of individual children. Teachers assess children's social, emotional, and physical development as well as their intellectual growth—just as a pediatrician assesses a child not only by weighing and measuring him and checking his visual acuity, his hearing, and his reflexes, but also by observing his ability to walk and his relationship to his parents. Similarly, programs are assessed by measuring not only the success of the children enrolled in them but also parents' satisfaction with their children's progress and teachers' feelings of accomplishment. Assessment is sometimes formal and sometimes informal. In contrast to testing, assessment is ongoing. A test is a sample of behavior or knowledge taken at a specific time. Assessment covers a much longer time frame and attempts to sample a much broader spectrum of behavior or knowledge.

Assessment is defined as collecting and evaluating information about the performance of an individual, the quality of a program, or the effectiveness of an activity. Testing may be one component of collecting data for assessment purposes, but it is only in the evaluating of data that assessment happens. Webster's defines *assessment* as the action or instance of assessing. *Assess* comes from the French word *assidere,* meaning to sit beside or assist. Thinking of assessment as assisting or coaching creates a mindset about the purposes and uses of assessment that focuses on the positive results of good assessment.

Assessment is vital to good teaching; it is necessary to assess both the program and the progress of individual children. Good teachers would be involved in assessment even if there were no external requirements to do so; they want to know how well children are doing, and they want to know about the effectiveness of their programs. They even assess their assessment programs. Good assessments not only help teachers plan instruction, but also empower both children and teachers, as children become more aware of their accomplishments and teachers feel confident about their ability to guide children' learning. In addition, good assessment helps facilitate communication so that teachers and parents can talk about children and programs in meaningful ways.

Assessment alone does not improve children or programs—just as measuring a child's height and weight does not make the child grow. Only when assessment has a purpose and is used to help make decisions about curriculum, about individual children, and about programs can it help a child or a program grow.

Types of Tests

Tests vary considerably in the purposes for which they were designed. The following definitions are based on the NAEYC's "Position Statement on Standardized Testing of Young Children 3 through 8 Years of Age" (1988):

Achievement test—A test that measures the extent to which a person has mastery over a certain body of information or possesses a certain skill after instruction has taken place

Criterion-referenced test—A test that evaluates a test taker in relation to a specified performance level (as distinguished from a test that compares the test taker's score to the performance of other people, which are norm-referenced tests)

Developmental test—An age-related, norm-referenced assessment of a child's skills and behaviors compared to those of children of the same chronological age; sometimes used incorrectly as screening tests

Norm-referenced test—A test that compares the test taker's performance to the performance of other people in a specified group

Readiness test—A test that assesses a child's level of preparedness for a specific academic or preacademic program

Reliability—The degree to which test scores are consistent, dependable, or repeatable; that is, the degree to which test scores can be attributed to actual differences in test takers' performance rather than to errors of measurement

Screening test—A test used to identify children who may be in need of special services; such a test focuses on the child's ability to acquire skills and may also be called a *developmental screening test*

Standardized test—A test composed of empirically selected items that is to be used in a specific way, is based on adequately defined norms, and is backed by data on reliability and validity

Validity—The degree to which a test measures what it is supposed to measure; also, the degree to which a certain inference from a test is appropriate or meaningful (p. 45)

As a student, you have probably had experience with all these kinds of tests. For instance, you probably took achievement tests while you were in elementary school, or you might have taken one in order to be admitted to the teacher-education program you are in now. You might also have to take an examination in order to become a certified teacher in your state. Generally, achievement tests are norm referenced and standardized. You have also likely

Parents AND Assessment

■ Make assessment the focus of one parent meeting. Explain the differences between *assessment* and *testing*. Also provide parents with examples of various kinds of tests, and explain how each could best be used in a program for young children.

taken tests in your college classes. These tests are usually criterion referenced, as the teacher determines the correct answers, and, in theory, everyone could get a perfect score.

Testing Young Children

Young children are routinely given **screening tests.** Screening tests vary considerably, but most attempt to determine a child's ability to learn skills. Many of these tests ask children to identify objects, words, and numerals that are common in some environments. Developmental screening tests are designed to determine what children can do compared to other children their age. These tests often involve drawing geometric figures, bouncing balls, balancing on one foot, and repeating series of numerals or words. *Readiness tests* ask young children to recognize letters and numerals, to find objects that go together, and to recognize objects that are not the same as other objects in a set. These tests are supposed to predict a child's success in coping with an instructional program.

Meisels (1987) argues that in most cases screening tests lack reliability and validity. Further evidence of the problems of reliability and validity comes from a large-scale study conducted in Minnesota (Thurlow, O'Sullivan, and Ysseldyke 1986), in which every preschool child in the state was given a developmental screening test. Some districts found a problem with every child, and some found no problems at all. These results probably reflect the inadequacies of the tests themselves, the way in which they were administered, or the way in which the results were interpreted. In sum, the study makes clear one of the real dangers of using standardized tests, which is that decisions may be made on the basis of faulty information.

Standardized tests should be considered one of many avenues available for collecting information about a child, not the only avenue. Kamii and

Having children read aloud is one way of assessing their reading skills.

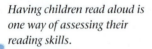

Kamii (1990) argue that standardized achievement tests encourage teachers to teach in ways that do not promote autonomous learning and that the tests do not tap children's thinking processes. Martin (1988) disapproves of the use of standardized screening tests to homogenize the children in any program. She maintains that a flexible program "can accommodate a wide diversity in children's backgrounds, maturity, temperaments, interests, talents, abilities, and skills" (p. 489). Screening tests, she believes, are symptoms of the schools' refusal to accept differences.

The report of a task force of the National Association of State Boards of Education (NASBE 1988) echoes this view. The authors state that "developmental or readiness tests should not be used to determine placement in what may be perceived as homogeneous groups. We think that early childhood classrooms should contain a heterogeneous mix of children with various levels of skills and abilities" (p. 14). It is true that pressures on schools to achieve are enormous and that some schools try to limit differences so that they can show more gains on tests. Only knowledgeable teachers, administrators, and parents can break this cycle.

The following guidelines, which are based on the NAEYC's "Position Statement on Standardized Testing of Young Children 3 through 8 Years of Age" (1988), will help teachers determine if and when a standardized test should be used with young children:

NAEYC

1. Standardized tests must be used only for the purposes for which they were intended.

2. The use of standardized tests must be restricted to situations in which testing provides information that will clearly contribute to improved outcomes for children.

3. Test content should *not* determine the school's curriculum. Rather, the school's curriculum should guide teachers and others in the selection of tests.

4. Test givers must be qualified to administer the tests and sensitive to the developmental needs of young children.

5. Teachers and administrators must be knowledgeable about testing and able to interpret test results accurately and cautiously to parents, school personnel, and the media.

6. The younger the child, the more difficult it is to design tests that are reliable and valid. Nevertheless, all standardized tests used must be reliable and valid according to technical standards of test development.

7. Day-to-day instructional decisions must depend primarily on teacher observation. Standardized tests cannot provide information for planning day-to-day instructional activities.

8. Because standardized tests are not useful for day-to-day instructional decisions and student appraisal, taking time to administer the tests takes away from instructional time. Therefore, before teachers devote substantial

classroom time to administering standardized tests, they should establish the purposes of the test data and determine whether the time and expense involved are warranted.

9. Student appraisal decisions should be based primarily on teacher observation and should reflect the goals of the classroom.

There are some valid reasons for using standardized tests, such as to collect data for research studies that allow broad-based comparisons that can help make schools better places for children. Some tests may also help in diagnosing children who need special services. The responsibility for using tests in ways that benefit children lies with teachers and administrators.

High-Stakes Testing

You are probably familiar with the term *high-stakes testing* and know that it means tests on which major decisions are based. For example, in many states now a student cannot graduate from high school without passing a state exam. You may also be experiencing high-stakes tests on a personal level because you probably have to pass a test in order to be certified to teach, regardless of your grades in classes or your performance in a field experience. There is the threat of high-stakes tests even for very young children, and early childhood educators must do all they can to make sure that young children are not tested inappropriately.

Strategies for Assessment

One of the hallmarks of the Reggio Emilia schools discussed in Chapter 2 is the incredible amount of time teachers spend documenting children's thinking and work. Most U.S. teachers do not have the time to provide that constant level of documentation. Nonetheless, *all* teachers need to assess the children in their programs—as well as the effectiveness of their programs—as part of good teaching. Leonard (1997) states that observation helps teachers get to know children as individuals with unique personalities, provides a basis for making educational decisions, and generates the data needed to help parents see and understand their children's progress. And Helm, Beneke, and Steinheimer (1997) suggest that carefully documenting children's work has many advantages for teachers of young children. In addition to being able to respond to demands for accountability, teachers who document children's work in a variety of ways are able to plan for active learning experiences and are able to meet special needs.

Figure 7.1 is a web diagram of the many types of successful documentation. As shown in the figure, teachers have many strategies from which to choose in making assessments of their children and their programs. In choosing which strategy or strategies to use, teachers must first decide what they

Figure 7.1 Documenting Children's Work

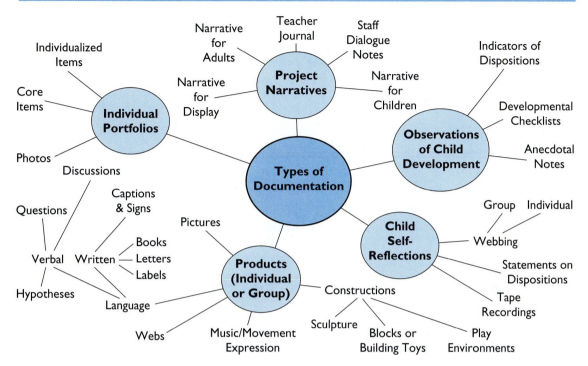

Source: J. H. Helm, S. Beneke, and K. Steinheimer, "Documenting Children's Learning," *Childhood Education* 73 (April 1997): 200–205. Reprinted by permission of Judy Harris Helm, Sallee Beneke, and Kathy Steinheimer, and the Association for Childhood Education International. Copyright © 2000 by the Association.

need to know and how that information will be used. Not all strategies are equally useful, and not all are manageable in the time available to teachers. The following sections will define and illustrate the various strategies available to early childhood teachers. Some of these strategies will require help from paraprofessionals or other professionals. For example, a specific tally cannot be recorded by the teacher who is trying to manage the behavior; rather, it must be done by an observer who is not intervening in the behavior.

Time–Activity Samples

A *time–activity sample* is simply a chart of the various areas or activities in the classroom that is marked to indicate the children working in each area at a certain time. A time–activity sample may provide information about the daily activities of an individual child or patterns for the entire group (see Figure 7.2). If the teacher has been concerned that a particular child is participating in only

Figure 7.2

Time–Activity
Samples

Observer ___Linda Reynolds_____ Date ___April 1___

Time ___9:15 A.M._____

Student	Art Area	Writing Area	Discovery Area	Water Play Area
Sara	✗			
Addie			✗	
Robert				✗
Juan	✗			

Observer ___Linda Reynolds_____ Date ___April 1___

Time ___9:30 A.M._____

Student	Art Area	Writing Area	Discovery Area	Water Play Area
Sara	✗			
Addie				✗
Robert				✗
Juan		✗		

one kind of activity, then doing a time–activity sample might help the teacher confirm whether that is, in fact, the case. Conducting a whole-group time–activity sample might help the teacher think about the activities provided and which ones are not attracting children (see Figure 7.3). Once the teacher has collected the information from several such samples (i.e., a sufficient number on which to base instructional decisions), then she can decide how to help the child or children engage in other activities or how to change the activities currently offered.

Figure 7.3

Whole-Group
Time–Activity
Sample

Observer Linda Reynolds			Date April 1	
Time	Art Area	Writing Area	Discovery Area	Water Play Area
9:15 A.M.	////	/	///	//
9:30 A.M.	//	///		//
9:45 A.M.	/	/		///
10:00 A.M.	///	//		//

Tallies

It is difficult to help a child change an inappropriate behavior without knowing exactly how often the behavior occurs. A *tally* provides a record of behaviors over a period of time. To mark each observed occurrence—for example, each incidence of aggressive behavior—the teacher would simply make one tally mark. The total tally count would provide some baseline data against which the child's improvement could later be judged. However, it would not provide information about the kind of aggression or the circumstances in which it occurs. A more specific tally would be more useful, perhaps including the time each incident occurred and a quick note describing the specific behavior (see Figure 7.4).

Observer Linda Reynolds   Date April 1

Child Observed Taylor Thomas

Time	Observation
8:30	Hit Sarah as she came into room
8:35	Pinched Jeremy as she sat down at puzzle table
8:42	Pushed Shawn away from puzzles
9:00	Pulled Trish's hair at water table
9:06	Grabbed a toy from Alex
9:30	Kicked Greg when he walked near her

Figure 7.4

Specific Tally

Running Narratives or Logs

A *running narrative* or *log* records the activities of the day (see Figure 7.5). It may help the teacher recall how often and when an activity has been offered and provide a general record for children and parents, who may enjoy recalling a certain day or activity.

Incident Records

An *incident record* documents the details of an isolated incident (see Figure 7.6). The amount of information provided by such a record is limited, but there are times when it is useful. For example, suppose a child has never been able to choose a book independently and look at it for any length of time, but then one day, she does. An incident record would provide information about when and how this behavior occurred. Obviously, any time a behavior is observed for the first time, an incident record is a useful tool.

Figure 7.5

Running Narrative

Observer ___Linda Reynolds___

April 1   All children were present today. Took a walk looking for signs of spring. Recorded signs on chartpaper when we returned. Each child contributed one thing to be recorded. Children chose their favorite song of the year ("Looby Lou"). We sang and danced it four times.

April 2   Tony and Liza were absent. It rained today, so we put out our rain gauge to measure how much. Wrote a class poem about the rain. Tara and Pete wanted to write their own poems. The class poem and Tara and Pete's poems are on the chart stand. We will read them again tomorrow.

April 3   Tony was absent again. Liza is back and feeling well. Favorite art activity today was easel painting. Ten children made paintings. Three made paper sculptures. The music teacher helped us learn a new song, "Round and Round the Village." This is a singing game, so we played and sang it several times.

April 4   Georgio brought three tadpoles to school, which his mother helped him catch in a pond near their house. Found a book in the library about frogs and toads. Watched a video about the growth of a frog from the egg to an adult frog. Drew pictures of tadpoles for our science journals.

Figure 7.6

Observer ___Linda Reynolds___	Date ___April 1___	
Child Observed ___Nicole Byers___	Time ___9:30 A.M.___	

Nicole selected a book from the library shelves. She took it to a beanbag chair and looked at it intensely for 10 minutes. During this time, she looked at the book all the way through two times. She turned to one page and pointed to each word as she told the story.

Figure 7.6

Incident Record

Narratives

A *narrative* can describe the behavior of one child or a group of children at a particular time, such as arrival time or snack time (see Figure 7.7). Although narratives are usually general in nature, they can provide useful information on which the teacher can base decisions about the program or individual children. For example, in Figure 7.7, which is a narrative about arrival time, there is a lot of information about how the children come into the room and select activities. For the child who is typically late and hesitates to come into the classroom, the teacher should investigate that behavior or consider whether enough choices are available for the children.

Observer ___Linda Reynolds___	Date ___April 1___
Time ___Arrival Time: 8:30 A.M.___	

Thomas, Nathan, and Cheryl arrived first and came into the room together. They hung up their coats and went to the blocks area. Theresa arrived next. She threw her coat on the floor and went to the easel and grabbed a smock. Freddie and Joe arrived next. They went to the blocks without hanging up their coats. Jason arrived next. He stepped into the room and stood barely inside the door for 5 minutes. Angelina and Edward walked past him to get into the room, but he did not move. They hung up their coats and went to the dramatic play center to get out the dolls and doll clothes. Jason took off his coat but held it in his arms while he walked over to Mrs. Jolie and asked her to help him hang it up. He then walked over to the blocks but only stood and watched. He made no effort to join the group playing.

Figure 7.7

Narrative

Anecdotal Records

When teachers observe children's behavior and record their observations, they produce *anecdotal records*. Kept over a period of time, these records are likely to reveal patterns of behavior that will suggest strategies for helping an individual child become more competent or supporting the child's obvious growth. Irwin and Bushnell (1980) state that anecdotal records help teachers "test hunches about reasons for a child's behavior or learning style, . . . identify what conditions may be reinforcing behavior, and . . . gain feedback about what children have learned from a particular curriculum unit or presentation" (p. 23).

One key to making an anecdotal record is to record the information without interpretation—just the facts, please! For example, if the teacher observes Sally push Leon so hard that he falls backward into the sandbox, the teacher should record the act, not make a statement such as "Sally was aggressive." This may be the only incidence of pushing all year—Sally may be reacting to the fact that Leon pulled her hair. If Sally pushes several children and each incident is noted in the anecdotal record, then the teacher might interpret from the series of observations that Sally needs help in controlling her impulse to push people. A record stating that Sally was aggressive does not help the teacher focus on her behavior and find its causes. Any interpretation of behavior included in anecdotal records must be clearly labeled as such.

If possible, the teacher should record what happens just prior to an observation and also what happens after it. For example, if Leon pulls Sally's hair, that should be noted as part of the observation. What Sally does next should also be part of the recording. Knowing whether Sally runs away after pushing Leon, apologizes and helps him up, or sits down to play with him is valuable for the teacher in assessing Sally's behavior.

The bias of the observer is always an issue in anecdotal records. Even though the observer may record an incident exactly as it happened, with no

Keeping anecdotal records can help teachers chart children's development throughout the schoolyear.

evaluative or interpretive comments, the choice of incidents to record, the frequency of recordings, or the lack of recordings may all reflect the bias of the observer.

Another key to making helpful observations is to observe children in many different situations and activities. Children who never initiate conversation inside the classroom may talk nonstop outdoors and single-handedly organize half the class for an activity. Observations should also focus on the total development of the child. Records of the child's physical, social, emotional, and intellectual development help the teacher put together a clear picture of the whole child. Katz (1984) suggests looking at preschoolers in terms of their range of affect, variations in play, curiosity, response to authority, friendship, interest, spontaneous affection, and enjoyment of life.

Various educators' guidelines for collecting anecdotal records (Bentzen 1985; Boehm and Weinberg 1987; Irwin and Bushnell 1980) are summarized here:

1. Record the incident as soon as possible after it occurs.
2. Include the setting, time, and activity.
3. Record the exact words of the participants when possible.
4. Record the actions and words of other people in the incident.
5. Make each record as objective, accurate, and complete as possible.

In addition, Boehm and Weinberg (1987, p. 17) recommend limiting discussion to one incident; separating interpretive comments from factual reporting; and considering supportive information in order to accumulate the most useful records.

Making anecdotal records is time consuming. Unfortunately, this kind of information often stays in the teacher's head, rather than being put on paper. One technique for making note collecting easier is to prepare a loose-leaf notebook with a page for each child. The teacher might carry a pad of sticky notes or computer labels in her pocket and jot down observations on individual notes; at the end of the day, these notes can be stuck on the appropriate child's page and the teacher won't have to recopy the information. Additional notes can be added as trends or patterns are observed (Hill and Ruptic 1994; Reardon 1991).

Teachers should make an effort to observe two or three children daily. Over time, they will have accomplished observations on every child. (Sometimes, a teacher may choose one or two children and observe them for a week or two. Usually, these are children the teacher feels need special help because they have either behavior or learning problems.)

Checklists and Rating Scales

Teachers can use checklists to make quick notes of what children actually do in the classroom. This information is valuable for determining which children are interested in which activities or which children have accomplished given tasks. Teachers can use the information obtained from checklists for evaluating learning areas and for reporting to parents.

Most checklists are constructed by teachers and used in a variety of activities, although some may be supplied by the district, state, or other administrators. Consider a checklist of children's physical skills. The skills to be observed would be listed across the top of the page and the children's names down the side of the page. If "Skipping" were one of the skills listed and a teacher observed a child skipping, he would enter the date beside the child's name. Other abilities are also relatively easy to record on a checklist: working puzzles, constructing patterns with beads or pattern blocks, cutting with the right or left hand, using counting as a problem-solving strategy, choosing a book and looking at it for five minutes, playing in a group for ten minutes, and so on. Most teachers who use checklists find that it is most helpful to have a variety of such lists in the areas where the activities would be most likely to be observed. Table 7.1 identifies possible skills and abilities that can be noted on checklists.

McAfee and Leong (1997) have identified the following advantages of using checklists:

1. *Large amounts of information are recorded quickly.*
2. *Checklists are flexible and versatile. They are easily analyzed, interpreted, and quantified.*
3. *Other people, such as aides, can be trained to use checklists.*
4. *Checklists do not have to be completed in the day or week they are begun; they are ongoing.*
5. *Checklists keep track of a child's progress as well as achievement at a specific time.* (p. 89)

Rating scales are similar to checklists except that the behaviors are marked in terms of frequency (always, sometimes, never) or quality (above average, average, or below average) (see Figure 7.8). Rating scales can also provide useful information for teachers as they plan learning experiences. It is most appropriate to use rating scales to compare children's current behaviors to their previous behaviors. Teachers can get caught in the trap of comparing children to one another if they are not judicious in their use of rating scales.

Records of Conversations, Conferences, and Interviews

Records of conversations, conferences, and interviews with children can serve a variety of purposes. Notes from conversations can document a child's abilities with productive language (vocabulary, fluency, articulation of sounds), with concepts (explaining why fish do not sleep), and with processes (how a paper snowflake is cut out). Records of conferences and interviews are more formal in that the teacher designs a set of questions and records the child's responses. Figure 7.9 is an example of a reading–writing conference record. Any of these records can be useful for making instructional decisions for that child.

Table 7.1   Skills and Abilities That Can Be Noted on Checklists

Physical Development	Social–Emotional Development	Intellectual Development
■ Develop large muscles: run, hop, skip, gallop, balance, walk backward, throw and catch a ball ■ Develop small muscles: cut, paste, clap, button, zip, tie, stack ■ Manipulate tools ■ Copy simple shapes ■ Assemble puzzles ■ Draw, pretend write, write ■ Play games ■ Wash, use the toilet, dress without assistance ■ Visually follow a line of print from left to right and top to bottom and return ■ Distinguish sounds and symbols	■ Experience success at school ■ Interact with other children ■ Listen to and follow directions ■ Make choices ■ Initiate and complete activities ■ Accept responsibility ■ Express thoughts in a variety of ways ■ Show appreciation for and sensitivity to others ■ Explore and experiment ■ Practice social skills ■ Enjoy school ■ Maintain self-control ■ Talk ■ Play ■ Respond positively to adult authority ■ Share ■ Help clean up ■ Approach tasks positively and stay with tasks ■ Work independently ■ Cooperate ■ Respond to humor	■ Know and recite personal information: first and last name, age, address, birthdate, telephone number ■ Explain simple pictures ■ Show interest in print and desire to read and write ■ Differentiate between fantasy and reality ■ Speak in sentences of five or more words ■ Recognize colors ■ Recognize numbers ■ Count ■ Demonstrate one-to-one correspondence ■ Recite alphabet ■ Recognize upper- and lowercase letters ■ Write first name ■ Identify patterns and basic shapes ■ Recognize likenesses and differences ■ Measure ■ Ask questions ■ Brainstorm ■ Make lists ■ Classify objects and topics

Asking questions in a conversation, conference, or interview is also a good way to gather information about how children feel about different activities and the things that interest them most. Often, these questions are intended to be open ended. For example, the teacher might ask, "What is your favorite thing to do in the classroom?" or "What is your favorite thing to do outdoors?" Some types of records are designed to gather information by asking children to mark responses to given questions.

Figure 7.10 shows an example of the type of form a teacher might complete during an open-ended interview with a child. Records such as these can help teachers make planning decisions. For instance, if the teacher determines

Figure 7.8

Rating Scale

Observer Linda Reynolds		Date April 1			
Child Ramon Martinez			Frequently	Sometimes	Not Yet
Uses language effectively				✓	
Solves problems in arithmetic with sums to 10			✓		
Participates in group discussions					✓
Participates in singing experiences				✓	

that children are feeling uncomfortable about certain learning experiences, then those can be modified so that the children's attitudes about school might be improved. These records can also provide teachers with clues about experiences that would be of interest to the children and would therefore likely be the basis for successful learning experiences.

Figure 7.9

Reading–Writing
Conference Record

Teacher _____ Date _____

Child _____

What are you reading (or writing) today?

Are you having any problems?

Would you read your favorite part to me (or what you have written)?

Positive specific comments:

What are you going to learn next?

Figure 7.10

Teacher Linda Reynolds   Date   April 1

Child Mary Ricard

1. Do you have a pet?

    A cat named Selena

2. What is your favorite toy?

    My Molly doll

3. What do you like to do best when you play outside?

    Hang on the monkey bars

4. Who do you like to play with?

    Cara, who lives next door

5. What do you like to do best here at school?

    Painting pictures

6. What is your favorite book or story?

    Color Zoo

Parent Questionnaires

When Hill, Ruptic, and Norwick (1998) asked primary-grade teachers what assessment tools gave them the most information, one of the answers was *parent questionnaires*. Harp (2000) also recommends parent questionnaires as a useful tool for promoting cooperation between the parents and the school. Parents can be asked what they have done to prepare their child for school, how their child feels about coming to school, how they would describe their child as a learner, and so on. The answers to these questions can help teachers communicate better with parents during conferences and plan activities that will involve parents.

Self-Evaluations

Even very young children can begin to evaluate themselves. They can describe orally what they learned while they were involved in the activities of the day, or they can tell how they learned to do something. Older children can decide with the teacher which things they are learning are most important and record those in a booklet or on a checklist they have constructed.

Primary children might be encouraged to complete short, written evaluations of selected pieces of their work to share with others. For example, they might complete the sentence "I think this is my best writing because _____" or "I want to share this art because _____."

An Expert Speaks

Ann Benjamin
University of Massachusetts Lowell

Assessment in Early Childhood Education

Despite the call for developmentally appropriate assessment and evaluation practices in early childhood education (NAEYC 1988), policymakers and politicians have increasingly pushed for more standardized testing of children at younger and younger ages. Most teachers know intuitively that testing children under the age of seven or eight yields questionable results. Nonetheless, the "testing craze" ("Why the testing craze" 1999) is likely to continue, and teachers are well advised to prepare themselves to respond.

How do novice teachers equip themselves for a challenge that many veterans find daunting? Teachers who have successfully navigated their way through the complex world of assessment and evaluation offer the following advice:

1. Familiarize yourself with an array of assessment tools and techniques—there are many, and each type serves a different purpose (Airasian 2001; Harp 1996; Irwin and Bushnell 1980; Krechevsky 1998; Meisels et al. 1993).

This will help you construct a rich understanding of learning and development, with test scores being only one component of a complex, multifaceted description of each child.

2. Learn the language of assessment and evaluation—make sure you understand terms such as *objective* and *subjective, reliable,* and *valid.* Know the difference between formative and summative assessment. Become familiar with terms such as *portfolios, performance assessment, work samples, rubrics,* and *authentic assessment* (Airasian 2001; Brandt 1992; Woolfolk 2001).

3. Develop keen observation, recording, and reporting skills—worthwhile assessment depends on the teacher's ability to observe children systematically across a variety of learning situations and to summarize her observations for parents and colleagues (Beaty 1986; Carlevale 1991; McNeely 1997; Nicolson and Shipstead 1994; Schweinhart 1993).

4. Use ongoing assessment to help plan the daily and weekly curriculum. Effective teachers know

Part of the process of self-evaluation should include what needs to come next, so as children think about what they have done well, they should be encouraged to think about what they need to learn, too. For instance, if a child has learned to print his first name, he should be acknowledged for that achievement and then asked if he wants to learn to print his last name (or perhaps the name of a friend or some other word of interest). If a child can read a given text successfully, then he might be encouraged to read a more difficult text or a text from a different genre. Self-evaluation should be linked to personal goal setting.

Strategies for Organization

Records alone do not constitute assessment; they must be evaluated by the teacher. If the teacher has collected various behavioral records over a period of weeks, he can then decide how much and in what ways a child's behavior has changed. The records he has kept should provide evidence for his conclusions.

what children need to learn *before* they decide what to teach (Worthen 1996).

5. Involve children in the assessment process by designing age-appropriate self-evaluations or instruments that help children understand what they must do to produce quality work (Flagg 1998).

6. If you must grade children, insist that grading legends be clearly defined and linked to samples of children's actual work.

7. If you are required to test young children, prepare them to do their best—involve their families by urging a good night's sleep, supportive attitudes, and a nutritional breakfast. Communicate honestly with students, telling them that the test is an opportunity to show what they have learned. Don't pretend that the results are not important.

Conferences are critical in communicating with parents; teachers must prepare carefully for conferences. Try to meet the parent before the conference so that your first meeting is not at the conference. Try to structure the conference so that you accomplish your goals in the allotted time. Encourage parents to plan their questions in advance. If you need a translator, make arrangements for one. As you speak to parents, try to put yourself in their place. Would you be glad you made the effort to attend the conference? Would you return for the next conference? Do parents leave the conference knowing what they can do to support their child's continued growth? Have you shared worthwhile suggestions for at-home activities? Finally, have you discovered what is special about the child? Do parents recognize that you appreciate their child's unique qualities? Have you shared with parents what is truly wondrous about their child (Benjamin 1993, 1997)?

When all is said and done, do parents tell you how the information you provided might help them make decisions on their child's behalf? Assessment succeeds only if the results help *each family* decide what is best for *their child's* educational future. Test scores alone will never accomplish that purpose.

And in order to be useful in documenting and reporting those conclusions, the records must be organized. One popular choice for organizing observations is the portfolio.

Portfolios

Paulson, Paulson, and Meyer (1991) define a **portfolio** as "a purposeful collection of student work that exhibits the student's efforts, progress, and achievements in one or more areas. The collection must include student participation in selecting contents, the criteria for selection, the criteria for judging merit, and evidence of student self-reflection" (p. 60).

Purpose

Portfolios are popular with teachers. But before teachers decide to use a portfolio system, they must decide the purpose the portfolio will serve: Will it be

used to communicate with parents? Will it be used to determine the child's individual progress? Will it be used for teacher accountability? Will it be used for
all these purposes?

In deciding purpose, teachers should understand that a portfolio alone
is not an assessment; rather, it is a collection of materials that can be used to
assess progress. Thus, a portfolio is not especially useful until the materials
have been evaluated by the teacher or others. A collection of materials such as
writing samples and artwork, for instance, is only that—a collection. It becomes an assessment tool when it has been used to determine a child's
progress and needs.

Portfolios can be invaluable in communicating with parents. When a
child receives a letter grade of A or C for an entire year's performance in a
subject, parents have no way of knowing exactly what the child has learned or
how much progress she has made since the beginning of the term. Flood and
Lapp (1989) suggest a comparison portfolio strategy that is especially helpful
in communicating a child's growth to parents. They suggest selecting writing
samples, reading samples, and other pertinent information (such as the number of books read, how often reading is chosen as a free-choice activity,
changes in attitudes, and so on) that will demonstrate the child's growth in an
area. Teachers should make sure that parents are aware of how pieces were selected for a portfolio: Are they the child's best work? work that demonstrates a
particular competency? work that is in progress? Parents also should be invited to offer suggestions for portfolio entries or deletions.

Sometimes, portfolios are used to provide evidence for teacher accountability. For instance, items in portfolios could be used to document that given
activities were provided for children. Teachers might also exchange three or
four portfolios with peers in order to validate their own opinions about the instruction provided and the children's achievement. If teachers choose to exchange portfolios, the selection of the portfolios for examination should be
clearly understood. For example, if four were to be exchanged, one might be
from a child showing outstanding performance, two from children showing
average performance, and one from a child having difficulties of some kind.
Teachers might even want to submit portfolios of selected children's pieces to
their administrators in order to demonstrate effectiveness in fostering children's achievement.

Content

Portfolios can be valuable for documenting children's growth, for communicating with parents, and for validating the quality of instruction. However,
their usefulness depends on how and what materials are selected and how
they are organized.

A variety of items could be included in a portfolio—drawings or paintings the child has made, photos of block constructions he has made, photos or
videos of him climbing on outdoor equipment, notes about or videos of him
throwing or catching a ball, records of books he has read (or listened to the

teacher read), stories he has written or dictated, samples of his classification activities, and notes about his social growth.

Of course, portfolios may also contain teacher observations and notes. If, for example, a piece of writing is selected for inclusion in a child's portfolio, the teacher might add some observation about the selection—perhaps noting that the child worked on the piece over a period of four days but was reluctant to make any changes after a conference with the teacher. The same sort of comment might accompany art samples or other work. Work samples, when used along with other information collected by the teacher, clearly demonstrate the child's growth and the effectiveness of the program.

Organization

The most logical organization for a portfolio that will be used to determine a child's individual progress is to create a section of the portfolio to match each of the major program goals. For example, Meisels (1993, p. 36) suggests the categories of personal–social development, language and literacy, mathematical thinking, scientific thinking, social studies, art and music, and physical development.

The High/Scope program (Schweinhart 1993) recommends the following organizational categories:

- **Initiative**—expressing choices, engaging in complex play
- **Creative representation**—making, building, pretending
- **Social relations**—relating to adults, making friends
- **Music and movement**—exhibiting body coordination, imitating movements to a beat
- **Language and literacy**—showing interest in reading, beginning reading, beginning writing
- **Logic and mathematics**—sorting, counting objects, describing time sequences (p. 32)

Teachers of younger children might find different categories more appropriate for their students, whereas teachers of eight-year-olds might need more specific categories for mathematics, reading, and writing.

Once the major categories have been determined, one or two core items can be collected and dated in fall, winter, and spring. *Core items* are work samples that are common to all children. For example, all children in the first grade would be expected to complete some writing and reading. Other items can be added in each category that reflect the child's individual interests or activities.

Multiple Intelligence Categories   Another strategy for organizing the information gathered about a child is to use Gardner's (1983) multiple intelligences as categorical headings and record information under them, perhaps one category per page. For example, behaviors related to language and print would be recorded under "Linguistic Behaviors" and mathematical experiences under "Logico-Mathematical." The primary advantages of this organizational system are that it reveals the child's strengths at a glance and indicates whether a balance of activities has been offered.

In addition to observing children's strengths in the intelligences, Krechevsky (1998) suggests that teachers observe children's working styles. For example, is the child easily engaged in activities? persistent in solving problems? planful? focused or easily distracted? Knowing how a child works can help the teacher plan activities for the child and teach her valuable work strategies.

Developmental Areas   Using the four areas of child development is another organizational strategy. The teacher's observations can be organized to reflect the child's physical development, social development, emotional development, and cognitive development. Observations that fit into more than one category should be duplicated so they can be included in the second category, as well. One advantage of this means of organization is that it enables the teacher to quickly determine which developmental areas are receiving a lot of attention and which are perhaps being ignored.

Overview of Portfolios

Whatever system is used to organize observations and assessments, a portfolio should include a table of contents or summary sheet listing the materials included and the dates they were collected. Two or three times a year it will be helpful to summarize the data in the portfolio. Such a summary will help teachers determine where their information is too thin and to use what information they have more fully in planning learning experiences. Including some sort of summary will also help prevent the portfolio from becoming a jumble of materials over time.

Most teachers prefer to collect portfolio items in large, expandable folders or loose-leaf binders. However the materials are collected, they should be stored in a place that is easily accessible to both children and teachers. Often, children like to review what they have done already and add items that are especially significant to them. And teachers will certainly want to add to the portfolios on a regular basis.

A portfolio of work samples with careful summaries can be an accurate measure of a child's performance (Meisels et al. 1995). Because such a system is just as valid and provides much more information than achievement tests, it certainly seems reasonable to replace achievement testing with a well-developed portfolio system. Stone (1995) summarizes the differences between portfolio assessment and more traditional assessment in Table 7.2.

Portfolios are most useful when they are built into the instructional day and help teachers make good instructional decisions (Stone 1995). In schools and classrooms in which the use of portfolios for assessment is most successful, teachers and children work to describe good products. Then they think about how the portfolio entries demonstrate growth toward worthwhile goals. Finally,

Table 7.2 Portfolio Assessment versus Traditional Assessment

Portfolio Assessment	Traditional Assessment
Uses multiple forms of assessment	Uses one form of assessment
Gives complete picture of child's learning	Gives narrow view of child's learning
Makes assessment within contexts	Makes assessment in contrived learning context (i.e., test)
Is child centered	Is curriculum centered
Is ongoing	Conducts one-time test on particular task
Supports the process of learning	Represents isolated task separate from the process of learning
Focuses on what children can do	Focuses on what children cannot do
Evaluates child's past achievements and potential	Evaluates by comparison to norms
Benefits children by supporting their growth	Labels, sorts, and ranks children
Provides teachers with information to extend child's learning	Provides little information teacher can use to help child
Provides opportunity for child to evaluate own learning	Uses only teacher evaluation

Source: From S. Stone, *Understanding Portfolio Assessment: A Guide for Parents* (Wheaton, MD: Association for Childhood Education International, 1995). Reprinted by permission of S. Stone and the Association for Childhood Education International. Copyright © 1995 by the Association.

teachers, parents, and children use the portfolios to celebrate achievements, to set new goals, and to reflect on the process of learning together. Barclay and Breheny (1994) found that reporting to parents was much more effective when they kept portfolios of children's work to share at conference time.

Electronic Portfolios

There are several sites at which teachers can produce portfolios based on checklists and comments for each child and then make these available to parents. These sites include Creative Curriculum (www.creativecurriculum.net), where fifty objectives are grouped under the categories of social/emotional development, physical development, cognitive development, and language development. Each objective is explained through many examples so that both teachers and parents will know what the objective means. This site suggests that the checklists be completed three times a year.

Another site is Work Sampling Online, a system developed by Sam Meisels (1993) at www.worksampling online.com. At this site, teachers can enter the data on each child in their class by entering a rating on many objectives grouped into the categories of personal and social development, language and literacy, mathematical thinking, scientific thinking, social studies, the arts, and physical development and health. This site also recommends entering the information on each child three times a year.

Another site is the Early Learning site, based on the assessment system developed by High/Scope, at www.earlylearner.net. The teacher is asked to complete questions, three times each year, grouped under the categories of initiative, social relations, creative presentation, music and movement, language and literacy, and logic and mathematics. Once the observations on each child are recorded, suggested activities for each area are displayed. If the teacher clicks on these activities, the site provides an explanation for these activities and what can be learned from each. It also provides suggestions for what to look for next in the child's development.

Each of these sites (1) features a place in the portfolio of each child where the teacher can make comments and provide explanations; (2) compiles the individual information into a group record and offers resources for the teacher, such as articles about children, curricula, and assessment; and (3) provides a forum through which teachers who are using the systems can talk with one another and share their successes and any problems. Teachers can scan samples of artwork, photos of constructions, or photos of children involved in activities and post these on a website that is available to parents. The individual profiles of students on all the sites are available only by special password so that parents can see only the record of their child. Electronic portfolios are relatively easy to construct and provide one more means for teachers to keep in touch with busy parents. However, all portfolio systems are only as good as the information recorded in them, and teachers will need to continue to engage in daily observations of their children, even if the portfolios are officially completed only three times a year.

Strategies for Reporting

Reporting to parents is an important aspect of the job of the early childhood teacher. Parents have a right to know about their child's performance and behavior in school. Teachers have an obligation to be as honest as they can with parents, but this honesty must be leavened with tact and sensitivity. Nothing is as important to parents as their children; honesty does not have to be brutal or hurtful. Reports to parents usually take the form of report cards, conferences, narratives, telephone calls, casual conversations, newsletters, or videotapes.

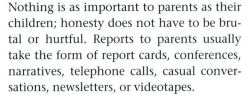

Parents AND *Reporting*

■ Ask parents to help create newsletters that include items specifically of interest to them. Also ask parents to help create or edit videotapes of school activities.

Report Cards

Although many schools require report cards for children in kindergarten or the primary grades, report cards are frustrating to both parents and teachers of young children. Many parents and most educators question the information conveyed on report cards: What does a grade mean? Does an A in mathematics mean that the child knows a given set of concepts or that the child can complete a given number of computations correctly? Grades are notoriously unreliable and useless in conveying what young children have or have not learned (Culbertson and Jalongo 1999; Robinson 1997).

Many schools have done away with letter grades on report cards for kindergarten (and some for primary grades), but often letter grades have been replaced by checklists of skills mastered, such as "Speaks in complete sentences" or "Counts to 100." These checklists have some of the disadvantages of letter grades and leave the impression that the program consists of teaching isolated skills.

A report card is not the best choice for reporting to parents. If teachers must use report cards, however, they should try to mediate the information for parents by enclosing written summaries of children's progress or at least comments that help parents understand the grades. Some schools have adapted their report cards so that they reflect more about what the child can do and depend less on letter grades. For example, rather than posting a grade in reading, some parts of a developmental checklist might be on the report card, such as "Self-corrects errors that change meaning." A report card might also have spaces for the child, teacher, and parents to record their goals for the next grading period. Another strategy is to have a conference with the parents to discuss the child's progress and to review the report card.

Conferences

The most effective way of reporting to parents is face to face in a conference. A conference should not be conducted so that the parents sit passively while the teacher tells them about their child. Both parents and teachers (and sometimes children) should participate; each should learn from the other, and both should have the opportunity to share information.

During a parent conference, the teacher should provide access to the child's work and her own observational records.

Effective conferences require advance preparation. All the observational records, information gathered from checklists, information from inventories or interviews, and portfolios of work will need to be assembled and organized. Teachers must not withhold information from parents; all records should be open to them. Preparation should also include writing a summary of the child's progress in all areas of development and thinking about the implications of assessments for future planning for the child. The teacher's role is also to seek information from the parents by asking for their observations as well as their plans and expectations for their child.

During a conference, the teacher should be prepared to answer questions from parents. Parents will likely want to know what they can do at home to help their child, what interests and abilities the teacher has observed in their child, how their child gets along with other children, who are their children's friends at school, and what kinds of things are difficult for their child.

A conference may allow the teacher to share information about the program with parents as well as information about their child. The inverse of this sharing is eliciting the feelings and understandings of the parents about the program. A well-planned conference provides for sharing information and for keeping the lines of communication open between teachers and parents (Gelfer and Perkins 1987).

Effective follow-up to a conference will be helpful in planning the next conference and will increase the parents' trust. All agreements made during a conference should be summarized in writing, and copies should be made for both the teacher and the parents. If the conference ends with an agreement that the teacher will perform certain tasks, then these tasks should be completed promptly and the information should be entered in the conference file. For example, if the parents request that the teacher observe their child for a specific behavior in the next two weeks and report to them, the teacher should make the observations, record them, and share them with the parents.

Evaluation of the conference is a component of follow-up activities. Canady and Seyfarth (1979, pp. 49–50) suggest some questions that will assist in evaluating the conference:

- Could the conference be described as a problem-solving session?
- Was there an equal distribution of power among all persons present during the conference?
- Was the emotional climate of the conference positive?
- Was the tone of the conference constructive?
- Were the goals of the conference understood by all persons present?
- Were the goals met?
- Were facts and all information related to the conference adequately handled?

Follow-up should be considered as carefully as preconference planning.

Narrative Reports

Another effective way of reporting to parents is through a narrative report. Narratives include basically the information that the teacher would share with parents in a conference. Statements in a narrative should be supported by evidence from the various records that the teacher has accumulated. One method of organizing the information is to focus on each area of development (intellectual, social, emotional, and physical). The narrative should also include what the teacher considers to be implications of the information and plans for the future.

A good narrative is a summary of the information from other records. For example, in summarizing a child's growth in social abilities, the narrative might read:

> Since the beginning of the year, Denise has gained in her ability to communicate her needs and wants with words most of the time. On three occasions, she has been observed asking a child for a toy that she wanted. She is also able to share classroom materials. She has been observed willingly sharing toy trucks and blocks with other children.

Note the objectivity of these remarks. They are specific observations, not judgments or generalizations. Statements such as "Jediah is unhappy" and "Samantha does not function at the level of her peers" have no place in a narrative report.

Telephone Calls

Generally, telephone calls are most useful for sharing with parents information about specific incidents. If, for example, Carly used words to express her frustration for the first time rather than hit someone, a telephone call to report that progress would be appropriate. Telephone calls should not be used to relay negative information about a child unless there is absolutely no alternative. Telephone calls should be brief and to the point and made at times that likely will be convenient for parents.

Casual Conversations

Sometimes, parents prefer to have casual conversations with the teacher when they are picking up or delivering their child. These conversations do not substitute for conferences, but teachers can help keep parents informed by reporting on progress or interesting anecdotes from the day. Again, these are not the times to report negative information. If a problem needs to be shared, a conference should be scheduled.

Newsletters

Although newsletters are not commonly listed as a means of reporting to parents, they can help keep parents informed about what is going on in the

Teachers should follow these guidelines for appropriate assessment in planning instruction and communicating with parents:

1. Curriculum and assessment are integrated throughout the program; assessment is congruent with and relevant to the goals, objectives, and content of the program.

2. Assessment results in benefits to the child, such as needed adjustments in the curriculum or more individualized instruction and improvements in the program.

3. Children's development and learning in all domains—physical, social, emotional, and cognitive—and their dispositions and feelings are informally and routinely assessed by teachers' observing children's activities and interactions, listening to them as they talk, and using their constructive errors to understand their learning.

4. Assessment provides teachers with useful information to successfully fulfill their responsibilities: to support children's learning and development, to plan for individuals and groups, and to communicate with parents.

5. Assessment involves regular and periodic observation of the child in a wide variety of circumstances that are representative of the child's behavior in the program over time.

6. Assessment relies primarily on procedures that reflect the ongoing life of the classroom and typical activities of the children. Assessment avoids approaches that place children in artificial situations, impede the usual learning and developmental experiences in the classroom, or divert children from their natural learning processes.

7. Assessment relies on demonstrated performance during real, not contrived, activities, for example, real reading and writing activities rather than only skills testing (Engel 1990; Teale 1988).

8. Assessment utilizes an array of tools and a variety of processes, including, but not limited to, collections of representative work by children (artwork, stories they write, recordings of their reading), records of systematic observation by teachers, records of conversations and interviews with children, and teachers' summaries of children's progress as individuals and as groups (Chittenden and Courtney 1989; Goodman, Goodman, and Hood 1989).

9. Assessment recognizes individual diversity of learning and allows for differences in styles and rates of learning. Assessment takes into consideration children's ability in English, their stage of language acquisition, and whether they have been given the time and opportunity to develop proficiency in their native language as well as in English.

program. Some newsletters use reports that children write or dictate about field trips, visitors, or other events to provide interesting information to parents. Newsletters need not be formal productions that require a lot of time. Kindergarten and primary children can write items to be included in newslet-

10. Assessment supports children's development and learning; it does *not* threaten children's psychological safety or feelings of self-esteem.

11. Assessment supports parents' relationships with their children and does not undermine parents' confidence in their children's or their own ability, nor does it devalue the language and culture of the family.

12. Assessment demonstrates children's overall strengths and progress, what children *can* do, not just their wrong answers and what they cannot do or do not know.

13. Assessment is an essential component of the teacher's role. Since teachers can make maximal use of assessment results, the teacher is the *primary* assessor.

14. Assessment is a collaborative process involving children and teachers, teachers and parents, school and community. Information from parents about each child's experiences at home is used in planning instruction and evaluating children's learning. Information obtained from assessment is shared with parents in language they can understand.

15. Assessment encourages children to participate in self-evaluation.

16. Assessment addresses what children can do independently and what they can demonstrate with assistance, because the latter shows the direction of their growth.

17. Information about each child's growth, development, and learning is systematically collected and recorded at regular intervals. Information such as samples of children's work, descriptions of their performance, and anecdotal records is used for planning instruction and communicating with parents.

18. A regular process exists for periodic information sharing between teachers and parents about children's growth and development and performance. The method of reporting to parents does not rely on letter or numerical grades but rather provides more meaningful, descriptive information in narrative form.

Source: From S. Bredekamp and T. Rosegrant, "Reaching Potentials through Transforming Curriculum, Assessment, and Teaching," in *Reaching Potentials: Transforming Early Childhood Curriculum and Assessment,* vol. 2, edited by S. Bredekamp and T. Rosegrant, 5–22 (p. 17) (Washington, DC: National Association for the Education of Young Children, 1995). Reprinted with permission from the National Association for the Education of Young Children.

ters. Even threes and fours can write items (these may need to be translated for the parents) or dictate items to be shared with families. A review of the week's events and a list of plans for the next week will help parents know what their children are learning and doing. Many parents will engage their children in activities at home that relate to topics at school if they are kept informed through a newsletter.

Videotapes

Another general means by which teachers can keep parents informed about the school program is to make a videotape of a typical schoolday and encourage parents to check it out. After everyone has had a chance to view the video, the teacher should make a new one. The first video might provide general information about the program, and later videos might concentrate on specific topics: new themes, areas added to the classroom, classroom pets, story time, music and movement activities, and so on. The teacher should ensure that every child is included in class videos.

Observation, Assessment, and Reporting

It is hard to fathom why any educator would bother to institute a comprehensive program of observation and assessment if the information was not to be shared with others—administrators, parents, and other teachers. It is also difficult to imagine attempting to report to parents about their children without having a strong, ongoing program of observation and assessment.

In the process of collecting information and preparing for reporting, teachers can evaluate their assessment programs: Are some pieces of information missing? Are there areas in the child's development about which more information is needed? Are there more effective ways of gathering the needed information? Parents, too, will offer assessment information. For example, they may let the teacher know that the child is transferring the information being learned in school to other situations. Effective observation, assessment, and reporting are mutually supportive activities.

> **Parents AND Assessment**
>
> ■ Write a letter to parents in which you explain two or three of the principles presented in the Developmentally Appropriate Practice box (pages 226–227) that you think are critical to good assessment. Include examples from children's work to support and illustrate your explanation.

Children with Special Needs

In planning assessment strategies for children with special needs, teachers must think about performance strategies that focus on the strengths of these children rather than the limitations. Lowenthal (1996) suggests that assessment for young children with special needs should involve much more than simply standardized tests. She notes, however, that some standardized tests have adaptations for children with specific disabilities. Teachers of special-needs children should use whatever means are available to help make the best decisions about each child's progress and future needs. Sampling systems, play observations, anecdotal records, and portfolio assessment can be invaluable in highlighting children's abilities.

Every child who has been identified as having special needs will have an *individualized education plan* (*IEP*) or *individualized family service plan* (*IFSP*), depending on her age. The development and implementation of these plans is specified by federal law. Each plan must contain the following information:

1. A statement of the child's present levels of educational performance, including academic achievement, social adaptation, prevocational and vocational skills, psychomotor skills, and self-help skills.
2. A statement of annual goals that describes the educational performance to be achieved by the end of the schoolyear under the child's Individualized Education Program.
3. A statement of short-term instructional objectives, which must be measurable intermediate steps between the present level of educational performance and the annual goals.
4. A statement of specific educational services needed by the child (determined without regard to the availability of services), including a description of:
   a. All special education and related services which are needed to meet the unique needs of the child, including the type of physical education program in which the child will participate
   b. Special instructional media and materials needed
5. The date when those services will begin and length of time the services will be given.
6. A description of the extent to which the child will participate in regular education programs.
7. A justification of the type of educational placement that the child will have.
8. A list of the individuals who are responsible for implementation of the Individualized Education Program.
9. Objective criteria, evaluation procedures, and schedules of determining, on at least an annual basis, whether the short-term instructional objectives are being achieved. (*Federal Register,* 30 December 1976, pp. 56966–56998)

Each child's IEP or IFSP is written by a team of specialists, including his classroom teacher and parents, who specify what goals are to be achieved and how. But it is often the task of the classroom teacher to monitor the child's progress toward achieving those goals. Ongoing monitoring may lead to revisions in the initial plan and/or the curriculum. Assessment and curriculum are closely related for children with disabilities (Wolery and Wilbert 1994).

Lowenthal (1997) recommends that children with special needs can benefit from assessments based on play behaviors, family interviews, and the multiple intelligences. Observations of play behaviors can indicate fine and gross motor development, social–emotional development, and intellectual develop-

Parents AND Assessment

■ Parents of children with special needs often require additional support in terms of providing information about assessment as it relates to their children or their placements. Invite specialists from the community to meet with parents and answer their questions about assessment.

ment as children climb, take turns, and solve problems. Teachers should approach interviews with parents with the mindset that the parent is a partner who can share observations about the child's interests and behaviors at home. Teachers' observations conducted over time can provide information about children's strengths in different kinds of knowing. One of the gifts of Gardner's (1983) theory is that it prompts teachers to discover learning strengths that they otherwise might not have expected to find. Looking for strengths can only be positive for special-needs children.

Celebrating Diversity

Good assessment for all students involves strategies that help students recognize their progress toward clearly defined goals and standards. In order to be culturally responsive, assessment must allow for variations in language, cognitive and communicative styles, and beliefs and values. For example, children who know about clipping grocery store coupons from newspapers might be asked to demonstrate how to group the coupons rather than to recall nursery rhymes that might be unfamiliar to them, given cultural differences. Adapting activities in ways like this allows children to demonstrate what they do know without being penalized for what they do not know about things that are culturally foreign to them.

A portfolio can be a valuable tool for encouraging dialogue with parents and community members about what children are learning and how it can best be assessed. Creating a culturally responsive portfolio requires that the curriculum also must be responsive to cultural differences and values. For example, what constitutes proper behavior for children may be defined differently in some communities than in others. To address these differences, parents and teachers can talk about the need to have certain behaviors in school. Parents also can help teachers understand how to help their children achieve certain goals or help the school modify the goals in light of cultural concerns. For example, suppose the school wants each child to attempt performing a new skill before having mastered it, whereas the cultural community advocates having the child observe the skill, practice it without an audience, and perform it only when he has decided that he is ready. In light of this cultural value, the school might need to think about curriculum and assessment differently. If each child is asked to cut on a line, create a poem, or the like, then classroom procedures should allow him to follow his own pattern of learning. Assessment would still evaluate the child's ability to perform the skill, but it would be initiated by the child. The work that is documented in a portfolio does not have to be the same for every child, nor does it have to be collected on the same schedule for every child.

Portfolio assessment focuses on issues that are specific to the child and therefore is more culturally sensitive than some other strategies for assessment. For example, portfolio entries can include work the child does in her first language. Moreover, input from the child's parents is valued, so they can offer suggestions that will be culturally appropriate for the child. Portfolio assessment gives every child the same chance at being successful at school (Farr and Trumbull 1997).

Chapter Summary

- Assessment is much more than testing; it involves ongoing data collection that leads to curriculum and planning decisions.

- Assessment of children should reflect as much information about them as possible, should serve a clear purpose, should be age appropriate, should be as much as possible like the everyday work that children do, should reflect the teacher's knowledge, and should be ongoing.

- Standardized tests are one tool for gathering assessment information about children. However, such tests should never be used to deny services to or make placement decisions about a child.

- The most common standardized tests given to young children are screening tests and readiness tests. These tests are often used inappropriately; critics of such tests also argue that they are not as valid and reliable as they should be.

- When testing young children, teachers should use tests only for the purposes for which they were intended and only when their use will clearly benefit children; select tests that are appropriate for the curriculum; allow only qualified people to administer tests; ensure that they and the school's administrators are knowledgeable about tests; choose only reliable and valid tests. Careful consideration should be given to the value of the tests in terms of the time consumed in administering them.

- Strategies for observation include time–activity samples; tallies; running narratives or logs; incident records; narratives; anecdotal records; checklists and rating scales; records of conversations, conferences, and interviews; parent questionnaires; and self-evaluations.

- In order to be useful, observations must be organized. One popular approach to organizing assessment information is the portfolio. Portfolios can be organized around the High/Scope key experiences, the Project Construct goals, the multiple intelligences, or the child developmental areas.

- Reporting to parents is an important component of the job of the early childhood teacher. The most common reporting methods include report cards, conferences, narrative reports, telephone calls, casual conversations, newsletters, and videotapes.

- Report cards do not provide meaningful information about young children. The best choice for effective communication between the teacher and parents is a conference. A written narrative is another effective approach.

- Telephone calls, casual conversations, newsletters, and videotapes can keep parents informed about day-to-day happenings and the general nature of the school program, but they are not appropriate for sharing in-depth information about individual children.

- Children with special needs may require types of assessment that are specified in their IEPs or IFSPs. The focus of assessment should always be on the strengths of the child.

- Some adaptations in assessment may be necessary in culturally diverse classrooms so that children will not be asked to perform tasks that are not relevant to their backgrounds and values. All children should be assessed through means that are fair and that demonstrate the value placed on each individual's culture and language.

Theory INTO Practice

Examine a standardized screening test for young children. Carefully read the information on norming samples, reliability, and validity. Compare this test with the screening measures used by your local schools to evaluate children before they begin kindergarten. What elements are similar? Which means of assessment is likely to yield the most useful information? Why?

Make a plan for sharing fair and accurate information about testing with the general public. Discuss this plan with a small group of your peers. Is the information currently available to the general public adequate? What would you want the parents of your students to know about testing? Why?

Prepare a presentation for your local school board in which you provide a rationale for eliminating standardized testing of any children before the fourth grade. Be sure to include what assessments you would recommend in place of standardized tests.

Interview two or three teachers of young children. How do they observe and assess the children in their classrooms? How do they report their evaluations to parents? Do they have control of this process, or must they use a system implemented by the school district or board?

With a partner, role-play a parent–teacher conference in which you, as the teacher, must communicate with a parent about his or her child's learning or behavior problems. What kinds of information would you gather and organize before the conference? How would you arrange the physical setting for the conference? Would you include the child? Why or why not?

Visit each of the three electronic portfolio sites. Evaluate them in terms of the inclusion of objectives that you think are important, the ability to communicate clearly with parents, and the value to you as a teacher in terms of the time invested in creating these portfolios.

Assessment Practices for Primary-Age Children

"Miss G., you always ask us hard questions. Now we ask ourselves and each other hard questions, too." —Ryan, age 7

Ryan is right: I do ask hard questions so that all of us in the class community will learn to think, question, and reflect on the learning we do each day. Now my "bottom line" is this question to myself: Why am I doing what I am doing?

Public school often requires testing or assessment. It sometimes helps me learn about my children, but more often, the evaluation and assessment decisions made by my students and me are more meaningful. It is productive for us to determine what will best capture our strengths, interests, and goals.

We keep portfolios. They are not collections of papers that sit in a file cabinet. The items placed in our portfolios are documents that represent what we can do and where we want to direct our attention. Last year, my class put together a portfolio checklist of documents that were important for us to consider for inclusion:

■ *Reading:* Monthly goals, copies of running records (and a piece of writing that described what the reader did to change and improve the use of strategies), a list of the books the child read independently, and photos or samples of book projects (play, poster, letter to the author, etc.)

■ *Writing:* Monthly goals, monthly writing samples with attached self-assessments that described what the samples demonstrated in terms of the writer's growth and change, self-edit checklists, writing samples from prompts, rubrics, and any other materials the student selected

■ *Science:* Samples from science and nature logs, photos, written explanations, and samples of experiments/results

■ *History/Social Studies:* Log entries, list of things studied/researched, photos, and samples

■ *Math:* Math log entries, examples of work done, list of demonstrated concepts understood by the individual, goals, and interests

■ *Physical Education/Art/Music:* List of pieces studied, strengths, interests, goals, samples, tapes, and written responses

Portfolios make it easy to organize student-led conferences held at the end of the year. Each child prepares a conference for his or her family. Other people may be included in the conferences (the Reading Recovery teacher, siblings, administrators, teachers from previous years, etc.). The portfolios and conferences represent the strong commitment to student involvement in the record-keeping and assessment procedures. The assessment model also keeps evaluation in sync with day-to-day learning and teaching.

I am busy maintaining records of children's academic, emotional, and social growth and change. My daily teaching plans come from what I observe the children doing as they work. Checklists do not work for me. They are more paperwork to transfer information. I now streamline my information to maintain a reasonable record-keeping system. Keeping folders or a notebook of running records helps me watch patterns and changes in students' reading behaviors over time. I also maintain notes on writing work, and I make conference notes as I work with individuals and groups. For work selected by students, I either concur with their choices or I pull other samples that I feel better represent their learning and work.

To be able to maintain the quality of teaching I want, my evaluation practices must be well thought out and simple. I observe the learners, evaluate their work, make teaching decisions, and reassess the growth. Assessment is ongoing, cyclical, and specific. To maintain that quality forces me to question my practices and get at the real issues.

CHAPTER 8

Working with Parents and Paraprofessionals

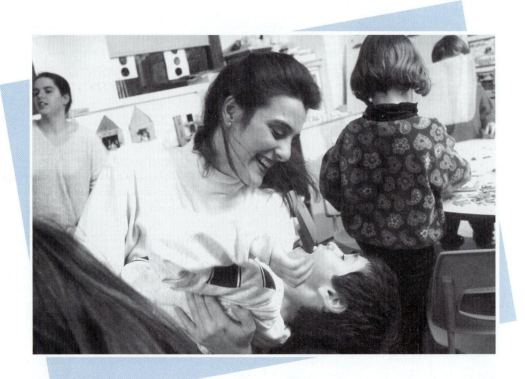

- Develop effective programs that encourage parent participation.
- Plan for effective communication with parents.
- Plan for the involvement of paraprofessionals in the program.
- Define the roles and responsibilities of volunteers in the program.
- Create strategies for relating effectively to families from diverse backgrounds.

Your observation this week was not what you had expected. You went to a school for children from ages three to five or six. Some of the children in this school had been identified as having special needs and were entitled to services provided by the school district. You expected to see teacher aides with these children, and your expectations were accurate in some instances—for example, interpreters were working with children who are deaf and aides were helping children in wheelchairs. What surprised you was the number of classrooms in which the teachers and aides were working together as a team. You knew that the teachers were ultimately responsible for all instruction in the classroom, but you also saw aides busy instructing small groups and tutoring individual children. Your only previous experience with teacher aides had been with some who supervised the playground and lunchroom.

You were also surprised at the number of parents who were volunteering. You knew that today most parents work outside the home, so you had thought that the days of "room mothers" and "room helpers" were over.

What does the teacher do to keep all these adults working together smoothly so that the children benefit from the extra hands, extra ears, and extra eyes?

Need for Parent Involvement

Research continues to support the importance of parent involvement in the success of children in school (Feuerstein 2000; Jones 2001; Marcon 1999). Even parents who participate infrequently in school activities can make a big difference in their children's academic lives compared to those who do not participate at all (Hampton and Mumford 1998). Henderson and Berla (1994) found that when parents were involved in their children's schooling, children achieve higher grades, have better school attendance, have more positive attitudes and behaviors, graduate from high school at a higher rate, and are more likely to enroll in higher education. There is no question that parent involvement pays off in better educational outcomes for children.

Realities of Parent–Teacher Relationships

There are good reasons for involving parents in the education of their children. In reviewing what we know about parent involvement programs, Epstein (1991) offers these conclusions:

- Parents and teachers are more similar than different—they have many goals in common and a need to share information.
- Programs must continue through the elementary and high school years, not stop after the early childhood years.
- Programs must include all families.
- Programs make the teacher's job easier.
- Program development takes time.

Parent–teacher relationships are not as simple as many articles lead us to believe. New teachers could mistakenly come to think that parent volunteers are common and that all parents will attend parent conferences if they are invited to do so. However, teachers of young children need to recognize that although parent involvement is very important, it is not always easy for the teacher, the school, or the parents to facilitate.

Pressures on parents today are tremendous due to changing family structures, economic conditions, and lack of support for the nuclear family. Many children live with single parents, in two-parent working families, or in blended families created by remarriages, and many live with relatives other than their parents or with people who are not related to them.

The plight of children in the United States continues to be serious. Nearly one child of every six is living below the poverty line ($13,738 for a family of three or $17,603 for a family of four). We have more poor children than we had twenty to thirty years ago. The overall average number of poor children in this country is 16.6 percent, although the rate is much higher in some states. Louisiana, Alabama, and Mississippi have the highest rates of child poverty, whereas New Hampshire has the lowest rate. Seventy-seven percent of the children living in poverty have at least one person in the family working; the percentage of working poor is the highest since records have been kept. About 43 percent of the children living in poverty live in families that have incomes of less than half the already low levels that designate poverty. Even though the percentages are higher for Black and Hispanic children, there are actually more poor White children. Many poor children live in suburbs and rural areas; child poverty is not confined to urban areas (Children's Defense Fund 2001).

The Children's Defense Fund (2001) states that

> *poor children are at least twice as likely as non-poor children to suffer stunted growth or lead poisoning, or to be kept back in school. Poor children score significantly lower on reading, math, and vocabulary tests when compared with otherwise similar non-poor children. More than half of poor Americans (55 percent) experience serious deprivations during the year (defined as lack of food, utility shutoffs, crowded or substandard housing, or lack of a stove or refrigerator). Poor households are more than 15 times as likely to experience hunger. . . . Each year spent in poverty adds more to a child's risk of failing to finish high school on time than does living in a single parent home or being born to a teenage parent, according to data from the U.S. Department of Education.*

The structure of the family has changed, as well, diverging from the typical "Dick and Jane" family of the past. In 1990, Cline found that only 5.9 percent of Americans lived in a family in which the father worked outside the home and the mother worked at home to care for the children. And with 70 percent of mothers of school-age children working outside the home, the percentage of such families grows smaller every day (Washington and Andrews 1998).

The enormous number of mothers in the workforce reflects economic conditions that make it ever more difficult for a family to survive economically. Many mothers work because they are the sole source of support for their children. These economic stresses in turn make it more difficult than ever before for parents to have choices about child care, to spend energy nurturing and educating their children rather than just trying to survive, or to become involved in the formal education of their children.

In addition to these pressures on the family, today's nuclear family does not have the support from the extended family that was available to past generations. Families often live long distances from other relatives and must depend on outsiders for child care and advice or support. Many parents are isolated; they have no one to help them cope with all the demands of caring for children and maintaining their daily lives.

Implications for Teachers

One of the first rules for teachers who want to establish good relationships with all parents is to adopt a **nonjudgmental attitude** toward them. Parents who have been labeled "hard to reach"—usually those who have low incomes, are members of ethnic minorities, and have limited formal education—are often presumed to have little concern about education or to place little value on school. However, research indicates that this is not the case. Chavkin and Williams (1993) found that 90 percent of such parents were concerned about their children's education and wanted to be actively involved in it. Some believed that it was the teacher's duty to get parents involved; even so, these parents were interested in their children's school experiences.

The vast majority of parents are interested in their children's education but rely on teachers to initiate contact.

There are many reasons parents do not get involved in school. Some may have had negative experiences in school, so that any contact with the school revives their own feelings of inadequacy; others may be overwhelmed with the pressures in their lives and unable to cope with one more demand; still others may not know what they can do to help their children in school. For some parents, it would be culturally inappropriate to be other than passive in their involvement with the school. In some cultures, teachers are highly respected figures of authority. For parents from such cultures to take an active role in school would be perceived as an infringement on the teacher's authority.

One of the responsibilities of teachers is to maintain relationships with the parents of the children in their care. Most teachers want parents to be involved, but they may have a narrow vision of what that involvement should look like. Especially with Latino parents, many schools operate on what Delgado-Gaitan (1991) calls a deficit model: "Deficit perspectives depict inactive parents in the schools as incompetent and unable to help their children because they have a different language, work long hours away from home, belong to different ethnic groups, or are just not interested" (p. 22). Her research says that this perception is simply not true; these parents often are very interested in their children's education and they do support it, but not always in ways recognized by the school.

New teachers must expect to be involved in major efforts to restructure family and school relationships. Expecting all families to meet middle-class standards for involvement in schools is unrealistic. It is also unrealistic to believe that only one model for family involvement is possible. Teachers who have such high but unattainable expectations may become frustrated and give up. A reasonable goal might be to get parents more involved this year than in previous years or to get more parents involved on a regular basis. Families and schools must learn new ways of interacting. Karr and Landerholm (1991) state the goal well: "Programs must meet the needs of the parents they serve rather than demand that the parents meet the needs of the program" (p. 6).

Teachers of young children must be especially sensitive to the needs of children from different family structures, and this sensitivity should be reflected in the language used to discuss families. The phrase *broken home,* for example, is inappropriate. A child's parents may be divorced and she may be living in a single-parent family, but there is nothing inherently wrong or deprived about such a family structure. Similarly, teachers must avoid planning activities in which the child is to make gifts for parents or events that are labeled "father–son" or "mother–daughter." Activities involving gifts or family events should be presented as opportunities to share with someone special in a child's life—a foster mother, a grandparent, or any other person—rather than being specifically labeled for mothers and fathers. When using photographs of families, teachers should make sure that a variety of family structures is illustrated and that discussions are not limited to families made up of Mother, Father, and children.

Although it is not directly the responsibility of the teacher, it is important that all school employees treat parents with respect and consideration. There are many sad stories of the school secretary or other staff treating parents poorly when they come to school, such as when they enroll their children. If a problem with parental treatment is apparent, teachers should suggest that the school board of directors provide sensitivity workshops for all school employees.

Encouraging Parent Involvement

Many studies have looked at effective parent involvement strategies, but they have provided no easy answers. Teachers who want parents to participate in school activities must begin by examining their own goals and feelings about having parents involved.

Teachers should encourage parents to visit frequently and to drop in without an appointment. Teachers can also provide guidance to parents in how to help young children learn at home. Some teachers have made kits to send home so that parents can help their children develop a variety of skills and abilities. For example, the kit could be about colors, letters, shapes, or numbers and contain materials such as a book, a tape for musical activities, and some suggested follow-up activities. This approach encourages active learning rather than workbook-type activities (Gorter-Reu and Anderson 1998).

Parents can prove to be strong allies in supporting developmentally appropriate programs if teachers take the time to help them understand how activities are selected and why certain teaching decisions are made (Stipek, Rosenblatt, and DiRocco 1994). Sending home appropriate activities that will involve parents with their children is also useful in helping parents understand that learning is not limited to drills on basic skills. Some research has indicated that the largest gain in children's achievement attributed to parent involvement

NAEYC

comes from participation in well-designed home activities (Jones 2001). Teachers must give thought to designing these home activities. Pena (2000) describes a workshop that teachers provided for parents in how to make little books for their children to use at home. These parents had low literacy skills themselves and did not know how to do what the teachers wanted them to do. More thought might have resulted in a workshop in which the school provided the little books and demonstrated how they could be used even by those with low literacy skills. Assigning pages of workbook-type assignments will not involve the family, but asking parents to listen to their child read, play a board game, or conduct a scavenger hunt in their home for objects that begin with the same sound can promote parent–child interactions.

Parent involvement will not simply happen and it will not happen if teachers and schools do not make a concerted effort to make it happen. Schools should contact parents at least monthly, and they should avoid contacting parents with only negative reports. When schools contact parents with only negative information, parents are likely to develop negative attitudes and give the school low ratings (Pena 2000). Two key elements for getting parents involved are to feed them and to put their children on stage (Jones 2001). Providing food, either snacks or meals, is easy and provides for interaction as people eat. Putting children on stage should be done in developmentally appropriate ways (singing songs they sing every day in class, acting out a story as they do on a regular basis in class, and so on), but the point is that parents love to see their children showcased in positive ways. We know that parents do not like to hear data about test scores, and they do not like to be harangued about getting other parents involved (Nichols-Solomon 2000). What they do want is to feel that the school respects them and that their contributions to the education of their children are recognized by the school.

Furlow (1999) suggests that teachers who want to involve parents in their children's education use these strategies:

1. Meet parents in a comfortable setting: their own home. Making home visits can be time consuming and even stressful, but it is a great way to build trust between parents and teachers. Visiting the home is often the only successful way to reach parents who do not have phones.

2. Cover all of the languages spoken by children and their parents. Many schools that enroll students from diverse cultures provide school materials in several languages. Some schools have even hired support personnel to reach out to immigrant families in their own languages and help them adapt to a new culture and a new school.

3. Involve parents in the school's decision-making process. Ensure that they are aware of school issues and events by making personal contacts, not just by sending home flyers. Also give them opportunities to provide feedback and make suggestions. By becoming involved in its decision making, parents take on some ownership for the school.

4. Make schools "parent friendly," starting with the front office. Parents who are new to a school (or perhaps weighed down by unpleasant mem-

ories of the schools they attended) can be uplifted by a front office that looks cheerful and is staffed by welcoming individuals who can help new parents navigate the school process. Clear signs that will help parents find their way around the building are important, too. Some schools provide parents with their own room or another space in which to meet and discuss school plans.

Kieff and Wellhousen (2000) suggest that as teachers plan any kind of meeting or activity for parents, they try to anticipate what barriers might make participation difficult for some parents. In Figure 8.1, they provide a list of possible modifications to overcome potential barriers.

Parent Roles

Parents may take on a variety of roles in the school. At one end of the continuum of parent involvement are parents who never participate in any school activities, although they are active in the sense of sending their children to school; one level higher are parents who participate in passive roles that only require them to listen. Further along the continuum are parents who participate by attending events at school or volunteering their time to help teachers in the classroom; even further along are those parents who get involved in decision making at the school or district level and who assist in teaching. Parents of children in cooperative schools usually are at this point. Some parents take total responsibility for their children's education and make the commitment to educate their children at home.

Many parents do not see how their involvement at school could possibly benefit their children. Teachers need to supply specific information about *why* parent involvement is important. For example, teachers often suggest that parents read to their children but do not share with the parents why reading will help the children become more literate. Parents who have specific information are much more likely to become involved. Coleman (1997) points out several benefits of teachers seeking common ground with parents and families. Doing so can lead to the feeling that parents and teachers are colleagues, maintain an open dialogue with families, and help both parents and teachers find ways to help each other.

Parents who choose not to be involved in their children's school cite as reasons health problems, economic differences between themselves and teachers, and work responsibilities. Some teachers, on the other hand, believe that parents are not more involved because of their unrealistic expectations of the school's role; an attitude that school is not important enough to warrant taking time from work; jealousy of teachers; teachers' lack of trust of parents; and a lack of activities to draw parents to school (Leitch and Tangri 1988).

Swick and McKnight (1989) found a cluster of characteristics in kindergarten teachers that strongly supported parent involvement, including belonging to a professional association and adhering to a developmentally oriented philosophy; they also found that administrative support for parent involvement was vital. Galinsky (1988) found that teachers who had more

Figure 8.1

Common Barriers and Possible Modifications Checklist

Barriers	Modifications
Time	☐ breakfast meetings ☐ weekend events ☐ one event scheduled over a number of days ☐ open invitations
Transportation	☐ school bus or van ☐ car pool arranged by teacher or parent volunteer ☐ buddy system among families
Child care	☐ school-provided child care ☐ child care provided by parent organization ☐ buddy system among families
Decorations/ celebrations	☐ artwork created by children in the art center ☐ artwork generated during a theme/project study
Curriculum	☐ opportunities for children to make multiple gifts and cards and to pick their recipients ☐ family members share expertise and culture ☐ bias-free curriculum
Food	☐ multiple menus available ☐ buffets ☐ picnics
Printed material	☐ translate copies ☐ make audiotapes ☐ make telephone calls ☐ use voice mail or e-mail
Special guest	☐ guest not specified by role ☐ a pal or friend ☐ open invitations to extended family members or a noncustodial parent
Expense	☐ support provided by community businesses underwriting the event or materials needed
Misunderstanding the role as parent volunteer in the classroom	☐ volunteer training sessions ☐ specific routines created ☐ recorded or printed instructions
Misunderstanding the parental role in home-extension learning activities	☐ specific routines created for home-extension learning activities ☐ parent workshops to explain activities ☐ demonstration tapes ☐ demonstrations during home visits
Discomfort in school situations	☐ alternative home visits or neighborhood meetings ☐ buddy systems among families ☐ small-group meetings

Source: Judith Kieff and Karyn Wellhousen, "Planning Family Involvement in Early Childhood Programs." *Young Children* 55 (May 2000): 18–25. Reprinted with permission from the National Association for the Education of Young Children.

Working with Parents and Paraprofessionals

Parent involvement has long been one of the most important factors related to student success. However, this information did not become nationally recognized until President Bill Clinton signed into law in March 1994 the bill for Goals 2000: Educate America Act, a program made up of eight goals aimed at helping students reach new heights in academics and occupational skills. Goal 7 was that "every school will promote parental involvement in children's education." While goal 7 was originally focused on parent involvement with school-age children, there were also programs to help parents prepare their children in the early years for school.

While there was no controversy over the need to provide parent involvement in the schools, there was disparity on how to implement this goal. Interpretations ranged from having parents and paraprofessionals work in the classrooms to having whole schools designed around the concept of parent involvement. Many schools have parents participate in school events, and others have parents on advisory boards and run various school programs. Some schools have their own employment and education programs for parents. While most parent help is welcomed, many teachers are not trained in utilizing parent support and therefore shy away from it. In addition, many parents have had bad school experiences of their own and therefore avoid coming to their children's school.

Paraprofessionals work in the system in varying degrees on all levels. Without formal training or educational backgrounds, they get specific training to meet needs in the classroom or school. Schools, often overcrowded and shorthanded, usually welcome their valuable contribution.

In 1997 studies showed large numbers of young children had two working parents or single parents. Welfare-to-Work was the solution for the poor, and child care was the solution for everyone else. Parents had less and less time to spend with their young children. By 1998 research related to the impact of the first three years of development began to surface. The much ignored 1994 multimillion dollar Carnegie Corporation Study began to make an impact. Results showed that millions of young children living in poor family environments were at risk of having tragic lives because of their lack of nurturing love, guidance, support, protection, and educational stimulation. Then the new brain research exposed the irreversible effects to the brain of early abuse and neglect.

By the year 2000 there were major improvements in the workplace with programs like flextime, child care at the business site, and parent education. Although not universal by any means, real help was starting to emerge. Then 2002 brought it to another level—a bill was passed for At-Home Infant Care (AHIC) programs for up to ten states to help the poor receive funding to stay at home with their young children. The current administration is responding by creating major early childhood initiatives that include parent involvement components.

education and were parents themselves were more likely to have positive perceptions of parents. She explained that it is not being a parent per se that leads to positive perceptions but "the ability to put themselves in the parent's shoes and to be empathetic" (p. 8). If teachers feel that parental involvement is important, they will work to overcome the barriers that they perceive are keeping parents out of the school.

Field trips provide a great opportunity for getting parents involved in school activities.

Every parent who wants to be involved should have the opportunity to do so. Teachers need to find out from parents how they would like to be involved. The most direct way of determining how parents feel and what they would like to do is to ask them—during a home visit or during a conference early in the year. Another way is to have them respond to a questionnaire. Figure 8.2 is an example of an interview form that teachers can use in determining the kind of involvement parents need or want.

Activities for Involving Parents

Many activities can be arranged to involve both parents who choose to be active and those who choose more passive roles. A number of levels of participation are possible:

NAEYC

1. Family reading, family math, or family science nights are evenings when the children and their families are invited to school and participate in reading, math, or science activities that are developmentally appropriate and that help parents understand why such activities are provided in school.

2. Potluck dinners offer a way to celebrate holidays by inviting families to share social evenings together. If the children can make part of the meal to share, so much the better.

3. Parent education workshops can range from sessions in which outside speakers talk about child development, discipline, or some other topic of general interest to meetings of small groups who want to discuss specific issues such as sibling rivalry with other parents.

4. Formal organizations of parents such as Parent–Teacher Associations can provide programs for parents and teachers.

5. Committees of parents can discuss school issues, including curriculum decisions, school policies, and hiring of staff.

Figure 8.2

Parent's Name _____ Date _____

Child's Name _____ Phone Number _____

1. **How would you like to be involved in our school's activities?**

   A. In the classroom:
   - ☐ Helping with art activities?
   - ☐ Helping with cooking activities?
   - ☐ Helping with woodworking?
   - ☐ Supervising water play?
   - ☐ Supervising sand play?
   - ☐ Reading to individual children or to small groups?
   - ☐ Taking a small group on a nature walk?
   - ☐ Helping children with the care of classroom pets?
   - ☐ Driving or supervising on field trips?
   - ☐ Making a classroom video?
   - ☐ Other: _____

   B. At home:
   - ☐ Typing a parent newsletter?
   - ☐ Sewing a costume for the dramatic play area?
   - ☐ Collecting and organizing teaching materials (such as prop boxes)?
   - ☐ Calling parents to remind them of meetings?
   - ☐ Bringing refreshments for a parent meeting?
   - ☐ Repairing damaged or torn books for the classroom library?
   - ☐ Making a classroom web page?
   - ☐ Making tape recordings of stories or poems?
   - ☐ Other: _____

2. **What topics would you like us to cover in a program for parents?**
   - ☐ Literacy activities to do at home?
   - ☐ Testing issues for young children?
   - ☐ Family services available in the community?
   - ☐ Places to take your child that are worthwhile and inexpensive?
   - ☐ How to select appropriate toys or how to make toys?
   - ☐ How to help my child with English when I am not a native speaker of that language?
   - ☐ Other: _____

6. Parents can become members of teams involved in making recommendations for children with special needs.

7. Parents and teachers can attend workshops in which they make instructional materials for use in the classroom.

8. Chapman (1991) suggests that parents can help produce videotapes that focus on lessons and explain the "whys" of the lesson (why certain materials, teaching strategies, responses to wrong answers are used) or that teach other parents specific techniques for helping their children, such as how to motivate them.

Communication with Parents

It is the teacher's responsibility to keep the lines of communication with parents open. Communication with parents can be divided into two categories: communication *about the program* and communication *about the individual child*. Parent conferences, newsletters, and telephone calls are all avenues for communication, but they are used more to talk about an individual child than about the program. Home visits, parent visits to the school, school handbooks, letters and notes, and a teacher who is prepared with good written information about community resources will supplement the above-mentioned communication methods and keep parents informed about the school's program.

Cattermole and Robinson (1985) asked parents what they considered the most effective forms of communication they received from school. Their first choice was information they received from their children—followed by school newsletters, report cards, parent–teacher conferences, visits to school, notes or phone calls from teachers, and formal meetings and informal contacts with friends.

School Handbooks

School handbooks are especially useful for sharing basic information about programs. A handbook should include the school calendar; the hours of each session; school policies such as procedures for getting refunds of tuition payments, celebrating birthdays at school, or handling sick children; a class list for each class; a list of the staff (with perhaps a short professional biography of each); and statements of the school's philosophy (Bundy 1991). The school handbook might also list the goals and objectives for the children, emergency procedures, bus routes, and other information useful to parents.

Home Visits

Although not as common as they once were, **home visits** are still an important means of establishing solid parent–teacher relationships. Some parents are much more comfortable in their own homes than at school. However, teachers should be sensitive to the fact that some parents may find a home visit from the teacher uncomfortable or intrusive, for any number of reasons. The information gained about the child, the parents, and the home environment are well worth the investment of time and energy required to complete home visits.

If a home visit can be arranged before school starts, the child and teacher can get to know each other individually before having to relate to each other in a group setting. Parents will also appreciate meeting the teacher before school begins and having a chance to ask questions about the program and discuss expectations for their child.

Home visits can be effective if teachers plan and prepare for them. The following suggestions may help in planning visits:

1. Schedule the visits well in advance. Send a written reminder of the visit. Let the parents know how long you expect the visit to last. Arrive and leave on time.

2. Make sure that parents know the purpose of the visit. Assure parents that they do not need to make any special preparations for your visit.

3. Be a gracious guest. If the parent offers something to eat or drink, accept it politely. Respect the parents and the home.

4. Do not make snap judgments about the home environment. If the physical surroundings do not match your image of a home, do not conclude that the home is not a good environment for the child.

5. Be prepared to talk about the program and your plans for the children in an informal manner. Listen, ask questions, and listen some more.

Often, teachers like to take something when they visit—materials for making a nametag for the child, a camera for photographing the child, a photograph album of activities from the previous year, a puppet, a wooden puzzle, a book that can be returned to the classroom later, or paper and crayons for drawing. Taking something can provide openings for sharing information and opportunities for observations (Johnston and Mermin 1995).

It is also helpful for the teacher to take an information sheet for the parents that gives his name and phone number, a school calendar with holidays and special events marked, information about snacks if parents will be providing them, and a list of rules for celebrating birthdays and for bringing objects to share at school. The teacher might also take along a list of materials that he needs at school. Teachers in one school district hand out a list of "beautiful junk"—egg cartons, oatmeal boxes, assorted nuts and bolts, baby food jars, old paint brushes, wood scraps, bottle caps, used magazines, and the like—that most households accumulate and that even families of limited means can contribute.

During a home visit, the teacher may want to discuss the special needs and interests of the child, any allergies or health problems that the teacher needs to be aware of, and the expectations the parents have for the child in the program. If it seems appropriate, the teacher can also discuss how the parents would like to be involved in the program. Parents may also want to know about the teacher's background, training, and experience. She should be prepared to discuss the program, how decisions are made about what to study, and how she plans to deal with discipline problems.

If the teacher is unable to visit two or three parents at home, he might try inviting them to a special meeting at school, where he shares the information he would have shared in a home visit. Kieff (1990) found that parents of children labeled at risk by their school district preferred meeting in small groups with the teacher. These parents did not feel comfortable in large, formal parent meetings.

It is important that all parents understand how much they teach their children and how important they are in their children's education. Hohmann, Banet, and Weikart (1979) suggest that teachers help parents

> realize that . . . parenting is teaching, . . . they already know a lot about child development in general and about their own children in particular, and . . . teachers are not purveyors of knowledge but rather people who wish to support and extend the learning that's already going on at home. (p. 20)

If parents cannot or will not come to school and the teacher cannot visit them at home, the teacher might try inviting the family to meet at a park, library, or other public place. Meeting on neutral ground may help the parents feel more comfortable. If such a plan is impossible, then the teacher should try to contact the parents by phone or by letter to share the information. The teacher should make her contacts with them nonthreatening and nonjudgmental. It is vital that the teacher continue to reassure parents that she is interested in their child and will welcome their questions.

A real partnership between schools and families is possible only if both truly believe that the other has something valuable to bring to the relationship, that the common goal is the welfare of the child, and that there is a sense of shared responsibility (Workman and Gage 1997).

Parent Visits to School

Some parents can arrange to visit the school during school hours and should always be welcomed. Parents who come to observe the program and their children's participation in it should be invited to sit and watch or to join in activities, whichever they feel most comfortable doing. Every parent who comes to observe should be invited to schedule a conference so that any questions or concerns can be discussed. Teachers can use a checklist such as that shown in Figure 8.3 to prepare for conferences with parents.

One school sends a special invitation to each parent to attend school on a given day, beginning a few weeks before regularly scheduled conferences. The invitation indicates that if parents cannot come on the stated day, they can come any time. With a little persistence, teachers in this school get almost 100 percent of the parents to visit the school, and conferences are much more successful after parents have seen the program in action.

Parents can be invited to participate in holiday celebrations that the children have planned or invited to visit when the children are involved in a

Figure 8.3

Parent–Teacher
Conference
Checklist

Parent's Name _____

Child's Name _____

☐ Arrange the time and place: _____.

☐ Gather all relevant information (e.g., assessments, samples of child's work, portfolio, anecdotal observations, checklists, and so on).

☐ Organize materials so they can be presented either by subject or by developmental area.

☐ Invite the parent to voice any changes observed since the last conference; make note of comments.

☐ Share information gathered with the parent.

☐ Ask for the parent's input about goals for the next learning period. (Perhaps set goals after each area of development is discussed.)

☐ Thank the parent for his or her interest and observations.

group activity so that they can observe their child's behavior in a group setting. Rather than having children put on performances, it is advisable to ask parents to visit when the children are involved in normal classroom activities, such as singing, playing musical instruments, or dramatizing stories. These activities do not require practice by the children but do allow the parent to feel good about their children's abilities.

The teacher might want to prepare an observation guide for parents so that they can see some of the important aspects of the program during their visit. Figure 8.4 is an example of such a guide, which can be adapted to fit the teacher's own needs.

Sometimes, parents who cannot attend school during the day can be invited for an evening visit. The children can come, too, and get involved in some of their usual school activities so that parents can learn more about what their children do at school.

A **parent place** in a corner of the classroom can help parents feel that they are important and needed. A table and a small bulletin board are all that is necessary to provide such a corner for parents. Parents can use the bulletin board to communicate with one another (notes about car pools, child care, and so on). The teacher can post photographs of parents working with the children or creating materials or games for the classroom, notices of special events of interest to families, lists of items that are needed in the classroom, and so on. The table can hold a small resource library for parents, providing copies of articles and books that parents might find helpful; pamphlets, magazines, and brochures such as those published by the National Association for

Figure 8.4

Observation Guide
for Parents

Welcome to XYZ School!

We are always pleased to have parents visit our programs! This sheet may serve as a guideline for observing your child as he or she interacts with others in school. We encourage you to schedule an appointment with the teacher to discuss your observations. You may use any part of this form, or you may turn it over and write down some questions that you want to ask the teacher later. Please do whatever is most comfortable for you. Enjoy your visit!

Check or circle whatever items are appropriate.

Setting:
Indoors

Outdoors

Activity:
Choice time (individual)

Whole group

Small group directed by teacher

Social Interactions:
With other children

With adults

Materials, Equipment, or Activities Selected:
List here

Did your child use material or equipment as it was designed to be used? or did he or she use the material or equipment to make up a game?

Time Spent in Each Activity:
Estimate here

Types of Interactions:
Solitary activities (played alone)

Small-group activities (joined or formed a small group)

Hosting a parent reading program is another way to get parents involved in the classroom.

the Education of Young Children (NAEYC) and the Association for Childhood Education International (ACEI) on a variety of topics; and other materials. Some larger schools provide "parent rooms" where parents can meet other parents, wait to pick up their children, or find information about parenting. Epstein (1991) lists making room (literally) for parents as an important component of parent involvement programs.

When parents cannot visit school or stay long enough to observe, notes and photographs of their children engaged in activities help communicate what is going on in class. A videotape of a day in the class that parents can borrow may also help to communicate with some parents. Greenwood (1995) reported very positive results when she created a video of children's activities that she circulated among parents. She made several videos during the year and also volunteered to make copies for parents, if they sent blank tapes.

Letters and Notes

Parents appreciate letters that give them information about school programs and their children, in particular. Instead of newsletters, some teachers like to send form letters that may include suggestions for things the parents could do at home to complement what the children are learning in school. Adding a personal note about the child at the bottom of each parent's letter makes this practice even more effective. Brief notes that communicate the child's progress are an important way of letting parents know that the teacher is aware of their child and her accomplishments.

Notes should always be positive. A note saying that "Sebastian succeeded in tying his shoes today" or that "Nancy read a complete book independently" will help parents feel that the teacher is staying in touch with them. Most teachers keep a list of parents and jot down the date when they send each parent a note. When all parents have been contacted, the teachers start over. Some schools even have notepaper printed with captions such as "Good News" or "Happygram."

D'Angelo and Adler (1991) suggest the following guidelines for preparing effective written communication for parents:

- *Keep sentences short. Try to keep sentences to ten or fewer words, and never allow them to include more than twenty words.*
- *Keep paragraphs short. Try to keep paragraphs to an average of six lines.*
- *Use easy words. Let the short, familiar words bear the main burden of getting your point across. Use big words or technical terms when only those words will express a message accurately.*
- *Get to the point. State the purpose of your message up front and omit irrelevant information.*
- *Write things in logical order. The newspaper formula of "who, what, where, when, why, and how" is helpful as an organizing device.*
- *Be definite. Don't hedge. Be careful with such words as* seems, may, perhaps, possibly, generally, usually, *and* apparently. *Give a clear picture of what you want to say.*
- *Be direct. Speak to each reader. Say "you should" or "please do" instead of "parents should."*
- *Use the active voice more often than the passive. Put the subject at the beginning of the sentence. For example, write "Please sign and return the consent slip if you want your child to go on the trip to the zoo," rather than "A consent slip must be signed by the parent in order for the child to attend the field trip to the zoo."*
- *Know your audience. Ask yourself, For whom is the material being written, and how well does the audience read? If you aren't sure, test your materials on a few people representative of the target audience. When in doubt, assume that there are at least some poor readers in your audience.*
- *Know yourself. Be yourself. Write as you would talk, and write to express—not to impress.*
- *Write and rewrite. Write a draft, then read it over. How long are the sentences? How many long words have you used? Have you used the passive voice a great deal? Are there unexplained technical words? Have you used jargon or abbreviations that your audience may not know? Can you say the same thing more clearly, more succinctly, or more interestingly? Ask someone else to read what you've written. Then rewrite it. (p. 354)**

In addition to these suggestions, make sure that your communications to the parents say something personal (if you are sending a form letter, add

*From Diane A. D'Angelo and C. Ralph Adler, "Chapter I: A Catalyst for Improving Parent Involvement," *Phi Delta Kappan* 72 (January 1991): 350–354. Reprinted with permission of the authors.

something personal), that they are positive, and that you think about the skill level of your audience.

Telecommunication

Some centers use technology to make communication with parents quick and easy. Bauch (1990) reports that one center uses a computerized calling system to call parents and deliver messages about the program. These systems allow the calls to be placed at the times that are convenient for parents and in the language the parents prefer.

A similar use of current technology is to equip each teacher's room with voice mail or an answering machine on which the teacher records a short message like the following, which any parent can hear by calling:

> Today, we went to the zoo to look for patterns. We found patterns on the animals, in the enclosures, and in the pathways. You could help your child find patterns in your home. We printed patterns with junk items in art, and we read a patterned book, *Brown Bear, Brown Bear.* Your child has a copy of this book, and you could read it or let him or her read it to you. If you have a chance this weekend, encourage your child to look for patterns in numbers, such as the pattern of house or apartment numbers on your block.

Providing a voice mail or answering system for each teacher allows parents to leave messages or ask questions about their child, helping them feel more connected. In addition to a summary of current activities, the outgoing message might also remind parents of upcoming meetings, programs, and so on. Some schools have found it useful to set up a hotline, which provides someone to help parents with questions about their children's homework or other activities.

Many schools now have websites with pages for individual classrooms, on which teachers can post photos of various activities or other information about daily classroom activities. Many of these sites are on intranet systems, which are open only to the school and its parents. Some schools are preparing electronic portfolios with postings of student work on a website that can be accessed with a personal identification number for security.

Whatever system is used, it should be accessible to parents beyond normal school hours. Many parents find it difficult to call the school during the day, and it is closed by the time they get home from work. Providing a message system, website, or hotline can help parents feel they are keeping in touch with the school.

Parents of Children with Special Needs

Parents of children with special needs are by necessity more involved in their children's education than some parents because legal requirements specify that they be consulted and informed about decisions made about their children.

Meetings to plan educational programs for children with special needs must include the parents. Communication with these parents may take the same forms it does with all other parents, but it may need to be more specific and more frequent. Teachers should check with their program administrators or principals about the legal requirements for communicating with parents of children with special needs.

Parents of children with special needs may themselves need support from the teacher. Spidel (1987) notes that the parent of a child who is exceptional often expects the child's teacher to do the following:

1. Understand his child's assets as well as his deficiencies.
2. Appreciate his child's accomplishments whenever and however they appear.
3. Help the parent (and the child) live without guilt or blame.
4. Tell his child how it really is. (The truth about himself may be difficult for a child who is learning disabled but not as difficult as the bewilderments and heartaches he experiences from half-truths and evasions.)

Shriver and Kramer (1993) found that most parents of students with special needs are satisfied with the services their children receive in the schools and with the teachers they have.

Community Resources

Finally, many parents need information about resources available to them in the community. Teachers are not expected to be child psychologists or marriage counselors, but they can help by keeping on hand a supply of brochures that describe the services offered by various community agencies and provide contact and referral information.

Volunteers in the Classroom

Volunteers in the classroom are very important, especially as resources continue to shrink and schools cannot afford to hire enough adults to maintain adequate adult–child ratios. Volunteers can be parents or others from the community. Community volunteers can be recruited from colleges, service groups, senior citizen groups, church groups, and the like. These volunteers often bring many skills and abilities to share with children—talents in music, storytelling, woodworking, art, or other areas that can enhance the program. Many teachers are especially interested in recruiting older volunteers in order to promote the intergenerational contact that is so often missing in the lives of today's children.

Both community and parent volunteers must be screened and trained before working in the classroom. Some schools have volunteer coordinators who are responsible for interviewing prospective volunteers and determining their suitability for working with children. In other situations, teachers themselves interview volunteers. Whoever conducts the interviews should try to determine what the person has to offer the children, his expectations about volunteering, and his ability to communicate with and nurture children. If a volunteer seems unsuitable for working directly with the children, he can be asked to perform tasks that do not involve the children, such as typing materials, mounting artwork, placing the children's work in their portfolios, and so on.

Training for volunteers should clearly describe the philosophy of the program, goals for the children, activities that are appropriate for volunteers, discipline in school, and school policies and procedures. Such training is important, as every person who works in the classroom models behavior for the children and teaches by example.

Volunteers should always feel that the work they do is of real benefit to the children. They must perceive that the tasks they are asked to do in the classroom are a value added to the regular program. For example, if volunteers are asked to correct papers, they may see that task as something the teacher would do anyway and believe that they are not really adding to the quality of the program. It would be more appropriate to ask volunteers to do tasks that the teacher simply could not do without their help. Any special experience that can be added because the volunteer is available to help will make it clear to the parent or community volunteer that she is needed to provide this experience for the children.

Here are some examples of appropriate activities for mature and well-trained volunteers:

1. Reading to children (individually or in small groups)
2. Supervising small groups in outdoor play
3. Taking a small group for a walk around the schoolgrounds (looking for signs of changing seasons, collecting natural materials, observing surface differences, and so on)
4. Supervising children in an area that could not be used without additional help (cooking, water, music, tumbling, sewing, and so on)
5. Playing board games with children or helping them learn to play checkers, chess, or other such games

It is important to take the time to help volunteers understand what they can do in the classroom and how to do it most easily. Although many parent and community volunteers are quite able to work with one child at a time, they may not have especially good group-management abilities. Specific instructions allow those who are not specially trained in working with groups of young children to feel more secure. If a volunteer were going to supervise the

Figure 8.5

Instructions for a
Volunteer

Supervising the Art Area

➤ Children may choose to do art activities between 9:15 and 10:15.

➤ Choices available to the children: paint and easels, modeling clay, crayons and drawing paper, swatches of fabric for collage.

➤ Any child who chooses easel painting should wear a painting smock. The smocks are on the hooks beside the sink. Children should be encouraged to get their own smocks and to replace them when finished. Completed paintings are to be placed on the drying rack to the left of the sink. All children should be encouraged to clean up and put away the materials they used.

➤ We are emphasizing the concepts of texture. Please use texture words such as *rough, smooth, grainy, splintery, nubby, bumpy,* and so on when talking to the children about their work.

➤ Some children will need help labeling their work with their names. You can write their names and the date in one corner of their work. If they want you to write something about their work, please write exactly what they say.

Thank you so much for your help! We could not offer so many choices to the children without it!

art area, for example, the instructions shown in Figure 8.5 would be helpful. A planning sheet such as the one shown in Figure 8.6 would guide a volunteer in supervising a cooking experience. Another approach is to develop a file of cards listing suggestions for different activities and to laminate the cards for durability.

Teachers should always take the time to thank volunteers for their help. Immediate positive verbal feedback is important. Written thank-you notes are also invaluable in helping volunteers feel appreciated. These need not be expensive—a small note that the teacher can send home with a child for his parent or mail to a community volunteer is appropriate.

More elaborate displays of appreciation for volunteers are often planned once or twice a year. Some schools like to have a tea, a luncheon, or a breakfast to honor those who have contributed volunteer time. If teachers can get publicity in the local paper for special contributions by volunteers, they should do so—public praise is always welcome. Articles in newsletters that go out to all the parents can note the work that volunteers are doing at home and at school.

Cooking Planning Sheet

Project ___Fruit Salad___   Date ___3/25___

Type: (Individual)   Small group

Purpose:

To help children learn about:

(new foods)   similarities and differences in color

other cultures   similarities and differences in size

texture changes   similarities and differences in weight

changes in smell   effects of heat

To develop:

(small muscle skills)   eye–hand coordination

other _____

Skills to be emphasized:

pouring	sorting	dipping	mixing	spreading
rolling	cracking	beating	juicing	grinding
slicing	grating	peeling	(cutting)	other _____

Ingredients needed:

___apple___   ___walnut___

___orange___   _____

___banana___   _____

___pineapple___   _____

Procedure:

1. Prepare stations for each step of the recipe.

2. Supervise children as needed as they complete each step
   of the recipe.

_____

_____

_____

_____

Figure 8.6

Planning Sheet
for a Volunteer

Developmentally Appropriate Practice

NAEYC

Think about all you have learned about DAP and reflect on those principles when applied to working with parents and teacher aides. Adults should be treated in developmentally appropriate ways, just as children should be. For example, adults need choices about what and how they will learn, and they need to be able to apply what they know to new information. When thinking about DAP, consider the importance of volunteers and teacher aides in programs:

- Are volunteers and aides given choices as much as possible?
- Are parents and teacher aides talked to and treated in ways that are respectful of their skills and abilities?
- Do the programs planned for parents allow choices and recognize the importance of parents as the first teachers of their children?
- Are parents' cultural and ethnic differences not only recognized but also celebrated?
- Are the individual differences in parents considered when planning activities for parents?

Working with Paraprofessionals

Most classroom teachers are delighted to have **paraprofessionals,** or teacher aides, to work with in the classroom. Teacher aides can add immeasurably to the quality of the program; they can provide individual attention, increased supervision, scheduling flexibility, and assistance in instruction. (In most states, it is illegal for a teacher aide to *teach,* meaning that aides are not responsible for planning instruction and making instructional decisions.)

Paraprofessionals fill many different roles. For example, instructional aides teach under the supervision of the teacher; special-needs aides may be assigned to work with one child with special needs, such as an interpreter for a child with hearing impairment; some aides supervise the playground, cafeteria, or bus loading and unloading but do not teach; other aides perform clerical duties for teachers, such as making copies, but do not interact with children. Clearly, the roles and responsibilities of paraprofessionals vary a great deal, and the training and supervision needs of the people in these roles also varies.

Paraprofessionals' levels of training and experience vary a great deal. Some will have completed programs of preparation to become paraprofessionals; others will have had no training at all. In most schools, paraprofessionals must at least have high school diplomas and be age eighteen or older.

After the teacher knows about the background and experience of the aide, she can make plans for training or orientation. Ashbaker and Morgan

www.ablongman.com/brewer5e

(2000/2001) recommend creating written job descriptions for teacher aides. Such descriptions can help in defining the roles of paraprofessionals, in promoting job satisfaction, and in guiding evaluation. Teachers can help children by encouraging schools and school boards to offer needed training for aides. Love and Levine (1992) found that training increased the effectiveness of teacher aides, which should not be surprising.

Working successfully with an aide requires some planning on the teacher's part and some ability to communicate well with adults. The following guidelines will help:

1. Take the time to discuss your philosophy, the program, what you consider appropriate discipline, and other pertinent information with the aide. Even if the aide has training and experience, it is important that you agree on how the class should be handled.

2. If the aide lacks training, provide it. This is not always easy because the aide may be paid by the hour and may not be willing to stay longer or come earlier without extra pay. Try to arrange for your aide to be paid for the time spent in training. Provide written information, explain why you do things the way you do, and then model the behaviors that you expect in the classroom. Take a few minutes for discussion each day.

3. Do not assign the aide all the "dirty" chores in the classroom. No one wants to clean the gerbil cage and the painting area all the time and never get a chance to do some of the more interesting classroom tasks, such as supervising a small group on a walk or in an art activity.

4. Make sure that paraprofessionals are included in professional development programs offered by the school.

5. Make sure that paraprofessionals have a mailbox in the school and that they are invited to participate in faculty meetings.

6. Paraprofessionals who are involved in teaching should also be involved in parent conferences with parents of the children with whom they work.

7. Ask the principal to provide training for supervision of paraprofessionals. Most teachers report that their only knowledge of how to supervise is "real life experience" (French 2001).

If the law states that aides are not to teach, what are they supposed to do? Generally, teacher aides can do almost everything that teachers do, with the exception of planning learning experiences and being responsible for assessment and reporting. However, aides can certainly contribute their observations of children or activities, which the teacher can communicate to parents and use in planning future activities. Assignments for aides should be determined by their level of skill and experience. A teacher could not expect an aide with no experience to work with the whole class during music time, for example.

Paraprofessionals can take on certain types of duties, including the following:

Instructional Duties

1. Reading to individual children or small groups or listening to children read
2. Providing individual help for children completing tasks
3. Providing small-group instruction that is planned by the teacher
4. Teaching children a song or a fingerplay
5. Working with a small group with manipulatives for mathematics or with materials for science investigations

Supervisory Duties

1. Supervising learning areas
2. Supervising outdoor play experiences (some states require one certified teacher on the playground during recess)
3. Supervising children on field trips
4. Supervising children as they move from one part of the building to another
5. Supervising children as they complete routines (hanging up coats, using the toilet, and so on)

Classroom Maintenance Duties

1. Preparing classroom displays and bulletin boards
2. Setting up and helping serve snacks
3. Helping to keep the classroom and materials clean and ready for use
4. Setting up and running audiovisual equipment
5. Gathering materials from the library or other resources

As the teacher and aide work together, it is important that the teacher maintain good communication with the aide, discussing what needs to be done and the priorities for the day. The teacher should be sensitive to adults' need to be involved in making decisions and should plan to involve the aide in choosing tasks to be done. The teacher and the aide must also evaluate the process as they work together: Is the aide learning new skills so that different activities are now appropriate? Does the aide feel appreciated? Is the aide comfortable with the tasks that he does routinely? Do the teacher and the aide agree on most issues? Does the aide want to learn new techniques for working with the children? Are both the teacher and aide satisfied with the communication between them?

Working successfully with aides requires that teachers provide frequent positive feedback and praise for a job well done. Notes of appreciation to aides, notes to principals or administrators or in newsletters specifically commending aides, and any other special recognition that is deserved can make teacher–aide relationships more positive and assure that good work continues.

Celebrating Diversity

Families can serve as resources for helping all children learn about and respect cultures that are different than their own. For example, all the children's families could be invited to contribute to the classroom some play items that are significant in their cultural traditions. Even families of limited means can contribute items such as empty food containers from traditional meals (Clark 1995). Having children bring in cultural items for sharing time is also useful in terms of celebrating diversity (Neuman and Roskos 1994). Families can become resources as food, songs, and stories from different cultures are studied.

It is very important for the school and its teachers to acknowledge children's cultures and help their families feel comfortable in the school. Both parents and children need to understand that speaking a language other than English is not unacceptable, so they need not feel embarrassed. Pena (2000) found that Hispanic parents were more likely to cite language barriers and the attitude of teachers and school administrators as reasons for their lack of involvement in schools. Community translators are often willing to help schools communicate with parents who do not speak English. Families respond well to activities such as potluck suppers, field days that include picnics or cookouts, and other activities that provide an atmosphere of acceptance and a chance to get to know other parents.

Chapter Summary

- Parent–teacher relationships are complex. Changing family structures, economic conditions, and isolation of the nuclear family all contribute to stresses on families that sometimes make parent involvement in the school difficult.

- A teacher must approach families with a nonjudgmental attitude and be sensitive to the needs of children from many types of family structures.

- Family involvement is important for children's self-esteem and achievement. Parents may choose not to be involved, to be involved only passively, or to be actively involved in their children's education.

- Activities for involving families include family nights at school, potluck dinners, parent educa-

tion programs, meetings of parent organizations, and committee meetings.

- Home visits by teachers can provide a wealth of information about children, their families, family interactions, and how children learn at home. Home visits must be carefully planned if they are to contribute to establishing good parent–teacher relationships.

- Inviting parents to visit and observe the program in action can open lines of communication between parents and teachers. It is important to make arrangements for parents who cannot visit during the regular schoolday to visit at some other time and see how the program works.

- Setting aside a corner of the classroom for parents will communicate to them that teachers value their presence and believe that their involvement is important.

- Teachers should be prepared to offer assistance to parents who need help in meeting their basic needs; teachers must be informed about community resources, whom to contact for help, and the referral process.

- Parent or community volunteers in the classroom can enhance the program for children. Volunteers need to be screened and trained to be most effec-tive and should be given tasks that benefit the children directly.

- Teacher aides can make vital contributions to programs for young children. Although they are not supposed to teach, aides can assume responsibilities for instruction, supervision, and classroom maintenance tasks. Teacher aides need carefully planned orientation and training.

- Everyone on the school staff should respect the cultural diversity of the students. Families can be wonderful sources of artifacts, food, clothing, and music that will enrich any program offered to children.

Theory INTO *Practice*

Interview several parents of young children. Ask them if they are involved in their children's school activities. If they are, ask them to tell you what they do. If they are not, ask them why not. If they would like to be involved, ask them what they would like to do.

Interview several teachers of young children to determine how they feel about having parents involved in school programs. How have they tried to get parents involved? What do they consider their most successful strategies for doing so?

Work with a small group of your classmates to plan a parent evening centered on literacy, math, or science. Your plan should outline activities for parents and children and include any written information you would share with parents about the purpose of the activities.

With your classmates, compile a list of community agencies that offer services to parents. Find out the procedure for referral to each agency and whom to contact. If possible, include the brochures and pamphlets that describe these agencies.

As an entire class, prepare a handbook for assisting teacher aides in the classroom. To do so, split the class into small groups. Each group should select one topic (e.g., the importance of play, the classroom environment, or supervising a center) about which to prepare guidelines. Compile each group's section of guidelines into a handbook.

Interview a paraprofessional to determine what she likes and dislikes about her job. What does she feel could be improved about her working conditions?

The Relationship between Teachers and Teaching Assistants

I teach kindergarten in a suburban school district. During the course of my twenty-year career, I have had the opportunity to work with various teaching assistants. I have strived to make this a beneficial experience for both the children and myself.

The most important point is to establish a good working relationship with your assistant. While it is not imperative that you become social acquaintances, a sincere yet professional rapport should be created for a positive experience. This will also make it easier to resolve any difficulties.

Before school starts, meet with your assistant—perhaps for lunch or a cup of coffee. Ask about family, past work experiences, hobbies, trips—just as you would when meeting a new colleague, neighbor, or friend. Share some of your personal background, including some of your strengths as a teacher. Use this time to show a sincere interest in her as a person and discover interests or strengths that your assistant might share in the classroom at some point.

It is important to set a framework. If your district doesn't have a job description for your assistant, then you need to create one. Include the amount of time she will be working with the children versus doing clerical duties, delegation of authority in the classroom, work schedule, evaluation system, and confidentiality expectations. It is also wise to share your educational philosophy and style of discipline.

It is essential to show your assistant respect in the classroom:

- Notice the good things and give sincere compliments, when they are deserved.
- Share important school memos about upcoming events, policies, school newsletters, and the like.
- Create a working space in the room for your assistant to keep notes, binders, books, and other school-job-related materials.

- Post her name next to yours on doors, bulletin boards, and so on.
- Introduce your assistant to parents via your newsletter, open house, or other means.
- Make sure your assistant is part of the class photo for the school memory book.
- Keep the lines of communication open—ask about her weekend, ask for an opinion about a classroom situation, and so forth.
- Share articles from professional journals or notices about upcoming conferences that might be of interest.
- Be realistic in your expectations. If your assistant doesn't understand a concept or method, model the technique in a nonthreatening manner.
- Let your assistant know your daily plans for the classroom in an informal planning session or in a written memo.

If a problem does arise, be honest and set time to talk things over. State the problem and listen to her response, but make sure your views are known, too. If the problem cannot be resolved, call in a third party, such as your principal. In the rare circumstance that an aide performs an undesirable behavior that is harmful to the children, make sure to document it as accurately and objectively as possible.

If your district requires a formal evaluation of your assistant, discuss the procedure with her. Be sure to provide reasons for your ratings and give your assistant a chance to respond.

I have been fortunate to have my present assistant for the past five years. The children see us as a unified team. It takes time and commitment to make our relationship work, but it is well worth the energy. It makes both of our jobs more satisfying. In turn, we feel that we are providing our students with the best teaching possible. And isn't that the point of education?

CHAPTER **9**

Celebrating the Magic
of Language

After reading this chapter, you will be able to do the following:

- Define the term *language*.
- Describe the typical sequence of language learning.
- Describe the three major models of language learning: behaviorist, linguistic, and constructivist.
- Observe the language learning of children more skillfully.
- Plan for language learning in a classroom environment.
- Describe language learning for children with special needs.
- Plan strategies for celebrating diversity in language use.

This week, your observation at a preschool focused on children's language. You observed a two-year-old, a three-year-old, and a five-year-old.

The two-year-old was a boy who was excited about dinosaurs and named several types of dinosaurs while showing you models of them. He also talked about dinosaur tracks; he rolled out a piece of Play Doh and pushed the feet of one of the dinosaur models into it to show you how tracks are made.

The three-year-old, a girl, was very quiet and did not initiate any conversation with you. You watched her play outdoors with the other children, but she never uttered a word; she just smiled and nodded when asked questions.

The five-year-old, another girl, was also quiet in the classroom, but when she was outdoors, she asked several children to play a game of tag with her and explained all of the rules to them. You noticed that she spoke Spanish and English and seemed quite competent in both languages.

When you returned to your classroom, you found that many of your peers had similar experiences. Now all of you have questions about the extraordinary variations found in children's language development. How do children learn language? What sort of program is best for helping them become more proficient users of language? Are published materials available to aid children in developing language abilities? What is the role of the teacher in planning for children's language development?

Language Development

One of the most exciting moments in parenting is when Baby says that first word—when he puts together sounds that communicate meaning. Parents share that moment with all who are close or can be reached by telephone, and the word is dutifully recorded in the baby book.

One of the characteristics that makes us human is our language, which gives us the ability to share with others our ideas, thoughts, dreams, discoveries, and knowledge. That children achieve the ability to communicate so rapidly and seemingly so effortlessly is a marvel to all who observe the process. The ability to communicate with others is learned so rapidly that it almost seems magical. Come celebrate this magic, the wonderful world of children's language.

Two premises underlie this chapter and should be kept in mind as you read. One is the belief, articulated by Goodman et al. (1987), that language is not acquired externally but rather is part of a process of personal development and emerges in the context of social use (p. 38). That is not to say that language is not present in the child's environment but that learning language is a more complex process than simply adopting language that is outside oneself. Therefore, in this chapter, the term that will be used to describe the learning of language is *language development* rather than *language acquisition*.

The other premise is that language, both oral and sign, is not developed in isolation; language is always related to cognitive development. Each system of language is also supported by learning more about the other system of language. For example, if a child is learning about printed language, that may influence her oral language development, and certainly oral language development supports learning about printed language. One would never say that a child could not be exposed to printed language because she did not possess a given oral language vocabulary.

Definition of Language

For the purposes of this chapter, *language* is defined as a system of communication used by humans that is either produced orally or by sign and that can be extended to its written form. Language also has characteristics that define it further. One characteristic is that language is rule governed. The rules of a given language are learned intuitively by those people who speak it; only speakers who make a scientific study of the language are likely to be able to verbalize these rules. An example of one of these rules is the placement of words denoting number, color, and size in descriptive phrases. For example, in describing *one big red balloon,* we would never say "red one big balloon."

Another characteristic of language is that it is arbitrary. There are no logical connections between the sounds that we use to label objects and the objects themselves. Social groups merely agree to use a particular combination of sounds to represent an object. Actually, very few words sound like what they represent, such as *buzz* or *hiss*. Words such as *table, chair, bottle,* and so on have no logical connections with their referents.

Language is also changing. New words are constantly entering our lexicon, and others are being discarded. Meanings, too, are changing. With a little thought, you could probably list thirty or forty words that have been added to the English language within the last five years and ten or so that have changed meaning. Even young children use words that were once uncommon (*rewind*), that did not exist a short time ago (*CD*, for *compact disc*), or that have changed meanings recently (*tape* or *videotape* as either a noun or a verb).

Parents AND *Language*

■ Encourage parents to talk to their children and celebrate their language achievements. Suggest that parents keep journals of special words that their children enjoy.

Language Systems

Every language is a set of systems: phonology, morphology, syntax, semantics, and pragmatics. *Phonology* is the system of sounds that make up the language; it includes the sounds that are used to make words, the rules for combining the sounds, and the stress and intonation patterns that help to communicate meaning. Different languages use different sounds and allow different combinations of sounds in words. In some languages, for instance, words can begin with the "ng" sound, but not in English. The task of the child is to learn to distinguish differences in sounds and intonation patterns that signal different meanings.

A second system of language is *morphology,* which deals with the meanings of sounds. A *morpheme* is the smallest unit of sound that carries meaning. Some words are morphemes; some are combinations of morphemes. *Tiger* is an example of a word that is a morpheme. The plural, *tigers,* is a combination of the free morpheme *tiger* and the bound morpheme *s.* The *s* is bound because it signals meaning but cannot carry meaning alone. Other morphemes signal changes of tense, person, and number rather than meaning. Mastering English morphology includes learning how to form possessives, plurals, and past and progressive verb tenses. For example, in English we say "one apple," but we must say "eight apples." Many other languages signal the number change with the number word only and do not require pluralization of the noun *apple.*

Syntax is a third system of language. In simple terms, the syntax of a language contains the rules for combining words into phrases and sentences and for transforming sentences into other sentences. Syntax provides information about word meanings based on their places in sentences. If you heard *A crad was zagging wickily,* you would know that the action described occurred in the past and that *wickily* described how the *crad* was *zagging.* You would also know that more than one *crad* existed because the article *a* signifies one of something. Children mastering syntax learn how to construct negatives, questions, compound sentences, passives, imperatives, and eventually complex sentences that include embedded clauses.

Semantics is the fourth system of language. Learning semantics means acquiring vocabulary and meanings associated with words. Some words are probably learned by repeated association, such as *bottle*. The word and the object are presented to the child simultaneously, again and again. Other word usages reflect the child's growing ability to categorize. A very young child may begin by using *doggie* to refer to any four-legged animal but then learns more specific terms, such as *horse* and *cow*. A child's system of meanings is constantly developing and changing as a result of experience and maturation. Cognitive abilities are reflected in a child's speech. For example, a child will begin to use *gone* about the same time that he learns the concept of object permanence. Mastering the semantic system requires that a child learn word meanings and relationships between and among words.

In addition to learning all the other systems of language, the child must learn the rules for using language in social interactions. *Pragmatics* is the use of language to express intention and to get things done. Speakers must learn to adapt their language to achieve their communication goals in different situations and to do so in socially acceptable ways. Pragmatics includes the rules for appropriate language in church, on the playground, and at the dinner table. A speaker of any language would not be considered competent in its use until she had mastered the basic rules for language use in various social contexts. Children reflect their understanding of pragmatics when they learn to say *please* or when they speak more simply to a baby than they normally speak.

Table 9.1 provides a summary of the language development of children in the systems of phonology, semantics, grammar, and pragmatics. Note that the grammar system contains elements of morphology and syntax, which are discussed as separate systems in the previous paragraphs. **Communicative competence** means the ability of a speaker to use language appropriately in a communication experience. Children may know more language than they are able to use at a given point in time, but how much they know and are able to use is constantly changing. Figure 9.1 illustrates the idea that linguistic competence (the language one knows) and communicative competence (the language one can use in actual communication experiences) are not totally overlapping sets.

Sociolinguistics, the study of language in a social context, is closely related to pragmatics. Sociolinguists ask: "What are the key aspects of a communication encounter and how do they influence one another? How do we adapt the language to various social contexts? And how does the language style used affect the social context itself?" (Lindfors 1980, p. 6). Anyone who has ever studied a foreign language should be familiar with the concept of knowing more language than can be used effectively. Early lessons in Spanish, for instance, will include learning words for foods, places, colors, numbers, and so on. The learner's ability to communicate, however, will be quite limited until he knows some of the systems of that language (for example, that adjectives follow nouns) and has experience in applying them. Similarly, a child learning

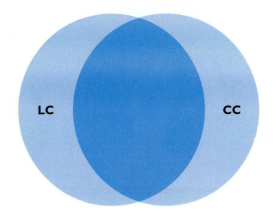

Figure 9.1

Linguistic and Communicative Competence

LC = Linguistic competence
CC = Communicative competence

Source: Celia Genishi and Anne Haas Dyson, Eds., *Language Assessment in the Early Years* (Norwood, NJ: Ablex, 1984). Reprinted with the permission of Ablex Publishing Corporation.

a first language will know words that he cannot use effectively; competence will come with experience. The learner's ability to communicate also will be quite limited until he knows some of the rules for putting together sentences and speaking in different situations. Children learning language may use phrases such as "Will you do me a favor?" or repeat patterns such as knock-knock jokes without fully understanding what a favor is or what makes a knock-knock joke funny.

Sequence of Language Development

Language development follows a sequence, which is fairly predictable even though there are many individual variations. Most children move from differentiated crying (crying that sounds different in response to different stimuli: being pricked by a pin, feeling cold or wet, and so on) through cooing and babbling to expressive jargon and one-word sentences. Some children learn the names of objects before other words. Nelson (1973) classifies children's language as *referential* or *expressive*. Common nouns are referential; social words are expressive. Many children develop *idiomorphs* (not real words), which they apply to objects that they evidently find related. For example, when shown flowers or pictures of flowers, the child may make a sniffing sound. For a period of time, this sound will represent anything to be smelled. Soon the child will develop longer utterances and learn to produce negatives and questions. Then the child's language consists of some mature forms and

Table 9.1   Language Development Milestones

From Laura E. Berk, *Child Development,* 5/e. Published by Allyn and Bacon, Boston, MA. Copyright © 2000 by Pearson Education. Reprinted by permission of the publisher.

Age	Phonology	Semantics
Birth–1 year	■ Categorical speech perception is present. ■ Speech sounds become organized into phonemic categories of native language. ■ Intonations and sound patterns of babbling begin to resemble those of native language.	■ Preference for sound pattern of native tongue is evident. ■ Sensitivity to stress patterns and phoneme sequences in words of native language develops. ■ Preverbal gestures develop.
1–2 years	■ Systematic strategies to simplify word pronunciation appear.	■ First words are produced; vocabulary builds to several hundred words. ■ Object words are emphasized first; action and state words follow soon after.
3–5 years	■ Pronunciation improves greatly.	■ Word-coinage forms expand. ■ Metaphors based on concrete, sensory comparisons appear.
6–10 years	■ Pronunciations signaling subtle differences in meaning are mastered.	■ At school entry, vocabulary includes about 10,000 words. ■ Meanings of words are grasped on the basis of definitions. ■ Appreciation of multiple meanings of words enhances understanding of metaphors and humor.
11 years–adulthood	■ Changes in syllabic stress after certain difficult words take on endings are mastered.	■ Vocabulary builds to over 40,000 words and includes many abstract terms. ■ Understanding of subtle, nonliteral word meanings, as in irony and sarcasm, improves.

some immature forms. By the time children are eight to ten years old, their language is mostly mature. At the same time, the child's comprehension of language is developing rapidly.

Language development is not complete at the end of infancy; it continues throughout one's lifetime. Children continue to make rapid gains in vocabulary during the early childhood years. Three- and four-year-olds learn to con-

Grammar	Pragmatics
■ Sensitivity to natural phrase units develops.	■ Joint attention with caregiver is established. ■ Ability to engage in vocal exchanges and turn-taking games develops.
■ Two-word utterances, in the form of telegraphic speech, appear. ■ First grammatical morphemes are added.	■ Conversational turn taking and topic maintenance are present.
■ Sentences clearly reflect an appreciation of adult grammatical categories. ■ Grammatical morphemes continue to be added in a regular order. ■ Many complex grammatical structures are added.	■ Conversational strategies, such as the turnabout, appear. ■ Grasp of illocutionary intent is present. ■ Ability to adjust speech in accord with social expectations develops.
■ A few complex grammatical structures, such as passive voice and infinitive phrases, continue to be refined.	■ Advanced conventional strategies, such as shading, appear. ■ Understanding of illocutionary intent expands. ■ Referential communication in unfamiliar, highly demanding contexts improves.
■ Refinement of complex grammatical structures continues.	■ Referential communication—especially detection of unclear messages received—continues to improve.

struct questions and negatives. "Why he no go?" changes to "Why isn't he going?" and "Me no do it" becomes "I didn't do it." Children also begin to use and understand more complicated sentences, such as "The dog under the table is mine." By the time a child begins kindergarten, she will have mastered most of the basic forms in her native language, although some immature forms, such as "gots" and "goed," will be present in her speech. Even children of eight and nine can be confused by such sentences as "The boy was bitten by the dog," because they respond to sentences as if the first noun named is doing the acting.

Older primary children are learning vocabulary and learning to use more complex sentence forms correctly. They are also becoming more aware of their audience. Very young children assume that their listeners share their context; older children can take the point of view of the listener and not assume a shared context. They gain skill in giving directions and relating stories in a sequence. They also gain abilities to use language that is not context bound and to discuss objects, events, and some abstract ideas, such as love.

Language play begins in infancy as children play with sounds and continues as young children create rhyming words or make up preposterous names or other silly words. The play of older children usually depends on changes in word forms or meanings. Children may create secret languages, such as Pig Latin, and a host of sayings for all types of situations, such as lying, cheating, name calling, begging, telling the truth, using table manners, and so on.

Older children and adults continue to learn language. People learn the vocabulary related to their professions and their hobbies, and they learn to use more formal speech when it is appropriate. Even the most literate person discovers new vocabulary words or new expressions as he listens and reads; language development does not end as long as a person is mentally active and an environment for learning is available.

Models of Language Learning

Three major models attempt to explain the development of children's language: the *behaviorist* model, the *linguistic* model, and the *constructivist* model (Berko-Gleason 1985; Butler 1974; King 1987). Each model will be examined briefly.

Behaviorist Model

The behaviorist model of learning language describes the process as consistent with the rules of operant conditioning, based on a stimulus-response model. In the simplest terms, infants are presented with language, they imitate the language, they are rewarded for their imitations, and they continue to repeat what they have heard. Imitation does not have to be exact or immediate in order for children to make use of it in learning language.

Behaviorist explanations fail to account, however, for the fact that much of children's language is constructed in ways that have never been modeled by mature speakers. For example, a child may say, "Higher the swing!"—a construction not used by any other speaker in the child's experience. Behaviorists also have difficulty explaining regressions in children's language. Typically, a young child will use the correct form of a past-tense verb, such as *went*. But as the child matures and generalizes the rules for constructing past-tense verbs, he replaces *went* with *goed*. Later, as the child learns that some words are exceptions to the general rules, *goed* is replaced by *went*.

The difficulty of modifying language through adult input is another problem for behaviorists. According to the stimulus-response model, the child should respond to adult correction of her language use. But as anyone who has attempted to correct a young child knows, this does not always happen. Literature on this subject contains many stories of adults' attempts to correct young children's language (McNeill 1966). The fact is, children do not change the forms of their language easily.

On the other hand, the behaviorist point of view does have some validity. Children obviously speak the languages of their homes. Any human child can learn any human language. No human language can be said to be more complex or more difficult than other languages. Children learn to produce the sounds needed in their native languages and to eliminate the sounds that are not required. Children also learn to repeat words and phrases that they hear around them, even when they do not know what they mean.

Linguistic Model

Another explanation for the development of language is the linguistic, or nativistic, model. Linguist Noam Chomsky (1965) was instrumental in developing this model. The theory holds that language is inherent in the child at birth and needs only be triggered by social contact with speakers in order to emerge.

When the linguistic explanation for language acquisition was developed, the study of language was dominated by behaviorist thinking. Some theorists began to question whether children could learn language as quickly as they obviously did solely through interactions based on stimulus and response. These theorists reasoned that language must be part of children's human inheritance. Chomsky (1965) theorized that humans were equipped with a *language acquisition device*—a structure in the brain that made possible the learning of language.

Evidence in support of this theory is that humans are the only species to acquire language, which they use to communicate ideas and pass on to other generations knowledge they have gained. Linguistic theorists also point out that language development is almost universal among humans. Only humans who have experienced severe trauma or mental retardation are unable to use language; the vast majority of humans use language at some level of competence. Linguistic theorists have contributed to the field of language development by forcing researchers to examine their models and more carefully observe what children actually do in learning language.

Constructivist Model

A third theory for explaining language development is that of the constructivists. This group of theorists—represented by Jean Piaget (1959), Jerome Bruner (1983), and Lev Vygotsky (1962)—believes that children learn language quickly because human brains seek patterns and order in language, just as they constantly seek patterns and order in the environment. For evidence, these theorists point to examples of language that is produced when there has been no previous model; to the uniqueness of language (the fact that except for clichés, we may never hear exactly the same sentence used in the same context more than once); and to the obvious reliance of the child on the rules of language, which are rarely taught but which are abstracted from examples presented to the child.

Learning language is not an effortless process. Children make a conscious effort to learn the names of things, feelings, and actions. The constructivist model views the learner as vital in the process of learning language. The learner is active in seeking and constructing meaning and in seeking communication with others (Bruner 1983; Jaggar and Smith-Burke 1985; Shuy 1987). Learning to discriminate and correctly label a cat or a dog illustrates the active nature of language learning. If a child sees a dog and says "Doggie," the caregiver will likely respond, "Yes, it's a dog." If the child labels the animal "Kitty," the response will likely be, "No, it's a dog." The child is left on his own to determine the features of each animal that are distinctive, because it is difficult to describe the features verbally in a way that has any meaning for a very young child.

Children learning language produce hypotheses and test them with the speakers in their environments. They try different combinations of sounds and words in different situations. Constructivists believe that this problem-solving behavior is very important in learning language. They also believe that the errors in children's speech reflect new knowledge about language rules.

Constructivists also recognize the importance of social interactions in the development of language. Many of the words learned first, such as *bye-bye* and *hi,* have meaning only as parts of interactions with others. For constructivists, many factors affect language learning. These factors (social, maturational, biological, cognitive) interact and modify one another as a child learns language (Berko-Gleason 1985). Many constructivist researchers believe that infants control much of their interaction with adults in their environments by smiling, making sounds, and repeating adult sounds to continue the interactions.

Bruner (1983) describes the language acquisition support system that adults create for children who are learning language. The support system is "scaffolding" that provides a framework and supports the child until she has mastered language forms at a given level; the scaffolding is moved to a higher level when the child's language forms become more complex. For example, when a very young child in a high chair drops a cereal bowl to the floor, her parent says, "Uh-oh." When the child has learned to say that phrase each time she drops something, the parent begins to say, "Down" or "Gone" each time. As the child's language abilities increase, the parent begins to use longer sentences when something is dropped, such as, "Please don't drop your cereal bowl on the floor."

Whitmore and Goodman (1995) point out that the *functions* of language—why we use it—precede the *forms.* For instance, children use sounds that are not recognizable as words to convey meanings such as "Turn the page," "Read," and "Pick me up."

Table 9.2 Comparison of Features across Models

Feature	Behaviorist	Linguistic	Constructivist
Environment	X	X	X
Reward	X		
Imitation	X	x	x
Grammar		X	X
Social Interaction	x	X	X
Teaching	X		
Problem Solving		X	X

X = Dependent feature
x = Minor feature

Comparison of Models

Table 9.2 compares the primary features of the three major models of language learning. A large *X* means that the model depends on that feature, and a small *x* means that the feature plays only a minor role in learning language. As you can see, the greatest similarity among the three models is that they all place a great deal of emphasis on the language environment of the learner. All three focus on imitation as well, but linguistic and constructivist thinkers place less emphasis on imitation than do behaviorists.

Creating an Environment for Learning Language

Because almost all children learn language and can use it to satisfy their communication needs, observations of what parents and caregivers do naturally to encourage language development is helpful when planning for successful language learning. Parents and other caregivers teach language informally, focus on the intent or meaning of the child's utterances rather than on the form, expect success, recognize that language learning is wholistic, and celebrate the child's unique, creative uses of language.

Use an Informal Approach

Adults and older children in an infant's environment do not teach language formally. What they do is talk to the child about the environment and happenings in the environment. Long before an infant can produce language, speakers around the child will be talking to her: "Oh, are you thirsty? Here is a bottle of water" or "It's time for your bath now." They also make attempts to talk about what is interesting to the child. If the baby is looking at something, the adult will attempt to determine what has caught the child's interest and talk about it. As the child grows and becomes mobile, the parent's or caregiver's language is more controlling, but it is still closely related to the context (for example, "Play here with your ball. Roll the ball on the floor."). Parents do not plan language lessons each day. They just talk to their children as they make cookies, repair the sink, wash the car, cook dinner, and go through the daily household routines. Language is learned through meaningful interactions, not by talking about it or analyzing it.

In school settings, teachers can attempt to follow the child's lead in conversations and talk about topics that are meaningful and interesting to the child. Sometimes teachers are so determined to follow the given curriculum or their own agenda that they fail to respond to children's interests or to concentrate on topics that are actually important to children. It is not as easy to follow the child's lead at school as it is at home, where only one or two children are present, but teachers do need to think about children's needs and interests in communication experiences.

Focus on the Speaker's Intent

Learning language is a self-generated process. It is controlled by the learner and is not dependent on external rewards. Achieving communication with significant others seems to be reward enough to keep the child learning. Parents and other adults seem to know this intuitively, because the majority of their responses to a child's language are focused on the child's intent, rather than on perfection of the utterance. Even parents who do correct their children's speech are much more likely to correct content than form. If the child runs into the house and shouts, "Daddy gots a new car!" the adult is more likely to respond, "No, Daddy has borrowed that car" than to instruct the child to say, "Daddy *has* a new car." In fact, if Daddy does have a new car, the response is likely to be "Let's go see it!"

In the early childhood classroom, teachers can make a real effort to focus on what children are trying to say rather than the form they use. Teachers should concentrate on providing new objects and new experiences to help build the young child's vocabulary. Efforts to correct grammatical structures are relatively useless with this age group. A study that compared teachers trained to repeat the child's incorrect utterance in correct form and those trained to extend the conversation based on the child's utterance showed that extension is more useful in helping children achieve language growth (Cazden 1965). If a child says, "See red car," the teacher using extension would say, "Yes, I see a red car and a blue car going down the street." These responses are much more closely related to what parents do in responding to the meaning rather than to the form of utterances. In primary classrooms, teachers can help children learn the vocabulary of topics that interest them, provide opportunities to express their own ideas, and continue to focus on children's meanings. Strategies for encouraging language growth include the following:

- **Expansion** involves using the child's utterance but adding to it grammatically. If the child says, "Red truck," the teacher might respond, "The red truck is going fast."

- **Extension** has the teacher add meaning to the child's utterance but not necessarily change it grammatically. For example, if the child says, "Red truck," the teacher might respond, "I see a red truck, a blue truck, and a yellow truck."

- **Repetition** has the teacher take part of the child's utterance and repeat it. The child might say, "Down" when going down the slide. The teacher might then say, "Everyone is going down. Everyone is going down."

- **Parallel talk** is most often used in play when the teacher describes the child's actions. If the child says, "Going fast" while riding a tricycle, the teacher might repeat, "Going fast. Going very fast. Going faster."

- **Self-talk** is also used most frequently in play—for example, when the teacher is building with the blocks and says, "I am going to need a larger block for this space. I will need a long block here."

- **Vertical structuring** involves the teacher responding to the child's utterance with a question that will encourage a longer response. For example, if the child says, "I want to go" (pointing to where she wants to go), the teacher would ask, "Where do you want to go?"

- **Fill-in** has the teacher using structured sentences and having the child fill in the last word or phrase. For example, if the child says, "She hungry," the teacher might offer, "Does she want something to _____?" and pause for the child to complete the thought. Fill-ins are often used with children during read-alouds, when the teacher pauses at the ends of the lines to allow the children to complete them (especially with a rhyming or repetitive text) (Kratcoski and Katz 1998).

In sum, you should note that *all* these strategies depend on the teacher using the child's utterance. Drilling children on the use of any element of language is not recommended.

Expect Success

If you went to the local hospital and interviewed parents of newborn infants about their expectations of whether their babies would learn to talk, you would probably get emphatically positive answers (along with strange looks for asking such a question!). Parents expect that their children will become mature speakers. When the baby makes errors, they know it is a normal part of the process in learning language. They do not expect that their child will be able to say, "My bowl of cereal has fallen to the floor" when he drops his oatmeal off the high chair. They do know that their child's language will mature over time and that immature forms will be replaced by more mature and more complex forms.

In early childhood classrooms, teachers can also expect success as children are learning language. Teachers who view errors such as the use of irregular plurals (*mouses, feets*), adding *-ed* to form the past tense of verbs (*goed, runned*), and the use of incorrect verb forms as indicators of the child's growing mastery of the rules of English will treat those errors differently than teachers who view them as mistakes to be corrected. Language is learned through active exploration of the systems, not by direct imitation of models. Errors are indications of the active nature of language learning as well as growth and maturation.

Emphasize the Holistic Nature of Language Learning

Children learn language, language functions, and how to use language in social interactions all at the same time (Halliday 1982). Parents do not set out to teach language to their children by limiting their children's learning to one piece of the complex system of language. They help their children learn language by conversing with them in meaningful contexts and in social situations. They present language as a whole, within a context, and within a social milieu. Few parents would drill their children by asking them to learn a list of nouns, followed by a list of verbs, and then some adjectives. They would not expect their children to practice language outside a real context. The idea of a parent asking a child to go to his or her room and practice saying, "I would like a drink of water" is ludicrous.

Teachers of young children can also preserve the wholistic nature of language learning by not breaking language into bits and pieces for study in school. Words in isolation—or worse, sounds in isolation—have no meaning that can be constructed. Children do not need to practice isolated elements of language; they do not learn the parts and then put them back together and use them. They do need to use language in a variety of situations and with a variety of speakers. They need to talk about topics of interest to them and to learn to adjust their language to meet the requirements of the speaking situation. Real talk provides young children a chance to practice their developing language.

Celebrate Creativity

Goodman et al. (1987) describe a child learning language as always creative or inventive and at the same time pulled back into conformity. Children are always creating new words and phrases, but when they find that their words fail to communicate what they intended, they conform more to the usual social forms. This inventiveness in language is important. We could not create new terms when they were needed if we lost our capacity to be inventive language users. Parents and others tend to celebrate some of the creative language of children. For example, many people have nicknames that were invented when they were children by younger siblings who could not pronounce their real names. Almost all families use special words that were either errors in pronunciation or words invented by their children.

In the classroom, teachers can celebrate children's unique expressions by recording them to share later or by posting them on a chart or bulletin board. Some of the expressions children use are very poetic. Teachers can also celebrate children's language by not changing it. If a child uses a dialect, these expressions can also be celebrated and recorded. There are appropriate times and strategies for helping young children develop skill in speaking effectively in different contexts, but for very young children the focus should be on their unique ways of expressing that meaning. Children need to have their language accepted and valued.

Recognize Language Achievements

Children have made such amazing progress in mastering their native language before entering preschool that teachers sometimes fail to recognize how much they have accomplished. Children's linguistic competencies include the ability to select meaningful parts of a message, to recognize differences in linguistic contexts, and to use syntactic rules. If you say to a very young child, "Your father has gone to the office to work," the child will respond, "Daddy gone." Obviously, the child knows what is significant in the message. Children adapt their language to listeners when they are very young. This is particularly noticeable in children from bilingual families, who sort out which language they should speak with which people. Children also use correct syntactical rules from the time they begin to use sentences of more than one word. They say, "More milk" as opposed to "Milk more," for example.

Daniels (1994) found that children learning sign language along with spoken language were more advanced than their age peers in language development and that they had no trouble with code switching (knowing when to use sign versus oral language). In short, children are efficient users of language and able to use whatever is in their environment to communicate.

In summary, children learn language when they are in environments where language is used and when they interact with others. They learn best when meaning, rather than form, is stressed. Parents set the stage for successful language learning by using language in real-life situations, by dropping specific intentions to teach language, and by accepting approximations that gradually become closer to adult models. Parents also take delight in their child's progress and celebrate her imaginative and poetic uses of language.

Parents AND Language

■ Be sure that parents understand that so-called errors in their children's speech, such as adding -ed to verbs, are signs of language growth. Giving children opportunities to learn vocabulary in meaningful ways is the most useful strategy for helping them develop their language abilities.

WWW

Children's vocabulary and ability to use language changes and grows as they find new situations in which to practice.

Observing Language Learners

Yetta Goodman (1985) has coined the term *kidwatching* to describe how teachers should pay attention to children—to what they are thinking and saying and how they are responding—which is extremely important in assessing language development. Teachers have to learn how to observe children's language and how they use it. Teachers must also learn how to provide the environments that foster children's growth in language abilities and what specific activities can be most helpful to a given child at a given time (Goodman 1985).

The following guidelines will be helpful as teachers observe the language of young children:

1. Always observe a child's language in a variety of contexts before drawing any conclusions about the child's abilities. Some children who are almost nonverbal in school settings will be extremely verbal on the playground. Some children will not contribute to conversation even in small groups but can communicate effectively one to one with a child or an adult.

2. Look for competence in using language for a variety of purposes. For example, how does the child share information, get what is needed or wanted, or use imaginative language? Can the child communicate both with adults and with other children?

3. Look for effectiveness in communication rather than for specific abilities, such as "The child speaks in complete sentences." Often, the most effective communication does not require the use of complete sentences. What teachers need to know is whether children can adapt their language to the requirements of different speaking situations.

4. Look for signs of growth in the child's knowledge of language systems. For example, are there changes in the child's use of inflectional endings and clauses?

5. Look for growth in vocabulary. As a child participates in the activities provided in the classroom, are labels for objects and actions becoming a part of his vocabulary?

Careful observation of children's language will provide insights that will help teachers plan activities and structure the environment to foster growth in language. The teacher who observes that a child does not know the language for expressing emotions, for example, will help by providing some of the labels for feelings when the child needs them. Other children may need more opportunities to recount incidents in sequential order. The teacher may guide by asking, "What came first?" or "Then what happened?" and so on. Plans and guidance that meet children's individual needs can be provided only on the basis of careful observation. Without knowledge of children's language, effective instruction is almost impossible.

Language Development in School Settings

Commercial Programs

Encouraging the development of language is always one of the primary goals of teachers of young children. Toward this goal, various commercial programs are available, often consisting of a teacher's guide, pictures of objects in various categories, and sometimes plastic models of objects. These materials may also be accompanied by audiotapes or computer programs designed to allow children to practice repeating words or phrases.

Commercial programs designed to teach children language are objectionable for several reasons. One, of course, is that these programs ignore the interactive and active nature of language learning. Another objection is that most programs are designed for small-group instruction, yet it would be rare to find a group in which all the children needed to learn the same words or phrases. A third objection to commercial language programs is that most of the actual production of language is done by the teacher, rather than by the children. Finally, most of these programs are expensive.

Using a commercial program is not the answer for promoting children's language growth. Setting up an environment that encourages language growth and that is responsive to children's language *is* the answer. Language is learned best when children use it for meaningful purposes. In the best classrooms, children have many opportunities to talk with one another and with adults. Children playing with clay, sand, water, blocks, and other classroom materials are encouraged to talk about their experiences. As adults move around the play areas, they listen to the children's language, make observations, and expand on

NAEYC

the children's language in meaningful interactions that are developmentally appropriate. If a three-year-old is playing with the sand, the adult might offer the language to describe what is taking place by remarking, for example, "You are making a tunnel in the sand." An eight-year-old playing with water and boats might be encouraged to use the vocabulary connected with boating: *deck, port, stern, aft, dock,* and so on.

Wells (1986) reached several disturbing conclusions following an extensive longitudinal study of the language of children in Bristol, England. For *none* of the children studied was the language used in the classroom as linguistically rich as that used at home, which was self-motivated, spontaneous, unstructured, and supported by adults. Wells concluded that several factors made language development at school much more difficult than it was at home: a large number of students per teacher, a curriculum dominated by norm-referenced tests, and the fact that many teachers did not believe that talking was important for learning.

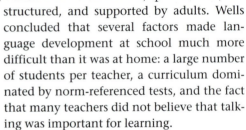

Parents AND *Language*

■ Invite parents to observe the language that children use in the classroom and to talk with you about the differences they observe between classroom language and that used at home.

WWW

Activities That Encourage Language Growth

Almost everything that happens in the early childhood classroom will contribute to children's language development. If children are arguing over a toy, the teacher can help them use language that is appropriate for disagreeing and for solving the problem. If an adult visits the class, the children can have opportunities for interaction with the visitor, who serves as another model of language use. If the children go on a field trip, they will have the opportunity to learn the vocabulary connected with what they are observing. Language development goes on all through the schoolday.

The activities described in the following sections are merely suggestive of the opportunities teachers have for helping children develop more competency as language users.

Literature

Language in children's books is very important. When an entire book contains only three hundred words, an author cannot waste words but must choose the best ones to convey the ideas. Martin (1986); Harste, Woodward, and Burke (1984); and Blackburn (1985) point out that everyone stores up all the words, phrases, and story elements they hear and that this language becomes theirs after a time. Books help children fill up their storehouses of beautiful words. Even simple stories can do this.

In *Whose Mouse Are You?* (Kraus 1970), when the little mouse is asked about his brother, he replies, "I have none." That is probably not the way most children would respond nor is it the language most children would hear at home, but it is elegant. Sometimes we choose books or stories just because the words sound so wonderful. The elephant's child says, "Good-by. I am going to the great, gray-green greasy Limpopo River all set about with fever trees to find out what the Crocodile has for dinner" ("The Elephant's Child," in Kipling 1965, p. 132). We read such language because we love to hear the sound of it. Children, too, love the sound of language, whether they understand the meaning of every word or not. The language in books allows teachers to expand children's language in supportive and creative ways. Books with simplified vocabularies are somewhat useful for beginning readers, but for all other purposes, books should be chosen because they have beautiful language.

Narrative Stories Children's literature often serves as a focus for learning new vocabulary or new ways of expressing ideas and can provide the foundation for countless activities, including the following:

1. Compare the words used in different versions of familiar folk stories. For example, several words are used to label the woodcutter in versions of "Little Red Riding Hood." Children might discuss what they think is the best choice of words and what pictures the different words bring to mind.

2. Dramatize stories or rhymes. Actually speaking the words and performing the actions that go with them help children make vocabulary real and personal.

3. Have children retell stories in their own words and/or use puppets to recall stories.

4. Ask children to create new versions of stories by selecting words to fit the patterns in repetitive books. For example, in *Someday* (Zolotow 1965), the pattern is "Someday I'll _____." Children can think of what they will do "someday."

5. Encourage children to tell their own original stories and record them either in writing or on audiotape. Having children tell their own stories results in more complex language use and more detailed stories than is the case when children are asked to tell stories about a picture or wordless picture book (Hough, Nurss, and Wood 1987).

Storytelling Telling stories can also aid in children's language development. Storytelling has the advantage of being a direct communication between the listener and the teller. Children listening to a story are required to be active listeners. If they tune out, the story will go on; there will be no instant replay. Storytelling also invites children to become active by participating in the story, repeating phrases or words or creating voices or gestures for the characters.

Storytelling is also flexible. If the audience gets restless, the storyteller can add more drama to the voices, shorten the story, end the story immediately, or whatever is required to make the session successful. Of course, this requires that the storyteller pay close attention to the audience and respond accordingly.

Stories told to children should contain language that they can understand from context so that the storyteller will not have to stop for explanations. Stories for children should also be about topics and situations that appeal to them; if the children are not interested in what the story is about, they will tune out and become restless.

The storyteller should invite participation in the tale, especially after the first telling. Possible activities include these:

1. Invite children to dramatize a story as you tell it. For example, "The Turnip," a Russian folktale, works very well (Morgan 1990).

2. Provide materials so that children can retell stories during activity periods. Make available flannelboard pieces, wooden characters, fingerpuppets, or puppets, depending on the age and experience of the children.

3. Encourage children to tell their own stories. Older children can write and produce their stories in many forms: a skit for TV, a scroll story, a flannelboard story, and so on.

4. Encourage children to join the storytelling by repeating certain phrases or sounds.

Poetry/Chants/Rhymes/Songs   Fingerplays and choral readings help children learn new vocabulary words and new sentence patterns that add to their repertoires. Teachers should plan activities such as the following:

1. Create new versions of song lyrics or rhymes by selecting words that fit the rhymes. For example, after learning *Alligator Pie* (Lee 1974), children can write or dictate new versions.

2. Dramatize rhymes or song lyrics. When children participate in drama, their actions indicate comprehension of the words. For example, the words of the various versions of "Bear Hunt" describe different actions; children can do the actions to demonstrate that they understand the words.

3. Dramatize concepts in science or social studies—such as the attraction and repelling of magnets or the arrival of a famous explorer—so that the language has real meaning for children.

Sharing Time

Sharing time can have many positive benefits for language development if managed appropriately. For instance, sharing time should be conducted in small groups so that children do not have to sit for long periods while each person has a turn. Objects should be displayed to the group, rather than passed around. Teachers should also help children learn how to begin and end

Rhyming and singing activities encourage language growth.

presentations, and sessions should be structured so that children are not required to stand up or come to the front of the class in order to participate (Oken-Wright 1988).

Teachers should also control sharing time so that it does not turn into a session in which children show off their latest possessions. The following activities may help achieve that control:

1. Sharing can be organized so that children describe the details of the process for making objects they have created in class. For example, a child might share how a textile print or clay object was made. Cooking experiences and building with blocks are other activities that provide interesting topics for sharing.

2. Children can bring objects from home that are related to a theme or topic of study. For example, they might bring something square when the class is learning shape concepts.

3. Children can share personal experiences that are important to them. They might talk about a special trip or an exciting event that occurred at home, such as the birth of kittens.

4. Sharing time can be used as a brainstorming session for solving class problems and planning class activities.

Teachers must also consider children's ages in planning activities for sharing time. For instance, younger children might be asked to offer suggestions for classroom or playground safety, and older children might be asked to think about the room arrangement and how it might be altered for better traffic patterns. In planning themes and projects, older children might be asked to persuade others that a topic of study that interests them would be a good choice for the next class theme.

Classroom Centers and Activities

Classroom centers such as the blocks area, where several children work together, tend to encourage more language use than centers where the activities are more solitary. It follows that teachers who want to encourage children's language development and use will arrange learning areas so that children can talk to one another and will prompt children to work together.

Materials will also need to be interesting and novel enough that children will want to talk about them. Several research studies (Anen 1991; Dyson and Genishi 1991; Isbell and Raines 1991) have verified the commonsense knowledge that children who are encouraged to participate in active and interesting activities are more likely to use language and produce more language than children who are asked to complete skills activities. A classroom environment in which teachers and children use language for many purposes will contribute to the communicative competence of the children.

Language development also can be enhanced through thematic instruction (Bergeron et al. 1996). Themes that present real experiences and real materials to manipulate will certainly help children expand their vocabularies in meaningful ways.

Children with Special Needs

Most children learn to use language. For those few who cannot learn to use language in the usual ways, some specialized assistance may be required.

Children with disabilities may need special help in communicating effectively in the classroom. Many devices are available for assisting communication; some are very expensive and others are inexpensive. Parette, Dunn, and Hoge (1995) describe some low-cost devices such as communication notebooks, communication vests, communication boards, communication aprons, and communication wallets. **Assisted communication** is becoming more commonplace for children with special needs. We can expect the technology in this field to continue to change, making such assistance more readily available.

Most schools offer programs for children with disabilities beginning at age three, and learning to communicate is a major goal of these programs. Full-inclusion classrooms (previously called *mainstreaming*) provide positive settings for promoting the language development of all children. Moreover,

Children with language and hearing impairments may need help from aides in the classroom.

such classrooms provide the opportunity to include children with special needs in experiences that are not drill-and-practice sessions on words or phrases. For some children, teachers will need to ask for help from school language specialists to determine the most effective means of assisting the children in efforts to communicate.

Children with Language Delays

A **language delay** results in a child's using language that is noticeably deficient for his age (Dumtschin 1988). Sometimes, delays in language can be attributed directly to specific causes, including physical problems (such as loss of hearing or structural problems in the speech-producing organs) or disease (for example, cerebral palsy); mental retardation; or emotional problems (such as autism) (Cole and Cole 1989). Other delays in language have no apparent cause; the child seems normal in other areas, but his language is not typical for his age group.

General indicators of developmental language disorders include these characteristics:

- Absence of spoken words by age eighteen months
- Absence of two-word phrases with messages by age two years
- Inappropriate responses to questions
- Echoing of speech
- Poor intelligibility (unclear speech)
- Undeveloped play skills

- Poor understanding or use of adjectives and prepositions
- Problems with word finding
- Dependence on gestures to follow directions
- Need for frequent repetition of directions
- Poor social interactions with peers
- Poor school performance (Willig 1998)

One of the first steps in providing for the needs of a child with a language delay is to make a referral to diagnose or rule out any underlying cause for the delay. Some schools have speech and language therapists who can be consulted. If the center or school does not employ a therapist, the referral may be to a therapist in private practice. If no professional can be located, the National Association for Hearing and Speech Action can provide assistance. If a cause for the delay can be identified, the therapist will make recommendations for activities or strategies that will be helpful to the teacher and parents. If no cause for the delay can be identified, the teacher will want to provide as much support for the child's language growth as possible.

A child's failing to talk on the normal schedule may lead to stress on the family and problems in peer relationships. When children are unable to communicate adequately with their peers, they may be excluded from their play groups and therefore have even less chance to learn to talk.

Research has shown that conversation between children and adults can be helpful in assisting children with language delays (Cross 1984; Lasky and Klopp 1982). As noted earlier, most adults respond to the meaning of a child's speech and continue conversations on topics introduced by the child. Children whose language is less mature than that of age peers may need even more conversation with adults that focuses on their meanings and intentions. Teachers need to be especially careful not to assume that children cannot understand normal conversation just because they cannot produce language typical of age-mates. Restricting a child's language environment is not appropriate. Although children with specific language impairments may use the same language patterns as younger children, they have more communicative competence. In other words, they are able to use what language they have more effectively (Rollins et al. 1994).

Researchers have also found that children with language delays have more interactions with adults who are critical of their language productions than do children who are making normal progress (Bondurant, Romeo, and Kretschmer 1983). Teachers should respond to children by supplying the correct labels for objects or actions without being negative. For example, if a child

Parents AND Language

- Help parents find the assistance they need for their exceptional children: a speech therapist, a language specialist, communication devices, or other services.

- Help parents appreciate the value of helping children build broad vocabularies through real experiences.

is looking at a book of zoo animals and mistakenly calls the tiger a lion, the teacher might respond, "This tiger is very large. Tigers and lions are both in the zoo."

Teachers should also be aware of their use of controlling language with children who have language delays. Girolametto, Hoaken, Weitzman, and von Lieshout (2000) found that children with language delays experienced more directive language from adults than did children whose language development was normal. Language that is controlling fails to help children develop positive interaction patterns or increase their vocabulary. For example, consider the message delivered by the command "Pick these up now!" with that of the direction "Please help me pick up the large blocks and put them on the top shelf."

Children who are late talkers seem to benefit somewhat from intervention strategies (Robertson and Weismer 1999). However, a number of experts suggest that these children be observed carefully but not treated, as many catch up with their peers in language use by age three. Studies have not been able to show the long-term gains sought by intervention strategies (Tallal and Rice 1997).

Jones and Warren (1991) make several suggestions for working with children with language delays. First, the teacher should follow the child's lead, establishing dialogue and planning novel activities that reflect the child's interests. The teacher should also provide support for the child's language by commenting on the child's utterances but not necessarily expecting a response.

Finally, teachers also need to be aware of the amount of talking by adults and the amount of talking by children encouraged in classrooms. If children are constantly involved in teacher-directed activities, in which listening and following directions are the accepted behaviors, then little time will be left for active language production (Hough, Nurss, and Goodson 1984). Children need to talk to adults and to other children if their language is to improve. Most of the children's day should be structured so that language is an integral part of activities. Teachers should make every effort to talk *to* children, not *at* them, and to accept children's language. All children need the same conditions in order to achieve maximum growth in language: an accepting environment, interesting things to talk about, and adults with whom to engage in meaningful conversations.

Ideas for the Classroom

Teachers who want to help all children develop their language abilities will encourage children to use language in classroom settings. This is especially true for those children whose language development is atypical. The following strategies may be useful in planning activities that enhance language development:

1. Encourage children to retell stories that you have read or told. A flannel-board may encourage older preschoolers to be more confident in their retellings.

2. Encourage children to use puppets to tell stories or to carry on conversations among puppet characters.

3. Involve children in learning fingerplays, song lyrics, chants, and choral readings.

4. Plan cooperative classroom activities in which children use language freely, such as card games or board games or building projects.

5. Be sure that children with language delays are not "talked down to" by anyone in the classroom and that their participation in activities is not limited.

Celebrating Diversity

Language is one obvious and easily observable difference among the cultures of the children in any typical classroom. Suggestions for celebrating children's language in the classroom include the following:

1. Post signs and announcements in as many of the languages spoken in the class as possible.

2. Arrange for regular classroom use of books and recordings in the languages represented by students.

3. Encourage the parents of bilingual children to read to them frequently.

4. Share special words with children who speak other languages.

5. Share the feeling of accomplishment when children learn new vocabulary or forms in their native languages or new languages.

6. Buy good-quality books and computer programs that use the languages spoken by the children in the classroom.

Children Who Use Dialects

A **dialect** is a systematic variation of the common language spoken by a particular group. All of us speak dialects of some sort. There are regional dialects, social class dialects, and cultural/ethnic dialects. By definition, a dialect is rule governed and consistent.

Children who speak dialects are not merely making errors in their grammatical constructions; they are following the rules of their dialects. The most important thing for teachers to remember is that children who speak dialects are not less capable of learning language than other children, nor is the dialect less effective for communication than more standard English. When judgments are made about the correctness of children's speech, these judgments are usually social, not linguistic (Jaggar 1980).

Dialects may differ in terms of vocabulary, syntax, and morphology. Vocabulary differences include all the various terms used to describe, for example, the parts of a car, the seed in a peach, or an ice cream drink. Vocabulary differences may also include some verb usages, such as the use of *carry* for *take* (as in "He will *carry* you to town"). Syntactical differences often include deleting some words. In some dialects, the correct form of "He is working today" is "He be working," which indicates that the subject is presently working. Morphological differences include dropping some inflectional endings so that possessives are formed differently ("That girl shoes") or tense or number are indicated differently ("He go there yesterday"). The differences in dialects and more standard speech are usually only minor, surface differences.

Teachers of young children who speak dialects that are different from the dialect of the majority should be especially sensitive to each child's use of language and be prepared to honor the child's ability to learn language. The child's dialect is certainly effective for communicating in her home or neighborhood. Exposure to literature and to models of other, more standard dialects may give the child alternative ways of expressing needs and thoughts over a period of time, but the teacher's goal should not be eradication of the dialect.

Ideas for the Classroom

Children who speak dialects need teachers who accept and respect their speech. The ideas that follow offer ways to help children develop their language skills in standard English while maintaining their dialect when it is appropriate:

1. Involve children in drama. They can dramatize stories and role-play various speaking situations.

2. Invite speakers to the classroom who are skilled in both the children's dialect and standard English.

3. Read children's books that use dialects.

4. Record the speech of several children saying essentially the same thing, and compare the words used.

5. Record what children say in standard spelling, but allow them to read what you have written in dialect.

6. Provide opportunities for children to talk to many different speakers.

English-as-a-Second-Language (ESL) Children

In the typical U.S. classroom today, many children do not speak English as their native language. To facilitate communication with these **English-as-a-**

Developmentally Appropriate Practice

As you think about language development and developmentally appropriate practice, reflect on the following:

NAEYC

- Many children learn to use language differently than middle-class White children. These differences are not just dialectal but reflect culturally appropriate uses of language in telling stories or entertaining groups. In a developmentally appropriate classroom, what goals and standards should be set for children's language use? For example, should all children be expected to achieve the middle-class model of language use? Why?

- Language is best learned when it is used for a real purpose; thus, contrived activities to practice language skills are rarely effective. How should real language be used in activities for children of different ages—say, preschoolers versus primary-grade children?

- The teacher must accept and respect the language of all children in a DAP classroom. How can the teacher demonstrate acceptance and respect for a student who speaks English as a second language?

- The best environment for learning language includes the critical elements of DAP, such as choice, active involvement, age and individually appropriate expectations, and so on. How do these elements enhance learning language?

second-language (ESL) children,* a number of approaches may be used: Some schools offer special bilingual programs for students who do not speak English; other schools provide tutors whose goal is to help children learn English; and some schools expect classroom teachers to provide for ESL children in the regular classroom context. Because most teachers will have ESL children in their classrooms, they should be aware of some of the research on second-language learning and its implications for instruction.

The controversy about bilingual education continues to be played out in the popular press, but bilingual programs offer benefits to children that are often not apparent to the general public (Krashen 2000a). If at all possible, children whose native language is not English should be enrolled in a good bilingual program; however, with so many languages represented in many of our schools, a bilingual program is often not a possibility for the children. There is no evidence that fluency in a first language interferes with learning English (Shin and Krashen 2001).

To learn a second language successfully requires the same conditions that foster learning a native tongue (Krashen 1981, 2000a). Specifically, the ESL learner needs someone with whom to talk as well as support for attempts

*In some school systems, ESL students are referred to as having *limited English proficiency* (*LEP*).

at communication. Language is learned best within a social context in which success at communication is expected. Because second-language learners use the strategies of simplification and overgeneralization, which are also common in original-language development, they will benefit from encouragement rather than correction during the early stages of learning English. For example, ESL learners may simplify all verbs to one tense and depend on context to help communicate the real message. Finally, second-language learners pick up more details in order to make their communication more effective. They learn to say, "I went there yesterday in the afternoon" rather than "I go there." For young children, this process may take only a few months; for older children, it may take longer.

Tabors (1998) has identified a sequence for learning English by children who are native speakers of other languages. At first, children will use only their home languages. When they want to communicate with English speakers, they will enter a nonverbal but not a noncommunicative period. In this stage, children may whine, point, mime, or cry in order to communicate. The next stage is telegraphic and formulaic speaking in the target language. Children learning a second language will use the same telegraphic speech used by native speakers of that language when one or two words will capture the meaning of a longer utterance. Formulaic speaking involves the use of common catch words and phrases, such as "ok," "uh-oh," "bye-bye," "mine," and "I don't know." Using these words and phrases can help children continue to play or interact with others even though their language skills are minimal. Finally, children achieve productive use of the new language. This stage will be marked with errors because the children are no longer depending on memorized phrases but are beginning to combine elements into real utterances.

> ## Parents AND Language
>
> ■ Arrange for parents whose first language is not English to share some of their native language with the class; children might like to learn greetings, counting words, or days of the week in another language. Also, ask bilingual parents to help you translate some favorite stories into their native language and then share them with the children. Finally, encourage parents to support their child's use of his first language and not to feel that it will be a detriment to his success.
>
> *WWW*

The following guidelines will help teachers of bilingual speakers be more effective:

1. *Get as much information as possible about the child's language background. Try to determine if the child is a talker or shy at home. Find out what languages the child's playmates speak.*
2. *Be careful about the conclusions you draw from the information you gather. Assuming a child who does not speak much does not know much about language can be very dangerous.*
3. *Compare the child's language only to other similar bilingual children.*
4. *Understand that second-language learners will make grammatical errors. There are common generalizations made by second-language learners that are not made by first-language speakers.*

Few educational issues in North America have become as volatile or as ideologically loaded as the debate on the merits or otherwise of bilingual education. Organized campaigns against bilingual education have resulted in referenda in states such as California and Arizona that have placed major restrictions on the extent to which languages other than English can be used for instructional purposes. The public controversy about bilingual education contrasts with the considerable consensus among applied linguists regarding the outcomes of such programs. The research on bilingual education supports the following conclusions:

1. **Bilingual programs for minority- and majority-language students have been successfully implemented in countries around the world.** As documented in an enormous amount of international research, students educated for part of the day through a minority language do not suffer adverse consequences in the development of academic skills in the majority language. As one example, there are more than 300,000 English-background students in various forms of French–English bilingual programs in Canada.

2. **The development of literacy in two languages entails linguistic and perhaps cognitive advantages for bilingual students.** There are more than 150 research studies carried out since the early 1960s that report significant advantages for bilingual students on a variety of metalinguistic and cognitive tasks. Bilingual students get more practice in learning language (by definition), and this seems to sharpen their awareness of subtleties of linguistic meaning and form.

3. **Significant positive relationships exist between the development of academic skills in L1 (first language) and L2 (second language).** This is true even for languages that are dissimilar (e.g., Spanish and Basque, English and Chinese, Dutch and Turkish). These crosslingual relationships provide evidence for a common underlying proficiency that permits transfer of academic and conceptual knowledge across languages. This transfer of skills and knowledge explains why spending

5. *Be aware that second-language learners may lose some of their competence in their first language. For example, a child may move away from the environment in which the first language was used regularly and therefore lose some ability to use that language.*

6. *Know it is normal for second-language learners to use both languages to communicate.* Linguistic borrowing *describes what happens when a word from one language is inserted into a sentence of the other language.* Code switching *is switching back and forth between languages, but not necessarily single words. Both are normal for bilinguals.*

7. *Learn as much as possible about the cultures represented in the classroom. Make sure this information is both for traditional and contemporary lifestyles.*

instructional time through a minority language entails no adverse consequences for the development of the majority language.

4. **The most successful bilingual programs are those that aim to develop bilingualism and biliteracy.** Most bilingual programs implemented in the United States have provided some first-language instruction as a short-term bridge to mainstream English-only programs. However, these short-term programs are less successful, in general, than programs that continue to promote both L1 and English literacy throughout elementary school. Particularly successful are dual-language programs that serve English-background students in the same classes as minority-language students, with each group acting as linguistic models for the other.

5. **Bilingual education, by itself, is not a panacea for underachievement.** Underachievement derives from many sources, and simply providing some first-language instruction will not, by itself, transform students' educational experience. Effective instruction will affirm student identities and build on the cultural and linguistic knowledge they bring to the classroom.

6. L1 loss among minority-language students is extremely common among second generation students and first generation students who arrive at an early age. Research shows that fewer than 20 percent of second generation students maintain fluency in their home language. This can cause communication problems within the family and represents a loss of linguistic resources for the nation. Furthermore, students who become fully bilingual report better relations with their families, greater self-esteem, and higher educational aspirations than those who lose their L1.

In short, there are compelling reasons why educators in both English-only and bilingual programs should be proactive in acknowledging the linguistic accomplishments of bilingual students and encouraging them to fully develop this personal and social resource.

Use this information in order to determine if any test used to evaluate bilingual speakers is biased. (Piper 1993, pp. 210–211)*

Burnett (1993) stresses that appropriate assessment of ESL learners is crucial. He recommends setting up an assessment center that is more friendly than the usual testing office and conducting multiple assessments before decisions are made about any child.

*From *Language for All Our Children* by Piper, T., © 1993. Reprinted by permission of Prentice-Hall, Inc., Upper Saddle River, NJ.

Classroom teachers can begin to assess the language development of children whose first language is not English by engaging children in writing an autobiography (photos and drawings may be more prominent than writing), keeping a journal in their first language, keeping a dialogue journal (the teacher may need help in translating), and organizing themes such as "Our Family Roots" in which all the children study the places from which their families came to the States (Peregoy and Boyle 2001).

In summary, the best environment for ESL learning includes support, encouragement, meaningful purposes for communication, and an expectation that children will talk with others who speak the language to be learned. "For a learner to be free to learn another language, the learner must be able to trust others to respond to the messages communicated and not be laughed at or singled out. In addition, a learner must be active in seeking people to talk with" (Urzua 1980, p. 38).

Ideas for the Classroom

Teachers who want to help ESL children achieve competence in English will be thoughtful about the classroom environment and activities that make learning English as much like learning a first language as possible. The following suggestions may stimulate teachers' thinking:

1. Plan for activities that require children who speak English and children who are learning English to work together (Hester 1987). This is one of the best strategies for helping children learn English. In the early childhood classroom, it is not difficult to arrange for such cooperative experiences.

2. Encourage ESL children to share their native languages through songs, fingerplays, or books.

3. Share (or find someone to share) with the class stories or poetry in another language and then in English.

4. Be careful not to separate non-English-speaking children or to exclude them from activities that you feel they will not understand. ESL children learn language by listening, watching, and following examples.

5. Writing and reading activities can be based on children's growing vocabulary in English. At first, children can make books of the words that they are learning. After only a few weeks, teachers will find that most children are learning too rapidly to use this technique.

Teachers should also help parents appreciate the importance of continuing use of the home language even after the child becomes fluent in English. Research indicates that children do better in acquiring English if the home language is maintained (Collier 1987). In interviews with parents of ESL children, most reported that they appreciate the bilingual programs at their children's schools and many believed it was important to read in the children's native languages. However, some Hispanic parents were not interested in having the school teach their children to read in Spanish because the parents wanted to teach the children this at home. One group of Hispanic parents reported that writing the alphabet, sounding out words, and learning the sounds of letters were the most important skills to be taught in a school program. But a group of Khmer parents emphasized writing the alphabet, listening to stories, and learning simple words. All parents from both groups reported working with their children at home on letters and sound–letter relationships. None of these parents advocated giving up their native language in favor of English (Brewer 1998b).

Chapter Summary

- Language is composed of the systems of phonology, semantics, syntax, morphology, and pragmatics. Each of these systems offers a challenge to the learner.

- Children all over the world learn language in a similar sequence, although with individual variations. The basic sequence begins with crying and moves through cooing, babbling, and echoing to the use of single words, multiple words, and then complete sentences.

- Three different models explain the process of learning language: behaviorist, linguistic, and constructivist. The constructivist view is based most directly on observations of children learning language and using it to communicate.

- Observations of children learning language reveal that it is learned informally; that adults should focus on the intent of the learner; that adults should expect success; that language learning is wholistic; and that language is creative.

- The language achievements of young children are quite remarkable. By the time children are five or six, they have mastered most of the basic forms of their native languages and have an extensive vocabulary.

- Observing language development is important for planning activities and strategies that will help each child maximize language development. Observers should not merely look for discrete skills from a checklist but should also observe children carefully in a variety of language contexts.

- Activities that foster the growth of language take place in the classroom every day. Children need opportunities to talk with other children and with adults. They need something interesting to talk about, and they need teachers who celebrate their use of language.

- Some children do not achieve language competence at the same rate as their peers. Children with language delays need teachers who are aware of the strategies that research has shown to be most important in helping them achieve growth in language.

- Children who speak dialects other than the dialect of the majority and children for whom English is their second language (ESL) can be helped by knowledgeable teachers who structure supportive learning environments.

Theory INTO Practice

Tape-record the language of a two-year-old and a six-year-old engaged in a similar activity, such as molding clay or playing with another child outdoors. Listen to the tapes and compare the differences in the children's language in terms of vocabulary, sentence length, number of adjectives, and so on. What conclusions can you draw?

Interview the caregivers of three two-year-old children to learn about the vocabulary of each child. Make a list of the words that each caregiver reports. Compare these lists. Do they contain similar words or classes of words? Based on your observations, what conclusions can you draw about the typical vocabulary of a two-year-old?

Observe an adult reading the same book to a two-year-old and then a four-year-old. How does the language of the adult differ in the two readings? Does he ask more questions or different kinds of questions when reading to the different children? Does he expect more responses or different kinds of response from either child? Explain your observations.

Tape-record four twenty-minute samples of one child's use of language. Make sure that the samples are collected in different situations, such as being at school, playing outdoors, being at home with the family, and playing with a friend. Compare the samples you record in terms of mean length of utterance, use of monosyllabic words, and functions of language employed. Explain how this sampling technique provides a clearer picture of the child's language development than is possible with a single sample.

Observe the home language and the school language of a five- or six-year-old child for about twenty minutes in each situation. Do the numbers and kinds of verbal interactions differ in the two situations? Do they differ in ways you would have predicted? Explain your observations.

Plan an experience for children whose first language is not English. Explain how it will help them become more competent speakers of English.

A Teacher Speaks

Jennifer Rosholt

Stevenson Elementary School
Seattle, Washington

Teaching Content and Language Together

My kindergarten/first-grade classroom welcomes students who come from many backgrounds and who speak many different languages at home. In our classroom, English is the bridge language. It bridges my students to each other and their learning while, at the same time, their first languages are honored and respected. Because my students are at all levels of understanding and use of English, I need to establish language objectives for each lesson as well as content objectives. I do not teach English instead of content. I teach both together in meaningful, interactive ways.

A kindergarten classroom is the perfect ESL (English-as-a-second-language) environment. It is *language rich* and involves many opportunities for social interaction. *Language rich* means a classroom filled with hands-on materials that students are using daily; pictures tagged with written words all around the room; and poems, songs, and books that are repetitive and fun. It encompasses all of the things that children touch and experience with infinite opportunities for them to talk and draw pictures about everything in their own way, at their own pace. Students are learning language by using language—speaking, listening, reading, and writing.

Our current study of insects in the classroom is one example of my ongoing instructional strategy of teaching content and language together. Students rotate among three different activities called *centers*. During this time, I bring together objectives in math, science, social skills, following directions, reading, writing, and English. I assess students' counting skills, numeral recognition skills, and fine motor skills on paper as well as observe social skills and insect knowledge.

One center is an insect lotto game. The students at this center each have a board with nine insect pictures. One student holds a stack of cards with matching pictures; that student shows one card at a time. Students look at their boards to see if they have matches. The game is played until all of the boards are filled. Students are cooperating, matching, recognizing insects, and using the newly introduced vocabulary (insect names, *please, thank you,* and so on).

At another center, students use clay and various materials to create insects. Each must have three body parts, six legs, and two antennae. Students are introduced to and have knowledge of these characteristics of insects prior to the centers. Students make their insects and draw pictures of them to show their work. They are demonstrating their knowledge about insects by using new vocabulary (body parts, legs, insect names, antennae), using fine motor skills to draw, and having the opportunity for creative expression.

At the last center, I interact with students. We each have a sheet of paper with pictures of some insects (ladybug, butterfly, caterpillar, grasshopper, bee, ant). Next to each picture is a box. Together, we clap out the name of the insect. Each clap corresponds to a single syllable. Students record the number of syllables in the box. They are becoming aware of the sounds in words, counting, and using new vocabulary words.

People who can speak more than one language experience many advantages. They enjoy a rich understanding of language as a concept. Their opportunities are broad. Children who walk into our class speaking little or no English bring many gifts to share with us. They want to learn what we offer to teach, and we must deliver this in the most effective and meaningful ways.

CHAPTER 10

Developing Literacy

After reading this chapter, you will be able to do the following:

- Define the terms *literacy, emergent reading, phonemic awareness,* and *phonics instruction.*
- Describe the processes of learning to read and write.
- Plan appropriate literacy instruction for young children.
- Create a classroom environment that supports young children's development of literacy.
- Plan the assessment of young children's literacy development.
- Adapt literacy instruction for children with special needs.
- Celebrate diversity in the classroom.

You and your classmates were anxious to observe this week. After reading so much about literacy, you wanted to see what kinds of literacy instruction were taking place in the schools.

Your visit was to a local school that deliberately selects students to maintain a ratio of about one-half English speakers, one-fourth Khmer speakers, and one-fourth Spanish speakers. Children begin in this program at age three and can continue through the fourth grade.

You spent most of your time in the classroom with three- and four-year-olds. You observed them listening to stories on tape (playing with puppets that are appropriate to the stories), listening to the teacher read (sometimes in all three languages), and playing with letters and word cards. The children also were encouraged to write using markers, whiteboards, paper, and other readily available writing materials. Their classroom contained many of the play areas common to preschools, such as a dramatic play area and a blocks area.

When you walked through the classrooms for older children, you saw many webs, word walls, word lists, and other indications that the children were focusing on word study. You also observed illustrations and other projects related to books. Second graders were working on posters explaining the life cycles and characteristics of insects they had selected to learn about. The children were reading reference books, using the computer to check websites, and making their own observations of insects.

Back in your own class, you were not surprised to hear about so many varia-
tions in the observations of your classmates. Some observed in classrooms where no
word study was apparent; others observed in classrooms where the literacy instruction
was a scripted program. After all that you have read and heard about phonics and
reading instruction, you are anxious to learn more about literacy instruction for
young children.

Popular Debate about the Development of Literacy

Reading instruction has always been important to Americans. In colonial times, the Puritans of Massachusetts passed laws requiring parents to teach their children to read. And in our own times, legislation has been passed that dictates what kind of reading instruction will be offered to children in public schools. So from Puritan times to the present, how to teach reading has continued to generate discussion on the front pages of newspapers and in the features of magazines. Moreover, you can be certain that the debate about reading and writing instruction is not likely to end soon.

Clearly, how well you teach children to read and write—and how well you communicate to parents what you are doing in terms of the literacy development of their children—will be critical to your success as a teacher. What is required of you as a professional teacher is that you pay careful attention to the research, that you learn to carefully observe the children you teach, and that you continue to learn about children and the development of literacy for as long as you teach. Pay close attention to legitimate research, and ignore those articles on the Internet and in print sources that are typically presented without an author's name or source references. Recently, a piece quoted Marie Clay, a recognized authority on literacy, as having said that 30 to 50 percent of children would not make adequate progress in learning to read in a meaning-based approach. No source was cited to allow readers to check the accuracy of the claims. (The article was written by someone supporting a commercial tutoring service.) What Clay actually said was that less than 10 percent of children in a good meaning-based program will need extra help in order to become proficient readers (Clay 1991, 1993a, 1993b). Also be aware that the press tends to publish opinion pieces as if they were fact. Not long ago an article written by a lawyer appeared in a local paper, touting phonics instruction as the only way in which children can learn to read. This person had no qualifications that made him an authority on how children learn to read nor any experience in teaching children to read.

Whenever you read articles such as these, ask these questions:

1. Who wrote the article and what are his or her qualifications?
2. What was the author's purpose in writing the article?

3. Was this person's work reviewed by a body of peers (i.e., other experts in the field)?

4. Who would benefit from following the recommendations in the article?

Also consider that there is a problem with reporting program results about literacy teaching. Children usually learn to read in many ways and from many sources. So beware of programs that claim certain success rates from their specific instruction. It is difficult to determine exactly what is being learned in school about literacy. In school, children may learn from each other as they take records in the "doctor's office," watch their friends write words under their drawings, or listen to the names of their classmates. At home, children may play "school" with older siblings, listen to adults read to them, observe signs and other print in their neighborhood, and learn common words such as *exit* and *men* and *women* as they go about their lives. All of these activities and more contribute to the development of literacy. The exact benefit of planned instruction is difficult to isolate.

Current Thinking about Literacy Instruction

Views of literacy have changed over the years. It was once considered a skill that someone did or did not master. Today, the development of literacy is considered a continuum, beginning when the child learns to use language and continuing through adulthood with no ending point (Harp and Brewer 1996). No one can ever reach the point where he has nothing left to learn about reading and writing.

What educators know about children and how they learn to read and write has also changed drastically over the last few years. We once considered children to be "blank slates" when they came to school, knowing nothing about reading or writing. We now know that children know a great deal about literacy and have had numerous experiences with literacy events long before they come to school.

Educators today also know that learning to read is not a single, linear process. As observers began to look more carefully at what young children were doing as learners of reading and writing, the term *emergent reading* was coined to describe a child's growing capacity to make sense of printed words. For example, children may recognize **environmental print**: stop signs, logos, product names, and so on. They may also explore print as they use markers, crayons, or chalk to create letter forms or their names.

Emergent literacy is a broad concept that describes what a child knows about reading and writing at a given point in time. The teacher's responsibility is to determine what a child knows and then choose the experiences that will help the child move along the continuum toward becoming an ever more skilled reader.

Goals of Literacy Instruction

All literacy instruction must be founded on these basic goals:

1. To continue the oral language development of each child
2. To help each child learn how print is decoded
3. To ensure that each child feels that he can achieve success in literacy learning
4. To ensure that each child will have the disposition to continue learning about literacy

In the study that was supposed to put an end to the debates about reading instruction (Snow, Burns, and Griffin 1998), the goals of initial reading instruction were condensed to the following:

Use reading to obtain meaning from print,
have frequent and intensive opportunities to read,
be exposed to frequent, regular spelling-sound relationships,
learn about the nature of the alphabetic writing system, and
understand the structure of spoken words. (p. 2)

(As you can see, these goals are included in goals 1 and 2 above.)

These goals for literacy instruction are most likely to be met in an interesting and safe environment where children can play and work together and where adults help children learn. None of these goals can be met by engaging children in isolated practice activities that are designed to teach specific skills.

Developing a Supportive Classroom Environment

Classrooms that foster the development of literacy have several distinguishing characteristics: They are interesting and full of activity, they allow for participation in many different experiences, and they connect reading and writing to children's experiences. Classrooms where literacy emerges are also print rich: They contain a wide variety of reading, writing, and listening materials that are accessible to children.

In a stimulating, active environment, children will be encouraged to participate in a wide variety of experiences. Such a classroom will not be a quiet place! Children developing new concepts should want to talk about them, read about them, and write about them. For example, as a science activity, children might observe hatching silkworms. This activity would require research about when silkworms hatch, when the mulberry leaves that they eat are available, what will happen to the silk if the larvae are allowed to mature, and how to preserve some eggs so that another generation of silkworms can be grown. This activity might also involve gathering food for the larvae and observing the metamorphosis of the larvae into silkworms. Children involved in such experiences will be constantly talking about their observations, reading from a variety of sources, listening to others read, and writing about their experiences and feelings. Children also engage in dramatic play that is book related (Rowe 1998), which helps develop concepts about books and reading. Activities that encourage thinking, talking, reading, and writing should be part of every schoolday.

Several studies have found that adding selected materials to the play environment and guiding their use can encourage children to participate in more literacy activities in their play (Christie 1990; Morrow and Rand 1991; Neuman and Roskos 1993). Christie (1990) notes that giving children time to play is simply not enough. Teachers must also intervene to promote literacy activities, perhaps thinking about what literacy materials could be added to play areas, encouraging children to play in theme centers where literacy is a natural response to a theme, or modeling literacy behaviors in play areas. For example, a teacher might set up an "office" or a "grocery store" or invite children to write labels for their block constructions. Theme areas that involve literacy experiences include a "doctor's office," a "shoe store," a "restaurant," a "home" (making lists, checking the TV guide, reading the newspaper, reading to babies, and so on), and a "post office."

Neuman and Roskos (1993) recommend using real literacy objects rather than pretend objects. An "office" might be equipped with real file folders and forms. The materials selected should be familiar to the children from their real-world experiences. Morrow and Rand (1991) suggest that literacy materials be kept in clearly marked places, that they be changed frequently to keep children's interest in them high, that teachers model the uses of materials as

Classrooms that promote the development of literacy make a wide variety of reading, writing, and listening materials available to children.

needed or suggest possible uses when appropriate, and that all levels of development be accepted for the most positive results.

Brian Cambourne's work in defining the conditions under which literacy is learned most easily led to a model of learning that describes both the physical environment and the social or psychological environment. Based on his observations, he formulated the model shown in Figure 10.1. In this model, Cambourne (1995) stresses the importance of *immersion* and *demonstration*. This means that the learner sees and hears those people who are important in her life using reading and writing. *Expectation* that the learner can become a successful user of print is vital, as students usually learn what is expected of them. According to the model, the learner takes *responsibility* for her own learning in that she chooses the pieces to be attended to in any experience, not the teacher. To illustrate this point, consider that a child will sit in her crib and practice sounds and sound combinations, but it would never work to send a toddler to her room to practice sounds.

Employment means that the learner can actually use the information he is learning in real and meaningful activities—for instance, learning how to make cookies by reading the directions. *Approximations* in literacy learning are as necessary as they are in learning to speak. We would not expect a child to use the mature form of *cookie* on his first attempt to communicate the desire for a snack. Every literacy learner will also make mistakes, but these mistakes can be extremely useful to the teacher in uncovering what the child knows and can use about printed language. Finally, the learner must receive a *response,* or feedback from his efforts. Do not confuse *feedback* with *praise;* feedback can simply be recognition of the meaning that the child attempted. For example, the child who writes *pst* on the supply list at school will get feedback if the teacher responds, "Oh, yes, we do need paste. I'll get some from the supply closet."

Learning to Read

We have learned a great deal about the process of reading in the last few years. Researchers have been trying to develop a model that would explain the process of reading and could then be used to help children engage in that process. *Reading,* by definition, means gaining meaning from print, not just pronouncing the words. As a reader tries to make sense of print, she predicts

Figure 10.1   The Conditions of Learning: A Model of Learning as It Applies to Literacy

Source: Figure 1 from Brian Cambourne. (1995, November). "Toward an Educationally Relevant Theory of Literacy Learning: Twenty Years of Inquiry." *The Reading Teacher,* 49(3), 182–202. Reprinted with permission of Brian Cambourne and the International Reading Association. All rights reserved.

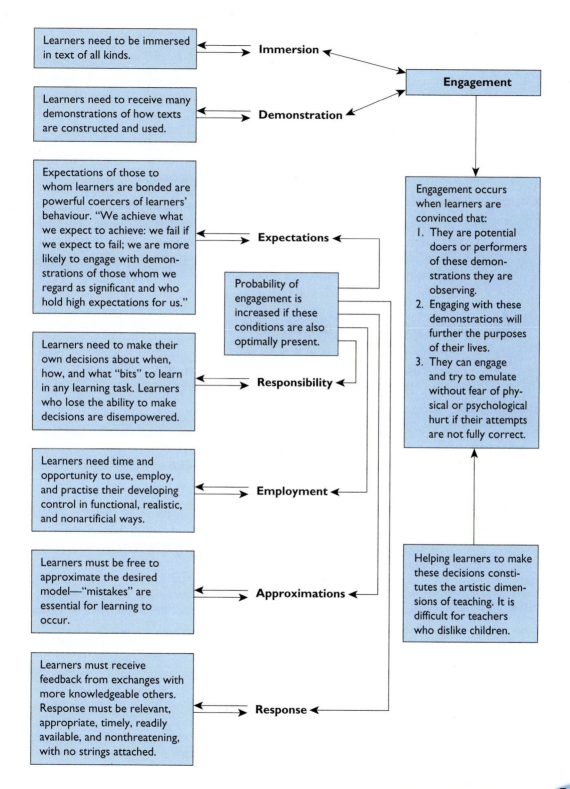

Learners need to be immersed in text of all kinds. → **Immersion**

Learners need to receive many demonstrations of how texts are constructed and used. → **Demonstration**

Engagement

Expectations of those to whom learners are bonded are powerful coercers of learners' behaviour. "We achieve what we expect to achieve: we fail if we expect to fail; we are more likely to engage with demonstrations of those whom we regard as significant and who hold high expectations for us." → **Expectations**

Probability of engagement is increased if these conditions are also optimally present.

Engagement occurs when learners are convinced that:
1. They are potential doers or performers of these demonstrations they are observing.
2. Engaging with these demonstrations will further the purposes of their lives.
3. They can engage and try to emulate without fear of physical or psychological hurt if their attempts are not fully correct.

Learners need to make their own decisions about when, how, and what "bits" to learn in any learning task. Learners who lose the ability to make decisions are disempowered. → **Responsibility**

Learners need time and opportunity to use, employ, and practise their developing control in functional, realistic, and nonartificial ways. → **Employment**

Learners must be free to approximate the desired model—"mistakes" are essential for learning to occur. → **Approximations**

Helping learners to make these decisions constitutes the artistic dimensions of teaching. It is difficult for teachers who dislike children.

Learners must receive feedback from exchanges with more knowledgeable others. Response must be relevant, appropriate, timely, readily available, and nonthreatening, with no strings attached. → **Response**

what the print will say, uses cues from the print to confirm or reject her prediction, and moves on if her prediction is confirmed. If it is rejected, she must recycle through the prediction-confirming or prediction-rejecting phase again, this time using more or different cues. At the same time, the reader is matching the meaning to what she knows about the topic. If what she knows matches, then she goes on; if it does not match, again she must reread (K. Goodman 1996; Y. Goodman and Burke 1980). Then the information is integrated into what the learner knows, and the cycle is repeated.

The true wonder of this process is that it happens so rapidly that good readers are not aware of doing it. Even beginning readers often apply several parts of the process simultaneously. What we know is that reading is not simply looking at the letters of the word, sounding them out, blending them, saying the word, and then repeating that process. Readers use **cueing systems** in the reading process, including the sound–letter relationship of the print itself, their background knowledge, their knowledge of language, cues from the illustrations (if the material is illustrated), and any number of other signals that are personal to them.

Cues That Readers Use

The print itself offers cues, as there are many words that we recognize instantaneously (our *sight-word vocabulary*). However, print cues sometimes fail us. For instance, when we read the word *tear*, does it mean "water falling from our eyes" or "a rip in our clothing"? Nonetheless, sound–letter relationships do provide information as we read. For example, if we are reading a text about big cats and come to a word that we do not recognize, the *p* at the beginning of the word would cue us that the word is not *tiger* but *panther*. If we know that *mother* and other common words end with the sound represented by -*er,* that will also help us decode the word. We might also know the word *pan* and use that knowledge to determine the first part of the unknown word *panther.*

Parents AND Literacy

■ Plan a family literacy night, during which you use a "big book" demonstration to explain how you are helping the children learn to read. See Cairney and Munsie (1995) for ideas.

WWW

In addition to knowledge of sound–letter relationships, readers also use what they know about how language works. Language cues include *semantics*—knowledge of word meanings and the relationships between and among words. Meanings are rarely exact, but all language users have developed meanings for words. When several readers see the letters *c a t*, each may picture a different cat, but there will be enough shared meaning to communicate.

Another language cue is provided by the *syntax* of the sentence—the order in which the words and phrases are arranged. If, for example, the reader sees *the,* he will know that a noun will follow. Syntax is specific to a given language. In English, adjectives usually are placed before the nouns they modify, but in Spanish, adjectives are placed after the nouns.

Other cues include what we know about the world. If we read *A hurricane spawned a _____ when it came ashore,* we use our knowledge of weather to help us fill in *tornado.* We would not think that the word *spawned* had anything to do with laying eggs in this context.

Illustrations offer cues to readers if they correspond with the text and provide accurate information. Beginning or early readers often use pictures as cues to predict new or unknown words.

In summary, readers use a variety of cues to create meaning. Moreover, readers bring to the reading process a wealth of information about language, topics, story structure, and words represented by squiggles.

Stages of Reading

The International Reading Association and the National Association for the Education of Young Children (IRA/NAEYC 1998) developed and published a joint position statement that defines developmentally appropriate practices in literacy instruction for young children. This continuum of literacy development, shown in Figure 10.2, describes five phases and grade levels. As stated in the note at the top of the figure, however, not all children at any grade will function at the same level in terms of literacy or any other area of development.

The information in Figure 10.2 can help teachers plan goals for their literacy programs and plan instruction for individual children. A preschool teacher of children who have not had many literacy experiences will need to begin with activities based on what the children know. For example, if a child has no experience in listening to books being read, then perhaps the teacher will need to tell him short and interesting stories. The next step might be to tell him stories using a flannelboard or a puppet. After the child has some experience with stories, then the teacher can begin to read to him from books. Once the child is engaged with book reading, the teacher can help him recognize how print works by demonstrating directionality and discussing the differences between the information that can be obtained from illustrations versus print. To begin such a child with drilling on letters and sounds before he knows about books and stories would make no sense.

Instruction for children with limited literacy experiences will require more individual story time, more story repetitions, and more talking about books individually and in small groups than might be required by more advantaged children. However, the results will be well worth the effort. Mem Fox (1999) argues that a child who knows four nursery rhymes by heart by the age of four will probably learn to read without difficulty. Knowing these rhymes indicates the child has experience with words and sounds and pays attention to remembering them. If a child lacks that experience, then the teacher must supply it.

For every child, the goals must be to help her find satisfaction in literacy experiences and to encourage the disposition to continue learning. Any program that fails to achieve these goals is not appropriate for young children.

Note: This list is intended to be illustrative, not exhaustive. Children at any grade level will function at a variety of phases along the reading/writing continuum.

Phase 1: Awareness and exploration (goals for preschool)

Children explore their environment and build the foundations for learning to read and write.

Children can

- enjoy listening to and discussing storybooks
- understand that print carries a message
- engage in reading and writing attempts
- identify labels and signs in their environment
- participate in rhyming games
- identify some letters and make some letter-sound matches
- use known letters or approximations of letters to represent written language (especially meaningful words like their name and phrases such as "I love you")

What teachers do

- share books with children, including Big Books, and model reading behaviors
- talk about letters by name and sounds
- establish a literacy-rich environment
- reread favorite stories
- engage children in language games
- promote literacy-related play activities
- encourage children to experiment with writing

What parents and family members can do

- talk with children, engage them in conversation, give names of things, show interest in what a child says
- read and reread stories with predictable texts to children
- encourage children to recount experiences and describe ideas and events that are important to them
- visit the library regularly
- provide opportunities for children to draw and print, using markers, crayons, and pencils

Phase 2: Experimental reading and writing (goals for kindergarten)

Children develop basic concepts of print and begin to engage in and experiment with reading and writing.

Kindergartners can

- enjoy being read to and themselves retell simple narrative stories or informational texts
- use descriptive language to explain and explore
- recognize letters and letter-sound matches
- show familiarity with rhyming and beginning sounds
- understand left-to-right and top-to-bottom orientation and familiar concepts of print
- match spoken words with written ones
- begin to write letters of the alphabet and some high-frequency words

What teachers do

- encourage children to talk about reading and writing experiences
- provide many opportunities for children to explore and identify sound-symbol relationships in meaningful contexts
- help children to segment spoken words into individual sounds and blend the sounds into whole words (for example, by slowly writing a word and saying its sound)
- frequently read interesting and conceptually rich stories to children
- provide daily opportunities for children to write
- help children build a sight vocabulary
- create a literacy-rich environment for children to engage independently in reading and writing

What parents and family members can do

- daily read and reread narrative and informational stories to children
- encourage children's attempts at reading and writing
- allow children to participate in activities that involve writing and reading (for example, cooking, making grocery lists)
- play games that involve specific directions (such as "Simon Says")
- have conversations with children during mealtimes and throughout the day

Phase 3: Early reading and writing (goals for first grade)

Children begin to read simple stories and can write about a topic that is meaningful to them.

First graders can
- read and retell familiar stories
- use strategies (rereading, predicting, questioning, contextualizing) when comprehension breaks down
- use reading and writing for various purposes on their own initiative
- orally read with reasonable fluency
- use letter-sound associations, word parts, and context to identify new words
- identify an increasing number of words by sight
- sound out and represent all substantial sounds in spelling a word
- write about topics that are personally meaningful
- attempt to use some punctuation and capitalization

What teachers do
- support the development of vocabulary by reading daily to the children, transcribing their language, and selecting materials that expand children's knowledge and language development
- model strategies and provide practice for identifying unknown words
- give children opportunities for independent reading and writing practice
- read, write, and discuss a range of different text types (poems, informational books)
- introduce new words and teach strategies for learning to spell new words
- demonstrate and model strategies to use when comprehension breaks down
- help children build lists of commonly used words from their writing

What parents and family members can do
- talk about favorite storybooks
- read to children and encourage them to read to you
- suggest that children write to friends and relatives
- bring to a parent-teacher conference evidence of what your child can do in writing and reading

- encourage children to share what they have learned about their writing and reading

Phase 4: Transitional reading and writing (goals for second grade)

Children begin to read more fluently and write various text forms using simple and more complex sentences.

Second graders can
- read with greater fluency
- use strategies more efficiently (rereading, questioning, and so on) when comprehension breaks down
- use word identification strategies with greater facility to unlock unknown words
- identify an increasing number of words by sight
- write about a range of topics to suit different audiences
- use common letter patterns and critical features to spell words
- punctuate simple sentences correctly and proofread their own work
- spend time reading daily and use reading to research topics

What teachers do
- create a climate that fosters analytic, evaluative, and reflective thinking
- teach children to write in multiple forms (stories, information, poems)
- ensure that children read a range of texts for a variety of purposes
- teach revising, editing, and proofreading skills
- teach strategies for spelling new and difficult words
- model enjoyment of reading

What parents and family members can do
- continue to read to children and encourage them to read to you
- engage children in activities that require reading and writing
- become involved in school activities
- show children your interest in their learning by displaying their written work
- visit the library regularly
- support your child's specific hobby or interest with reading materials and references

Source: From a Joint Position Statement of the IRA/NAEYC, adopted 1998 (October). "Learning to Read and Write: Developmentally Appropriate Practices for Young Children," *The Reading Teacher* 52(2): 193–216. Reprinted with permission of the International Reading Association. All rights reserved.

Learning How Print Is Decoded

Developing Phonemic Awareness

Phonemic awareness is a set of skills defined by Ehri and Nunes (2002) as the ability to "focus on and manipulate phonemes in written words" (p. 111). Tasks to determine phonemic awareness include asking learners to isolate a sound (tell me the first sound in *paste*); to identify a sound (tell me the sound that is the same in *bike, boy,* and *bell*); to categorize a sound (which word does not belong—*bus, bun,* or *rug*?); to blend sounds to create a word; to segment sounds in given words; and to delete sounds (what is *smile* without the *s*?) Phonemic awareness falls under the umbrella of phonological awareness, which is the ability to recognize larger spoken units such as syllables, onsets, and rimes.

Several studies have concluded that phonemic awareness is highly correlated with success in beginning reading experiences (Hoffman et al. 1998; Lundberg, Frost, and Petersen 1988). Phonemic awareness is not a single skill but a cluster of skills that develops over time. For example, recognizing rhyming words is one level of phonemic awareness, being able to distinguish the beginning sound of a word from the rest of the word is another level, and completely segmenting the word is another. The skills that constitute phonemic awareness are developed as a result of children's experience with oral and written language.

Many common preschool and kindergarten activities help children become more aware of sounds in words—for instance, clapping the beats in the children's names, having the children complete the rhyming line of a nursery rhyme that the teacher starts, reading aloud books with rhyming words and a wide variety of alphabet books, making a list of words that begin with the same sound as a given word, and dictating sentences in which all the words begin with the same sound (Novick 1999/2000). For a child who needs additional practice with sounds, the teacher might use an activity such as the Elkonin boxes (Elkonin 1973). The child is given a card with three boxes drawn on it along with some markers, such as pennies or plastic chips. He is instructed to place a marker in a box for each sound he hears in a given word. (The markers are for sounds, not letters.) A four-letter word such as *cake* would mean marking three boxes.

The National Reading Panel report (2000) suggests that skill in phonemic awareness is one of the best predictors of reading success. However, in their analysis of studies of phonemic awareness, they found that studies in which the children attached letters to sounds were more effective in aiding children's reading and spelling skills. In other words, these were studies of phonics instruction rather than phonemic awareness.

Cunningham and Cunningham (2002) state that children do need phonemic awareness, but they also need other skills if they are to learn to read successfully. They oppose spending large portions of class time on phonemic awareness programs without regard for what children know and can do. "Such single level instruction can only bore and even confuse those who already have or would learn phonemic awareness without it" (p. 93).

Most children develop phonemic awareness without specific instruction. They only need to take part in interesting language activities and have teachers who help them focus on the sounds of words from their oral language and how sounds are recorded in print.

Phonics Instruction

Phonemic awareness is often confused with phonics. To clarify, *phonemic awareness* is the child's awareness of sounds, not the relationship between sounds and the letters used to represent them. *Phonics* is learning how to decode the print symbols used to represent language sounds.

Much has been written in the professional and popular press recently about phonics instruction and its place in helping children learn to read. The debate is not about whether children should learn sound–letter relationships; everyone agrees that knowing such relationships is a critical skill. Instead, the debate is over when and how such instruction should take place. Advocates of the "phonics first" approach believe that children should master sound–letter relationships before actually reading meaningful material. Others argue that children should have rich experiences with meaningful literature, and when they have achieved a workable sight vocabulary, then they should learn sound–letter relationships to help them decode unfamiliar words.

Research on Phonics Instruction

Many of the research studies that claim to prove that phonics instruction in a direct and systematic program results in higher reading achievement than alternate methods of reading instruction have been criticized by other researchers. For example, Taylor (1998) examined a study by Foorman et al. (1998) that supported direct phonics instruction for African American children and found that some of the results were based on a sample size of only five children (p. 46). Certainly, no valid generalization can be made from such a small sample. Others have found problems with research studies sponsored by the National Institute of Health (Krashen 1999; McQuillan 1998; Smith 1999; Stahl, Duffy-Hester, and Stahl 1998). Many of these studies were conducted on children with special learning needs, so their findings cannot be generalized to all children. Other research was conducted by individuals aligned with specific programs of instruction that would obviously benefit from supportive findings. Studies that used the reading of isolated words as the measure of success have drawn criticism because there is no research to connect the success of reading isolated words with real reading of connected text. Clay (1991), among others, cautions against using word lists as measures of reading competency.

None of this criticism is to say that phonics instruction is not important. Good teachers have always taught children phonics and will continue to do so. The issue in some of the studies just cited is that they call for *systematic* phonics instruction—a "one-size-fits-all" approach.

After an analysis of studies examining the effectiveness of "systematic phonics instruction," the National Reading Panel (2000) found that phonics instruction was useful in helping children become more skilled readers. They found that kindergarten and first-grade learners benefited more from the instruction than did older children. Even so, the teacher need not follow a lockstep program for every child. She can keep records of the work done with individual children and make sure that every useful sound–letter relationship and the strategies for applying them have been covered over a period of time. Phonics can certainly be taught without a commercial program (Routman 2000).

In an extensive study of eight first-grade classrooms that met stringent criteria for whole-language instruction, Dahl et al. (1999) found that children were gaining skill in using phonics information through their reading. In sum:

> *Findings demonstrated that whole language classrooms included a more complex and varied mix of phonics instructional events encompassing direct instruction, individualized instruction, and instruction embedded in ongoing reading and writing activities. . . . This was accomplished by teachers making informed instructional decisions based on the literacy development and progress of each student.* (p. 338)

Problems with Planning Phonics Instruction

One problem that confronts teachers planning phonics instruction is children's dialects. Goodman (1996) points out the difficulty of deciding what pronunciations will make sense to children. Bear et al. (2000) recommend that teachers allow children to participate in phonics activities without trying to make them all hear or say the same sound; such slight variations will not be harmful to word study.

From what we know about language, a **dialect** is not an incorrect or inferior form of speech but a rule-bound variation of English. Therefore, if children in one region of the country pronounce a vowel in a certain way, it is phonetically correct, even if it varies from the pronunciation used in another region. For example, consider the words *pen* and *pin*. In the South, there is no difference in the pronunciations of these words. Children learn how to spell these words to indicate their different meanings in writing and know that context will help their listeners determine which word is being used in oral language. In some parts of the country, *idea* is pronounced with an *r* sound added to the end. No dialect indicates more or less intelligence or skill in language use than another dialect.

A second problem with planning phonics instruction is that there is no one way of teaching every child to read. Cambourne (1999) believes that the slogan "explicit and systematic teaching of reading" can be dangerous if such teaching is "mindless and decontectualised" (p. 127). In addition to the labels *direct* and *systematic, balanced* is another word that is currently prominent in the literature on reading instruction. However, *balanced* is not an appropriate description of the best instruction in literacy. It implies that equal amounts of time and instruction are provided for learning phonics skills and for doing meaningful reading. A balanced program could not possibly be appropriate for every child, every day.

What is needed in literacy instruction is an intelligent teacher who is knowledgeable about how children learn to read and write, who can organize a day so that there are always good reasons for children to engage in literacy tasks, and who can provide the needed instruction for every child. Duffy and Hoffman (1999) recommend that we replace the search for a

> *perfect method concept with a commitment to developing independent, problem-solving, and spirited teachers who understand that their job is to use many good methods and materials in various ways according to students' needs.* (p. 15)

Greenberg (1998a, 1998b, 1998c) agrees, adding that the issue must be what each child knows, not whether teaching phonics is appropriate. This is not a "pie in the sky" view. Millions of teachers do exactly this every day.

A third problem with planning phonics instruction is that it should not be provided for children who do not need it. When a child knows a sound–letter relationship, he does not need to have instruction on that relationship. Just as in any other kind of teaching, the professional teacher should decide what instruction will make sense to the learner and provide it at the appropriate time. To illustrate this concept, imagine this scenario in a first grade classroom:

> There are twenty-two children. Four of them are able readers of many texts. Three more can read many common words and indicate that they know many sound–letter relationships because they write them in their journals. Five of the children do not speak English as their first language. They are learning English rapidly as they play with their fellow students and engage in interesting activities, such as caring for a pet rabbit. These children learn the vocabulary of the activities in English with help from their teachers as well as their peers. Three other children have limited vocabularies, even though their home language is English. They, too, are learning new vocabulary and how to listen and respond to stories. The seven remaining children have just begun to find satisfaction in recognizing common sounds in the names of their classmates, to read the jobs chart, and to want to write stories on their own. These children delight in learning about words that begin with *b* and are anxious to use them in their writing. For the other students, such a lesson would produce either boredom or confusion.

Those children who already know sound–letter relationships will be bored and soon conclude that school is not interesting and not able to teach them very much. (These children can be found in every grade.) Those children who will be confused will learn what Katz (1986) calls *learned stupidity*—that they are not capable of performing the tasks required of them at school. (These children can be found in every grade, too.)

So, what can the teacher of these twenty-two children do to make phonics instruction appropriate for her class?

Appropriate Phonics Instruction

In their article entitled "Everything You Wanted to Know about Phonics (but Were Afraid to Ask)," Stahl et al. (1998) provide seven principles for good phonics instruction. Namely, good phonics instruction should do the following:

1. Develop the alphabetic principle.
2. Develop phonological awareness.
3. Provide a thorough grounding in the letters.
4. Avoid teaching rules, using worksheets, dominating instruction, and boring learners.
5. Provide sufficient practice in reading words.
6. Lead to automatic word recognition.
7. Be one part of reading instruction (pp. 339–343).

Other reasonable suggestions for phonics instruction come from the Center for the Improvement of Early Reading Achievement (Hiebert et al. 1998), which has compiled a suggested list of phonics accomplishments for children from kindergarten to second grade:

- ■ *Kindergarten:* Children should know many sound–letter relationships and begin to understand that the sequence of letters in a written word represents the sequence of sounds in a spoken word.

- ■ *First grade:* Children should be able to decode phonetically regular one-syllable words in texts and monitor their own reading to self-correct if the word they have identified does not fit with the other cues provided in the sentence.

- ■ *Second grade:* Children should be able to decode one-syllable words not yet known through sound–letter knowledge, through recognition of phonograms, or by analogy to rhyming words and be able to decode multisyllabic words through phonic and structural analysis.

Taking these suggestions into account, let us now return to the first grade class discussed in the previous section. How can the teacher of that class meet the diverse needs of her students? Figure 10.3 shows a page from her plan book, in which she develops various activities based on reading aloud one book.

Such planning clearly illustrates the principles of good phonics instruction. This approach is supported by the work of Strickland (1998), who describes a whole-to-part-to-whole plan. As in the plan in Figure 10.3, the teacher starts with a text, uses a part of it for instruction, and then concludes with the whole. Moustafa and Maldonado-Colon (1999) describe a similar idea based on the rhyme "The Eensy, Weensy Spider." Many other teachers use this model on a daily basis, perhaps choosing a different text for each group of children. Regardless, the point is to plan instruction that meets the needs of all children and helps them feel that they are successful literacy learners.

Figure 10.3

Literacy Activities
from the Teacher's
Plan Book

Whole group:
Read aloud One Duck Stuck (Root 1998). Take pleasure in the words and repeat some of them, encouraging the children to join in when they can.

Children who are reading exceptionally well:
Encourage them to write their own stories following the pattern established in the duck story. (The moose is stuck in the muck on the final endpaper, but this is not mentioned in the text.) After their stories are completed, ask the children to share them with the class. If a child does not choose this activity, she can choose another writing project.

Children who are strong beginning readers:
Review the text with these children, and find all the rhyming words they can read (duck, muck, luck, stuck; fish, swish; moose, spruce; crickets, thickets). Call attention to the rhyming words that are not spelled with the same pattern (moose and spruce). Using several sets of words, help children apply the strategy of using a rhyming word they know to decode a new word. Make a book of rhyming words to use as a reference or to share with the class.

ESL children/Children with limited vocabulary:
Make sure that these children understand what all the words mean, including the invented words ("The crickets leap to the duck. Pleep, pleep."). Read the book in a shared reading experience, and encourage the children to join in when they can. Draw attention to the clues on the page for the number words (a numeral and the illustration). Let each child select a favorite page and help lead the others as that page is read again. Talk about the invented words that the author selected or created to describe the movements of the animals. Ask the children what words they would use to describe the movements of different animals. Enjoy the book one more time. Encourage the children to choose a word or words for their word banks.

Children making good progress:
Review the text with these children, and help them identify the repetitive patterns ("Help! Help! Who can help?" and "We can! We can!"). Use the /an/ from can and help the children create new words by changing the c to r, f, d, m, p, t, and v. If the children understand this activity, repeat it using another word from the text. If they do not know the /fr/, /sk/, or /tr/ sounds as onsets, then select words from the book with these onsets and ask the children to think of other words that begin with the same sounds. Help the children use their knowledge of these onsets to decode new words; write them on a whiteboard. Reread the book, stressing the patterns and words discussed. Encourage the children to write about their favorite parts of the book.

As you reflect on your own experience in learning to read and what you know about developmentally appropriate practice, think about these statements:

NAEYC

- Literacy is a continuum of learning that begins at birth. The teacher's task is to find where each child is on that continuum and what she wants and needs to know next.

- Adding play materials that will encourage literacy activities does not necessarily make the classroom less playful.

- Isolated skill instruction (such as teaching the names of letters and how to recognize sight words) is rarely developmentally appropriate.

- Literacy is not the whole focus of instruction in a developmentally appropriate classroom.

A Final Word on Phonics

Even the strongest advocates of the "phonics first" approach recognize that children need to develop a sight vocabulary because of the large number of common words in English that are not phonetically regular (Blachman 1991). Phonics advocates also recognize that children need interesting texts to read (Adams 1990). Lyon (1998) states that from the beginning, children need to be "playing with language through nursery rhymes, storybooks, and writing activities" and to have "as early as possible experiences that help them understand the purposes of reading, and the wonder and joy that can be derived from reading" (p. 12). Teachers must not be overwhelmed by the "phonics first" arguments without considering what they can do to help children enjoy reading experiences and develop a strong disposition to engage in literacy experiences.

Learning to Write

In the past, teachers and parents assumed that children would learn to write after they learned to read and that this learning would take place primarily in a school setting. That view of writing dominated the instructional literature for years. Then in 1971, Carol Chomsky made a radical departure from the traditional view when she advocated that nonreaders should be writing and that reading instruction should begin with writing. Since that time, there has been a flurry of research activity focusing on young children and their writing. The resulting information has greatly expanded the view of writing—what it is, how it develops, and how best to teach it.

The more traditional view defined writing in terms that were mostly limited to handwriting. Children were expected to copy letters until they

Mary Renck Jalongo
Indiana University of Philadelphia

Becoming Literate

Becoming literate is a complex task for young children. They pay attention to the language around them and can read environmental print, such as their favorite food labels or billboards. Most young children will attempt to write things that matter to them, such as printing their own names and those of their family members and pets. They usually pretend to write and read as fluently as adults do, for instance, scribbling rapidly to imitate the literate adult's handwriting or talking while looking at a newspaper. Young children often pretend to read a picture book by telling a story using the pictures as a prop. Their retellings incorporate words and phrases from the text of the book, and often they will memorize the entire text of a favorite book. But it isn't just having books around, as important as that is, that invites children into the world of literacy.

Language is a social instrument and is fundamentally interactive. In fact, it is the interaction that surrounds significant pieces of print—whether it is a grocery shopping list, a story on computer, or an e-mail message from family or friend—that urges children to invest the effort and concentration necessary to learn to read and write at a level that is acceptable to their dominant culture. What counts as being literate varies from one culture to the next, depending on what types and levels of literacy are required to participate fully in life and work and have a voice in community and society.

Many of the things that very young children are taught in the name of literacy are exceedingly difficult for them to understand. One kindergarten teacher's manual, for example, includes a lesson on helping five-year-olds to determine which syllable is emphasized in the words that they hear. In order to accomplish this task, the child would first need to understand what a syllable is and would also need to have sufficient auditory discrimination to hear the emphasis. Yet, in reality, many five-year-old children are baffled by this level of word analysis. They cannot always tell where the flow of speech that they hear is separated into words, much less syllables.

In helping children become literate, there are fundamental differences of opinion about how best to achieve success. Some experts make the part-to-whole argument in which young children first learn the alphabet, then connect letters with sounds, then begin building words, then progress to simple sentences, and finally are able to read paragraphs and books. In this skills-based approach, teachers tend to rely on direct instruction of skills and concentrate on giving students practice with these skills. In contrast, the whole-to-part approach argues that, under normal conditions of repeated exposure to favorite picture books, many young children learn to read. Using this literature-based approach, the emphasis is on oral language.

Best practices in early literacy combine the two approaches. This approach is called "balanced literacy" because it seeks to capitalize on the strengths of a literature-based approach such as child-initiated writing, self-selection of reading materials, and individualization, and, at the same time, utilize the strengths of direct instruction, such as systematic instruction in phonics and opportunities for guided practice in basic skills.

As you work with young children, it is important to keep their inexperience in mind and to build on their assets in oral language. It is also important to maintain a balanced literacy program capable of optimizing the potential of every child in the diverse groups of learners found in early childhood programs.

could reproduce close approximations of the teacher's model. Then they were expected to copy sentences. Teachers often gave children exercises in a handwriting text to copy or began the schoolday by writing a poem or a quotation on the board for the children to copy. Children's attempts at writing on their own were basically ignored or perhaps even punished—certainly not encouraged (Atkins 1984). In light of the research conducted since the 1970s, however, writing is generally defined more broadly today to include children's efforts at making marks on paper—beginning with scribbles.

We now recognize that children construct their understanding of written language in a developmental sequence that is observable and very similar in all children. The stages of writing development have been described by Temple et al. (1993), Clay (1975), and Ferreiro and Teberosky (1982). These stages are outlined in the following sections.

Development of Writing

Scribbling Stage

Writing begins with scribbling, as illustrated in Figure 10.4. A scribble may seem to be only random marks on a paper. But in this example, note that the child (who is three years, six months old) has begun to make some lines (the up-and-down marks at the top) that are more like writing and has contained the major part of the scribble in a box. This scribble indicates increasing control of the writing instrument and increasing knowledge of letter shapes. This child says he has written *Milk, hotdogs, and mustard.*

Parents and teachers of scribblers should provide them with a variety of materials, such as paint, books, paper, and crayons. Parents and teachers should label the children's scribbling as "writing" and model writing just as they model reading for their children. Parents can model writing in everyday situations, for instance, saying, "We are almost out of milk. We should write it on our grocery list," or "I am writing a letter to Aunt Sue. Would you like to write something to her?" or "I am going to leave a note for Daddy so he will

Figure 10.4

Scribbling

know where we are," and so on. Parents should also read aloud and encourage children to talk to one another and to adults.

Linear Repetitive Stage

The next stage in writing development is the linear repetitive stage. In this stage, children discover that writing is usually horizontal and that letters appear in a string across a page. Children in this stage think that a word referring to something large has a longer string of forms than a word referring to something small (Ferreiro and Teberosky 1982; Schickedanz 1988). In other words, children look for concrete connections between words and their referents.

Figure 10.5 is an example of linear repetitive writing. Given a form, the child completed it with linear scribbles. Such examples of writing provide opportunities to observe children's knowledge of print as they use it in different ways. Figure 10.6 shows how the child (three years, six months old) made shapes in a linear pattern. The longer (bottom) scribble translates to *mustard*, and the shorter (top) scribble is *milk*.

Children in the linear repetitive stage need the same support that scribblers need from parents and teachers. Adults might also begin watching for the emergence of letter forms.

Random-Letter Stage

The next stage is the random-letter stage, in which children learn which forms are acceptable as letters and use them in some random order to record words or sentences. Children produce strings of letters that have no relation to the sounds of the words they are attempting to record. They may also include some forms that are not recognizable as letters because their repertoire of letters is so limited.

Figure 10.5   Linear Repetitive Writing

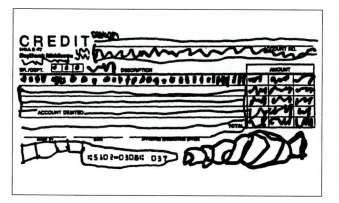

Figure 10.6   Linear Repetitive Writing

The five-year-old child who created Figure 10.7 wrote *This is a ghost*. But the five-year-old who created Figure 10.8, when asked what it said, responded, "I don't know what it says. I can't read." Perhaps he was merely making a list of letters that he knows or experimenting with letter shapes and had no intention of saying anything with this writing. If this child does not write to communicate a message at least occasionally, his teacher should stress to him the communicative nature of print. An example would be to attach a note on the cracker basket at snack time that says "2 Ritz crackers, 1 Vanilla wafer." Such a purposeful use of print can be applied all through the day.

Figure 10.9 is an example of a common feature in children's early writing: using a set of letters that they know (often the letters of their name) by writing them again and again and saying that they carry a message. This child wrote *Once upon a time two little girls liked to play outside. I like to play outside, I said. Let's go see your snowman, said sister. The end.*

Teachers and parents should encourage children's attempts to write. Children need the adults around them to respond to the intent of their writing, not to correct their form. If the people around them honor their attempts to write and treat their writing as important, children's writing skills will grow. Just as we know that a child who is saying "goed" is actually making progress in learning language, we know that a child who has discovered letters and understands that they stand for thoughts has made progress in learning about written language.

Figure 10.7   Random-Letter Writing

Figure 10.8   Random-Letter Writing

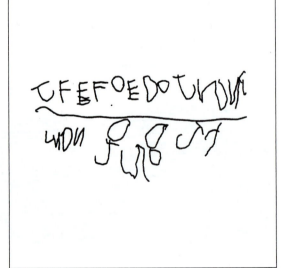

Figure 10.9

Random-Letter
Writing

Letter-Name, or Phonetic, Writing

The next stage of development is that of early phonetic writing, in which children begin to make the connection between letters and sounds. The beginning of this stage is often described as *letter-name writing* because children write the letters whose names and sounds are the same. For example, they write the word *you* with the letter *u*. They begin to represent words with graphemes that reflect exactly what they hear.

   Figure 10.10 is an example of early phonetic writing. In this sample, the child (five years old) has used dots to mark the spaces between words, which is a common feature in beginning writing. These words say *Sweater, socks, hats, jacket.* Note the reversed *j* and the mark at the top of the *K,* indicating that the child closed the top and then could not erase the writing when she realized that a *K* should be open at the top. Figure 10.11 is an example of late phonetic writing, when the child has mastered many print conventions, such as the spaces between words, but spells many words phonetically. With a little prac-

Figure 10.10

Early Phonetic
Writing

Figure 10.11
Late Phonetic Writing

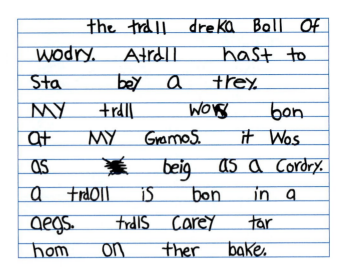

the trdll dreKa Ball of wodry. Atrdll hast to Sta bey a trey. MY trdll wo⊠ bon at MY Gramos. it Wos as ✗ beig as a Cordry. a trdOll iS bon in a aegs. trdlS Carey tar hom on ther bake.

tice, one can read phonetic writing. This sample says *The turtle drinks a bowl of water. A turtle has to stay by a tree. My turtle was born at my grandma's. It was as big as a quarter. A turtle is born in an egg. Turtles carry their home on their back.*

Transitional Spelling

As children learn more about the written language system, they begin to learn the conventions of written language. They begin to spell some words in conventional ways, even though their spelling up to this point has been phonetic. A good example is the word *love*. Because children are exposed to this word so often, they begin to spell it in its conventional form very early. *The* is another common example. This stage of spelling is called *transitional* to indicate that children are moving from phonetic spelling to more standard or conventional spelling.

Figure 10.12 is an example of transitional spelling. Much of the writing is correct by conventional standards. Note the spelling of *they* (*thay*) using a pattern that works with other English words, such as *day, pray,* and so on. This child will learn that *they* is an exception to the usual pattern. In the line that begins *The smoning,* the child probably meant to put the *s* on *the* (for *this*) but put it with *moning* (*morning*). Teachers should ask children to read back their writing so that they learn to catch these errors themselves. Children's writing is less automatic than that of adults, so their thinking gets ahead of their production.

Parents AND Literacy

■ Use examples from the children's work in class to explain the stages in writing development to parents. Also let parents know that you will send home a brief note when their child passes one of the developmental milestones in writing.

WWW

Teachers and parents can foster independence in writing at this stage by asking children how they think words are spelled, by supplying needed information, and by encouraging children to help one another in the writing process. Instruction in spelling as an isolated subject is not necessary at this point. Children will learn to spell conventionally the words they need for writing. In Figure 10.12, much of the writing is correct. Teachers should focus on how much children know at this stage, rather than correcting spellings they do not yet know.

Conventional Spelling

Finally, children achieve mostly conventional spelling. Just as children move slowly from babbling to adult speech, they need time to learn the conventions of written language. Adult speech is not mastered without considerable time and effort from the learner and support from sensitive adults. Children deserve the same support as they move from scribbling to mature writing.

Figure 10.13 is an example of conventional spelling, written by a child in the summer after first grade. Note that this child spells all the words conventionally and has also mastered apostrophes. She makes a line to indicate a substitution for a word that she marked out. The spacing makes the line "I like

Figure 10.12   Transitional Spelling

> One deay I promist
>
> Emily M.   that I would
>
> ploy with her. And the
>
> day befor that I promist
>
> Grace I word play with
>
> her. The smoning they came
>
> up   to me!

Figure 10.13   Conventional Spelling

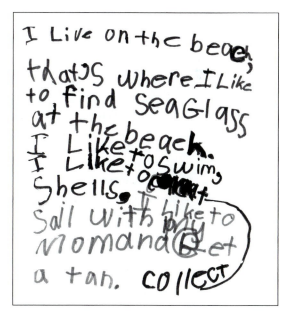

to sail with my mom and get a tan" a little more difficult to read, but generally the spacing is appropriate.

Conventions of Written Language

Children must learn other elements of written language that are not related to representing sounds with specific letters or combinations of letters. One of these elements is *directionality:* the **convention** that in English, writing begins on the left and moves to the right. Other conventions include the use of space around words and the use of abbreviations. Children must also learn to arrange words on a page and in a book. Children may temporarily ignore what they know about directionality if they cannot fit a word on a page or line. Through experience, they learn to carry words over to the next page or to put extra words on the backs of pages. Graves and Stuart (1985) observed that the space around words was negative space and that learning what to do with it was a difficult concept for young children. Some children attempted to fill up negative space by placing periods between the words. They recognized spaces but tried to make them positive rather than negative.

In order to make all these discoveries about written language, children need experience exploring writing, opportunities to make hypotheses about how print works, and feedback that verifies their guesses. Teachers and parents who recognize that children are exploring the flexibility of written language and constructing an understanding of what is possible will be able to foster growth in children's writing. They will offer many opportunities for writing, will recognize most mistakes as explorations of the written language system, and will be able to celebrate the growth that they can observe in the children's understanding.

The Writing Process with Young Children

Much has been written in recent years about the writing process and means of implementing it across the curriculum so that elementary children can achieve competence in writing. The work of Graves (1994) and Calkins (1986) has been helpful to teachers of older elementary children who want to create an environment that promotes writing skills and to take the time necessary to implement the process. The whole point of emphasizing the process of writing is to help teachers move away from giving children isolated bits and pieces of instruction in the conventions of printed language and toward helping children learn those conventions while engaging in relevant and meaningful writing activities.

Helping younger children write meaningfully requires providing the necessary tools (paper, writing instruments) and helping children appreciate the usefulness of writing. Even very young children should be encouraged to keep journals in which they can record their experiences and feelings. Young children may begin by drawing pictures and talking about them. As they participate in classroom activities, they may begin to use letters or words and phrases to aid in expressing their ideas. Gradually, the amount of writing will increase. Teachers of young children should be aware that not all children will choose to write in journals. Children are to be encouraged but not forced to write in their journals regularly.

Figure 10.14 shows three samples of writing taken from a first-grade child at one-month intervals. Note the progress this child has made with only two months of school experience as a writer. Green (1998) kept a record of children's writing by asking three- and four-year-olds to sign in each day. She recorded the changes in how they wrote their names from September to April and classified them into the following categories: *controlled scribbles, controlled scribbles and mock letters, one or two letters of name, full first name letters out of order,* and *full first name letters in order.* For the four-year-olds, she added the categories *first and part of last* and *first and last, complete.* Green learned much about the children's development as writers from this activity and had oppor-

Figure 10.14   First Grader's Writing at Three-Month Intervals

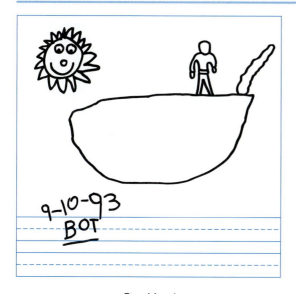

First Month

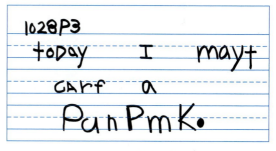

Second Month

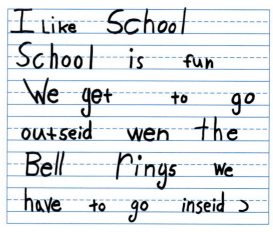

Third Month

With the help of his teacher, this boy is writing a description of the story that was just read to him.

tunities to observe their discoveries about print, such as spacing, letter reversals, and so on. Teachers need to find their own systems for observing children's writing carefully.

Helping Children Feel Successful as Literacy Learners

The teacher who wants children to feel successful as literacy learners will provide many opportunities for them to choose their own literacy activities and will help individual children choose tasks that are appropriate. The key is to find the interest of each child and build literacy experiences around it. For example, if the child is interested in playing trucks in the sandbox but shows no interest in words or books, the teacher should choose some books about trucks, construction vehicles, and sand to share with that child and make available for browsing. Another option is for the teacher to take dictation as the child tells what he has done that day with the blocks. The teacher should be sure to read the narrative back to the child so he can agree that it says what he said. Teachers should also include these dictated experiences in notes to the child's parents or in compilations of class activities.

A child's interest in words might be aroused by focusing on her name and the names of her classmates for activities, such as taking attendance and assigning classroom tasks. Art projects might be another way to stimulate interest, perhaps by having the teacher take dictation about the child's product or the process of creating it or by supplying books about art in the art center. Whatever the child's interests, the instruction provided must be pleasant and successful. It must focus on the child's interests and help her begin to use literacy for her own needs. Many teachers have recognized that a child *was* paying attention to literacy upon catching her moving her name to the job she wanted to do on the classroom job chart!

It is also important that the teacher not treat reading and writing as the only important activities in which children are involved. Children need to be involved in play, art, music, and so forth, and the teacher must value these experiences for themselves, without always tacking on a reading or writing component to legitimize the experience. To do otherwise would send children the subtle message that only reading and writing are important.

The communication skills—speaking, reading, listening, and writing—should permeate all instruction in every subject. But each child's efforts in these areas should be natural—resulting from his own inclination and growing ability in each area. The artificial separation of learning into distinct instructional subjects must be avoided. When instruction is separated from experience, children develop the misconception that learning takes place only in school. Ideally, education is entering an era in which teachers will refocus on children's learning, rather than on defining education in terms of instruction.

If we honor children's attempts to read and write, they will continue to engage in these behaviors. That means keeping the children's work, paying close attention to their developing control of written language, encouraging role-play reading before children can actually read text, finding texts of interest as children move into independent reading activities, and helping children create their own texts frequently. Honoring children's efforts also means learning more about what each child knows about literacy every day and planning instruction for that child that will be satisfying and encouraging. Only by continuing to read and write will a child get better at doing them.

Urging children to write and "publish" their own books is a good way to honor their attempts at writing.

➤ Read a selection of the many books about families. The following list includes only a few examples:

The Always Prayer Shawl (Oberman 1994)

Aunt Flossie's Hats (and Crab Cakes Later) (Howard 1991)

The Carrot Seed (Krauss 1993)

Charlotte's Web (White 1999)

Ira Sleeps Over (Waber 1987)

Less than Half, More than Whole (Lacapa and Lacapa 1992)

Lily's Purple Plastic Purse (Henkes 1996)

The Lotus Seed (Garland 1993)

Mama Cat Has Three Kittens (Fleming 1998)

The Runaway Bunny (Brown 1977)

Sarah, Plain and Tall (MacLachlan 1985)

The Secret Garden (Burnett 1987)

Song and Dance Man (Ackerman 1988)

Stellaluna (Cannon 1993)

The Stray Dog (Simont 2001)

Sylvester and the Magic Pebble (Steig 1969)

They Were Strong and Good (Lawson 1940)

Three Cheers for Catherine the Great! (Best 1999)

Too Many Tamales (Soto 1993)

➤ Also see books by Beverly Cleary, Judith Viorst, Rosemary Wells (Max and Ruby books), other books by Kevin Henkes, and other books by Patricia MacLachlan.

➤ Tell or read traditional folk stories with family structures such as "The Three Bears," "Three Billy Goats Gruff," and "Three Pigs."

➤ Act out traditional folk stories such as those listed above.

➤ Read some stories about grandparents such as *Kevin's Grandma* (Williams 1975), *Our Granny* (Wild 1993), *Grandma's Records* (Velasquez 2001), *The Friday Nights of Nana* (Hest 2001), *The Days of Summer* (Bunting 2001), and *Grandpa's Face* (Greenfield 1988). Children could write about their own grandparents. If their grandparents are not part of their lives, the children might choose to write about any relative.

➤ Compile children's family stories into a class book.

➤ Write a letter to someone in the family who lives far away and tell them the family news.

➤ Write and illustrate a book as a gift for a family member.

➤ Write a biography of someone from the community who has made an important contribution.

➤ Write invitations and thank-you letters to various community members who could visit your class.

Planned Activities for Fostering the Development of Literacy

Read-Alouds

Reading aloud to children—as individuals, in small groups, or as a whole class—is an absolutely essential part of literacy instruction. Not only does reading aloud provide children with a pleasurable experience, a positive emotional response to reading, and a means of getting "book" language in their heads, but it also offers distinct opportunities to become more literate. Reading aloud also produces these benefits:

1. The teacher can demonstrate the nature, pleasures, and rewards of reading, which will increase the children's interest in books and their motivation to read for themselves.

2. Children learn the ways in which language can be recorded.

3. Children realize that some of their own experiences and thoughts are like those that have been recorded by the authors they have read.

4. Children who listen to stories can compose narratives in their own heads and want to create and record their own texts.

5. Children refine their understanding of the elements of language: patterns, sounds, rhythms, and styles.

6. Listening to stories they already know allows children to confirm their predictions about how the episodes are arranged to make the story work. Listening to known stories also allows children to discover new levels of meaning in a story.

7. Children who have had extensive experience in listening to stories are better able to edit their own stories in their heads.

8. Children need to be challenged by reading material that is beyond their independent reading level.

9. Reading aloud a variety of different texts throughout the schoolday helps children understand that reading goes well beyond any lesson or school activity (adapted from Mooney 1990, pp. 21–24).

Interactive reading aloud—in which children can ask questions, make comments, answer questions posed by the reader—is extremely valuable for

Listening to audiotapes in a classroom reading center is an efficient way for students to experience a story being read aloud.

young children but difficult to manage with large groups (Collins and Shaeffer 1997). Therefore, at least some read-aloud experiences need to be conducted with individuals or very small groups. Most teachers manage this kind of reading by using volunteers, teacher aides, or older children (Klesius and Griffith 1996).

Shared Reading

Shared reading—an instructional strategy in which the teacher takes primary responsibility for the reading but involves the children actively in the process—is another important experience that supports the young child's developing literacy. Shared reading is often done with books in a large format ("big books") and print, which all the group can see. Although this approach certainly adds to the effectiveness, successful shared reading can be done with small groups and regular books.

In shared reading, the teacher introduces the book by reading the title, showing the children the front of the book, and asking them to predict what the story will be about. Once these predictions have been made and discussed, the teacher usually reads the name of the author and discusses other books by that individual (if appropriate). Then the teacher reads aloud the book, passing her hand or a pointer under the print as she reads it. On the second and other repeated readings of the story, the children can be asked to join in the reading of repetitive phrases. The teacher might then call attention to some elements of the print, perhaps capital letters, punctuation, illustrations that do or do not match the print on the page, the author's use of a specific word, the style of the story (folktale, realistic, personal narrative, and so on), or other features that will be meaningful to the children. Often, the children themselves call attention to features of the print on successive repeated readings. They may notice rhyming patterns, spelling patterns, page numbers, or any number of other features (Clements and Warncke 1994; Stewart 1995).

Eventually, of course, the children will have memorized the story and be able to "read" it successfully. At that point, the teacher can suggest that the children write their own stories based on the pattern of the original, that they draw their own illustrations, that they write sequels, and so on, depending on the needs and abilities of the individual children. Some children may want to read the story independently, whereas others may want to play with the blocks and not do anything related to the story at the moment. Offering a choice of responses is extremely important (Fallon and Allen 1994). Thus, assigning every child to create a caterpillar from an egg carton after having read *The Very Hungry Caterpillar* (Carle 1969) would not be appropriate; however, mak-

Parents AND Literacy

■ Send parents a newsletter that lists some of the children's favorite books, words to chants, and lyrics of songs that the children know by rote so that parents can enjoy reading or singing with their children. You should keep this newsletter short and make it reader friendly. Some teachers reproduce the covers of books, along with their titles, to help those parents who might not read themselves. Also encourage parents to tell family stories, and celebrate some of those in the newsletter (Buchoff 1995; Harding 1996).

WWW

ing the materials available if children want to make caterpillars would be appropriate.

Guided Reading

Guided reading is a teaching strategy often used with beginning independent readers. It is usually done with first- and second-grade students, although the strategy would be appropriate for some kindergartners, as well. Guided reading requires that the teacher select a text for a specific group of readers and guide them through the reading of it. The group is usually no larger than six children. After selecting the text, the teacher decides on a reading strategy that will be emphasized in this lesson and where to stop reading before discussing the text with the children. Guided reading differs from shared reading in that the children have the primary responsibility for the reading.

Once the teacher has selected an appropriate text and called the group together, he asks the children to make predictions about the content of the story from the cover illustration. These predictions are recorded. Then he may introduce the story using some of the vocabulary that might be difficult for the readers but not quoting the sentences in the text exactly. Sometimes teachers use a "picture walk" in the introduction, which means that children turn the pages of the text looking at the illustrations and discussing what might be happening in the text. Next, the children read to the designated spot while the teacher observes their reading closely. The discussion at each stop will focus on strategies the readers used to figure out unknown words as well as the meaning of the passage.

Guided reading is an effective strategy, but the teacher must be skilled in selecting the appropriate text, planning strategy instruction, and leading the discussions. Fountas and Pinnell (1996) describe guided reading in great detail.

Journals

Providing journals and a time for writing in them is a strategy that will be successful for some four-year-olds and most five-year-olds. Journal writing may begin with drawing pictures and eventually move to writing messages and then to recording ideas. A journal in which the entries are dated and the teacher has sometimes recorded what the child has "read" from her writing will serve as an excellent record of the child's progress in writing. When milestones are reached, copies of significant pages can be made and sent home to parents. Some primary-grade children may want parts of their journals to remain private, and teachers should respect their wishes.

More Examples of Literacy Activities

- Construct a word wall by adding cards on which are printed the onsets and rimes familiar to the children. For example, the children might learn the word *cat* from a storybook. The /at/ rime could be added to the word wall, and then other words with that rime could be constructed and spelled by using analogy (*fat, sat, bat,* and so on). Have children keep their own word banks of words that they know and can use to decode or learn other words (Gaskins et al. 1997).

■ Have children participate in cooking experiences in which they read the recipe cards and complete the activities. One card can be made for each step of the cooking. Worobey (1999) suggests making recipe cards, packaging them in bags, and encouraging parents to check them out and make the foods at home.

■ Create songbooks with the lyrics of the children's favorite songs. These books can be illustrated by the children and read together, used to learn about sound–letter relationships, and used to provide other skill instruction, perhaps spelling patterns or punctuation conventions. Some children can write new lyrics for familiar melodies; others will want to share these books with their families. Finally, some children will want to create their own picture books for songs after they have seen various examples such as *What a Wonderful World* (Weiss and Thiele 1995); *Mockingbird* (Ahlberg 1998); *Frog Went a-Courting* (Catalano 1998); *Miss Mary Mack* (Hoberman 1998); *Old MacDonald* (Schwartz 1999); *The Farmer in the Dell* (Wallner 1998); and *This Land Is Your Land* (Guthrie 1998).

■ Help the children construct a "restaurant" after a visit to a local restaurant. They can create menus and order forms for the "servers" to use along with signs to advertise their restaurant. As the children play going to eat in the restaurant, the "servers" can write orders and deliver them to the "cooks." They can also create bills for the "customers" to pay. If the teacher has recorded the children's visit with photographs, they can use the photographs to illustrate a dictated book telling about the restaurant.

■ Help the children prepare reader's theater productions of common folk stories, such as "Three Billy Goats Gruff," "Goldilocks and the Three Bears," and "The Three Little Pigs." Reader's theater requires repeated reading as the children practice their performance, and reading for a production can be an aid to fluent reading. The children can perform these stories for their classmates.

■ Reads aloud poems from Hopkins's (1996) *School Supplies* and Shields's (1995) *Lunch Money and Other Poems about School.* Have the children choose some aspect of their own school experience and write about it. They do not have to write poems, but they could be encouraged to put their thoughts in poetic form after they have completed their first drafts.

■ After a visit to a pet store and a veterinarian's office, maintain the children's interest by reading books about animals. Visit the school library and have the librarian help the children find books and videos about animals and their care. Some of the children may choose to give oral reports about what they have learned. Others may make posters to share their information. Still others may get together to make an alphabet book about pets and their care.

- When the children are learning how to multiply, encourage them to create story problems in which multiplication is needed for the solutions. Also have the children keep math journals in which they record how to solve problems requiring multiplication. These math writings will help the children use literacy skills to remember how to solve problems and to share their learning process with others.

- Have the children bring in labels from toothpaste, milk, cereal, and so on, and use these items to create a "big book" of environmental print. Help the children notice that all the toothpaste labels have the word *toothpaste* on them somewhere. They can look for other similarities and differences in the labels and realize that the print can be separated from the design and still be read.

Programs for Literacy Instruction

Programs for reading instruction have existed for many years. Many of these programs are based on basal readers for which a publishing company produces a set of graded materials, including pieces of text, workbooks, skills pages, assessment schemes, and other materials that are intended to be used for reading instruction. These materials are accompanied by a detailed teacher's manual that specifies what the teacher is to do in detail. Until recently, most of these materials did not contain a preschool program, so they did not have as much impact on early childhood programs as they did on elementary programs. Most of these programs now have materials for preschool, and many schools have adopted them as their primary instructional material. Basal readers are intended to be a resource, but often they become the curriculum. Teachers whose districts have adopted a basal reader program must be aware of the philosophy of the series and know that they must take personal responsibility for literacy instruction regardless of what program has been adopted. Following a published program mindlessly will not result in good instruction.

Another type of instructional material is the scripted program. These programs are so prescriptive that the teacher is given no choice in presenting material. The teacher must follow the program exactly as it is written, including sticking to a rigid time schedule for activities and presenting the activities in an exact order. One such program is Success for All (Slavin 1996). This program presents research that supports program claims of reading achievement when compared to other types of reading instruction, but other researchers not affiliated with the program have not been able to replicate the research findings (Pogrow 2000).

Another approach intended to help teachers find balance and include all the elements of a literacy program is Four Blocks (Cunningham, Hall, and DeFee 1991). This program was designed to give teachers a framework for including guided reading, writing, word study, and independent reading during each instructional day. The time blocks are prescribed, but the content of each block is determined by the teacher based on what the children know and need to know. Four Blocks is not a published program or a basal reading program. The teacher must supply the materials for instruction and make the decisions about how and when to teach the elements of reading.

Assessing Literacy

NAEYC

The IRA/NAEYC (1998) position statement on reading and writing makes this assertion about assessing literacy:

> Sound assessment should be anchored in real-life writing and reading tasks and continuously chronicle a wide range of children's literacy activities in different situations. Good assessment is essential to help teachers tailor appropriate instruction to young children and to know when and how much intensive instruction on any particular skill or strategy might be needed. . . .
>
> Teachers need to regularly and systematically use multiple indicators—observations of children's oral language, evaluation of children's work, and performance at authentic reading and writing tasks—to assess and monitor children's progress in reading and writing development, plan and adapt instruction, and communicate with parents. (pp. 206, 210)

As a teacher, you will not be able to plan activities that will support a given child's development of literacy without knowing what he understands about reading and writing now. In her book *An Observation Survey of Early Literacy Achievement*, Clay (2002) describes in detail several strategies for observing the literacy development of a child. Three of these techniques are critical for teachers of young children: (1) observing the child's writing, (2) determining his knowledge of books and print, and (3) observing his reading behaviors.

Observing Writing

As a child writes, the teacher needs to observe the process the child follows on a regular basis and keep samples of her products on at least a biweekly basis. Observing the process will provide information about how many letters the child can use in writing, what she knows about the directionality of print, how she solves problems such as spelling unknown words, and how she works at writing. (Is it with pleasure, or does it seem to be a struggle?) Observing the products of writing can produce information about what the child knows about letters, sound–letter relationships, and punctuation and other conventions of writing (Button, Johnson, and Furgerson 1996). Such observations can help in judging the zone of proximal development for that child. For example, if a child spells *friend* as *frend,* then a little assistance will enable her to spell the word in the conventional way. If, however, the child spells *friend* as *frd,* then it seems likely that she is hearing the beginning and ending sounds of words and recording them accurately, but trying to teach the conventional spelling of *friend* would probably not be useful at this time (Taylor 1996).

Determining Knowledge of Books and Print

In observing how children handle books and what they know about print, the teacher may ask each child individually to show her the parts of the book (such as the front and back), where to start reading, what to do when finished reading one page, and where the top of the page is. The teacher might also ask the child to point to an uppercase letter, to point out a certain word, and so on. The teacher may also observe the children's behavior with books as they choose them from the classroom library shelves. Observing younger children will reveal if they know how to hold a book, which way is right side up, or how to turn the pages. Observing older children will provide information about how they determine which book to read and what they are interested in (Harp 2000).

In addition, the teacher will want to know how many letters children can recognize, whether they can distinguish lowercase and capital letters, what concept they have of *word,* and so on. Much of this information can be gained from careful observations of the children's writing. If more information is needed, then the Concepts about Print test described in *An Observation Survey* (Clay 1993a) can be administered.

Observing Reading

Many effective techniques are available for observing children's reading behaviors. For instance, keeping running records or miscue inventories is an excellent means of learning what children know and can do as readers. Each of these records is taken as the child reads aloud a selected text. For younger children, this text is often their own writing. As the child reads, the teacher marks exactly what the child does and says. Clay (1993a) has developed a set of conventions for marking such records so that they can be shared with others. Goodman and Marek (1996) have also developed a system for recording and analyzing reading behaviors. Please consult these sources for details on marking and analyzing reading behaviors.

Listening carefully to a child read can reveal what kinds of errors she makes, how often the child corrects her own errors, and other reading behaviors such as finger pointing and reading word for word. Each of these recording systems also includes checking the child's comprehension of the text. The value of such records is that over time, the child's growth as a reader can be documented and appropriate instruction can be planned.

Children with Special Needs

Certain children may need special help in becoming successful users of printed language. Although some schools place all students with disabilities in very structured, direct instruction programs, more and more special educators are finding that these students respond to the principles of developmentally appropriate practice just like their classmates do. Special-needs students need choices, chances to follow their own interests, and opportunities for success as much as any other children.

One approach that may be helpful in teaching children with special needs is for the teacher to spend extra time with them in techniques such as assisted reading. Giving these children more specific strategy instruction in the context of authentic reading experiences may also prove beneficial (Sears, Carpenter, and Burstein 1994). Teachers must also use observational strategies to discover children's understanding of the reading and writing processes before attempting to help them learn successive steps.

Children with physical disabilities, such as sight or hearing loss, may need special materials to make their encounters with print successful. Teachers may need to provide materials printed in braille or very large print for children with vision limitations. Teachers may need to learn to sign or to have an interpreter present to take dictation from children who use sign rather than spoken language. Children who cannot hold ordinary writing instruments may need an adult or older child to act as a scribe for them; children who have difficulty with controlling pens or pencils can learn to use typewriters or computers to communicate.

Some children may require more specialized equipment in order to engage in literacy activities with other learners and become literate. Langone, Malone, and Kinsley (1999) state that **assistive technology** is not only beneficial in helping children become as independent as possible but that it is mandated by law when appropriate. Such assistive technology devices as portable keyboards, touch screens, speech synthesizers, and voice recognition devices can help children with disabilities participate in all classroom activities—from composing stories to completing research on topics of their choice.

Beyond these special materials and devices, children with sight or hearing challenges need teachers who assume that they will be successful, who determine what they know (even though it may take some outside help to do so), and who support their learning. It is important to remember that these children need to read and write about what is meaningful to them and to learn what they want to learn at the time, not what the teacher may have planned. Ruiz (1995) documented the stages that her child who was deaf went through in learning to write. One of the outcomes of this study was to verify that children do not need a perfect, overlearned mastery of sound–letter relationships in order to be successful readers and writers. Ruiz's daughter learned to read and write with very little sound knowledge at all but in stages that roughly parallel those of hearing children.

Children who have not achieved the oral language skills typical of their age group may need more opportunities to learn and practice oral language forms. When words are introduced in print, some children may need more background experiences in order to develop meanings for these words. Teachers should arrange for children who have language delays to interact with other children as much as possible and to talk with adults, as well.

Celebrating Diversity

Most classrooms have some students who are bilingual or who represent various cultural and ethnic groups. Helping these children continue to develop as readers and writers is an extremely important task. Recall Cambourne's (1995) condition of expectation and the concept of engagement, as discussed earlier in this chapter. Teachers must expect that all children are users of literacy in some way and try to discover what they know about print and how print is used in their homes. Teachers must also consider how to engage children and take steps to see that the classroom activities are appropriate and meaningful for all children, not just those from mainstream cultural groups or whose first language is English. As Schmidt (1995) states, "Schools may actually interfere with children's literacy learning if educators do not work to understand the diverse backgrounds of the children in their classrooms. Schools must take the first steps toward connecting with the children's cultures" (p. 411).

Activities that are arranged around meaningful themes may help children who speak English as their second language (ESL) become more skilled as readers and writers and speakers of English (Ernst and Richard 1995; Twiss 1996). For example, as children study houses, they can draw pictures of the houses they live in now and the houses they lived in before in their native countries. Sharing these children's pictures with the class provides opportunities for meaningful oral experiences and writing and reading experiences, whether in English or in students' native languages.

Learning to use what children know—such as how to recite street rhymes or classify grocery coupons—can help children feel that the literacy of their households is important and valued. Families can be encouraged to keep their own albums of literacy activities, perhaps using some materials provided by the school (Clements and Warncke 1994). Teachers can also use sharing time to help children present objects and events that are important to them and their families.

As noted earlier, teachers of children who speak dialects need to value the children's language and encourage them to develop their dialectal abilities while providing models of standard English when appropriate. For example, a child may communicate more effectively in his dialect on the playground but need a model of standard English when he has the opportunity to interview a guest speaker. Teachers who value children's language will not correct the use of dialects but will acknowledge them as an acceptable form of communication. When taking dictation from a child who speaks a dialect, the teacher should record the words in conventional spelling but not change the syntactical structure of the child's utterances. As a child reads from charts or books, the teacher should not correct the child who reads the text "My mother is going to work" as "My mama be going to work." Such a child has demonstrated an understanding of the printed text, and that is much more important than an absolutely perfect rendering of the text at this point.

ESL children need many opportunities to interact with English-speaking children and adults. The worst possible approach would be to isolate such children from the other children in order to give them special help in learning English. Children who play and talk with other children who speak English will learn the language quickly. Teachers should allow children to use their native languages when necessary for communication. In past years, schools often limited children's use of native languages in order to force them to speak English more quickly (Watts-Taffe and Truscott 2000). That approach does not facilitate more rapid learning of English; rather, it does much harm to children's self-concepts and feelings of acceptance and actually hinders language development. The goal is not to eliminate children's first language but to help them achieve competence as speakers of a second language.

Ideally, all children would learn to read in their first languages and then be taught to extend their skills in English (Snow et al. 1998). Obviously, this is not always possible; even so, teachers can help children learn English and can use the children's native languages as much as possible in the classroom. Signs, posters, announcements, and other print can be posted in more than one language.

Freeman and Freeman (1999) urge teachers to be very careful when planning step-by-step instruction in literacy for bilingual speakers. They state, "Never have we seen so much emphasis placed on testing students and putting them into leveled groups. This word-recognition approach specifically targets poor and minority students" (p. 247). Such programs may lead to more failure for these children.

The concerned teacher will also learn enough about a child's native language to recognize where the child might have particular difficulties with English. For example, some sounds used in English, such as the *sh* at the beginning of *sheep*, are rare in Spanish; there are differences in syntactical patterns between the two languages, as well. Chapter 9 mentioned the differences in placement of adjectives in Spanish sentences; Spanish also allows redundancy. A Spanish-speaking child might say, "My mother, she," which is acceptable in Spanish. Some languages, such as Chinese, are not alphabetical; for Chinese children, teachers can provide experiences with sound–letter relationships in meaningful contexts. As a child begins to learn words in English, the teacher will record those words in print for the child and will make sure that the child has many opportunities to write and explore English (Brewer 1998).

Finally, using literature that represents the cultures of the children in the school in an authentic manner is an extremely effective means of celebrating diversity. Teachers should try to find books printed in the languages of the children and use them for read-alouds, perhaps bringing in parents or volunteers. All children need to be able to find positive images of themselves in books and other print media. Finding just the right book or story can help a child see the importance of his culture and its literacy. For young learners especially, Opitz (1999) suggests that teachers attend to the supports in the texts of culturally appropriate books as well as to their cultural content. *Supports* are defined as rhyming texts, texts with repetition, familiar events or sequences, and illustrations that readers can use.

Chapter Summary

- The goals of literacy instruction include helping children develop their oral language skills, helping children learn how print is decoded, making sure that each child feels that he can achieve success in literacy learning, and making sure that each child will have the disposition to continue to learn about literacy.

- Phonemic awareness is an important ability in learning to read but does not usually require direct instruction. Most children achieve phonemic awareness by learning rhymes, by listening to poems and stories, and by participating in other common tasks in the early childhood classroom.

- Every child needs to know how to use sound–letter relationships to decode new words, but these relationships can be learned in ways other than drill-and-practice on the isolated sounds. And although teachers should be accountable for teaching children to use sound–letter relationships, such instruction need not be based on any commercial program.

- How reading develops is best described along a continuum. As teachers identify the children's current abilities and skills, they can plan instruction that will encourage children to move along the continuum toward becoming more skilled readers.

- The child's control of the form of written language progresses through a number of stages: from scribbling, linear repetitive writing, random-letter writing, letter-name (or phonetic) writing, transitional spelling, to conventional spelling. How the child uses written language provides the teacher

with an understanding of what the child knows about written forms that is invaluable in planning literacy experiences for her.

- The development of literacy is best achieved in an interesting, active classroom where a wide variety of activities are available to the children. Children who are involved in interesting activities can be encouraged to use print in connection with these activities in meaningful ways.

- Exercises in isolated skills are not appropriate for young children. Children cannot practice skills out of context and then apply what has been learned to actual literacy experiences.

- Teachers cannot plan instruction without knowing what children know, so assessing children's progress is vital to good planning. Teachers can observe literacy behaviors in many everyday activities and can plan more detailed assessments of children's knowledge of print and books and of their reading and writing behaviors.

- In order to become literate, children with special needs should be offered choices in the materials they are expected to read, materials that match their interests, and opportunities for success in reading and writing.

- Teachers should expect that *all* children will become literate. Being from a family that is poor or belongs to a racial or ethnic minority does not have to mean failure in school. All children need an environment that honors their knowledge of literacy and encourages their attempts to learn more about printed language.

Theory INTO Practice

Collect and then analyze writing samples from four kindergartners. What understandings do these children seem to have about print? Write two statements that you could tell the parents of each child about what she knows. Also write at least one instructional goal for each child.

Observe the children in a preschool and in a second-grade class as they select books for reading. What do you notice about their selections? Ask two or three children in each grade why they selected the books they did. How can you use this information in selecting books for your own classroom library?

Choose an age group (preschool through second grade), and select a book that you think would be appropriate for reading aloud. Then plan a skill activity for a group of children who are very able readers for their age, an activity for a group of less-experienced readers, and a group who is just meeting expectations for growth in literacy.

Administer the Concepts about Print test (from *An Observation Survey*, Clay 1993a), or create a running record of a child's oral reading skills. (A description of how to mark a running record can be found in the same source.) What did you learn about the child's abilities that will help guide planning instruction for him?

A Teacher Speaks

Sandy Bjorklund

Madison Camelview School
Phoenix, Arizona

Reading in the Literacy Classroom

I teach 26 second graders in an urban school. My classroom includes about 40 percent non- or limited-English speakers and 80 percent subsidized lunch students. Student abilities in reading range from emergent to fluent, and many of my students lack language experience. I strive to make every minute count!

The formal literacy time in my classroom occurs over a two-and-a-half-hour block. My goal is to immerse my students in literacy (reading and writing) during this time. In order to do this, I plan each day based on assessments of individual student needs. Ongoing daily assessments include such things as running records, samples of student writing, observations made during rove time, and monitoring notes. Monitoring notes can be formal (i.e., when taken during a reading group) or informal. I use these notes, along with student draft books, for parent conferences and progress reports.

Learners are grouped in both reading and writing based on individual strengths and their next teaching point. Groups change often—in some cases, daily—to meet the learners' needs. Short, focused teaching is used during these times with the whole group, small groups, and individuals.

In order for me to have the opportunity to work with learners individually or in small groups, students need to be able to work independently. To achieve this, each student is given a daily plan. This plan provides the literacy activities students should be working on when not working with me. The plan sheet changes over the course of the year, but children are expected to write, read from independent book boxes, practice spelling, and work on handwriting. After these four parts of the plan are completed, they can choose language activities around the room from their plan, such as listening center, exploring books, alphabet games and puzzles, whiteboards, buddy reading, word-building activities, and chalkboard.

My plan of the day is built to include a number of short pieces of instruction interspersed within literacy time. I call this the "Yo-Yo" method of instruction,

as I constantly pull the kids back to the whole group for short instructional objectives. The rest of the literacy block is divided as follows:

- *Write to . . .* (10–15 minutes): I model some piece of the writing process. This might be shared writing with the students helping me compose the piece, depending on my focused teaching objective.
- *Students work on their daily plans* (35 minutes): I pull two small groups for reading and/or writing instruction and move between meeting with the groups and working with individuals.
- *Read to whole group* (20 minutes): I read to the children from a book that meets a focused objective. Often this objective is linked to the writing process, and thus we read like writers, discussing what good writers do.
- *Students work on their daily plans* (20 minutes): I work with one small group and rove among individual students.
- *Skills instruction with whole group* (15 minutes): This lesson may cover phonics, word study, or the mechanics of writing. The lesson is always based on teacher observation/assessment and is always taken from whole to part in order to show the skill in the context of meaning.
- *Students work on their daily plans* (20 minutes): I rove and support students in checking that they have accomplished their plans for the day.
- *Status of class* (10 minutes): Students open their draft books on their desks with their daily plans visible. I check to make sure they have met the expectations for that day and guide students in what they will do the next day.
- *Share published works* (10 minutes): Students may choose to share any work they have published before giving it to the intended audience.

This is an overview of the literacy time block in my classroom. It did not happen quickly but evolved as my understanding grew. I suggest that a new teacher begin slowly and stay focused on a smaller piece of the process until it is working successfully.

Manipulation and Discovery through Mathematics

After reading this chapter, you will be able to do the following:

- Describe how children learn mathematics.
- Define the *strands* of mathematics, as articulated by the National Council of Teachers of Mathematics.
- Plan appropriate mathematics experiences for young children.
- Recognize the qualities of materials that are appropriate for mathematics instruction.
- Assess the mathematical understanding of young children.
- Plan for connections between mathematics and literacy.
- Adapt mathematics instruction for children with special needs.
- Celebrate the diversity of mathematics learners in your classroom.

When you were assigned to observe mathematics instruction this week, you thought you would see young children working the simple addition problems you remembered from your own childhood. You visited a kindergarten classroom and observed the children playing. The teacher helped you see the geometry they were learning in block play and in playing with pattern blocks, the patterns they were creating in art, the measuring they were doing as they compared the sizes of three pumpkins, the counting they were doing as they prepared and ate their snack, and the computations they did to solve the problems of how many more sunny days they had recorded than cloudy ones and how many children wanted a rabbit for a pet versus how many wanted a gerbil. You were impressed; these children were really mathematical thinkers.

During your discussion of your observations, many of your peers shared your observations of mathematics embedded in the curriculum, but others had observed children engaged in completing worksheets as part of a formal math curriculum. These children were able to add and subtract numbers totaling ten or less, and a few were able to regroup and work with numbers larger than ten.

When you heard these reports, you were anxious about mathematics instruction. What is the best way to help children learn about math? What kind of experiences are most valuable for young learners? You know that math is a major part of the state tests and wonder what kind of instruction will help children be successful on those tests?

Definition of Mathematics

This chapter and the next, on mathematics and science, are titled "Manipulation and Discovery" because young children learn mathematics and science from their manipulation of objects and their discovery of relationships and patterns in their environments. *Mathematics* means much more than just *arithmetic*. Perhaps when you were a child, math meant practicing arithmetic: working addition, subtraction, and multiplication problems on reams of ditto sheets. If you think of math for young children as limited to such simple equations as 1 + 1 = 2, observe young children for a few minutes while they play. You will become aware of both their interest in mathematics and the scope of mathematics itself: "You got a bigger cookie than me!" "I am taller than you." "I have more clay than you." "I gots five pennies."

Many topics that seem relevant to mathematics activities are also relevant to science activities. As children learn to classify and group and as they think about functions and relationships, they are learning both math and science. In fact, it is often difficult to separate math and science in the early childhood classroom.

The dictionary defines *mathematics* as "the science of numbers and their operations, interrelations, combinations, generalizations, and abstractions, and of space configurations and their structure, measurement, transformations, and generalizations." But for young children, mathematics is a way of viewing the world and their experiences in it. It is a way of solving real problems. It is an understanding of number, operations on number, functions and relations, probability, and measurement. It is much more than the pages of simple equations that you may remember working as a child. Children are mathematical thinkers outside school. The challenge is to keep that interest, enthusiasm, and curiosity alive in the school setting.

How Mathematics Is Learned

Piaget (1970) describes three ways that human beings learn. They learn from these sources:

1. *The physical world*—Concepts such as *hot, cold, rough, smooth,* and so on
2. *The social world*—Socially transmitted information such as *language, religion, superstition,* and so on
3. *The construction of mental relationships*—Concepts such as *counting, seriation, numeration, conservation,* and so on

Piaget calls the construction of mental relationships *logico-mathematical learning.* This type of learning will be our focus in this chapter (DeVries and Kohlberg 1987a; Elkind 1998; Kamii and DeClark 1985; Kamii and Joseph 1989; Piaget 1970).

Logico-mathematical thinking requires the learner to create categories and hierarchies of objects without regard to their physical properties. For example, if you hold three yellow, wooden pencils in your hand, you will observe that they are made of wood and that they are inflexible. Those are physical facts. You cannot decide those characteristics. However, that there is a set of three pencils is a mental construct. They are physically separate objects, but their forming a set of three is a mental relationship. Think about the concept of *threeness*. It is not dependent on the physical properties of the objects to which you are applying it. You could have three houses, three whales, three mustard seeds, three amoebas, and so on. In sum, the physical characteristics of the objects (including size, shape, color, texture, and temperature) do not determine that there are three; your placing them in a relationship is what makes that determination.

As learners, children abstract certain information from their experiences. For example, children learning color names learn to ignore other properties of objects and to focus on the property of color. Piaget (1970) calls this **simple abstraction** (also known as *empirical abstraction*). Although theorists do not agree on exactly how simple abstraction is accomplished, most believe that children abstract the concept of color from repeated experiences with objects that someone labels as blue, red, yellow, or other color names. It is sophisticated learning for the child to be able to label as blue all the many tints and hues of color that we call blue. Children also make abstractions about the rules that govern language use from repeated experience with language.

However, logico-mathematical concepts cannot be abstracted from experience. If, for example, a child plays with three dolls, he must reflect on the relationship he has created among the dolls; he cannot merely abstract the concept *three* because there are three dolls. We know this is true because we can think about millions, billions, and trillions even though we have probably never had any experience with sets of this magnitude. We are able to think in these terms because we understand the hierarchical nature of the

Working with manipulatives helps children construct basic mathematical concepts.

number system; that is, we understand that millions, billions, and trillions are made up of thousands, hundreds, tens, and ones.

Piaget (1970) explains that we construct ideas by means of logico-mathematical learning by a process called **reflective abstraction.** This process works as follows: The learner manipulates objects and then reflects on the results. This reflection leads to reorganizing her mental constructs. Once this reorganization has taken place, it is impossible for the learner to think in exactly the same way again.

To illustrate the process of reflective abstraction, consider an example from mathematics. Most young children lack number conservation skills. Suppose a young child is presented with two identical sets of objects, such as plastic chips. In one of the sets, the chips are arranged in a row so closely that they almost touch one another; in the other set, the chips are arranged so that there are large spaces between them. Observing these two sets of chips, the young child will believe that the set that occupies the most space contains the most chips. After experience with manipulating sets and reflecting on the number of items in sets arranged in various physical configurations, the child will learn that the physical arrangement has no bearing on the number of objects in the set. This observation will produce a mental reorganization, so the child will never again think that physical configuration influences number.

Even very young children can recognize the difference between numbers of items in small sets—for instance, 2 cookies compared to 5 cookies. Piaget (1970) calls these *perceptual numbers.* But with numbers larger than 8 or so, perceptions are no longer reliable and a system of numbers must be constructed. This system must be based on the relationship among numbers: that 1 is included in 2, 2 in 3, and so on. When a child has created this system, he can begin to understand operations on numbers, such as addition, subtraction, multiplication, and division. Children can be taught that 2 + 3 = 5, but *"they cannot be taught directly the relationships underlying this addition"* (Kamii and DeClark 1985, p. 14; italics in original). These relationships must be constructed by the learner, based on his observations.

When we count objects, we have to order them so that each is counted only once. Creating that order is a mental operation. When we order objects from largest to smallest, for instance, we create a relationship among the objects. Concepts of *size, time,* and *geometry* must also be constructed by the learner.

Applied to mathematics, Vygotsky's (1978) view would prompt teachers to think about what children might be on the verge of discovering and to provide the materials and assistance that would enhance making those discoveries. Vygotsky's view would not support a step-by-step curriculum that fails to take into account the individual achievement of each child.

Think once again about your own experiences with math and math teachers. Most students have been in the situation of having a math teacher who truly understood geometry or calculus but could not teach students what he knew. If math could be taught directly from one person to another, then students could learn what was in the teacher's head. Obviously, that is not the case.

If we accept the thesis that mathematical concepts must be constructed by each learner, based on observations with real-life materials and situations, then what are the responsibilities of the teacher? One responsibility is to supply the language for the concepts that the child is constructing. A child can discover the concept *five* but must have the label "five" supplied. Teachers should use the language that mathematicians use, even with young children. It is no more difficult for children to learn the correct terminology than it is to learn some made-up version. Moreover, using the correct terminology from the start will eliminate the need to change terminology in the future (Monroe and Panchyshyn 1994/1995; Tracy 1994).

Another of the teacher's responsibilities is to arrange the environment so that the materials that best represent a concept are available for manipulation and to provide time for manipulation. When children are involved physically, the teacher must also involve them mentally by engaging them in reflective thinking; this can be accomplished simply through asking questions about what the children observe and then guiding their observations.

We can conclude, then, that mathematics instruction must be based on the hands-on manipulation of objects by learners and that symbols should be introduced after concepts are well in place.

Teaching Mathematics

Use these descriptors as guidelines for developing objectives and planning learning activities focused on mathematics. Programs in which these goals are achieved can help all children become mathematically literate and able to use mathematics in solving real-life problems. Moreover, the children in these programs will feel they are capable learners of mathematics.

Mathematics in the Classroom

The new National Council of Teachers of Mathematics (NCTM 2000) standards for preschool through second grade (Pre-K–2) include five content standards and five process standards:

Content Standards	*Process Standards*
1. Number and operation	1. Problem solving
2. Patterns, functions, and algebra	2. Reasoning and proof
3. Geometry and spatial sense	3. Communication
4. Measurement	4. Connections
5. Data analysis, statistics, and probability	5. Representation

Developmentally Appropriate Practice

The National Council of Teachers of Mathematics (NCTM) position statement (2000) declares that "All students, regardless of their personal characteristics, backgrounds, or physical challenges, must have opportunities to study—and support to learn—mathematics." In the joint position statement (2002) from NAEYC and NCTM on mathematics instruction for young children, they make the following statement about instruction in mathematics:

In high-quality mathematics education for 3- to 6-year-old children, teachers and other key professionals should

- Enhance children's natural interest in mathematics and their disposition to use it to make sense of their physical and social worlds

- Build on children's varying experiences, including their family, linguistic, and cultural backgrounds; their individual approaches to learning; and their informal knowledge

- Base mathematics curriculum and teaching practices on current knowledge of young children's cognitive, linguistic, physical, and social-emotional development

- Use curriculum and teaching practices that strengthen children's problem-solving and reasoning processes as well as representing, communicating, and connecting mathematical ideas

- Ensure that the curriculum is coherent and compatible with known relationships and sequences of important mathematical ideas

- Provide for children's deep and sustained interaction with key mathematical ideas

- Integrate mathematics with other activities and other activities with mathematics

- Provide ample time, materials, and teacher support for children to engage in play, a context in which they explore and manipulate mathematical ideas with keen interest

- Actively introduce mathematical concepts, methods, and language through a range of appropriate experiences and teaching strategies

- Support children's learning by thoughtfully and continually assessing all children's mathematical knowledge, skills, and strategies.

However, it is not possible to separate these standards for content and process in designing mathematics experiences for young children. The standards are interconnected and interwoven throughout the curriculum. For example:

> Children recognize patterns of all sorts in the world around them and gradually begin to use patterns as a strategy for solving problems. Both number and geometry are used in measurement, for example, as children answer questions such as "How

heavy?" "How big?" and "How tall?" The ability to gather, organize, represent, and use data to answer questions is likely to involve all of the process standards. Skills are acquired in ways that make sense to children. Teachers must continually attend to maintaining a balance between emphasis on conceptual and procedural [skill] aspects of mathematics. Children whose skills and strategies are based on understanding of fundamental mathematical concepts are more likely to retain and be able to expand their knowledge and understanding in later years. (NCTM 2000, p. 3)

Children need to employ a variety of strategies to answer questions and solve problems. If the teacher supplies the strategy, it may not make sense to the child. For example, suppose that just before beginning an art activity, the teacher poses the question: How many pieces of paper are needed in order for every student to have one? Some younger children will need to get a piece of paper, bring it to a classmate, and repeat this procedure until everyone has a paper. Others may be able to count the number of children in the class and get the corresponding number of papers. Some first and second graders will pass out the papers without counting the number needed in advance. Some children will be able to use the attendance figures to calculate how many classmates are absent from the class; others will need to count and may not know how to find the number who are missing. According to Schwartz (1995), authentic mathematics occurs in the classroom when children work like this with attendance figures, as well as with learning center choices and distribution of snacks or materials.

Kamii and DeClark (1985) cite an example of first graders who were voting. The class included twenty-four students, and when the vote for the first choice was thirteen, one child said they did not need to vote for the other choices. Even after hearing the child's explanation of having a majority vote, the other children did not understand why this could be so and needed to continue the vote. Similarly, some children will be able to measure the size of a game and find an appropriate storage space; others will have to use trial and error. Children will be in many stages of understanding; they must use their own thinking to make sense of problems.

Math instruction should be part of the children's play time. Children can play games with cards, dominoes, or dice that help them think about math. (In some communities, such gaming materials might be unacceptable, and teachers will need to be creative in selecting other materials that encourage the same kinds of thinking.) Children in play also group, sort, classify, and seriate objects. They construct sets of blocks, beads, crayons, and other materials. Attendance records and weather charts provide many opportunities for thinking mathematically. As children play "grocery store" or participate in cooking activities, they can weigh, measure, and count in meaningful situations. Almost any topic of study lends itself to helping children develop

Parents AND Mathematics

■ Ask parents to observe their children's use of mathematics at home and to keep weekly records of what they see. By doing so, parents will become more aware of how mathematics is used in their children's lives and thus more able to help children make connections between math at school and math at home.

WWW

mathematical concepts in addition to other knowledge. For example, if the class is studying shells or leaves, then classification, seriation, graphing, counting, and measuring will be integral parts of the study.

Andrews (1995) suggests that teachers who look for activities that meet the NCTM standards can find them in play activities with water, blocks, and art. Finding these activities, however, requires teachers to think much more broadly about mathematics than might have been the case several years ago. For example, young children learn very little about the calendar as it is typically taught in mathematics programs (e.g., days of the week: "Today is _____; Yesterday was _____; Tomorrow will be _____"; date of the month: repeats similar sequence; months of the year: repeat months in order). Schwartz (1994) suggests that the calendar can be useful if it is used to record or plan for events. She suggests beginning with a daily plan (a schedule) and then adding a weekly plan and a multiple-week plan when doing so is necessary and will make sense to the children. For instance, a weekly plan would be needed to schedule for a field trip or classroom visitor, and keeping records of sprouting plants or hatching eggs would require a multiple-week plan. Teachers should try to think of how the children can really use the information from a calendar, rather than simply having them repeat words about concepts that mean nothing to them.

Instruction in mathematics should focus on providing experiences and activities for young children and asking questions to guide children's reflections. Children should be encouraged to think of mathematics as real problems to solve, not simply as calculations to complete. Burns and Richardson (1981) have identified the problem of teaching arithmetic first:

> We teach the abstract processes of arithmetic first and then hope that children will learn to use these processes to solve problems. . . . The emphasis on problems must come first; it's the starting place for developing arithmetic understanding and for establishing the need for computation. (p. 39)

The Strand Model

The strand model is one way of conceptualizing the important elements of mathematics instruction (see Figure 11.1). Each of the *content strands*—Algebra (Patterns and Functions), Geometry, Measurement, and Data Analysis and Probability—is represented on the model; Number and Operations are at the center because they are used to solve problems in all the strands. The *process strands*—Problem Solving, Communication, Connections, Reasoning and Proof, and Representation—surround the content strands because good instruction embeds the content within the framework created by the process strands.

NAEYC

In an early childhood program, these strands must be interpreted in ways that are developmentally appropriate. For example, one teacher (Meriwether 1997) made menu cards that indicated how many crackers or slices of fruit each child could have for a snack. When yogurt appeared on the snack tray, the children had to learn how to indicate a serving of what they called "wet stuff." They had always measured milk and juice by the glassful, so they

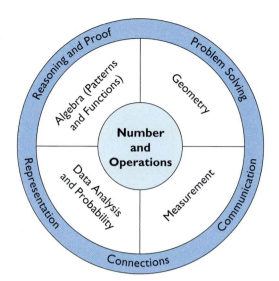

Figure 11.1

The Strand Model

decided to measure "wet stuff" by the container. Different kinds of crackers offered opportunities to talk about shapes and the relationships between them. For instance, a square of graham cracker can be broken into two rectangles, and a sandwich can be cut into triangles, rectangles, or squares. Children making menu cards for the group also discovered the concept of *zero* and thought it was a fine joke to mark that each person could take zero of something. These experiences covered the geometry strand, the number strand, the measurement strand, and the reasoning strand while being embedded in problem solving. And when the children learned to write the menu cards, they were learning representation and communicating their understandings.

Another teacher (Hinnant 1999) found that engaging children in growing a garden presented many opportunities for mathematical and scientific learning. The ideas for creating webs shown in Figure 11.2 provide a "garden full" of graphic possibilities.

Both these example illustrate the many ways in which mathematics can be integrated into daily activities. Depending on the children's understandings and the strategies they have developed for solving problems, the teacher can introduce mathematical symbols and algorithms that will make sense to the learners. Problem solving is not a set of standard procedures that children memorize and apply in given situations. Most real-world problems are not clearly defined; they do not lend themselves to solution by memorized strategies. Number and Operations are at the center of the model because they can be used to find and record solutions to real problems in all the strands of mathematics.

As children gain skill in computing by using objects, they gradually shift to paper and pencil to record their thinking. For example, a second-grade class wanted to solve the problem of how many cars would be needed to take all the

Figure 11.2   Math Webbing Ideas for Kindergarten through Second Grade

Mental Math

- The number of seeds in a package
- Which plants will grow taller
- How many flowers will bloom on each plant
- The color that yields the most plants or flowers
- The number of days in summer, fall, winter, and spring
- The number of colors in a rainbow

Number and Operation

- How many flower seeds were planted
- The stages of a garden from preparing the earth to flowers blooming
- The number of leaves on new plants and later on mature plants
- The number of plants of each variety in the garden
- A database to keep track of seeds and bulbs ordered in one year
- The number of weeds pulled in a week

Measurement

- Area of the garden
- Circumference of a flower
- Heights of the plants
- Distance apart plants should be planted
- Depth in the ground that seeds should be placed
- Amount of water needed daily and weekly

Geometry and Spatial Awareness or Sense

- Construct a map of a garden using Unifix cubes, pattern blocks, or other shapes.
- Design a dress or shirt based on flower symbols.
- Use carpet squares to plan a garden.
- Arrange artificial or pretend flowers in rows any direction or configuration to invent a garden of the future.
- Design a solar greenhouse.
- Use the computer to draw parts of a garden.

Time and Money

- How long did it take each type of plant to sprout?
- What is the length of a season—months, days, hours, minutes?
- When should we start our garden each year?
- How much did our garden cost us?
- Compare the cost of bulbs to other seeds.
- Do some plants require more sun?

Patterns and Relationships

- Growing times
- Different flowers and plants for blooming and growing
- Colors of rows of flowers
- How flowers are planted—differences in other regions or countries
- Differences in sizes, shapes, and colors of garden plants and flowers
- Order of planting and blooming

Statistics and Probability

- Outline weather patterns.
- Graph the growth of the garden, charting each set of flowers and plants.
- Predict how many flowers will bloom from the seeds planted.
- Predict which variety of plant will produce the most flowers.
- Graph the types of bugs found in the garden.
- Predict how many flowers and plants will grow in each row of the garden.

Source: Excerpted from H. A. Hinnant, "Growing Gardens and Mathematicians: More Books and More Math for Young Children," *Young Children* 54 (February 1999): 24–25. Reprinted with permission from the National Association for the Education of Young Children.

second graders on a school field trip. There were seventy-three second graders, and each car would hold five children. The work of three children is shown in Figure 11.3. As you can see, two of them counted by fives; the other started with seventy-three tally marks, circled five marks at a time, and then counted the circles. Also notice that two of the children added wheels to their boxes to make their representations more concrete.

It is not necessary to restrict young children to solving problems using the conventional algorithms. If the strategies they use make sense and are accurate, they do not need to change them. Allowing such diversity of strategies also provides opportunities for discussions and for learning that problems can be solved in more than one way.

Thinking about each strand can help teachers plan balanced programs of mathematics. Effective mathematics teaching requires understanding what students know and need to learn and then challenging and supporting them to learn it well. The following sections provide specific examples of mathematics instruction in a developmentally appropriate classroom.

Figure 11.3

Three Students' Approaches to Problem Solving

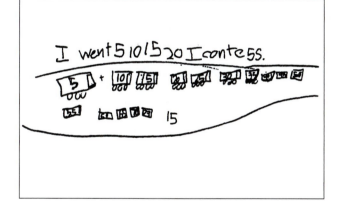

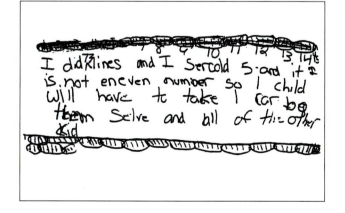

The Content Strands

Number and Operations   As noted earlier, number and operations are at the center of the model, and like problem solving, they are part of every strand of mathematical thinking. Young children can use basic arithmetic concepts in solving problems. Arithmetic includes the concepts of one-to-one correspondence, counting, number, place value, operations on whole numbers, and fractions.

Children's concept of number develops fairly rapidly between the ages of about three and six. In their investigation of children's concepts of the magnitude of the first nine numbers in the counting string, Murray and Mayer (1988) found that most three-year-olds recognized 1 as a small number and other numbers as large but did not make other discriminations. Four-year-olds were able to discriminate between small and medium-sized numbers and small and large numbers, but they had trouble comparing medium-sized and large numbers. Five-year-olds could categorize all the numbers correctly.

Number can be explored without computation in many ways. Threes and fours can make books of numbers that relate to them: their measurements, ages, shoe sizes, clothing sizes, birthdates, number of teeth, and so on. Fives and sixes can explore how numbers are used in or on buildings. The teacher might ask the children to talk about what they learn from how the rooms are numbered, how the seats in an auditorium are numbered, or how the houses on a street are numbered. The teacher might also have children look for as many other uses of numbers as they can find (Turkel and Newman 1988). Sevens and eights can continue to look for numbers in the environment and explore larger numbers.

Developing a sense of numbers and their relationships to one another (numbers can be less than, more than, or part of other numbers) is basic to being able to carry out operations on whole numbers (Van de Walle 1988). Primary children should have many opportunities to explore numbers and their relationships to one another before they are introduced to formal addition and subtraction exercises.

One-to-One Correspondence   One-to-one correspondence is the concept that one object can be related to another object. Thousands of pages of workbook exercises have been filled with pictures of rows of dogs and rows of bones, with directions to the child to draw a line from one dog to one bone. Worksheets like these are supposed to help children recognize that if there is a bone for each dog, then the sets are equivalent.

In fact, these practice sheets are not very effective in helping children understand one-to-one correspondence because children need to create their own sets and construct their own understanding of equivalency. Providing

---

Parents AND *Mathematics*

■ Ask parents to assist their children in determining the numbering patterns of the streets and houses in their neighborhoods. For example, some streets follow a numerical order. Some houses are numbered with odd numbers on one side of the street and even on the other side; some systems skip numbers between houses. Apartments usually follow a system of numbering floors and then the apartments on each floor.

them with sets that someone else has constructed does not allow them to develop the concept. For those of us who are no longer preoperational thinkers, it seems obvious that equivalency of sets can be established by counting. But for preoperational children who do not conserve number, counting is not a reliable strategy.

Some teachers have tried to teach children one-to-one correspondence by having them physically attach one element of each set to an element in another set. Even these physical connections are not as effective in helping children develop the concept as are repeated experiences in creating sets of their own. What children must do is create sets and then think about the relationships that exist between the sets. Children create sets that help them understand one-to-one correspondence when they place one chair at the table for each person, put one brush in each jar of paint, pass out one sheet of paper for each person, or give each person a carton of milk. Teachers can help guide children's reflections by asking them if they had too few, enough, or too many chairs, brushes, papers, or cartons of milk. One-to-one correspondence also figures in seriation tasks, as children relate items in one series to items in another.

Counting If you asked the next three or four people that you met on the street what young children should learn first about mathematics, it's likely they would all say counting. Some program goals include counting to 10 as appropriate objectives for fours and counting to 100 as an appropriate objective for fives or sixes.

Counting can be either rote counting or rational counting. *Rote counting* is naming the numbers in order without making any connection between numbers and sets of real-life objects. *Rational counting* is the ability to order and enumerate objects in sets. Rote counting is often encouraged by parents and teachers, but when children learn to count by rote it is *social knowledge* (that is, things children learn merely because they are told to do so by an adult) and not really related to mathematical understanding.

Learning to count proceeds in stages: The child knows that each object must have a distinct tag (counting word); the child knows that the list of tags must have a particular order; and the child makes the connection between counting and number. Teachers of young children can appreciate these stages, just as they appreciate stages in learning to walk or to write (Price 1989). Two-year-olds have a concept of counting and often attach number words to objects, even though it is almost impossible for them to count correctly. Researchers (Bullock and Gelman 1977; Gelman and Tucker 1975) have found that very young children can attach number tags to objects in ascending order (1, 5, 7) long before they can count accurately.

Counting is, of course, a useful problem-solving strategy. It is best if the child discovers the strategy rather than has it imposed by the teacher or parent. For example, rather than saying, "Count the plates and get a napkin from the cupboard for each one," a parent or teacher might say, "Make sure that we have enough napkins for each plate." Discovery of counting as a problem-solving strategy takes some time, but it is worth it to the child.

Teachers will find many opportunities for helping children develop the concept of counting. Threes and fours are likely to be able to count only a limited number of objects correctly; therefore, counting activities should be individualized to match each child's abilities. Threes and fours can count these items:

- Pieces of paper needed for art
- Place settings needed in the housekeeping center
- Blocks used to build a structure
- Chairs or mats needed for the group
- Dolls in the doll center
- Trucks and cars

Most counting experiences for fives and sixes will involve larger numbers, such as the number of papers needed for the whole class, and will involve recording and comparing different numbers. Fives and sixes can become involved in these activities:

- Counting the pieces of equipment taken outdoors and recording the number of items so that everything can be put away later
- Keeping score in games
- Counting the number of children absent each day and comparing the records over a month
- Counting the number of pieces of paper needed for a class project and multiplying to find how many would be needed for two projects
- Counting by twos, fives, and tens

Sevens and eights can continue to count, record, and compare numbers that have meaning for them in their daily lives and also learn to count by threes and fours.

Place Value Children obviously need to know that 12 and 21 do not represent the same number. Traditionally, place value has been included in the first-grade curriculum and again in the second-grade curriculum before children begin working on two-digit addition problems that require regrouping. Kamii and DeClark (1985) and Kamii and Joseph (1989) recommend that place value not be taught at all in first grade but that it be included in second grade when children use it to solve two-digit addition problems. They cite extensive research and classroom observations in which less than half the children below fourth grade understood that the 1 in 16 represents 10. In traditional mathematics texts, children are taught to write the answers to two-digit problems beginning with the ones column. Kamii believes that this is also social knowledge (as defined earlier). Real understanding of place value is not achieved until children are solid conservers and can understand the part-

Doing math problems in pairs and groups helps children learn to articulate how they "worked through" a problem.

whole relationships involved in place value. Building an understanding of tens requires extensive experience in doing arithmetic; teachers cannot foster that understanding simply by supplying materials bundled into tens to help the child see the tens and ones in a problem.

Operations on Whole Numbers   Threes and fours can begin to develop the concepts necessary for addition, subtraction, multiplication, and division, even though these problems are not presented to them symbolically or formally. Children can observe many meaningful examples of operations on whole numbers at home or in school settings:

■ They see that when objects from two separate sets are combined, one larger set is created. While playing in the blocks center, children may put the blocks from two piles together and create one larger pile. They may pick up the crayons from each place at the table and put them together.

■ They observe subtraction when they see a set reduced as elements are taken away. If a plate of crackers for snack time is passed around, children see the number reduced as each child takes a portion. After they spend some pennies, they know that they have fewer.

■ They observe multiplication when the teacher counts materials by sets or when they count groups such as place settings rather than individual pieces.

■ They observe division when materials must be shared in equal portions. Often, it is a child's responsibility to determine how to divide food or play materials so that everyone has an equal share.

Instruction in addition and subtraction should not be attempted formally for fives and sixes until the children have achieved reversibility in thinking and understand subtraction as the inverse of addition. Instruction in multiplication and division should continue informally as they are needed to solve real problems; these operations can be presented as repeated addition or repeated subtraction. Fives and sixes can improve their arithmetic understanding by observing adults recording equations for arithmetic operations, recording the equations themselves, counting the sets of shoes worn by the children in the class, or passing out cards for a game by sets of two.

Sevens and eights will continue the use of addition and subtraction to solve problems. Teachers can begin more formal instruction in multiplication and division with children of these ages.

Each child should have numerous experiences working both multiplication and division problems with manipulative materials before she is asked to use the symbols. Children should not be asked to work problems without access to manipulative materials with which the problems can be solved. As addition, subtraction, and multiplication facts become familiar to children, they may not use the manipulatives on every problem, but they should always be available. Every child should view a problem involving operations as something to be worked out, not as something that will be unsolvable if she forgets a fact.

Arithmetic is basic, but it should always be a tool for solving problems, not simply an end in itself. Achieving expertise in computation should be secondary to achieving the thinking and reasoning skills that are possible through all the strands of mathematics.

Fractions   As in other areas of mathematics, the symbols for fractions should not be introduced until the concept is fully understood. Teachers of young children can use fractional terms (*one-half, one-fourth*) when they are relevant to children's experiences: one-half of a graham cracker, one-half cup of water, one-fourth of the paper, and so on. But the symbol ½ should not be introduced until second or third grade. Fractions can indicate either how many of a set of equal-sized parts are being considered or a number. For children who are just developing a stable concept of whole numbers, formal fractions will be difficult.

Manipulatives for helping children learn about fractions include pattern blocks, fraction tiles, and teacher-made materials such as cardboard circles, squares, and rectangles cut into various fractional parts. Even for second and third graders, work with fractions should involve oral problem solving with manipulatives. Goals of instruction in fractions should include helping children know what halves, thirds, and fourths mean; know the difference between unit fractions (elements of a set) and nonunit fractions (parts of one whole); and recognize equivalent fractions.

Reasoning and Proof   One of the process strands in the model is reasoning and proof. Any time children are faced with problems that require sorting and classifying, they must use reasoning. Because *number* is one category of classification, sorting and classifying are important in creating mathematical categories. (Recall the three pencils mentioned at the beginning of the chapter;

they can be classified as writing tools, wooden objects, painted objects, and so on as well as by number.) Here are some appropriate activities to help threes and fours learn to reason:

- Putting all the sand toys in one container
- Sorting the dishes in the housekeeping area into storage areas for plates, silverware, cooking utensils, and so on
- Classifying the unit blocks into different sizes for storage
- Sorting all the crayons, markers, and pencils into containers
- Comparing sets and using categories such as *more* and *less*

As you can imagine, this list could go on for pages and pages, as almost all the play materials in the classroom must be sorted and classified for storage each day. As children do these tasks or help teachers do them, teachers can talk to them about what they are doing and the criteria they are using for sorting and classifying. As children mature in their understanding, teachers should refine the criteria for classification so that items are sorted on the basis of increasingly complex criteria.

Fives and sixes engage in reasoning when they sort materials, define the criteria for classifications, and seriate objects. Here are examples of problems for fives and sixes:

- Sorting buttons, keys, or other objects into groups and then explaining the criteria by which the classifications were made—The teacher might then encourage children to think of other criteria by which the same objects could be grouped. If the children had already grouped buttons by color, then they might group them by size, by number of holes, by whether they are shanked or unshanked, or by what they are made of.
- Creating Venn diagrams with yarn circles—If one circle contains objects that are blue and the other contains objects that are square, the intersection of the circles will contain square, blue objects—yet another category.
- Sorting models of zoo animals and farm animals for storage—As each is placed in the container, the child makes a tally mark and then compares the sizes of the sets of animals. This is a meaningful and logical extension of classification into arithmetic.
- Going on a "circle hunt" to find as many circles as possible while on a walk—Groups record and then compare the numbers of circles they find. These numbers can be recorded and compared to the numbers of squares or triangles found on other hunts.
- Playing card games (Old Maid, Rummy, Go Fish, and so on)

Sevens and eights can continue to classify objects and compare sets that are created. Tasks for sorting and classifying can be extended to sets of numbers;

for most tasks, children can use arithmetic to record the operations. Teachers can stimulate sorting and classifying skills in the following ways:

- Asking questions—"If all these numbers are even numbers, can 7 be included in this set?"
- Getting children to think about what pieces of information are needed to solve problems—"We know that our classroom is forty tiles long and thirty tiles wide and that it has eight windows. How many tiles cover the floor?"
- Posing "if-then" statements—"If you double your score and then find half of it, what will you have?"
- Asking children how many ways they can think of to get an answer to a problem
- Having children solve problems and defend their solutions

Seriation   Seriation tasks are inherent in the play experiences of even very young children. Seriation requires keeping in mind the characteristics of one element while comparing it to another element. Most very young children can compare two objects and determine which is larger and which is smaller. When asked to create a series based on size from a set of items, most four-year-olds will pick up two items at a time, compare them, determine the larger of those two, and then pick up two more items without considering the previous item. In their play, threes and fours will begin to place objects such as cans on the grocery store shelves in some kind of order, but seriating a large number of items is not an appropriate task. Appropriate seriating tasks for threes and fours include arranging dolls in the doll bed; arranging pairs of objects from the classroom (crayons, spools, spoons, plates, and so on) into sets of larger objects and smaller objects; arranging trucks in the blocks center by size; and arranging sets of three or four blocks into series.

Most fives can complete a simple seriation of more than three items. As children become more skilled, the numbers of objects to be seriated can be increased. Some classroom problems involving seriation for this age group include arranging stacks of paper by ascending size on the art shelves; arranging blocks in the unit blocks area by ascending or descending size; arranging strips of paper that represent the heights of class members; and arranging stacks of blocks in ascending order (one block, three blocks, five blocks, and so on).

Sevens and eights can accomplish the following kinds of seriation tasks: arranging sets of numbers in order or in patterns (a seriation task similar to arranging stacks of blocks); finding missing items in a series; and creating double series (a set of balls to match a set of bats).

Measurement   Measurement is a third strand in the model. Measurement experiences for young children must be based on their ability to conserve length and area. Many children are interested in measuring, and some measurements are meaningful to them. For instance, children are usually quite interested in their own heights, weights, ages, and so on.

Threes and fours can take part in activities such as the following:

- Exploring measurement through materials such as balance scales
- Finding a block of the proper length to fill a given space
- Measuring each other for new shoes or new clothes
- Using different-sized containers in the sand and water areas—Children can use one container to fill another and thereby develop concepts of *larger* and *more.*
- Using blocks to build walls or towers with lengths and heights equal to those of other objects

Fives and sixes still do not have stable understandings of linear measures, but they can begin to use nonstandard and some standard measures to measure objects of interest to them. Children of this age are still usually most interested in measuring themselves. The following kinds of measurement are appropriate:

- Measuring their heights with strips of paper or yarn and hanging the strips on the wall for comparison
- Measuring their tables with their hands or some other personal item such as their shoes
- Measuring the classroom by counting how many steps it takes to cross it
- Determining the number of pieces of paper that are required to cover their tables—If each group is given a different size of paper to use, the children can begin to recognize the need for standard measures.
- Measuring the cloth needed to cover the doll bed
- Using containers in the sand and water that are standard measuring cups or metric measures—The children can count how many cups are required to fill a quart or half-gallon milk carton.
- Measuring ingredients required in cooking experiences—Remember that a container that holds one-quarter cup is still one cup to the preoperational child; therefore, a real understanding of fractions usually will not be gained from cooking experiences.
- Estimating the sizes of objects using strings—The children can cut strings that they think will fit around their heads or their waists and then try them out to check their predictions. They can use this same technique for estimating the girth of their Halloween pumpkins, a watermelon, or their teacher.
- Measuring the heights of their block constructions or determining how many tiles their constructions cover on the floor

Sevens and eights can continue to use nonstandard linear measurements. Some children may be able to make the transition to standard measures, especially when a task does not require repeated measures. Here are some appropriate measurement tasks for this age group:

- Choosing the appropriate measuring device for measuring a piece of paper for a book cover or a piece of wood for something they are building in the woodworking area
- Accurately measuring given quantities of liquid, such as cups, pints, quarts, liters, and so on
- Using units (squares of paper or wooden blocks) to measure surface areas and making comparisons with arithmetical computations

As always, the emphasis should be on meaningful measurement tasks; the transition to standard measurements should be based on individual development.

Time   Time is a component of measurement that is often emphasized in programs for young children. However, children do not have the ability to quantify and integrate durations of time until about age ten (Levin, Wilkening, and Dembo 1984). Preschoolers are certainly aware of time, as they hear adults talk about time for a snack, time for outdoor play, time to get ready to go home, and so on, but they believe that they can influence the passage of time.

Teaching young children to tell time is not an appropriate goal. Preschoolers can be shown the clock face when it is time for certain events in their day, but they should not be expected to tell time. For a preschooler, a digital clock is easier to read than an analog clock because he only needs to recognize the numerals. A dial requires that the child translate the numbers 1, 2, 3, and so on to 5, 10, and 15 to indicate minutes, while also remembering that the numbers stand for the hour. Reading the time from a digital clock does not mean that the

Although young children may be aware of the concept of time, actually learning to tell time for the purpose of measurement should be reserved for older children.

child understands time; it just means he can recognize the numerals and read them in two parts.

Fives and sixes may attach more meaning to the passage of time, but learning to read time is still only appropriate for individual children who are ready for the information. Some sevens and eights will begin to make the transition to a stable view of time and will need to learn to tell time. For other children, time still will not be a stable concept and they will need to know only the times that are important in their daily schedules.

Money   The money system is another component of measurement that is often included in curriculum plans. Remember that for young children, *bigger* means "more." It is difficult for a young child to understand that a dime is worth more than a nickel when a nickel is physically larger than a dime. Money should be a topic in the curriculum only if children have a real use for the knowledge. Preschool children certainly do not have a concept of how much money is needed to buy objects. Some preschoolers think that if you need more money, you need only write a check or go to a cash machine.

Preschoolers can begin to explore the ideas of money as they play "grocery store," "shoe store," or "riding on the bus." Teachers may make play money available for the children. Some fives and sixes may need more knowledge of money if they receive a small allowance and save money for special purchases. Sevens and eights can begin to use computations that involve money and change if the problems are real. For example, they might learn about change if some of them buy lunch at school: What amount of money did each student bring to buy lunch? Is it enough? Will there be change? If there is change, how much will it be? Can anyone buy an extra carton of milk today? How much more must the teacher pay for lunch?

Geometry and Spatial Sense   A fourth strand of mathematics is geometry and spatial sense. Geometry involves more than Euclidean shapes. It includes topology (the connectedness of objects) and concepts of how shapes and forms are related to each other. The sequence of development of geometric concepts includes recognition of familiar shapes such as spoons, recognition of figures as open or closed, and recognition of Euclidean shapes such as squares and triangles (Copeland 1984). Very young children have difficulty recognizing the differences between shapes such as squares and rectangles. The emphasis for young children should be on experiences that help them develop concepts of space and the relationships of objects in space. Some examples of activities to encourage geometric understanding follow.

> ### *Parents* AND *Mathematics*
>
> ■ Ask parents to help their children look for geometric patterns and shapes. They should find as many shapes as possible in their houses or apartments and record their findings.
>
> *WWW*

Threes and fours can use two- and three-dimensional objects of various shapes in their play and discover the properties of these shapes. At this age, children do not necessarily need to learn the names of shapes. They can build with blocks and begin to discover how space can be enclosed with lines and that objects can be inside or outside these lines.

Fives and sixes can do activities such as playing with blocks; playing with pattern blocks and exploring these shapes and their relationships; constructing a square from four smaller squares; and discovering that a regular hexagon can be divided into two regular trapezoids.

At any age, the emphasis should be on manipulation and on reflecting on what has been constructed, rather than on learning labels. Some children will be interested in labels and will want to know them, but drill and practice are not appropriate for children of this age.

Teachers can encourage sevens and eights in the following kinds of tasks:

- Continuing to explore both two-dimensional and three-dimensional shapes

- Exploring area and volume of different shapes—Children can fill hollow three-dimensional shapes such as cylinders, cubes, rectangular prisms, and spheres with sand or water and determine how they could compute the volume of each.

- Exploring spaces on a geoboard and constructing various shapes and repeating or rearranging them

- Using geometry and measurement in planning room arrangements that will fit everything, use space to the best advantage, and allow for the best movement patterns

- Applying their growing knowledge of geometry to problems in arranging the furniture in their rooms at home

Algebra (Patterns and Functions)   The fifth strand of mathematics is algebraic patterns and functions. *Patterns* are visual, auditory, spatial, numerical, or combinations of these. The base 10 system is organized in patterns of ones, tens, hundreds, and so on, and patterns are evident in all the strands of mathematics. Promoting recognition of patterns is extremely important in helping young children develop mathematical concepts (Burton 1982; Ditchburn 1982). Recognizing and creating patterns helps children learn to order, predict, and estimate. Children can make patterns with beads, blocks, tiles, pattern blocks, pieces of paper, shoes, their bodies, leaves, flowers, seeds, and numerous other materials. Children can be helped to recognize patterns on the calendar, in blocks, in games, and in art materials.

Functions are the patterns created when certain actions are performed on objects or numbers. When a piece of paper is folded once, the result is two sections of paper; when it is folded twice, the result is four sections; and so on. When preschoolers can begin to observe how many sections are created when they fold pieces of paper or that there are two shoes for every one person, that is functional thinking. Some ideas for encouraging functional thinking in threes and fours include having children observe the number of shoes per person when they take off their shoes for a movement experience; observe the number of crayons or pencils per person; and fold paper and observe the number of sections created.

Fives and sixes can record their findings about activities in function tables. For example, if every person has two shoes, a function table of this information would look like this:

People	Shoes
1	2
2	4
3	6
4	8

The children should be encouraged to find patterns among numbers in the table. Function tables could be created for a variety of activities.

Sevens and eights can work on creating more involved function tables. A child might create a table of a mathematical operation, such as multiplying by 4, and let a partner determine the function illustrated. Tables could be created for addition, subtraction, multiplication, or division problems from the children's experiences. (Note that this is *not* a suggestion to teach children mathematical operations formally.)

Guess the Function

2	8
3	12
4	16

Data Analysis and Probability   Another strand in the model is data analysis and probability. Data analysis is an appropriate topic in the early childhood classroom when it is defined as comparing and analyzing information. Many activities in the classroom involve relationships that can be compared and analyzed.

Fives and sixes can carry out these kinds of tasks:

- Creating graphs of information, such as their choices at snack time
- Graphing how many children walk, ride the bus, or come by private car to school
- Graphing how many children have on certain types of shoes
- Voting for their favorite books and recording the results with tally marks
- Collecting and analyzing data on such topics as birthdates (Curcio and Folkson 1996)

Sevens and eights can work with information that is important to them by completing these kinds of activities:

- Graphing how many children eat the school lunch and how many bring their lunch each day for a month—Children can then try to determine why the choices were made. (Were there more children eating the school lunch when hamburgers were served as opposed to meat loaf?)
- Surveying the school to determine the students' favorite play equipment
- Tallying the number of books checked out of the class library, comparing the information for several weeks, and trying to determine the reasons for any variations

In the process of solving these problems, children use computation and logical thinking as well as statistics.

Children do not develop a firm concept of probability until they are in the concrete operational stage of thinking. However, sevens and eights can begin some interesting activities with probability involving small numbers. For example, they might flip a coin for a given number of times and record the numbers of heads and tails. Or they might draw colored cubes from a bag containing ten cubes: seven red and three blue. As each draw is completed, the child tallies the color of the cube and then returns the cube to the bag. After ten draws, the child predicts how many cubes of each color are actually in the bag. Drawing, tallying, and predicting can be repeated several times.

The Process Strands

Refer again to Figure 11.1 (on page 353) and note the outer ring, which makes up the process strands: Problem Solving, Reasoning and Proof, Communication, Connections, and Representation. The process strands surround the content strands because good instruction embeds the content within the framework created by these processes.

Problem Solving   As discussed earlier in this chapter, problem solving provides a context for mathematical activities and thinking throughout the day. Thus, the additional process strands are related to problem solving and to the content of the other strands.

Reasoning and Proof   The reasoning and proof strand calls for teachers to help children recognize and value the habits of thinking clearly and checking new ideas against what they already know, making and investigating mathematical conjectures, developing and evaluating mathematical arguments, and selecting and using various types of reasoning and methods of proof. For example, a child observing a classmate creating a pattern might ask for an explanation of the pattern or might suggest a different explanation for the pattern. In the earlier example of the children solving the number-of-children-per-car

Let's Face the Facts

Imagine that you are a new teacher who has just been hired to teach second grade. When interviewed, you impressed the principal with your knowledge and enthusiasm for reform mathematics. You enjoy helping young children solve problems and gain skills by thinking about what they are doing. During the first week of school, a veteran teacher reminds you that the school policy is that grades one through four give timed tests every Friday. The timed math tests begin in first grade with one-digit addition and continue in second grade with more difficult addition and subtraction facts (e.g., 14 – 6). In grade three they give tests on multiplication, and in grade four they test on division facts. There are about thirty written facts to complete in three minutes in grades one and two. There are one hundred multiplication/division facts to complete in five minutes in grades three and four. What are you going to do?

Now imagine that you are a parent of a second-grade child who attends this school. Your son works so hard to learn these facts and do the right thing, but he cannot perform under these time constraints. The teacher puts large red slash marks on any problem that is missed or wrong, and then puts a big red percentage on the top of the paper. Your son cannot achieve the 95 percent needed to pass these tests. Both of you dread Fridays. You know efficiency is important, and systematic practice will help achieve it, but at what cost to your child's self-esteem and self-confidence?

As a teacher you can talk with your colleagues about what you learned in your college courses. Children follow a developmental sequence as they approach a problem. If you build on what they already know, they will learn their facts much more

quickly. The rate at which young children accomplish the goal of efficiency varies greatly. Some researchers found that emphasizing speed for speed's sake actually can hinder student progress (Isaacs and Carroll 1999).

It *is* important to practice once a week. For motivation you may wish to give each child a sturdy chart where he can color in each fact as it is mastered. Make a cardboard rectangle with the type of fact listed in the left-hand column and the actual facts written in squares across the grid. For example, the top line would say: "The number +1" . . . 0 + 1, 1 + 1, 1 + 2, etc. Use the order that has been researched by several authors (Smith 2001). Each child will need triangle flashcards with the types of problems he is working on. A triangle flashcard uses a fact family where the sum is in the top corner and each addend occupies a corner. To practice addition, cover up the top corner. To practice subtraction, cover up one of the bottom corners. Individual testing is needed. Perhaps you can use peer tutors from the upper grades, or you can quiz several children each day during your free moments. A general rule of thumb is that when a child gets a fact correct within a few seconds five times in a row, he can color it on his chart. How do you know that he really knows it? With a young child, you can watch his or her face. If he frowns and starts to count on his fingers or pause to think, it isn't committed to memory. It is important to test both orally and in the written form. To give a written quiz, just draw triangles on a worksheet and leave one corner of each triangle blank for the child to fill in.

Early childhood passes so quickly. We can make a difference in the way children feel about mathematics.

problem, they discussed their methods of solving the problem, explained their reasoning, and offered proof that they were correct.

Teachers can also help children develop the language of logic (e.g., *not, and, or, all, some, if/then,* and *because*) through the many different experiences of a schoolday. For instance, the teacher might say, "*If* you choose one toy now, *then* you can choose another later."

Communication   Children have to learn to organize their mathematical thinking in order to communicate it to others. For young children, such communication may be in the forms of drawings, gestures, and body movements. And then gradually children will be introduced to the conventions of using mathematical symbols. For example, if preschool or kindergarten children create a graph of the kinds of shoes worn by the class members, the graph could be constructed using pictures of the shoes. Older children could construct a comparable graph using colored squares and then finally using the numerals and bars of a typical bar graph. The process of making a model of mathematical information should begin with real objects and then gradually move to mathematical symbols. The goal is to help children learn to think about how they can communicate their mathematical findings and knowledge to others. At the conclusion of any math activity, the teacher should help the children find ways to communicate their learning with one another and with those outside the classroom.

Connections   The connections strand is included to help teachers focus on the logical connections among mathematics and the other subject areas in the curriculum. For example, in reading, children learn the concepts of number and seriation through page numbers, chapter numbers, and the use of ordinal numbers to signify the order of events in a story. In physical education, children learn about measurement when they compare the distances they can throw or the number of times they can bounce a ball. In music, children learn about patterns and the values of the notes used to represent music in its written form.

Teachers who are aware of these connections can help children realize them, as well, by recording some of the information from other subject areas using mathematical symbols the children already know. For example, if the book the children are reading does not have page numbers, the teacher might help the children determine why this convention was not followed and how page numbers could be added.

Representation   Representation is the skill of finding ways to illustrate one's understandings in communication, reasoning, and problem solving so that the information can be preserved, referred to, remembered, and discussed. Obviously, as children gain skill in representation, their communication about math concepts will be more accurate and they will make more use of traditional mathematical symbols. Children need to develop a repertoire of basic representation skills—such as model building, making drawings and graphs of various types, and creating symbols—as they move toward the more conventional forms of representation.

Process Skill Instruction

All the process skills are intended to be used in a natural, integrated fashion in the early childhood classroom. Teachers are not expected to plan lessons on, say, representation or communication. Rather, they should aim to help children use their growing skills and understandings in ways that promote the view of mathematics as a natural, comfortable way of looking at and describing the world around them. In order to meet the goals of mathematical instruction, teachers must be alert to the variety of mathematical learning that is possible in many ordinary experiences throughout every day.

Materials for Instruction

Many excellent materials for helping children make discoveries about mathematical concepts are available today. Both commercial and teacher-made materials can be useful in good math programs. Commercial materials such as Unifix cubes, pattern blocks, geoblocks, and base 10 blocks are basic for a sound manipulatives-based program. Teacher-made manipulatives might include bean sticks, boxes of junk to be sorted and classified, glass beads on strings in sets from one to ten, geoboards, and so on. Most of these materials can also be purchased if not made by the teachers. When creating manipulative materials, teachers should ensure that mathematical concepts are presented accurately and that the materials do not distract from the concept to be learned. One does not bring in an elephant to teach the concept *gray*.

Some materials—such as Cuisenaire rods, Dienes blocks, and Montessori rods—are not good choices for helping young children develop concepts of number. Remember that most of these children do not yet conserve number or length. When given a Cuisenaire rod that is supposed to represent 5 because it is five times as long as the 1 rod, most preconservers will say that this rod is one (and it is one rod). According to Piaget (1952a):

> Cuisenaire rods . . . are open to the most totally opposed methods of using them, some of them genuinely operative if the child is allowed to discover for himself the various operations made possible by spontaneous manipulations of the rods, but the others essentially intuitive or figurative when they are limited to external demonstrations and to explanations of the configurations laid out by the teacher. (p. 73)

Better representations of number are individual objects such as Unifix cubes, chips, or beans. Once when observing a group of gifted kindergartners, the author saw a child build a square pyramid with Cuisenaire rods. To determine how many units had been used to construct the structure, she still counted each of the different-sized rods as one unit, even after several explanations by the teacher about how to count each rod.

➤ Survey the children in one grade level to determine what work their parents do. Make a graph to illustrate the findings.

➤ Compare the population figures for your town/city from the 1990 census and the 2000 census. How much has the population changed? Are more or fewer people living in your town/city now than in 1990?

➤ Invite a mathematician to visit the class and discuss his or her work. Some children might not be aware that mathematics can be a career choice.

➤ Children can measure their rooms at home (whether they have a room alone or share it).

➤ How many children attend your school? How many are there in each grade? Compare the grade levels to determine the largest and smallest classes.

➤ How much space does your city/town cover? How will you find out? Who keeps the records of area within the city limits?

➤ How much area does your school cover? What is the area of the building? What is the area of the playground? What is the area of the parking lot? Compare these areas. Which is more? Which is less?

➤ How many children who attend your school (or are in your class) live close enough to walk to school? How many children ride buses? How many children get to school in other ways? Make a graph to report the comparisons.

➤ How many books are in your school library? How many books are there per student? How many books are checked out of your library each week? Are more books checked out now than last year?

➤ What is the average height of children in your class?

➤ What is the average number of children in families represented in your class? in your school? in your community?

Other materials may also prove less effective in helping children develop concepts. For children who do not yet conserve length, a counting line is not the best strategy for promoting understanding of addition and subtraction. It is also important to be careful when choosing materials for representing fractional parts of a whole. Objects that cannot be divided accurately are not appropriate for developing fractional concepts. Pattern blocks and fraction tiles are better representations of fractions than apples and pies, which cannot be cut accurately into fractional pieces.

Some teachers continue to use worksheets and workbooks rather than manipulatives. They may believe that manipulatives are too expensive, that manipulatives take up too much time, or that parents expect to see paper-and-pencil evidence of children's work (Stone 1987). Some manipulatives are expensive, but materials of good quality will last indefinitely, and many manipulatives can be constructed by teachers for very little cost. Using manipulatives does take time, but covering the topics without achieving understanding is not efficient teaching. Taking the time initially to make sure that children understand will save time eventually because the same topics will not have to be taught again and again.

Calculators, Computers, and Young Children

Most young children have had some experience with calculators (Pagni 1987). Many households have one or more calculators that children have observed being used, and many young children have their own calculators.

It is reasonable for children to use calculators to solve arithmetic problems and to check their own and their peers' solutions to problems. But a calculator cannot substitute for real experience as a way of developing a concept of number or appropriate counting strategies. Thinking about the problem and how it can be solved should be the focus of instruction. Teachers should not be so concerned about developing children's basic skills that they do not use calculators. Calculators can be useful in computation.

Young children should be allowed to explore calculators. They may enjoy pushing the buttons and watching the numbers change. Older children can begin using calculators to solve equations and learn the importance of entering the numbers correctly. By the time children are seven or eight, they can use calculators in computation and for exploring functions and relationships among numbers.

Many young children may also be familiar with computers and the variety of tasks they can do. Some computer software can enhance a good manipulatives-based math program. Children who have had real experience with geoblocks and geoboards can extend their experiences with a program called Logo, especially if they are able to manipulate the turtle. Yelland (1995) found that children using Logo worked in a collaborative environment to solve problems and that their reasoning and logic skills were enhanced. Other programs are being developed almost daily. Many are simply drill-and-practice on arithmetic problems, but more and more programs ask children to interact with different situations and to think logically about outcomes. Teachers should evaluate software carefully and choose programs that allow children to think, rather than simply practice algorithms.

The Reading–Writing Connection

Teachers can help children use reading and writing to record their questions, their discoveries, and their solutions to problems. Many teachers (especially those in the primary grades) provide each child with a notebook in which to write his questions and solutions. The teacher responds to the child's work in the notebook, writes questions, and presents new problems to be solved. Children are also encouraged to read one another's notebooks and to discuss their solutions and discoveries.

In describing the reading and writing experiences of her class, Richards (1990) noted that children made books of ways they had solved problems and that their writing about mathematics was quite varied. They wrote summaries, descriptions, definitions, reports, instructions, notes, evaluations, explanations, and personal responses to math. Scott, Williams, and Hyslip (1992) suggest that mathematics is best conceptualized as communication and reasoning, not as a series of mysterious rules and symbols. They found that second graders responded well to journal-writing experiences in the math curriculum, including stories, pictures, and diagrams to explain their understandings.

Whitin (1997) kept a clipboard that was designated as the data-collection board. Children used it to take surveys of anything that interested them, and they learned to write or draw the conclusions they reached in ways that others could interpret. Brown (1997) encouraged first graders to keep journals of mathematics experiences both inside and outside school, noting when they used math in some way. Kroll and Halaby (1997) helped children use math journals to record their problem-solving strategies and found that doing so helped the children learn both mathematics and written communication skills.

Literature and Mathematics

Literature can also contribute to the instructional program in mathematics. The most obvious types of literature to use are counting books and rhymes. Many excellent counting books are available. In addition, problems in classification, ordering, and the basic operations can be introduced through literature (see Figure 11.4). As described by Whitin (1994), "Books portray mathematics not as a sea of symbols and potentially frustrating mental tasks that have no meaning for children but as a tool for making decisions and solving problems" (p. 10).

In selecting books that support the development of math concepts for young children, teachers should remember that the authors of children's books are not math teachers—nor do they need to be. Well-written books grow from their authors' appreciation of mathematical concepts as they appear in the real world. Teachers should avoid using books that are basically math workbooks in disguise. Children do not want to find practice problems in their literature.

Assessment

When assessing their knowledge of mathematics, it is not enough to find out what children can *do*—it is important to know what children *understand*. Historically, educators assumed that if children could do things such as counting and adding, they understood what they were doing. Research has proven otherwise.

Richardson (1988) found that children who could count often had no concept of number and some who could do place-value problems in their

Figure 11.4   Books with Mathematical Content

Counting

Arlene Alda's 1 2 3: What Do You See? (Alda 1998)
City by Numbers (Johnson 1998)
Counting Wildflowers (McMillan 1986)
Count with Maisy (Cousins 1997)
The Handmade Counting Book (Rankin 1998)
More, Fewer, Less (Hoban 1998)
1 is for One (Wheatley 1996)
One Less Fish (Toft and Sheather 1998)
12 Ways to Get to 11 (Merriam 1993)
Two Ways to Count to 10 (Dee 1988)

Multiplication

Bunches and Bunches of Bunnies (Mathews 1990)
Counting by Kangaroos (Hulme 1995)
Two of Everything (Hong 1993)

Division

The Doorbell Rang (Hutchins 1986)
One Hundred Angry Ants (Pinczes 1993)
A Remainder of One (Pinczes 1995)

Reasoning

Who Sank the Boat? (Allen 1982)

Fractions

Eating Fractions (McMillan 1991)
Give Me Half! (Murphy 1996)

Geometry

The Hole Story (Merriam 1995)
Shapes, Shapes, Shapes (Hoban 1986)
So Many Circles, So Many Squares (Hoban 1998)

Money

Alexander, Who Used to Be Rich Last Sunday (Viorst 1978)
Bunny Money (Wells 1997)

Measurement

Biggest, Strongest, Fastest (Jenkins 1995)
How Big Is a Foot (Myller 1990)
If You Hopped Like a Frog (Schwartz 1999)
King Bidgood's in the Bathtub (Wood 1985)
Measuring Penny (Leedy 1998)
Twelve Snails to One Lizard (Hightower 1997)

More Complex Problems

Bats on Parade (Appelt 1999)
How Much Is a Million (Schwartz 1993)
The King's Chessboard (Birch 1993)
Math Curse (Scieszka 1995)
One Grain of Rice (Demi 1997)
Sea Squares (Hulme 1991)
Window (Baker 1991)

Note: Full bibliographical information is provided in the References section (pages 525–528).

workbooks could not use place-value information to solve real problems. Labinowicz (1980) reported similar findings: Only about half the children who could work out equations such as 5 + 4 could work out the same problem logically when presented with real objects to add. In a later work, Labinowicz (1985) reported that children who had completed drills of number combinations could not automatically recall the correct answers. In interviews about how they solved problems, many children reported that they had taught themselves other ways of thinking about the number combinations in order to make sense of the problems. Children who can do tasks assigned by teachers but who do not understand them may not have enough time to engage in the experiences needed in order to develop the concepts. They may simply continue to do more tasks for which they memorize procedures.

The most effective type of assessment presents the child with a problem and has the teacher observe carefully the strategies the child uses in solving that problem. For example, to assess counting abilities, the child should be presented with real objects to count; the number of objects should be larger than the teacher estimates the child can count. To check a child's understanding of place value, the teacher should try to determine how she organizes objects in a large set for counting and question her about her strategies to try to reveal her thinking processes. Problems in creating patterns, in classification, and in basic operations should be presented with manipulative materials that the child can use to find solutions. Paper-and-pencil tests may help determine what a child can do, but only by giving a child real problems to work can a teacher uncover what she understands (Sgroi et al. 1995).

Teachers will need to assess children's abilities to conserve number and length in order to plan experiences. If children cannot conserve, it does not mean that the teacher must wait until they can before offering them mathematics instruction. Problems and tasks must be evaluated in terms of the kinds of thinking required to solve them; appropriate experiences can be selected based on children's levels of thinking. Children learn a great deal about mathematics before they can conserve number and length (McClintic 1988).

Teachers should not limit themselves to assessing children's computation abilities or problem-solving skills. Teachers should also assess how children feel as learners of mathematics, how children view mathematics, and what abilities children have to apply mathematical thinking to everyday problems. Micklo (1997) found that using a math portfolio in the primary grades can help teachers assess children's mathematical understandings and provide information about individuals' strengths and needs that letter grades cannot. Using portfolios will also help teachers reflect on the activities and experiences provided for the children in terms of their developmental appropriateness and their contribution to mathematical understanding.

Parents AND Mathematics

■ Share examples of problem-solving strategies (similar to those shown in Figure 11.3, page 355) in a newsletter to parents with the goal of helping them understand that their children learn standard algorithms at given times. Stress that in school math focuses on understanding, not memorization.

Children with Special Needs

In mathematics, as in any other curriculum area, the teacher must take responsibility for making sure that children with disabilities have access to the materials they need to help them understand the concepts, as well as the time they need to explore those materials. Some materials may have to be modified, such as making tactile materials and providing braille numerals for students with visual challenges. Adaptations can make it possible for children with motor problems to roll dice or spin spinners—for instance, providing cups for the dice and easy-to-grasp handles on the spinners. Adaptations also may be needed for computers and calculators so that children can manipulate them easily. For example, some computers can produce very large print or can read aloud materials on screen.

Celebrating Diversity

Most cultures employ the same concepts of number, counting, and the like that are employed in the United States. Thus, children who do not speak English as their first language often do well in math because they know the concepts and have only to learn new labels for the numerals and operations. Teachers can take advantage of the knowledge these children have when planning working groups that will solve problems involving mathematics. These children should also be encouraged to write their own story problems in their native languages and to share what they know about math with their classmates. For example, a child could tell about the money used in his home country, and it could be compared to the money used in the United States. Counting words from the various languages represented in the class could be used for counting experiences or for labeling sets. Most teachers are aware that children like to learn how to count in other languages.

Teaching the history of mathematical learning in other cultures may not be appropriate for young children; it would be appropriate, however, for the teacher to mention contributions to mathematical knowledge made by cultures other than European Americans.

Chapter Summary

- Mathematics is more than just arithmetic. Mathematics includes classification, seriating, grouping, relationships, statistics, probability, fractions, geometry, and arithmetic.

- Mathematics is not a subject at which someone is innately good or poor. Neither is knowledge of mathematics transmitted from a person who knows to one who does not. Each individual learns mathematics by constructing understanding. Mathematical relationships are mental constructs.

- Mathematics in the classroom setting should be based on real problems that children are interested in solving. Some problems will involve the use of arithmetic; others will not.

- Instruction in mathematics should focus on helping children understand mathematical concepts before mathematical symbols are introduced.

- Writing down their questions, discoveries, and solutions can be very helpful to children learning mathematical concepts.

- Some mathematical concepts can be introduced through children's literature. Counting books and rhymes may interest children, and other books may introduce the basic operations, classification, or ordering.

- Assessment in mathematics should focus on the child's understanding, thought processes, and attitudes about mathematics.

- All children, including those with disabilities, need access to materials and time to explore them in order to understand mathematical concepts. Modifications may be needed for some materials in order for children to use them easily.

- Experiences that help children develop mathematical understanding do not usually depend on skill in language abilities. Thus, mathematics can be the subject area in which all children have an equal chance to succeed.

Theory INTO *Practice*

Observe mathematics instruction in a primary-grade classroom. If the instruction is individualized or integrated into themes, can you identify the goals and objectives? Pay close attention to the children's behavior during instruction. Do they seem interested? Do you think they like math? Explain your answers.

Plan an experience that will help threes and fours develop the concept of *number*. Be sure to include the materials you will use and how you will interest the children in the experience.

Research has revealed that children spend as much as one-third of their schoolday in computation activities. How much of the time devoted to mathematics instruction should be devoted to computation? Discuss your position with a group of your peers.

Choose a children's book with content that is related to mathematics. Plan how you would use the book with young children. How would you bring the mathematical elements to the children's attention if they did not mention them? What manipulatives could you use to illustrate the concept presented in the book?

Plan a Family Math Night. Include plans for the activities you would include, the materials you would need, the demonstrations you would give, and any handout materials you would provide for parents.

Many of the students preparing to become teachers are not very comfortable with their own mathematics abilities. If you have found mathematics difficult, discuss why with a group of your peers. As a teacher, how will you take a positive approach to those elements of instruction that were negative in your own education?

Karen Yourd

Bon Meade Elementary School
Moon Township, Pennsylvania

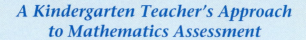

A Kindergarten Teacher's Approach to Mathematics Assessment

Mathematics filters into almost every aspect of the day in my kindergarten classroom. The children become mathematicians magically, without even being aware that it is happening. Positional and directional words are used daily in many situations. Sorting and patterning activities are part of play, calendar, and snack times. Adding and subtracting take place long before the children can put words to their actions. The mathematical activity adds excitement to the classroom and provides many opportunities for me to assess the learning of each student.

Assessment is an ongoing process, a collection of data that are then used for planning and instruction. Anecdotal records can provide useful information for planning instruction. One strategy for collecting these records is to use computer labels on which notes are recorded. When a label is full, it is transferred to a file for that child.

Another technique is to keep a growth-over-time piece for each child. The tasks completed should be fairly consistent so that growth can be demonstrated. Begin with a piece of paper divided into quadrants; write a direction in each square. Read the directions to the children. The four directions might include, "Write your name," "Draw a picture of yourself," "Draw a picture of your house," and "Draw five things." As the year progresses, the last direction might change to "Show a set with one more/less than 5," "Write the numeral 5," or "Write an addition equation."

I call another activity *silent sorting*. I send two children with black shoes to one corner, two children with white shoes to another, and two children with sandals to another. Then each child in the remainder of the group tries to find where she belongs. The criteria for the sorting can be any number of factors.

Graphing is a skill that can be introduced to young children and that they generally enjoy. The most basic form of graphing is to use the children themselves, lined up according to some given criteria, such as height. Then objects can be used, like the children's shoes, if determining the most popular shoe color, or fruit, if determining the children's fruit preferences. The next step is to transfer the results to a paper or chart graph. Results should always be discussed and observations noted. Self-stick notes are wonderful for attaching children's observations directly onto the chart. Eventually, individual charts can be made. Children especially like manipulatives that are edible, such as cereal or candy. I use this type of activity to assess sorting skills, reasoning skills, and counting ability as well as the ability to create and interpret a graph.

Whatever the task, it is important that children explain how they came up with their answers. Their explanations provide insight into the approaches and ways of thinking they use to solve problems. Information from observations, tasks, daily activities, and explanations all help determine a child's strengths and what can be done to help her grow in mathematical thinking.

CHAPTER 12

Manipulation and Discovery through Science

After reading this chapter, you will be able to do the following:

- Define the term *science* as it relates to early childhood education.
- Explain the scientific process.
- Plan an appropriate science program for young children.
- Develop appropriate science experiences for young children.
- Plan for the integration of science and literacy activities.
- Adapt science experiences for children with special needs.
- Celebrate the diversity of young learners.

*Y*our observation task this morning in the child-care center was to look for children engaged in scientific learning. You chose to observe a group of three- and four-year-olds for the first hour and a group of seven-year-olds for the second hour. In observing the younger children, you expected to see play and language learning, but you did not expect to see much "science." After all, threes and fours cannot really be expected to do experiments, can they?

Once you reviewed your notes, however, you found that children were engaged in many activities that could be labeled "science." Some children compared the textures of sand in different containers; other children tried to sink little wooden barges in water. You also found that many of the children's expressed interests were related to science. You overheard two children asking the teacher what had happened to the orange they had brought for snack several days ago—it was covered with mold. You noticed that the teacher did not throw the orange away but left it out for the children to see and smell.

In the second hour, you watched as seven-year-old children were instructed to take out their science books. They were provided with the materials to complete an experiment described in their textbooks: They were to observe the results of mixing unknown powders with water. At the end of the experiment, the teacher guided the children's discussion of their observations. Then they read the discussion in the text about dissolving.

After observing these two classrooms, you are left with the question: What is science? Is science the informal learning that was taking place in the class of younger children, or is it the more formal guided learning in which the older children were participating?

Definition of Science

In general terms, *science* is the process of observing, thinking, and reflecting on actions and events. Kilmer and Hofman (1995) define *science* more specifically as the "knowledge about specific phenomena, . . . the processes used to collect and evaluate information, . . . and as a recently added aspect, [*technology* when defined as] the application of science to problems of human adaptation to the environment" (p. 43). Children engaged in scientific thinking are constructing a framework of relationships within which factual information can be organized into meaningful and useful concepts. Science is an attitude exemplified by curiosity and interest in the world. Science is problem solving. Science is not learning facts and memorizing formulas.

Science in early childhood education is encouraging children to explore their environments and reflect on their observations and discoveries. Ideally, science is not a time set aside from other experiences; it is part of an ongoing integrated approach in which children think and construct basic understandings about the world. Broadly speaking, a child at the easel follows the basic scientific process when he hypothesizes (predicts that the paint is ready to apply to paper), collects data (paints), revises the prediction (determines that the paint is too runny or too thick), and draws conclusions about how paint reacts under given conditions. He may also discover the interactions of primary colors and explore those interactions very scientifically.

Kilmer and Hofman (1995) use the criteria listed in Table 12.1 to define *science,* identifying both what it is and is not. Raper and Stringer (1987) also have pointed out what science is not:

> *Science is not book learning. We can learn a good deal from books, of course, and there is no other way that we can learn about the lives and discoveries of the great men and women of science except by reference to recorded information. But, fundamentally, the processes of science can only be understood by actively using them. Teachers need to be discouraged from seeing book learning as a substitute for practical activity.* (p. 47)

Many teachers report that they feel less prepared to teach science than any other subject-matter area (Wenner 1993). Perhaps such feelings are a result of teachers' misconceptions that science requires complicated materials and is a hard subject to master. This view of science is changing as more teachers at all grade levels are encouraged to think about science as exploring and inquiring rather than learning specific facts.

Sciencing, a term popular with early childhood teachers, implies not only the active nature of science experiences but also the idea that both children and teachers are involved in the process of learning science—as opposed to having the teacher teach the children. *Sciencing* also implies that the whole classroom is used for learning rather than setting aside one area as a science area (McNairy 1985).

Table 12.1   Criteria for Defining Science

For Children 3 through 8, Developmentally Appropriate Sciencing . . .	
Is	**Is Not**
Actively participating	Memorizing a lot of facts
Handling materials	Watching the teacher do most of the demonstrating
Controlling their own actions	and handling of objects
Investigating familiar phenomena	Studying content with no link to their knowledge or experience
Reflecting on teachers' open-ended questions	Being restricted by closed, single-right-answer questioning or being told what to expect
Observing the results of their own actions	Lacking opportunities to observe the results of their own actions
Experiencing both planned and spontaneous opportunities	Experiencing science only as teacher-planned activities
Investigating and working individually or in small groups	Participating in science activities only in a large group
Investigating the range of basic concepts	Learning about only one or two concepts
Exploring a variety of content from life, earth, and physical sciences	Learning only limited content
Having their knowledge and skills assessed in multiple ways	Having their knowledge and skills assessed only by written tests

Source: S. J. Kilmer and H. Hofman, "Transforming Science Curriculum," in *Reaching Potentials: Transforming Early Childhood Curriculum and Assessment,* vol. 2, edited by S. Bredekamp and T. Rosegrant, 43–63 (p. 62) (Washington, DC: National Association for the Education of Young Children, 1995). Reprinted with permission from the National Association for the Education of Young Children.

Learning Science

Just as children learn mathematics through manipulation and discovery, they learn science by manipulation, observation of the results of their manipulations, and discovery of relationships and effects. The role of experience in science is primary—science cannot be done without touching, tasting, feeling, smelling, pushing, pulling, rotating, mixing, comparing, and so on (McIntyre 1984).

Learning in the area of science involves primarily *physical knowledge* and *logico-mathematical knowledge.* When children explore the properties of materials, they are gaining knowledge from the materials themselves, which is physical knowledge. When they create relationships among materials, as in classifying leaves, their learning is logico-mathematical. As Chaille and Britain (1991) explain:

> *Constructivism is based on the idea that children are actively engaged—naturally and without the aid of direct instruction—in building theories about the world and*

the way it works. From a constructivist perspective, children are natural scientists and, given the opportunity, will engage on their own in experimentation and problem solving. (p. 23)

If a teacher believes that children must construct their own knowledge, then she will not make the mistake of *telling* them about concepts in science. Even so, believing that children must construct their own understandings does not free the teacher of the obligation to help children learn science. The teacher's role, then, is to plan appropriate activities, select appropriate materials, present challenges, provide time for experiences, and ask questions to guide children's thinking. Teaching science requires thoughtful planning and reflection.

The Scientific Process

The **scientific process** is a cycle of forming hypotheses, collecting data, confirming or rejecting the hypotheses, making generalizations, and then repeating the cycle. The basic skills used in the scientific process include observing, classifying and comparing, measuring, communicating, experimenting, relating, inferring, and applying. Because inferring and applying require more abstract thinking, young children should not be expected to be competent in these skills in a formal sense. Each of these skills, as it applies to an early childhood science program, is discussed in a following section. Keep in mind, however, that these skills are important in learning generally. They do not apply *only* to learning science.

Parents AND Science

■ Help parents understand the nature of scientific learning by including reports of science investigations (such as freezing and melting) in the parent newsletter. Encourage parents to do science with their children during everyday experiences, such as taking a walk to look for patterns and shapes (or shades of color, plants, animals, and so on).

Observing

Looking and *observing* are not the same thing. Teachers need to provide guidance in observation techniques. Children can be encouraged to look carefully for specific actions or information. For example, children can be encouraged to observe the behavior of a bird on the ground—does it walk or hop? Observation is certainly not limited to visual input; it should involve all the senses—seeing, hearing, smelling, tasting, and feeling.

Classifying

Classifying is a basic process skill used in organizing information. In order to classify objects or information, children must be able to compare and contrast the properties of objects or information. Very young children begin to classify by function, color, and shape. Older children can classify on the basis of specific characteristics or properties, but multiplicative classifications, in which objects fit into multiple categories, are difficult for children in the early childhood years. Children must be able to think in concrete operational terms before they can think of objects as belonging to several categories at once, and most children are not concrete thinkers in the early childhood years. Teachers can encourage children to classify objects and to explain how objects have been grouped. Children can classify blocks by shape, group the materials that are stored in the art area, or sort buttons, leaves, shells, or other collections.

Comparing

Comparing is the process of examining objects and events in terms of similarities and differences. It usually involves quantifying, counting, measuring, and closely observing. Comparing is important as children observe, for example, the behavior of a mouse and a guinea pig and then determine what is alike and different about them. Another example would be having children compare the petals on a daisy with those of a rose.

Measuring

Measuring is a basic process skill necessary for collecting data. Measurement does not refer only to using standardized measures. Children can measure the hamster's food by scoops, cut a piece of string the height of their bean plant, compare the sizes of seeds or rocks, or use a beaker to collect snow and observe the amount of water produced when the snow melts.

Communicating

Communicating is another basic process skill. Children can be encouraged to share their observations and their data collections through a variety of means. They can talk about their findings, make pictorial records, produce charts and graphs, or write narratives in order to share information, data, and conclusions. The communication process is important, as children begin to understand how knowledge is created in the field of science.

Experimenting

Experimentation is not a new process for young children. They have been experimenting since they first picked up a rattle or threw a cereal bowl off the high chair tray. In the scientific process, experimenting means controlling one or more variables and manipulating conditions. Teachers can help children think of their play activities as experiments by skillful questioning and encouraging children to reflect on their actions and the results of their actions. When children try to balance one block on a tower of blocks, drop food coloring into glasses of water, or plant several seeds in different soils, they can be guided to think of these activities as experiments.

Relating, Inferring, and Applying

Young children will use the process skills of relating, inferring, and applying only in very informal ways:

- **Relating** is the process of drawing abstractions from concrete evidence. For example, children who observe water freezing may not be able to relate that observation to the abstract idea that given liquids become solids at given temperatures.

- **Inferring** is the ability to determine cause-and-effect relationships or explanations for phenomena when the processes are not directly observable. Examples of such unobservable phenomena include electricity and magnetism.

- **Applying** is using information from experiences to invent, create, solve new problems, and determine probabilities. Children can be involved in applying scientific knowledge but not in a formal, analytical sense. For example, if children can observe the behavior of water when it is dropped on waxed paper, blown across waxed paper with a straw, or left outside on a winter night, they can apply some of these observations to other liquids and make predictions about what will happen to them under the same conditions. It is unreasonable, however, to expect children to analyze results and apply them without having provided concrete experiences to think about.

You will notice that the steps in the scientific process outlined in Figure 12.1 are not always linear. As a learner observes some phenomena, she may decide to compare her observations to the observations of others, she may decide to set up an experiment that will allow her to measure the results of adding more water to a solution, she may communicate her findings to others at this point, or she may decide to repeat the experiment but to vary it by adding salt water, and so on. Experimenting will require more observations, which may lead to more comparisons or more measurements, which may lead to more observations, so the cycle is usually recursive, not linear.

Planning an Early Childhood Science Program

The National Science Education (NSE) standards are an invaluable resource in planning a science program for children of any age. A federally sponsored initiative developed by teachers, scientists, and others, this document describes what it means to be a scientifically literate person and establishes what should be taught at specific grade levels (Abruscato 2000). The unifying concepts and

Figure 12.1 The Cycle of Scientific Exploration

Observing

Classifying

Relating
Inferring
Applying

Comparing

Experimenting

Measuring

Communicating

processes that cross all grade levels and all areas of scientific study include the following:

> *Systems, order, and organization*
> *Evidence, models, and explanation*
> *Constancy, change, and measurement*
> *Evolution and equilibrium*
> *Form and function* (Rakow and Bell 1998, p. 166)

These concepts provide a broad framework for science instruction. Early childhood educators must determine what content areas are developmentally appropriate for young children within this framework. Rakow and Bell (1998) have summarized the major content areas deemed appropriate for young learners by the NSE standards in the areas of the physical sciences, life sciences, and earth/space sciences. Science programs should also cover the areas of science and technology, science in personal and social perspectives, and the history and nature of science, according to the NSE. Later in this chapter, specific goals for each area will be listed along with suggestions for instruction (see pages 396–404).

NAEYC

WWW

Based on the work of Lev Vygotsky, a constructivist approach to teaching science would include the following elements:

- *Active engagement with phenomena*
    - *Students ask questions*
    - *Students mindfully interact with concrete materials*
- *Use and application of knowledge*
    - *Teachers and students use prior knowledge*
    - *Students identify and use multiple resources*
    - *Students plan and carry out investigations*
    - *Students apply concepts and skills in new situations*
    - *Students are given time for reflection*
- *Multiple representations*
    - *Teachers use varied evaluation techniques*
    - *Students create and revise products or artifacts to represent understanding*
    - *Students use language as a tool to express knowledge*
- *Use of learning communities*
- *Authentic tasks* (Krajcik, Czerniak, and Berger 1999, pp. 37–38)

Barclay, Benelli, and Schoon (1999) suggest that teachers use questions and comments to promote scientific thinking, as illustrated in Figure 12.2.

Figure 12.2 Questions and Comments to Promote Scientific Thinking

- What do you think will happen if . . . ?
- I don't know, either. Let's see if we can find out.
- This looks interesting. What are you trying to do?
- Tell me about _____.
- What can you do to make that happen?
- Let's see who can _____.
- What did you mix together? What happened?
- Put together all the things you think belong together.
- Tell me how you put your group of objects together.
- Tell us something about the _____'s size and shape.
- What did you do first? What did you do next? When did this happen? What happened afterward?
- Does _____ look the same today as it did yesterday?

- How are these alike? How are they different?
- How does it feel/look/smell/sound/taste (if safe)?
- Where have you seen something like this before?
- How did you do that?
- I wonder how _____ works?
- It *does* look like magic. How do you suppose that magic works?
- What else can you think of that works like/does that?
- What can you change to try to make _____ work/happen?
- What have you found out?
- How can you use what you learned?
- Draw a picture of what you see.

Source: K. Barclay, C. Benelli, and S. Schoon, "Making the Connection! Science and Literacy," *Childhood Education* 75 (Spring 1999): 145–149. Reprinted by permission of Kathy Barclay, Cecelia Benelli, and Susan Schoon, and the Association for Childhood Education International. Copyright © 2000 by the Association.

Planning Balanced Content

Children's interest in biological science is so strong that teachers often emphasize it and fail to help children explore the areas of physical or earth sciences. But the basics of all areas of science can be developed in the early childhood years.

With guidance, children learn about botany as they sow seeds, eat plants, pull weeds, and smell flowers. They learn about zoology as they observe animals at the zoo, feed a puppy, hold a snake, and bury a goldfish. They learn about physics as they try to lift a heavier friend on the other end of the teeter-totter, observe the gears in a clock, watch someone jack up the family car, throw balls at targets, and feel the heat of a city sidewalk. They learn about chemistry as they watch sugar disappear in lemonade and feel the fizz when they place lozenges in their mouths. They learn about geology as they fill their pockets with stones, find fossils in rocks, pour water on sand, and mark the sidewalk with a rock. They learn about astronomy as they observe the sun, the moon, the stars, and the seasons.

The rule for planning a balanced science program for early childhood is simple: Do not try to teach children concepts about phenomena that cannot be touched, tasted, seen, or heard. If children cannot explore a concept through real materials, then the concept is too abstract and is not appropriate for the early childhood years. Children develop concepts over many experiences and explorations.

Vygotsky (1962) supports this notion, stating that "practical experience . . . shows that direct teaching of concepts is impossible and fruitless. A teacher who tries to do this usually accomplishes nothing but empty verbalism, a parrotlike repetition of words" (p. 83). Howe (1993) agrees: "The effort to teach concepts that are not accessible to children through their own experience and thinking is inappropriate in preschool and the primary grades" (p. 232).

Electricity is an example of a topic often presented in early childhood classrooms. However, the outcomes of experiences involving electricity usually reflect the child's preoperational thinking and often are not what is expected when the experiences are planned. Usually, children are supplied with batteries, small bulbs, and wires. The goal is to attach the wire to the battery and light the bulb. The expected outcomes are that children will develop an understanding that electricity is energy and that energy can be stored in a battery, channeled through a conduit (the wire), and released as the bulb lights.

What usually happens is that the teacher must verbalize these concepts. The children may learn to repeat them, but their explanations of why the bulb lights up include that "It wants to light up," that "It lights up because we want light," or that "It is magic." Electricity is a very abstract concept; even when children can be active in attaching the wires to the battery, what they learn from manipulating the objects is rarely what teachers expect them to learn. Unless an abstract concept can be made concrete, it is not appropriate for study by young children.

In planning experiences that will help children develop concepts, teachers must also examine the materials they select to make sure that the concepts children learn with them are not erroneous. For example, if all the tall containers in the water play area hold more than the short containers, children might assume that tall containers always hold more. The same sort of erroneous reasoning might result if children who are exploring floating and sinking find that all the materials that float are small and all the ones that sink are large (Benham et al. 1982).

A science program, like a math program, consists of the children's everyday experiences supplemented by some planned experiences that will spark their interest and help them explore new materials and objects. Children's everyday observations will make them aware of what happens to milk when a carton is inadvertently left out overnight; to a carrot when it is left out in the room for a few days; to the volume of rice when it is cooked; to water left outdoors on a freezing night; to a snowball when it is brought into the classroom; and so on.

Planned experiences to supplement these observations require some preparation by the teacher. Planned experiences might involve bringing various animals into the classroom; bringing in assortments of natural materials for sorting and classifying; or providing levers and gears for children to explore. In each case, the teacher should help the children observe, hypothesize, collect data, and draw conclusions. A balanced science program, then, includes both types of experiences and activities to help develop concepts in the life sciences, physical sciences, and earth sciences.

In addition to thinking about the concepts that are appropriate for children to learn, teachers who are planning for science experiences must provide an environment that is safe for exploration, teach children how to explore and investigate safely, and encourage them to enjoy science and learn some basic concepts and attitudes that are not specific to any one experience.

Providing a Safe Environment

It is the responsibility of the teacher to examine the environment for any hazards to young children. As children mature and become more skillful, safety rules may change. Here are some general safety rules:

1. Equipment should be sturdy and in good repair. Although glass may be the best choice for some activities (such as making an aquarium), most materials provided for the children should be unbreakable. Metal materials should not have torn places or rough edges. Tubs and bins should not be cracked or torn.
2. Use of all heat sources should be well supervised. All electric outlets should have safety covers; electric cords should be taped against walls.
3. Plants in the classroom should be nonpoisonous.
4. Tubs and pools of water should be closely supervised.
5. Tools such as knives and hammers should be in good condition, and their use should be supervised carefully.

Teaching Children to Explore and Investigate Safely

Once the environment has been made safe, teachers need to think about rules to help children safely explore materials, objects, animals, and plants. These general guidelines will help ensure safe explorations:

1. No material should be tasted or eaten unless the children know that it is edible or safe to taste. If, for example, the teacher provides powder for the children to explore, children must be taught not to taste the powder without instruction to do so. Children should be taught never to taste any unfamiliar substance.

2. Plants also should not be tasted or eaten unless the children know what they are or an adult says they are safe to eat. For instance, children should never eat leaves, berries, or roots unless they know they are safe. Children should be aware of safety precautions even when eating commercially obtained foods.

3. Children should be taught how to smell any unfamiliar substance. A child who plunges his face into a container could irritate his eyes or nose. Teachers can demonstrate how to hold and sniff any substance without danger of inhaling the substance or burning membranes.

4. Children should be taught not to touch or handle unknown animals. Every child should know not to touch wild animals and how to hold any pet or classroom animal without hurting or frightening it.

The art is in teaching children to be properly cautious without dimming their enthusiasm. Teachers should make sure that children understand the necessity for these precautions while encouraging safe explorations and discoveries.

Encouraging Children to Enjoy Science

Children delight in their scientific discoveries. They may be cautious about touching a toad for the first time, but once they have, they will not be able to wait to share that experience with their families. Teachers of young children may need to relearn some attitudes about science themselves in order to enjoy and guide children's explorations.

Science should be nonbiased. Many adults feel that science is more appropriate for boys than for girls. In fact, all children should be encouraged to participate in a variety of activities and their interests should be respected, regardless of their sex or socioeconomic status. Children involved in a science-based curriculum gain observation skills and classification skills. They may also be encouraged to pursue careers in science. This encouragement is especially important for girls and children from ethnic and cultural minorities, who continue to be underrepresented in the science professions.

Science can be the hub around which other learning experiences are organized. One first grader refused to read about hats and bears in his basal reader but would struggle to read anything about science. He dictated the following story:

> I like science. I'll tell about science. If you want to know about making sparklers. You need some aluminum filings and you need charcoal powder. You need sulfur and potassium nitrate. You buy these things at a pharmacy. You mix all these chemicals together to make sparklers. You put the stuff on wires like those in plant holders. You wait a night and a day.

Parents AND Science

■ Invite parents whose work involves science or technology to visit the classroom and describe what they do. If possible, arrange worksite visits (Sprung 1996).

WWW

This boy's story illustrates the interest many children have in learning about the world and the importance of building curriculum experiences around those interests. The point is not to make sparklers but to build on children's interests while teaching them literacy and other skills.

"Messing about" can be extremely important in developing scientific concepts. Not everything about science is neat and tidy. Sometimes, children's explorations do not end with neat answers. When a four-year-old beats the soap bubbles in a tub of water with a rotary beater until they get smaller and smaller, she doesn't necessarily come up with answers about how the bubbles get smaller, but her curiosity to try things out is sustained. Many discoveries have been made when specific outcomes were not planned.

Finally, teachers must be flexible in planning so that unexpected events can be appreciated. If a child brings in a pet iguana, the teacher should be able to leave his carefully planned study of tree rings for another day.

Teaching Basic Concepts and Attitudes

Basic concepts and attitudes are important as children learn about science:

- *Conservation*—Children should begin learning early about the importance of conserving the world's limited resources. Most of this teaching can be done through modeling. For example, teachers should arrange for children to wash vegetables in a pan of water rather than under running water. By recycling all paper used in the classroom, teachers will help children learn not to waste paper. Lights should be turned off when they are not needed. Food should be used only to eat; use junk for printing, rather than potatoes or other vegetables. Collages can be made with inedible weeds rather than edible seeds (Holt 1989).

- *Respect for life*—Teachers can help children learn to respect life and not destroy it. For example, insects and spiders can be captured and released outdoors, rather than killed. Care should be taken that proper food and habitats are provided for any animal visitor to the classroom.

- **Respect for the environment**—Children can become aware of pollution, including litter. They can be taught not to litter and to recycle the materials used in the classroom.

Planning the Sequence of Activities

Kamii and DeVries (1993) have outlined some principles to follow in planning activities through which children can develop physical and logico-mathematical understandings. They suggest that teachers consider various levels of acting on objects when selecting activities:

- **Acting on objects to see how they react**—Young children engage in actions such as rolling, squeezing, and pushing objects. Teachers can ask children what will happen if they squeeze an object and so on.

- **Acting on objects to produce desired effects**—Children also act on objects not simply to explore them but intentionally to make things happen. They may pour the milk from their cup onto the high chair tray so they can splash it. The teacher might ask children to blow on a spool to move it across the floor and so on.

- **Becoming aware of how an effect is produced**—Many children can produce effects without knowing how they achieved the results. The teacher might ask a child to tell someone else how an effect was achieved. If the child is unable to do so, the teacher will know that the request was inappropriate for the child's level of development.

- **Explaining causes**—Most young children cannot explain the causes of many effects that they observe and should not be asked to give explanations.

Introducing the Activity

- **Principle I**—The teacher should introduce the activity in a way that maximizes children's initiative. An activity can be introduced by putting out material to which children will naturally gravitate; by presenting the material and telling them, "See what you can think of to do with these things"; or by proposing a specific problem to be solved with the materials.

- **Principle II**—The teacher should begin with parallel play. Because teachers want children to do things with materials, they must make sure that each child has her own materials. (If, however, several children want to play together, they should of course be encouraged to help one another with questions, comparisons, and so on.)

During the Activity

- **Principle I**—The teacher should figure out what the child is thinking and respond sparingly in his terms. Figuring out what the child is thinking is sometimes quite difficult. The teacher may get clues from the child's actions or from his questions. The direction to "respond sparingly" may force the teacher to drop his own agenda and follow the child's, at least for the time being. Teachers can help children with practical problems to facilitate experimentation and observation, offer materials to encourage comparisons, or model new comparisons.

- **Principle II**—The teacher should encourage children to interact with other children.

- **Principle III**—The teacher should offer the child activities that increase her physical knowledge and that exercise her current social, moral, and motor abilities.

After the Activity

Teachers should encourage children to reflect on activities briefly after they have been completed. This can be accomplished through questions about what they did, the results of what they did, what they noticed, what other children did, the problems they encountered, and so on. The point is not to get all children to arrive at one right answer but to allow children to think about what they did.

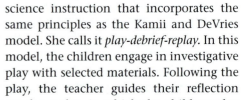

Parents AND Science

- Invite parents to observe their children engaged in play activities with science content. Provide parents with a checklist of the science processes to help them recognize these processes while watching the children play.

Wasserman (1988) describes a model for science instruction that incorporates the same principles as the Kamii and DeVries model. She calls it *play-debrief-replay.* In this model, the children engage in investigative play with selected materials. Following the play, the teacher guides their reflection through questions and sets the stage for replay, in which the children play with the same materials again, either to duplicate their previous results or to explore further.

An example of these principles in action might be a bubble-blowing activity for young children. Because most children are fascinated by bubbles, just making the materials available will be motivational. To begin, each child should have his own bubble wand and access to bubble solution. As the children blow bubbles, the teacher should try to get them to think about the force needed to make bubbles. After a time, the teacher should offer the children bubble wands that are not round but square, triangular, or rectangular and perhaps of different sizes, as well. The children should be guided to observe the sizes and shapes of the bubbles blown with different wands and then to draw conclusions about those observations. To follow up, the children might make bubbles again but be encouraged to find different materials to use in the bubble solution—their hands, cheesecloth, and so on. In this replay activity, the children can apply what they learned from the first bubble activity.

An example of a play-debrief-replay scenario with primary-grade children might involve mechanics. Children could be invited to take apart an old toaster and observe the mechanical parts. As they worked, the teacher would

Science education is an often neglected portion of the curriculum in elementary school, particularly during the primary grades. If science is taught, it is often reduced to a compilation of facts that are not meaningful to a young child. This shortchanges both the students and their teachers. If teachers would take a meaningful learning approach to science, they would be able to tap into children's natural curiosity about their surrounding world. One way to accomplish this would be by integrating science and literacy.

Studies with literacy have shown that if reading can be related to a child's everyday life, it becomes more meaningful for the child, as he understands its practical use and is eager to gain a skill he sees adults use daily (Goodman 1986; Purcell-Gates 1996; Roskos and Neuman 1994; Strickland 1990). Teachers already use ideas such as mock post offices and student book creations to make literacy more meaningful. Teachers could also use science, such as the recording of data from simple experiments, to emphasize literacy as a useful tool in yet another area. Using the natural world to teach science would make young students aware that typical student questions such as "Why is the sky blue?" are the types of questions "real" scientists ask. If more meaningful science were incorporated into the curriculum, students would view science as a way to satisfy their curiosity and answer their questions about the natural world. Thus, rather than viewing science as a difficult, unfriendly subject consisting of a sterile, impractical collection of facts, students might have a more positive attitude toward it.

The teachers are the primary gatekeepers of early childhood education. In order to achieve a meaningful learning approach, teachers must be willing to include science in their curriculum. While early childhood educators have many choices in their curricula, two constants remain: literacy and math education. It would seem ideal if early childhood educators could be persuaded to integrate science into either their math or literacy curricula. For instance, the literacy program could gain meaning through the integration of science, and the children would be exposed to a vital topic that will continue to impact their lives through high school and beyond.

try to determine what they were thinking about how the machine worked. After the children had a chance to examine the materials carefully, the teacher could provide other levers, springs, and gears for investigation. After reflection on the activity, the children could play with the materials again and perhaps invent their own simple machines.

A similar line of thinking led Dever and Hobbs (1998) to describe the sequence of activities in science as the *learning spiral*. This spiral begins with engagement followed by investigation, sharing, and assessing. To illustrate this approach, the authors brought in stuffed owls and allowed the children to explore the owls and develop questions that they wanted to answer. As the children developed the questions, they were guided by teachers and peers in finding the answers. They then found ways to share their answers with the other children. Assessment was ongoing, as teachers noted children's prior knowledge about owls and observed their applications of literacy and math skills during the investigation and sharing experiences. The authors found that the children's knowledge of content (owls) increased along with their skills in other areas, such as reading, writing, and problem solving. The keys to this approach are to provide interesting objects for engagement and then to guide individual children in investigating. The sharing experiences should help the children organize and consolidate their knowledge.

Additional criteria for selecting science activities come from Jeffries (1999). She suggests that teachers evaluate activities in terms of the interest and enjoyment they will evoke from children, their relevance to the children's experiences, the degree to which they involve the senses, the extent to which they encourage connections and active learning, and their ability to promote inquiry.

Finally, teachers should keep in mind that not every child has to participate in every experience. Children should be allowed to choose those elements of an experience that are of interest to them or to choose another experience entirely. They can learn the same basic scientific skills from many different experiences.

Suggestions for Experiences in the Classroom

Many science experiences can also be labeled math, art, or language arts experiences. In reading the following suggestions for appropriate science activities, keep in mind the discussion of an integrated model of curriculum in Chapter 4 and remember that science should not be separated from ongoing classroom experiences.

Life Sciences

The NSE standards for the life sciences include these goals for content knowledge:

- *The characteristics of organisms*
- *The life cycles of organisms*
- *Organisms and environments* (Rakow and Bell 1998)

In a constructivist classroom, the teacher's role in helping children connect with nature will not be exactly the same as it is in teaching the earth sciences or physical sciences. In those areas, the teacher may provide the children with materials and time so they can experiment in order to find answers to their questions. But as Chaille and Britain (1991) remind us, such experimentation is not possible with most questions about the natural world. Children cannot be allowed to experiment in ways that may harm other creatures, even if doing so will answer their questions.

Therefore, to help children learn about the natural world, the teacher will assist them in active observation, model respect for all living creatures, and serve as a resource person in answering questions. Wilson (1995) suggests

This kindergartner is practicing a skill that is important in the life sciences: observing a living being!

bringing nature into the classroom. Adding materials in learning centers and taking children outdoors as often as possible (but with a focus on the beauty and wonder of nature, not in naming every plant and animal) are two ways of helping children gain appreciation for the natural world.

Threes and Fours

Science experiences for three- and four-year-olds should be playful. Teachers should be alert to the discoveries that children are making as they play and should be ready to guide the children's thinking as they participate in the following kinds of activities:

- Observing animals—Small animals that can be held are ideal, such as rabbits, guinea pigs, and snakes. Teachers may want animals to visit for short periods of time rather than be permanent residents. Fish, birds, insects, spiders, and reptiles are also interesting to children.
- Observing simple ant farms or beehives—Some schools have specially prepared beehives that attach to windows so that children can observe the bees safely from inside the room.
- Observing spiderwebs, bird nests, or other animal homes
- Providing some care for classroom pets, such as feeding the fish or filling the rabbit's water container
- Collecting and observing tadpoles from the local pond
- Observing the life cycles of butterflies or moths
- Examining the different textures found in natural items such as tree bark
- Sprouting sweet potatoes, pineapple and carrot tops, grapefruit or orange seeds, and so on—With care (and a little luck), the children may actually be able to eat the results of their work.

Fives and Sixes

Science experiences for five- and six-year-olds should continue to be based primarily on play experiences. Teachers will want to record or encourage children to record their discoveries on charts and in reports. Many print materials can be provided to extend children's interests in science topics, and more planned experiences are appropriate as children mature. Activities for fives and sixes can include the following:

- Making a collection of seeds to sort—Most seeds sold commercially are treated with substances that are poisonous when ingested, so if the class uses commercially prepared seeds, the teacher should ensure that children do not put them in their mouths and that they wash their hands carefully after handling the seeds.

- Conducting an ongoing study of animals—During the course of the year, many different animals can be introduced into the classroom: hamsters, goldfish, lizards, gerbils, crayfish, turtles, garter snakes, and land snails. With some guidance (and some good library resources), children can help construct habitats for these animals, study their life cycles, and focus reading and writing experiences around these visitors. Teachers are cautioned not to use a human family analogy when studying animals. The animals should be referred to as "male" and "female" rather than as "Mommy" and "Daddy." If a family analogy is used and the male gerbil eats the offspring, the teacher will have some explaining to do about what daddies do! The important concepts that children should learn are that it takes a male and female of the same species to produce offspring, that the amount of care animals provide for their young varies, and that each animal needs food, water, and protection in order to survive.

- Starting and maintaining a class garden—If creating one is possible, a garden plot outdoors is ideal. If weather and space limit outside gardening options, an inside garden can be planted in tubs or old wading pools. Children can help prepare the garden with pebbles or sand for drainage, soil for planting, and organic material for fertilizer. Children can learn about appropriate plants, plant seeds, and sprouts and care for the plants. They can also cook and eat the products of a garden.

- Conducting an intensive study of the life cycles of selected insects or amphibians—To learn about life cycles, children might study silkworms, butterflies, moths, frogs, or other creatures. The life cycles must be readily observable in the classroom so that children can record changes and keep scientific records of the stages.

- Hatching eggs—Many classrooms hatch eggs in the spring. Ideally, eggs should be hatched by a mother hen at school, but an incubator is the next best choice. Hatching eggs can stimulate many reading and writing projects. Children can describe the development of the embryo or care of the eggs. Teachers should keep in mind that no hatching experiences should be undertaken without planning for what will be done with the baby animals after they have been hatched. It is not appropriate to teach children that life is expendable.

■ Making collections of natural materials for sorting and classifying, such as leaves, pinecones, and seashells—What to choose depends on the environment and the children's experiences. Print materials such as posters, books, and magazines can be added to displays of natural materials, and experiences can be extended from these collections.

■ Building a bug—After they have observed insects, ask children to choose material (clay, paper, cardboard, wire, pipe cleaners, and so on) to build an insect of their choice. Provide a field guide of insects to help them. "The goal is not for the child to create a scientifically accurate rendering of the insect, but to construct the insect as he or she sees it, to internalize how it fits together, which features are important, and how the parts relate to the whole" (Danoff-Burg 2002, p. 44–45).

■ Extending play experiences—Ross (2000) suggests activities built on children's play experience, such as a disassembly line, a windy day party, a digging experience, and playing with roly-polies.

Sevens and Eights

Experiences for sevens and eights should continue to be based on their interests and their home and school environments. More of their experiences should involve experimenting and employing the scientific process. Activities for children of this age include the following:

■ Studying plants—Children might learn the names and purposes of parts of plants and seeds and experiment with different conditions for sprouting seeds and growing plants while controlling environmental elements (light, soil conditions, amount of water, and so on). The teacher could introduce children to some plants that are not green (fungi, mushrooms) and plants that reproduce without seeds (ferns).

Parents AND Science

■ Prepare a set of activities based on kitchen science (things to do with common kitchen materials) or backyard science (things to do in the backyard or park) that can be sent home with children periodically.

WWW

■ Studying the characteristics of different animals and performing classifications based on these characteristics—Rule and Barrera (1999) found that examining collections in object boxes helped children understand the characteristics used to classify each set of items. For example, the class collected several boxes of bird-related materials. One was a collection of tools that students could compare to bird beaks, another was a set of cards of bird pictures and objects related to their food, and another was a collection of bird shapes or representations (toys, baskets, and so on) that could be matched to a set of descriptive adjectives.

- Studying birds in the local environment—Activities might focus on adaptations in feet, bills, wings, and so on to meet environmental demands and on the place of birds in ecosystems.

Physical Sciences

The value of children learning the physical sciences comes not from memorizing specific concepts and facts but from having opportunities "to act on objects and see how objects react—to build the foundation for physics and chemistry" (Kamii and DeVries 1993, p. 12). For young children, activities in physics should meet these criteria:

1. *Children must be able to produce the movement by their own action.*
2. *Children must be able to vary their action.*
3. *The reaction of the object must be observable.*
4. *The reaction of the object must be immediate.* (Marxen 1995, p. 213)

The NSE standards for content knowledge in the physical sciences include the following:

- *Properties of objects and materials*
- *Position and motion of objects*
- *Light, heat, electricity, and magnetism* (Rakow and Bell 1998)

Threes and Fours

Physical science experiences, like all school experiences for very young children, must be based on play experiences and everyday classroom activities. Some possibilities include the following:

- Manipulating modeling clay and observing its properties—Can it be rolled? stretched? pushed? Children can compare the properties of Silly Putty and Play Doh to those of clay.
- Using pull toys with removable wheels to discover the difference between moving toys with wheels and moving toys without them
- Painting with tempera paints—Children can observe how paint drips and runs, what consistencies paints have, and how colors mix.
- Playing with water—Teachers should provide a variety of containers, tubes, funnels, and so on for explorations with water (Bird 1983).
- Playing with blocks—Children learn about gravity, balance, and support as they build structures.
- Blowing activities with straws—Children can explore wind and air pressure (blowing) as forces to move different objects.
- Rolling balls toward targets from various distances and angles (Kamii and DeVries 1978)

- Using rollers and boards for moving materials, balancing themselves, and so on (Kamii and DeVries 1978)
- Observing light and shadows—Very young children often believe that shadows are parts of the objects that cast them. Activities need not include technical explanations of shadows.

Fives and Sixes

Teachers of fives and sixes can begin to introduce some activities to help the children develop specific concepts and can extend their experiences through reading and writing tasks. Children might share some of what they learn orally as a way of evaluating their daily activities in addition to recording some of their discoveries in their journals. The following activities are appropriate for this age group:

- Playing with water—Children can explore floating and sinking with a variety of materials. They can sort the materials into categories and then try to modify the materials that float so that they sink and vice versa. Modifications might include adding materials or making boats out of different materials.
- Moving objects across water by blowing on them through straws—Children can have races (Kamii and DeVries 1978).
- Blowing bubbles—Children can mix and compare bubble solutions and record the best mixtures. They can also experiment by dipping different shapes into bubble solutions and record their findings (shapes of bubbles, which bubbles last longer, which shapes produce the most bubbles, and so on).
- Finding gears, levers, and planes in the environment—Children can take apart old appliances to examine their parts.

This teacher is using an engaging, hands-on experiment to explain the concept of solids and liquids to these first graders.

- Learning about clamps, vises, and levers at the woodworking table (Schiller and Townsend 1985)
- Creating elevators during block play; using pulleys
- Experimenting with different weights in different positions on balance scales or teeter-totters
- Experimenting with sound using different materials and different ways of vibrating the materials
- Controlling the variables for some physical changes in matter—Is there a way to make ice or snow melt faster or water evaporate more quickly?
- Making paper airplanes and paper helicopters—Do different folds in the paper produce different results?
- Cooking—Children can observe changes in matter (melting, hardening, expanding, shrinking, and so on).

Sevens and Eights

The physical science exploration of sevens and eights can be extended by reading and writing tasks associated with keeping careful records and recording discoveries:

- Playing with water—Experiences should be extended to exploring the properties of water and beginning activities that focus on water cycles. Children can record the results of rate-of-flow experiments on sand in the sandbox or changes in evaporation rates of water and other liquids.
- Dissolving and heating substances—Children can observe different reactions of matter by finding substances that dissolve in water or testing the effects of heat and cold on different materials.
- Changing states of matter (solid, liquid, vapor)—Children can observe matter in these states, record their observations, and form hypotheses about the causes of the changes.
- Inventing machines—Children can invent machines using gears, levers, inclined planes, or pulleys. Kuehn (1988) suggests that humorous inventions (balloon poppers, dog feeders, and so on) are appropriate because the children learn invention strategies without having to produce serious machines.
- Exploring magnets—Children can explore magnets by creating structures with magnetic building pieces and testing which materials will or will not be attracted by magnets. They can also explore magnetic forces using different materials: Will iron filings be attracted through paper? plastic? wood? thin metal? (Harlan 1980).
- Studying sources of light and shadows—Children can measure the shadows of the same object at different times of day and record the results. Children can also create shadow plays or make silhouettes from shadows of children.

- Cooking experiences—More complex activities are appropriate, during which children can explore the reactions of different combinations of ingredients, temperatures, or other conditions of cooking. An example is separating biscuit dough into two portions, adding baking powder to one portion only, and then cooking and comparing the two portions.

Earth/Space Sciences

The NSE standards for content knowledge in the earth/space sciences include the following:

- *Properties of earth materials*
- *Objects in the sky*
- *Changes in the earth and sky* (Rakow and Bell 1998)

Threes and Fours

As in other areas of science, basic concepts of scientific thinking about the earth and space are developed while young children play. For threes and fours, such concepts are developed when they play with different mixtures of sand and water and different textures and colors of sand; observe rain, snow, or other precipitation; or watch snow melt or water freeze or evaporate.

Fives and Sixes

Earth/space science experiences for fives and sixes might include these activities:

- Classifying rocks by size, shape, color, density, and hardness—Children can experiment with rocks by scratching them with nails, using eye droppers to drop vinegar on their surfaces, weighing rocks of approximately equal size, chipping rocks with a rock pick (if safety goggles are supplied), or comparing polished and unpolished rocks of the same kind. The teacher can read *Everybody Needs a Rock* (Baylor 1974).

- Making simple maps of the school property that show all the different surface coverings (grass, asphalt, gravel, and so on)

- Examining the different compositions of soil collected in the children's yards or from different places on the schoolgrounds—Are there differences in color, smell, and texture? What happens when water is added? Children can put each sample through a screen and compare what they find or plant seeds in each sample and record the results.

- Recording weather daily over the course of the year—What is the most common type of weather in any given month? Some children may be able to start taking some weather measurements with a large thermometer, a wind sock, and a rain gauge.

- Observing the change of seasons by noting the weather, plants, and animals in the local environment during each season

- Exploring the wind with kites, pinwheels, bubbles, and their own bodies

Think about what you have read and what you have experienced in regard to science instruction as you reflect on these questions:

NAEYC

- What elements of a science program are essential for DAP? Why?

- In comparison to traditional science programs, will developmentally appropriate programs produce more people who are scientifically literate? Why or why not?

- Why are some teachers more successful at traditional science instruction than others? Is it motivation? intelligence? experience? Are any of the reasons for that success relevant to developmentally appropriate practice? If so, how?

- Should learning scientific facts ever be part of a developmentally appropriate program? If so, for what age group?

Sevens and Eights

The following activities are appropriate for seven- and eight-year-old children:

- Learning about air and air pressure through experiments such as blowing up balloons, creating bubbles in water, or moving materials with air

- Observing the weather—A simple weather station allows children to take their own measurements and record them. Weather studies can be extended into a study of light, air, wind, and clouds (Huffman 1996).

- Becoming familiar with the relationship of the earth, the moon, and the sun—Children might make models or observe the position of the moon in the sky for one complete phase.

- Learning about land features in the region—Children might observe land features such as ponds, lakes, mountains, rivers, and deserts and study the characteristics of these features as habitats for people and animals.

- Comparing temperatures in full sun and in the shade, holding other conditions constant

- Placing different materials in the sun and measuring their temperatures to begin understanding the differential heat absorption rates of different materials

- Learning about gardening—Invite a guest whose hobby is gardening to talk about plants and gardening techniques suitable for the area.

- Learning from speakers—Write invitations and thank-you letters to speakers. Write reports as a group or as individuals using the information learned.

Other Content Areas

In addition to the three basic content areas of science, the NSE standards include science and technology, science in personal and social perspectives, and the history and nature of science. For young children, the science and technology goals can be met through helping children use technology in their activities and distinguish between natural and human-made objects. The content goals for science in personal and social perspectives can easily be met through experiences focused on personal health and through social studies experiences that help children learn about changes in their environments and changes in populations. To address the standards in the history and nature of science, the children need to learn that science is a human endeavor. This goal can be met by inviting scientists to visit the classroom on a regular basis, by reading biographies of scientists, and by making sure that children are aware of the inventions and discoveries that contribute to their daily lives.

Using Textbooks

Many science programs for primary children are based mainly on materials in textbooks. A more appropriate approach would be to organize science experiences for children and then use science textbooks as resources, much as we would choose other appropriate books to enhance study of a topic. For example, suppose a teacher organizes classroom activities around the topic of insects. If a science textbook included information about insects or photographs that could help children, then it should be used. But students should not study insects simply because the topic is in the textbook, nor should a textbook be regarded as a program of science instruction.

Integrating Science throughout the Day

Science is so much a part of the youngest children's play experiences that teachers rarely need help in integrating science. Teachers of primary children are often required to teach a certain number of minutes of science each day and to document that they have planned and implemented science instruction.

One strategy for meeting the requirements for science instruction while integrating it with the other classroom activities is to plan thematic units that lend themselves to interesting science activities. Many topics that are appropriate for primary children emphasize science. In selecting a topic, the teacher must remember that it should be interesting to both the children and himself, important enough to be taught, and appropriate to the children's level of development and environment. Science topics include trees, fish, birds, patterns, and cycles, among others, as well as the more traditional topics of senses, colors, and seasons.

Science activities for preschool children should be fun, but the teacher should always be ready to guide their learning.

Math and science are so closely related that it is often difficult to label activities as "math" or "science." For example, seriation activities may help children construct both scientific and mathematical concepts. Pearlman and Pericak-Spector (1994) suggest that learning about seriation should involve much more than ordering items by length. Activities should be provided that have children seriate by width, size, and thickness; by color; by texture; by sound; and by taste. Children with more experience in seriating can order a set of rubber bands by the pitch each produces when twanged or a set of containers by the estimated volume each holds. Measurement is another area in which science and math overlap. Children can explore materials and quantities that will balance on a double-pan scale or the volume of a given amount of popped corn and the amount of water needed to fill the spaces around it in a container (Lehman 1994).

Clearly, any topic in science can be expanded by reading and writing experiences that are real and meaningful to the children. Science experiences can also be extensions of literature experiences. Butzow and Butzow (1988) argue that scientific and technological literacy are becoming increasingly important and that the issues related to science and technology should be introduced early in a child's experience. Many issues can be introduced through literature experiences, and follow-up activities can be planned to help children gain information and develop problem-solving skills along with increasing literacy skills.

The Reading–Writing Connection

Because most children find science such an interesting topic of study, science plays an important role as a unifying topic for literacy experiences. Children can increase their literacy skills in the process of learning about science topics. For example, consider the activity mentioned earlier, in which children were growing plants in soda bottles. As they make observations of their plants, the children can keep journals to record what happens to their plants each day. These journals serve as authentic reasons for engaging in literacy experiences. Children could participate in any number of literacy activities based on the topic of plants.

Children should also be encouraged to write about science in ways other than recording experiments. Again, having children keep science journals allows them to record their findings and discoveries with pictures and text. For example, children might write narratives explaining how an orange molded or how a carrot dried up when left out long enough. Feely (1993) suggests that children should write procedural texts (how to do something) and explanations (how something works) and draw accompanying flowcharts. They can also create word webs, concept webs, and KWL charts. (A KWL chart lists what children Know about a topic, What they want to learn, and, when the study is completed, what they Learned [Ogle 1989].)

Rillero, Cleland, and Conzelman (1999) found that writing haiku poetry helped children increase their observation skills. A *haiku* is by definition about nature, and careful observation is required in order to write such a poem. These authors note that the typical 5-7-5 syllable pattern of haiku should not be the emphasis of the writing experience; instead, the description of nature should be the focus of the children's efforts. Another popular form of structured poetry, called a *cinquain,* is also useful in encouraging children to express what they know in a poetic form. A cinquain follows this pattern:

First line: Two syllables announcing the topic (A cinquain usually has no title)

Second line: Two adjectives that describe the topic

Third line: Three action words that are associated with the topic (*-ing* words)

Fourth line: Four words that express a feeling about the topic

Fifth line: A synonym for the topic word

And here is a sample cinquain:

Tadpole
Soft, translucent
Swimming, growing, changing
Can live in water
Baby frog

Teachers should also make use of the variety of children's information books that are available. In fact, it is difficult to imagine a scientific topic that children would study for which no such books could be found. Books can be used to introduce a topic, to expand children's knowledge of it, and to aid children in consolidating

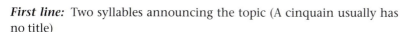

Parents AND Science

- Some teachers have been successful in using a "science backpack" that children take home on a rotating basis. The backpack contains a letter explaining the purpose of the activity, an information book and perhaps a narrative story that are related to the activity, and all the materials necessary for completing the activity (Kokoski and Downing-Leffler 1995; Patton and Kokoski 1996).

➤ Learn about the systems of the body (digestive, pulmonary, circulatory, skeletal, reproductive).

➤ Learn the names of body parts and their functions.

➤ Demonstrate how a muscle can move a bone.

➤ Learn about the chemical composition of the human body.

➤ Examine a hair, a fingernail clipping, or a fingerprint under a microscope. Compare hair from two different people.

➤ Create a set of fingerprints for each child and compare them. How are the police able to use fingerprints to identify who touched something at a crime scene?

➤ Bones: Invite a radiologist to bring an X ray of a bone and explain how an X ray is taken. Ask the butcher shop to slice up a leg bone from a cow so that children can examine how a bone is constructed.

➤ Find out how many jobs in your community are directly connected to science. Invite several scientists from different fields to speak to the class about their work.

➤ Ask children to find three objects in their homes that are the result of scientific studies. Compile a list for the class.

---

their knowledge. For example, to interest children in spiders, the teacher could read *Spiders Spin Webs* (Winer 1998). As the study continued, the teacher might want to read *Spectacular Spiders* (Glaser 1998), and reading *Spiders Near and Far* (Dewey 1992) might be useful to help children recall what they know. (Winer's book contains lists of books and websites about spiders that can be accessed through the publisher's web page.)

Read-alouds of books with science content can be interesting and informative, and many good information books are available. Each year, a committee from the National Science Teachers Association selects outstanding science trade books and publishes the list in the journal *Science and Children*. These books are judged for content, illustration, and presentation for the intended audience. They are listed by category, and the NSE standards that could be addressed when using each book in the classroom are indicated. The books are also labeled to indicate the grade levels for which they would be appropriate.

Language is important when learning science. Owens (1999) suggests that children need to have experiences to talk about, to trust that adults will not laugh at their incomplete ideas, and "blocks of time to devote to wondering about their world without adult constraints concerning subject matter, curricular areas of study, or the mastery of factual content" (p. 7). In other words, children need interesting things to do, the time to talk about them with their peers and with adults who value their ideas, and the freedom to follow their own interests without adults telling them what to do. Children will learn science in such an environment!

Children with Special Needs

Some adaptations of materials may be necessary to help children with disabilities develop concepts in science—for instance:

- Helping children with visual impairments sort and classify objects using tactile cues
- Helping children with hearing impairments experience sound through tactile means—For example, children can feel the vibrations of tuning forks, guitar strings, and rubber bands stretched across cigar boxes.
- Arranging materials so that children with physical disabilities can work with them easily and as independently as possible

As in other areas of study, teachers will want all children to participate fully and will adapt materials when necessary to make that possible. "Multisensory instruction with a variety of activities provides the experiential background necessary for concept formation for all students. It also allows students with sensory limitations to profit from more activities" (Cain and Evans 1984, p. 233).

Multisensory activities are also appropriate for children who are gifted. Follis and Krockover (1982) recommend that programs for such children be discovery based and designed to foster independent learning. Teachers of children who are gifted must be careful not to emphasize the verbal facility of these children so much that they fail to involve them in manipulative learning experiences.

Celebrating Diversity

Teachers should be sure to include the contributions of various cultures when they discuss inventions and materials that make everyone's lives safer and more pleasant. When visitors are invited to the classroom to demonstrate or talk about science, they should not all be white males. Children need to know that people from both genders and all ethnic and cultural groups have contributed to the world's storehouse of scientific knowledge.

In addition, teachers should make sure they know enough about the cultures of students in their classrooms that they do not engage the students in activities that will be offensive. For example, people from some cultures would find playing with cornmeal on a sand table offensive. Others would be disturbed by studies of plants or animals that have symbolic meanings in their particular cultures. The key is to understand the various communities of the children well enough to avoid offending them.

Chapter Summary

- Science *is* process, thinking, and an attitude of curiosity and interest in the world. Science *is not* memorizing facts and formulas.

- The scientific process is a cycle that includes forming hypotheses, collecting data, confirming or rejecting the hypotheses, making generalizations, and repeating the cycle. Process skills for young children include observing, classifying, comparing, measuring, communicating, and experimenting. Other process skills that are used less often by young children include relating, inferring, and applying.

- One goal of science instruction is to get children actively involved in exploring and manipulating a variety of materials or phenomena. Other goals include helping children acquire factual knowledge and encouraging their curiosity and interest.

- A balanced science program includes the everyday, playful activities of children that can lead to scientific understandings as well as experiences planned by the teacher. Science instruction should include activities that focus on the life sciences, physical sciences, and earth/space sciences.

- The National Science Education (NSE) standards are an invaluable resource in planning a program of science instruction that meets the needs of young children. Following the standards will en-

sure that all areas of scientific learning will be addressed in the program.

- Concepts in science must be constructed by the learner. Very little knowledge in science can be simply transmitted from teacher to learner.

- Teachers planning science experiences must provide a safe environment for exploration, must help children learn to investigate safely, and must help children enjoy science.

- Topics in science can easily be extended to promote literacy by having children create and read charts, reports, journals, and literature.

- Most topics in science can be the focus of a thematic organization; classroom experiences in all subject-matter areas can revolve around the science topic.

- Children with special needs can benefit from a multisensory, hands-on approach to teaching science. Teachers may have to make minor adaptations in materials to meet the needs of special learners.

- Children should be provided with examples of the work of scientists from many cultures to help illustrate the contributions these people have made to our daily lives. Teachers should ensure that no activities will be offensive to the cultural groups represented in the classroom.

Theory INTO Practice

Observe for at least one hour each in a preschool and a primary classroom. Record everything you see that you think is science. With your group, discuss what you observed and why you labeled it "science." Is there agreement about what science is? Explain your answer.

Plan a science experience for a small group of threes and fours, fives and sixes, or sevens and eights. Then use the evaluation criteria on page 383 to review your activity. If it does not meet certain criteria, how can you change your plan to comply?

Plan a theme based on a science topic that would be suitable for preschool or primary children. How have you connected science with social studies, mathematics, and literacy activities? Be specific.

Examine a commercial program for science instruction, and evaluate it using the list of elements that should be included in a constructivist approach (see page 388). Would you use this program in your classroom? Why or why not?

A Teacher Speaks

Pamela Pottle

Happy Valley Elementary School
Bellingham, Washington

Engaging First Graders in Science

According to Webster's *Beginning Dictionary, science* is "Knowledge about things in nature and the universe. Science is based on facts that are learned from experiments and careful study." The first-grade students in my classroom, like many young children, have extensive background knowledge about topics that are of interest to them, such as nature and animals. Young learners are naturally curious, willing to explore, and excited to share what they have discovered. As a teacher of science, I need to ensure how and what children learn about earth science, life science, and physical science is made as concrete as possible.

Several roles come to mind when I think about teaching science. My primary role is to provide a model for how the scientific process works. This process can be modeled through reading, writing, talking, building, and drawing. My goal is to provide my students with opportunities to become scientists themselves.

During our recent study of a wetland located near the school, I identified the process skills of observing, communicating, collecting, and interpreting data in addition to possible inferences my first graders could make based on their learning experience as the desired outcomes of this area of study. Initially, I had the students draw pictures of what they believed a wetland was. This was an assessment sample that helped me see what knowledge my students possessed about wetlands. These illustrations were also posted to create a bulletin board entitled "Is this a wetland?" As the students explored and learned more about wetlands, they replaced their first-impression drawings with realistic drawings reflecting their observations of wetlands.

In order to build opportunities for conversations about the wetlands, I posed this question to my students: *What habitat differences can you find within a wetland?* We took our clipboards on our walk along established trails in order to record our observations. As we discovered a habitat difference, we stopped and discussed what we noticed and wondered about it. Young learners are very skilled at collecting information. My job is to guide them toward interpreting what they have learned to ensure that science is more than just observing and communicating.

We then brought our findings from the walk back to the classroom. I worked with the students to come to some conclusions as to what we noticed about differences in habitats. Having conversations about the differences in habitats led to another question: *How might this habitat support life for certain animals?* I allowed students to explore and create paper models of the animals that might be found in this habitat. At the conclusion of this unit, my students had learned what a wetland actually was and what kinds of life could survive in it.

When I teach science, I try to consider how to make the real world accessible to my first graders' senses. I must take an abstract concept and provide opportunities to see, touch, smell, feel, hear, and do. This allows my students to represent their learning through charts, graphs, illustrations, diagrams, and maps. Once my students have created a picture in their minds, they begin to use the scientific process in a meaningful way.

CHAPTER 13

Encouraging the Creative Arts

- Plan appropriate visual arts experiences for young children.
- Plan appropriate music and movement experiences for young children.
- Plan appropriate dramatic experiences for young children.
- Explain ways to integrate the arts into content-area experiences.
- Plan for collaborating with arts specialists in your building.
- Plan arts experiences for children with special needs.
- Plan arts experiences that celebrate diversity.

Today you visited a first-grade/second-grade combination class with the objective of observing arts instruction. You wanted to know how the classroom teacher incorporated the arts into the daily program and what the specialists at the school did in their classes.

Your observations were very interesting. You saw children painting at easels, cutting paper for illustrating a story they had written, and creating clay objects that were going to be fired and given as gifts. A little later, as the children gathered for story time, they participated in singing several songs. The teacher had the lyrics to these songs printed on large charts, and one child used a pointer to point to the words as they were sung. After reading a story, the teacher encouraged three or four children to spend some time planning what they could do to act out the story on another day.

The teacher worked with the specialists on the staff to select experiences that would enhance topics of study in the classroom. The specialists planned experiences for their time with the children in conjunction with the classroom teachers.

When you met with your peers to debrief your observations, you found that instruction in the arts varied a great deal. For example, in one school there was no art at all because the specialist was responsible for four schools, and each school got only one nine-week period of art per year. Some teachers had been observed teaching children art lessons in perspective following a model in a children's book. In yet another school, the entire curriculum rotated around art experiences.

You have many questions about instruction in the arts and the place of the arts in an early childhood curriculum. Should the classroom teacher plan for art activities, or should the art specialist be responsible for all art instruction? How can participation in the arts be evaluated? When there is so much emphasis on test scores, can a teacher afford the time for the arts?

Importance of Arts Experiences

The arts are vital to a good early childhood program. Who can imagine a program for young children in which there is no music? no painting? no movement or dance? no drama? Children sing and dance and draw as part of their daily lives, whether they are in school or at home. If children are natural participants in the arts, then obviously the arts are important in any program for young children.

The Consortium of National Arts Education Associations (1996) explains the importance of arts education as follows:

- *The arts are worth studying simply because of what they are. Their impact cannot be denied. Throughout history, all the arts have served to connect our imaginations with the deepest questions of human existence. . . .*
- *The arts are used to achieve a multitude of human purposes: to present issues and ideas, to teach or persuade, to entertain, to decorate or please. Becoming literate in the arts helps students understand and do these things better.*
- *The arts are integral to every person's daily life. Our personal, social, economic, and cultural environments are shaped by the arts at every turn. . . .*
- *The arts offer unique sources of enjoyment and refreshment for the imagination. They explore relationships between ideas and objects and serve as links between thought and action. Their continuing gift is to help us see and grasp life in new ways.*
- *The arts help students develop the attitudes, characteristics, and intellectual skills required to participate effectively in today's society and economy. The arts teach self-discipline, reinforce self-esteem, and foster the thinking skills and creativity so valued in the workplace. They teach the importance of teamwork and cooperation. They demonstrate the direct connection between study, hard work, and high levels of achievement.*

An early childhood program would be much the poorer without music, art, and drama.

Definitions of **creativity** vary considerably. For the purposes of this chapter, *creativity* is defined as "the proactive, purposeful impulse to extend beyond the present, characterized by originality, imagination, and fantasy" (Edwards 1990, p. 8). To foster creativity, the teacher of young children must help them express themselves and avoid teaching them that their interpretations of their world are not "correct" or "good." Young children are willing to draw and sing and dance without self-consciousness. They do not worry that the colors they use are not the colors of the things they are representing in real life. Nor do they worry that what they have drawn does not look like what they say it is. They believe in themselves and their abilities. The challenge is to maintain their belief in themselves while working in a group setting.

The arts can serve as an integrating force that helps children make connections with their experiences. The arts help young children put together what they know about topics in science, social studies, health, math, literature,

Art in the Curriculum

There are several approaches to the arts in U.S. schools. First, in the Nurture the Natural approach (see McArdle 2001), arts practice is based on the belief that the child is the center of the program and that most learning should occur through free, playful, spontaneous, and unstructured experiences. Art is valued because it provides opportunities for the child's self-expression of thoughts and feelings, and although it is deemed appropriate for adults to observe children's processes of expression and to gently discuss a child's artwork in order to grasp a deeper understanding and appreciation of the child, to *teach* the child in the arts would be seen as inappropriate, as it could potentially stifle his or her creativity and sense of self. The teacher's role is one of simply providing developmentally appropriate materials and then essentially standing back and letting children's creativity unfold. However, the program can have a tendency to become laissez-faire, and anything that the child creates is considered beautiful, charming, spontaneous, and unique. The negative aspect of this is that children do not learn how to discern and strive for quality within their own arts experiences and are not given any guidance to go beyond their current level of competence.

Second, in the Polish the Product approach (Gardner 1997b; Wright 1997), it is believed that the development of technique and skill is more important than free expression and that creativity and self-expression cannot develop if children don't have adequate mastery of the discipline (i.e., music, dance, drama, art). The ease of full-group instruction can lead to mass-production art activities, such as stencils (e.g., twenty-five identical colored-in green apples), templates (e.g., egg carton caterpillars), and gimmicks (e.g., painting with feather dusters). Music, dance, and drama can become focused almost exclusively on events such as an end-of-year performance, where it is expected that the teachers and children present a product that is as polished as possible. The message to children can be that the works produced by children are not as valued as those provided by adults and that children should look to adults for artistic inspiration rather than find it from within.

Finally, an approach that takes the best from those presented above is the Free the Discipline approach, which brings together both the child's freedom of expression and creativity and his or her artistic mastery and refinement of the discipline. In other words, arts education should integrate both Nature and Polish. What a child is born with should be more than simply nurtured, it should be cultivated. Clearly, children cannot learn without assistance in any of the disciplines, including the arts. Just how much and what type of assistance is the key to good early childhood arts education.

Through the arts, children participate in meaning-making through visual–spatial imagery and the use of the body, and they turn action into representation using the unique symbol systems of the arts—still and moving 2-D and 3-D images; movement, gesture, dance, and dramatization; and the use of the voice, musical instruments, words, and sound effects (Wright 2003). In a Free the Discipline approach, adults assist young children to develop the "grammars" of the arts and the ability to not only create but also "read" or interpret a range of texts—visual, aural, bodily-kinesthetic, spatial, intrapersonal.

and so on. The arts are also important for personalizing education. "There is an increasing awareness among educators that the development of instructional approaches that integrate the student's affect and unique personal experiences with course content can increase student motivation, participation, and learning" (Edwards 1990, p. 5).

As noted in Chapter 2, probably the most discussed early childhood programs in the world in recent years are the preschools of Reggio Emilia in northern Italy. Arts are the major focus of the school experience in these programs, and the curriculum is project based. Projects generally grow out of children's play and interests, although some are initiated by teachers in response to observed needs of the children. Children express what they are learning and observing in their environment through the arts. For example, children might be encouraged to create images of themselves using many different media. These images and the discussions about them might lead to explorations of body movements. The environment is also visually stimulating in ways that encourage pondering, wondering, and remembering.

The goal of these preschools is to enhance children's creative and intellectual development, and the arts are believed to be central to that development (New 1990). Gandini (1993) states that teachers in Reggio Emilia view art as only one of the child's means of expression: "Children's expression through many media is not a separate part of the curriculum but is inseparable from the whole cognitive/symbolic expression in the process of learning" (p. 8).

Even though many people and organizations have made statements about the importance of the arts, they are still neglected in many school systems. Moreover, the arts are the first area to be cut whenever schools have budget problems. Engel (1995) suggests that the difficulty of assessing art skills and performance is one of the reasons the arts are not especially valued in schools.

Visual Arts

The term *visual arts* usually refers to graphic arts, such as using crayons, chalk, and paint and creating sculpture or collage. From the constructivist point of view, as children grow and develop, their representations with graphic materials change in predictable and unvarying stages. Every child moves through the same sequence of stages, but every child moves through them at an individual rate. As teachers observe these stages, they can make inferences about the child's cognitive development and thinking processes. The following are brief descriptions of the stages in drawing.

Stages in Development

Many art educators have tried to describe the stages in the development of children's drawing. Lowenfeld and Brittain (1982) have identified these stages as scribbling, preschematic, schematic, and drawing realism. The first stage, *scribbling,* usually begins at about thirteen months of age. Before that age, children put the crayons or pencils in their mouths. At about thirteen months, children begin to mark with crayons and pencils. The first scribbles are generally zigzags, not distinct shapes. Kellogg (1970) has examined children's scribbles and concluded that they usually fall into distinct patterns, which can be identified by an educated observer. By around three years of age, children begin to include distinct shapes, mostly circles, in their scribbling. Figure 13.1 is an example of scribbling.

At about four years of age, children begin to make attempts to represent objects that are familiar in their environment. This stage is the *preschematic* stage. Children in this stage typically draw human figures with very large heads and legs coming out of heads. Kellogg (1970) points out that these first drawings of humans derive from the circles and lines that children have created in their scribbles. Children may also draw other objects that are part of their experience, such as animals, using basically the same forms. Colors used in children's drawings are not realistic, and figures tend to be placed randomly on a page. Figure 13.2 is an example of a drawing by a child in the preschematic stage.

At about seven years old, children move into the *schematic* stage, in which they develop definite forms representing their environment. Children will repeat basically the same forms, again and again—drawing people or trees or birds with the same forms or symbols. Figures or objects are often arranged on a baseline, rather than placed at random on the page; however, the baseline itself may be placed randomly or at an angle to the edge of the paper. Children in this stage often represent objects in space from a point of view that is much different from the adult point of view. Children may use an "X-ray" perspective so that viewers can see the inside and outside of a house at the

Figure 13.1

Scribbling

Figure 13.2

Preschematic Drawing

same time. They may also draw objects from different views in one picture. The drawings in Figure 13.3 are representative of the schematic stage.

At around nine, children enter the stage of *drawing realism*. They begin to make their drawings much smaller and include much more detail; they are also no longer eager to share their work with adults. Some children in early childhood classrooms may be making the transition into this stage. The drawing in Figure 13.4 is typical of the drawing realism stage. Observe how the horse's legs are drawn not touching the ground and the several attempts to get the stirrup just right. The horse was also colored brown in the original drawing.

Another approach to describing children's art development is that of Engel (1995, 1996), who believes that teachers can view children's drawings from two perspectives: one, a descriptive perspective and the other, a developmental perspective. In looking at children's drawings from a descriptive perspective, teachers should keep the following questions in mind:

1. *Materials, context: What is it made of? And, if the information is available, when and under what circumstances was it made? . . .*
2. *Basic elements, techniques: What can the observer see? . . .*
3. *Character of communication: What does it represent? . . .*
4. *Aspects of organization, meaning: How is the picture organized? . . .*
5. *Function, intent: What is it about? . . .*
6. *Sources, origins: Where does the idea come from? . . .* (1995, pp. 31–34)

In viewing children's drawings from a developmental perspective, teachers should consider the descriptors outlined in Table 13.1, which presents a developmental continuum.

Figure 13.3   Schematic Drawing

How young children draw does not seem to reflect training. Brittain (1969) reported his experience in trying to teach nursery school children to draw squares. After many experiences with squares, the children began to draw them at around four years of age. As Brittain put it, children accomplish the task of drawing a square at about the same time with or without instruction.

Even though instruction may not result in changes in children's drawing, children can learn the vocabulary of art. Dixon and Tarr (1988) demon-

Figure 13.4

Realistic Drawing

Table 13.1   Developmental Continuum in Children's Drawings

Preschool (ages 2–5)	Early Primary (ages 4–6)	Middle Primary (ages 5–8)	Late Primary (ages 7–10)
■ scribbles, loops, zigzags, wavy lines, jabs, arcs—often partially off the paper at first ■ chance forms or shapes ■ trying out different effects ■ meaning in the act itself, not in results or product ■ experimenting with leaving a mark, with colors and motions to leave a sign or have an effect ■ reflecting motion of hand/arm ■ separate lines, circlelike shapes, combined straight and curved lines ■ other basic forms, controlled marks, first schematic formulae, mandalalike shapes *Sources:* physical act of moving a hand and arm, basic concepts such as the circle, exploration of possibilities of line	■ shapes combined, becoming schemas; intentional image repetition of schemas; development of preferred schemas ■ beginnings of representation, often of people; letterlike forms; basic forms represented consistently—houses, flowers, boats, people; animals in profile ■ meaning (subject matter) increasingly readable ■ repertory or symbolic forms repeated, practiced, and new elements added ■ beginnings of individual style (e.g., typical way of drawing a house) ■ figures isolated, no context or baseline; each discrete (no overlapping of whole or of parts); size and details according to perceived importance or interest (e.g., long arms) ■ several figures on the page; beginning representing of events or narratives; schematic figures placed in a larger concept, for example, knowing an elephant is a four-legged animal with a trunk, the child uses a well-established routine or schema, for drawing animals—cats, dogs, and so forth—and adds a trunk *Sources:* child's concepts and knowledge about the world, which take precedence over direct perception (as in the elephant example above)	■ elaboration and variation of schematic figures and experimentation; repetition of imagery, practicing "set pictures" (always drawn the same way), such as racing cars ■ details often traditional or formulaic, such as windows with tie-back curtains, chimneys with smoke coming out at an angle, girls defined by skirts and long hair ■ narrative, illustrative, inventive; baselines often multiple; "see-through" houses; most figures in own space, without overlapping *Sources:* copying conventional renderings by other children, imagination, book illustrations, TV, cartoons, and so on	■ increased differentiation —of kinds of animals, flowers, buildings, and so on; practiced drawing of favorite subjects—battle scenes, princesses, characters from TV, comics, books; pictures often telling detailed stories ■ interest in drawing from nature ■ figures sometimes in profile, with limbs bent, props added to indicate roles (e.g., cowboy hat and rope); increasing demand for looking real ■ color more naturalistic; scenery, overlapping, shadows, beginning perspective, and shading; more realistic use of scale; distance, elevations, and perspective added ■ backgrounds: landscapes, seascapes, sky, underground, under the sea; figures more logically interrelated; elevations, consistent viewpoints given ■ action: eye still seeing one relationship at a time, the mind having to put them together on the page to solve problems; fine control of line *Sources:* observation, imagination, book knowledge, copying, and so forth

Source: B. S. Engel, *Considering Children's Art: Why and How to Value Their Works* (Washington, DC: National Association for the Education of Young Children, 1995), p. 35. Reprinted with permission from the National Association for the Education of Young Children.

strated that children could be taught to recognize elements of art. In a unit on lines, the children moved to music to create lines with their bodies; looked at examples of lines in art; and used lines in their own art with straws, strips of paper, and markers. After these experiences, the children could identify lines as elements of art. Schirrmacher (1986) recommends that teachers point out the elements of color, line, mass or volume, pattern, shape or form, space, and texture when discussing art with young children.

Aylward et al. (1993) found that preschoolers were able to classify works of art by style after a course of study that specifically introduced abstract art and artists. In addition, the teachers observed that the children were more involved in their own art projects during and after this study. Epstein (2001) recommends that teachers ask children questions about their own art experiences that will help them think more about the content of art. For example, she suggests that when a group of children has finished an art experience, the children could be asked why their products are so different when they all used the same materials, or they could be asked to think about why some artists would want to make large pictures and some want to make small pictures.

Davis and Gardner (1993) suggest that teachers respond to children's art not by asking them to tell about their pictures and then writing on them (usually just labeling the components) but by demonstrating their own perceptions. For example, the teacher might say, "Look at the action in this line; this figure is indeed scribbling around on this page" or "This is a nicely balanced drawing; see how you have placed these large figures over here; it makes your drawing very strong" (p. 202). Such statements help children realize that the symbols of art can indeed communicate and that the symbols need not be accompanied by words in order to be valuable.

Goals of Visual Arts Experiences

The expected outcomes of art instruction are much more process oriented than product oriented. In other words, goals are likely to be general—involving children in art experiences and helping children become aware of the elements of art—and are unlikely to include having each child complete a certain product. Other important goals of visual arts experiences in the early childhood classroom include the following:

1. Encouraging children to explore a wide variety of materials
2. Providing activities that give sensory pleasure to the participants
3. Allowing children to make discoveries about color, shape, and texture
4. Helping children gain control of fine muscles and practice eye–hand coordination
5. Helping children feel comfortable with their ability to express themselves through art
6. Introducing children to the work of the world's artists

Visual arts activities provide unique opportunities for children to explore their own thoughts and feelings.

Clearly, these goals are very broad; they do not focus on specific skills, such as mastering perspective. The purpose of art in the early childhood years is to help children express what they know and feel and to begin to recognize how others express themselves through art. One teacher summed up this approach by saying, "I never thought of children's art as something to decorate the hallways. My main task is to keep children thinking, experimenting, trying, changing, and moving things—going beyond what's obvious to seeing and expressing relationships" (Dighe, Calomiris, and Van Zutphen 1998, p. 4.).

Suggested Visual Arts Experiences

Colbert and Taunton (1992) suggest that children need many opportunities to create, look at, and talk about art; they also need to become aware of art in their everyday lives. The activities described in the following sections will help achieve these objectives.

Graphic Art   Children can draw with pencils, crayons, chalk, and markers. A variety of papers of different colors, surface textures, and shapes can add interest to drawing activities. Patterns, dittos, and coloring books carry the message that the child cannot produce acceptable representations for herself; these should therefore be avoided. If the goal is for a child to learn to control the marker or chalk in order to fill in spaces, the child can fill in her own spaces, achieve the goal, and maintain a feeling of competence by drawing her own shapes and figures.

Painting   Young children can paint with tempera at easels or on tables, or they can fingerpaint. Children painting at easels have freedom to move their arms and can use more muscles than they can sitting at tables, where the muscular movements tend to be confined to the hands. When painting at easels, children can learn to control the paint drips, explore the results of using paints of different thicknesses, and stand back to look at their work from eye level more easily than when painting at tables. Fingerpaint invites children to explore texture and to risk the messiness. Children can be encouraged to use the sides of their hands and their palms as well as their fingers in the paint.

Teachers may want to offer other paint experiences, such as rolling paint from a roll-on bottle; spatter painting; blowing paint with a straw; dropping paint on paper; using objects other than a brush to apply paint (sponges, crumpled paper, aluminum foil, and so on); or rolling a small ball or marbles in paint and then on paper placed on the bottom of a box.

Printing   Printing can range from quite simple experiences, such as dipping a sponge or a piece of junk into paint and then pressing it onto paper, to complex projects, such as preparing a print form, rolling ink on it with a brayer, and then printing with it. Most kindergarten and primary children can make simple prints. Younger children tend to smear the paint when they try to press objects on paper. In addition to junk prints, kindergartners and primary children can make prints by gluing yarn, fabric scraps, or pieces of natural material onto cardboard or cylinders and then printing with these. Or they can combine media by doing a crayon rubbing and then printing over it.

Sculpture   Children enjoy sculpting with a variety of media; modeling clay is most commonly used. Clay should be available to children regularly. Clay experiences can be varied by using potter's clay that will harden; then children can paint their creations. Other variations include mixing clay with collage materials so that objects are embedded in the clay to achieve three-dimensional creations. Paper is also a popular medium for sculpting—it can be folded, torn, crumpled, or glued into three-dimensional forms. Cardboard tubes and small boxes are useful, too. Wood sculpture is also popular; children can glue wood scraps to create extraordinary shapes and designs. (Cabinet shops will often save wood scraps for teachers. Hardwood scraps usually have interesting shapes.)

Parents AND the Arts

■ Send home supplies for arts activities that can be done by families—for example, clay that can be molded, dried, and painted; some cut paper strips for paper sculptures (glue only the ends of the strips to a base sheet, twist strips over and under other strips, fold them, and so on).

WWW

Collage   Collages can be made with tissue paper; natural materials, such as bark and seeds; fabrics; and a variety of found materials. Collage gives children opportunities to develop an appreciation for texture and appealing arrangements of objects that are not possible with other media. Another advantage of collage is the use of glue. Paste and glue offer unique sensory experiences, and children will want to explore the stickiness, adhesive qualities, and spreadability of different adhesives.

Sewing and Weaving   Very young children can sew on styrofoam trays with holes punched in them or on net stretched in a frame. Kindergartners can sew on burlap with yarn. If children have trouble tying knots, the ends of the yarn can be taped on the back of the burlap with masking tape. Older children can sew with a variety of fabrics, either to create soft sculptures or to decorate the fabrics. Primary children can produce simple projects on circular or straw looms. They can also weave paper or fabric strips into interesting designs.

Combining Techniques   Teachers will think of many other experiences that are appropriate for young children and many ways to combine basic techniques. For example, children might paint on fabric; dye fabric; create simple batiks using crayons and dye on fabric; create puppets using paper, clay, or fabrics; use yarn to create a string design on cardboard and then print with the cardboard; fingerpaint on a table top and then make a print of the design by covering it with paper and rubbing lightly; create a crayon resist by drawing with wax crayons and painting over the drawing with tempera; or color with crayons, cover the colors with black crayon, and then scratch a design through the black crayon. The list of ideas is almost endless. Keep in mind, however, that as Wachowiak (1977) notes, children often do not enjoy or appreciate a new process or media until they become involved in it.

Viewing and Talking about Art   Schiller (1995) describes her experiences with bringing examples of fine art into her preschool classroom. Although she received very little response from the children at first, over time they began to discuss the artworks during group times and to choose their favorite pieces. Adding appropriate artworks that relate to topics of interest to the children is the key to getting them to talk about and look at art more closely.

Art versus Craft Activities

Art and craft activities are not the same. *Art,* as it is being defined in this chapter, is an opportunity for children to explore media with no external product goals. Although children may indeed create products as part of an art experience, they have control of their products, and the process of creating is more important than the products that result. *Craft* activities, on the other hand, generally require that children produce something, and most of the products will be very similar or even exactly the same. Some craft activities, such as making pencil holders for gifts, are acceptable if children have a choice about whether to participate. Such craft activities can be made more appropriate for children if the materials and designs for decorating the cans are selected by the children rather than dictated by the teacher. The planning, decision making, and self-expression that are so important in art are rarely found in craft experiences, in which the outcome is predetermined.

Many activities presented to young children as art are neither art nor craft. When children are given patterns for making owls or spiders at Halloween or flowers in the spring, what they learn from these cut-and-paste activities is to follow the teacher's directions, to wait until they are told what to do with materials, and to make their products look exactly like the teacher's model. Such activities meet none of the goals of art. Justifying these experiences with the claim that they teach children to follow directions is questionable—children can learn to follow directions in other activities. The negative learning and frustration that often accompany these projects outweigh any advantages in learning to follow directions.

Both art and craft activities have important places in an integrated curriculum. When provided with needed materials, children can paint a mural of snow activities, build a birdhouse or bird feeder, or illustrate a class book on a topic they have studied (Dever and Jared 1996). Certainly, it is not difficult for teachers to think of art and craft activities that might accompany certain topics of study. However, teachers must stay focused on allowing children to choose the activities they want to do and to express themselves as they participate in art and craft activities that enhance instruction in other areas.

Taking Art Seriously

Art education should be viewed as a serious undertaking for young children, not a curricular "frill" that can be omitted without harm. Teachers who believe in the value of art in the early childhood curriculum will offer "children sufficient experiential motivation so that they will have something to express and psychological safety so that they will feel free to do so" (Seefeldt 1995a, p. 44). These teachers will also believe that simply putting out materials is not enough—that teachers need to talk with children about their art and help them consider and reflect

> ### Parents AND the Arts
>
> ■ Plan a session to help parents look at and respond to their children's art products in positive terms. Make sure parents do not feel they have to be artists to be involved with the arts.
>
> WWW

on their expressions, in the same manner that they would talk to children about their writing. In addition to providing an outlet for self-expression, art experiences encourage critical thinking when children are allowed to choose how to express themselves and communicate with others through their art (de la Roche 1996).

Music

Music, like art, is a basic way of learning, experiencing, and communicating. All children deserve a rich musical environment in which to learn to sing, to play music, to move, and to listen. Music is also a valuable tool for helping children gain content knowledge and make sense of their experiences.

Music is a pervasive influence in our lives. We hear music when we worship, exercise, relax, drive, and attend baptisms, weddings, and funerals (Merrion and Vincent 1988). Planned musical experiences should not be delayed until children can participate in group singing or until they can keep an accurate beat. Because research indicates that children respond to music very early, McDonald (1979) suggests that "the starting time for learning about music is the same as the starting time for any learning. Music is one facet in the total education of the child. It must emerge with the nature and needs of the child, from birth onward" (p. 4).

Goals of a Music Program

An early childhood music program should focus on achieving these goals:

1. Teaching children to sing tunefully
2. Encouraging children to experiment with tempo, volume, and quality of sound
3. Encouraging children to express themselves through singing, movement, and playing simple instruments
4. Giving children opportunities to listen to music
5. Exposing children to a wide variety of types of music

In addition, teachers planning musical experiences for young children should keep in mind the beliefs articulated by the National Association for Music Education (1999):

- *All children have musical potential.*
- *Children bring their own unique interests and abilities to the music learning environment.*
- *Very young children are capable of developing critical thinking skills through musical ideas.*
- *Children come to early childhood music experiences from diverse backgrounds.*
- *Children should experience exemplary musical sounds, activities, and materials.*
- *Children should not be encumbered with the need to meet performance goals.*
- *Children learn best in pleasant physical and social environments.*
- *Diverse learning environments are needed to serve the developmental needs of many individual children.*
- *Children need effective adult models.* (n.p.)

For very young children, music need not necessarily be a group experience, although very short group experiences may be successful. More frequently, music is an individual or small-group activity. As children go about the day's activities, they and their teachers can sing and chant about what they are doing. A wide variety of songs and rhythms should be used, and children should be guided to move rhythmically to the beat and melodic direction they hear. Teachers can also provide safe toys with musical sounds the children can control (MENC 1994).

Also, music need not be limited to actual songs—it is *sound* that brings pleasure and helps children express feelings or thoughts. A child crooning a lullaby while rocking a doll or splashing rhythmically in water is making music a part of everyday experience.

Singing

Learning to sing is a developmental process. Young children need a supportive and encouraging environment for singing. Their ability to sing is closely related to their growing abilities in other areas of development. From research, we know that most children can sing by age two, that songs with a limited range are easier for children to sing, that play contributes to the development of singing, and that young children often enjoy listening to favorite songs again and again (McDonald 1979). Primary children increase their repertoire of songs and can often learn to sing in parts, such as singing a round. Singing, like other skills, is learned through singing, and all children should be considered singers (Neely 2002).

Selecting Songs

In choosing songs for children, teachers must consider the pitch range, the intervals, and the subject of the song. The range must be one in which most children are comfortable singing, which includes approximately the A below middle C to the G or A above middle C. As children mature, the range can be increased; children in the primary grades who are comfortable singing can be introduced to songs with greater ranges. Songs with descending intervals and few wide skips in the melody are more easily sung by young children. Songs should also be repetitious, both in melody and rhythmic patterns. Children enjoy a wide variety of songs about animals, themselves or their friends, and some nonsense rhymes and jingles (McDonald and Simons 1989).

Gilbert (1981) lists the following points to consider when choosing songs to teach:

1. *The song should* appeal to the children. *It may be the tune itself or the rhythm that is attractive; whatever it is, if children like the song and can remember it easily, they will enjoy singing it.*
2. *The song should* not be too long *and, in general, the younger the child the greater the need for repetition and for a predictable pattern within each verse.*
3. *Songs with* a chorus *encourage even shy children to join in.*
4. *Songs which lend themselves to* movement *often have greater potential with young children.*
5. *Avoid tunes with* very high notes *or difficult leaps.*
6. *Choose songs with words that the children* understand. *Sometimes it is necessary to explain a particular word; at other times it is better to substitute another word or phrase. Always try out new words to see how they "sing."* (p. 16)

A surprising number of songs fit the criteria described above. Some examples include "Go Tell Aunt Rhody," "Twinkle, Twinkle Little Star," "Where Is Thumpkin?" "Baa, Baa Black Sheep," and many other nursery songs. Older children will enjoy folk songs ("Michael Row Your Boat Ashore" and "This

Land Is Your Land"), humorous songs (such as the songs from *Mary Poppins*), and songs from other cultures. Teachers will know that songs are good choices if the children sing them spontaneously or ask to sing them in group music times.

Not only is singing a delightful experience, but children learning songs and creating words to melodies are also learning phonemic awareness and phonics skills (Smith 2000). If you make charts of the songs they know or make song booklets, the children can match the words they know to the words in print.

Presenting Songs

Teachers who are not confident of their singing voices can begin by learning a few simple folk songs and singing them with individual children or small groups before singing with the whole group (Jalongo and Collins 1985). What children need most is a teacher who loves music and shares that interest and enthusiasm; young children are appreciative of the teacher's singing and are not music critics. Jalongo (1996) believes that "teachers who have limited musical backgrounds can do as well in teaching music as do teachers with extensive musical backgrounds, but only if nonmusicians are conscientious and enthusiastic about following a daily musical curriculum featuring high-quality music" (p. 6).

Teachers who play the piano or feel comfortable about their own singing voices usually introduce songs by playing or singing them several times for the children and then encouraging children to sing along with them. Teachers who cannot play the songs can use recordings to introduce music quite successfully.

After presenting the whole song several times, the teacher may want to sing a line if the children are having difficulty learning it, but each experience should end with the children singing the whole song through again. This routine will need to be repeated several times over a period of days before the children will be comfortable with a new song.

Musical experiences can be opportunities for problem solving, as children invent new words to songs or new ways of moving to music. Singing games such as "Hokey Pokey" and "Punchinella" lend themselves naturally to problem solving, as children must create their own movements. Children can also create new words to familiar songs. They might substitute any five-letter name in "B-I-N-G-O" and make up a verse about that person. Problem solving is encouraged when children are free to explore and play and when their efforts are supported (Hildebrandt 1998).

Chants such as "The Bear Hunt" are also valuable in the music program, as children learn the rhythms and patterns of language. Many chants lend themselves to instrumentation or body percussion sounds; children can add claps, snaps, or clicks to the rhythm of the chant. Buchoff (1994) suggests that many poems and jump-rope rhymes are appropriate for classroom use. After the children have learned a chant, they can add physical accompaniments, such as clapping, snapping their fingers, tapping their fingers or toes, and so on. Putting the words to a chant on a poster or in a booklet or newsletter can also help children share the chant with their peers and parents.

Playing Instruments

Today's approach to playing instruments with young children focuses on their exploration of sound and rhythm. Even very young children like to produce sounds by banging on pots and pans. Such interest usually continues, and they are eager to explore sound with drums, bells, xylophones, and shakers. Even though the focus is on exploration, the teacher can help individuals or small groups with instruction in how to hold an instrument or how to strike it to get a more satisfactory sound. As children become able to keep a beat, they can invent simple accompaniments to familiar songs. Primary children can begin to learn to play simple instruments such as recorders.

Studies of children's use of musical instruments and the implications for teachers can be summarized as follows:

1. Children should have many opportunities for free exploration with instruments before any structured activities are attempted.

2. Teachers should attend to children's interests and needs when providing any instruction on how to play an instrument.

3. Children need to express rhythm through physical movement before instruments are introduced.

4. Exploration with instruments can help children learn about pitch, timbre, rhythm, and melody.

Teaching should focus on helping children achieve the technical skills needed to express creative ideas (McDonald and Simons 1989).

Parents AND the Arts

■ Teachers can help parents encourage the musical development of their children by making the music accessible to parents, helping parents understand that the music needs to be beautiful for optimal effect, and ensure that parents feel comfortable sharing music with their children as they grow.

WWW

Listening Experiences

Children can be encouraged to listen to a variety of music. Guided listening experiences for younger children should be very short. As children mature, the pieces of music selected for listening can be longer and the children can be expected to hear more complex patterns. Teachers should select classical music, folk music, and music from a variety of cultures and ethnic groups. Listening experiences are most effective if the children are comfortable, both physically and psychologically, and if new experiences are based on the children's previous experiences. Children also need guidance in what to listen for, such as repeated phrases or passages that create moods or images.

Listening experiences can be created through games and other everyday experiences. Children can be encouraged to listen to environmental sounds, both inside and outside the room. Games can include guessing what produced a given sound, clapping back a pattern produced on a drum by the teacher or another student, or recognizing voices (as in "Doggie, Doggie, Who Has the Bone?").

Older preschoolers and primary children can benefit from listening to short, live performances. Often, local symphony orchestras or high school groups prepare special programs for young children. Some of these programs introduce the instruments of the orchestra and help children listen for their sounds; others present musical stories that children will enjoy. Suthers (1993) found that introducing children to musical selections in advance of a program greatly enhanced their ability to listen to and appreciate the performance of an orchestra. To achieve this, teachers were provided with teaching kits consisting of plans for musical activities and recordings of the music to be played.

Whether to use music in the background when children are engaged in other activities is a question that teachers will have to answer for themselves. Some teachers argue that children ignore background music; this makes it difficult for them to learn to listen to music attentively. Others argue that providing carefully selected background music at quiet times of the day can be a way of exposing children to music when there might otherwise be no time to do so. No one advocates playing music that adds to the noise level when the children are engaged in noisy activities. Many teachers choose to make records and tapes available for children to use at listening stations during the activity times of each day. Such stations allow children who wish to listen to music the opportunity to do so without disturbing other children.

Movement and Dance

Movement to music begins very early—children often sway and nod to music they hear. Emile Jaques-Dalcroze (1865–1950), a Swiss composer and teacher, believed that movement was the best way to help children learn to love and appreciate music. He believed that training in moving in response to music should begin in the first year of life (Jaques-Dalcroze 1921). (We will return to Jaques-Dalcroze in the section on Dalcroze Eurhythmics, page 432.)

Fundamental motor abilities are learned and mastered during the preschool years; it therefore makes sense to focus on the *process* of movement instruction during this time, rather than on the *product*. Most children have mastered the basic movements by the time they enter first grade, but as Malina (1982) notes, "The quality of performance continues to improve as the fundamental patterns are refined and integrated into more complex movement sequences" (p. 215). Seven- and eight-year-olds continue to gain skill and control in motor development. They can add a beat to music, keep a beat with an instrument while singing, and learn simple folk dances.

Movement experiences should be planned to include both creative and more structured movements. Creative movement activities are those in which children interpret instructions in their own ways; their movements may not necessarily match the beat of the music. Examples of creative movement activities are having children move in a given direction and then change direction when the music changes; use movements that are heavy or light; move fast or slow; and so on. More structured movement experiences include asking children to learn to keep a beat and move to a beat.

A typical structured movement experience is clapping to simple rhythms. Teachers often have children clap the syllables in their own and their classmates' names. Teachers might also ask children to walk to a drumbeat or walk to the beat of music played on the piano or a recording. As children gain more control and are able to keep the beat more accurately, they may be asked to learn simple dance steps.

Sullivan (1982) recommends another simple movement exercise, "Clap, Clap, Clap Your Hands." With the children sitting down, the teacher plays:

C   C   G   F   E   C   C   D   E D   low G
Clap, clap, clap your hands. Clap your hands to-geth-er.

C   C   G   F   E   E   E   D   D D   C
Clap, clap, clap your hands. Clap your hands to-geth-er.

Children can be encouraged to think of other movements, such as tapping their knees, tapping their elbows, shaking their hands, shaking their heads, and so on.

Primary children can be encouraged to keep the beat and explore movement through such exercises as "Copycat." The children find their own space. The leader improvises a movement on the count of one, and the children imitate the movement on the count of two. A drum may be used to help keep the beat. In another exercise, the children stand in a long line across the room and are numbered off by threes. Together, they walk forward for eight counts, backward for eight counts, and then turn in their original spot for eight counts. When this pattern has been mastered, the "1s" perform the routine alone, followed by the "2s" and then the "3s." The whole pattern is repeated several times (Findlay 1971).

Dance education, defined by Koff (2000), is important in helping children learn to express themselves through movement. According to Koff, "Dance education can be described as the sequential development through the exploration of time, space, and energy in order to express oneself" (p. 28). Dance training, on the other hand, prepares children to perform as dancers. Dance education, then, is a movement program that can help children learn and can balance their need for movement against the more sedentary activities of most schooldays. Dance education can be integrated into the curriculum as students learn story elements and the parallel dance elements, or the understanding of culture, through the medium of dance. Dance provides children with the opportunity to learn nonverbal communication skills that can help many students solidify their understandings of the other communication skills that get so much attention in the typical curriculum.

Approaches to Music Instruction

Three approaches to musical instruction for young children will be described briefly in the following sections: Dalcroze Eurhythmics, the Kodály method, and the Orff approach.

Dalcroze Eurhythmics

Emile Jaques-Dalcroze (1865–1950) developed an approach to teaching music based on the belief that rhythm was the fundamental force in music and that children should develop an awareness of music through body movement. Jaques-Dalcroze believed that sequence was important in teaching children music and that the simplest of rhythmic experiences should be first, followed by more difficult and complicated activities, followed by instrumental study. This method—called *eurhythmics*—emphasizes the importance of an immediate physical response to music and of having children dramatize music with their bodies.

Findlay's *Rhythm and Movement: Applications of Dalcroze Eurhythmics* (1971) is a good source for teachers; it contains a brief explanation of the child's need for a rhythmic response and a wealth of ideas and activities that any teacher of young children will find interesting and helpful. Dalcroze training for teachers is also available at many universities across the United States.

The Kodály Method

Zoltán Kodály (1882–1967), a Hungarian composer, was a contemporary of Jaques-Dalcroze. He believed that the most important instrument in a child's music education was her own voice. Kodály relied heavily on children's games, nursery songs, and folk music in helping children learn to sing. He believed that accompaniments to songs should be simple and that a child should learn to "appreciate music as a pure, unadulterated melody emanating from himself, this appreciation being achieved through ear-training exercises" (Bayless and Ramsey 1991, p. 218). The Kodály method is not complicated, and most teachers can implement the program without special training or special equipment.

The Orff Approach

Carl Orff (1895–1982), a German composer, developed his method from work with young dance students in his school. Orff is most commonly associated with the pitched instruments that bear his name. (Most catalogs of musical instruments for children include the Orff instruments.) The Orff program involves structuring a musical environment and then helping children improvise within the environment. Important elements of the Orff method include rhythm, body percussion (stamping, slapping the thighs, clapping, and finger snapping), dramatic movement, melody, and the use of instruments (both percussion instruments and pitched instruments). Orff advocated that activities progress from speech to rhythmic activities to song and then to playing musical instruments. Although Orff instruments are fairly expensive, many schools use them, and Orff training is available to teachers who are interested in learning the approach (McDonald and Simons 1989).

Crinklaw-Kiser (1996) found that the Orff-Schulwerk approach to music is very compatible with a developmentally appropriate curriculum. (The word *schulwerk* in the title means "schoolwork.") This approach begins with what children like to do—sing, clap, dance, and so on. Starting with the rhythm of a song, first the words are added, and then activities are added to expand on that knowledge, such as word cards, charts, booklets, and so on.

NAEYC

Drama

Drama in the early childhood classroom is defined as experiences in which children play, pretend, role-play, or create characters or ideas. McGregor, Tate, and Robinson (1987) state that the essential characteristic of drama is acting out. In acting out,

> there is an agreement to suspend the normal social roles with each other in identifying with the new imagined roles. There is an agreement to make a different use of the environment. In this case a desk becomes a dining table laden with food, a chalk box becomes a cigar box, and so on. This different use of the environment includes a shift in the conventions of time. Events may be telescoped to give them greater or less significance. The usual conventions of space and time may be suspended during acting out. (p. 12)

Drama in early childhood education is not the production of plays in which children memorize lines and act given roles. Such productions are often appropriate for older children but are not appropriate for the early childhood years. Creative drama usually refers to spontaneous productions in which children create or recreate stories, moods, or incidents without learning lines or practicing their roles.

Parents AND the Arts

■ Encourage parents who are interested to participate with their children in creative dramatics or other arts experiences.

WWW

Drama in the classroom can contribute to the general goals of early childhood programs, fostering the development of skills such as these:

1. Critical-thinking and problem-solving skills
2. An ability to work cooperatively with others
3. An increased ability to understand the perspectives of others
4. An ability to communicate more effectively
5. The integration of ideas from many sources into a meaningful whole

Of course, drama experiences provide another avenue for self-expression and developing creativity that is as important as their contributions to other curriculum goals.

Encouraging Drama

Most experiences with drama occur spontaneously in children's play or in response to music, songs, stories, or other experiences. Teachers will want to encourage and support these dramatic activities, but they may also plan for specific experiences in drama. Teachers can encourage children's play and help them add or extend dramatic elements. For example, a teacher observing children choosing roles for dramatic play might help a child think of a role or imagine how someone might act in a given role or provide a prop or costume to help the child conceptualize the role more fully.

Most teachers of young children have observed that drama, like other creative arts experiences, is a natural response that arises in a supportive classroom environment with teacher encouragement. Children returning from a trip to the zoo often assume the roles of the people or animals they encountered there. After hearing a story, children will often act out the roles of some of the characters. Even very young children will imitate voices or pretend to be as sad or as scared as one of the characters in a story.

Planned drama experiences may be incorporated into movement, music, and literature experiences. If the children are exploring movement patterns, they might be asked to move in a way that represents a given character or mood—to tiptoe quickly to represent the movement of mice, for example. Children might also use drama to demonstrate their understanding of the lyrics of songs they are learning. (If they are asked to glide and they flap their

Children's literature provides an excellent foundation for drama activities.

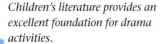

arms, the teacher can assume that they do not understand the term *glide*.) After listening to a story, children often want to retell it through dramatic representations. If, after listening to *Where the Wild Things Are* (Sendak 1963), they can act out Max's anger, the power of the "wild things," and Max's relief when he returns to his very own room, there will be no need to ask them comprehension questions.

Roser (2001) notes that drama is an underused response to reading or hearing a story read. Often, teachers turn first to writing and art, but drama can play an important role in helping children clarify their understandings of text by acting it out.

Other planned drama experiences can extend children's concept knowledge. Fox (1987, pp. 59–60) describes a dramatic activity that she calls "Caterpillars and Butterflies." (If the class were studying insects or caterpillars, these activities would not only add interest but would also give the teacher a chance to observe the children's understanding of concepts.) Fox suggests that children begin by observing how real caterpillars move. After these observations, the children crawl around, imitating the movements of the caterpillars (perhaps to music). After hearing the teacher read *The Very Hungry Caterpillar* (Carle 1969), some children can form a tight circle to create an orange, and others can crawl through the orange (eating a hole in the orange). Then the children can think about what happens to the caterpillar after it has eaten all the food. They can curl themselves into cocoons and then pretend to nibble out and spread their butterfly wings. It is helpful if the children can observe the movements of a real butterfly or watch a film of a butterfly in slow motion before they imitate the butterfly movements. Children might also create butterfly wings with scarves or tissue paper and use them in their movements.

Dyer and Schiller (1993) suggest that dramatic performances be approached as problem-solving opportunities instead of the usual memorize-and-rehearse activities. Children should be allowed to figure out how to present to an audience different elements of a story or different interpretations of an event. When this problem-solving experience is part of preparing for a performance, the results will be children's intellectual growth as well as greater audience interest.

Cline and Ingerson (1996) provide the following tips for successful drama experiences:

- *Keep story lines and sessions short.*
- *Focus initially on action instead of dialogue.*
- *Use many characters (even inanimate objects can be played). Create new ones if you need to.*
- *Encourage children to be specific ("If Humpty is fat, how can he move to show it?").*
- *Always keep a distinct physical boundary between the stage and the house (audience), even if it is just a line of tape on the floor. . . .*
- *Rotate players and audience frequently. . . .*

➤ Write a guide for the public art in your community. Note its location, the name of the artist, when it was installed, and so on.

➤ Survey families to determine how many participate in the arts in some way, either professionally or as a hobby. Invite the artists to demonstrate their art for the class or invite artists from the community to demonstrate their art.

➤ Learn and perform a folk dance from each of the countries of origin represented in the class.

➤ Examine the art in picture books produced by the Pinkney family.

➤ Learn and sing a song from each of the countries of origin represented in the class.

➤ Write and illustrate a book about a family adventure.

➤ Each child can create a decoration for her own room and then explain the process used to produce the piece. This can be a decoration for the wall or something that sits on a table or desk.

➤ Display art in many forms: sculpture, textile art, paintings, furniture decoration, calligraphy, and so on. Change the exhibits often.

➤ Display prints of famous pieces of art and discuss how they were made.

➤ If families own musical instruments, ask them to bring them to class, play them, and discuss how music is produced with them.

➤ Invite musicians from the community to play for the children. Make sure that you invite people from many different ethnic groups.

- *Narrate the stories during rehearsals and performances until the children become more proficient. . . .*
- *Interject comments or questions (side coaching). . . .*
- *Respect and encourage children's decisions. . . .*
- *Do not introduce the story with a movie, video, or play. These performances irrevocably become the "right" way and short-circuit the children's creativity.* (p. 8)

Roles of Specialists

Teachers who are privileged to teach in schools that have specialists in art, music, or physical education on staff should not hesitate to call on these people. They can be excellent resources. However, specialists do not relieve classroom teachers of the responsibility for teaching, music, or movement.

The best situation is for specialists and classroom teachers to work together to achieve mutual goals. Because art, music, and movement are integral to most content-area instruction, the classroom teacher's role is to inform the specialist of the concepts that she is seeking to help the children develop; the specialist's role is to advise the teacher of activities that would be appropriate for those concepts. For example, if the focus in the classroom is on small animals, an art specialist might suggest having children create torn-paper collages of animals or tempera paintings of animals.

An art specialist can help the classroom teacher not only by suggesting appropriate activities but also by helping the teacher recognize the language of art that is important for the children to learn and by helping the teacher develop other concepts. The art specialist is also a good resource person for the teacher who wants to present the works of other artists to young children. Exposure to fine art can serve as a stimulus to creative experiences and can increase awareness of aesthetic elements (Bowker and Sawyer 1988). The art specialist can also aid the classroom teacher in helping children learn to look at and talk about art. Unless the teacher and art specialist provide opportunities for this kind of art appreciation, it may never occur (Cole and Schaefer 1990).

Similarly, the music specialist can help the classroom teacher incorporate music into daily classroom activities. He can help the teacher select songs that are appropriate for the group and provide guidance in choosing movement experiences or instruments appropriate for the specific theme the teacher is using. For a theme of small animals, the music specialist might help the children learn songs about the small animals in the classroom; listen to animal sounds; distinguish pitch in animal sounds; and produce rhythm patterns to represent various animals.

The physical education specialist can also provide assistance for the classroom teacher of young children. The specialist can help select appropriate movement experiences and provide opportunities for motor activities that can contribute to children's learning in other areas. To extend the theme of small animals, the physical education specialist might help children reproduce the movement patterns of the animals in the classroom. These movements could further the objectives of the physical education program by promoting body control and integrating patterns of motor abilities.

The classroom teacher can take advantage of the expertise of specialists by keeping them informed about topics of interest in the classroom and needs that have been observed. Each specialist has much to offer that will expand children's experiences and further the collaborative development of the best program possible for each child.

Assessing Experiences in the Arts

Assessment of children's performance in the arts must be individualized. One cannot give a grade to a child's drawing, but one can note whether the child chooses to participate in drawing activities and keep samples of the child's drawing in order to document the child's development. In assessing music, the teacher must also observe individual children as they participate in activ-

It is hard to conceive of a developmentally appropriate program that fails to include the creative arts. For young children, the arts provide many opportunities to explore materials and techniques, to make choices, to express themselves, and to gain social and cognitive skills. Think about the arts in these terms:

■ *Allowing each child to choose her own activity and within that activity, to choose how to complete the activity*—For example, a child might choose to paint at the easel and then choose which colors to use, how to place the elements of the composition on the paper, and how long to work on the painting.

■ *Providing intellectual challenge*—A child can continue to learn new techniques and continue to explore new media. The arts are never learned in the sense of learning facts; every experience with the arts is new and challenging.

■ *Providing opportunities for growth in all domains*—While participating in the arts, children gain physical skill (control of body and fine motor skills), grow intellectually (making decisions, planning, organizing), gain social competence (work with others, have responsibility for materials, share space and materials), and develop emotionally (expressing feelings, gaining empathy for the feelings of others, and so on).

ities, become able to sing in tune, and keep the rhythm of a piece of music. Drama and movement activities must also be observed on an individual basis. It is important to know that children are learning to modulate their voices and control their body movements, but there is no need to compare one child to another. Assessment in the arts requires the development of a portfolio for work samples and anecdotal records of progress. A child's performance is always compared to his own earlier work, not to the work of other children. The goal is for children to learn through the arts and to enjoy their arts experiences without fear that they will be criticized or made to feel less than adequate for their work.

Connecting the Arts and Other Subject-Matter Areas

Although the goals and objectives of a creative arts program are important enough to stand alone, the arts also contribute to other curriculum areas in powerful ways. Children learning concepts in science, math, health, and social studies can express their understandings through art, music, movement, and drama. The following sections provide a few examples of the many possible ways the arts can be integrated into different themes or subject-matter areas:

- *Shadows*—Movement possibilities include having children attempt to make their shadows move in certain ways, move without touching the shadows of the other children, and so on. Primary children can make shadow characters and produce a shadow play. Children might also create a stage for the shadow play from a large carton and decorate it. Children can select or create background music for their shadow plays.

- *Birds*—Children can imitate the movements of different birds on the ground and in the air. They can listen to birdsongs and learn to recognize a few distinctive calls as well as melodic or repeating patterns. Birds can be represented through graphic art, collage, or sculpture. Bird nests can be made from natural materials. Primary children can note color patterns of birds and perhaps chart common colors and patterns.

- *Seashells*—Children can notice ocean sounds and the regularity of waves. Children can be challenged to represent the movements of different sea creatures, such as anemones and snails. They can sort shells by shapes and note the patterns of seashells. Paintings and drawings of seashells as well as objects (buttons, jewelry) made from seashells can be introduced. (Note, however, that the craft of making creatures from seashells is not art.)

- *Literature*—Given a piece of fabric, children can make a little overcoat for Joseph (*Joseph Had a Little Overcoat,* Taback 1999) and tell the story as they make each of the smaller and smaller things from the overcoat fabric. Children can act out the story of *The Hatsellers and the Monkeys* (Diakite 1999). Stories such as this one have the advantage of providing as many roles as needed because there is no given number of monkeys. Another story to act out, especially for older children, is *Chato's Kitchen* (Soto 1995). This story provides the opportunity to learn some Spanish words in retelling the story. Another good choice is *Say Hey! A Song of Willie Mays* (Mandel 2000). The refrain in this story/song lends itself to active participation in the reading of the book and to modeling for other oral responses. Some first and most second graders would enjoy participating in a reader's theater production (children read without memorization or costumes) of a simple story with good dialogue, such as the well-known folk story "Three Billy Goats Gruff." Many scripts are also available on the Web that would be suitable for young readers.

- *Reading and writing*—After children have learned the lyrics to a song, they can put them on a chart or on sentence strips. Primary children can write new lyrics or substitute words in the lyrics. Jalongo and Ribblett (1997) suggest that song picture books can support emerging literacy because the children can "read" the words after they know the song. Moreover, song picture books provide repetition and predictability along with opportunities for critical thinking, problem solving, and expanding vocabulary.

Children with Special Needs

NAEYC

Many experiences in the arts can be modified or adapted to make participation by children with special needs possible. Children with developmental delays may not be ready for group work or for some of the cognitive tasks in the arts program. Teachers will have to determine which experiences are developmentally appropriate for individual children and provide alternative experiences when necessary.

Because most art activities are planned for individuals, most children can participate in art at their own levels without adaptations; work surfaces or materials may have to be adapted for children with orthopedic disabilities. Examples of adaptations include providing work surfaces that are accessible for children in wheelchairs and providing sturdy materials that are easy to grasp so that children can draw and paint. Some children who do not have much control of their arms and hands might benefit from creating computer art; a computer program allows them to control color and so on. Children with visual impairments can paint, fingerpaint, create collages, and sculpt.

Teachers may need to seek expert advice about planning activities for children with specific types of hearing impairments. Some children are able to hear or feel many sounds—especially percussion or rhythmic elements. Gfeller (1989) makes these recommendations for adapting activities for children with hearing impairments:

1. Children who use hearing aids may hear better if background noises can be minimized.

2. If children use sign language, incorporate signing into singing activities.

3. Use visual aids to help children recognize patterns and other musical information that they may not be able to hear.

4. Placement in the group should make lip reading or watching or feeling instruments possible.

5. Using quality sound equipment that does not distort the sound helps children with some residual hearing.

6. Some children can hear better in the lower frequencies; therefore, instruments with lower pitches should be selected.

7. Rhythmic and percussive elements should be emphasized.

Children with delays in motor development may require instruments that do not have to be grasped, such as bells on a strap that can be fastened around the child's wrist or ankle; stands that hold instruments so that the child can play them are also helpful. During group movement sessions, children can be encouraged to move their heads, arms, legs, or whatever body parts they can control; they need not feel left out just because they cannot manage whole-body movements.

Experiencing music is something that can be enjoyed by all *students.*

Singing may be difficult for some children with speech disabilities, and teachers may need to use more chants and rhythmic speech experiences with them. The teacher may need to consult with a speech specialist to determine the best course of instruction for such children.

Brown (1991) suggests that signing can be added to many drama activities. She recommends that teachers use the following techniques for adapting drama for children with special needs:

1. *Use pictures to visually represent new vocabulary and concepts.*
2. *Break the drama lesson up into a series of short segments.*
3. *Use repetition to reinforce new language and concepts.*
4. *Allow children to imitate as a starting point.*
5. *Sequence the activities, building from the simple to more complex.*
6. *Begin the activities with warm ups and end with a closing.*
7. *Introduce techniques to maintain focus and control. (pp. 173–174)*

Brown (1991) goes on to suggest that having children sing during drama is a good way to involve those individuals who cannot physically participate in activities:

While some children become frogs hopping from log to lily pad, other children may carry out the action with a puppet-frog and environment created from signs and gestures. Give children in wheelchairs a special role by using the chair as an integral part of the activity. Wheelchairs make great spaceships and train engines. Children with limited movement can be given the role of the tree in the middle that the other children's hand/leaves fall from, or the Indian chief who must call back braves from a hunt. (p. 178)

As with all children, exposing children with special needs to the arts is a matter of thinking about what they can do, providing materials that are appropriate for them, and providing guidance in helping each child achieve his own goals.

Celebrating Diversity

The creative arts offer teachers invaluable opportunities for celebrating the diversity of their classrooms and communities. When choosing examples of fine art to share with children, teachers should make sure that the pieces represent many cultures. Moreover, pieces should include traditional styles from various cultures, which may not be used by contemporary artists but will help children appreciate the various ways humans have represented forms that were important to them. For example, the traditional carvings of the Maori people of New Zealand represented the animals and plants around them; these patterns became stylized and were used in carvings and on fabric. The traditional art of the American Indians of the Pacific Northwest represented the animals that were important in the stories of the tribes.

Parents AND the Arts

■ Encourage parents who are engaged in the arts—whether vocationally or avocationally—to share their art with the children.

www

In addition to the visual arts, many cultural groups have rich histories of music, drama, and dance. Find videos or photographs of such arts. Learn some traditional songs and dances with the help of local members of the culture, if possible.

Creative arts also offer children with language differences opportunities to be successful. Difficulties with a dialect or learning a second language will not affect a child's ability to create a painting or sculpture. Cultural and ethnic differences can be honored in musical and dance experiences and in sharing art from many cultures.

The arts provide excellent avenues for children to work together and appreciate the strengths of learners from many cultural backgrounds. Teachers can also gain an understanding of what children know in the content areas through the arts and can use the achievement in the arts as a form of alternative assessment. Ivey (1999) says it well when he states that "Democracy offers the promise of equal participation to hundreds of cultural traditions that shape our landscape—Native American, Asian, European, Black, and Hispanic—and this promise translates into an endless process of negotiation and accommodation. Art represents a place in which borrowing, blending, and sharing can really work."

Bilingual and limited English speakers have more opportunities to express their understandings through the arts when their language is not yet sufficient to express them in English (Goldberg 2001). It is difficult to think of any part of the curriculum in which cultural diversity can be celebrated more easily than in the arts.

Chapter Summary

- The arts are very important in early childhood programs. Children need to learn to express themselves and what they know in a variety of ways; the arts provide multiple avenues for expression.

- Children's drawing develops through predictable stages: scribbling, preschematic, schematic, and drawing realism.

- Program goals in the visual arts include helping children explore a wide variety of materials, engage in pleasurable activities, gain control of fine muscles, express themselves, and learn about the work of other artists.

- Music is a basic mode of learning, experiencing, and communicating. The goals of a music program include helping children learn to sing and encouraging them to experiment with tempo, volume, and quality of sound; express themselves; listen to music; and appreciate many kinds of music.

- Young children's singing ability develops over time as they gain control of their voices and learn to match the pitch of others.

- Songs selected by the teacher must be evaluated in terms of range of pitch, musical intervals, and content.

- Children should have many opportunities to explore simple musical instruments. Instruction in playing instruments should focus on helping individual children achieve their own musical objectives.

- Listening experiences are an important component of a music program. Children need guidance in listening and opportunities to listen to many types of music.

- Movement experiences should include both creative and more structured movements. Movement experiences can be planned to help children feel and move to a musical beat and to allow children to express their ideas.

- Drama in the early childhood classroom is a creative activity in which the children act out their ideas, impressions, and moods.

- Drama contributes to the overall goals of a program by helping children develop critical-thinking and problem-solving abilities, helping them work cooperatively with others, increasing their ability to understand the perspectives of others, learning to communicate more effectively, and helping them integrate concepts from subject-matter areas.

- Specialists in art, music, and physical education can help classroom teachers achieve objectives in subject-matter areas and can collaborate with teachers in promoting goals specific to art, music, and physical education.

- Activities in the arts can help integrate topics of study from the sciences and the social studies and can extend literary experiences.

- Activities in the arts can be modified so that children with special needs can participate and benefit from the experience.

- Many opportunities exist to share the arts of other cultures with children. Even very young children can learn to appreciate that it is not only acceptable to express knowledge and feelings in many ways but desirable, as well.

Theory INTO *Practice*

Interview a specialist in art, music, or physical education in the primary grades. How much planning does she do in collaboration with classroom teachers? If there is little or no collaboration, would this specialist like to collaborate? What ideas does she have for facilitating collaboration?

Choose a topic that is common in the preschool and the primary curricula, and plan arts experiences based on it. Make sure the experiences will actively involve the children and enhance their concept of the topic.

Select an art medium that is new to the children, such as clay (i.e., potter's clay, not modeling clay). Plan how to introduce this medium to a small group. What types of artworks will you expect the children to make? Why?

Select a picture songbook, and plan how you could use it with primary children to strengthen literacy goals as well as music and movement goals.

Observe the paintings of a three-year-old and a seven-year-old. What do the artworks have in common? What are the differences in their paintings? What can you say about the developmental stage of each child? What does knowing this mean in terms of planning future experiences for these two children?

Integrating Art and Social Studies

My second-grade class is heterogeneously grouped and quite culturally diverse. Some students have recently immigrated to the United States; others have always lived in the United States, and their families are very much involved in the traditions and customs of their own cultural community as well as the U.S. community. While teaching a unit on communities as part of our social studies curriculum, I find that integrating works of art into discussions and activities allows the students to observe and discuss how various communities from different time periods and cultures are alike and different.

I have adapted an integrated fine arts program called Art Tells a Story about Communities (Fitzpatrick and Parrish 1995) into my unit on communities. By looking at five paintings that depict various aspects of community life, the students make predictions about what they see in the paintings and the artists' motivations to paint the scene, answer questions asked by their peers and me, and observe and discuss five attributes common to all communities. I introduce each concept through one painting. Then I provide a variety of read-alouds, literature-based activities, role-playing simulations, art projects, and guest speakers to enhance and build on the community focus we originally discussed and observed in each of the paintings.

Each student completes an independent self-study of the painting by answering questions, writing his own questions, and making predictions about the people, places, things, and activities he sees in the painting. Finally, the class discusses their ideas about the painting as a group. After we have discussed their ideas, I give them some information about the artist, the style of the painting, and the story behind the painting. The students' favorite part of the discussion is sharing the title they would give the painting. I cover up the real title before we look at the painting, and after they have shared their predictions I reveal the title that the artist gave the painting.

We look at Norman Rockwell's *Norman Rockwell Visits a Family Doctor* to focus on community helpers and Grandma Moses's *Sugaring Off* to develop the concept of people in communities working together. We use Diego Rivera's *Piñata* to explore the concept of communities celebrating together and *Snap the Whip* by Winslow Homer to focus on the concept of communities playing together. Finally, we use *View of Paris with Furtive Pedestrians* by Jean Dubuffet to explore the idea that communities have important places. Art activities such as making books and posters are included in the study of each concept about communities.

The majority of primary students learn most effectively with visual aids. By studying community concepts through works of art, the students are able to make visual connections to the features that all communities share. The paintings motivate them to make comparisons to what they see and experience in their own U.S. community as well as communities they are familiar with from around the world. It allows them to see how communities of the past functioned similarly to present-day communities and how people help communities grow and change for the good of their citizens. Integrating the fine arts into a social studies unit is a great way to bring new ideas, points of view, and experiences to the students in your classroom.

CHAPTER 14

Living Together: The Social Studies

After reading this chapter, you will be able to do the following:

- Consider several approaches to social studies instruction for young children.
- Plan a social studies program for young children.
- Plan appropriate holiday celebrations for young children.
- Plan a curriculum that includes appropriate multicultural experiences.
- Plan for connections between social studies and literacy learning.

Your instructor began this week's class by asking you and your classmates what you remembered about social studies as part of your own school experience. Almost all of the responses were negative. Some students recalled reading chapters in a textbook and answering the questions at the ends of the chapters. Others told about memorizing lists of names, dates, and places. (Some were still memorizing historical facts.) A few of your classmates had learned to like history by reading biographies and historical novels. Others admitted being somewhat embarrassed by their lack of knowledge about geography and historical events.

You wondered what social studies instruction was like in today's schools. And what you found when you observed in a first-grade classroom really surprised you: The children were investigating problems in their school and neighborhood and learning how to solve those problems. For instance, the class you visited was concerned that the schoolyard was always littered with paper and trash. With the teacher's guidance, the children determined the source of the litter, wrote letters to the offending neighbors, petitioned the principal to place more trash receptacles on the playground, and started an antilitter campaign in their school. They presented their antilitter skit to all the classes in the school and put up antilitter posters and slogans near all the school exits. The teacher told you that these activities had developed over several weeks and that the children had decided that the next problem they would address was the lack of play equipment on the playground.

Back in your own class, your classmates had much to report about the social studies instruction they had observed. Some had found children studying heroes and heroines, and others had found children memorizing the famous speeches of various Americans. In some schools, the social studies curriculum was organized around holidays, and in others, social studies was based on the notion of learning to live together in harmony. At this point, you and your classmates are thoroughly confused about what instruction in social studies should involve.

Approaches to Teaching the Social Studies

The term *social studies* has been used for many years to label the social sciences taught in early childhood and elementary programs. The social sciences include history, political science, economics, anthropology, psychology, sociology, and geography. In programs for children, these separate subject areas are combined to form the social studies. Beyond that, however, there is little agreement about the nature of the social studies and what content should be covered by social studies instruction.

Multiple Views of the Social Studies Curriculum

Programs for young children use several approaches to social studies:

- One approach is to integrate social studies into the daily lives of the children. Proponents of this approach believe that social studies need not be a content area for young children. They believe that as children learn to settle disputes, work out systems for taking turns, and establish other arrangements for living and working together responsibly, they are learning the most important concepts of social studies.

- Another approach is to treat social studies as a content area with a body of knowledge that should be learned by all young children. Proponents of this view believe that social studies content is important and that young children could be learning much more than is commonly taught in preschools and primary grades.

- A third approach combines these two views of social studies, so that children learn content in social studies but do so while learning the skills of interacting in groups.

Proponents of all three views believe that social studies is important because world conditions are changing and citizens must be prepared to participate effectively in government and society. Education as a cornerstone for participation in democracy is not a new idea. The focus of American schools following the Revolutionary War was on educating citizens to participate in the new democratic government. Thomas Jefferson (1743–1826) stated, "If a nation expects to be ignorant and free, in a state of civilization, it expects what never was and never will be" (qtd. in Butts 1960). To be successful, a representative democracy requires a citizenry capable of examining the issues and making decisions that will benefit the nation.

John Dewey (1859–1952) also emphasized the importance of learning to live in a democratic society. He believed that classrooms should be democratic and that children should learn to participate in the decision-making process as part of their school experience (Dewey 1916). His thinking was considered to be radical in his time because schools of that era were so authoritarian.

The Expanding Curriculum

The organizational pattern for social studies in elementary schools—called the **expanding curriculum**—was developed from the ideas of Lucy Sprague Mitchell (1878–1967). The expanding curriculum typically begins in kindergarten or first grade with a focus on the individual; the focus then moves to the individual in a group, a community, a state, a nation, and finally, the world. Mitchell believed that children learn social studies by participating in real experiences. She described how children learn geography, for example, from field trips during which they can examine the real features of the region around them (Mitchell 1928). Mitchell believed that in order to learn, children must have experiences, see relationships, and make connections and generalizations. She expected teachers not merely to supply information but to arrange activities that would enable children to gain information through experience.

In their 1994 position statement, the National Council of Social Studies (NCSS) defines social studies as follows:

> Social studies is the integrated study of the social sciences and humanities to promote civic competence. Within the school program, social studies provides coordinated, systematic study drawing upon such disciplines as anthropology, archaeology, economics, geography, history, law, philosophy, political science, psychology, religion, and sociology, as well as appropriate content from the humanities, mathematics, and natural sciences. The primary purpose of social studies is to help young people develop the ability to make informed and reasoned decisions for the public good as citizens of a culturally diverse, democratic society in an interdependent world. (Executive Summary, p. 1–2)

The National Council of Social Studies lists ten themes as important in constructing curriculum in the social studies. These themes are culture; time, continuity, and change; people, places, and environments; individual development and identity; individuals, groups, and institutions; power, authority, and governance; production, distribution, and consumption; science, technology, and society; global connections; and civic ideals and practices. The following example illustrates how these themes are incorporated in planning a topic of study for the early grades:

> *"Culture."* For the early grades, the standard (stated first, in a sentence) and its performance expectations (listed in alphabetical order) are as follows: Social studies programs should include experiences that provide for the study of culture and cultural diversity, so that the learner can: *a. explore and describe similarities and differences in the ways groups, societies, and cultures address similar human needs and concerns; b. give examples of how experiences may be interpreted differently by people from diverse cultural perspectives and frames of reference; c. describe ways in which language, stories, folktales, music, and artistic creations serve as expressions of culture and influence behavior of people living in a particular culture; d. compare ways in which people from different cultures think about and deal with*

their physical environment and social conditions; e. give examples and describe the importance of cultural unity and diversity within and across groups.

One of the classroom activities describes the experiences of a teacher, Carlene Jackson, who uses a new program to develop geographic understanding in her first grade class. Before the first day of school, Jackson looks over her class list, inferring that she will have students of Mexican, Vietnamese, and Korean ancestry, as well as of African-American and European-American backgrounds. Jackson and her students decide to study how families meet their basic needs of food, clothing, and shelter in five places: their community; Juarez, Mexico; Hanoi, Vietnam; Lagos, Nigeria; and Frankfurt, Germany. The class reads books and stories, looks at photos and slides, watches videos, and talks to speakers from their cities. Students sharpen their reading, writing, and speaking skills and learn new geography skills such as map reading. For each city, they read and discuss something about its location, climate, region, and people. This activity is designed to address performance expectations a, b, and d. (pp. 6–7)

This example illustrates how social studies can be an integrating discipline in the classroom and how teachers can draw on content from many disciplines to help children develop concepts in the social studies. At this time, the NCSS is working on new themes and standards. The number of themes will probably be reduced and the number of standards certainly will be.

Current Expectations

In recent years, the teaching of social studies has been widely criticized in the popular press. Critics have pointed to the lack of factual knowledge and skills exhibited by students, especially high school graduates, who lack geographic knowledge and often cannot even locate North America on a map. Critics also find that very few Americans have what they consider an adequate knowledge of U.S. history.

In response to this criticism, the current focus of social studies in many states is on learning history and facts. Proponents argue that other approaches have failed to teach students the basic knowledge needed to be an informed American citizen. To some degree, they are right; young children can learn much more than some social studies programs have offered. On the other hand, memorizing facts without understanding the concepts that underlie them is not an acceptable approach in early childhood education. In the rush to produce higher achievement, some of the new standards have failed to take into account what is known about child development and how children can learn in meaningful ways (Seefeldt 1995b).

It is clear that teachers do have responsibilities in the area of social studies instruction other than to help children learn to interact in groups, but it is equally clear that social studies need not be a separate subject or divorced from other activities in children's experiences. An early childhood teacher must plan for experiences in which the children can be active and that will help children gain meaningful knowledge, skills, and attitudes important in the social studies.

A Constructivist View of Social Studies Learning

As they do in any other area of learning, children construct their understandings of concepts in the social studies over a period of time. The following figures provide a graphic illustration of these changes in understanding.

Figure 14.1 is a map drawn by a four-year-old. A visiting grandmother had volunteered to drive the child to school and asked her mother to draw a map of the route, but the child wanted to draw the map herself. As shown in the figure, her concept of *map* is that it is something with many lines and squiggles. The small circle outside the larger circle may be the child's home.

Figure 14.2 is a map drawn the next year by the same child, who now needed to be driven to kindergarten. Note that it has many fewer lines and scribbles and that some are quite identifiable. For instance, her house is the square with the four small squares inside it (windows). The long lines that encircle the house are roads; they are connected to the circular lines at the top of the page by a narrow rectangular box divided by lines indicating a railroad crossing. The small rectangle (at the left side) indicates a four-way-stop intersection.

Figure 14.1 A Four-Year-Old's Map

Figure 14.2 A Five-Year-Old's Map

Figure 14.3

A Six-Year-Old's Map

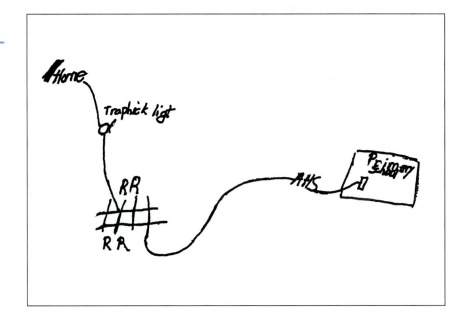

The third map, Figure 14.3, was drawn by the same child in the summer between kindergarten and first grade to give directions to her primary school. This map looks much more like a map that you would draw to help a friend find your house. It contains only the necessary information, not every cross street and building. It shows a traffic light (where one should go straight) and a railroad crossing (which is carefully marked). And the street actually did make a wide curve before the schools. The *AHS* stands for the high school building that must be passed before coming to the primary school. The door on the school designates the entrance where parents were supposed to drop off their children.

What can we conclude about the child who has drawn these maps? In sum, she has developed concepts through many experiences and those concepts have been refined over time with more experiences. The initial concept of *map* might have come from observing her parents using a street or highway map, from watching adult friends draw maps as part of giving directions to different locations, and from hearing her parents talk about directions to various locations. With more experience and some instruction, the child's concept of *map* will be expanded beyond road maps to include many kinds of maps and be refined to a more sophisticated understanding. Knowledge about maps cannot be mastered through lessons, however; it must be developed over time. Similarly, other important concepts in the social studies must be learned through the same developmental stages. A child might be taught that George Washington was the first U.S. president, but it will take time to fully develop the concept of *president* and what it meant to be the *first president*.

Planning Social Studies Education

Goals

The position statement of the NCSS (1989) remains the best available set of guidelines for creating social studies programs in which children gain the following knowledge, skills, and attitudes. Those guidelines identify three sets of goals for social studies education:

- **Knowledge goals**—Knowledge goals focus on concepts, including concepts that reflect the content of the social studies, such as:
  —Each person is unique.
  —People are interdependent.
  —The earth is covered with water and land.
  —Land forms determine where people live and affect how they live.
  —Social groups must solve problems.
  —Each person has responsibilities.

  Other knowledge goals focus on concepts based on the structure of the social science disciplines, such as:
  —We can learn about the past from evidence left by others.
  —Records can help us recall what has happened.
  —Groups can make decisions that affect each individual.
  —Individuals can help determine how problems are solved.

  Finally, some knowledge goals focus on concepts based on children's interests, such as:
  —Change is continuous.
  —Different social groups solve problems differently.
  —People in neighborhoods help one another.

- **Skill goals**—Skill goals are furthered by activities that emphasize the ability to record and communicate simple data; the ability to interact in socially acceptable ways with family, peers, and adults; and the ability to solve problems of a social nature.

- **Attitude goals**—Attitude goals emphasize helping children recognize the importance of each individual; respect the feelings of other individuals; and cultivate a continuing interest in learning about the people, places, and systems that are integral to the social studies.

Classroom Experiences

Threes and Fours

Appropriate experiences in the social studies, like any experiences for children who are three and four, cannot be separated from play. Just as in math and science, teachers will want to provide not only play materials that help children learn some social studies concepts but also time to use them. In developing topics for organizing curricula, teachers should make sure that social studies concepts are included when they are appropriate. The following descriptions may suggest other possibilities:

- Toys related to methods of transportation can be included in play areas. Trucks, cars, buses, trains, airplanes, and helicopters can be added to the blocks area, and boats and barges can be added to the water play area. The teacher can help children focus on the concept of the necessity of transporting goods and people.

- Children can take short walks in their neighborhood and identify different types of structures (houses, businesses, churches, and so on).

- Children can be led to observe changes in their immediate environments, such as changes in the room, on the playground, or in the school building.

- Children can be encouraged to create structures with blocks that represent what they know of their neighborhood or community. They might construct a fire station if they live near one or if the school is near one, an airport (if it is part of their experience), a gas station, a harbor, or other structures.

- Children can work together to move toys or materials that need to be moved or to clean up the materials and play areas.

- Teachers can keep a large scrapbook with records of important events in the children's experiences. Reviewing it with the children will teach them that we can keep records of events and that these records help us to recall the events accurately.

- Teachers can develop multicultural and gender-neutral prop boxes that help children explore similarities and differences in people. Boutte, Van Scoy, and Hendley (1996) recommend gathering the props needed to recreate a shoe store, bakery, hair salon, department store, grocery store, and restaurant. Making available materials that reflect a wide variety of cultural and ethnic differences will provide opportunities for discussion and active participation in learning about people. Prop boxes can be enhanced by adding music, literature, foods, art, cultural artifacts, and items for special needs.

Fives and Sixes

Social studies for the school beginner should continue to be based on play experiences and meaningful activities. The teacher will want to plan some experiences that help children develop specific concepts, but this does not imply that lessons in the social studies should be isolated from other experiences. Here are some suggested activities:

- Children can continue to learn about change by observing any changes in their neighborhood or community (such as buildings being constructed or torn down). The children can record their observations in their journals, or the teacher can help them record their observations on experience charts. Photographs of the sequence of the changes can help children keep records. Children can also learn about change in themselves by bringing in baby pictures or baby clothes and comparing them with their current looks and clothing.

- Children can celebrate the diversity of family structures in which they live. The teacher can find pictures to represent the family structures in the class, and the children can write or dictate lists of common features and positive attributes of families.

- Children can begin to explore racial and ethnic differences by examining differences in skin color, hair texture, and eye shape. After selecting paint chips or mixing paint to match their individual skin colors, they can create a chart illustrating the range of colors in the class. They can create another chart of hair textures and eye colors. With guidance from the teacher, kindergarten children can discuss the advantages of physical characteristics under different environmental conditions—for example, dark skin provides more protection from the sun (Derman-Sparks and ABC Task Force 1989).

- Children can begin to categorize objects or goods as "wants" or "needs." They can develop the concept that people are paid for their work and that the money is used to acquire goods.

- Children can create three-dimensional maps of their classroom and their neighborhood. Photographs can be attached to models of buildings or

Modeling clay is a fun way for children to recreate the topical features found on relief maps.

other structures in the neighborhood. These maps can be created with blocks, milk cartons, cereal boxes, and so on.

- Children can trace the route taken by the milk that is served every day in the classroom from the dairy farm to the dairy, the distributor, the delivery truck, and the cafeteria. They can make books of their observations and learn about the animals that provide milk and the people who process and deliver it.

- Children can create lists or pictures of items that can and cannot be bought with money. The items can then be reclassified as "wants" and "needs."

- Children can compare the rules at school with those at home in terms of who makes the rules, why the rules are needed, and how the rules can be changed.

- Children can create personal timelines by recording the important events of their lives, such as moving, having a new baby in the family, going to preschool, and so on. The timelines can be illustrated with drawings or photographs to indicate changes.

Sevens and Eights

Sevens and eights can do more with maps and learn more about economics and politics than younger children; however, they still need real experiences. Teachers should not expect sevens and eights to learn from textbooks alone or to be able to handle abstract concepts that are not part of their experience. Activities for this age group include the following:

- Children can map their school and perhaps their neighborhood by constructing three-dimensional maps and then transferring the information to a two-dimensional form. They can create legends for the two-dimensional maps.

- Children can learn about elections and voting. They can visit a polling place and see how the records are kept and how the ballots are marked. They can invite people who are running for local office to visit and explain why they want to be elected. They might interview several different people to determine how people make decisions about voting or why they do or do not vote. They can participate in classroom and school elections and make classroom decisions by voting.

- Children can survey others in school to find out what kinds of jobs their parents hold. This information can be presented on charts and graphs. (The teacher can use the work done by parents as a source of topics—for example, factory production or service industries.) If some parents are unemployed, on welfare, on strike, or laid off from their jobs, teachers can help children learn some of the reasons for these conditions in their neighborhoods.

- The class can survey the community to determine local natural resources and how they are used. They can determine who in the community makes decisions about resources and interview those people about their long-term goals. The teacher can help children obtain information on conserving natural resources from books, speakers, films, and so on. Children can make lists of what they can do to conserve resources.

- Children can determine who is responsible for all the services provided in the community and create Venn diagrams of government and private responsibilities.

- Current events can provide learning experiences for this age group if they are related to the children's interests and experience. Interesting pictures or stories from newspapers can be posted on a bulletin board as a catalyst to spark discussion or further explorations.

- Children can compare the tools they use in school to those used by children in the past and learn about the inventors of the tools that are new.

- Students can create timelines to record the important events and people they learn about. For example, after reading *Minty: A Story of Young Harriet Tubman* (Schroeder 1996), they could place a picture of Harriet Tubman on the timeline to indicate that she lived after the Pilgrims and after Charlotte Haines, a Revolutionary War character (*Charlotte,* Lunn 1998), but before Rosa Parks (*If a Bus Could Talk: The Story of Rosa Parks*, Ringgold 1999) and Ruby Bridges (*The Story of Ruby Bridges*, Coles 1995).

Social Development

The social studies curriculum offers many opportunities for children to develop social skills. For example, learning to take turns when talking about a topic in a group, learning to abide by a group decision without undue complaining, and learning that not everyone has the same perspective are basic elements of social studies instruction. The children need modeling and direct instruction in order to continue their social development. Teachers should model respect for all children and all cultures in terms of how books are selected for the library corner, how parents are invited and accepted into the classroom, and how responses are given to the children. As the children make group decisions, the teacher may need to use discussion and role-play to help them understand how to handle disappointment when the group's choice is contrary to theirs. The teacher will also need to help children learn that other people have other perspectives. Holiday celebrations, in which the children can share how their families celebrate, should be planned along with other activities that help children understand cultural differences and similarities.

Katz and McClellan (1997) offer suggestions for helping children gain social skills in three areas that seem particularly significant in social studies:

1. *Helping children participate appropriately in discussions:* Teachers should help individual children learn to be more patient with their peers and to judge what might interest their peers by making specific suggestions or through puppet play.

The Social Studies

Under great pressure to prepare young children for later academic success, far too many teachers claim they have no time for the social studies. "In our school we alternate between social studies and science every other semester," said a teacher. Others claim, "The curriculum is already overcrowded, and with the focus on reading and math there's just no time for frills like social studies."

Yet the study of the social sciences is critical. If our democracy is not only to persist, but to continue to change and improve, the development of the knowledge, skills, and attitudes required of citizens of a democratic society must begin in the early childhood classroom. Teachers who claim they have no time for social studies do not understand the true meaning of the social studies.

Here, children begin developing an understanding of an essential, if difficult, principle of democracy, that of giving up some of their needs, wants, and freedom for the good of the group. In the classroom, young children automatically give up some of their individuality. Once in a group setting, children face the hard reality of having to share. They must learn to share the attention of the adults who care for and teach them, as well as materials, play yard equipment, toys, and easels. Their wants—to continue to build with blocks, for example—are balanced by the needs of the group—to stop their work to eat lunch.

Within the democracy of the classroom, choice making is encouraged. Children choose which center they want to begin working in, what they will do once in the center, whether to work by themselves or with others, and when they are finished and ready to move to another center. Choice making extends to developing initial abilities to vote. At first children vote between two choices, such as do you want to play Duck, Duck, Goose or

Cross Over the Bridge? Progressing from these initial voting experiences, by age five or so, children can vote and then accept the will of the majority.

Children's here-and-now world is rich in learning resources. Think of the transportation, communication, and other social systems and institutions in children's worlds. Beginning with the center or classroom, children can study people and their jobs, where water comes from, where the trash goes, and myriad other social, economic, and scientific entities. Three-year-olds studying babies made graphs of foods they ate and that babies ate, weighed and measured themselves and a baby, tried on baby clothes, dictated and drew stories—meeting every academic standard yet developed for young children and many more. Second and third graders, using *Journey North* (www.learner.org/jnorth), studied the migration of monarch butterflies. Tracking the migration of the butterflies, children planted milkweed seeds, watched butterflies lay a single egg on each plant, tagged butterflies, and, through the Internet, kept track of their flight north.

No time for the social studies? Think again. The social studies, which enable young people to develop the ability to make informed and reasoned decisions for the public good as citizens of a culturally diverse, democratic society in an interdependent world (NCSS, 1998), are integral to and integrated within the total curriculum. To say there is no time for the study of an interdependent world, beginning during the earliest years and building throughout a lifetime, is ludicrous. Rethink the basics. Begin with the social studies, and the academics fall into their proper places, becoming necessary tools for children to learn ever more about the world in which they live and their role in improving that world.

2. *Helping children learn to negotiate and compromise:* Teachers should offer language models and direct instruction in these skills.

3. *Helping children assert their own preferences more gracefully:* Teachers should offer children appropriate language examples. For example, a child may need to learn to state his reasons for his choices or to soften his rejections of other children's ideas.

Another area of social development that is critical to good social studies instruction is *conflict management* or *conflict resolution*. The goals of conflict resolution overlap several of the knowledge, skill, and attitude goals just listed. Drew (1987) identifies the major concepts of conflict resolution as "accepting self and others, communicating effectively, resolving conflicts, and understanding intercultural differences" (p. 1). Teachers who focus on conflict resolution will help children learn alternate responses to social situations, learn about other people, and learn how to communicate their feelings and expectations in ways that lead to peaceful solutions to problems.

Kreidler (1994) reminds us that teachers must consider children's developmental levels when planning conflict resolution activities. For example, problem solving and point of view may be difficult concepts for young children to grasp, but they can work on concrete examples. Children also need to learn about cause and effect as part of conflict resolution. For example, if a child concludes that hitting is the solution when someone takes the toy she is playing with, then she must learn the consequences for hitting another person. Children also need help in expanding the choices that are available to them for solving conflicts.

Luke and Myers (1994/1995) and Kreidler (1994) suggest that using carefully selected literature, in which the characters solve their problems in a positive manner, is an effective means of teaching children about conflict resolution. Proponents of teaching conflict resolution skills hope that more people will learn to apply them and that eventually even nations will use these techniques to solve problems rather than resorting to violence or war.

Celebrating Holidays

In some programs for young children, instruction in social studies centers on holidays. Some schools move from one holiday to another without much in between, justifying the emphasis on holidays as important to the cultural heritage of the children. Such a rationale is logical only if the children share the culture in which the holiday originated. It is acceptable to celebrate holidays appropriately with young children, but social studies should certainly be more than completing worksheets about Lincoln's birthday.

Planning appropriate holiday celebrations seems to be a difficult task in some school settings. Holiday planning should be approached with the same

Parents AND Social Studies

■ Invite parents to school to ask them how they feel about celebrating holidays in the classroom. In your invitation, make sure that you describe the cultural diversity of your school so that parents can think about how others might feel about holidays.

Developmentally Appropriate Practice

Achieving DAP in social studies instruction, in which topics are fairly abstract, may seem more complicated than in math or science instruction, in which real things can be manipulated and observed. Teachers of young children will be especially challenged in planning appropriate social studies activities. In deciding what is developmentally appropriate, teachers should consider the following:

- Can children understand the concepts to be learned? If the concepts depend on being able to understand historical times or places far from children's experience, then children will be unlikely to understand them.

- Are the concepts related to children's real-life experiences? Learning about a harbor may not be appropriate for children who live far inland.

- Can meaningful activities in which children are involved be planned around the concept? Field trips, resource people, and real objects to explore may bring concepts to life for young children; completing dittoed worksheets and coloring pages, however, will not promote concept development.

- Can the concept be integrated into other areas of the curriculum? For example, can the concept be developed through activities in which children sing songs, learn dances, read stories, and create art?

- Do the activities honor the diversity of the children and their families?

- Will stereotypes be reduced rather than increased through participation in social studies activities?

careful considerations for developmental appropriateness of various activities and determination of goals that are applied in other curriculum areas. Bisson (1997) suggests that teachers follow these guidelines in planning for holidays:

- Talk about some holidays rather than celebrate each one. For example, the class might talk briefly about Presidents' Day, but it will have little meaning for young children. Perhaps invite a family to tell about a holiday they celebrate that is not selected for a school celebration.

- As much as possible, fit holiday celebrations into regular routines. Do holiday art projects as part of "choice time," or invite families to join the children in singing holiday songs they have learned. An elaborate production that involves practice and pressure is not an appropriate response to a holiday.

- Avoid basing classroom themes on holidays. A holiday should not be the focus of the curriculum for an extended period of time.

- Avoid materials and activities that scare the children, such as certain costumes and masks. Instead, have children create their own masks and costumes from dress-up clothes.

- Offer activities that calm the children and focus them on a process. For example, creating a center for making holiday cards and adding holiday colors to sand and water play will help children be creative without also feeling pressure. A variety of open-ended materials can be made available so the children can choose and create what is satisfying to them.

- Offer a choice of holiday-related activities or other activities that meet curriculum goals but are not holiday related.

Also consider these suggestions for holiday planning:

- Evaluate what the children will learn if the holiday is acknowledged in the curriculum. Each holiday should be evaluated in terms of the curriculum goals of the program (Dimidjian 1989; Timberlake 1978).

- Determine what the children think the holiday means and what they know about it.

- Remember that the children should have the most important role in deciding how the holiday should be celebrated. Involve them in planning and implementing the celebration. Is the celebration something they can really do themselves, or is it so elaborate that an adult must do it for them?

- Keep in mind that some commercial holiday materials are stereotypical. Thanksgiving might be a good time to help children understand why stereotypical images of American Indians are not appropriate and to help them learn what can be done to combat these stereotypes, such as writing letters of complaint to the company or refusing to buy such materials. Holiday celebrations should help children gain knowledge, show respect for others, and develop a deeper understanding of the similarities and differences among people.

The following suggestions for specific holiday celebrations are based on ideas in two books: *Anti-Bias Curriculum: Tools for Empowering Young Children* (Derman-Sparks and ABC Task Force 1989) and *Celebrate! An Anti-Bias Guide to Enjoying Holidays in Early Childhood Programs* (Bisson 1997).

Thanksgiving

- The children can focus on the harvest aspects of the holiday by visiting a farm, harvesting their own garden, or finding evidence of harvest in the community.

- The teacher can help the children find information about other harvest festivals and how they are celebrated.

- The teacher can help the children relate the eating of a meal to the celebration of the harvest.

- The teacher should supply *accurate* information about contemporary American Indians using books, pictures, and guest speakers. The teacher can help children critique greeting cards and TV specials for images of

American Indians and the authenticity of the portrayals of the first Thanksgiving. In the words of author and American Indian rights activist Michael Dorris, "It must be communicated to educators that no information about Native peoples is truly preferable to a reiteration of the same old stereotypes, particularly in the early years" (cited in Derman-Sparks and ABC Task Force 1989, p. 88).

■ The children can help cook some foods typical of Thanksgiving celebrations, such as cornbread, squash, and cranberries.

Halloween

■ The teacher can help children recognize the harvest aspects of Halloween (scarecrows, pumpkins, and so on).

■ Children can learn to recognize the similarities between jack-o'-lanterns and other cultures' representations of human figures with food. They can create some "vegetable people" from squash, turnips, or ears of corn. The vegetable people can be washed and eaten after the activity.

■ Children can explore costumes for different purposes (theater, other entertainment). Younger children can be encouraged to explore the concept of being the same person even though they look different in costumes.

■ A maker of masks can be invited to share his collection and help the children understand some of the cultural uses of masks or show slides of different masks from around the world. Involve the children in mask making. In order to avoid having them associate the color black with

Holiday planning requires the same careful consideration involved in planning activities in other curriculum areas. What issues should teachers consider in planning Halloween celebrations?

scary things, children can be encouraged to make masks that are scary but not black and others that are black but not scary.

- Teachers can help children explore scary feelings. Children can create paintings, songs, or dances that help them express their feelings. They can find scary things in books such as *Where the Wild Things Are* (Sendak 1963) and *There's a Nightmare in My Closet* (Mayer 1968) and talk about how the characters responded to being scared.

- Children in communities that still maintain the tradition of going from house to house at Halloween can explore how that tradition is carried on in other celebrations. Teachers can help children understand the trick in *trick or treat* by sharing "trickster" stories from the southwestern American Indian tradition and inviting children to plan some tricks.

- Older children can trace the origins of symbols used in Halloween celebrations.

Mother's Day and Father's Day

- Celebrate Family Day instead, hosting a program or open house to which children's families are invited.

- Have the children make cards or gifts for anyone in their families.

- Invite grandparents and other elderly relatives to the classroom to tell stories about when they were young children.

Valentine's Day

- Focus activities on the idea of friendship.

- Have materials available so each child can make a card for one special friend at home or at school.

- Involve parents and children in planning a friendship celebration that does not involve commercial valentines or decorations.

Martin Luther King Day

- List and discuss things that are fair and unfair—say, on the playground or in the lunchroom.

- Read a short book about the life of Dr. King.

- Talk about King's efforts to change unfair laws using peaceful means.

- Be sure to plan what you will tell the children about Dr. King's death so as not to frighten or upset them.

Social Studies Themes

As with other subject-matter areas, a thematic approach to social studies offers opportunities for children to do meaningful tasks that can help them acquire important knowledge, skills, and attitudes. A list of possible topics that would

Parents AND Social Studies

■ Keep parents informed about social studies activities by including information about them in the class newsletter. Solicit parental involvement by making a list of needed materials, asking for volunteers for field trips, and suggesting the sharing of skills such as cooking or sewing costumes.

be useful for developing social studies concepts would be nearly endless. Teachers could focus on the family; justice; change; the neighborhood; the city; celebrations; historical places in the community; parks; interdependence; workplaces; bread—and this is by no means an exhaustive list. Suggestions for developing three such topics are described in the following lists.

Immigration

■ Read aloud the following books about immigration:*
American Wei (Pomeranc 1998)
Anushka's Voyage (Tarbescu 1998)
The Butterfly Seeds (Watson 1995)
The Dream Jar (Pryor 1996)
From Far Away (Askar 1995)
Lights for Gita (Gilmore 1995)
A Picnic in October (Bunting 1999)
The Silence in the Mountains (Rosenberg 1999)
The Tangerine Tree (Hanson 1995)
A Very Important Day (Herold 1995)
When I First Came to This Land (Ziefert 1998)
When Jessie Came across the Sea (Hest 1997)

■ After finishing each book, talk about people's reasons for immigration. Record these reasons on a chart.

■ Have children interview their parents and grandparents to learn their immigration stories. Compile the stories to create a book of family stories.

■ If possible, ask families to come to school to share family treasures they brought with them when they came to the United States. And if appropriate, ask them to tell about what they left behind.

■ Ask several recent immigrants to come to class to share their experiences. What do they expect from their new lives in the United States?

Transportation

■ Have the children think of as many ways of transporting people and goods as possible. Make a list of these kinds of transportation, and then categorize them as land, air, and sea vehicles.

■ List all the possible ways children get from home to school. Make a graph that shows how many students get to school in each way.

■ If possible, take the class on a trip on a train or subway. Find out how traveling by train or subway (as opposed to traveling by personal car) benefits the community.

*Full bibliographic information is provided in the References (pages 505–528).

- If possible, visit a port to observe the unloading of a ship. Find out what kinds of goods are transported by ship. Also find out where these goods go after being unloaded from the ship. Most ships are loaded with containers that go directly to trains or trucks.
- Visit a local supermarket and determine how foods have been shipped to the market and from where. Locate the points of origin on a map or globe.

Communication

- Have the children interview family members to determine how many ways they communicate with others. Make a graph of the results for the class.
- Determine how many languages are spoken in the homes of the children in the class. Together, learn how to say the word *school* in each of these languages.
- Ask a person who signs to demonstrate sign language and teach the children some common signs. As a class, learn how to sign a short poem or song.
- Create a timeline that shows the ways people have communicated throughout history. Have the children add drawings or cutout pictures of the various types of communication.
- Make a list of all the reasons people need to communicate at school.
- Visit local businesses that are involved with communication: TV stations, radio stations, the newspaper office, the telephone company, and so on. Ask people about the jobs they do at these businesses.
- Make a list of the rules for communication in the classroom. Make another list of the rules for communication at home. Make a third list of the rules for communication in public places. Discuss how and why these three sets of rules vary.
- Write to a pen pal in another part of the world using e-mail or regular mail. Find out if communication is equally accessible to all people everywhere.
- Research inventions and inventors related to communication. Talk about how people's lives would be different without these inventions.

Multicultural Education

Multicultural education and **antibias curriculum** are terms used to describe educational programs that attempt to teach children respect for all people and their cultures. Multicultural education involves learning about one's own and other cultures in an integrated way. A multicultural or antibias curriculum is not achieved by superficial lessons; it is achieved by sensitive and knowledgeable teachers who help children learn in a context in which all cultures are appreciated.

The National Council for Accreditation of Teacher Education (1987) defines *multicultural education* as a perspective that recognizes "(1) the social,

Integrating the Curriculum

The theme of *Who Are We?* is a social studies theme in that most of the theme work will be related to the social sciences. Possible activities include:

➤ Ask families to share with the class any traditional clothing that they or their ancestors might wear or have worn.

➤ Ask families to help create a class cookbook with a favorite recipe from each child.

➤ Determine how many people work in the school and what their jobs are.

➤ Find out about the history of the school and make a timeline to represent events in the school's history. Children may want to draw pictures of various events and place the pictures on the timeline.

➤ Learn about the history of your own family as much as possible.

➤ Learn about the history of your town/city. When was it established? Who settled first? Why did the first settlers come to this place? Are there geographical features that influenced the location of your town?

➤ Determine the population groups in your town/city. If you have a population of recent immigrants to the United States, find out why they came to this town/city.

➤ Create a map that illustrates the country of origin of each family represented in the class.

➤ On a map of your town/city, locate the school and other important places such as city hall, the post office, the fire stations, and so on.

➤ Find out what family recreational facilities are in your town/city. Make a guide to recreational facilities that could be given to new residents.

➤ Invite members of the city government (such as city council members, chief of police, building inspector, parks and recreation director, and so on) to speak to the class about their responsibilities.

➤ Find people in your community who have lived there a long time, and invite them to tell the children about the changes they have witnessed.

➤ What kinds of businesses are in your community? Are the businesses the same as many years ago or have they changed?

political, and economic realities that individuals experience in culturally diverse and complex human encounters and (2) the importance of culture, race, sex and gender, ethnicity, religion, socioeconomic status, and exceptionalities in the education process" (p. 57).

The effort to eliminate racism and prejudice by making students and teachers more aware and accepting of the cultural diversity in the United States is relatively new. Recent U.S. demographic information indicates that cultural and ethnic minority populations are growing rapidly; consequently, multicultural education is also gaining importance.

Whaley and Swadner (1990) argue for beginning multicultural education in infant and toddler programs. Very young children learn to discriminate differences and classify things and feelings; they can also learn to be more empathetic than was once believed. Programs that support multicultural education are important as very young children begin to learn about people

Art projects can provide great opportunities for children to explore other cultures.

other than family. Teachers of preschoolers can make sure that materials (books, music, dolls, and so on) represent a variety of cultures, use pictures of different cultural and ethnic groups involved in a variety of experiences, and take every opportunity to help children learn to care for one another.

Basic Assumptions

The basic assumptions of multicultural education have been articulated by Hernandez (1989):

1. It is increasingly important for political, social, educational, and economic reasons to recognize that the United States is a culturally diverse society.
2. Multicultural education is for all students.
3. Multicultural education is synonymous with effective teaching.
4. Teaching is a cross-cultural encounter.
5. Traditionally, the educational system has not served all students equally well.
6. Multicultural education is synonymous with educational innovation and reform.
7. Next to parents, teachers are the single most important factor in the lives of children.
8. Classroom interaction between teachers and students constitutes the major part of the educational process for most students (pp. 9–11).

Several classroom implications follow from these assumptions. One is that lessons limited to teaching children about a single aspect of one other culture are inappropriate. For example, teachers sometimes attempt to teach about Hispanic culture by making and serving tortillas. More appropriate experiences would continue over a period of several days, during which children would discover that each cultural group has bread of some kind and participate in making and eating bread from each cultural group represented in the classroom. These experiences could reveal to children that people of all cultures buy bread at markets, that some cultures do not have traditional breads at all, and that others bake traditional breads only on special occasions. Finding the common elements in how people from different cultures cook, eat, dress, live in families, and carry on daily activities is an important goal.

Multicultural education is not just learning about other cultures. Teaching facts alone will never erase stereotypes and bias. As Phillips (1988) stresses:

> We must struggle to truly understand how culture is a source of group power and strength, and to examine how to allow groups to retain their cultural integrity while they gain the skills to function in the larger society. This perhaps is the central struggle we face as adults responsible for preparing today's children and tomorrow's leaders in a society that may de-value them by demanding that they give up their culture in order to achieve. (p. 46)

For too many children, success in school depends on learning in only one way and giving up other ways of learning and acting. Many American Indian educators believe that American Indian students drop out of school as soon as they can legally do so because they have to be "White" in order to succeed at school. Teachers of young children can provide students with many choices of learning activities and with many avenues for expressing what they know and are learning.

Another implication of Hernandez's (1989) assumptions is that effective teaching must be individualized, based on the child's development and relevant to the child's experience. Memorizing facts about other cultures, pasting a sombrero on a ditto sheet of a Hispanic man sitting under a cactus, and learning about American Indians of long ago are activities that do not meet the criteria for effective teaching. Children will develop concepts about other people as they interact with real people at school and in their neighborhoods. Thomson (1989) believes that experiences in which children can actively participate are the most valuable for helping them develop understanding and tolerance. She suggests that experiences such as role-playing Rosa Parks or discussing children's feelings on encountering discriminatory signs foster the active learning that is necessary for young children.

A third implication of Hernandez's assumptions is that teachers must take individual responsibility for learning about the children in the class and for helping all children learn to appreciate one another. Children learn how to appreciate others from observing and participating in interactions with the teacher. No commercial multicultural education program can relieve the teacher of learning about the children, including their cultural backgrounds, and planning experiences that will help them learn about each other in positive ways.

Goals

As summarized by Banks and Banks (1997), "Multicultural education incorporates the idea that all students—regardless of their gender and social class and their ethnic, racial, or cultural characteristics—should have an equal opportunity to learn in school" (p. 3). Ramsey (1998) states the specific goals of multicultural education as follows:

1. *Children will develop a strong identity of themselves, as members of a group, and as living beings on this planet.*
2. *Children will develop a sense of solidarity with all people and the natural world.*
3. *Children will become critical thinkers.*
4. *Children will be confident and persistent problem solvers.*
5. *Children will gain the academic skills that will give them access to the knowledge of our society and power to make a difference.* (pp. 6–7)

As children learn about others in their class and the world around them, teachers should respond to their questions in ways that reduce their fears (Baker 1994; Derman-Sparks 1993/1994) and help them understand individual and cultural differences. Thomson (1993) helped children understand discrimination by posting signs in various areas of the classroom that showed the international symbol for *no*. (These signs might forbid wearing tie shoes, plaid clothing, or other nonpersonal, changeable items.) After some experience with not being allowed to participate, the children talked about what it felt like.

Education that is multicultural will be reflected in the teacher's choices of books and literature, in the signs posted in the classroom, in holiday celebrations, and in planned activities—in short, throughout the curriculum. For example, children can learn about different languages and different systems of writing through language arts activities (Saracho and Spodek 1983). They can learn about foods contributed to their diets by North and South American cultures (corn), Eastern cultures (rice), and European cultures (wheat).

Children's families also are a valuable source of information and support for a multicultural or antibias curriculum. Teachers can bring families into the classroom to share traditions, expectations, and stories (McCracken 1993; Neuman and Roskos 1994; Swick et al. 1995; Swick, Boutte, and Van Scoy 1995/1996; Wardle 1996). A study of American Indians would be appropriate in the multicultural curriculum for young children. Brophy (1999) found that kindergarten and first-grade children typically have cartoonlike images of American Indians and believe that American Indians are mean and violent. By second grade, the children have usually abandoned the cartoonlike image but believe that native peoples adopted European ways once they were exposed to them. In order to rid children of their stereotypical images and help them develop a more accurate view of native peoples in today's world, Haukoos and Beauvais (1996/1997) suggest that teachers select one *nation* (which is the preferred terminology as opposed to *tribe*) for in-depth study, focus on the commonalities of native people from one region, use authentic children's literature, and learn about contemporary native peoples.

Teachers should plan all activities with an eye for including a multicultural dimension. Figure 14.4 is a checklist designed to help teachers analyze their classrooms and provide education that is multicultural.

Assessing Program Quality

Derman-Sparks (1999) states that a program with the following characteristics is well on the way to providing quality multicultural/antibias education:

- *Staff actively incorporate their children's daily life experiences into daily curriculum.*
- *Staff tailor curriculum and teacher-child interactions to meet the cultural, as well as individual, developmental needs of their children, actively using parents' or family caregivers' knowledge about their home cultures.*
- *Daily classroom life and curriculum incorporate diversity and justice issues related to gender, disabilities, socioeconomic status, and the many ways of being a family, as well as issues related to ethnicity and culture.*
- *Staff use a variety of strategies to involve parents actively and regularly in the program, including provisions for languages other than English.*
- *Staff intentionally encourage children's development of critical thinking and tools for resisting prejudice and unfair behaviors directed at themselves or others. Parents and other neighborhood people share what they do to improve the quality of life and social justice in their communities.*
- *Staff reflect the cultural and language diversity of the children and families they serve and the communities of their centers and schools.*
- *Staff engage in intentional and regular reflections about their practice and the influences of their cultural backgrounds, and they openly help each other uncover and change biases and hurtful (even if unintentional) behaviors.* (p. 43)

Parents AND *Social Studies*

- After parents visit the classroom or contribute significant items from their cultures, be sure to acknowledge them in newsletters, on bulletin boards, and in displays.

The ability of children now in early childhood classes to cope with life in this century may well depend on the quality of their educational experiences. Quality education must include multicultural experiences.

Connecting Social Studies with Reading, Writing, and Literature

Children want to know about the people and the relationships in their world. Teachers should use this natural curiosity to prompt exploration of a variety of social studies topics. Many of these topics can be introduced, studied, and summarized through meaningful literacy experiences using stories, nonfiction, and poetry. One valuable source of information about new books is the bibliography of notable social studies trade books for young people that is published each year in the journal *Social Education*. Figure 14.5 provides a checklist for analyzing bias in children's books. Teachers should use these guidelines to help them make the best selections of literature for their classrooms.

Figure 14.4 Multicultural Checklist

Use this checklist to help you focus on individual aspects of your classroom environment, take a closer look at your curriculum, and highlight areas that need improvement. Try to answer each question as it pertains to your classroom.

Curriculum Area	Question	Yes	No
Language Arts	1. Does your classroom have a wide variety of age-appropriate and culturally diverse books and language arts materials? Look for examples.	☐	☐
	2. Are the cultures in your class and community represented in your books and materials?	☐	☐
	3. Are there any books that speak of people of diverse cultures in stereotypic or derogatory terms? What are they? Should they be removed, or is there a way to use them with children to broaden their concepts and encourage them to share their experiences?	☐	☐
	4. Are the pictures of people on the walls representative of a multicultural community?	☐	☐
Social Studies	5. Does the curriculum help children increase their understanding and acceptance of attitudes, values, and lifestyles that are unfamiliar to them? If so, how? If not, what can you do to change it?	☐	☐
	6. Are materials and games racially or sex-role stereotypic? If so, how can you change your collection to give strong, positive images?	☐	☐
Blocks	7. Are the accessories in the blocks area representative of various cultural groups and family configurations? If not, how can you change them?	☐	☐
	8. Are the people blocks accessories stereotypic in terms of sex roles? If so, how can you change them?	☐	☐
Dramatic Play	9. Is there a wide variety of clothes (everyday garments, not exotic costumes) from various cultural groups?	☐	☐
	10. Are the pictures on the walls and the props representative of a diversity of cultures?	☐	☐
	11. Are the dolls representative of the major racial groups in our country, not just in colors but in features?	☐	☐
Music and Games	12. Do music experiences reinforce children's affirmation of cultural diversity? How?	☐	☐
	13. Do you use fingerplays, games, and songs from various cultural groups?	☐	☐
Cooking	14. Do cooking experiences encourage children to experiment with foods they aren't familiar with?	☐	☐
	15. Are these experiences designed to give children a general notion of the connections between cultural heritage and the process of preparing, cooking, and eating food? If so, how?	☐	☐

Source: Adapted from Frances E. Kendall, Ph.D., "Creating a Multicultural Environment," *Pre-K Today* (November/December 1988): 34–39. Reprinted with permission of the author.

Figure 14.5   Evaluation Criteria for Analyzing Bias
in Children's Literature

Literary Criticism: Multicultural Literature

1. Are the characters portrayed as individuals instead of as representatives of a group?
2. Does the book transcend stereotypes?
3. Does the book portray physical diversity?
4. Will children be able to recognize the characters in the text and illustrations?
5. Is the culture accurately portrayed?
6. Are social issues and problems depicted frankly, accurately, and without oversimplification?
7. Do nonwhite characters solve their problems without intervention by whites?
8. Are nonwhite characters shown as equals of white characters?
9. Does the author avoid glamorizing or glorifying nonwhite characters?
10. Is the setting authentic?
11. Are the factural and historical details accurate?
12. Does the author accurately describe contemporary settings?
13. Does the book rectify historical distortions or omissions?
14. Does dialect have a legitimate purpose and does it ring true?
15. Does the author avoid offensive or degrading vocabulary?
16. Are the illustrations authentic and nonstereotypical?
17. Does the book reflect an awareness of the changing status of females?

Source: From Donna Norton and Saundra Norton, *Through the Eyes of a Child: An Introduction to Children's Literature,* 6th ed., by Norton, Norton, and McClure, © 2003. Reprinted by permission of Pearson Education, Inc., Upper Saddle River, NJ.

The following list is a sampling of the books available on the topic *families* that would be suitable for young children:*

Always My Dad (Wyeth 1997)

Amazing Grace (Hoffman 1991)

Black, White, Just Right (Davol 1993)

Boundless Grace (Hoffman 1995)

Celebrating Families (Hausherr 1997)

A Chair for My Mother (V. Williams 1982)

Daddies (Greenspun 1992)

Everett Anderson's Goodbye (Clifton 1995)

Families Are Different (Pellegrini 1991)

Fathers, Mothers, Sisters, Brothers: A Collection of Family Poems (Hoberman 1993)

*Full bibliographic information is provided in the References (pages 505–528).

First Pink Light (Greenfield 1991)

How My Parents Learned to Eat (Friedman 1984)

The Iguana Brothers (Johnston 1995)

In Daddy's Arms I Am Tall: African Americans Celebrating Fathers (Steptoe 1997)

Less Than Half, More Than Whole (Lacapa and Lacapa 1992)

Lots of Dads (Rotner and Kelly 1997)

Loving (Morris 1990)

Ma Dear's Aprons (McKissack 1997)

The Relatives Came (Rylant 1991)

The Table Where Rich People Sit (Baylor 1994)

Tar Beach (Ringgold 1991)

When Mama Gets Home (Russo 1998)

Working Cotton (S. A. Williams 1992)

These books could be used for read-alouds, for shared reading experiences, or for independent reading, depending on the abilities of the children. These books could also be used to prompt children to write stories about their own families. Children could write reports on their families, contribute to a class book on families, or make invitations asking families to come to the school for a special event. Children could also choose books to share with their families, which would give them another opportunity to read or have someone read to them.

Many other opportunities are possible for meaningful literacy experiences as children explore social studies topics of interest. For example, if children are studying the work of their parents or of school personnel, they could write reports of their findings from their surveys, read more about some of the occupations that especially interest them, write entries for an ABC book of jobs, write letters inviting speakers to class and thank-you notes to speakers who have shared information, and so on. The children might also create charts, reports, books of various kinds, narrative stories, and poetry. For example, if the children have been exploring the cultures of the children in their class, they could create journals in which they record their responses to foods they have tried, pictures of articles of clothing, or their personal responses to something they learned. The class might create a "big book" with photographs and reports they have dictated, which could be reviewed often.

There are many ways of recording and summarizing what children learn. Such documentation allows children to present and reflect on what they learn. It is also useful to teachers in reporting to parents and administrators the concepts that children are developing and their growing literacy abilities and understandings in the social studies. Literacy activities can help teachers meet their goals of having all children develop pride in their own cultural heritages, appreciate the contributions of people of diverse backgrounds to the larger society and culture, and demonstrate respect for the cultures of diverse groups.

Chapter Summary

- Several approaches to teaching social studies can be found in programs for young children. Some approaches stress learning facts, and some stress learning to live together successfully in group settings. Others attempt to combine these two approaches.

- The goals of social studies instruction focus on strengthening knowledge, skills, and attitudes. Children's experiences should help them develop concepts related to social studies, skills in collecting and presenting data, and attitudes that are important in a democracy.

- Teaching social studies as a series of lessons is not as effective as integrating it into a variety of classroom activities.

- A constructivist view of social studies learning holds that children's learning of content must always be considered developmental and will change with the experiences gained in and out of school.

- When celebrating holidays, teachers should determine what children will learn from celebrations;

include different cultural perspectives; involve the children in making decisions about holiday celebrations; reduce the amount of stress surrounding holidays to a minimum; and choose appropriate learning experiences for the age and developmental level of the children.

- An important strategy for integrating social studies with other curriculum areas is to use themes. As always, teachers should select topics that are meaningful to the children and that provide real reasons to apply skills.

- Education that is multicultural is more important than ever in the United States and the world. A multicultural point of view should permeate all instruction and not be limited to isolated lessons designed to teach one cultural group about another.

- Multicultural education should begin with infants and toddlers and should help children learn to respect and care for one another.

- Literacy experiences are a natural way of introducing, exploring, and concluding topics related to the social studies.

Theory INTO Practice

Choose a concept in the social studies and plan a developmentally appropriate experience for each age group: threes and fours, fives and sixes, and sevens and eights. Try to make these experiences as active as possible.

Plan a holiday celebration for either threes and fours, fives and sixes, or sevens and eights. Be sure to make the goals of the celebration clear, to involve the children in the planning stage, and to assess your plan for the impact it may have on those children whose families do not celebrate this holiday.

Many state curricula now call for children to memorize famous historical speeches beginning in kindergarten. In a small group, assess such an activity in terms of its appropriateness for young children and its contribution to the development of concepts in social studies.

Select a topic in social studies. Find at least three children's books that you could use to introduce the topic, to develop some aspect of the topic, or to provide a concluding experience for the topic. Try to find a fictional story, a poem, and a nonfiction book that would be appropriate. Create a plan for using the literature you find.

In a small group, develop a web for a topic that would be appropriate for social studies instruction for young children.

Promoting the Home–School Connection

Social studies—or the study of societies and their interdependence on one another—by definition means learning about our place and the places of others in the world. In order for young children to make sense of this concept, we must start with that which is most important to youngsters: their families. They know their families, and they know they belong to their families.

As a teacher, I further promote the home–school connection in all other topics, as well, so that we—the children and I—may embark on our family discovery adventures together. I've used several methods of making the connections:

1. *Sending a family survey letter home to the parents and asking them to complete it together, if at all possible*—This survey letter includes questions relating to family names, number of people in the family, pets, occupations, interests, hobbies, and special traits of individuals in the family. Students are asked to return the surveys and share their information with the class. Translations of the letters are sent in the languages needed.

2. *Having children construct a bulletin board of the classroom "family," which is made up of individual students' families*—This bulletin board includes any information the students desire to share about themselves and their families using any chosen media: poetry, artwork, songs, chants, pictures, and the like. Children's literature is used as a springboard for discussions about family configurations, dynamics, and traditions. Students develop skits about their roles in their families and/or their classrooms. Parents, grandparents, and other available family members are invited to the classroom to share stories about their cultures or occupations. Many discussions occur about how families are the same and different, again illuminating the common bond of humanity.

3. *Encouraging students to keep journals*—These journals are used to record interviews with various family members, comments about what families do together, any traditions they have shared, as well as ideas the children would like to incorporate into the classroom community.

This unit or topic extends for approximately one month, culminating in a presentation to families about the discoveries students have made about themselves and each other. The presentation often includes songs, artwork, portfolios, and/or collages depicting each student in the middle of a sheet of paper surrounded by the meaningful people, objects, or hobbies in her life. The success of this unit is due to young children's self-absorption and their need to make sense of the world around them. This unit on families is a simple, exciting, challenging way to incorporate and involve all youngsters in an awareness of the external world.

This unit is the central thread in the cultural tapestry woven throughout the year, as the children learn about themselves. Having this knowledge increases their self-esteem, and as their self-esteem increases, they learn and care about other cultures, their relation to them, and their interdependence on each other. The result is an understanding and clear awareness of the importance of each unique individual in the human family.

CHAPTER 15

Promoting Wellness:
Motor Development,
Health, and Safety

- Describe the goals for young children's physical development.
- Describe appropriate activities for encouraging young children's physical development.
- Integrate health and safety education in the early childhood curriculum.
- Plan experiences that will help children develop healthy nutritional habits.
- Involve children with special needs in activities to encourage physical development.
- Celebrate diversity through activities aimed at developing a healthy child.

Your assignment this week, to observe for instruction in health and wellness, motor development, nutrition, and safety, seemed so broad. You thought you were not likely to see all these areas addressed in any one day, but in the kindergarten you visited, you did see some aspects related to all these topics. For example, as the children played outdoors, you saw the teacher encouraging children to participate in activities such as jumping over ropes on the ground. When the children had their snack, you noticed that the teacher talked about the value of eating vegetables and that the snack was a tray of cut-up vegetables from which children could select one or two to try. You knew the class was going to make vegetable soup the next day. During the circle time, a police officer visited the class and the children participated in a bicycle safety program.

As you talked to the teacher, you realized that not all these topics would be included every day but that safety, nutrition, and health were integrated into the regular curriculum as much as possible. Motor development was the focus of outdoor play planned by the teacher or physical education planned by a specialist. The children had physical education at least three days a week with the specialist. Both teachers planned jointly for these activity periods.

You are glad that you saw so much focus on physical development because you believe that physical development should not be ignored any more than social or intellectual development. However, your peers' observations ran the gamut. In some schools, no specialist was available for physical education, some schools did not require physical education, and some schools had eliminated recess in order to get more time for academic topics. Some schools had a safety or nutrition lesson once a week, but there was no effort to integrate these lessons with the curriculum.

You have many questions about what kind of physical education is appropriate for primary children and how to integrate health and safety into an appropriate curriculum.

Encouraging Motor Development

In this era when physical fitness is of such concern to many adults, the media continue to report that U.S. children are neither as fit as they once were nor as fit as they should be. Many more children than ever before are obese, have limited capacity to perform physical tasks, or have hypertension and cardio-vascular disease. The solution to this problem lies in educating children to make more healthful choices in their lives—choices that include active exercise and a healthy diet. The list of fitness facts in this chapter emphasizes the need to develop the habit of healthy exercise in young children.

Young children need the opportunity to develop **fundamental motor skills.** Motor fitness is defined in terms of

1. Agility—The ability to change the movement direction of the entire body in space, both rapidly and accurately
2. Balance—The maintenance of equilibrium while either stationary or moving
3. Coordination—The ability to perform motor skills smoothly and accurately
4. Power—The ability to transfer energy into force at a fast rate
5. Reaction time—The time elapsed between stimulation and the beginning of a reaction to that stimulation
6. Speed—The ability to perform a movement in a short period of time (Corbin and Lindsey 1996)

Motor fitness can be achieved through regular opportunities to run, jump, hop, slide, gallop, and skip. Controlling these movements, as in running to the beat of a drum or changing the lead foot when they hear a signal while they are galloping, can help children gain motor control and can be accomplished with nothing but some space and a whistle or drum.

Corbin and Pangrazi (2003) have suggested several guidelines for appropriate physical activity. These guidelines include the following:

1. *Children should accumulate at least 60 minutes, and up to several hours, or age appropriate physical activity on all, or most days of the week.*

2. *Children should participate in several bouts of physical activity lasting 15 minutes or more each day.*
3. *Children should participate each day in a variety of age appropriate physical activities to achieve optimal health, wellness, fitness, and performance benefits.*
4. *Extended periods (periods of two hours or more) of inactivity are discouraged for children especially during the daytime hours* (p. 8–9).

There are many good reasons children should participate in vigorous physical activity each day. Such activity helps to prevent chronic disease and obesity and helps in optimizing growth and development. Of course, physical activity helps children develop motor skills, which are useful all through life. Cognitive functioning can be improved through physical activity, and such activities do not detract from academic achievement. Finally, physical activity encourages wellness of the body as a whole (Corbin and Pangrazi 2003). It is obvious that full inclusion of all students would be a hallmark of good programs and that no physical activities would be used as punishments.

These guidelines are for grades K–12 and do not mention pre-K. Preschool children certainly do need to participate in physical activity every day, and planning for vigorous physical activity is very important. Many children will participate in active play without any more planning than giving them time and a playground, but observations have revealed that a percentage of children will stand around and talk on the playground rather than do anything. It is for these children that the teacher has to do careful planning to get them moving and participating.

Teachers know that motor development is important and can contribute to children's development in other areas. The psychomotor domain is stimulated by activities that require thought and deliberate movement, such as bouncing a ball, hitting a target with a ball, or hitting a ball with a bat. This area of development includes fundamental motor skills such as walking and running, which are necessary for participation in games and sports throughout life. Seefeldt (1984) notes that "the rudimentary skills which make up the components of our games and sports can be learned by children in an enriched environment before they are six years of age" (p. 35). He goes on to state that opportunities both for practice and motivation are at their highest levels in the early childhood years.

Although physical fitness for young children is more difficult to define than fitness for older populations (Seefeldt 1984), with a minimal level of physical fitness young children will be able to perform physical tasks such as walking and running. Fitness is also defined by cardiorespiratory function, relative leanness, abdominal endurance, lower-back flexibility, and upper-body strength and endurance (Gober and Franks 1988; Leppo 1993; Ross and Pate 1987). Children younger than age ten have been included in national studies of children's fitness only recently; however, standards now exist, beginning with six-year-olds. Standards for the different levels of fitness—presidential, national, and health fitness—are available on the Web at www.indiana.edu/~preschal. This site also provides information about modifying these standards for students with disabilities.

Teachers must not overlook physical education activities in their efforts to balance a program, so that every area of a child's development is fostered. Physical education activities can contribute to a child's social and intellectual development as well as to her physical development. For example, through sports and games, children learn to interact with others in positive ways. They may learn the importance of interdependence and the feeling of belonging that being part of a team can offer. A child's self-concept may be enhanced as she becomes physically skillful. Children gain intellectual skill by creating games and movements, expressing themselves as they negotiate in games, and solving problems related to physical goals. Working puzzles, cutting, and pushing buttons to operate teaching equipment all require not only thinking but physical skills, as well. Children need both physical skills and cognitive abilities to feel good about themselves. Emphasizing only cognitive abilities may strengthen a child in one area while undermining her ability in another. Weiller and Richardson (1993) state the case well: "Regular, appropriate physical activity is the responsibility of all educators. It is crucial that children acquire appropriate skills, develop a sound fitness level, and feel positive about their movement abilities" (p. 137).

Goals of Physical Development Programs

Current recommendations suggest that children should engage in moderate physical activity at least sixty minutes each day (Pangrazi, Corbin, and Welk 1996). This hour need not occur in one time block but can be spread over the day. However, because many children do not have opportunities to be physically active at home, teachers need to make sure that a large portion of that sixty minutes is completed at school.

The goals of physical development programs for young children include having children participate in a variety of activities that will foster motor development; helping children develop gross motor skills; helping children develop a positive attitude toward active movement experiences; and helping children develop fine motor skills. These goals, like goals in other areas of curriculum, are broad and can best be met by a balance of planned and spontaneous activities. Activities designed for specialized skill development should never overshadow, replace, or serve as the primary purpose of general physical education (Gallahue 1981). However, teachers must make a concerted effort to involve children in active physical experiences. One study (Miller 1978) found that children in free-play situations often spent the time playing quietly and spent very little time in vigorous physical activities. Participation in vigorous activity can be increased through planned activities, teacher modeling and participation, and careful observation of children to ensure their involvement.

A developmentally appropriate program of physical education is based on three principles: "(1) motor skill development is sequential and age-related; (2) children progress through similar sequences of motor development; and (3) the rates at which children progress through sequences of motor development varies" (Grineski 1992, p. 33). Table 15.1 provides an overview of the gross motor development of young children.

Gabbard (1995) agrees that children need to participate in age-appropriate activities and adds that gender should not determine participation in activities, that activities should be noncompetitive, and that equipment should match the size, confidence, and skill of the children. Primary-age children should be involved in activities designed to help them develop movement awareness and basic motor skills. As in any other area of the curriculum, the teacher has to ob-

Table 15.1 Milestones in Gross Motor Development in Early and Middle Childhood

Age	Gross Motor Skills
2–3 years	■ Walks more rhythmically; hurried walk changes to run. ■ Jumps, hops, throws, and catches with rigid upper body. ■ Pushes riding toy with feet; little steering.
3–4 years	■ Walks up stairs, alternating feet, and downstairs, leading with one foot. ■ Jumps and hops, flexing upper body. ■ Throws and catches with slight involvement of upper body; still catches by trapping ball against chest. ■ Pedals and steers tricycle.
4–5 years	■ Walks downstairs, alternating feet; runs more smoothly. ■ Gallops and skips with one foot. ■ Throws ball with increased body rotation and transfer of weight on feet; catches ball with hands. ■ Rides tricycle rapidly, steers smoothly.
5–6 years	■ Increases running speed to 12 feet per second. ■ Gallops more smoothly; engages in true skipping and sideways stepping. ■ Displays mature, whole-body throwing and catching patterns; increases throwing speed. ■ Rides bicycle with training wheels.
7–12 years	■ Increases running speed to more than 18 feet per second. ■ Displays continuous, fluid skipping and sideways stepping. ■ Increases vertical jump from 4 to 12 inches and broad jump from 3 to over 5 feet; accurately jumps and hops from square to square. ■ Increases throwing and kicking accuracy, distance, and speed. ■ Involves the whole body in batting a ball; batting increases in speed and accuracy. ■ Dribbling changes from awkward slapping of the ball to continuous relaxed, even stride.

Source: From Laura E. Berk, *Child Development*, 5/e. Published by Allyn & Bacon, Boston, MA. Copyright © 2000 by Pearson Education. Reprinted by permission of the publisher.

Note: These milestones represent overall age trends. Individual differences exist in the precise age at which each milestone is attained.

serve the children carefully in order to know when to increase the difficulty of the task and when to provide more time for development of individual skills.

Planned Activities

Physical education programs should include experiences with movement and games and activities that help to foster skill development. In each of these areas, activities must be matched to children's developmental levels and to the needs of individuals. Some children will be able to jump from a standing position or catch a ball while others will still be learning to walk backward or to go down steps by alternating feet.

When planning for individual differences, teachers can accommodate a wide variety of skill levels in the way that directions are given. For example, rather than ask all children to do headstands, teachers could ask all children to "Find a way to balance using three parts of your body" (Petersen 1992, p. 37). As you read the following ideas for planned experiences, keep in mind that all activities must be evaluated in terms of their appropriateness for individual children.

Movement   In planning movement activities, emphasize the exploration of space and how the human body can move in space. Many movement activities can be enhanced with the addition of music or rhythmic accompaniment.

Jumping   Lay two ropes on the ground about ten inches apart, and allow children to practice a standing broad jump over them; as children's skills increase,

Physical fitness activities foster motor development, physical skill development, and self-esteem in young children.

move the ropes farther apart. Place hula hoops in a pattern across the floor or on flat ground so that children can jump from one to another. Position a sturdy bench or box so that children can jump off it safely. Encourage children to explore how they can turn while jumping or how they can stretch their bodies or make them as small as possible while jumping.

Climbing on Apparatus   Encourage children to think of different ways to hang, move, stretch, or curl and to find different ways to get on and off the apparatus safely. To determine how high children should be allowed to climb, Readdick and Park (1998) suggest following this rule of thumb: Allow about one foot of height for each year of age until about age five. After that, the children's competence and the teacher's own comfort level should guide decisions about height.

Following an Obstacle Course   Build an obstacle course with materials in the classroom. For example, create a path to follow that requires children to crawl under a table, climb over a sturdy bench, jump through a series of hula hoops placed on the floor, and crawl through a tunnel created with a quilt and chairs. Invite children to move over, around, under, and through obstacles in as many ways as possible.

Rolling and Tumbling   If you have a grassy slope that children can roll down, use it. If not, encourage children to roll and find ways to turn their bodies on mats.

Using a Parachute   Preschool children will enjoy stretching a parachute and moving it up and down. They will also enjoy getting under it. Older, more well-coordinated children will enjoy games in which they bounce objects on the parachute, take turns running under it, and use it in stretching and rhythmic activities.

Games   Games such as circle games, in which only one person is "It," often require all other participants to sit or stand and wait for most of the play period. Better choices are games that involve the whole group. Teachers can invent games of Tag with multiple "Its" for kindergarten and primary children.

Staley and Portman (2000) note that the research clearly demonstrates the need for making sure that children are engaged in vigorous activity at least thirty minutes a day (although it does not have to be all at one time). Games as part of the curriculum must therefore get everyone moving and have very little waiting and watching time.

For preschool children, one game that keeps everyone moving is Soap Bubbles, in which all the children move within a marked space without touching anyone else. If children touch, they "burst" and must make themselves as small as possible. (Children who have been touched can move outside the space and continue moving.) The game begins with a very large space, but the teacher moves the space markers so that there is less and less space until most children have been touched. This game can be accompanied by music (Pangrazi and Dauer 1992).

Many games for primary children involve an entire group in movement activities. One example is Back-to-Back, for which there must be an uneven number of children. Children pair off and stand back-to-back; the child left over claps her hands and calls out a movement ("run," "hop," "skip," "slide," "gallop," or "jump"). Following the command, each child must move forward a certain distance and then turn and find a new partner; the one left over becomes the leader for the next round. In a similar game called Stop and Start, the children are spaced far enough apart to move freely. The leader calls out a movement, such as "skip." All the children move until the leader signals them to stop. Any child who moves after that must wait on the sidelines for one round.

Parents AND *Wellness*

■ Get parents involved in their children's physical development by sending home descriptions of activities that the whole family can enjoy together—for example, bowling with a ball and empty soda containers.

WWW

Skill Activities

Throwing and Catching   Very young children should practice throwing with relatively large, soft balls. Balls about six inches in diameter are easiest to catch. Threes and fours can begin to catch with their arms extended. A yarn ball or a Nerf ball is good for these children. Children can be encouraged to throw a ball as high as possible, to roll it on the ground, and to stop the ball with their feet or other body parts while it is rolling. Children can also toss the ball with two hands, with one hand, and play catch with a partner. Tossing bean bags or tossing and rolling small balls at a target (a bowling pin or an empty bleach bottle) are also appropriate activities.

Kicking and Batting   Primary children can begin to learn to kick a ball. To learn how, they should begin with a stationary ball and be encouraged to tap the ball with their feet, to tap it so that it goes to a partner, and to kick the ball to a target area. Batting a ball should also begin with the ball stationary, perhaps on a cone. Children should be encouraged to think of as many ways to hit the ball as possible.

Benelli and Yongue (1995) suggest making a bat from a two-liter plastic bottle and a wooden dowel. The handles of most bats are too large for small hands and the hitting surfaces are too small.

Children with Special Needs

Children with special needs can participate in outdoor play and physical education activities with some adaptations in equipment and in activities. The teacher must consider the developmental level of the individual child and the

An Expert Speaks

Judith Kieff
University of New Orleans

The Immediate and Long-Term Benefits of Recess

Young children think and learn differently than older children and adults. Therefore, best practice for programs serving young children will include specific teaching and learning strategies designed to fit their unique learning styles and abilities and promote optimal development. Recess is one such strategy. Traditionally, recess is a fifteen- to twenty-minute break from formal classroom instruction that provides opportunities for young children to freely engage in activities that simultaneously promote health, cognitive and social development, and emotional well-being. Therefore, recess can be seen as a strategy that has both immediate and long-term benefits related to school success.

The immediate benefits of recess include the opportunity for children to escape the formality of classroom instruction and do what children do naturally: run, climb, hop, dance, walk, talk, and bounce freely in the outdoor environment. These may not seem like remarkable activities, but the combination of whole-body movement with fresh air and sunshine provides children with a mental break from sustained periods of concentration and focus, thus allowing their brains time to process information. Children return to the classroom with a renewed sense of focus and mental energy. Another immediate effect of recess is the feeling of pleasure and control that comes from having choices in activities and interacting with peers and adults in an informal setting. The resulting sense of value and well-being can sustain a child's persistence when he or she is later faced with challenging academic tasks.

The long-term benefits of recess result from the multiple opportunities it provides for sustained play and social interactions. Play is a primary vehi-

cle for the development of physical and logico-mathematical knowledge, social competency, and perceptual-motor skills during childhood. Play offers children the opportunity to explore and discover facts about their environment, practice and consolidate previously learned academic skills, and apply language and communication skills in authentic contexts. Sociodramatic play episodes often provide children with negotiating and problem-solving challenges. While children are playing, they are freed from the stress of "being wrong," so they often function at their highest cognitive level. The cumulative effect of functioning at a high level of play during recess will ultimately benefit children's academic achievement.

Certainly, to be effective, recess must take place on well-maintained playgrounds where equipment is safe, abundant, and age appropriate. Recess should be supervised by multiple staff members who are both well acquainted with the children they supervise and trained not only to interact with children, but also to foster children's positive interactions with one another. When these high standards are met, recess becomes a time- and cost-effective strategy that promotes long-term academic gains.

Policymakers, administrators, and sometimes even parents may call for the limitation or abolishment of recess on the grounds that children need more time to work at structured academic tasks. Unfortunately, they do not understand the young child's unique style of learning. Early childhood professionals are charged with the responsibility of advocating for and demonstrating the effectiveness of strategies that support the optimal learning environment for children. Recess is one such strategy.

child's abilities when planning for physical experiences. Children with mental retardation can participate in most outdoor activities, but they may need more encouragement and more praise than other children. Teachers may have to help children with retardation establish motor patterns by moving them into positions or by modeling behaviors again and again. These children may also make less rapid progress, and teachers should be aware that children may have to repeat activities many times before mastering them.

Children with visual disabilities can participate in many climbing, swinging, and sliding experiences without adaptations. For skill activities for these children, the teacher will need to be attentive to lighting conditions and equipment choices. For example, Pangrazi and Dauer (1981) recommend that when teaching a child with visual limitations to catch a ball, the area should be well lighted and a yellow ball should be used. In certain games, children with visual limitations can get help from other children; the teacher can make sure that tactile information is provided to help children identify home base, boundary lines, and so on.

Auditory disabilities rarely prevent children from participating fully in physical activities. Such children should be placed in front of the teacher so they can read lips and have the best opportunity for hearing directions. Children with auditory disabilities may need interpreters in order to follow the directions in games and may need visual signals to supplement some auditory signals. For example, if children were playing Stop and Start, described earlier, the teacher could wave a flag when the group was to stop moving.

Teachers who want to involve children with orthopedic disabilities in programs of physical education should first consult with the child's physician or case manager to determine the level of activity recommended. A physical education specialist can help the teacher make the adaptations that will benefit each child. Some will need modified equipment—for example, a bat with straps that enable the child to hold it. Others will need to use larger or softer balls or to participate in activities that involve upper-body strength if their legs are immobile. Every child needs to interact as much as possible with other children, and physical education should not be inaccessible to children with disabilities.

Pangrazi and Dauer (1992) recommend that teachers think about modifications for youngsters lacking strength and endurance by lowering or enlarging goals, softening balls, reducing the distance balls must be thrown, and using lighter balls and bats. If coordination is a problem, teachers should have children begin with stationary objects when learning to strike an object; throw for velocity without concern for accuracy when learning to throw; and use soft, lightweight objects for catching, such as beach balls and balloons. For children who lack ability in balance, teachers might increase the width on balance beams; suggest learning to balance with as many body parts touching the floor as possible; provide assistance with balance, such as a cane or chair; and think about play surfaces so that children are not playing on slick floors with slick shoes.

Health, Nutrition, and Safety

Helping children develop their physical abilities and encouraging them to be physically active is certainly important. It is also important to help children learn to make good choices in health practices, nutrition, and safety. Young children, of course, do not make these choices without guidance from parents and teachers, but they can begin to develop healthy habits.

Health Education

Historically, health care was an important goal of early preschool programs. In today's world of more personal responsibility for health, education for health-ful choices continues to be important; however, it tends to be overlooked in many programs (Bruhn and Nader 1982). Because children and young adults do not perceive themselves as vulnerable to illness (Gochman and Saucier 1982), health educators have recommended that programs in health educa-tion be developed and implemented for children as young as two or three (Kingsbury and Hall 1988).

Personal Routines

Health education is not a lesson to be taught on a schedule. It must be inte-grated throughout the day and made a part of many activities. Children learn about good health habits in many ways: observing parents and teachers (espe-cially those who take time to explain why they are making the decisions they make); listening to stories; and making regular visits to the doctor and dentist. For example, as children wash their hands after using the toilet and before eat-ing, the teacher can mention the importance of cleanliness in staying healthy; as children brush their teeth after eating, the teacher may demonstrate how to hold the brush and point out that brushing down over the teeth is best. Brush-ing teeth can be encouraged if the children can reach their own toothbrushes and the sink so that they can be independent about the task. A visit by a den-tal hygienist to demonstrate the correct procedures for brushing and flossing will remind children to brush on a regular basis. The children might also visit a dentist's office and get a chance to sit in the chair and look at the tools and equipment. A flashlight and a chair will probably be all the children need to play "dentist" after such a visit. When a child loses a tooth, the teacher is given a perfect opportunity for discussing and reading about teeth—how they grow and the importance of caring for them.

A significant portion of health education in early childhood programs will be taught as daily routines are established. Children will learn to wash their hands after using the toilet or blowing their noses or before eating and to brush their teeth after eating. As they participate in these routines, they can be taught the reasons these behaviors are important. Although young children are not able to understand the causal relationships between germs and disease,

Developmentally Appropriate Practice

Think about your readings, your observations, and your experiences as you respond to the following statements about developmentally appropriate practice in physical education and health:

- A developmentally appropriate physical education program offers children a challenge at the level of their individual abilities.

- An outside play period is *not* sufficient for physical education in a developmentally appropriate program.

- Some areas of health education require direct instruction, which does not normally fit a developmentally appropriate program.

- The guidelines for DAP state that teachers of young children are responsible for children's total development, not just academic or intellectual development.

they can understand that regular hygiene routines contribute to their staying well and feeling healthy.

Teachers also must be aware of sanitary procedures that will help prevent illness. Teachers of infants and toddlers must be careful to wash their hands thoroughly after diapering or assisting children at the toilet. Often teachers of young children must help them blow their noses or clean their faces after a sneeze. Teachers should scrub their hands after every such incident. Teachers must also model the importance of washing their hands carefully before either serving or cooking food. Changing tables and tables where food is served should be scrubbed and disinfected regularly.

Medical Procedures

The health education program should also include helping children become more comfortable and accepting of medical procedures, health care professionals, and hospitals. Parents should be involved in planning these particular activities, as they can provide specific information about their children's experiences and possible fears. Many activities in the classroom—such as playing with puppets, listening to stories, playing with toy medical equipment (or real equipment, if that is possible and appropriate), and meeting health care professionals—can help children understand and feel more positive about medical care. Field trips to the offices of health care professionals and to hospitals can also be arranged. These trips must be planned carefully, but most hospitals have programs for educating even very young children about being in the hospital.

Children can learn some simple first aid procedures. One program uses puppets to dramatize stories in which first aid is required (Marchand and McDermott 1986). Children learn first aid procedures and why they are necessary. They also learn to select the most appropriate procedure from the alternatives available and how to use the telephone to get help in an emergency.

Substance Abuse and HIV/AIDS

Two relatively new facets of health education for young children are substance abuse programs and programs to educate children about HIV (human immunodeficiency virus) and AIDS (acquired immunodeficiency syndrome). In many public schools, such programs are now required. With so much about drugs and HIV/AIDS on television and in the conversations of adults, teachers in preschool settings must be able to answer children's questions and understand their fears. Early childhood educators are in a unique position to contribute to preventing drug abuse and educating the public about HIV and AIDS, because both problems affect many children's lives directly and because early childhood educators can work with parents in ways that have positive results over long periods of time.

In a longitudinal study that followed a group of children from the time they were five until they were eighteen, Shedler and Block (1990) found that young adults who were frequent users of drugs were relatively maladjusted as children of seven years old. The frequent users were described at age seven as

> not getting along well with other children, not showing concern for moral issues (e.g., reciprocity, fairness), having bodily symptoms from stress, tending to be indecisive and vacillating, not planful or likely to think ahead, not trustworthy or dependable, not able to admit to negative feelings, not self-reliant or confident, preferring nonverbal methods of communication, not developing genuine and close relationships, not proud of their accomplishments, not vital or energetic or lively, not curious and open to new experience, not able to recoup after stress, afraid of being deprived, appearing to feel unworthy and "bad," not likely to identify with admired adults, inappropriate in emotive behavior, and easily victimized and scapegoated by other children. (p. 618)

Based on these findings, Shedler and Block (1990) recommend that resources for prevention of drug abuse be focused on intervening in the development of the personality syndrome that underlies drug use, rather than on campaigns such as "Just Say No." The research highlights the importance of positive experiences for children at home and at school that will develop stronger self-concepts, more skill in social interactions, and more prosocial behaviors.

Even young children know about HIV/AIDS and may fear that they or people close to them will become infected. Children see programs, news stories, and commercials on television aimed at educating the public about HIV and AIDS, but they rarely understand what they see and hear. Teachers who feel the need to provide information about HIV and AIDS must consider the children's cognitive development and needs when making decisions about what to say.

Teachers of young children can be prepared to answer children's questions in positive ways. For example, they can say that HIV is the virus that causes the disease called AIDS but that children who do not have the virus or the disease are not likely to catch it and that children cannot get it from touching a person who has it. Most children asking such questions are seeking reassurance that they are safe; they do not need a lesson on adult sexual behavior or drug use. Parents also may need guidance in what to say when children ask them questions. Primary-grade children are likely to encounter some sort of planned instruction that is aimed at making children aware of the dangers of HIV/AIDS. The goals of most programs for primary children are limited to having the children understand that they cannot contract HIV or AIDS by being with or touching someone who has it.

When making a decision about what to tell children when one of their classmates is HIV positive or has AIDS, teachers will have to exercise their own judgment, based on knowledge of the children and how much they have heard from parents. If the children know that a child is ill and ask questions, the teacher should answer as honestly as possible while helping children feel safe from the disease.

Even though young children do not need to know much about HIV and AIDS, teachers *do* need to know. In particular, teachers must be able to sort out the facts from the myths about HIV and AIDS. The National Education Association has published a handbook of information entitled *The Facts about AIDS* (Bauer et al. n.d.). Because many teachers will have children who have HIV/AIDS in class or will know of parents who do, they will be faced with providing information to other parents; thus, teachers need accurate, up-to-date information. They also need to work together to determine the best alternatives for teaching children about HIV/AIDS and the best information to provide to parents (Fetter 1989).

Nutrition Education

Food is not only basic to life, but it is also closely related to people's social and cultural lives. Food is an integral part of family, religious, and cultural celebrations. Many aspects of food are culturally determined: what people think is appropriate to eat; how they eat it (with fingers, pieces of bread, chopsticks, or forks); with whom they eat (with other men, with women and children, or in family groups); and when they eat during the day. How food is used socially is also culturally determined. Many people offer guests something to eat or drink as soon as they are in their homes, and food is often central to social gatherings. For years, business was conducted over lunch—now people even have "power breakfasts"! Teaching children to make healthy choices in the food they select is certainly a worthwhile goal and one that will affect their lives through adulthood.

Nutrition education is important because children commonly have problems related to nutrition. Although children do not often have control over what they are offered to eat, they do make choices from the food offered to them. The choices provided for them in a school setting should be nutritious and should help them learn about food and nutrition. Physical problems related to nutrition include tooth decay, obesity, iron deficiency anemia, and hypersensitivity to foods. Teachers need to focus on providing nutritious snacks; controlling the amounts of sugar, salt, and fiber in children's school diets; and establishing good food habits.

Learning about the food groups helps children understand what foods are essential for a healthy body.

Appropriate goals for nutrition education with young children would include helping children learn to eat a variety of foods; increasing children's awareness of their reasons for selecting certain foods; and helping children develop positive attitudes about food.

Notice that these broad goals do not include teaching children to recite the four food groups on cue. Primary children might find it meaningful to classify foods according to their contributions to a healthy diet, but Herr and Morse (1982) believe that classifying foods into four groups requires more skill in generalization than should be expected from young children. They recommend that foods be categorized into ten groups: milk, meat, dried peas and beans, eggs, fruits, vegetables, breads, pastas, cereals/grains/seeds, and nuts.

The goals of teaching children sound eating habits can be achieved in the classroom by offering nutritious snacks and meals and through food preparation experiences. Teachers are responsible for the quality of food that children are offered; children can then choose if and how much they are going to eat. The following foods are appropriate for snacks:

Raw Vegetables

Celery	Cauliflower flowerets
Peas in pod	Turnip sticks
Cucumber wedges	Jicama sticks
Tomato slices	Broccoli flowerets

Fresh Fruits

Apple wedges	Pineapple cubes
Orange segments	Pear or peach slices
Banana slices	Kiwi
Strawberries	Papaya
Blueberries	Mango

Other Snacks

Unsweetened fruit juice	Cottage cheese
Dried fruit	Peanut butter
Milk	Muffins
Milkshakes made from milk and fruit	Dry cereals (unsweetened)
Lowfat yogurt	Whole-grain crackers
Cheese	

In programs in which children are offered lunch or both breakfast and lunch, teachers should follow the guidelines of the U.S. Department of Agriculture (USDA 1999/2000) or the guidelines in the accreditation standards of the National Association for the Education of Young Children (NAEYC 1998) describing the nutritional and caloric requirements for children.

Teachers of children younger than three will want to be especially careful not to offer children food they cannot chew easily, such as raw carrots or peanuts, or bite-sized pieces of food that they can swallow without chewing. Foods such as raisins and popcorn can easily cause choking. Unless the children can be supervised carefully while they eat, other foods are better choices.

Teachers and parents must work together in order to achieve the goals of nutrition education. If parents know what teachers are trying to do with nutrition information, they can help reinforce the ideas. For example, teachers who work in schools where children bring their own snacks to school can ask parents to cooperate in sending only nutritious snacks for the children. A letter explaining the importance of reducing the sugar in children's diets (Rogers and Morris 1986) and a list of suggested snacks will aid parents in choosing snack foods that are appropriate.

One strategy for helping children learn to eat a variety of foods is to offer new foods at snack time. Rothlein (1989) suggests these ways to make adding new foods to a child's diet relatively easy:

1. *Introduce only one new food at a time.*
2. *Serve the new food with familiar foods.*
3. *Serve only small amounts of the new food—begin with one teaspoon.*
4. *Introduce new foods only when the child is hungry.*
5. *Talk with the child about the new food—taste, color, texture, and shape.*
6. *Encourage the child to taste the new food but do not force the child to eat it. If the food item is rejected, accept the refusal calmly and try again in a few weeks. As foods become more familiar, children more readily accept them.*
7. *If the child rejects the food, try to determine why she didn't like it. Often children will accept a food if it is prepared and presented in a different way. For example, raw carrots may be accepted although cooked carrots are refused.*
8. *Provide cooking experiences. When children are involved in preparing the food, they have more of an interest in tasting it.*
9. *Be a model! If children observe adults eating and enjoying new foods, they are more likely to enjoy them. Remember that young children often imitate the eating habits of their parents, and that the child's food habits—likes and dislikes—*

frequently reflect the parents'. Children can learn to accept foods disliked by a parent if they are presented positively and if Mom and Dad take a few bites themselves! Help parents see the wisdom of doing this. As a caregiver or teacher, model a curious approach to new foods yourself.

10. *Finally, keep trying. . . . A child's fear of a new food can be reduced by simply increasing exposure to the food. (p. 34)**

To help older children learn to appreciate new foods, involve them in cooking experiences as part of their social studies or science studies, ask parents or volunteers to share special cultural or ethnic dishes, and taste foods that are mentioned in stories that they read or hear. For example, if the teacher reads the Paddington books aloud to the class, he could have children taste marmalade and could explain its place in a healthy diet.

Fuhr and Barclay (1998) suggest that teaching units on various kinds of food can also help children learn to appreciate new foods and to gain experience with trying them. These authors developed units on bread, fruit, protein, potatoes, milk, and vegetable soup that included reading, art, music, and cooking activities.

> ## *Parents* AND *Wellness*
>
> ■ If school snacks are supplied by parents, ask them to send nutritious foods. Be on the lookout for simple, healthy snack ideas that you can share with parents.
>
> ■ If food allergies in some children make certain snack foods dangerous, contact parents and seek their cooperation. They can help reinforce the idea of not sharing foods or simply not send foods to school that are dangerous for some children.
>
> WWW

Cooking Experiences

Many teachers involve children in preparing foods for snacks or meals to be eaten at school. Even very young children can spread peanut butter or cheese on their crackers, sprinkle topping on their toast, or make simple sandwiches. Older children can peel vegetables, cut fruit, squeeze oranges to make juice, make English muffin pizzas with cheese and pizza sauce, and cut up apples for applesauce. Kindergarten and primary children can read and follow simple recipes for a variety of foods. Teachers should follow these basic guidelines for cooking experiences:

1. Cook only nutritious foods.

2. Let the children do the cooking. Watching while the teacher measures the ingredients and then getting to stir does not give children a feeling of being involved. In planning a cooking experience, consider the maturity and skills of the children. Can they do what is required—measure, cut, mix, and so on? How many children can participate in the activity? Experiences should be planned for individuals or very small groups.

3. Plan for the children's safety, particularly if an experience involves heat or cutting. Make sure children are carefully supervised when using

*From Liz Rothlein, "Nutrition Tips Revisited: On a Daily Basis Do We Implement What We Know?" *Young Children* 44 (September 1989): 30–36. Reprinted with permission from the National Association for the Education of Young Children.

sources of heat. Tape electrical cords of appliances to the wall so that children cannot trip over them and pull appliances off the table; position appliances so that spills land on the table rather than on the floor. Make sure that children understand how to use cutting tools and sources of heat safely.

4. Be attentive to cleanliness. Are the children's hands and the utensils clean? In some areas of the United States, hepatitis has been a problem and teachers have been asked not to cook at school. Check local policies before cooking in the classroom.

Teachers will of course want to anticipate the learning outcomes that will be possible from cooking experiences. Children will be able to relate content from other subject-matter areas to cooking experiences. The following are only a few examples of the possibilities:

- *Science*—Observing changes in matter such as melting, congealing, shrinking (greens before and after cooking), expanding (rice before and after cooking), and transformation of water into steam
- *Language*—Learning cooking vocabulary, such as *boil, simmer, roll, knead, dice, shred,* and *grate,* as well as the names of foods and utensils
- *Mathematics*—Comparing quantities, measuring
- *Social Studies*—Working cooperatively, learning about people involved in food production, preparing or tasting ethnic or cultural foods, and learning about food customs
- *Literacy*—Reading recipes or charts, connecting food experiences to stories (for example, making blueberry muffins after reading *Blueberries for Sal* [McCloskey 1948]), writing shopping lists, writing recipes, collecting and illustrating booklets of favorite recipes

Safety Education

Teachers of young children need to address questions of fire safety, traffic safety, water safety, poison safety, and personal safety. The teacher is responsible for checking the classroom and the play yard for any safety hazards, planning for emergencies, teaching children safe behaviors and what to do in an emergency, and supervising children closely. Pickle (1989) demonstrated that even preschoolers can benefit from instruction in safety education; primary children can also benefit from such instruction.

Fire Safety

Most elementary schools have a fire safety program that includes visits from local firefighters, poster contests about fire prevention, instructions about what to do if there is a fire, and regular fire drills. A fire safety program should help children recognize the danger of fire and learn to treat fire with caution; prepare children to respond appropriately during a fire through regular fire drills; and teach children how to call the fire department.

Every classroom should have a written plan of action in case of fire that specifies the duties and responsibilities of each person (who will check the restroom, who will be responsible for children who are disabled, who will carry the class list, and so on), the exits to be used, and the point of assembly outside. Every class should practice fire drills on a regular basis. In some drills, selected exits should be blocked; drills should be planned to occur at unpredictable times such as meal or nap times. Near each exit, the teacher should post a map showing all exits and routes for evacuating the building and a class list to be used to account for the children after the building has been evacuated. Finally, teachers should provide parents with information about the fire drill procedures at school and encourage parents to plan regular fire drills at home.

Asking a local firefighter to visit the classroom can help promote children's awareness of fire safety. Most fire departments have an educational specialist who is responsible for teaching children fire prevention and fire safety. These people are usually talented in communicating with young children; they can teach children the "stop, drop, and roll" technique and demonstrate the pieces of equipment used by firefighters. Some firefighters encourage children to touch or try on equipment so that it does not frighten them when they see it on a firefighter. If children do try on firefighting gear, the firefighter can talk to the children about how different they look when they wear it. It is important that children recognize and not be afraid of firefighters in full gear in case they should ever have to be rescued from a fire. Teachers should preview any presentation to ensure that it is appropriate for their children.

All children should be taught that in the case of a fire, they should leave the building or house first and then call the fire department. In the dramatic play area, a toy telephone and a large poster with the numbers to be dialed can help children practice dialing "0" or "911" to call the fire department in an emergency. Primary children might benefit from reading *The 9 Lives of El Gato the Cat* (Consumer Product Safety Commission 1983), a comic book that reviews the most common causes of fires and burns and explains what to do in case of fire. The Consumer Product Safety Commission website has a kids page that offers games and safety tips that can be printed.

Traffic Safety

Teachers must share with parents the responsibilities for teaching children about traffic safety. The most frequent accidents involving children are those in which the child darts into the street, usually in the middle of the block. Goals of a traffic safety program include teaching children to stop before entering a street; teaching children how to cross a street safely; and teaching children to interpret traffic signals.

With repetition and the cooperation of parents, teachers can impress on children the importance of stopping at every curb. If there are no curbs on local streets, children should be taught to identify the boundary of the street and to stop there every time.

Children need direct experience in looking and listening for traffic and then walking—not running—across the street. Often, very young children do

Traffic safety can be practiced indoors in safe play areas.

not know what to look and listen for when they approach a street. With guidance from teachers and parents, they can learn to look and listen for approaching traffic and to cross carefully after the traffic has cleared. Children also must learn to make sure that drivers of stopped vehicles have seen them before crossing in front of the vehicles. Children may also need help understanding directions from crossing guards at school crossings. It may be prudent to teach children younger than four not to cross the street at all unless an adult tells them it is safe to do so.

Street crossings can be simulated in the dramatic play area so children can practice stopping, looking and listening for traffic, and walking carefully across the street. An area outdoors can be marked as a street, especially where children are riding wheel toys, and with guidance the children can practice crossing these "streets" carefully. The teacher might also mark some streets on the floor inside with masking tape and have the children role-play pedestrians and drivers of vehicles as they practice traffic safety. Teachers can make or purchase replicas of traffic signals for the blocks center and help the children set up their own streets, complete with signals, and practice safety procedures.

The third goal, teaching children to interpret traffic signals, can be furthered by constructing paper traffic signals or wiring a simple signal to a battery. Games such as Mother, May I? help children learn to move when the signal is green and stop when the signal is yellow or red. Teachers can invent other games based on Follow the Leader or Tag in which children must respond to traffic signals.

With help from a police officer and volunteers, the children can be taken to an intersection and helped to cross the street with the signals provided. At intersections in some communities, children must learn to read symbols or the word *WALK,* rather than traffic signals. Pictures or posters of these words and symbols will teach the children to interpret them.

Involve parents by explaining what you are trying to teach in traffic safety and seek their help in reinforcing the same rules when they are with their children. Both parents and teachers must model safe traffic behavior if children are to learn it.

Water Safety

Discussions of water play in this book have stressed that such play should be carefully supervised. Water play is enjoyable and important for meeting program goals, and teachers should not hesitate to include water play in their programs—but it must be supervised. In some areas where backyard swimming pools are popular, drowning has become the leading cause of death for young children. Children should never be left unsupervised when near swimming pools, lakes, or ponds. Even children in wading pools must have constant supervision.

Parents AND Safety

■ Keep parents informed about the safety lessons conducted at school so they can reinforce those lessons with their children at home.

No child should ever be allowed to swim alone, even if she is a capable swimmer. Swimming lessons do not make a child immune to danger, and supervision should not be relaxed simply because a child has had swimming lessons. The American Academy of Pediatrics (AAP 1988) recommends that only children three and older be given swimming lessons. The AAP's view is that the risk of contracting infectious disease or swallowing dangerous amounts of water during swimming lessons is too great for children younger than three.

Poison Safety

Teachers have a responsibility to make sure that school environments are poison free. Anything poisonous, including ornamental plants, should be removed. Cleaning compounds and other hazardous materials must be stored in locked cabinets, out of children's reach. All such materials must be carefully marked with poison symbols and never stored in old food containers.

Children must learn that they are never to eat any unknown substance or anything that is not food. Children younger than three or four cannot be expected to remember not to put objects in their mouths. Teachers of children this young need to take extra precautions to remove any dangerous items and to supervise the children closely.

Children should be taught to recognize the symbol for poison and to avoid containers that show it. Teachers should keep in mind that many household chemicals, such as automatic dishwasher detergent, are very dangerous if ingested yet are not marked with the poison symbol. Children must learn to recognize these dangerous items.

Personal Safety

Periodically, horror stories in the news remind us that the world is not always a safe place for children. Children must learn some rules of personal safety. In many police departments, officers are specially trained to communicate to children the importance of not talking to, accepting rides with, or taking treats from strangers. Many young children do not know what the word *stranger* means—they must be given practice in distinguishing strangers from people they know.

Identifying strangers might be made into a game, using pictures of familiar people and unfamiliar people so that children develop the concept that an unknown person is a stranger. Children might also role-play what to do if approached by a stranger offering treats or rides. Parents might be alerted to the dangers of having their child's name displayed on clothing or backpacks, which makes children identifiable; young children will be confused if a stranger knows their name.

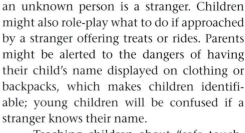

Parents **AND** *Safety*

■ Hatkoff (1994) suggests that parents should be informed about what community resources are available to help their children. Teachers and schools can help provide this information by sponsoring programs such as Kids on the Block, a national program that helps first through eighth graders learn self-protection strategies.

WWW

Teaching children about "safe touching" from people they know is also very important. In many communities, groups present puppet plays that help children understand the difference between "good touching" and "bad touching." Films and videos can also help teachers convey these messages to children, and children might role-play how to tell the appropriate person if they have been touched inappropriately.

Many primary-grade children are *latchkey children,* meaning that they stay alone after school until their parents return from work. Many communities offer special programs for helping these children learn rules for safety and for feeling more secure while they are alone. In the best of worlds, young children would not be left alone, but if they are, they need some guidance in answering the telephone and the door and in practicing fire safety and first aid. Efforts to keep children safe must involve the parents, the school, and the community.

The Internet poses a new source of danger for children, who may stumble on or be drawn into inappropriate chatrooms and websites. As discussed in Chapter 3 (page 97), children should be taught some basic guidelines about web safety—for instance, that they should never give out their real names, their parents' names, or their home addresses or phone numbers. The Web offers much to explore but also potential danger to children who fail to take these simple precautions.

Integrating Health and Safety Education

Many health and safety concepts can best be taught by establishing healthy routines, modeling healthy choices for the children, and incorporating discussions about health or safety procedures into the normal activities of the day. Children will learn nutrition lessons at snack and meal times by what is served and through conversations with the teacher. Traffic safety can be reviewed every time children go on a walk, although instruction should not be limited to

➤ Survey children's families to determine what kinds of physical activities they participate in on a regular basis (golf, tennis, jogging, biking, and so on).

➤ Make a list of the foods served at special times in each family. Have a tasting party for some of these foods.

➤ Make a list of the kinds of jobs in the community that are important to safety, such as police officer, firefighter, sheriff, lifeguards, and environmental police. Ask some of these people to visit the class and talk about safety (traffic safety, fire safety, stranger safety, water safety).

➤ Ask a dietician from the community to speak to the class about healthy eating.

➤ Survey the families of children in the class or the school to find out how many work in fields related to health, safety, or physical development.

➤ If your school has a physical education teacher, invite parents to a meeting at which they can demonstrate one or two fun activities that the whole family can do together.

➤ Learn to play a game that is important to each ethnic group represented in the classroom or school.

➤ Keep a record of the healthy foods served at snack time and vote each week on the favorite food of the week. Repeat the favorite food the next week.

these reviews. Some safety lessons can also be incorporated into other experiences. For example, if the focus in literacy were on reading environmental print, then poison signs and traffic signs could be incorporated into the experience. However, some safety instruction should be included in the curriculum even if it cannot be integrated with other classroom experiences. Teachers may choose to present short lessons on safety once a week or so throughout the year; this approach is more effective than focusing on a safety theme and concentrating all the instruction in a one- or two-week period.

Parents AND Wellness

■ Involve parents who work as health care professionals by asking them to share their work with the class.

Physical education and nutrition experiences are easier to integrate into the classroom routine than safety instruction. If, for example, the current topic were animals, children could imitate animal movements, learn what animals need to eat to be healthy, compare human food to animal food, and so on. If the topic focused on the neighborhood, children could determine how food is obtained and distributed in the neighborhood and identify facilities for physical activities (parks, jogging trails, exercise stations, courts for basketball or volleyball, and so on). Science activities can include growing food and observing changes in foods as they cook. Social studies experiences can include visiting producers or distributors of food; learning about what manners are considered appropriate in different cultures (in some cultures, people eat with their fingers; in other cultures, people do so only with certain foods or at specific times, such as at picnics); and learning about who prepares food in different cultures (men, women, or both).

Goldberg (1994) describes a health program that addresses the special needs of children with asthma and food allergies. The entire class learned about the medical procedures used in treating asthma and allergies through activities in the dramatic play area, which was equipped with masks and other medical supplies. She recommends that teachers contact local health care professionals to collaborate with them in planning medically oriented dramatic play. Involving health care professionals in planning programs will help ensure that both parents and children understand the medical needs of others and live more comfortably with any conditions of their own, as well. This is particularly important in classes and schools in which students or staff may have life-threatening conditions.

Physical education and nutrition education can easily be integrated into literacy experiences. In addition to tasting foods mentioned in stories, children can create ABC books or reference books of healthy foods, learn to read recipes, find foods mentioned in stories, write stories about special times when food is served in their homes, and find food words used in conversation (for example, "That's peachy," "He's a ham," "That car is a lemon"). They can create movements to tell stories, describe movements after they do them, write about how exercise makes them feel, keep records of their exercise, and find examples of movements and exercise in the books they hear and read.

Celebrating Diversity

To involve families in health, nutrition, and safety programs, teachers can invite them to participate in field days or other such outings in which adults and children can join in a variety of games and activities. Some of these might be traditional games of skill from the cultures represented in the classroom or games from earlier historical periods, such as rolling a hoop.

Families can also be wonderful resources for sharing foods that they enjoy or that are served at special times in their cultures. Teachers should help children understand that people from many cultures eat essentially the same things on a daily basis but that their special foods may vary. Having tasting parties with foods from different cultures may help make this clear. For instance, a study of breads from around the world might help children understand how all cultures have some special foods, even though they have many other foods in common, such as fruits and vegetables.

Chapter Summary

■ Planned physical education programs should include movement, games, and activities to foster skill development.

■ Physical activities can be adapted to allow children with special needs to participate as much as possible. Adaptations might include modifying equipment and structuring experiences so that children can achieve goals.

- Children learn health concepts best when they are integrated with daily classroom routines, such as washing hands and brushing teeth.

- Children need to learn the importance of cleanliness and to become more comfortable with medical procedures and health professionals.

- Today's teachers must be prepared to help children resist substance abuse, to communicate with parents, and to answer children's questions about drug abuse and HIV/AIDS.

- Children can begin to learn about healthful foods through snacks and meals served at school. They can also learn about nutrition through cooking experiences.

- Teachers of young children must incorporate lessons on fire safety, traffic safety, poison safety, water safety, and personal safety into their programs. Parents should be involved in these efforts.

- Teachers should incorporate games, activities, and foods that are special to families from those cultures represented in the classroom. All children should know that their special family traditions are not only acceptable but important in the life of the school.

Theory INTO Practice

Work with a physical education specialist to plan several movement experiences for a selected age group: threes and fours, fives and sixes, or sevens and eights.

Plan a cooking experience for a selected age group. Create a card with directions that would enable a paraprofessional or parent volunteer to supervise this experience. Think about the children's abilities and interests and how everyone can be actively involved in the experience. What academic skills can be enhanced through this experience?

Investigate Internet resources that provide information about young children's health and health education. Be sure to consider the credibility of the information and the sources cited.

Discuss with your group the importance of teaching children safety guidelines for using the Web. How is doing so similar to teaching children about strangers? Is web safety a concern at school or only at home? At what age should web safety become a matter of concern?

In small groups, collect information about safety instruction resources available in your community. What programs and materials are offered by the police and fire departments? What other community agencies or services offer safety instruction?

With a partner, role-play an exchange between a teacher and a parent whose ideas about food and nutrition do not agree. Playing the role of teacher, how can you be culturally sensitive to the parent's beliefs yet still insist on what you consider appropriate nutrition? What foods could you introduce at school that might help children eat more healthily at home?

Discuss with your group the importance of having the teacher of young children model good food choices.

Teaching Young Children about Health and Safety

Young children love to pretend. Having been a kindergarten teacher for over nineteen years, I have found that one of the best and most meaningful ways to teach health and safety is by letting my students use their imaginations and their love of drama. Together, in the safety of my classroom, we take a walk into the dangers of the world around us. As a group, we problem-solve, test our theories, and choose the best solutions.

I begin by telling a story about a child or some children faced with a dangerous or potentially dangerous situation. I end the story at the point where the character has to make some kind of decision. The following is an example of a short safety story:

One cold winter day, Sara took a walk to the duck pond. When she got there, she was very surprised to see that the pond was frozen. Sara had always wanted to ice skate and thought that this would be a great chance to see what it would feel like to glide across the ice.

I end the story here and ask my class, "What would you do?" We discuss and record several ideas. Some responses to the story have been "I would do it"; "I would step on the ice first to see if would break"; "If the ice was hard enough, I would skate on it"; and "I would go ask my mom if I could ice skate."

To help dramatize this story, I tape bulletin board paper over some of my big blocks to represent the pond, making sure to place the blocks far enough apart so that the weight of a child walking over these areas will cause the paper to break. I always play the role of the adult figure and choose the students to play the roles of the characters who make the decision. We act out each possible solution and discuss the results. Of course, when an actor or actress falls through, it always gets a big laugh, but the children really listen when we discuss what would happen if someone *really* fell through. I always take advantage of my adult role, so when my young actor or actress comes to ask for permission to skate on the pond, I have everyone's full attention as I tell about the dangers of a frozen pond.

This particular story is very important for the students in the part of the country where I live. Most winters are mild, but every once in a while, a pond will freeze over with a thin layer of ice. Using my method of teaching health and safety allows me the opportunity to teach what is truly important in the lives of my students. We reinforce the lessons by writing in our journals, using centers to recreate the story, and doing experiments with freezing water. It really helps students understand the dangers of a frozen pond when they see that ice develops around the *edge* of the bowl first.

Whenever possible, I use community resources to help with different areas of safety concerns: a firefighter for my stories about fire safety; a mother to help with stories involving babies; medical workers for stories about medicine, drugs, or accidents; a police officer for stories about getting lost or stranger dangers. This method of teaching health and safety integrates many other areas of the curriculum, but most important, it helps make safety real for my students.

GLOSSARY

absorbent mind A phrase describing Montessori's belief that the child is able to absorb information long before he can be taught certain concepts.

antibias curriculum A curriculum aimed at eliminating bias of all types by teaching children to respect people regardless of their sex, age, race/ethnicity, or other traits.

assessment Use of a comprehensive evaluation system to determine the quality of a program or the progress of a child.

assisted communication Communication through means other than speech or sign, such as computers, special boards, and so on.

assistive technology Devices such as portable keyboards and speech synthesizers that allow children with disabilities to communicate.

autoeducation The child's ability to organize her own thinking when engaged in certain activities.

behaviorist A theory suggesting that behavior can be shaped by rewards and punishments.

child care Care for children in a group, usually for the entire working day; the term *day care* was used previously.

cognitive development The development of the ability to think and reason.

communicative competence The ability to use language to achieve your needs, regardless of the social correctness of the utterances.

constructivist A theory suggesting that children learn by constructing their own understanding; based on the work of Piaget and Vygotsky.

convention A rule of written language that is determined by social agreement, such as the use of capital letters.

corporal punishment Physical punishment such as spanking, pinching, or slapping.

creativity Purposeful behavior or ideas that extend beyond the present and are original and imaginative.

cueing systems What a reader uses to get information about print, such as the graphophonic system, the syntactical system, the semantic system, and the schematic system.

curriculum A written plan for learning experiences.

developmentally appropriate practice (DAP) Practice that is age and individually appropriate for each child in a program.

dialect A systematic variation from the common language that is used regularly and shared by a social group. The variation can be in word order, meaning, or pronunciation.

direct instruction Instruction in which the teacher presents information directly to the children.

discipline Guidance aimed at helping children gain self-control of their behavior.

egocentric thought patterns Thought patterns in which the individual fails to consider the viewpoints of others.

emergent literacy The concept that children are learning about printed language beginning in infancy rather than at one point in time.

emerging curriculum An approach to curriculum development in which the teacher follows the lead of the children.

English as a second language (ESL) A term describing speakers whose native language is not English.

environmental print Print that occurs in the everyday environment, such as stop signs and candy labels.

expanding curriculum An organizational pattern for social studies in which the focus of activities moves from the individual to the family, the neighborhood, the city, the state, the nation, and the world.

freedom The principle that dictates that the child, not the teacher, should choose activities for learning.

fundamental motor skills Basic motor skills such as moving, running, jumping, throwing, and so on.

Head Start A program started in the 1960s to help young children who are disadvantaged prepare for success in school.

home visit A planned visit to a child's home by a school staff member such as a teacher, counselor, or principal.

incidental learning Learning that occurs in addition to what is written into the learning plan.

instructional materials Materials selected to help children develop specific skills or learn specific concepts.

language delay A delay in the development of an individual child's language ability that results in his skills not matching what is typical of his peers.

learning areas Areas in a classroom where certain activities can take place and certain materials are stored.

learning plan A comprehensive plan of learning experiences for children.

least restrictive environment (LRE) The educational setting that is the least restrictive for an individual with given characteristics; the setting that provides the best educational opportunity for a child who is disabled.

mainstreaming A placement approach in which children with disabling conditions are included in regular classrooms; now more frequently referred to as *inclusion*.

mandated goals Goals set by a school director or written into the school curriculum.

maturationist A theory suggesting that children will "unfold," or develop to their full potential, given optimal conditions.

metaknowledge Knowledge of what one knows.

multicultural education An approach to education that encourages children to understand and respect all people and cultures.

nonjudgmental attitude An attitude of acceptance; a refusal on the part of a teacher to criticize parents.

operant conditioning A form of conditioning that rewards behavior that moves closer to target behavior.

paraprofessional A paid assistant in the classroom.

parent place A special area of the classroom or a room in the school set aside for parents.

phonemic awareness The ability to examine language separate from meaning and manipulate its component sounds.

portfolio A collection of artifacts and anecdotes that document a student's efforts and achievements.

practice play Play in which the player explores the nature of objects or materials with no other play goals.

prepared environment A learning environment structured to promote the development of given concepts in a child's mind.

progressive education movement A model that rejects methods involving memorization and recitation and provides experiences that are more active and engaging for learners.

punishment Removal of privileges or physical punishment designed to change children's behavior.

reflective abstraction Thinking about the results of personal manipulations of objects.

room arrangement The arrangement of furniture and materials to meet the needs of the children and teacher.

scientific process A strategy for solving problems that includes making hypotheses, collecting data, testing hypotheses, and drawing conclusions.

screening test A test designed to determine whether a child is eligible for a particular program or needs special attention.

sensitive periods Times in a child's development when certain concepts are learned more easily.

shared reading Reading in which the teacher does most of the reading, but the children are actively involved in the process.

simple abstraction Abstracting a concept from repeated experiences with objects.

sociodramatic play Play in which children assume roles and act out episodes, such as putting a baby to bed.

sociolinguistics The study of language as it is used in a social context.

stimulus-response theory A theory that organisms will respond to given stimuli based on previous experience with the stimuli.

teaching strategies Methods of presenting instruction, such as demonstrations, lectures, and simulations.

thematic approach The organization of curriculum and learning experiences around a chosen topic.

transitions Periods of time between activities in the classroom.

volunteers Parents or community members who help in the classroom without pay.

zone of proximal development (ZPD) The gap between what a child can do independently and what he cannot do even with assistance.

REFERENCES

General Sources

Abruscato, Joseph. *Teaching Children Science: A Discovery Approach*. 5th ed. Boston: Allyn and Bacon, 2000.

Adams, Marilyn J. *Beginning to Read: Thinking and Learning about Print*. Cambridge, MA: MIT Press, 1990.

Airasian, P. W. *Classroom Assessment: Concepts and Applications*. Boston, MA: McGraw Hill, 2001.

Alger, Harriet A. "Transitions: Alternatives to Manipulative Management Techniques." *Young Children* 39 (September 1984): 16–26.

Alliance for Childhood. *Fool's Gold: A Critical Look at Computers and Childhood*. 2000. Available online: www.allianceforchildhood.net/htm.

Almy, Millie. "A Child's Right to Play." *Childhood Education* 60(5) (May-June 1984): 350.

Ambron, Sueann R. *Child Development*. 2d ed. New York: Holt, Rinehart and Winston, 1978.

American Academy of Pediatrics. *Safe Swimming for Your Young Child*. Washington, DC: AAP, 1988. (This leaflet is one in a series called "TIPP: The Injury Prevention Program.")

American Montessori Society. *Standards and Criteria for AMS School Accreditation*. ERIC Document Reproduction Service 2523040. New York: AMS, 1984.

Andersen, Susan R. "The Trouble with Testing." *Young Children* 53 (July 1998): 25–29.

Anderson, M. P. "ACT against Violence." *Young Children* 56 (July 2001): 60–61.

Andrews, Angela G. "The Role of Self-Directed Discovery Time in the Development of Mathematics Concepts." *Teaching Children Mathematics* 2 (October 1995): 116–120.

Andrews, A. G., and P. R. Trafton. *Little Kids—Powerful Problem Solvers: Math Stories from a Kindergarten Classroom*. Portsmouth, NH: Heinemann, 2002.

Anen, Judith. *Enhancing the Curriculum through the Addition of Rich and Diverse Language Development Activities*. ERIC Document Reproduction Service 329944. 1991.

Antler, Joyce. *Lucy Sprague Mitchell: The Making of a Modern Woman*. New Haven, CT: Yale University Press, 1987.

Ashbaker, Betty, and Jill Morgan. "Paraeducators: A Powerful Human Resource." *Streamlined Seminar* (Winter 2000/2001): 19. ERIC Document Reproduction Service 453573. 2000/2001.

Association for Supervision and Curriculum Development. *Developmental Characteristics of Children and Youth*. Alexandria, VA: ASCD, 1975.

Atkins, Cammie. "Writing: Doing Something Constructive." *Young Children* 40 (November 1984): 3–7.

Austin, Pat. "Math Books as Literature: Which Ones Measure Up?" *New Advocate* 11 (Spring 1998): 119–133.

Aylward, Kim, Scott Hartley, Tiffany Field, Jean Greer, and Nitza Vega-Lahr. "An Art Appreciation Curriculum for Preschool Children." *Early Child Development and Care* 96 (September 1993): 35–48.

Baker, Gwendolyn C. "Teaching Children to Respect Diversity." *Childhood Education* 71 (Fall 1994): 33–35.

Baker, Katherine Read. *Let's Play Outdoors*. Washington, DC: National Association for the Education of Young Children, 1966.

Banks, James A., and Cherry A. Banks, eds. *Multicultural Education: Issues and Perspectives*. 3d ed. Boston: Allyn and Bacon, 1997.

Barbour, Ann C. "The Impact of Playground Design on the Play Behaviors of Children with Differing Levels of Physical Competence." *Early Childhood Research Quarterly* 14 (January 1999): 75–98.

Barbour, Nita, Tupper Dooly Webster, and Stephen Drosdeck. "Sand: A Resource for the Language Arts." *Young Children* 42 (January 1987): 20–25.

Barclay, Kathy, Cecelia Benelli, and Susan Schoon. "Making the Connection! Science and Literacy." *Childhood Education* 75 (Spring 1999): 146–152.

Barclay, Kathy H., and Camille Breheny. "Letting the Children Take Over More of Their Own Learning: Collaboration Research in the Kindergarten Classroom." *Young Children* 49 (September 1994): 33–39.

Barnett, Lynn A. "Research Note: Young Children's Resolution of Distress through Play." *Journal of Child Psychology and Psychiatry and Allied Disciplines* 25 (1984): 477–483.

Bauch, Jerold P. "The TransParent School: A Partnership for Parent Involvement." *Educational Horizons* 68 (Summer 1990): 187–189.

Bauer, Nancy, Martin Botel, Helen O. Dickens, Kenneth D. George, Sol Levin, Aaron H. Katcher, and Irving E. Sigel. *The Facts about AIDS: A Special Guide for NEA Members*. Washington, DC: National Education Association Health Information Network, no date.

Bayless, Kathleen M., and Marjorie E. Ramsey. *Music: A Way of Life for the Young Child*. 4th ed. Columbus, OH: Merrill, 1991.

Bear, Donald R., Marcia Invernizzi, Shane Templeton, and Francis Johnson. *Words Their Way: Word Study for Phonics, Vocabulary, and Spelling Instruction*. Upper Saddle River, NJ: Merrill, 2000.

Beaty, J. J. *Observing Development of the Young Child*. Columbus, OH: Merrill, 1986.

Becker, H. J. *Findings from the Teaching, Learning and Computing Survey: Is Larry Cuban Right?* Revision of paper written for January 2000 Technology and Leadership Conference of the Council of Chief State School Officers, Washington, DC, July 2000.

Benelli, Cecelia, and Bill Yongue. "Supporting Young Children's Motor Skill Development." *Childhood Education* 71 (Summer 1995): 217–220.

Benham, Nancy Barbour, Alice Hosticka, Joe D. Payne, and Catherine Yeotis. "Making Concepts in Science and

Mathematics Visible and Viable in the Early Childhood Curriculum." *School Science and Mathematics* 82 (January 1982): 45–55.

Benjamin, A. C. "I Wish the Teacher Would Tell Me What Is Really Special about My Child." Paper presented at the annual conference of the Essex County AEYC, September 1997.

Benjamin, Ann C. "Observations in Early Childhood Classrooms: Advice from the Field." *Young Children* 49 (September 1994): 14–20.

Bentzen, Warren. *Seeing Young Children: A Guide to Observing and Recording Behavior.* New York: Delmar, 1985.

Bereiter, Carl, and Siegfried Engelmann. *Teaching Disadvantaged Children in the Preschool.* Englewood Cliffs, NJ: Prentice-Hall, 1966.

Bergen, Doris. "Pretend Play and Young Children's Development." ERIC Document Reproduction Service 458045. 2001.

Bergen, Doris. "Should Teachers Permit or Discourage Violent Play Themes?" *Childhood Education* 70 (Annual Theme 1994): 300–301.

Bergen, Doris. "Using a Schema for Play and Learning." In *Play as a Medium for Learning and Development,* edited by D. Bergen, 169–180. Portsmouth, NH: Heinemann, 1988.

Bergeron, Bette S., Sarah Wermuth, Melissa Rhodes, and Elizabeth A. Rudenga. "Language Development and Thematic Instruction: Supporting Young Learners at Risk." *Childhood Education* 72 (Spring 1996): 141–145.

Berk, Laura E. *Child Development.* 5th ed. Boston: Allyn and Bacon, 2000.

Berk, Laura E. *Infants, Children, and Adolescents.* Boston: Allyn and Bacon, 1996.

Berk, Laura E. "Vygotsky's Theory: The Importance of Make-Believe Play." *Young Children* 50 (November 1994): 30–39.

Berk, Laura E., and Adam Winsler. *Scaffolding Children's Learning: Vygotsky and Early Childhood Education.* Washington, DC: National Association for the Education of Young Children, 1995.

Berko-Gleason, Jean, ed. *The Development of Language.* Columbus, OH: Merrill, 1985.

Betz, Carl. "Beyond Time-Out: Tips from a Teacher." *Young Children* 49 (March 1994): 10–14.

Bigler, R. S., and L. S. Liben. "Cognitive Mechanisms in Children's Gender Stereotyping: Theoretical and Educational Implications of a Cognitive-Based Intervention." *Child Development* 63 (1992): 1351–1363.

Bigler, R. S., and L. S. Liben. "The Role of Attitudes and Interventions in Gender-Schematic Processing." *Child Development* 61 (1990): 1440–1452.

Bird, John. *Science from Water Play.* London: Macdonald Educational, 1983.

Bisson, Julie. *Celebrate! An Anti-Bias Guide to Enjoying Holidays in Early Childhood Programs.* St. Paul, MN: Redleaf Press, 1997.

Bjorkland, Gail. *Planning for Play: A Developmental Approach.* Columbus, OH: Merrill, 1978.

Blachman, Benita A. *Getting Ready to Read: Learning How Print Maps to Speech.* Timonium, MD: York Press/U.S. Depart-ment of Health and Human Services, Public Health Service, National Institutes of Health, 1991.

Black, S. M. "HIV/AIDS in Early Childhood Centers: The Ethical Dilemma of Confidentiality versus Disclosure." *Young Children* 54 (March 1999): 45.

Blackburn, Ellen. "Stories Never End." In *Breaking Ground: Teachers Relate Reading and Writing in the Elementary School,* edited by J. Hansen, T. Newkirk, and D. Graves. Portsmouth, NH: Heinemann, 1985.

Blair, Umbreit, and C. Kwang-Sun. "Analysis of Multiple Variables Related to a Young Child's Aggressive Behavior." *Journal of Positive Behavior Interventions* 2 (Winter 2000): 33–40.

Bloom, Benjamin S. *Stability and Change in Human Characteristics.* New York: John Wiley and Sons, 1964.

Bodrova, Elena, and Deborah J. Leong. *Tools of the Mind: The Vygotskian Approach to Early Childhood Education.* Englewood Cliffs, NJ: Prentice-Hall, 1996.

Boehm, Ann E., and Richard A. Weinberg. *The Classroom Observer: Developing Observation Skills in Early Childhood Settings.* 2d ed. New York: Teachers College Press, 1987.

Bondurant, J. L., D. J. Romeo, and R. Kretschmer. "Language Behaviors of Mothers of Children with Normal and Delayed Language." *Language, Speech and Hearing Services in Schools* 14 (1983): 233–242.

Bordner, Ginger A., and Mira T. Berkley. "Educational Play: Meeting Everyone's Needs in Mainstreamed Classrooms." *Childhood Education* 69 (Fall 1992): 38–40.

Boutte, Gloria S., Irma Van Scoy, and Susan Hendley. "Multicultural and Nonsexist Prop Boxes." *Young Children* 52 (November 1996): 34–39.

Bowker, Jeanette E., and Janet K. Sawyer. "Influence of Exposure on Preschoolers' Art Preferences." *Early Childhood Research Quarterly* 3 (1988): 107–115.

Boyd, Brenda J. "Teacher Response to Superhero Play: To Ban or Not to Ban?" *Childhood Education* 74 (January 1997): 23–27.

Brandt, Ron. "Educators Need to Know about the Human Brain." *Phi Delta Kappan* 81 (March 1999): 235–238.

Brandt, R. "On Performance Assessment: A Conversation with Grant Wiggins." *Educational Leadership* 49 (1992): 35–37.

Bredekamp, Sue, ed. *Developmentally Appropriate Practice in Early Childhood Programs Serving Children from Birth through Age 8.* Washington, DC: National Association for the Education of Young Children, 1987.

Bredekamp, Sue. "Reflections on Reggio Emilia." *Young Children* 49 (November 1993): 13–17.

Bredekamp, Sue. "Twenty-Five Years of Educating Young Children: The High/Scope Approach to Preschool Education." *Young Children* 51 (May 1996): 57–61.

Bredekamp, Sue, and Carol Copple, eds. *Developmentally Appropriate Practice in Early Childhood Programs.* Rev. ed. Washington, DC: National Association for the Education of Young Children, 1997.

Bredekamp, Sue, and Teresa Rosegrant. *Reaching Potentials: Appropriate Curriculum and Assessment for Young Children,* vol. 1. Washington, DC: National Association for the Education of Young Children, 1992.

Bredekamp, Sue, and Teresa Rosegrant. "Reaching Potentials through Transforming Curriculum, Assessment, and Teaching." In *Reaching Potentials: Transforming Early Childhood Curriculum and Assessment,* vol. 2, edited by S. Bredekamp and T. Rosegrant, 15–22. Washington, DC: National Association for the Education of Young Children, 1995.

Brett, Arlene. "Computers and Social Development of Young Children." *Dimensions of Early Childhood* 23 (Fall 1994): 10, 13, 48.

Brewer, Jo Ann. "Literacy Development of Young Children in a Preschool Setting." In *Facilitating Preschool Literacy,* edited by R. Campbell, 119–130. Newark, DE: International Reading Association, 1998a.

Brewer, Jo Ann. "A Study of the Literacy Preferences of Parents of Three Language Groups." Unpublished manuscript, 1998b.

Brewer, Jo Ann, and Judith Kieff. "Fostering Mutual Respect for Play at Home and School." *Childhood Education* 73 (February 1996/1997): 92–96.

Brittain, W. L. "Some Exploratory Studies of the Art of Preschool Children." *Studies in Art Education* 10 (1969): 14–24.

Bromer, Billi L. "Who's in the House Corner? Including Young Children with Disabilities in Pretend Play." *Dimensions of Early Childhood* 27 (February 1999): 17–23.

Brophy, Jere. "Elementary Students Learn about Native Americans: The Development of Knowledge and Empathy." *Social Education* 63 (January/February 1999): 39–45.

Brown, Mac H., Rosemary Althouse, and Carol Anfin. "Guided Dramatization: Fostering Social Development in Children with Disabilities." *Young Children* 48 (January 1993): 68–71.

Brown, Nancy, Nancy Curry, and Ethel Tittnich. "How Groups of Children Deal with Common Stress through Play." In *Play: The Child Strives toward Self-Realization,* edited by G. Engstrom, 26–38. Washington, DC: National Association for the Education of Young Children, 1971.

Brown, Sue. "First Graders Write to Discover Mathematic's Relevancy." *Young Children* 52 (May 1997): 51–53.

Brown, Victoria. "Integrating Drama and Sign Language: A Multisensory Approach to Learning for Children with Special Needs." In *Early Childhood Creative Arts: Proceedings of the International Early Childhood Creative Arts Conference,* edited by L. Overby. Reston, VA: American Alliance for Health, Physical Education, Recreation and Dance, 1991.

Bruer, John T. "In Search of Brain-Based Education." *Phi Delta Kappan* 80 (September 1999): 649–657.

Bruhn, John G., and Philip R. Nader. "The School as a Setting for Health Education, Health Promotion, and Health Care." *Family and Community Health* 4 (1982): 57–59.

Bruner, Jerome. *Child's Talk: Learning to Use Language.* New York: W. W. Norton, 1983.

Bruner, Jerome. *The Process of Education.* New York: Vintage Books, 1960.

Buchoff, Rita. "Family Stories." *Reading Teacher* 49 (November 1995): 230–233.

Buchoff, Rita. "Joyful Voices: Facilitating Language Growth through Rhythmic Response to Chants." *Young Children* 49 (May 1994): 26–30.

Bullock, Merry, and Rochel Gelman. "Numerical Reasoning in Young Children: The Ordering Principle." *Child Development* 48 (June 1977): 427–434.

Bundy, Blakely Fetridge. "Fostering Communication between Parents and Preschools." *Young Children* 46 (January 1991): 12–17.

Burnett, Gary. *The Assessment and Placement of Language Minority Students.* ERIC Document Reproduction Service 357131. 1993.

Burns, Marilyn, and Kathy Richardson. "Making Sense Out of Word Problems." *Learning* 10 (January 1981): 39–44.

Burton, Grace M. "Patterning: Powerful Play." *School Science and Mathematics* 82 (June 1982): 39–44.

Butler, Lester G. "Language Acquisition of Young Children: Major Theories and Sequences." *Elementary English* 51 (1974): 1120–1123.

Button, Kathryn, Margaret J. Johnson, and Paige Fergerson. "Interactive Writing in a Primary Classroom." *Reading Teacher* 49 (March 1996): 446–454.

Butts, R. Freeman. "Search for Freedom—The Story of American Education." *National Education Association Journal* (March 1960): 33–48.

Butzow, Carol, and John Butzow. *Science, Technology and Society as Experienced through Children's Literature.* ERIC Document Reproduction Service 294141. 1988.

Byrum, Donna, and Virginia L. Pierce. "Bringing Children to Literacy through Theme Cycles." In *Bringing Children to Literacy: Classrooms at Work,* edited by Bill Harp, 105–122. Norwood, MA: Christopher Gordon, 1993.

Cadwell, Louise Boyd. *Bringing Reggio Emilia Home: An Innovative Approach to Early Childhood Education.* New York: Teachers College Press, 1997.

Cain, Sandra E., and Jack M. Evans. *Sciencing: An Involvement Approach to Elementary Science Methods.* 2d ed. Columbus, OH: Merrill, 1984.

Cairney, Trevor H., and Lynne Munsie. "Parent Participation in Literacy Learning." *Reading Teacher* 48 (February 1995): 392–403.

Calkins, Lucy. *The Art of Teaching Writing.* Portsmouth, NH: Heinemann, 1986.

Cambourne, Brian. "Conditions for Literacy Learning." *Reading Teacher* 53 (February 1999): 126–127.

Cambourne, Brian. "Toward an Educationally Relevant Theory of Literacy Learning: Twenty Years of Inquiry." *Reading Teacher* 49 (November 1995): 182–202.

Canady, Robert Lynn, and John T. Seyfarth. *How Parent-Teacher Conferences Build Partnerships.* Fastback 132. Bloomington, IN: Phi Delta Kappa Educational Foundation, 1979.

Canter, Lee. *Assertive Discipline.* Seal Beach, CA: Canter and Associates, 1976.

Canter, Lee. "Assertive Discipline and the Search for the Perfect Classroom." *Young Children* 43 (January 1988): 24.

Caples, Sara E. "Some Guidelines for Preschool Design." *Young Children* 51 (May 1996): 14–21.

Carlevale, J. M. *Observing, Recording, Interpreting Child Behavior.* West Greenwich, RI: Consortium Publishing, 1991.

Carlsson-Paige, Nancy, and Diane E. Levin. "Can Teachers Resolve the War-Play Dilemma?" *Young Children* 50 (July 1995): 62–63.

Cattermole, Juleen, and Norman Robinson. "Effective Home/School Communication—From the Parents' Perspective." *Phi Delta Kappan* 67 (September 1985): 48–50.

Cazden, Courtney. "Environmental Assistance to the Child's Acquisition of Grammar." Doctoral dissertation, Harvard University, 1965.

Ceglowski, Deborah. "Understanding and Building upon Children's Perceptions of Play Activities in Early Childhood Programs." *Early Childhood Education Journal* 25 (February 1997): 107–112.

Chaille, Christine, and Lori Britain. *The Young Child as Scientist: A Constructivist Approach to Early Childhood Science Education*. New York: HarperCollins, 1991.

Chaille, Christine, and Steven B. Silvern. "Understanding through Play." *Childhood Education* 72 (Annual Theme 1996): 274–277.

Chapman, Warren. "The Illinois Experience: State Grants to Improve Schools through Parent Involvement." *Phi Delta Kappan* 72 (January 1991): 355–358.

Charles, C. M., and Karen Blaine Barr. *Building Classroom Discipline*. 3d ed. New York: Longman, 1989.

Chavkin, N. F., and D. L. Williams. "Minority Parents and the Elementary School: Attitudes and Practices." In *Families and Schools in a Pluralistic Society,* edited by N. F. Charkin, 73–119. Albany, NY: SUNY Press, 1993.

Children's Defense Fund. "Basic Facts on Poverty (December, 2001)." Available online: www.childrensdefense.org. Retrieved August 2002.

Chomsky, Carol. "Write First, Read Later." *Childhood Education* 47 (March 1971): 296–299.

Chomsky, Noam. *Aspects of a Theory of Syntax*. Cambridge, MA: MIT Press, 1965.

Christie, James F. "Dramatic Play: A Context for Meaningful Engagements." *Reading Teacher* 43 (April 1990): 542–545.

Christie, James F., E. Peter Johnson, and Roger B. Peckover. "The Effects of Play Period Duration on Children's Play Patterns." *Journal of Research in Childhood Education* 3 (1988): 123–131.

Christie, James F., and Francis Wardle. "How Much Time Is Needed for Play?" *Young Children* 47 (March 1992): 28–32.

Clark, Patricia. "Culturally Appropriate Practices in Early Childhood Education: Families as the Resource." *Contemporary Education* 66 (Spring 1995): 154–157.

Clark, Patricia. "Recent Research on All-Day Kindergarten. Eric Digest." ERIC Document Reproduction Service 453982. 2001.

Clay, Marie M. *Becoming Literate: The Construction of Inner Control*. Portsmouth, NH: Heinemann, 1991.

Clay, Marie M. *An Observation Survey of Early Literacy Achievement*. Portsmouth, NH: Heinemann, 1993a.

Clay, Marie M. *Reading Recovery: A Guidebook for Teachers in Training*. Portsmouth, NH: Heinemann, 1993b.

Clay, Marie M. *What Did I Write? Beginning Writing Behavior*. Portsmouth, NH: Heinemann, 1975.

Clements, Douglas H., Bonnie K. Nastasi, and Sudha Swaminathan. "Young Children and Computers: Crossroads and Directions from Research." *Young Children* 48 (January 1993): 56–64.

Clements, Douglas H., and J. Samara. "The Role of Technology in Early Childhood Learning." *Teaching Children Mathematics* 5 (2002): 340–343.

Clements, Nancy E., and Edna W. Warncke. "Helping Literacy Emerge at School for Less-Advantaged Children." *Young Children* 49 (March 1994): 22–26.

Clewett, Ann S. "Guidance and Discipline: Teaching Young Children Appropriate Behavior." *Young Children* 43 (May 1988): 26–31.

Cline, Dusty B., and David Ingerson. "The Mystery of Humpty's Fall: Primary-School Children as Playmakers." *Young Children* 51 (September 1996): 4–10.

Cline, R. K. J. *Focus on Families: A Reference Handbook*. Santa Barbara, CA: ABC-CLIO, 1990.

Colbert, C., and M. Taunton. "Developmentally Appropriate Practices for the Visual Arts Education of Young Children." National Art Education Association Briefing Paper. Reston VA: National Art Education Association, 1992.

Cole, David A. "Facilitating Play in Children's Peer Relationships: Are We Having Fun Yet?" *American Educational Research Journal* 23 (1986): 201–215.

Cole, Elizabeth, and Claire Schaefer. "Can Young Children Be Art Critics?" *Young Children* 45 (January 1990): 33–38.

Cole, Martha L., and Jack T. Cole. *Effective Intervention with the Language Impaired Child*. 2d ed. Rockville, MD: Aspen, 1989.

Coleman, Mick. "Families and Schools: In Search of Common Ground." *Young Children* 52 (July 1997): 14–21.

Collier, Robert G. "Reading, Thinking, and Play: A Child's Search for Meaning." In *Claremont Reading Conference 47th Yearbook,* edited by Malcolm P. Douglas. Claremont, CA: Claremont Reading Conference, 1983.

Collier, Virginia. "Age and Rate of Acquisition of Second Language for Academic Purposes." *TESOL Quarterly* 21 (April 1987): 617–641.

Collins, N. L. D., and M. B. Shaeffer. "Look, Listen, and Learn to Read. *Young Children* 52 (May 1997): 65–68.

Comenius, John Amos. *A Reformation of Schools*. 1642. Reprint, London: Scolar Press, 1969.

Consortium of National Arts Education Associations. *Summary Statement*. March 1996. Available online: www.menc.org/publication/books/summary/html.

Cooper, Carolyn S., and Mary A. McEvoy. "Group Friendship Activities: An Easy Way to Develop the Social Skills of Young Children." *Teaching Exceptional Children* 28 (March 1996): 67–69.

Cooper, Jaclyn L., and Martha T. Dever. "Sociodramatic Play as a Vehicle for Curriculum Integration in First Grade." *Young Children* 56 (May 2001): 58–63.

Cooper, K. J. "Study Says Natural Light Boosts Learning." *Boston Globe,* November 26, 1999, p. A33.

Coopersmith, Stanley. *The Antecedents of Self-Esteem*. San Francisco: W. H. Freeman, 1967.

Copeland, Richard W. *How Children Learn Mathematics: Teaching Implications of Piaget's Research.* 4th ed. New York: Macmillan, 1984.

Corbin, C., and R. Lindsey. *Concepts of Physical Education with Laboratories.* Madison, WI: W. C. Brown/Benchmark. Cited in Marjorie L. Leppo, Diane Davis, and Bruce Crim, "The Basics of Exercising the Mind and Body." *Childhood Education* 76 (1996): 142–147.

Corbin, Charles R., and Robert P. Pangrazi. *Guidelines for Appropriate Physical Activity for Elementary School Children, 2003 Update.* Reston, VA: American Alliance for Health, Physical Education, and Recreation, 2003.

Cordell, A. S. "Self-Esteem in Children." In *Enhancing Self-Esteem.* Littletown, edited by C. J. Carlock, 287–376. Littletown, PA: Taylor and Francis Group, 1999.

Council on Interracial Books for Children. *10 Quick Ways to Analyze Books for Racism and Sexism.* ERIC Document Reproduction Services 188852. 1974.

Crinklaw-Kiser, Donna. "Integrating Music with Whole Language through the Orff-Schulwerk Process." *Young Children* 51 (July 1996): 15–21.

Cross, T. G. "Habilitating the Language-Impaired Child: Ideas from Studies of Parent–Child Interaction." *Topics in Language Disorders* 4 (1984): 1–14.

Crosser, Sandra. "Managing the Early Childhood Classroom." *Young Children* 47 (January 1992): 23–29.

Cryan, John R. "The Banning of Corporal Punishment." *Childhood Education* 63 (February 1987): 146–153.

Cuban, L. "So Much High-Tech Money Invested, So Little Use and Change in Practice: How Come?" Paper prepared for Council of Chief State School Officers Annual Technology Leadership Conference, Washington, DC, January, 2000.

Culbertson, Linda Doutt, and Mary Renck Jalongo. "'But What's Wrong with Letter Grades?' Responding to Parents' Questions about Alternative Assessment." *Childhood Education* 75 (Spring 1999): 130–135.

Cunningham, Patricia M. *Phonics They Use: Words for Reading and Writing.* New York: Addison-Wesley, 2000.

Cunningham, Patricia M., and James W. Cunningham. "What We Know about How to Teach Phonics." In *What Research Has to Say about Reading Instruction,* edited by Alan E. Farstrup and S. Jay Samuels, 87–109. Newark, DE: International Reading Association.

Cunningham, Patricia M., D. P. Hall, and M. Defee. "Nonability Grouped, Multilevel Instruction: A Year in a First Grade Classroom." *The Reading Teacher* 44 (1991): 566–571.

Curcio, Frances R., and Susan Folkson. "Exploring Data: Kindergarten Children Do It Their Way." *Teaching Children Mathematics* 2 (February 1996): 382–385.

D'Angelo, Diane A., and C. Ralph Adler. "Chapter I: A Catalyst for Improving Parent Involvement." *Phi Delta Kappan* 72 (January 1991): 350–354.

Dahl, Karin L., Patricia L. Scharer, Lora L. Lawson, and Patricia R. Grogan. "Phonics Instruction and Student Achievement in Whole Language First-Grade Classrooms. *Reading Research Quarterly* 34 (July/August/September 1999): 312–341.

Daniels, Marilyn. "The Effect of Sign Language on Hearing Children's Language Development." *Communication Education* 43 (October 1994): 291–298.

Danoff-Burg, James A. "Be a Bee and Other Approaches to Introducing Young Children to Entomology." *Young Children* 57 (September 2002): 42–47.

Davidson, Jane, and June L. Wright. "The Potential of the Microcomputer in the Early Childhood Classroom." In *Young Children: Active Learners in a Technological Age,* edited by June L. Wright and Daniel D. Shade, 77–91. Washington, DC: National Association for the Education of Young Children, 1994.

Davis, Jessica, and Howard Gardner. "The Arts and Early Childhood Education: A Cognitive Developmental Portrait of the Young Child as Artist." In *Handbook of Research on the Education of Young Children,* edited by B. Spodek, 191–206. New York: Macmillan, 1993.

Day, Mary Carol, and Ronald K. Parker. *The Preschool in Action: Exploring Early Childhood Programs.* 2d ed. Boston: Allyn and Bacon, 1977.

Debord, K. *Appropriate Limits for Young Children: A Guide for Discipline, Parts One and Two.* ERIC Document Reproduction Service ED 403989. 1996.

de la Roche, Elisa. "Snowflakes: Developing Meaningful Art Experiences for Young Children." *Young Children* 51 (January 1996): 82–83.

Delgado-Gaitan, Concha. "Involving Parents in Schools: A Process of Empowerment." *American Journal of Education* 100 (November 1991): 20–46.

Derman-Sparks, Louise. "Empowering Children to Create a Caring Culture in a World of Differences." *Childhood Education* 70 (Winter 1993/1994): 66–71.

Derman-Sparks, Louise. "Markers of Multicultural/Anti-bias Education." *Young Children* 54 (September 1999): 43.

Derman-Sparks, Louise, and the ABC Task Force. *Anti-Bias Curriculum: Tools for Empowering Young Children.* Washington, DC: National Association for the Education of Young Children, 1989.

Dever, Martha T., and Deborah Hobbs. "The Learning Spiral: Taking the Lead from How Young Children Learn." *Childhood Education* 75 (Fall 1998): 7–11.

Dever, Martha T., and Elizabeth J. Jared. "Remember to Include Art and Crafts in Your Integrated Curriculum." *Young Children* 51 (March 1996): 69–73.

DeVries, M. W., and A. J. Sameroff. "Culture and Temperament: Influences on Infant Temperament in Three East African Societies." *American Journal of Orthopsychiatry* 54 (1984): 83–96.

DeVries, Rheta, and Lawrence Kohlberg. *Constructivist Early Education: Overview and Comparison with Other Programs.* Washington, DC: National Association for the Education of Young Children, 1987a.

DeVries, Rheta, and Lawrence Kohlberg. *Programs of Early Education: The Constructivist View.* New York: Longman, 1987b.

Dewey, John. *The Child and the Curriculum.* Chicago: University of Chicago Press, 1902.

Dewey, John. *Democracy and Education.* New York: Free Press, 1916.

Dewey, John. *The School and Society*. New York: McClure, Phillips, 1900.

Dighe, Judith, Zoy Calomiris, and Carmen Van Zutphen, "Nurturing the Language of Art in Children." *Young Children* 53 (January 1998): 4–9.

Dimidjian, Victoria Jean. "Holidays, Holy Days, and Wholly Dazed." *Young Children* 44 (September 1989): 70–75.

Dinkmeyer, D., and R. Dreikurs. *Encouraging Children to Learn*. ERIC Document Reproduction Service 447391. 2000.

Dinwiddie, Sue A. "The Saga of Sally, Sammy, and the Red Pen: Facilitating Children's Social Problem Solving." *Young Children* 49 (July 1994): 13–19.

Ditchburn, Susan J. *Patterning Mathematical Understanding in Early Childhood*. ERIC Document Reproduction Service 218008. 1982.

Dixon, Glen T., and Patricia Tarr. "Extending Art Experiences in the Preschool Curriculum." *International Journal of Early Childhood* 20 (June 1988): 27–34.

Dreikurs, R., B. Grunwald, and F. Pepper. *Maintaining Sanity in the Classroom*. New York: Harper and Row, 1982.

Drew, Naomi. *Learning the Skills of Peacemaking: An Activity Guide for Elementary-Age Children on Communicating, Cooperating, Resolving Conflict*. Rolling Hills Estates, CA: Jalmar Press, 1987.

Duffy, Gerald G., and James V. Hoffman. "In Pursuit of an Illusion: The Flawed Search for a Perfect Method." *Reading Teacher* 53 (September 1999): 10–15.

Dumtschin, Joyce Ury. "Recognize Language Development and Delay in Early Childhood." *Young Children* 43 (1988): 16–24.

Dyck, James A. "The Case for the L-Shaped Classroom. *Principal* 74 (November 1994): 41–45.

Dyer, Suzanne M., and Wendy Schiller. " 'Not Wilting Flowers Again!' Problem Finding and Problem Solving in Movement and Performance." *Early Child Development and Care* 90 (May 1993): 47–54.

Dyson, Anne Haas, and Celia Genishi. "Visions of Children as Language Users: Language and Language Education in Early Childhood." In *Handbook of Research on the Education of Young Children,* edited by B. Spodek. New York: Macmillan, 1993.

Dyson, Anne Haas, and Celia Genishi. *Visions of Children as Language Users: Research on Language and Language Education in Early Childhood*. Technical Report No. 49. ERIC Document Reproduction Service 335678. 1991.

Eaton, Mary. "Positive Discipline: Fostering The Self-Esteem of Young Children." *Young Children* 52 (June 1997): 47–52.

Edwards, Carolyn, Lella Gandini, and George Forman, Eds. *The Hundred Languages of Children: The Reggio Emilia Approach to Early Childhood Education*. Norwood, NJ: Ablex, 1993.

Edwards, Linda C. *Affective Development and the Creative Arts: A Process Approach to Early Childhood Education*. Columbus, OH: Merrill, 1990.

Edwards, Linda C., and Martha L. Nabors. "The Creative Arts Process: What It Is and What It Is Not." *Young Children* 48 (March 1993): 77–81.

Eheart, B., and R. Leavitt. "Supporting Toddler Play." *Young Children* 40 (March 1985): 18–22.

Ehri, Linnea C., and Simone R. Nunes. "The Role of Phonemic Awareness in Learning to Read." In *What Research Has to Say About Reading Instruction,* edited by A. E. Farstrup and S. Jay Samuels, 110–139. Newark, DE: International Reading Association, 2002.

Elicker, J., and S. Mathur. "What Do They Do All Day? Comprehensive Evaluation of a Full-day Kindergarten." *Early Childhood Research Quarterly* 12 (January 1997): 459–480.

Elkind, David. "Child Development and Early Childhood Education: Where Do We Stand Today?" In *Curriculum Planning for Young Children,* edited by Janet Brown, 4–11. Washington, DC: National Association for the Education of Young Children, 1982.

Elkind, David. *Educating Young Children in Math, Science, and Technology*. ERIC Document Reproduction Service 416993. 1998.

Elkind, David, and G. J. Whitehurst. "Forum: Young Einsteins: Much Too Early, Much Too Late." *Education Matters*. Summer 2001. Available online: www.edmatters.org.

Elkonin, D. B. "Reading in the USSR." In *Comparative Reading,* edited by J. Downing, 551–579. New York: Macmillan, 1973.

Ellis, M. "The Complexity of Objects and Peers." In *Play and Learning,* edited by Brian Sutton-Smith. New York: Gardner Press, 1979.

Engel, Brenda. *Considering Children's Art: Why and How to Value Their Works*. Washington, DC: National Association for the Education of Young Children, 1995.

Engel, Brenda. "Learning to Look: Appreciating Child Art." *Young Children* 51 (March 1996): 74–79.

Englemann, Sigfried. "How Sound Is High/Scope Research?" *Educational Leadership* 56 (June 1999): 83–84.

Epstein, Ann S. "Thinking about Art: Encouraging Art Appreciation in Early Childhood Settings." *Young Children* 56 (May 2001): 38–43.

Epstein, Joyce L. "Paths to Partnership: What We Can Learn from Federal, State, District, and School Initiatives." *Phi Delta Kappan* 72 (January 1991): 344–349.

Epstein, Joyce L., and Susan L. Dauber. *Teachers' Attitudes and Practices of Parent Involvement in Inner-City Elementary and Middle Schools*. Baltimore, MD: Johns Hopkins University Center for Research on Elementary and Middle Schools, 1989 (as quoted in Olson 1990).

Erikson, Erik. *Childhood and Society*. 2d ed. New York: Norton, 1963.

Ernst, Gisela, and Kerri J. Richard. "Reading and Writing Pathways to Conversation in the ESL Classroom." *Reading Teacher* 48 (December/January 1995): 320–326.

Fagot, Beverly I., and Richard Hagan. "Aggression in Toddlers: Responses to the Assertive Acts of Boys and Girls." *Sex Roles* 12 (February 1985): 341–351.

Fallon, Irmie, and JoBeth Allen. "Where the Deer and the Cantaloupe Play." *Reading Teacher* 47 (April 1994): 546–551.

Farr, Beverly P., and Elise Trumbull. *Assessment Alternatives for Diverse Classrooms*. Norwood, MA: Christopher Gordon, 1997.

Farver, Jo Ann. "Aggressive Behavior in Preschoolers' Social Networks: Do Birds of a Feather Flock Together?" *Early Childhood Research Quarterly* 11 (March 1996): 333–350.

Farver, Jo Ann, and Yoohim L. Shin. "Social Pretend Play in Korean- and Anglo-American Preschoolers." *Child Development* 68 (1997): 544–556.

Federal Register, 30 December 1976, pp. 56966–56998.

Federal Register, 18 June 1990, p. 24838.

Feely, Jenny. "Writing in Science." In *Science and Language Links,* edited by Johanna Scott, 27–37. Portsmouth, NH: Heinemann, 1993.

Ferreiro, Emilia, and Ana Teberosky. *Literacy before Schooling.* Portsmouth, NH: Heinemann, 1982.

Fetter, M. Patricia. "AIDS Education: Every Teacher's Responsibility." *Childhood Education* 65 (Spring 1989): 150–152.

Feuerstein, Abe. "School Characteristics and Parent Involvement: Influences on Participation in Children's Schools." *Journal of Educational Research* 94 (September/October 2000): 29–41.

Findlay, Elsa. *Rhythm and Movement: Applications of Dalcroze Eurhythmics.* Evanston, IL: Summy-Birchard, 1971.

Fitzpatrik, Shannon, and Genelle Parrish. *An Integrated Fine Arts Program: Art Tells a Story about . . . Communities.* Huntington Beach, CA: Creative Teaching Press, Inc., 1995.

Flagg, A. *Rubrics, Checklists, and Other Assessments.* New York: Scholastic, 1998.

Flood, James, and Diane Lapp. "Reporting Reading Progress: A Comparison Portfolio for Parents." *Reading Teacher* 42 (March 1989): 508–514.

Flynn, Linda L., and Judith Kieff. "Including Everyone in Outdoor Play." *Young Children* 57 (May 2002): 20–26.

Follis, Helen, and Gerald Krockover. "Selecting Activities in Science and Mathematics for Gifted Young Children." *School Science and Mathematics* 82 (January 1982): 57–64.

Foorman, Barbara R., David J. Francis, Jack M. Fletcher, and Christopher Schatschneider. "The Role of Instruction in Learning to Read: Preventing Reading Failure in At-Risk Children." *Journal of Educational Psychology* 90 (January 1998): 37–55.

Ford, Sylvia A. "The Facilitator's Role in Children's Play." *Young Children* 48 (September 1993): 66–69.

Forman, George E. "The Constructivist Perspective to Early Education." In *Approaches to Early Childhood Education,* 2d ed., edited by Jaipaul Roopnarine and James E. Johnson. New York: Macmillan, 1993.

Forman, George E., and David S. Kuschner. *The Child's Construction of Knowledge: Piaget for Teaching Children.* Washington, DC: National Association for the Education of Young Children, 1983.

Fountas, Irene C., and Gay Su Pinnell. *Guided Reading: Good First Teaching for All Children.* Portsmouth, NH: Heinemann, 1996.

Fowlkes, Mary Anne. "Gifts from Childhood's Godmother—Patty Smith Hill." *Childhood Education* 61 (September/October 1984): 45–49.

Fox, Mem. *Teaching Drama to Young Children.* Portsmouth, NH: Heinemann, 1987.

Fox, Mem. "Writing Picture Books for Young Children." Speech at National Association for the Education of Young Children National Conference, New Orleans, LA, November 10, 1999.

Frank, Lawrence K. "Play Is Valid." *Childhood Education* 44 (March 1968): 433–440.

Frank, Nancy K. "Supervising Paraprofessionals: A Survey of Teacher Practice." *Journal of Special Education* 35 (Spring 2001): 41–54.

Freeman, David, and Yvonne S. Freeman. "The California Reading Initiative: A Formula for Failure for Bilingual Students?" *Language Arts* 76 (January 1999): 241–248.

French, Nancy K. "Supervising Paraprofessionals: A Survey of Teacher Practices." *Journal of Special Education* 35 (Spring 2001): 41–53.

Froebel, Friedrich. *The Education of Man.* Translated by W. N. Hailmann. New York: D. Appleton, 1826.

Frost, Joe L., and Joan B. Kissinger. *The Young Child and the Educative Process.* New York: Holt, Rinehart and Winston, 1976.

Frost, Joe L., and Susan C. Wortham. "The Evolution of American Playgrounds." *Young Children* 43 (July 1988): 19–28.

Fuhr, Janet E., and Kathy H. Barclay. "The Importance of Appropriate Nutrition and Nutrition Education." *Young Children* 53 (January 1998): 74–79.

Fuqua, Beth Howard. "Exploring Math Journals." *Childhood Education* 74 (Winter 1997/1998): 73–77.

Furlow, Elaine. "Growing School/Home Partnerships: The Family Education Network." *Multimedia Schools* 6 (January/February 1999): 44+.

Fusaro, J. A. "The Effect of a Full-Day Kindergarten on Student Achievement: A Meta-Analysis." *Child Study Journal* 27 (1997): 269–277.

Gabbard, Carl. *Playground Apparatus Experiences and Muscular Endurance among Children 4–6.* ERIC Document Reproduction Service 288190. College Station, TX: Texas A&M University, 1979.

Gabbard, Carl. "P.E. for Preschoolers: The Right Way." *Principal* (May 1995): 21–24.

Galen, Harlene. "Increasing Parental Involvement in Elementary School: The Nitty-Gritty of One Successful Program." *Young Children* 46 (January 1991): 18–22.

Galinsky, Ellen. "Parents and Teacher-Caregivers: Sources of Tension, Sources of Support." *Young Children* 43 (March 1988): 4–12.

Gallahue, David L. *Fundamental Movement Experiences for Children: A Developmental Skill Theme Approach.* ERIC Document Reproduction Service 211459. 1981.

Gandini, Lella. "Fundamentals of the Reggio Emilia Approach to Early Childhood Education." *Young Children* 49 (November 1993): 4–8.

Gardner, Howard. "The First Seven . . . and the Eighth." *Educational Leadership* 55 (January 1997a): 8–14.

Gardner, Howard. *Frames of Mind: The Theory of Multiple Intelligences.* New York: HarperCollins, 1983.

Gardner, H. "The Key in the Key Slot: Creativity in a Chinese Key." *Journal of Cognitive Education* 6 (1997b): 15–26.

Gardner, Howard. "The Understanding Pathway." *Educational Leadership* 57 (March 1999): 12–15.

Garrison, C. G. *Permanent Play Materials for Young Children.* New York: Scribner's, 1926.

Gartrell, Dan. "Assertive Discipline: Unhealthy for Children and Other Living Things." *Young Children* 42 (January 1987a): 10–11.

Gartrell, Dan. "Misbehavior or Mistaken Behavior?" *Young Children* 50 (July 1995): 27–34.

Gartrell, Dan. "Punishment or Guidance?" *Young Children* 42 (March 1987b): 55–61.

Gartrell, Daniel. "Replacing Time-Out: Part I—Using Guidance to Build an Encouraging Classroom." *Young Children* 56 (November 2001): 8–16.

Gartrell, Daniel. "Replacing Time-Out: Part II—Using Guidance to Maintain an Encouraging Classroom." *Young Children* 57 (March 2002): 36–43.

Garvey, Catherine. *Play.* Cambridge, MA: Harvard University Press, 1977.

Gaskins, Irene W. et al. "Analyzing Words and Making Discoveries about the Alphabet System: Activities for Beginning Readers." *Language Arts* 74 (March 1997): 172–184.

Gelfer, Jeffrey I., and Peggy G. Perkins. "Effective Communication with Parents: A Process for Parent/Teacher Conferences." *Childhood Education* 64 (October 1987): 19–22.

Gelman, Rochel, and Marsha F. Tucker. "Further Investigations of the Young Child's Conception of Number." *Child Development* 46 (March 1975): 167–175.

Genishi, Celia, and Anne Haas Dyson, eds. *Language Assessment in the Early Years.* Norwood, NJ: Ablex, 1984.

Gerson, Bev. "Implementing the Reggio Emilia Curriculum at Salem State Preschool." Presentation at Salem State College, Salem, MA, April 3, 2000.

Gfeller, Kate. "Integrating the Handicapped Child into Music Activities." In *Musical Growth and Development: Birth through Six,* edited by Dorothy T. McDonald and Gene M. Simons, 113–140. New York: Schirmer Books, 1989.

Gilbert, Jean. *Musical Starting Points with Young Children.* London, England: Ward Lock Educational, 1981.

Ginott, Haim G. *Teacher and Child.* New York: Macmillan, 1972.

Girolametto, Luigi, Lisa Hoaken, Elaine Weitzman, and Riet van Lieshout. "Patterns of Adult–Child Linguistic Interaction in Integrated Day Care Groups." *Language, Speech, and Hearing Services in Schools* 31 (April 2000): 155–168.

Glasser, William. "A New Look at School Failure and School Success." *Phi Delta Kappan* 78 (April 1997): 597–602.

Glasser, William. "School Violence from the Perspective of William Glasser." *Professional School Counseling* 4 (December 2000): 77–81.

Glazer, Susan Mandel. "Oral Language and Literacy Development." In *Emerging Literacy: Young Children Learn to Read and Write,* edited by Dorothy S. Strickland and Lesley Mandel Morrow, 16–26. Newark, DE: International Reading Association, 1989.

Gober, Billy E., and B. Don Franks. "Physical and Fitness Education of Young Children." *Journal of Physical Education, Recreation, and Dance* 59 (September 1988): 57–61.

Gochman, David S., and T. F. Saucier. "Perceived Vulnerability in Children and Adolescents." *Health Education Quarterly* 9 (1982): 46–59.

Goffin, Stacie G., and Catherine S. Wilson. *Curriculum Models and Early Childhood Education: Appraising the Relationship.* Columbus, OH: Merrill, 2001.

Goldberg, Ellie. "Including Children with Chronic Health Conditions: Nebulizers in the Classroom." *Young Children* 49 (January 1994): 34–37.

Goldberg, Merryl. *Arts and Learning: An Integrated Approach to Teaching and Learning in Multicultural and Multilingual Settings.* New York: Longman, 2001.

Goodman, Kenneth. *On Reading: A Common-Sense Look at the Nature of Language and the Science of Reading.* Portsmouth, NH: Heinemann, 1996.

Goodman, Kenneth, E. Brooks Smith, Robert Meredith, and Yetta Goodman. *Language and Thinking in School.* 3d ed. New York: Richard C. Owen, 1987.

Goodman, Yetta. "Kidwatching: Observing Children in the Classroom." In *Observing the Language Learner,* edited by Angela Jaggar and M. Trika Smith-Burke. Newark, DE: International Reading Association/National Council of Teachers of English, 1985.

Goodman, Yetta, and Carolyn Burke. *Reading Strategies: Focus on Comprehension.* Katonah, NY: Richard C. Owen, 1980.

Goodman, Yetta, and A. M. Marek. *Retrospective Miscue Analysis: Revaluing Readers and Reading.* Katonah, NY: Richard C. Owens, 1996.

Goodman, Y. M. "Children Coming to Know Literacy." In *Emergent Literacy: Writing and Reading,* edited by W. H. Teale and E. Sulzby, 1–14, Norwood, NJ: Ablex Publishing Company, 1986.

Gordon, Ann, and Kathryn W. Browne. *Guiding Young Children in a Diverse Society.* Boston: Allyn and Bacon, 1996.

Gorter-Reu, Maralee S., and Jean Marie Anderson. "Home Kits, Home Visits, and More." *Young Children* 53 (May 1998): 71–74.

Gould, A. O. "Developing Specialized Programs for Singing." *Council for Research in Music Education* 17 (1969): 9–22.

Gowen, Jean W. "The Early Development of Symbolic Play." *Young Children* 50 (March 1995): 75–84.

Grangaard, E. M. "Color and Light Effects on Learning." ERIC Document Reproduction Service 382381. 1995.

Graves, Donald. *A Fresh Look at Writing.* Portsmouth, NH: Heinemann, 1994.

Graves, Donald. Presentation at a conference of the International Reading Association, Atlanta, Georgia, May 1990.

Graves, Donald, and Virginia Stuart. *Write from the Start.* New York: New American Library, 1985.

Gray, Dianne E. The *Teacher's Role in Understanding Aggression and Dealing with It Effectively in the Preschool Environment.* ERIC Document Reproduction Service 200334. 1981.

Greabell, Leon C., and Sonia D. Forseth. "Creating a Stimulating Environment." *Kappa Delta Pi Record* 17 (February 1981): 70–73, 75.

Green, Connie R. "This Is My Name." *Childhood Education* 74 (Summer 1998): 226–231.

Greenberg, Polly. "How and Why to Teach All Aspects of Preschool and Kindergarten Math Naturally, Democratically, and Effectively (For Teachers Who Don't Believe in Academic Programs, Who Do Believe in Educational Excellence, and Who Find Math Boring to the Max)—Part 1." *Young Children* 48 (May 1993): 75–84.

Greenberg, Polly. "Lucy Sprague Mitchell: A Major Missing Link between Early Childhood Education in the 1980s and Progressive Education in the 1930s." *Young Children* 42 (July 1987): 70–84.

Greenberg, Polly. "Some Thoughts about Phonics, Feelings, Don Quixoté, Diversity, and Democracy: Teaching Young Children to Read, Write, and Spell, Part 1." *Young Children* 53 (July 1998a): 72–83.

Greenberg, Polly. "Thinking about Goals for Grownups and Young Children While We Teach Writing, Reading, and Spelling (and a Few Thoughts about the 'J' Word), Part 3." *Young Children* 53 (November 1998b): 31–42.

Greenberg, Polly. "Warmly and Calmly Teaching Young Children to Read, Write and Spell: Thoughts about the First Four of Twelve Well-Known Principles, Part 2." *Young Children* 53 (September 1998c): 68–82.

Greenwood, Deborah. "Home-School Communication via Video." *Young Children* 50 (September 1995): 66.

Griffith, Priscilla L., and Mary W. Olson. "Phonemic Awareness Helps Beginning Readers Break the Code." *Reading Teacher* 45 (March 1992): 516–523.

Grineski, Steven. "Teaching and Learning in Physical Education for Young Children." *Journal of Physical Education, Recreation and Dance* 59 (May/June 1988): 91–94.

Grineski, Steven. "What Is a Truly Developmentally Appropriate Physical Education Program for Children?" *Journal of Physical Education, Recreation and Dance* 63 (August 1992): 33–35, 60.

Grubb, Norton. "Young Children Face the State Issues and Options for Early Childhood Programs." *American Journal of Education* 97 (August 1989): 358–397.

Gullo, D. F. "Integrating Computer Technology into the Early Childhood Curriculum: A Constructivist Approach." *Journal of Early Education and Family Review* 7 (May/June 2000): 7–15.

Gullo, Dominic F., Carol U. Bersani, Douglas H. Clements, and Kathleen M. Ramsey. "A Comparative Study of 'All-Day,' 'Alternate-Day,' and 'Half-Day' Kindergarten Schedules: Effects on Achievement and Classroom Social Behaviors." *Journal of Research in Childhood Education* 1 (1986): 87–94.

Gunsberg, Andrew. "Empowering Young Abused and Neglected Children through Contingency Play." *Childhood Education* 66 (1989): 8–10.

Halliday, M. A. K. "Three Aspects of Children's Language Development: Learning Language, Learning through Language, Learning about Language." In *Oral and Written Language Development Research: Impact on the Schools*, edited by Y. Goodman, M. Haussler, and D. Strickland. Urbana, IL: National Council of Teachers of English, 1982.

Hampton, Fredrick M., and Dawne A. Mumford. "Parent Involvement in Inner-City Schools." *Urban Education* 33 (September 1998): 410–428.

Harding, Nadine. "Family Journals: The Bridge from School to Home and Back Again." *Young Children* 51 (January 1996): 27–30.

Hardman, Michael L. et al. *Human Exceptionality: Society, School, and Family.* 4th ed. Boston: Allyn and Bacon, 1993.

Harlan, Jean. *Science Experiences for the Early Childhood Years.* 2d ed. Columbus, OH: Merrill, 1980.

Harms, Thelma. "Evaluating Settings for Learning." *Young Children* 25 (May 1970): 304–309.

Harp, B. *Handbook of Literacy Assessment and Evaluation.* Norwood, MA: Christopher-Gordon, 1996.

Harp, Bill. *The Handbook of Literacy Assessment and Evaluation.* Norwood, MA: Christopher Gordon, 2000.

Harp, Bill, and Jo Ann Brewer. *Reading and Writing: Teaching for the Connections.* Fort Worth, TX: Harcourt Brace, 1996.

Harper, Andrew, Marty Flick, Karen Taylor, and Renee Waldo. "Education Through Music: A Breakthrough in Early Childhood Education?" *Phi Delta Kappan* 54 (May 1973): 628–629.

Harste, J., V. Woodward, and C. Burke. *Language Stories and Literacy Lessons.* Portsmouth, NH: Heinemann, 1984.

Hartle, Lynn et al. "Outdoor Play: A Window on Social-Cognitive Development." *Dimensions of Early Childhood* 23 (Fall 1994): 27–31.

Hartup, W. *Having Friends, Making Friends, and Keeping Friends: Relationships as Educational Contexts.* ERIC Document Reproduction Service ED34584. 1992.

Hatkoff, Amy. "Safety and Children: How Schools Can Help." *Childhood Education* 70 (Annual Theme 1994): 283–288.

Haugland, Susan W. "What Role Should Technology Play in Young Children's Learning? Part 1." *Young Children* 54 (June 1999): 26–31.

Haugland, Susan W. "What Role Should Technology Play in Young Children's Learning? Part II. Early Childhood Classrooms in the 21st Century: Using Computers to Maximize Learning." *Young Children* 54 (July 2000): 12–18.

Haukoos, Gerry D., and Archie B. Beauvais. "Thoughts for Teaching about American Indians." *Childhood Education* 73 (Winter 1996/1997): 77–82.

Healy, J. M. *Endangered Minds.* New York: Simon & Schuster, 2000.

Heath, Harriet E. "Dealing with Difficult Behaviors—Teachers Plan with Parents." *Young Children* 49 (July 1994): 20–24.

Heath, Shirley B. *Ways with Words: Language, Life, and Work in Communities and Classrooms.* New York: Cambridge University Press, 1983.

Hektner, Joel M., Gerald J. August, and George M. Realmuto. "Patterns and Temporal Changes in Peer Affiliation among Aggressive and Nonaggressive Children Participating in a Summer School Program." *Journal of Clinical Child Psychology* 29 (2000): 603–615.

Helm, Judy Harris, Sallee Beneke, and Kathy Steinheimer. "Documenting Young Children's Learning." *Childhood Education* 73 (April 1997): 200–205.

Hemmeter, Mary Louise, Kelly L. Maxwell, Melinda Jones Ault, and John W. Schuster. *Assessment of Practices in Early Elementary Classrooms.* New York: Teachers College Press, 2001.

Henderson, Anne T., and Nancy Berla. *A New Generation of Evidence: The Family is Critical to Student Achievement.* Washington, DC. ERIC Document Reproduction Service 375968. 1994.

Henniger, Michael L. "Enriching the Outdoor Play Experience." *Childhood Education* 70 (Winter 1993/1994): 87–90.

Henniger, Michael L. "Learning Mathematics and Science through Play." *Childhood Education* 63 (1987): 167–171.

Henniger, Michael L. "Planning for Outdoor Play." *Young Children* 49 (May 1994): 10–15.

Herlein, Woodie S. "Teaching Tips for Learning Centers: Providing a Safe and Educational Outdoor Environment." *NHSA Journal* (Summer/Fall 1995): 41–45.

Hernandez, Hilda. *Multicultural Education: A Teacher's Guide to Content and Process.* Columbus, OH: Merrill, 1989.

Herr, Judith, and Winifred Morse. "Food for Thought: Nutrition Education for Young Children." *Young Children* 39 (November 1982): 3–11.

Hester, Hilary. "Peer Interaction in Learning English as a Second Language." *Theory into Practice* 26 (1987): 208–217.

Heyman, Mark. *Places and Spaces: Environmental Psychology in Education.* Fastback no. 112. Bloomington, IN: Phi Delta Kappa Educational Foundation, 1978.

Hiebert, Elfrieda H. et al. *Every Child a Reader: Applying Reading Research in the Classroom.* Ann Arbor: Center for the Improvement of Early Reading Achievement, University of Michigan School of Education, 1998.

Hildebrandt, Carolyn. "Creativity in Music and Early Childhood. *Young Children* 53 (November 1998): 68–74.

Hill, Bonnie C., and Cynthia Ruptic. *Practical Aspects of Authentic Assessment: Putting the Pieces Together.* Norwood, MA: Christopher Gordon, 1994.

Hill, Bonnie C., Cynthia Ruptic, and Lisa Norwick. *Classroom Based Assessment.* Norwood, MA: Christopher Gordon, 1998.

Hill, Carol B. *Creating a Learning Climate for the Early Childhood Years.* Fastback no. 292. Bloomington, IN: Phi Delta Kappa Educational Foundation, 1989.

Hill, David. "Order in the Classroom." *Teacher Magazine* (April 1990): 70–77.

Hill, Patty Smith. "The Home and the School as Centers of Child Life." *Progressive Education* 5 (July/August/September 1982): 211–216.

Hill, Patty Smith. "The Function of the Kindergarten." *Young Children* 42 (July 1987): 12–19. (Originally published in 1926)

Hill, Patty Smith. *Kindergarten.* ERIC Document Reproduction Service ED346995. 1992.

Hill, Winfred F. *Learning: A Survey of Psychological Interpretations.* 3d ed. New York: Thomas Y. Crowell, 1977.

Hills, Tynette W. "Assessment in Context—Teachers and Children at Work." *Young Children* 48 (July 1993): 20–28.

Hinchey, Patricia H., Sally Adonizio, Nan Demarco, and Kyra Fetchina. "Sketching a Self-Portrait of Skills Instruction: Classroom Research and Accountability." *Language Arts* 77 (September 1999): 19–26.

Hinnant, Hilari A. "Growing Gardens and Mathematicians: More Books and Math for Young Children." *Young Children* 54 (March 1999): 23–25.

Hirsch, Elisabeth S., ed. *The Block Book.* Rev. ed. Washington, DC: National Association for the Education of Young Children, 1984.

Hitz, Randy. "Assertive Discipline: A Response to Lee Canter." *Young Children* 43 (January 1988): 25–26.

Hoffman, James, Patricia M. Cunningham, James W. Cunningham, and Hallie Yopp. *Phonemic Awareness and the Teaching of Reading.* Newark, DE: International Reading Association, 1998.

Hohmann, Mary, Bernard Banet, and David P. Weikart. *Young Children in Action.* Ypsilanti, MI: High/Scope Press, 1979.

Hohmann, Mary, and David P. Weikart. *Educating Young Children: Active Learning Practices for Preschool and Child Care Programs.* Ypsilanti, MI: High/Scope Educational Research Foundation, 1995.

Holdaway, Don. *The Foundations of Literacy.* Portsmouth, NH: Heinemann, 1980.

Holt, Bess-Gene. *Science with Young Children.* Rev. ed. Washington, DC: National Association for the Education of Young Children, 1989.

Honig, Alice Sterling. "Compliance, Control, and Discipline." *Young Children* 40 (January 1985): 50–58.

Hough, D., and S. Bryde. "The Effects of Full-Day Kindergarten on Student Achievement and Affect." Paper presented at annual conference of American Educational Research Association, New York. ERIC Document Reproduction Service 395691. 1996.

Hough, Ruth A., Joanne R. Nurss, and M. S. Goodson. "Children in Day Care: An Observational Study." *Child Study Journal* 14 (1984): 31–46.

Hough, Ruth A., Joanne R. Nurss, and Dolores Wood. "Tell Me a Story: Making Opportunities for Elaborated Language in Early Childhood Classrooms." *Young Children* 43 (1987): 6–12.

Howe, Ann C. "Science in Early Childhood Education." In *Handbook of Research on the Education of Young Children,* edited by B. Spodek, 225–235. New York: Macmillan, 1993.

Hranitz, John R., and E. Anne Eddowes. "Priorities: Parents and the Home." *Childhood Education* 63 (June 1987): 325–330.

Hubbard, Ruth S. "Creating a Classroom Where Children Can Think." *Young Children* 53 (September 1998): 26–31.

Huffman, Amy B. "Beyond the Weather Chart: Weathering New Experiences." *Young Children* 51 (July 1996): 34–37.

Hunt, J. McVicker. *Intelligence and Experience.* New York: Ronald Press, 1961.

Hymes, Dell. *Foundations of Sociolinguistics: An Ethnographic Approach.* Philadelphia: University of Pennsylvania Press, 1974.

Ilg, Frances L., and Louise B. Ames. *The Gesell Institute's Child Behavior.* New York: Dell, 1955.

International Reading Association/National Association of Educators of Young Children (IRA/NAEYC). Joint Position Statement. "Learning to Read and Write: Develop-

mentally Appropriate Practices for Young Children."
Reading Teacher 52 (October 1998): 193–215.

Irwin, D. Michelle, and M. Margaret Bushnell. *Observational Strategies for Child Study.* New York: Holt, Rinehart and Winston, 1980.

Isaacs, A. C., and W. M. Carroll. "Strategies for Basic-Fact Instruction." *Teaching Children Mathematics* 5 (1999): 505–508.

Isbell, Rebecca, and Betty Exelby. *Early Learning Environments That Work.* Beltsville, MD: Gryphon House, 2001.

Isbell, Rebecca, and Shirley Raines. "Young Children's Oral Language Production in Three Types of Play Centers." *Journal of Research in Childhood Education* 5 (Spring/ Summer 1991): 140–146.

Isenberg, Joan, and Mary Renck Jalongo. *Creative Expression and Play in the Early Childhood Curriculum.* New York: Macmillan, 1993.

Isenberg, Joan, and Nancy Quisenberry. "Play: A Necessity for All Children." *Childhood Education* 64 (February 1988): 138–145.

Isenberg, Joan, and Teresa Rosegrant. "Children and Technology." In *Selecting Educational Equipment and Materials for School and Home,* edited by Joan Moyer, 25–29. Wheaton, MD: Association for Childhood Education International, 1995.

Ivey, Bill. "The Arts Are Basic." *Teaching Music* 6 (June 1999): 56–57.

Jacobs, Heidi Hayes, ed. *Interdisciplinary Curriculum: Design and Implementation.* Washington, DC: Association for Supervision and Curriculum Development, 1989.

Jaques-Dalcroze, Emile. *Rhythm, Music and Education.* Translated by L. F. Rubenstein. London, England: Hazell Watson and Viney Ltd. for the Dalcroze Society, 1921.

Jaggar, Angela. "Allowing for Language Differences." In *Discovering Language with Children,* edited by Gay Su Pinnell. Urbana, IL: National Council of Teachers of English, 1980.

Jaggar, Angela, and M. Trika Smith-Burke, eds. *Observing the Language Learner.* Newark, DE: International Reading Association/National Council of Teachers of English, 1985.

Jalongo, Mary Renck. "The Child's Right to the Expressive Arts: Nurturing the Imagination as Well as the Intellect. A Position Paper of the Association for Childhood Education International." *Childhood Education* 66 (Summer 1990): 195–201.

Jalongo, Mary Renck. "Using Recorded Music with Young Children: A Guide for Nonmusicians." *Young Children* 51 (July 1996): 6–13.

Jalongo, Mary Renck. "What Is Happening to Kindergarten?" *Childhood Education* (January 1986): 154–160.

Jalongo, Mary Renck, and Mitzie Collins. "Singing with Young Children! Folk Singing for Nonmusicians." *Young Children* 40 (January 1985): 17–21.

Jalongo, Mary Renck, and Deborah M. Ribblett. "Using Song Picture Books to Support Emergent Literacy." *Childhood Education* 74 (Fall 1997): 15–22.

Jeffries, Carolyn. "Activity Selection: It's More Than the Fun Factor. *Science and Children* 37 (October 1999): 26–29, 63.

Jensen, Eric. *Teaching with the Brain in Mind.* Alexandria, VA: Association for Supervision and Curriculum Development, 1998.

Johns, Kenneth M., and C. Espinoza. *Management Strategies for Culturally Diverse Classrooms.* Fastback #396. Bloomington, IN: Phi Delta Kappa Educational Foundation, 1996.

Johnston, Lynne, and Joy Mermin. "Easing Children's Entry to School: Home Visits Help." *Young Children* 49 (July 1995): 62–68.

Jones, Elizabeth. "Inviting Children into the Fun: Providing Enough Activity Choices Outdoors." *Child Care Information Exchange* 70 (December 1989): 15–19.

Jones, Elizabeth, and John Nimmo. *Emergent Curriculum.* Washington, DC: National Association for the Education of Young Children, 1994.

Jones, Hazel A., and Steven F. Warren. "Enhancing Engagement in Early Language Teaching." *Teaching Exceptional Children* 23 (Summer 1991): 48–50.

Jones, Rebecca. "Involving Parents Is a Whole New Game: Be Sure You Win!" *American School Board Journal* 88 (September 2001): 18–22.

Jones, Vernon F., and Louise S. Jones. *Comprehensive Classroom Management: Motivating and Managing Students.* 3d ed. Boston: Allyn and Bacon, 1990.

Kamii, Constance. *Number in Preschool and Kindergarten.* Washington, DC: National Association for the Education of Young Children, 1982.

Kamii, Constance, and Georgia DeClark. *Young Children Reinvent Arithmetic: Implications of Piaget's Theory.* New York: Teachers College Press, 1985.

Kamii, Constance, and Rheta DeVries. *Physical Knowledge in Preschool Education.* Englewood Cliffs, NJ: Prentice-Hall, 1978.

Kamii, Constance, and Rheta DeVries. *Physical Knowledge in Preschool Education: Implications of Piaget's Theory.* Rev. ed. Englewood Cliffs, NJ: Prentice-Hall, 1993.

Kamii, Constance, and Rheta DeVries. "Piaget for Early Education." In *The Preschool in Action: Exploring Early Childhood Programs,* 2d ed., edited by Mary Carol Day and Ronald K. Parker, 365–420. Boston: Allyn and Bacon, 1977.

Kamii, Constance, and Linda Joseph. "Teaching Place Value and Double-Column Addition." *Arithmetic Teacher* 35 (February 1988): 48–52.

Kamii, Constance, and Linda Joseph. *Young Children Continue to Reinvent Arithmetic—2nd Grade: Implications of Piaget's Theory.* New York: Teachers College Press, 1989.

Kamii, Constance, and Mieko Kamii. "Why Achievement Testing Should Stop." In *Achievement Testing in the Early Grades: The Games Grown-Ups Play,* edited by Constance Kamii, 15–39. Washington, DC: National Association for the Education of Young Children, 1990.

Karnes, M. B., A. M. Schwedel, and M. B. Williams. "A Comparison of Five Approaches for Educating Young Children from Low-Income Homes." In *As the Twig Is Bent . . . Lasting Effects of Preschool Programs,* edited by

Consortium for Longitudinal Studies. Hillsdale, NJ: Lawrence Erlbaum Associates, 1983.

Karr, Jo Ann, and Elizabeth Landerholm. *Reducing Staff Stress/Burnout by Changing Staff Expectations in Dealing with Parents.* ERIC Document Reproduction Service 351128. 1991.

Katz, Lilian. "Engaging Children's Minds: The Implications of Research for Early Childhood Education." In *A Resource Guide to Public School Early Childhood Programs,* edited by Cynthia Warger. Alexandria, VA: Association for Supervision and Curriculum Development, 1988.

Katz, Lilian. Keynote speech. Oregon Association of School Administrators Conference of Kindergarten Teachers and Elementary Principals, Salem, Oregon, 1986.

Katz, Lilian. *More Talks with Teachers.* Urbana, IL: ERIC Clearinghouse on Elementary and Early Childhood Education, 1984.

Katz, Lilian. "The Professional Early Childhood Teacher." *Young Children* 39 (September 1984): 3–10.

Katz, Lilian, and Sylvia C. Chard. *Engaging Children's Minds: The Project Approach.* Norwood, NJ: Ablex, 1989.

Katz, Lilian, and Diane E. McClellan. *Fostering Children's Social Competence: The Teacher's Role.* Washington, DC: National Association for the Education of Young Children, 1997.

Kellogg, Rhoda. *Analyzing Children's Art.* Palo Alto, CA: National Press Books, 1970.

Kendall, Frances E. "Creating a Multicultural Environment." *Pre-K Today* (November/December 1988): 34–39.

Kennedy, David K. "After Reggio Emilia: May the Conversation Begin!" *Young Children* 51 (July 1996): 24–27.

Kent, Judith F., and Jennie Rakestraw. "The Role of Computers in Functional Language: A Tale of Two Writers." *Journal of Computing in Childhood Education* 5 (1994): 329–337.

Kieff, Judith. "Preferences of Mothers of At Risk and Peer Model Children for Parent Involvement Strategies." Doctoral dissertation, Oregon State University, 1990.

Kieff, Judith, and Renee Casbergue. *Playful Learning and Teaching: Integrating Play into Preschool and Primary Programs.* Boston: Allyn and Bacon, 2000.

Kieff, Judith, and Karyn Wellhousen. "Planning Family Involvement in Early Childhood Programs." *Young Children* 55 (May 2000): 18–25.

Kilmer, Sally J., and Helenmarie Hofman. "Transforming Science Curriculum." In *Reaching Potentials: Transforming Early Childhood Curriculum and Assessment,* vol. 2, edited by S. Bredekamp and T. Rosegrant, 43–63. Washington, DC: National Association for the Education of Young Children, 1995.

King, Martha L. "Language: Insights from Acquisition." *Theory Into Practice* 26 (1987): 358–363.

Kingsbury, Nancy M., and Joan C. Hall. "Provision of a Health Education Program for Preschoolers: A Demonstration Project Using Volunteers." *Early Childhood Development and Care* 36 (July 1988): 91–100.

Klesius, Janell P., and Priscilla L. Griffith. "Interactive Storybook Reading for At-Risk Learners." *Reading Teacher* 49 (April 1996): 552–590.

Koff, Susan R. "Toward a Definition of Dance Education." *Childhood Education* 77 (Fall 2000): 27–31.

Kohn, Alfie. *The Schools Our Children Deserve: Moving beyond Traditional Classrooms and "Tougher Standards."* Boston: Houghton Mifflin, 1999.

Kokoski, Teresa M., and Nancy Downing-Leffler. "Boosting Your Science and Math Programs in Early Childhood Education: Making the Home-School Connection." *Young Children* 50 (July 1995): 35–39.

Kontos, Susan, and Amanda Wilcox-Herzog. "Teachers' Interactions with Children: Why Are They So Important?" *Young Children* 52 (January 1997): 4–12.

Kostelnik, Marjorie, Laura Stein, Alice P. Whiren, and Anne K. Soderman. *Guiding Children's Social Development.* 2d ed. Albany, NY: Delmar, 1993.

Koster, Joan B. "Clay for Little Fingers." *Young Children* 54 (March 1999): 18–22.

Krajcik, Joseph S., Charlene M. Czerniak, and Carl Berger. *Teaching Children Science: A Project-Based Approach.* Boston: McGraw-Hill, 1999.

Kramer, Rita. *Maria Montessori: A Biography.* New York: G. P. Putnam's Sons, 1976.

Krashen, Stephen. "Looking for Bilingual Answers." *American Language Review* 4 (January/February 2000a): 16–19.

Krashen, Stephen D. *Second Language Acquisition and Second Language Learning.* New York: Pergamon Press, 1981.

Krashen, Stephen D. *Three Arguments against Whole Language and Why They Are Wrong.* Portsmouth, NH: Heinemann, 1999.

Krashen, Stephen. "What Does It Take to Acquire Language?" *ESL Magazine* 3 (May/June 2000b): 22–23.

Kratcoski, Annette Manning, and Karyn Bobkoff Katz. "Conversing with Young Language Learners in the Classroom." *Young Children* 53 (May 1998): 30–33.

Krechevsky, M. *Project Spectrum: Preschool Assessment Handbook.* New York: Teachers College Press, 1998.

Kreidler, William J. *Teaching Conflict Resolution through Children's Literature.* New York: Scholastic, 1994.

Kritchevsky, Sybil, and Elizabeth Prescott. *Planning Environments for Young Children: Physical Space.* Washington, DC: National Association for the Education of Young Children, 1969.

Kroll, Linda, and Mona Halaby. "Writing to Learn Mathematics in the Primary School." *Young Children* 52 (May 1997): 54–60.

Kuehn, Christine. "Inventing: Creative Sciencing." *Childhood Education* 65 (Fall 1988): 5–7.

Labinowicz, Ed. *Learning from Children: New Beginnings for Teaching Numerical Thinking.* Menlo Park, CA: Addison-Wesley, 1985.

Labinowicz, Ed. *The Piaget Primer: Thinking, Learning, Teaching.* Menlo Park, CA: Addison-Wesley, 1980.

Langone, John, D. Michael Malone, and Tina Kinsley. "Solutions for Young Children with Developmental Concerns." *Infants and Young Children* 16 (April 1999): 65–78.

Lasky, E. Z., and K. Klopp. "Parent-Child Interactions in Normal and Language-Disordered Children." *Journal of Speech and Hearing Disorders* 47 (1982): 7–18.

Lasky, Lila, and Rose Mukerji. *Art: Basic for Young Children.* Washington, DC: National Association for the Education of Young Children, 1980.

Leatzow, Nancy, Carol Neuhauser, and Liz Wilmes. *Creating Discipline in the Early Childhood Classroom.* Provo, UT: Brigham Young University Press, 1983.

Lee, Fong Yun. "Asian Parents as Partners." *Young Children* 50 (March 1995): 4–8.

Leff, S. S., T. J. Power, P. H. Manz, T. E. Costigan, and L. A. Nabors. "School-Based Aggression Prevention Programs for Young Children: Current Status and Implications for Violence Prevention." *School Psychology Review* 30 (2001): 344–363.

Lehman, Jeffrey R. "Measure Up to Science." *Science and Children* 31 (February 1994): 30–31.

Leitch, M. Laurie, and Sandra S. Tangri. "Barriers to Home–School Collaboration." *Educational Horizons* 66 (Winter 1988): 70–74.

Leonard, Ann Marie. *I Spy Something! A Practical Guide to Classroom Observations of Young Children.* Little Rock, AR: Southern Early Childhood Association, 1997.

Leppo, Marjorie L. *Healthy from the Start: New Perspectives on Childhood Fitness.* Teacher Education Monograph 15. ERIC Document Reproduction Service 352357. 1993.

Levin, I., F. Wilkening, and Y. Dembo. "Development of Time Quantification: Integration of Beginnings and Endings in Comparing Durations." *Child Development* 55 (1984): 2160–2172.

Lillard, Paula P. *Montessori: A Modern Approach.* New York: Schocken Books, 1972.

Lindfors, Judith Wells. *Children's Language and Learning.* Englewood Cliffs, NJ: Prentice-Hall, 1980.

Love, Ida H., and Daniel Levine. *Performance Ratings of Teacher Aides with and without Training and Follow-Up in Extending Reading Instruction.* ERIC Document Reproduction Service 349294. 1992.

Lowenfeld, Viktor, and W. Lambert Brittain. *Creative and Mental Growth.* 7th ed. New York: Macmillan, 1982.

Lowenthal, Barbara. "Teaching Social Skills to Preschoolers with Special Needs." *Childhood Education* 72 (Spring 1996): 137–140.

Lowenthal, Barbara. "Useful Early Childhood Assessment: Play-Based, Interviews and Multiple Intelligences." *Early Child Development and Care* 129 (February 1997): 43–49.

Luke, Jennifer L., and Catherine M. Myers. "Toward Peace: Using Literature to Aid Conflict Resolution." *Childhood Education* 71 (Winter 1994/1995): 66–69.

Lund, Kathryn A., and Candace S. Bos. "Orchestrating the Preschool Classroom: The Daily Schedule." *Teaching Exceptional Children* 14 (December 1981): 120–125.

Lundberg, Ingvar, Jergen Frost, and Ole-Peter Petersen. "Effects of an Extensive Program for Stimulating Phonological Awareness in Preschool Children." *Reading Research Quarterly* 23 (Summer 1988): 263–284.

Lunzer, E. "Intellectual Development in the Play of Young Children." *Educational Review* 11 (1959): 205–217.

Lyon, G. Reid. "Overview of Reading and Literacy Initiatives." Statement to Committee on Labor and Human Resources. Washington, DC: National Institutes of Health, 1998.

Malaguzzi, Loris. "For an Education Based on Relationships." *Young Children* 49 (November 1993): 9–12.

Malina, R. M. "Motor Development in the Early Years." In *The Young Child: Reviews of Research,* vol. 3, edited by S. G. Moore and C. R. Cooper, 11–229. Washington, DC: National Association for the Education of Young Children, 1982.

Malkusak, Tony, Jean Schappet, and Bruya Lawrence. "Turning Accessible Playgrounds into Fully Integrated Playgrounds: Just Add a Little Essence." *Parks and Recreation* 37 (May 2002): 66–71.

Marantz, Mady. "Fostering Prosocial Behavior in the Early Childhood Classroom: Review of the Research." *Journal of Moral Education* 17 (January 1988): 27–39.

Marchand, Nancy E., and Robert J. McDermott. "'Mouse Calls': A Storytelling Approach to Teaching First Aid Skills to Young Children." *Journal of School Health* 56 (December 1986): 453–454.

Marcon, Rebecca A. "Positive Relationships between Parent School Involvement and Public School Inner City Preschoolers' Development and Academic Performance." *School Psychology Review* 28 (1999): 395–413.

Marion, Marian. "Guiding Young Children's Understanding and Management of Anger." *Young Children* 52 (November 1997): 62–67.

Marshall, Hermine H. "The Development of Self-Concept." *Young Children* 44 (July 1989): 44–51.

Martin, Anne. "Teachers and Teaching." *Harvard Educational Review* 58 (November 1988): 488–501.

Martin, Bill, Jr. "Celebrating Language." Seminar sponsored by the School of Education, Oregon State University, Corvallis, Oregon, Summer 1986.

Martin, Sue. *Developmentally Appropriate Evaluation: Convincing Students and Teachers of the Importance of Observation as Appropriate Evaluation of Children.* ERIC Document Reproduction Service 391601. 1996.

Marxen, Carol E. "Push, Pull, Toss, Tilt, Swing: Physics for Young Children." *Childhood Education* 71 (Summer 1995): 212–216.

Mason, Jana M., and Shobha Sinha. "Emerging Literacy in the Early Childhood Years: Applying a Vygotskian Model of Learning and Development." In *Handbook of Research on the Education of Young Children,* edited by B. Spodek, 137–150. New York: Macmillan, 1993.

Masselli, David et al. "Aggressive Behavior of the Preschool Child." *Education* 104 (Summer 1984): 385–388.

McAfee, Oralie, and Deborah Leong. *Assessing and Guiding Young Children's Development and Learning.* 2d ed. Boston: Allyn and Bacon, 1997.

McArdle, F. "Art in Early Childhood: The Discourse of 'Proper' Teaching." Doctoral dissertation, Queensland University of Technology, Brisbane, 2001.

McCarthy, Jan. "Reggio Emilia: What Is the Message for Early Childhood Education?" *Contemporary Education* 66 (Spring 1995): 139–142.

McClintic, Susan V. "Conservation—A Meaningful Gauge for Assessment." *Arithmetic Teacher* 35 (February 1988): 12–14.

McCracken, Janet B. *More Than 1, 2, 3—The Real Basics of Mathematics.* Washington, DC: National Association for the Education of Young Children, 1987.

McCracken, Janet B. *Valuing Diversity: The Primary Years.* Washington, DC: National Association for the Education of Young Children, 1993.

McDonald, Dorothy T. *Music in Our Lives: The Early Years.* Washington, DC: National Association for the Education of Young Children, 1979.

McDonald, Dorothy T., and Gene M. Simons. *Musical Growth and Development: Birth through Six.* New York: Schirmer Books, 1989.

McGregor, Lynn, Maggie Tate, and Ken Robinson. *Learning through Drama.* Portsmouth, NH: Heinemann, 1987.

McIntyre, Margaret. *Early Childhood and Science.* Washington, DC: National Science Teachers Association, 1984.

McKenna, Michael C., and Dennis J. Kear. "Measuring Attitude toward Reading: A New Tool for Teachers." *Reading Teacher* 43 (May 1990): 626–639.

McNairy, Marion R. "Sciencing: Science Education for Early Childhood." *School Science and Mathematics* 85 (May/June 1985): 383–393.

McNeely, S. L. *Observing Students and Teachers through Objective Strategies.* Boston: Allyn and Bacon, 1997.

McNeill, David. "Developmental Psycholinguistics." In *The Genesis of Language,* edited by Frank Smith and George Miller. Cambridge, MA: MIT Press, 1966.

McQuillan, Jeff. *The Literacy Crisis: False Claims, Real Solutions.* Portsmouth, NH: Heinemann, 1998.

Meisels, Samuel J. "High-Stakes Testing in Kindergarten." *Educational Leadership* 47 (April 1989): 16–22.

Meisels, Samuel J. "Remaking Classroom Assessment with the Work Sampling System." *Young Children* 48 (July 1993): 34–40.

Meisels, Samuel J. "Uses and Abuses of Developmental Screening and School Readiness Testing." *Young Children* 42 (January 1987): 4–6, 68–73.

Meisels, Samuel J., and others. "New Evidence for the Effectiveness of the Early Screening Inventory." *Early Childhood Research Quarterly* 8 (September 1993): 327–346.

Meisels, Samuel J., Fong-Ruey Liaw, Aviva Dorfman, and Regena F. Nelson. "The Work Sampling System: Reliability and Validity of a Performance Assessment for Young Children." *Early Childhood Research Quarterly* 10 (1995): 277–296.

Meriwether, Linda. "Math at the Snack Table." *Young Children* 52 (July 1997): 69–73.

Merrion, Margaret Dee, and Marilyn Curt Vincent. *A Primer on Music for Non-Musician Educators.* Fastback 270. Bloomington, IN: Phi Delta Kappa Educational Foundation, 1988.

Micklo, Stephen J. "Math Portfolios in the Primary Grades." *Childhood Education* 73 (Summer 1997): 194–199.

Midjaas, C. L. "Use of Space." In *Instructional Leadership Handbook,* edited by J. W. Keefe and J. M. Jenkins. Reston, VA: National Association of Secondary School Principals, 1984.

Miller, Cheri Sterman. "Building Self-Control: Discipline for Young Children." *Young Children* 40 (November 1984): 15–19.

Miller, S. "The Facilitation of Fundamental Motor Skill Learning in Young Children." Doctoral dissertation, Michigan State University, 1978.

Missouri Department of Elementary and Secondary Education. *Project Construct Goals.* St. Louis, MO: Author, 2001.

Mitchell, Anne, and Judy David. *Explorations with Young Children: A Curriculum Guide from the Bank Street College of Education.* Mt. Rainier, MD: Gryphon, 1992.

Mitchell, Lucy S. "Making Young Geographers Instead of Teaching Geography." *Progressive Education* 5 (July/August/September 1928): 217–223.

Mize, Jacquelyn, and Gary Ladd. "Toward the Development of Successful Social Skills Training for Preschool Children." In *Peer Rejection in Childhood,* edited by S. R. Asher and J. D. Cole, 338–361. New York: Cambridge University Press, 1990.

Monroe, Eula E., and Robert Panchyshyn. "Vocabulary Considerations for Teaching Mathematics." *Childhood Education* 72 (Winter 1994/1995): 80–83.

Montessori, Maria. *Dr. Montessori's Own Handbook.* New York: Frederick A. Stokes, 1914.

Mooney, Margaret E. *Reading to, with, and by Children.* Katonah, NY: Richard C. Owen, 1990.

Moore, Kimberly B. "Protecting Children Indoors and Out." *Early Childhood Today* 15 (April 2001): 12–13.

Moore, Lynn M. "Learning Language and Some Initial Literacy Skills through Social Interactions." *Young Children* 53 (March 1998): 72–75.

Morrow, Lesley M., and Muriel K. Rand. "Promoting Literacy During Play by Designing Early Childhood Classroom Environments." *Reading Teacher* 44 (February 1991): 396–402.

Morrow, Lesley M., Diane H. Tracey, Deborah G. Woo, and Michael Pressley. "Characteristics of Exemplary First-Grade Literacy Instruction." *Reading Teacher* 52 (February 1999): 462–476.

Moustafa, Margaret, and Elba Maldonado-Colon. "Whole-to-Parts Phonics Instruction: Building on What Children Know to Help Them Know More." *Reading Teacher* 52 (February 1999): 448–458.

Murray, Paula L., and Richard E. Mayer. "Preschool Children's Judgments of Number Magnitude." *Journal of Educational Psychology* 80 (June 1988): 206–209.

Music Educators National Conference (MENC). *The School Music Program: A New Vision.* Reston, VA: Author, 1994.

Myhre, Susan. "Enhancing Your Dramatic-Play Area through the Use of Prop Boxes." *Young Children* 48 (July 1993): 6–11.

National Association for Music Education. *The K–12 National Standards, PreK Standards, and What They Mean to Music Educators.* 1999. Available online: www.menc.org/publications/books/prek12st.html.

National Association for the Education of Young Children (NAEYC). *Accreditation Criteria and Procedures of the Na-*

tional Academy of Early Childhood Programs. Washington, DC: NAEYC, 1984.

National Association for the Education of Young Children (NAEYC). "Educating Yourself about Diverse Cultural Groups in Our Country by Reading." *Young Children* 48 (March 1993): 13–16.

National Association for the Education of Young Children (NAEYC). *Child Health Alert* 16 (1998): 5.

National Association for the Education of Young Children (NAEYC). *Helping Children Learn Self-Control.* Washington, DC: NAEYC, 1986.

National Association for the Education of Young Children (NAEYC). "NAEYC Position Statement: Technology and Young Children—Ages Three through Eight." *Young Children* 51 (September 1996): 11–16.

National Association for the Education of Young Children (NAEYC). "NAEYC Position Statement on Standardized Testing of Young Children 3 through 8 Years of Age." *Young Children* 43 (March 1988): 42–47.

National Association for the Education of Young Children/National Council of Teachers of Mathematics. "Early Childhood Mathematics: Promoting Good Beginnings." A joint position statement. Washington, DC: Author.

National Association of State Boards of Education (NASBE). *Right from the Start: The Report of the NASBE Task Force on Early Childhood Education.* Alexandria, VA: NASBE, 1988.

National Council for Accreditation of Teacher Education (NCATE). *NCATE Standards, Procedures, and Policies for the Accreditation of Professional Units.* Washington, DC: NCATE, 1987.

National Council for the Social Studies (NCSS). "Curriculum Standards for Social Studies: Expectations of Excellence." Washington, DC: NCSS, 1998.

National Council for the Social Studies (NCSS). *Position Statement on Interdisciplinary Learning, Pre-K–Grade 4.* 1994. Available online: www.ncss.org/standards.

National Council of Social Studies Task Force on Early Childhood/Elementary Social Studies. "Social Studies for Early Childhood and Elementary School Children: Preparing for the 21st Century." *Social Education* 53 (January 1989): 14–23.

National Council of Teachers of Mathematics (NCTM). *Curriculum and Evaluation Standards for School Mathematics.* Washington, DC: NCTM, 1989.

National Council of Teachers of Mathematics (NCTM). *Standards for Discussion.* 2000. Available online: www.nctm. org.

National Reading Panel. *Report of the National Reading Panel: Teaching Children to Read: An Evidence-Based Assessment of the Scientific Research Literature on Reading and Its Implications for Reading Instruction.* Washington, DC: National Institute of Child Health and Human Development/National Institute for Literacy, 2000.

Neely, Linda P. "Practical Ways to Improve Singing in Early Childhood Classrooms." *Young Children* 47 (July 2002): 80–83.

Neisworth, John T., and Thomas J. Buggey. "Behavior Analysis and Principles in Early Childhood Education." In *Approaches to Early Childhood Education,* 2d ed., edited by Jaipaul Roopnarine and James E. Johnson. New York: Macmillan, 1993.

Nelson, Katherine. "Structure and Strategy in Learning to Talk." *Monographs of the Society for Research in Child Development* 38 (1973): 149.

Nelson, R. G. "Which Is the Best Kindergarten?" *Principal* 79 (May 2000): 38–41.

Neuman, Susan B., and Kathy Roskos. "Bridging Home and School with a Culturally Responsive Approach." *Childhood Education* 70 (Summer 1994): 210–214.

Neuman, Susan B., and Kathleen A. Roskos. *Language and Literacy Learning in the Early Years.* Fort Worth, TX: Harcourt Brace Jovanovich, 1993.

New, Rebecca. "Excellent Early Education: A City in Italy Has It." *Young Children* 45 (September 1990): 4–10.

Nichols-Solomon, Rochelle. "Barriers to Serious Parent Involvement." *Phi Delta Kappa* 82 (September 2000): 19–21.

Nicolson, S., and S. G. Shipstead. *Through the Looking Glass: Observations in the Early Childhood Classroom.* New York: Merrill, 1994.

Norton, Donna. *Through the Eyes of a Child: An Introduction to Children's Literature.* Columbus, OH: Merrill, 2003.

Norton, Donna, and Saundra Norton. *Through the Eyes of a Child: An Introduction to Children's Literature.* Columbus, OH: Merrill, 2003.

Novick, Rebecca. "Supporting Early Literacy Development: Doing Things with Words in the Real World." *Childhood Education* 76 (Winter 1999/2000): 70–75.

Oden, S., L. J. Schweinhart, and D. P. Weikart. *Into Adulthood: A Study of the Effects of Head Start.* Eric Document Reproduction Service 444730. 2000.

Odoy, Hillary Ann, and Sarah Hanna Foster. "Creating Play Crates for the Outdoor Classroom." *Young Children* 52 (September 1997): 12–16.

Ogle, Donna M. "The Know, Want to Know, Learn Strategy." In *Children's Comprehension of Text,* edited by K. D. Muth, 205–223. Newark, DE: International Reading Association, 1989.

Ohanian, Susan. "Goals 2000: What's in a Name?" *Phi Delta Kappan* 81 (January 2000): 344–355.

Oken-Wright, Pamela. "Show and Tell Grows Up." *Young Children* 43 (1988): 52–58.

Opitz, Michael F. "Cultural Diversity + Supportive Text = Perfect Books for Beginning Readers." *Reading Teacher* 52 (May 1999): 888–890.

Owens, Caroline V. "Conversational Science 101: Talking It Up!" *Young Children* 54 (September 1999): 4–9.

Pagni, David. "You're Never Too Old (or Too Young) to Use a Calculator." *Elementary Mathematician* 1 (December 1987): 10–11.

Pangrazi, Robert P., C. B. Corbin, and G. J. Welk. "Physical Activity for Children and Youth." *Journal of Physical Education, Recreation, and Dance* 67 (April 1996): 38–40, 42–43.

Pangrazi, Robert P., and Victor P. Dauer. *Dynamic Physical Education for Elementary School Children.* 10th ed. New York: Macmillan, 1992.

Pangrazi, Robert P., and Victor P. Dauer. *Movement in Early Childhood and Primary Education.* Minneapolis, MN: Burgess, 1981.

Parette, Howard P., Jr., Nancy S. Dunn, and Debra R. Hoge. "Low-Cost Communication Devices for Children with Disabilities and Their Family Members." *Young Children* 50 (September 1995): 75–81.

Parker, Emelie L. et al. "Teachers' Choices in Classroom Assessment." *Reading Teacher* 48 (April 1995): 622–624.

Parten, Mildred B. "Social Participation among Preschool Children." *Journal of Abnormal and Social Psychology* 27 (July/September 1932): 243–269.

Patton, Mary M., and Teresa M. Kokoski. "How Good Is Your Early Childhood Science, Mathematics, and Technology Program? Strategies for Extending Your Curriculum." *Young Children* 51 (July 1996): 38–44.

Paulson, F. Leon, Pearl R. Paulson, and Carol A. Meyer. "What Makes a Portfolio a Portfolio?" *Educational Leadership* 48 (February 1991): 60–63.

Pearlman, Susan, and Kathy Pericak-Spector. "A Series of Seriation Activities." *Science and Children* 31 (January 1994): 37–39.

Peck, Charles A., Tony Apolloni, Thomas P. Cooke, and Sharon A. Raver. "Teaching Retarded Preschoolers to Imitate the Free-Play Behavior of Nonretarded Classmates: Trained and Generalized Effects." *Journal of Special Education* 12 (Summer 1978): 195–207.

Pellegrini, Anthony D. *Applied Child Study: A Developmental Approach.* Hillsdale, NJ: Lawrence Erlbaum Associates, 1987.

Pellegrini, Anthony D. "The Relationship between Kindergartners' Play and Achievement in Prereading, Language and Writing." *Psychology in the Schools* 17 (October 1980): 530–535.

Pellegrini, Anthony D., and Brenda Boyd. "The Role of Play in Early Childhood Development and Education: Issues in Definitions and Function." In *Handbook of Research on the Education of Young Children,* edited by Bernard Spodek, 105–121. New York: Macmillan, 1993.

Pena, Delores C. "Parent Involvement: Influencing Factors and Implications." *Journal of Educational Research* 94 (September/October 2000): 42–55.

Peregoy, S. F., and Owen F. Boyle. *Reading, Writing, and Learning in ESL.* New York: Addison Wesley Longman, 2001.

Perlmutter, Jane C., and Louise Burrell. "Learning through 'Play' as Well as 'Work' in the Primary Grades." *Young Children* 50 (July 1995): 14–21.

Perrone, Vito. "How Did We Get Here?" In *Achievement Testing in the Early Grades: The Games Grown-Ups Play,* edited by Constance Kamii, 1–14. Washington, DC: National Association for the Education of Young Children, 1990.

Pestalozzi, Johann Heinrich. *How Gertrude Teaches Her Children.* Translated by Lucy E. Holland and Francis C. Turner. Syracuse, NY: C. W. Bardeen, 1894.

Pestalozzi, Johann Heinrich. *Leonard and Gertrude.* Translated and abridged by Eva Channing. Boston: D. C. Heath, 1885.

Petersen, Susan C. "The Sequence of Instruction in Games: Implications for Developmental Appropriateness." *Journal of Physical Education, Recreation and Dance* 63 (August 1992): 36–39.

Phillips, Carol Brunson. "Nurturing Diversity for Today's Children and Tomorrow's Leaders." *Young Children* 43 (January 1988): 42–47.

Phyfe-Perkins, Elizabeth. "Children's Behavior in Preschool Settings: A Review of Research Concerning the Influence of the Physical Environment." In *Current Topics in Early Childhood Education,* vol. 3, edited by L. Katz et al. Norwood, NJ: Ablex, 1980.

Piaget, Jean. *The Child's Conception of Number.* London: Routledge and Kegan Paul, 1952a.

Piaget, Jean. "Development and Learning." In *Piaget Rediscovered,* edited by R. Ripple and V. Rockcastle. Ithaca, NY: Cornell University Press, 1964.

Piaget, Jean. *The Equilibration of Cognitive Structures: The Central Problem of Intellectual Development.* Chicago: University of Chicago Press, 1985.

Piaget, Jean. *The Language and Thought of the Child.* 3d ed. London: Routledge and Kegan Paul, 1959.

Piaget, Jean. *The Origins of Intelligence in Children.* New York: International Universities Press, 1952b.

Piaget, Jean. *Play, Dreams and Imitation in Childhood.* New York: W. W. Norton, 1962.

Piaget, Jean. *Science of Education and the Psychology of the Child.* New York: Orion Press, 1970.

Piaget, Jean, and Barbel Inhelder. *The Psychology of the Child.* Translated by Helen Weaver. New York: Basic Books, 1969.

Pickett, Anna L. et al. *Promoting Effective Communications with Paraeducators.* ERIC Document Reproduction Service 357586. 1993.

Pickle, Barbara. *Increasing Safety Awareness of Preschoolers through a Safety Education Program.* ERIC Document Reproduction Service 310880. 1989.

Piper, Terry. *Language for All Our Children.* New York: Merrill, 1993.

Pogrow, Stanley. "Success for All Does Not Produce Success for Students." *Phi Delta Kappan* 82 (September 2000): 67–80.

Ponick, F. S. "What's Happening in Early Childhood Music Education?" *Teaching Music* 7 (October 1999): 30–31.

Potts, R., A. C. Huston, and J. C. Wright. "The Effects of Television Form and Violent Content on Boys' Attention and Social Behavior." *Journal of Experimental Child Psychology* 41 (1986): 1–17.

Prescott, Elizabeth, Elizabeth Jones, and Sybil Kritchevsky. *Group Day Care as a Child-Rearing Environment.* Washington, DC: Children's Bureau, Social Security Administration, Department of Health, Education and Welfare, 1967.

Price, Gary Glen. "Research in Review: Mathematics in Early Childhood." *Young Children* 44 (May 1989): 53–58.

Purcell-Gates, V. "Stories, Coupons, and the TV Guide—Relationships Between Home Literacy Experiences and Emergent Literacy Knowledge." *Reading Research Quarterly* 31(4) (1996): 406–428.

Raffaele, Linda M. Knoff. "Improving Home-School Collaboration with Disadvantaged Families: Organizational Principles." *School and Psychology Review* 28 (March 1999): 448+.

Rakow, Steven J., and Michael J. Bell. "Science and Young Children: The Message from the National Science Education Standards." *Childhood Education* 74 (Spring 1998): 164–167.

Ramsburg, Dawn. "The Debate over Spanking." *ERIC Digest.* ERIC Document Reproduction Service ED 405139. 1997.

Ramsey, Patricia G. *Teaching and Learning in a Diverse World: Multicultural Education for Young Children.* New York: Teachers College Press, 1998.

Ransbury, Molly Kayes. "Friedrich Froebel 1782–1982: A Reexamination of Froebel's Principles of Childhood Learning." *Childhood Education* 59 (November/December 1982): 101–105.

Raper, George, and John Stringer. *Encouraging Primary Science: An Introduction to the Development of Science in Primary Schools.* London: Cassell, 1987.

Ratcliff, Nancy. "Use the Environment to Prevent Discipline Problems and Support Learning." *Young Children* 56 (September 2001): 84–88.

Readdick, Christine A., and Patricia Bartlett. "Vertical Learning Environments." *Childhood Education* 71 (Winter 1994/1995): 86–90.

Readdick, Christine A., and Jennifer J. Park. "Achieving Great Heights: The Climbing Child." *Young Children* 53 (November 1998): 14–19.

Reardon, S. Jeanne. "A Collage of Assessment and Evaluation from Primary Classrooms." In *Assessment and Evaluation in Whole Language Programs,* edited by Bill Harp. Boston: Christopher Gordon, 1991.

Reifel, Stuart, and June Yeatman. "From Category to Context: Reconsidering Classroom Play." *Early Childhood Research Quarterly* 8 (1993): 347–367.

Rettig, Michael. "The Play of Young Children with Visual Impairments: Characteristics and Interventions." *Journal of Visual Impairment and Blindness* 88 (September/October 1994): 410–420.

Reynolds, Gretchen, and Elizabeth Jones. *Master Players: Learning from Children at Play.* New York: Teachers College Press, 1997.

Richards, Leah. "Measuring Things in Words: Language for Learning Mathematics." *Language Arts* 67 (January 1990): 14–25.

Richards, Mary Helen. *Mary Helen Richards Teaches: The Child in Depth.* Portola Valley, CA: Richards Institute of Music Education and Research, 1969.

Richardson, Kathy. "Assessing Understanding." *Arithmetic Teacher* 35 (February 1988): 39–41.

Richardson, Kathy, and Leslie Salkeld. "Transforming Mathematics Curriculum." In *Reaching Potentials: Transforming Early Childhood Curriculum,* edited by S. Bredekamp and T. Rosegrant, 23–42. Washington, DC: National Association for the Education of Young Children, 1995.

Rillero, Peter, Jo Ann V. Cleland, and Karen A. Conzelman. "The Nature of Haiku." *Science and Children* 37 (October 1999): 16–20.

Rivkin, Mary S. "Problem Solving through Outdoor Play." *Early Childhood Today* 15 (April 2001): 36–42.

Robertson, Shari Brand, and Susan Ellis Weismer. "Effects of Treatment on Linguistic and Social Skills in Toddlers with Delayed Language Development." *Journal of Speech, Language & Hearing Research* 42 (October 1999): 1234+.

Robinson, Sandra L. "The Grading Ritual: Unreliable and Unsuitable—But Unalterable?" *Young Children* 52 (July 1997): 86–87.

Roeper, Annemarie. "Play and Gifted Children." In *Play as a Medium for Learning and Development,* edited by D. Bergen, 163–165. Portsmouth, NH: Heinemann, 1987.

Rogers, Cosby S., and Sandra S. Morris. "Reducing Sugar in Children's Diets: Why? How?" *Young Children* 41 (July 1986): 11–16.

Rogers, Dwight L., and Dorene D. Ross. "Encouraging Positive Social Interaction among Young Children." *Young Children* 41 (March 1986): 12–17.

Rogers, Fred, and Hedda B. Sharapan. "Helping Parents, Teachers, and Caregivers Deal with Children's Concerns about War." *Young Children* 46 (March 1991): 12–13.

Rollins, Pamela R., Barbara A. Pan, Gina Conti-Ramsden, and Catherine E. Snow. "Communicative Skills in Children with Specific Language Impairments: A Comparison with Their Language-Matched Siblings." *Journal of Communication Disorders* 27 (June 1994): 189–206.

Roopnarine, Jaipaul, and Alice S. Honig. "Research in Review: The Unpopular Child." *Young Children* 40 (September 1985): 59–64.

Roopnarine, Jaipaul L., and James E. Johnson. *Approaches to Early Childhood Education.* Columbus, OH: Merrill, 2000.

Rose, Lowell C., and Alec M. Gallup. "The 31st Annual Poll of the Public's Attitudes toward the Public Schools." *Phi Delta Kappan* 81 (September 1999): 41–56.

Rosenthal, David M., and Julanne Y. Sawyers. "Building Successful Home/School Partnerships: Strategies for Parent Support and Involvement." *Childhood Education* 72 (Summer 1996): 194–200.

Roser, Nancy L. "A Place for Everything and Literature in Its Place." *The New Advocate* 14 (Summer 2001): 211–249.

Roskos, K., and S. Neuman. "Play Settings as Literacy Environments: Their Effects on Children's Literacy Behaviors." In *Children's Emergent Literacy: From Research to Practice,* edited by D. F. Lancy, 251–264. Westport, CT: Praeger Press, 1994.

Ross, Dorothy G. *Stanley Hall: The Psychologist as Prophet.* Chicago: University of Chicago Press, 1972.

Ross, James G., and Russell R. Pate. "The National Children and Youth Study II: A Summary of Findings." *Journal of Physical Education, Recreation and Dance* 58 (November/December 1987): 51–56.

Ross, Michael E. "Science Their Way." *Young Children* 55 (March 2000): 6–13.

Roswal, Glenn, and Greg H. Frith. "The Children's Developmental Play Program: Physical Activity Designed to Facilitate the Growth and Development of Mildly Handicapped Children." *Education and Training of the Mentally Retarded* 15 (December 1980): 322–324.

Rothlein, Liz. "Nutrition Tips Revisited: On a Daily Basis Do We Implement What We Know?" *Young Children* 44 (September 1989): 30–36.

Rousseau, Jean-Jacques. *Emile.* Translated by Barbara Foxley. 1780. Reprint, New York: E. P. Dutton, 1950.

Routman, Regie. *Conversations.* Portsmouth, NH: Heinemann, 2000.

Rowe, Deborah W. "The Literate Potentials of Book-Related Dramatic Play." *Reading Research Quarterly* 33 (January/February/March 1998): 10–35.

Rubin, K., G. Fein, and V. Vanderberg. "Play." In *Carmichaels's Manual of Child Psychology: Social Development,* edited by E. Hetherington. New York: Wiley, 1983.

Ruiz, Nadeen T. "A Young Deaf Child Learns to Write: Implications for Literacy Development." *Reading Teacher* 49 (November 1995): 206–217.

Rule, Audrey C., and Manuel T. Barrera. "Science Object Boxes: Using Object Boxes to Promote Hands-On Exploration of Both Concrete and Abstract Science Topics." *Science and Children* 37 (October 1999): 30–37+.

Safford, Phillip L. *Integrated Teaching in Early Childhood: Starting in the Mainstream.* White Plains, NY: Longman, 1989.

Samaras, Anastasia. "Children's Computers." *Childhood Education* 72 (Spring 1996): 133–136.

Saracho, Olivia N., and Bernard Spodek, eds. *Understanding the Multicultural Experience in Early Childhood Education.* Washington, DC: National Association for the Education of Young Children, 1983.

Schickedanz, Judith. "Helping Children Develop Self-Control." *Childhood Education* 70 (Annual Theme 1994): 274–278.

Schickedanz, Judith. "Views of Literacy Development: Then and Now." Paper presented at the annual conference of the National Association for the Education of Young Children, Anaheim, CA, 1988.

Schickedanz, J. A., D. I. Schickedanz, and P. D. Forsyth. *Toward Understanding Children.* Boston: Little, Brown, 1982.

Schiller, Marjorie. "An Emergent Art Curriculum That Fosters Understanding." *Young Children* 50 (March 1995): 33–38.

Schiller, Pam, and Joan Townsend. "Early Childhood: Science All Day Long: An Integrated Approach." *Science and Children* 23 (October 1985): 34–36.

Schirrmacher, Robert. "Talking with Young Children about Their Art." *Young Children* 41 (July 1986): 3–7.

Schmidt, Patricia R. "Working and Playing with Others: Cultural Conflict in a Kindergarten Literacy Program." *Reading Teacher* 48 (February 1995): 404–412.

Schreiber, Mary E. "Lighting Alternatives: Considerations for Child Care Centers." *Young Children* 51 (May 1996): 11–13.

Schwartz, Sydney. "Calendar Reading: A Tradition That Begs Remodeling." *Teaching Children Mathematics* 1 (October 1994): 104–109.

Schwartz, Sydney L. "Authentic Mathematics in the Classroom." *Teaching Children Mathematics* 1 (May 1995): 580–584.

Schwartz, Sydney, and Helen F. Robison. *Designing Curriculum for Early Childhood.* Boston: Allyn and Bacon, 1982.

Schweinhart, Lawrence J. "Observing Young Children in Action: The Key to Early Childhood Assessment. *Young Children* 48 (July 1993): 29–33.

Schweinhart, L. J. "Recent Evidence on Preschool Programs." *Eric Digest.* ERIC Document Reproduction Service 458046. 2000.

Schweinhart, Lawrence J., and David P. Weikart. "The Advantages of High/Scope: Helping Children Lead Successful Lives." *Educational Leadership* 57 (January 1999): 76–77.

Schweinhart, Lawrence J., David P. Weikart, and M. B. Larner. "Consequences of Three Preschool Curriculum Models through Age 15." *Early Childhood Research Quarterly* 1 (1986): 15–46.

Scott, Deborah, Brenda Williams, and Kathy Hyslip. "Mathematics as Communication." *Childhood Education* 69 (Fall 1992): 15–18.

Sears, N. C., and L. L. Medearis. "Educating Teachers for Family Involvement with Young Native Americans." Manuscript, East Central University, Ada, OK, 1993.

Sears, R. "Relation of Early Socialization Experiences to Self-Concepts and Gender Role in Middle Childhood." *Child Development* 41 (1970): 267–289.

Sears, Sue, Cathy Carpenter, and Nancy Burstein. "Meaningful Reading Instruction for Learners with Special Needs." *Reading Teacher* 47 (August 1994): 632–638.

Seefeldt, Carol. "Art—A Serious Work." *Young Children* 50 (March 1995a): 39–45.

Seefeldt, Carol. "Transforming Curriculum in Social Studies." In *Reaching Potentials: Transforming Curriculum and Assessment,* vol. 2, edited by S. Bredekamp and T. Rosegrant. Washington, DC: National Association for the Education of Young Children, 1995b.

Seefeldt, Vern. "Physical Fitness in Preschool and Elementary School-Aged Children." *Journal of Physical Education, Recreation and Dance* 55 (November/December 1984): 33–37.

Sgroi, Laura A. et al. "Assessing Young Children's Mathematical Understandings." *Teaching Children Mathematics* 1 (January 1995): 275–277.

Shade, Daniel D. "Appropriate Use of Computers with Young Children." Paper presented at the NAEYC National Institute for Early Childhood Professional Development, Minneapolis, MN, 1996.

Shedler, Jonathan, and Jack Block. "Adolescent Drug Use and Psychological Health: A Longitudinal Inquiry." *American Psychologist* 45 (May 1990): 612–630.

Sheldon, Kristyn. " 'Can I Play Too?' Adapting Common Classroom Activities for Young Children with Limited Motor Abilities." *Early Childhood Education Journal* 24 (February 1996): 115–120.

Shepard, Lorrie A. "The Challenges of Assessing Young Children Appropriately." *Phi Delta Kappan* 76 (November 1994): 206–212.

Shepard, Lorrie A., Sharon L. Kagan, and Emily Wurtz. "Goal 1 of Early Childhood Assessments Resource Group Recommendations." *Young Children* 53 (May 1998): 52–54.

Shilling, Wynne A. "Young Children Using Computers to Make Discoveries about Written Language." *Early Childhood Education Journal* 24 (April 1997): 253–259.

Shin, Nguyen A., and Stephen Krashen. "Development of First Language Is Not a Barrier to Second Language Acquisition: Evidence from Vietnamese Immigrants to the United States." *International Journal of Bilingual Education and Bilingualism* 4 (2001): 159–164.

Shriver, Mark D., and Jack J. Kramer. "Parent Involvement in an Early Childhood Special Education Program: A Descriptive Analysis of Parent Demographics and Level of Involvement." *Psychology in the Schools* 30 (July 1993): 255–263.

Shure, Myrna B. "Bullies and Their Victims: A Problem-Solving Approach to Prevention." *Brown University Child & Adolescent Behavior Letter* 16 (October 2000): 1–3.

Shuy, Roger. "Language as a Foundation for Education: The School Context." *Theory Into Practice* 26 (1987): 166–174.

Slavin, Robert E. et al. "Success for All: A Summary of Research." *Journal of Education for Students Placed at Risk* 1 (January 1996): 41–76.

Smilansky, Sara. "Can Adults Facilitate Play in Children? Theoretical and Practical Considerations." In *Play: The Child Strives toward Self-Realization,* edited by G. Engstrom, 39–50. Washington, DC: National Association for the Education of Young Children, 1971.

Smith, Frank. "Why Systematic Phonics and Phonemic Awareness Instruction Constitute an Educational Hazard." *Language Arts* 77 (November 1999): 150–155.

Smith, John A. "Singing and Songwriting Support Early Literacy Instruction." *The Reading Teacher* 53 (May 2000): 646.

Smith, S. S. *Early Childhood Mathematics.* Boston, MA: Allyn and Bacon, 2001.

Snow, Catherine E., M. Susan Burns, and Peg Griffin. *Preventing Reading Difficulties in Young Children.* Washington, DC: National Academy Press, 1998.

Sorohan, Erica G. "Playgrounds Are Us." *Executive Educator* (August 1995): 28–32.

Spidel, Jo. "Working with Parents of the Exceptional Child." In *Parents as Partners in Education,* 2d ed., edited by Eugenia Hepworth Berger. Columbus, OH: Merrill, 1987.

Spodek, Bernard. *Early Childhood Education.* Englewood Cliffs, NJ: Prentice-Hall, 1973.

Spodek, Bernard, Olivia N. Saracho, and Michael D. Davis. *Foundations of Early Childhood Education: Teaching Three-, Four-, and Five-Year-Olds.* Englewood Cliffs, NJ: Prentice-Hall, 1987.

Sprung, Barbara. "Physics Is Fun, Physics Is Important, and Physics Belongs in the Early Childhood Curriculum." *Young Children* 51 (July 1996): 29–33.

Stahl, Steven A., Ann M. Duffy-Hester, and Katherine A. D. Stahl. "Everything You Wanted to Know about Phonics (but Were Afraid to Ask)." *Reading Research Quarterly* 33 (July/August/September 1998): 338–355.

Standing, E. M. *Maria Montessori: Her Life and Work.* New York: Academy Guild Press, 1957.

Standing, E. M. *The Montessori Method: A Revolution in Education.* Fresno, CA: Academy Library Guild, 1962.

Staley, Lynn. "Beginning to Implement the Reggio Philosophy." *Young Children* 53 (May 1998): 20–25.

Staley, Lynn, and Penelope A. Portman. "Red Rover, Red Rover, It's Time to Move Over!" *Young Children* 55 (January 2000): 67–72.

Steinfels, Margaret O'Brien. *Who's Minding the Children? The History and Politics of Day Care in America.* New York: Simon and Schuster, 1973 (as quoted in Grubb 1989).

Stewart, Janice P. "Teacher-Mediated Learning for Young Readers: Successful Strategies with Predictable Book Reading." *Reading Horizons* 36, no. 2 (1995): 131–147.

Stipek, Deborah, Linda Rosenblatt, and Laurine DiRocco. "Making Parents Your Allies." *Young Children* 49 (March 1994): 4–9.

Stone, Janet I. "Early Childhood Math: Make It Manipulative." *Young Children* 42 (September 1987): 16–23.

Stone, Sandra J. "Integrating Play into the Curriculum." *Childhood Education* 72 (Winter 1995/1996): 104–107.

Stone, Sandra J. *Understanding Portfolio Assessment: A Guide for Parents.* Wheaton, MD: Association for Childhood Education International, 1995.

Stoner, Sue, and Karyn Purcell. "The Concurrent Validity of Teachers' Judgments of the Abilities of Preschoolers in a Daycare Setting." *Educational and Psychological Measurement* 45 (Summer 1985): 109–116.

Strickland, Dorothy S. "Emergent Literacy: How Young Children Learn to Read." *Educational Leadership* 47 (March 1990): 18–23.

Strickland, Dorothy S. *Teaching Phonics Today: A Primer for Educators.* Newark, DE: International Reading Association, 1998.

Sullivan, Molly. *Feeling Strong, Feeling Free: Movement Exploration for Young Children.* Washington, DC: National Association for the Education of Young Children, 1982.

Sulzby, Elizabeth. "Roles of Oral and Written Language as Children Approach Conventional Literacy. In *Early Text Construction in Children,* edited by C. Pontencorvo, M. Osoline, B. Burge, and L. Resnick, 25–46. Hillsdale, NJ: Erlbaum, 1996.

Suthers, Louie. "Introducing Young Children to Live Orchestral Performance." *Early Child Development and Care* 90 (May 1993): 55–64.

Sutterby, John A., and Joe Frost. "Making Playgrounds Fit for Children and Children Fit on Playgrounds." *Young Children* 57 (May 2002): 36–41.

Sutton-Smith, Brian. "The Spirit of Play." In *The Young Child at Play: Reviews of Research,* vol. 4, edited by Greta Fein and Mary Rivkin, 3–13. Washington, DC: National Association for the Education of Young Children, 1986.

Sutton-Smith, Brian. "The Struggle between Sacred Play and Festive Play." In *Play as a Medium for Learning and Development,* edited by Doris Bergen. Portsmouth, NH: Heinemann, 1988.

Swick, Kevin J., Gloria Boutte, and Irma Van Scoy. "Families and Schools Building Multicultural Values Together." *Childhood Education* 70 (Winter 1995/1996): 75–79.

Swick, Kevin J., and Shirley McKnight. "Characteristics of Kindergarten Teachers Who Promote Parent Involvement." *Early Childhood Research Quarterly* 4 (March 1989): 19–29.

Swick, Kevin J. et al. *Family Involvement in Early Multicultural Learning.* ERIC Document Reproduction Service 380240. 1995.

Sylva, Kathy, Jerome S. Bruner, and Paul Genova. "The Role of Play in the Problem-Solving of Children 3–5 Years Old." In *Play: Its Role in Development and Evolution,* edited by Jerome S. Bruner, Alison Jolly, and Kathy Sylva, 244–257. New York: Basic Books, 1976.

Sylwester, Robert. *A Celebration of Neurons: An Educator's Guide to the Human Brain.* Alexandria, VA: Association for Supervision and Curriculum Development, 1995.

Syzba, Chris Mulcahey. "Why Do Some Teachers Resist Offering Appropriate, Open-Ended Art Activities for Young Children?" *Young Children* 54 (January 1999): 16–20.

Tabors, Patton O. "What Early Childhood Educators Need to Know: Developing Effective Programs for Linguistically and Culturally Diverse Children and Families." *Young Children* 53 (November 1998): 20–26.

Takenishi, Michelle, and Hal Takenishi. *Writing Pictures K–12: A Bridge to Writing Workshop.* Norwood, MA: Christopher Gordon, 1999.

Tallal, Paula, and Mahel Rice. "Fast Forword (Computer Software): Language Disorders." *ASHA* 39 (March 1997): 12–13.

Taylor, Denny. *Beginning to Read and the Spin Doctors of Science: The Political Campaign to Change America's Mind about How Children Learn to Read.* Urbana, IL: National Council of Teachers of English, 1998.

Taylor, Judy. "How I Learned to Look at a First-Grader's Writing Progress Instead of His Deficiencies." *Young Children* 51 (January 1996): 38-42.

Tegano, Deborah W., J. D. Moran III, A. J. Delong, J. Bricker, and K. K. Ramassinie. "Designing Classroom Spaces: Making the Most of Time." *Early Childhood Education Journal* 23 (March 1996): 135–141.

Temple, Charles A., Ruth G. Nathan, Frances Temple, and Nancy A. Burris. *The Beginnings of Writing.* 3d ed. Boston: Allyn and Bacon, 1993.

Theemes, Tracy. *Let's Go Outside! Designing the Early Childhood Playground.* Ypsilanti, MI: High/Scope Educational Research Foundation, 1999.

Thomas, A., and S. Chess. *Temperament and Development.* New York: Brunner/Mazel, 1977.

Thomason, Tommy. *Writer to Writer: How to Conference Young Authors.* Norwood, MA: Christopher-Gordon, 1998.

Thompson, Susan, Paula Knudson, and Darlene Wilson. "Helping Primary Children with Recess Play: A Social Curriculum." *Young Children* 52 (September 1997): 17–21.

Thomson, Barbara. "Building Tolerance in Early Childhood." *Educational Leadership* 47 (October 1989): 78–79.

Thomson, Barbara J. "This Is Like That Martin Luther King Guy." *Young Children* 48 (January 1993): 46–48.

Thurlow, Martha L., Patrick J. O'Sullivan, and James E. Ysseldyke. "Early Screening for Special Education: How Accurate?" *Educational Leadership* 44 (November 1986): 93–95.

Timberlake, Pat. "Classroom Holidaze." *Childhood Education* (January 1978): 128–130.

Tolman, Marvin N., and Garry R. Hardy. "Teaching Tropisms." *Science and Children* 37 (November/December 1999): 14–17.

Tracy, Dyanne M. "Using Mathematics Language to Enhance Mathematical Conceptualization." *Childhood Education* 70 (Summer 1994): 221–224.

Trawik-Smith, Jeffrey. "How the Classroom Environment Affects Play and Development: Review of Research." *Dimensions* 20 (Winter 1992): 27–30.

Tudor, Mary. *Child Development.* New York: McGraw-Hill, 1981.

Turkel, Susan, and Claire M. Newman. "What's Your Number? Developing Number Sense." *Arithmetic Teacher* 35 (February 1988): 53–55.

Twiss, Lindy L. "Innovative Literacy Practices for ESL Learners." *Reading Teacher* (February 1996): 412–414.

Urzua, Carole. "Doing What Comes Naturally: Recent Research in Second Language Acquisition." In *Discovering Language with Children,* edited by Gay Su Pinnell. Urbana, IL: National Council of Teachers of English, 1980.

U.S. Department of Agriculture. *Food and Nutrition* 22 (December 1992), nos. 1–2.

U.S. Department of Agriculture. *The Healthy Eating Index, 1999/2000.* Washington, DC: USDA.

U.S. Department of Agriculture. Leaflet 572, Human Nutrition Information Service. Washington, DC: USDA, August 1994.

Van de Walle, John A. "The Early Development of Number Relations." *Arithmetic Teacher* 35 (February 1988): 15–21.

Van Hoorn, Judith, Patricia Nourot, Barbara Scales, and Keith Alward. *Play at the Center of the Curriculum.* New York: Macmillan, 1993.

Veitch, Beverly, and Thelma Harms. *Cook and Learn: Pictorial Single Portion Recipes.* Menlo Park, CA: Addison-Wesley, 1981.

Vergeront, Jeanne. *Places and Spaces for Preschool and Primary (Indoors).* Washington, DC: National Association for the Education of Young Children, 1987.

Vygotsky, Lev. *Mind in Society: The Development of Higher Psychological Functions.* Cambridge, MA: Harvard University Press, 1978.

Vygotsky, Lev. *Thought and Language.* Cambridge: MIT Press, 1962.

Wachowiak, Frank. *Emphasis Art.* 3d ed. New York: Harper and Row, 1977.

Wadsworth, Barry J. *Piaget's Theory of Cognitive and Affective Development.* 4th ed. New York: Longman, 1989.

Ward, Christina D. "Adult Intervention: Appropriate Strategies for Enriching the Quality of Children's Play." *Young Children* 51 (March 1996): 20–24.

Wardle, Francis. "Proposal: An Anti-Bias and Ecological Model for Multicultural Education." *Childhood Education* 72 (Spring 1996): 152–156.

Washington, V., and J. D. Andrews. *Children of 2010.* Washington, DC: National Association for the Education of Young Children, 1998.

Wasserman, Selma. "Play-Debrief-Replay: An Instructional Model for Science." *Childhood Education* 64 (April 1988): 232–234.

Wasserman, Selma. "Serious Play in the Classroom." *Childhood Education* 68 (Spring 1992): 132–139.

Wasserman, Selma. *Serious Players in the Primary Classroom: Empowering Children through Active Learning Experiences.* New York: Teachers College Press, 1990.

Watts-Taffe, Susan, and Diane M. Truscott. "Using What We Know about Language and Literacy Development for ESL Students in the Mainstream Classroom." *Language Arts* 77 (January 2000): 258–265.

Weikart, Phyllis. *Teaching Movement and Dance: A Sequential Approach to Rhythmic Movement.* Ypsilanti, MI: High/Scope Press, 1998.

Weiller, Karen H., and Peggy A. Richardson. "A Program for Kids: Success-Oriented Physical Education." *Childhood Education* 69 (Spring 1993): 133–137.

Weinstein, Carol S. "The Physical Environment of the School: A Review of the Research." *Review of Educational Research* 49 (Fall 1979): 577–610.

Wells, Gordon. *Learning through Interaction: The Study of Language Development.* Cambridge, England: Cambridge University Press, 1981.

Wells, Gordon. *The Meaning Makers: Children Learning Language and Using Language to Learn.* Portsmouth, NH: Heinemann, 1986.

Wenner, George. "Relationship between Science Knowledge Levels and Beliefs toward Science Instruction Held by Preservice Elementary Teachers." *Journal of Science Education and Technology* 2 (1993): 461–468.

Whaley, Kimberlee, and Elizabeth Blue Swadner. "Multicultural Education in Infant and Toddler Settings." *Childhood Education* 66 (Summer 1990): 238–240.

Whitin, David J. "Collecting Data with Young Children." *Young Children* 52 (January 1997): 28–32.

Whitin, David J. "Literature and Mathematics in Preschool and Primary: The Right Connection." *Young Children* 49 (January 1994): 4–11.

Whitmore, Kathryn F., and Yetta M. Goodman. "Transforming Curriculum in Language and Literacy." In *Reaching Potentials: Transforming Early Childhood Curriculum and Assessment* 2, edited by S. Bredekamp and T. Rosegrant, 145–166. Washington, DC: National Association for the Education of Young Children, 1995.

"Why the Testing Craze Won't Fix Our Schools." *Rethinking Schools Online* (Spring 1999), www.rethinkingschools. org/archives/13-03/edit133.htm.

Willig, Sharon. "General Indicators of Developmental Language Disorders." *American Speech-Language-Hearing Association* 40 (Summer 1998): 43+.

Wilson, Ruth A. "Nature and Young Children: A Natural Connection." *Young Children* 50 (September 1995): 4–11.

Winter, Suzanne M., Michael J. Bell, and James D. Dempsey. "Creating Play Environments for Children with Special Needs." *Childhood Education* 71 (Fall 1994): 28–32.

Wittmer, Donna S., and Alice S. Honig. "Encouraging Positive Social Development in Young Children." *Young Children* 49 (July 1994): 4–12.

Wolery, Mark, and Jan S. Wilbert, eds. *Including Children with Special Needs in Early Childhood Programs.* Research Monograph of the National Association for the Education of Young Children, vol. 6. Washington, DC: NAEYC, 1994.

Wolf, Jan. "Singing with Children Is a Cinch!" *Young Children* 49 (May 1994): 20–25.

Woolfolk, A. *Educational psychology.* Boston, MA: Allyn and Bacon, 2001.

Workman, Susan H., and Jim A. Gage. "Family-School Partnerships: A Family Strengths Approach." *Young Children* 52 (May 1997): 10–14.

Worobey, Harriet S. "Recipe Cards to Share with Parents." *Young Children* 54 (September 1999): 34.

Worthen, S. C. *The Integrated Classroom: The Assessment-Curriculum Link in Early Childhood Education.* Englewood Cliffs: NJ: Merrill, 1996.

Wright, J. L., and D. Shade, eds. *Young Children: Active Learners in a Technological Age.* Washington, DC: National Association for the Education of Young Children, 1994.

Wright, S. "The Arts and Schooling: An Analysis of Cultural Influences." *Journal of Cognitive Education* 6 (1997): 53–69.

Wright, S. *The Arts, Young Children, and Learning.* Boston: Allyn and Bacon, 2003.

Wuertenburg, Jacque. Speech to Northern Arizona Reading Council, Flagstaff, Arizona, April 1993.

Yarrow, L. "Should Children Play with Guns?" *Parents* 58 (January 1983): 50–52.

Yelland, Nicola J. "Encouraging Young Children's Thinking Skills with Logo." *Childhood Education* 71 (Spring 1995): 152–155.

Zanandrea, M. "Play, Social Interaction, and Motor Development: Practical Activities for Preschoolers with Visual Impairments." *Journal of Visual Impairment and Blindness* 92 (March 1998): 176–188.

Zigler, Edward F., and Matia Finn-Stevenson. *Children: Development and Social Issues.* Lexington, MA: D. C. Heath, 1987.

Children's Books

Ackerman, Karen. *Song and Dance Man.* New York: Knopf, 1988.

Ahlberg, Allan. *Mockingbird.* Illustrated by Paul Howard. Cambridge, MA: Candlewick Press, 1998.

Alda, Arlene. *Arlene Alda's 1 2 3: What Do You See?* Berkeley, CA: Ten Speed Press/Tricycle, 1998.

Allen, Pamela. *Who Sank the Boat?* New York: Coward-McCann, 1982.

Appelt, K. *Bats on Parade.* New York: Morrow, 1999.

Askar, Saoussan. *From Far Away.* Illustrated by Michael Martchenko. Loganville, GA: Annick Press, 1995.

Baker, J. *Window.* New York: Greenwillow, 1991.

Baylor, Byrd. *The Desert Is Theirs.* New York: Charles Scribner and Sons, 1970.

Baylor, Byrd. *Everybody Needs a Rock.* New York: Atheneum, 1974.

Baylor, Byrd. *The Table Where Rich People Sit.* New York: Simon and Schuster, 1994.

Bentley, W. A. *Snow Crystals*. Mineola, NY: Dover, 1931.

Best, Cari. *Three Cheers for Catherine the Great!* New York: DK Publishing, 1999.

Birch, David. *The King's Chessboard*. Illustrated by Devis Grebu. New York: Puffin, 1993.

Brown, Margaret Wise. *The Runaway Bunny*. HarperTrophy, 1977.

Bunting, Eve. *The Days of Summer*. San Diego, CA: Harcourt, 2001.

Bunting, Eve. *A Picnic in October*. Illustrated by Nancy Carpenter. San Diego: Harcourt Brace, 1999.

Burnett, Francis H. *The Secret Garden*. New York: HarperCollins, 1987.

Cannon, Janell. *Stellaluna*. San Diego, CA: Harcourt, 1993.

Carle, Eric. *Pancakes, Pancakes*. New York: Scholastic, 1990.

Carle, Eric. *The Very Hungry Caterpillar*. New York: Scholastic, 1969.

Catalano, Dominic. *Frog Went A-Courting*. Honesdale, PA: Boyds Mills Press, 1998.

Clifton, Lucille. *Everett Anderson's Goodbye*. Illustrated by Ann Grifalconi. New York: Holt, 1995.

Coles, Robert. *The Story of Ruby Bridges*. Illustrated by George Ford. New York: Scholastic, 1995.

Consumer Product Safety Commission. *The 9 Lives of El Gato the Cat*. Washington, DC: CPSC, 1983.

Consumer Product Safety Commission. *Protect Someone You Love from Burns*. Project Burn Prevention. Washington, DC: CPSC, 1978.

Cousins, Lucy. *Count with Maisy*. Cambridge, MA: Candlewick, 1997.

Davol, Marguerite W. *Black, White, Just Right*. Illustrated by Irene Trivas. New York: Whitman, 1993.

Dee, R. *Two Ways to Count to Ten*. New York: Henry Holt, 1988.

Demi. *One Grain of Rice*. New York: Scholastic, 1997.

dePaola, Tomie. *The Cloud Book*. New York: Scholastic, 1975.

Dewey, Jennifer O. *Spiders Near and Far*. New York: Dutton, 1992.

Diakite, Baba Wague. *The Hatseller and the Monkeys*. New York: Scholastic, 1999.

Dragonwagon, Crescent. *This Is the Bread I Baked for Ned*. New York: Macmillan, 1989.

Eden, Philip et al. *DK Pockets: Weather Facts*. New York: DK Publishers, 1995.

Ehlert, Lois. *Color Farm*. New York: Lippincott, 1990.

Ehlert, Lois. *Color Zoo*. New York: Lippincott, 1989.

Evans, Lezlie. *Rain Song*. Illustrated by Cynthia Jabar. Boston: Houghton Mifflin, 1997.

Fleming, Denise. *Mama Cat Has Three Kittens*. New York: Henry Holt, 1998.

Friedman, I. R. *How My Parents Learned to Eat*. Boston: Houghton Mifflin, 1984.

Galdone, Paul. *The Gingerbread Boy*. Boston: Houghton Mifflin, 1985.

Galdone, Paul. *The Little Red Hen*. Boston: Houghton Mifflin, 1985.

Garland, Sherry. *The Lotus Seed*. San Diego, CA: Harcourt, 1993.

Gilmore, Rachna. *Lights for Gita*. Illustrated by Alice Priestley. Gardiner, ME: Tilbury House, 1995.

Glaser, L. *Spectacular Spiders*. Illustrated by Gay W. Holland. Brookfield, CT: Millbrook, 1998.

Greenfield, Eloise. *First Pink Light*. Illustrated by Jan S. Gilchrist. New York: Writers & Readers, 1991.

Greenfield, Eloise. *Grandpa's Face*. New York: Philomel, 1988.

Greenspun, Adele A. *Daddies*. New York: Putnam, 1992.

Guthrie, Woody. *This Land Is Your Land*. Illustrated by Kathy Jakobsen. Boston: Little, Brown, 1998.

Hanson, Regina. *The Tangerine Tree*. Illustrated by Harvey Stevenson. New York: Clarion, 1995.

Hausherr, Rosemarie. *Celebrating Families*. New York: Scholastic, 1997.

Henkes, Kevin. *Lilly's Purple Plastic Purse*. New York: Greenwillow, 1996.

Herold, Maggie R. *A Very Important Day*. Illustrated by Catherine Stock. New York: William Morrow, 1995.

Hest, Amy. *The Friday Nights of Nana*. Cambridge, MA: Candlewick Press, 2001.

Hest, Amy. *When Jessie Came across the Sea*. Illustrated by P. J. Lynch. Cambridge, MA: Candlewick, 1997.

Hightower, Susan. *Twelve Snails to One Lizard: A Tale of Mischief and Measurement*. Illustrated by Matt Novak. New York: Simon and Schuster, 1997.

Highwater, J. *Songs of the Seasons*. New York: Lothrop, Lee & Shepard, 1995.

Hoban, Russell. *Bread and Jam for Francis*. New York: HarperCollins, 1986.

Hoban, Tanya. *More, Fewer, Less*. New York: Greenwillow, 1998.

Hoban, Tanya. *Shapes, Shapes, Shapes*. New York: Greenwillow, 1986.

Hoban, Tanya. *So Many Circles, So Many Squares*. New York: Greenwillow, 1998.

Hoberman, Mary Ann. *Fathers, Mothers, Sisters, Brothers: A Collection of Family Poems*. Illustrated by Marylin Hafner. New York: Puffin, 1993.

Hoberman, Mary Ann. *Miss Mary Mack*. Boston: Little, Brown, 1998.

Hoffman, Mary. *Amazing Grace*. Illustrated by Caroline Binch. New York: Dial, 1991.

Hoffman, Mary. *Boundless Grace*. Illustrated by Caroline Binch. New York: Dial, 1995.

Hong, Lily Toy. *Two of Everything*. New York: Albert Whitman, 1993.

Hopkins, Lee Bennett. *School Supplies: A Book of Poems*. Illustrated by Renee Flower. New York: Simon and Schuster, 1996.

Howard, Elizabeth F. *Aunt Flossie's Hats (and Crab Cakes Later)*. New York: Clarion, 1991.

Hulme, Joy N. *Counting by Kangaroos: A Multiplication Concept Book*. Illustrated by Betsy Scheld. New York: W. H. Freeman, 1995.

Hulme, Joy N. *Sea Squares*. Illustrated by Carol Schwartz. New York: Hyperion, 1991.

Hutchins, Pat. *The Doorbell Rang*. New York: Greenwillow, 1986.

Jenkins, Steve. *Biggest, Strongest, Fastest*. New York: Tichnor & Fields, 1995.

Johnson, Stephen T. *City by Numbers*. New York: Viking, 1998.

Johnston, Tony. *The Iguana Brothers*. Illustrated by Mark Teague. New York: Scholastic, 1995.

Jonas, Ann. *Color Dance*. New York: William Morrow, 1989.

Kalbacken, Joan. *The Food Pyramid*. New York: Children's Press, 1998.

Kalman, Bobbie. *What Are Food Chains and Webs?* New York: Crabtree, 1998.

Keats, Ezra Jack. *The Snowy Day*. New York: Viking, 1962.

Kipling, Rudyard. *Just So Stories*. New York: Grosset and Dunlap, 1965.

Kraus, Robert. *Whose Mouse Are You?* New York: Macmillan, 1970.

Krauss, Ruth. *The Carrot Seed*. New York: HarperFestival, 1993.

Kunhardt, Dorothy. *Pat the Bunny*. Racine, WI: Golden Press, 1960.

Lacapa, Kathleen, and Michael Lacapa. *Less Than Half, More Than Whole*. Illustrated by Michael Lacapa. Flagstaff, AZ: Northland, 1992.

Landau, Elaine. *Apples*. New York: Children's Press, 1999.

Landau, Elaine. *Bananas*. New York: Children's Press, 1999.

Landau, Elaine. *Corn*. New York: Children's Press, 1999.

Landau, Elaine. *Sugar*. New York: Children's Press, 2000.

Landau, Elaine. *Wheat*. New York: Children's Press, 2000.

Lawson, Robert. *They Were Strong and Good*. New York: Viking, 1940.

Lee, Dennis. *Alligator Pie*. Toronto: Macmillan of Canada, 1974.

Leedy, Loreen. *The Edible Pyramid: Good Eating Every Day*. New York: Holiday House, 1996.

Leedy, Loreen. *Measuring Penny*. New York: Henry Holt, 1998.

Leonard, M. *Food Is Fun!* New York: HarperFestival, 2000.

Lewis, C. S. *The Lion, the Witch, and the Wardrobe*. New York: Macmillan, 1951.

Lionni, Leo. *Little Blue and Little Yellow*. New York: Astor, 1959.

Llewellyn, Claire. *Chocolate*. From the "What's for Lunch" series. New York: Children's Press, 1998.

Llewellyn, Claire. *Eggs*. From the "What's for Lunch?" series. New York: Children's Press, 1999.

Llewellyn, Claire. *Milk*. From the "What's for Lunch?" series. New York: Children's Press, 1998.

Llewellyn, Claire. *Oranges*. From the "What's for Lunch?" series. New York: Children's Press, 1999.

Llewellyn, Claire. *Peanuts*. From the "What's for Lunch?" series. New York: Children's Press, 1998.

Llewellyn, Claire. *Potatoes*. From the "What's for Lunch?" series. New York: Children's Press, 1998.

Lunn, Janet. *Charlotte*. Illustrated by Brian Deines. Toronto: Tundra Books, 1998.

Lyon, George Ella. *Come a Tide*. Illustrated by Stephen Gammell. New York: Orchard Books, 1990.

MacLachlan, Patricia. *Sarah, Plain and Tall*. New York: HarperCollins, 1985.

Mandel, Peter. *Say Hey! A Song of Willie Mays*. New York: Hyperion, 2000.

Martin, Bill, Jr., and John Archambault. *Listen to the Rain*. New York: Henry Holt, 1988.

Martin, Jacqueline Briggs. *Snowflake Bentley*. Illustrated by Mary Azarian. Boston: Houghton Mifflin, 1998.

Mathews, Louise. *Bunches and Bunches of Bunnies*. New York: Scholastic, 1990.

Mayer, Mercer. *There's a Nightmare in My Closet*. New York: Dial Books, 1968.

McCloskey, Robert. *Blueberries for Sal*. New York: Viking, 1948.

McElroy, Lisa T. *Meet My Grandmother: She's a Children's Book Author*. Brookfield, CT: Millbrook Press, 2001.

McKissack, Patricia. *Ma Dear's Aprons*. Illustrated by Floyd Cooper. New York: Simon and Schuster, 1997.

McMillan, Bruce. *Counting Wildflowers*. New York: William Morrow, 1986.

McMillan, Bruce. *Eating Fractions*. New York: Scholastic, 1991.

McMillan, Bruce. *The Weather Sky*. New York: Farrar, Straus & Giroux, 1996.

Merriam, Eve. *The Hole Story*. New York: Simon and Schuster, 1995.

Merriam, Eve. *12 Ways to Get to 11*. Illustrated by Bernie Karlin. New York: Simon and Schuster, 1993.

Morgan, Pierr. *The Turnip*. New York: Macmillan, 1990.

Morris, Ann. *Bread, Bread, Bread*. New York: Scholastic, 1989.

Morris, Ann. *Loving*. New York: Lothrop, Lee & Shepard, 1990.

Murphy, Stuart J. *Give Me Half!* Illustrated by G. Brian Karas. New York: Scholastic, 1996.

Myller, R. *How Big Is a Foot?* New York: Dell, 1990.

Numeroff, Laura J. *If You Give a Moose a Muffin*. New York: Scholastic, 1991.

Numeroff, Laura J. *If You Give a Pig a Pancake*. New York: HarperCollins, 1998.

Oberman, Sheldon. *The Always Prayer Shawl*. Honesdale, PA: Boyds Mills Press, 1994.

Paul, A. *Eight Hands Round*. New York: HarperCollins, 1991.

Pellegrini, Nina. *Families Are Different*. New York: Holiday, 1991.

Pinczes, Elinor J. *One Hundred Angry Ants*. Illustrated by Bonnie MacKain. New York: Scholastic, 1993.

Pinczes, Elinor J. *A Remainder of One*. Illustrated by Bonnie MacKain. Boston: Houghton Mifflin, 1995.

Polacco, Patricia. *Thundercake*. New York: Philomel, 1990.

Pomeranc, Marion Hess. *American Wei*. Illustrated by Dyanne Disalvo-Ryan. New York: Albert Whitman, 1998.

Pooley, Sarah. *It's Raining, It's Pouring: A Book for Rainy Days*. New York: Greenwillow, 1993.

Pryor, Bonnie. *The Dream Jar*. Illustrated by Mark Graham. New York: William Morrow, 1996.

Rankin, Laura. *The Handmade Counting Book*. New York: Dial, 1998.

Richard, David. *My Whole Food ABC's*. Illustrated by Susan Cavaciuti. New York: Vital Health, 1997.

Ringgold, Faith. *If a Bus Could Talk: The Story of Rosa Parks*. New York: Simon and Schuster, 1999.

Ringgold, Faith. *Tar Beach*. New York: Random, 1991.

Robson, Pam. *Banana*. From the "What's for Lunch?" series. New York: Children's Press, 1998.

Robson, Pam. *Corn*. From the "What's for Lunch?" series. New York: Children's Press, 1998.

Robson, Pam. *Honey*. From the "What's for Lunch?" series. New York: Children's Press, 1998.

Robson, Pam. *Rice*. From the "What's for Lunch?" series. New York: Children's Press, 1998.

Rockwell, Lizzy. *Good Enough to Eat: A Kid's Guide to Food and Nutrition*. New York: HarperCollins, 1999.

Root, Phyllis. *One Duck Stuck*. Illustrated by Jane Chapman. Cambridge, MA: Candlewick Press, 1998.

Rosenberg, Liz. *The Silence in the Mountains*. Illustrated by Chris K. Soentpiet. New York: Orchard Books, 1999.

Rotner, Shelley, and Sheila M. Kelly. *Lots of Dads*. New York: Dial, 1997.

Russo, Marisabina. *When Mama Gets Home*. New York: Greenwillow, 1998.

Rylant, Cynthia. *The Relatives Came*. New York: Simon and Schuster, 1991.

Saunders-Smith, Gail. *Eating Apples*. Richmond, CA: Pebble Books, 1997.

Sawyer, Ruth. *Journey Cake, Ho!* New York: Puffin, 1978.

Say, Allen. *Grandfather's Journey*. Boston: Houghton Mifflin, 1993.

Schroeder, Alan. *Minty: A Story of Young Harriet Tubman*. Illustrated by Jerry Pinkney. New York: Dial, 1996.

Schwartz, Amy. *Old MacDonald*. New York: Scholastic, 1999.

Schwartz, David. *How Much Is a Million?* New York: Mulberry, 1993.

Schwartz, David. *If You Hopped Like a Frog*. New York: Scholastic, 1999.

Scieszka, Jon. *Math Curse*. New York: Viking, 1995.

Sendak, Maurice. *Where the Wild Things Are*. New York: Harper and Row, 1963.

Shields, Carol Diggory. *Lunch Money and Other Poems about School*. Illustrated by Paul Meisel. New York: Dutton, 1995.

Shulevitz, Uri. *Snow*. New York: Farrar, Straus & Giroux, 1998.

Siera, July. *Counting Crocodiles*. Illustrated by Will Hillenbrand. San Diego: Harcourt Brace, 1997.

Simon, Seymour. *Storms*. New York: Mulberry Books, 1992.

Simont, Marc. *The Stray Dog*. New York: HarperCollins, 2001.

Soto, Gary. *Chato's Kitchen*. New York: Putnam, 1995.

Soto, Gary. *Too Many Tamales*. New York: Putnam, 1993.

Spier, Peter. *Rain*. Garden City, NY: Doubleday, 1982.

Steig, William. *Sylvester and the Magic Pebble*. New York: Simon & Schuster, 1969.

Steptoe, Javaka. *In Daddy's Arms I Am Tall: African Americans Celebrating Fathers*. New York: Lee & Low, 1997.

Taback, Simms. *Joseph Had a Little Overcoat*. New York: Viking, 1999.

Tarbescu, Edith. *Anushka's Voyage*. Illustrated by Lydia Dabcovich. New York: Clarion, 1998.

Toft, K., and A. Sheather. *One Less Fish*. Watertown, MA: Charlesbridge, 1998.

Trivas, I. *Emma's Christmas*. New York: Orchard, 1988.

Velasquez, Eric. *Grandmas's Records*. New York: Walker, 2001.

Viorst, Judith. *Alexander, Who Used to Be Rich Last Sunday*. New York: Atheneum, 1978.

Waber, Bernard. *Ira Sleeps Over*. Boston: Houghton Mifflin, 1987.

Wallace, Karen. *Eyewitness Readers: Whatever the Weather*. New York: DK Publishers, 1999.

Wallner, Alexandria. *The Farmer in the Dell*. New York: Holiday House, 1998.

Watson, Mary. *The Butterfly Seeds*. New York: Morrow/Tambourine, 1995.

Weiss, George, and Bob Thiele. *What a Wonderful World*. Illustrated by Ashley Bryan. New York: Atheneum, 1995.

Wells, Rosemary. *Bunny Money*. New York: Dial, 1997.

Wheatley, Nadia. *1 Is for One*. Illustrated by Darius Detwiler. Greenvale, NY: Mondo, 1996.

White, E. B. *Charlotte's Web*. HarperCollins, 1999.

Wiesner, David. *Sector 7*. Boston: Houghton Mifflin, 1999.

Wild, Margaret. *Our Granny*. New York: Tichnor & Fields, 1993.

Williams, Barbara. *Kevin's Grandma*. New York: Dutton, 1975.

Williams, Sherley Ann. *Working Cotton*. Illustrated by Carole Byard. San Diego: Harcourt, 1992.

Williams, Vera. *A Chair for My Mother*. New York: Greenwillow, 1982.

Winer, Yvonne. *Spiders Spin Webs*. Illustrated by Karen Lloyd-Jones. Watertown, MA: Charlesbridge, 1998.

Wisniewski, David. *Rain Player*. New York: Clarion Books, 1991.

Wood, Audrey. *King Bidgood's in the Bathtub*. New York: Harcourt Brace Jovanovich, 1985.

Wood, Audrey. *Quick as a Cricket*. New York: Child's Play, 1982.

Wyeth, Sharon Dennis. *Always My Dad*. Illustrated by Raul Colon. New York: Knopf, 1997.

Yolen, Jane. *Owl Moon*. New York: Philomel Books, 1987.

Yolen, Jane. *Snow, Snow: Winter Poems for Children*. Illustrated by Jason Stemple. Honesdale, PA: Boyds Mill Press, 1998.

Zemach, Margot. *The Little Red Hen*. New York: Farrar, Straus and Giroux, 1983.

Ziefert, Harriet. *When I First Came to This Land*. Illustrated by Simms Taback. New York: Putnam, 1998.

Zolotow, Charlotte. *Someday*. New York: Harper and Row, 1965.

INDEX

Note: **Bold** page numbers indicate key terms, which are defined in the Glossary.

language development in, 286–290
learning environments for, 93–94
literacy instruction for, 337–339
mainstreaming of, 286–287
mathematics instruction for, 376–377
physical education programs for, 484, 486
play and, 164, 166–167
playground adaptations for, 103–104
science instruction for, 409
Chinese jump ropes, 85
classical conditioning, 4
classification, in scientific process, 384–385
classroom centers, for language development, 286
climbing, in physical education programs, 483
cognitive development, 15, **26**–30
behaviorist program focus on, 55
curriculum and, 29–30
patterns of, 26–28
play and, 149–150
collage, 423
Comenius, John, 36
communication
assisted, **286**
of benefits of play, 159–161
congruent, 191
in mathematics instruction, 370
in scientific process, 385
communication with parents, 246–254
about assessment results, 222–228
of children with special needs, 253–254
about community resources, 254
conferences for. *See* parent conferences
developmentally appropriate practice for, 226–227
home visits for, 246–248
letters and notes for, 251–253
parent visits to school for, 248–251
school handbooks for, 246
telecommunication for, 253
communicative competence, **268**
community resources, informing parents about, 254
comparison, in scientific process, 385

competence, communicative, **268**
complex play units, 79
computers, 94–97, 98
children's use of World Wide Web and, 97
for mathematics instruction, 373
parents and, 94, 96
software selection for, 96–97
teaching and learning with, 94–97
concrete operational period, 26, 29
conditioning
classical, 4
operant, **4**–5
conferences
with parents. *See* parent conferences
recording to document children's work, 212–215
conflict management, 459
conflict resolution, 459
congruent communication, 191
connections, in mathematics instruction, 370
consequences, logical, 192
conservation, in science instruction, 392
constructivism, 383–384
constructivist programs, 55–66
goals of, 59–63
learning and, 57–59
overview of, 63, 66
typical day in preschool using, 64–65
constructivist theory/model, **6**–10, 11
for early childhood education, 55–66, 66, 67
of Gardner, 9–10
of language learning, 273–274, 275
of Piaget, 6–7
of social studies learning, 451–453
of Vygotsky, 7–8
convention, **326**
conventional spelling, 325–326
conversations
recording to document children's work, 212–215
for reporting assessment results, 225
cooking experiences, 493–494
cooperative play, 138, 139
corporal punishment, **172**
counting, 357–358

creative arts, 412–443
assessment in, 437–438
children with special needs and, 440–442
connecting with other subject-matter areas, 438–439
developmentally appropriate practice for, 438
diversity and, 442–443
dramatic, 433–436
importance of experiences in, 414, 416
musical. *See* music
outdoors, 99
parents and, 423, 425, 429, 433, 442
specialists' roles in, 436–437
visual. *See* visual arts
creativity, **414**
language development and, 278–279
criterion-referenced tests, 201
cueing system, **308**–309
Cuisenaire rods, 371
culture. *See* diversity; multicultural education
curriculum, 108–120, **109**. *See also specific subject areas*
antibias, **465**
developmentally appropriate, 112–120
emerging, **117**–118
expanding, **449**
integrated, 114. *See also* integrating the curriculum
organization of, 111
thematic approach to, **114**–120
curriculum planning, 109–111
cognitive development and, 29–30
developmentally appropriate practice and, 122, 226–227
diversity and, 132–133
emotional development and, 25–26
guidance and, 177–180
intellectual development and, 29–30
parents and, 110, 130, 132
physical development and, 13, 16
social development and, 23–24

Dalcroze eurythmics, 432
dance, 430–431

classrooms for, 304–307
current thinking about, 303
debate about literacy development and, 302–303
diversity and, 339–341
goals of, 304–306
helping children feel successful
at, 328–336
learning how print is decoded
and, 312–318
model of learning to read and,
306, 308–311
programs for, 335–336
literature
in art instruction, 439
connecting with social studies,
470, 472–473
for language development,
282–284
mathematics and, 374
log(s), for documenting children's
work, 208
logical consequences, 192
logico-mathematical intelligence, 9
logico-mathematical knowledge,
383–384
logico-mathematical learning,
346–348
Logo program, 373
Luther, Martin, 36

mainstreaming, **43,** 286–287
mandated goals, **122,** 124
manipulatives/games area, 85, 88
map drawing, 451–453
mastery learning, 41
materials
instructional. *See* Instructional
materials
for play, 155–156
mathematics, 344–378
arithmetic versus, 346
assessment of children's knowledge in, 374–376
definition of, 346
learning of, 346–349
parents and, 351, 356, 365, 376
play and, 162
mathematics instruction, 349–373
algebra in, 366–367
calculators and computers in, 373
for children with special needs,
376–377
communication in, 370
connections in, 370

content and process standards
for, 349–352
counting in, 357–358
data analysis and probability in,
367–368
for developmentally appropriate
practice, 350
diversity and, 377
fractions in, 360
functions in, 366–367
geometry and spatial sense in,
365–366
literature and, 374
materials for, 371–373
measurement in, 362–365
money in, 365
one-to-one correspondence in,
3560357
place value in, 358–359
play and, 351
problem solving in, 368
reading-writing connection and,
373–374
reasoning and proof in, 360–362,
370
representation in, 370–371
seriation in, 362
strand model for. *See* strand
model for mathematics in-
struction
time in, 364–365
whole numbers in, 359–360
maturationist theory, **5**–6, 11
measurement
in mathematics instruction,
362–365
in scientific process, 385
medical procedures, in health education, 488
metaknowledge, **7**
middle childhood. *See also specific
periods and ages*
development of play behaviors
during, 147–148
language development during,
270–271
play during, 153
mind, absorbent, **46**
minorities. *See* diversity; multicultural education
misbehavior, 192
mistaken behavior, 192
Mitchell, Lucy Sprague, 39–40, 55,
61, 449

modeler role of teachers, play and,
145
money, in mathematics instruction,
365
Montessori programs, 45–52, 66–67
goals of, 49–52
typical day in, 50–51
morphemes, 267
morphology, 267
"Mother rhymes," 37
motor development. *See* physical education programs
movement, in physical education
programs, 482
movement experiences, 430–431
multicultural education, **465**–470
assessment of program quality in,
470
basic assumptions of, 467–468
checklist for, 471
goals of, 469–470, 471
multiple intelligences, 9–10
as organizing strategy, 219–220
music, 425–433
goals of programs in, 426
instructional approaches for,
432–433
listening experiences and,
429–430
movement and dance and,
430–431
playing instruments and, 429
singing and, 427–429
musical intelligence, 9
music areas, 84–85

narratives
for documenting children's work,
209
for language development, 283
for reporting assessment results,
225
National Association for Nursery
Education (NANE), 38
National Association for the Education of Young Children
(NAEYC), 38
natural environment, respect for, in
science instruction, 393
naturalist intelligence, 10
negative reinforcement, 4
newsletters, for reporting assessment results, 225–228
nonjudgmental attitude, **347**
norm-referenced tests, 201

notes, for communicating with parents, 251–253
numbers, whole, 359–360
nutrition education, 490–494
    diversity and, 500

observation
    of language learners, 280–281
    of reading, 337
    in scientific process, 384
    of writing, 336–337
observation guides, for parents' school visits, 249, 250
observer role of teachers, play and, 144
obstacle courses, in physical education programs, 483
onlooker play, 138, 139
open-ended materials, 155
operant conditioning, **4**–5, 52
Orff approach for music instruction, 432–433
organization, of assessment records, 216–222
outdoor environments, 97, 99–102
    adaptations for, 103–104
    safety in, 102–104
outdoor play, 163–164

painting, 422–423
parachutes, in physical education programs, 483
parallel talk, for encouraging language growth, 277
paraprofessionals, **258**–261
    developmentally appropriate practice for working with, 258
    duties of, 260
    guidelines for working with, 259
parent(s)
    assessment and, 201, 228, 230
    communication with. *See* communication with parents; parent conferences
    computers and, 94, 96
    creative arts and, 423, 425, 429, 433, 442
    curriculum planning and, 110, 130, 132
    developmentally appropriate practice for working with, 258
    development and, 3, 23, 31
    guidance and, 174, 177, 189, 194
    language and, 267, 279, 282, 288, 293

learning environment and, 86
literacy and, 324, 332
mathematics and, 351, 356, 365, 376
play and, 143, 146, 147, 148, 164
playgrounds and, 97
reporting and, 222
reporting assessment results to, 222–228
safety and, 497, 498
school design and, 55, 67, 69
science and, 384, 392, 394, 399, 407
social studies and, 459, 464, 470
wellness and, 484, 493, 499
parent conferences
    checklist for, 248, 249
    for reporting assessment results, 223–224
parenting styles, self-concept and, 176–177
parent involvement
    activities for, 244, 246
    encouraging, 239–246
    lack of, reasons for, 238, 241, 242
    need for, 235–236
    parent interview form for, 244, 245
    parent roles and, 241, 243–244, 245
    parent–teacher relationships and, 236–239
parent places, **249,** 251
parent questionnaires, for documenting children's work, 215
parent–teacher relationships, 236–239
patterns, in mathematics instruction, 366
Peabody, Elizabeth, 42
permissive parents, 177
Perry Preschool, 68
personality development, 17–18
personal routines, in health education, 487–488
personal safety education, 497–498
Pestalozzi, Johann, 36
phone calls, for reporting assessment results, 225
phonemic awareness, **312**–313, 313
phonetic writing, 323–324
phonics, definition of, 313
phonics instruction, 313–318
    appropriate, 316–317

planning, problems with, 314–315
    research on, 313–314
phonology, 267
physical development, 12–13, 14, 16. *See also* physical education programs
    curriculum and, 13, 16
    patterns of, 12–13
    play and, 150–151
physical education areas, 85, 89
physical education programs, 478–486
    in children with special needs, 484, 486
    goals of programs for, 480–482
    planned activities for, 482–484
    skill activities for, 484
physical environment, structuring, 75
physical knowledge, 383
physical punishment, 172
physical sciences, in science instruction, 400–403
Piaget, Jean, 6–7, 8, 55
    on cognitive development, 26–27, 28–29
    on early education, 60
    on learning, 59–60
Pink Tower, 47
place value, 358–359
planner role of teachers, play and, 145–146
play, 136–138
    academic learning and, 161–163
    benefits of, 153–155
    for children with special needs, 164, 166–167
    communicating benefits of, 159–161
    definition of, 138
    developmentally appropriate practice and, 154
    development of, 146–148
    directed, 138
    diversity and, 164–165
    exploratory, 149
    free, 138
    guided, 138
    at home versus school, 151
    illicit, 152
    instrumental, 152
    materials for, 155–156
    with objects, 139–140
    outdoor, 163–164

parents and, 143, 146, 147, 148, 164
practice (functional), **139**
in primary grades, 153
purposes of, 148–151
roles in, 143–146
rule-governed, 149
in school settings, 151–161
social, 138–139
social development and, 19–29
sociodramatic, **141**–143
teacher's roles in, 144–146
as teaching strategy, 156, 158–159
Vygotsky's view of, 140–141
play crates, 100
play-debrief-replay, 394–395
playgrounds, 97, 99–102
adaptations for, 103–104
parents and, 97
safety on, 102–104
poetry
for language development, 284
for science instruction, 407
poison safety education, 497
portfolios, **217**–222
content of, 218–219
electronic, 221–222
organization of, 219–220
purpose of, 217–218
traditional assessment compared with, 220–221
positive behaviors, supporting, 185, 186
positive reinforcement, 4
practice play, **139**
pragmatics, 268
preoperational period, 26, 28–29
prepared environment, **46**
preschematic stage of drawing development, 417
preschoolers. *See also specific ages*
development of play behaviors during, 146–147
language development during, 270–271
phonics instruction for, 316
print
determining knowledge of, 336
environmental, **303**
printing activities, 423
proactive actions, 21
probability, in mathematics instruction, 367–368

problem solving, in mathematics instruction, 368
program assessment, 131–132
progressive education movement, **38**
Project Construct, 55
proof, in mathematics instruction, 360–362, 368, 370
prosocial behaviors, 20–21
proximodistal development, 13
Public Law (PL) 93-644, 44
Public Law (PL) 94-142, 43, 44
Public Law (PL) 99-457, 43–44
pull-out programs, 131
punishment, 4, **172**–173
corporal (physical), **172**
discipline versus, 172
effects of, 174

quiet areas, 89

random-letter stage of writing development, 321–323
rating scales, for documenting children's work, 212, 214
rational counting, 357
reactive actions, 21
readiness, 49
readiness tests, 201, 202
reading. *See also* literacy; literacy instruction
aloud, 330–332
in art instruction, 439
connecting with social studies, 470, 472–473
cueing systems in, 308–309
definition of, 306, 308
guided, 333
observation of, 337
phonemic awareness and, 312–313
phonics instruction and, 313–318
shared, **332**–333
stages of, 309–311
reading-writing connection
mathematics instruction and, 373–374
science instruction and, 406–409
reasoning, in mathematics instruction, 360–362, 368, 370
recess, 486. *See also* playgrounds
recognition
of language achievements, 279
for volunteers, 256
referential language, 269

reflective abstraction, **348**
Reggio Emilia schools, 55, 62–63, 118, 204
reinforcement, 4
reinforcement schedules, 52
relating, in scientific process, 386
reliability of tests, 201
repetition, for encouraging language growth, 277
report cards, 222–223
reporting
of assessment results, 222–228
parents and, 222
representation, in mathematics instruction, 370–371
respect for environment, in science instruction, 393
respect for life, in science instruction, 392
responses, for literacy instruction, 306–307
responsibility, for literacy instruction, 306–307
rhymes, for language development, 284
rolling, in physical education programs, 483
room arrangement, **74,** 76–78
rote counting, 357
Rousseau, Jean-Jacques, 5, 36
routines
personal, in health education, 487–488
simplifying, 129
rule-governed play, 149
running narratives, for documenting children's work, 208

safety, 102–104
parents and, 497, 498
for science instruction, 390–391
safety education, 494–498
diversity and, 500
for fire safety, 494–495
integrating with health education, 498–500
for personal safety, 497–498
for poison safety, 497
for traffic safety, 495–497
for water safety, 497
samples, from play activities, 160
sand and water tables areas, 88–89
sandboxes, 99
scaffolding, 27
scheduling, 124–131

storage, for outdoor materials, 100
storage areas, 90
storytelling, for language development, 283–284
strand model for mathematics instruction, 352–371
  content strands in, 356–368
  process strands in, 352, 368, 370–371
  webs and, 353, 354
stupidity, learned, 315
subject-matter approach to curriculum organization, 111
substance abuse, in health education, 489
success
  expectations of, for language teaching, 277–278
  helping children feel successful as literacy learners and, 328–336
Success for All program, 335
super play units, 79
symbols, in practice play, 139
syntax, 267–268
  as cue in reading, 308

tallies, for documenting children's work, 207
teacher(s)
  conferences with parents. *See* parent conferences
  discipline and, 174–175
  home visits by, 246–248
  relationships with parents, 236–239
  roles in play, 144–146
  specialist, roles in art instruction, 436–437
teacher aides. *See* paraprofessionals
teaching skills, guidance and, 181–182
teaching strategies, **156**
  play as, 156, 158–159
telecommunication, for communicating with parents, 253
telephone calls, for reporting assessment results, 225
telling, as teaching strategy, 156
testing, 201–204
  assessment versus, 200

high-stakes, 204
reliability and validity in, 201
standardized tests for, 202–204
types of, 201–202
textbooks, in science instruction, 405
thematic approach to curriculum organization, 111, **114**–120
  evaluating themes for, 118–120
  implementing themes for, 116–118
  for social studies, 463–465
  theme, selection of, 115–116
Thorndike, Edward, 4, 52
three-year-olds
  science instruction for, 397, 400–401, 403
  social studies instruction for, 453–454
time. *See also* scheduling
  in mathematics instruction, 364–365
time-activity records, 159, 160
time-activity samples, for documenting children's work, 205–207
time out, 173–174
traffic safety education, 495–497
transition(s), **128**–129
  guidance for, 184–185
transitional spelling, 324–325
tumbling, in physical education programs, 483

Unifix cubes, 371

validity of tests, 201
verbal skills, guidance and, 182
vertical structuring, for encouraging language growth, 277
videotapes, for reporting assessment results, 228
violence. *See also* aggression
  in schools, 22
visual arts, 416–425
  activities for, 422–424
  art versus craft activities and, 424–425
  goals of experiences in, 421–422

stages in development of drawing and, 416–421
  taking seriously, 425
  talking about, 424
  viewing, 424
volunteers, **254**–258
  displaying appreciation for, 256
  instructions for, 255
  planning sheet for, 255, 256
  training for, 255
Vygotsky, Lev, 7–8, 55
  on cognitive development, 27
  on learning, 59, 60
  on play, 140–141

water play, outdoors, 99
water safety education, 497
water table areas, 88–89
Watson, John B., 4
weaving, 423–424
Weikart, David, 55, 61
wellness. *See also* health education; nutrition education; physical education programs; safety; safety education
  developmentally appropriate practice and, 488
  parents and, 484, 493, 499
whole numbers, 359–360
withitness, 187–188
woodworking areas, 88
World Wide Web, children's use of, 97
writing, 318, 320–328. *See also* reading-writing connection
  in art instruction, 439
  connecting with social studies, 470, 472–473
  conventions of written language and, 326
  development of, 320–326
  observation of, 336–337
  process with young children, 326–328
written letters and notes, for communicating with parents, 251–253

zone of proximal development (ZPD), **8, 58**